# "Listen to this Voice"

# "Listen to this Voice"

## Selected Speeches of Governor Zell Miller

## Zell Miller

Mercer University Press
Macon, Georgia

ISBN 0-86554-641-X
MUP/H478


© 1998
Mercer University Press
6316 Peake Road
Macon, Georgia 31210-3960

10 9 8 7 6 5 4 3 2 1

∞The paper used in this publication meets the minimum requirements of American National Standard for Information Sciences—Permanence of Paper for Printed Library Materials, ANSI Z39.48-1984.

*Library of Congress Cataloging-in-Publication Data*

Miller, Zell, 1932—
"Listen to this voice": selected speeches of Governor Zell Miller:
[1991-1998] / Zell Miller
p. cm.
Includes index
ISBN 0-86554-641-X (alk. paper)
1. Georgia—Politics and government—1951- I. Title.
F291.2M55 1998
975.8′043′092—dc21
98-33971
CIP

# Contents

A governor makes many speeches. During his eight years, Zell Miller made over 1,800 of them. This is a selection of several complete speeches and excerpts from many others. These words helped shape his administration and give an insight into the man and his talent for communication.

One can see how aggressively he approached the financial crisis during his first year in office when Georgia and the nation were in a severe recession. His optimism, even in those times, shines through.

There are common threads woven all through these speeches: his all-encompassing reverence for education, his belief that personal responsibility comes with benefits, his love of the state's diverse environment, the importance he placed on job creation, his Marine-tough approach to crime and his inbred frugality show up time and time again.

Miller was one of the nation's most pro-active governors. Read these speeches and you will see what Zell Miller's administration was all about. Read them and you will see what this man from the mountains was all about. It's all here. In his words.

*"Listen to this voice.*

*It's a voice flavored by the Blue Ridge; a voice straight out of a remote valley hidden among the peaks and hollows of the Appalachian Mountains; a voice that's been described as more barbed wire than honeysuckle.*

*That this kind of voice could travel from a forgotten corner of Appalachia is a testament to the grace of God and the greatness of the Democratic Party."*

Zell Miller
Keynote Speech, Democratic National Convention
Madison Square Garden, New York
July 13, 1992


*"When I'm a very old man, if the Lord lets me live that long, and I'm thinking about the high points of my wonderful career for which I'm very grateful, in the late of the night, one of the things I will always remember is Zell Miller's voice at the New York Convention in 1992. I can give that speech about the house his mama built better than he can. But it captured the heart of America and the heart of what we're all about."*

President Bill Clinton
Atlanta, Georgia
July 9, 1998

With heartfelt thanks, this volume of words is dedicated to

> *Sarah Eby-Ebersole*, who has been my confidante, collaborator, editor, and speech writer for more than twenty years. What is between these covers is as much—or more—Sarah's as it is mine.

> *Stephen Grady Miller*, the father I never knew. But I believe it was his genes that gave me my passion for politics, history, and speeches.

> *Edna Herren*, the English teacher at Young Harris College who instilled in me the beautiful way that words may be strung together and the forcefulness of a well-turned phrase. It was also she who pushed (or lured) me onto a stage in front of an audience.

> *Shirley Carver Miller*, who has for more than forty years been my best listener, my most severe critic, and many times the audience of one who first heard these words roll off my tongue.

Throughout this multitude of words are words put there by some members of my most able staff: **Paul Begala**, **Rick Dent**, **Dan Ebersole**, **Ed Kilgore**, **Keith Mason**, and **Steve Wrigley**, among others.

*A Special Thanks*

Also lovers of words, my two sons, Murphy Carver Miller and Matthew Stephen Miller, have never known a world without their father's involvement in politics and controversy. Their patience, their love, and their steadfast support have been unflinching. For this I am grateful and very proud.

# 1991

# First Inaugural Address

*January 14, 1991*

Like seventy-eight other Georgians before me, five of whom honor us with their presence today, I have now taken a solemn oath of office as Governor of this state.

The succession of democratic government in Georgia reaches back across two centuries. So, in the first place, this is a day for tradition, a celebration of freedom conserved, sustained, expanded, and passed on from generation to generation.

That journey of freedom is not finished. The progress we have made was not always easy, and the history of the struggle is not some relic of the past, but the challenge and hope of our future. For each memory also points to the miles we still have to travel.

In the 18th century, James Edward Oglethorpe dreamed of establishing a colony in the New World where free and equal men could build new lives for themselves and their families. Today we know that dream must include women as well as men.

In the 19th century, Henry W. Grady dreamed of a New South where there would be a hundred homes for every one plantation. Today we know that dream must reach to the homeless as well as the middle class.

And in the 20th century, Martin Luther King, Jr. dreamed "that one day on the red clay hills of Georgia the sons of slaves and the sons of former slave owners will be able to sit down together at the table of brotherhood." Today we must keep alive that dream of the only son of Georgia ever to be honored with the Nobel Peace Prize.

Across this country, clouds of racial prejudice and division are gathering again. Here in this state, it is our special duty to reject racism. One of Dr. King's apostles—and my friend—Andrew Young made more history last year as a candidate for governor. And Georgia took another giant step toward racial harmony by conducting a campaign remarkably free from racial resentment.

We will not be divided in this state black against white. Sadly, that is an undeniable part of our past, but it is not and must not be any part of our future. And the future is the essence of this inaugural day.

We draw strength from our heritage, but we set our course on the horizon ahead. We are entering a time of change—not only change of administrations, but a profound change in the pattern of Georgia life and the way our people make a living.

The traditional cornerstones of our economy were cheap energy, farming and manufacturing. And while farms and factories will always be a real and special part of Georgia, our survival and success in the new economy will be determined not only by the productivity of our land, but by the productivity of our people; not only by the horsepower of our machinery, but the brainpower of our workers. Our future prosperity depends not just on strong backs, but on strong minds.

Georgia faces a choice: we can plow new ground, or we can let the weeds grow. So, rather than resist change, we Georgians welcome it. Indeed, let us become a catalyst for change. Let this new administration begin a new era of imagination and innovation, effort and growth.

The driving force, the engine of the Georgia that can be, is found in the first three words of the Federal Constitution I have just sworn to uphold: "We, the People." And our fundamental directive can be found in the Georgia Constitution: "All government, of right, originates with the people, is founded on their will only. Public officers are the trustees and servants of the people." That is government at its best, and that is the kind of Governor I will strive to be.

And so we dedicate this administration to the family farmer who plants his own crops and bales his own hay, to the small businesswoman who stays open late and calls her customers by their first names, to the bold entrepreneur who has built a better mousetrap or a smaller microchip.

We dedicate this administration to the senior citizen who opens her utility bill fearing that she will be forced to choose between being cold or being hungry, and to the young family just starting out, struggling to afford day care now and save for college later.

Listen to me: It is to every family that works and saves and sometimes comes up a little short at the end of the month that this administration is dedicated.

So what shall we do now with the power— and the responsibility?

We, the People, have the right, if we so choose, to fund bold, new education initiatives through a Georgia lottery devoted to our schools. We, the People, have the right to reach for the finest public schools in the history of this state, or anywhere in this nation.

In building a world-class school system, we will follow the advice of a part-time Georgian named Franklin D. Roosevelt, who once said, "Try something. If it works, try more of it. If it doesn't work, try something else. But for God's sake, try something."

The central purpose of the Miller Administration will be to prepare Georgia for the 21st century. Education is the most important part of that purpose. Without it, nothing else can save us. With it, nothing else can stop us.

We, the People, must advance on other fronts as well. Our government must be made leaner and cleaner, more open and more responsive. Our environment must be preserved from those who would trade our children's health and our fragile Earth for a quick buck.

Our streets and neighborhoods must be better protected against the rising tide of crime and drugs. Something is wrong when families hide behind home security bars, because criminals are released from behind maximum security bars. Our working families must be given relief from skyrocketing insurance rates, inadequate highways, and regressive taxes on the very food they eat.

We must do all this and more to strive, to seek, to find the Georgia that can be.

It is certain that our journey will not be completed in the limited time the people of Georgia have put this public servant in office. Nor will it be completed in the limited time the Lord has put this humble servant on Earth. But we take heart from the ancient Hebrew text: "The day is short, the work is great. It is not thy duty to complete the work. Neither art thou free to desist from it."

And so today, we take the first step of a thousand-mile journey. We launch a new administration, and we look to a new century.

By empowering our citizens, educating our children, building our prosperity, saving our environment, fighting crime, and demanding a government that works as hard as our people do, we will march toward the Georgia that can be.

A Georgia in which a little boy from a remote impoverished mountain valley, or a little girl in a dirty and dangerous urban slum can have his or her chance for greatness. A Georgia in which all of us have the opportunity to seek our destiny, seize that shining moment, and climb as far as strength and wit and perseverance will carry us; never to be blocked by barriers of race or barricades or region or gender or class.

By harnessing the two most powerful forces on earth—an educated people and an unshakable faith—let us now turn to the task of leading Georgia. And then let Georgia lead the nation into the twenty-first century.

God bless you, and God bless Georgia.

# State of the State Address

*January 16, 1991*

Mr. President, Mr. Speaker, members of the General Assembly of Georgia, distinguished guests, and my fellow Georgians:

It is my honor and my duty under our Constitution to report to you on the state of our state. But I want not only to discuss with you where we stand today, but also to begin to chart the course we must sail together in order to reach the Georgia that can be.

I have sat up here on this rostrum as your Lieutenant Governor, or out on the floor as a fellow legislator, and listened to six different Governors report on the State of the State. I am grateful for that perspective and for those years of preparation for the responsibility I now face.

I have spent countless hours presiding over the State Senate, and I see many lifelong friends from the Senate here today. Your friendship and support give me confidence that we can complete the journey before us.

I've also spent considerable time in this chamber, sometimes as the guest of the Speaker, sometimes as his adversary, sometimes as his student, but always with great respect. Respect not only for this strong leader, but also for the outstanding members who are the heart and soul of the House.

Most of you know that even before the crisis in the Middle East, our national economy was sliding into a recession that would have had a major impact on state finances and on this legislative session.

This will be a session of hard choices, hard thinking, and hard work. It must also be a session of teamwork and mutual respect for the executive role and the legislative role. For my part, I shall do everything in my power to make this administration one of cooperation, not confrontation. Let us remember that the hopes and dreams of more than six million Georgians converge under the Capitol dome in these 40 days we spend together. We must not hinder those hopes with political bickering, nor defer those dreams with political rifts.

On Friday I will report to you in detail on our financial situation, setting before you the budget that I have worked on almost every day since the election. The plain hard fact is that we face a difficult financial situation. Virtually every state government in the nation faces the same or a much more serious situation. There are two overriding reasons: the national recession and the New Federalism.

I have no crystal ball to tell me anything meaningful about the length or depth of the recession, but it is important that we all understand how New Federalism has affected the financial condition of this state and every other state.

You will recall that back in the 1970s we as a nation felt that too much power had gravitated to Washington, that federal regulation was becoming over-reaching and unworkable. Federal taxes were cut to stimulate the economy, and we fondly remember the economic boom of the 80s that followed.

But under New Federalism, the scope of many federal programs and their costs were not truly curtailed. They were simply shifted to the states. In the past ten years, the level of federal support through grants to state and local government went down 38 percent! Because we were in an economic boom, we did not give much attention to the shift of financial responsibility. Picking up the cost of programs as federal support was cut was not a great burden in those heady economic times. But now the upward spiral of state revenues has ground to a halt. The days of "drinking that free bubble-up and eating that rainbow stew" are gone.

I am not complaining about our new responsibilities. I believe in grassroots government. I believe government works better when it is closer to the people. But for you and me, it means our work is both more important and more difficult. The cautious, reserved approach to governing in the prosperous 80s is inadequate for the 90s. We cannot sit on the sidelines and wait for the economy to improve. We must act.

So I will bring to the General Assembly a legislative agenda that is a little different from the traditional approach for a new Governor. Today I want to briefly outline for you a blueprint to begin building the bridge between the Georgia that is and the Georgia that can be.

First, it should surprise no one here that my number one legislative initiative—and my top priority—is the Georgia Lottery for education. After traveling this state from Blairsville to Brunswick, I can tell you without any doubt that the people of Georgia want a lottery, and they want their lottery to finance new education programs.

I realize the lottery is an issue on which some of us disagree. I know there are strong and deeply held opinions on the subject. I want your input, but at the same time, I want you to know that I am adamant that the new lottery funds must not supplant existing funds for education. I hope you are too. Think about it; we cannot allow the lottery funds to be put in one pocket for our schoolchildren, while existing funds are taken from their other pocket.

That is why the constitutional amendment to create a Georgia lottery will place the proceeds in a special budget category—a budget category in which the lottery proceeds are clearly additional funds assigned to education.

Another hidden danger we must guard against is that the hundreds of millions of new dollars the lottery will raise will be used to simply buy more of the same mediocre, bureaucratic education programs. The people of Georgia will not stand for more of the same, and neither will I.

We've got a solid foundation with Quality Basic Education, but it's a foundation to build on, not to stand on. Among my education proposals for the year there are four programs which, if they prove successful, we should later fully fund with lottery proceeds. There may be others.

The four are: voluntary prekindergarten for four-year-olds, especially targeted at children who are at risk of becoming drop-outs when they get older; an expansion of the Governor's Honors Program for our gifted students; drug education, a doubling of the support we give to the DARE program—the partnership between law enforcement and education that is turning young lives around all over this state; and fourth, sex education. This is a difficult subject, I know, but if dealing with it makes you uncomfortable, ignoring it should make you ashamed. Georgia is eighth in AIDS cases, and fifth in infant mortality and teenage pregnancy. We have children having children, and we've got to stop it.

We must also begin delivering our programs more effectively. Along those lines, I have met at length with State Superintendent Werner Rogers, and we have agreed to work together to change the role of the State Department of Education. There will be an immediate restructuring of the Department of Education—a downsizing of the Department with more emphasis on providing service to local school systems and less bureaucratic monitoring.

I want to attract our best and brightest into the teaching profession. The State Superintendent and I also agreed to take action to reform an area I talked about in my campaign—teacher certification. We will take the certification program completely out of the Department of Education and place it in the Professional Standards Commission, a transfer of 40 employees. This action will allow a smaller agency to focus its energies and resources on removing the barriers that discourage qualified people from becoming teachers.

Next week I will appoint a task force to examine the most sensible way of implementing a system of paying our best teachers more. Teaching is the only occupation I know of where if you do a better job you don't get better pay. I want to change that, and I want you to help me.

One of the thorniest issues we face is Georgia's high dropout rate. It is time to act, to identify at-risk children, and to link what happens in the classroom to what happens in the family and community.

I have directed the Departments of Education, Human Resources, and Medical Assistance to create a plan for addressing the needs of children at risk, and to use the provisions of the state's Medicaid program for funding. I'll need your help in adding language to the appropriations act to allow these three agencies to pursue this program.

The third major area is as much a jobs issue as it is an education issue: literacy. You've heard the statistics: More than one out of every five adult Georgians is functionally illiterate. Over one million Georgians cannot read the warning on a medicine bottle, a letter from a loved one, or even read a bedtime story to their children.

If we are to compete for jobs in the new economy, we will have to invest more in our people. That is why I will ask you to adopt a tax credit for companies that provide literacy education. Such an approach will involve the private sector, strengthen the link between education and jobs, save money, avoid bureaucratic red tape, and make Georgia more attractive for companies who want to locate here.

The wisdom of the investment is even clearer when you read the studies that conclude that raising just 20,000 adults out of illiteracy will generate over $90 million per year in increased economic activity.

Literacy is so important to this former teacher that I'm deploying my most potent weapon to fight for it: First Lady Shirley Carver Miller. Shirley will make adult literacy her top priority, and will work with the Literate Community Program, which has such great promise, GED testing, and the whole range of programs in this important area.

As one who grew up and still calls home one of the most rural parts of our state, I pledge never to forget about rural Georgia. I have a long-standing commitment to improving transportation and will always continue to support economic development highways to open rural areas of our state to new industry.

This session I will introduce a major initiative to expand the state's economic development efforts, especially in rural Georgia. I will ask you to pass legislation changing the Georgia Residential Finance Authority to the Georgia Capital Finance Authority, a restructuring that will increase access to capital for business and industries that wish to relocate to Georgia. If you pass this legislation, we will have a new tool to attract small business firms to rural Georgia, where industrial financing is often difficult. I believe that the state has an obligation to promote growth in underserved areas.

One problem that we've been trying to solve for years, but on which we must do more, is crime. I have met with the chairman of the Pardons & Parole Board, and we can end Georgia's early release program. Beginning this July, we will start to phase out early release, and if you give me the boot camps I'm requesting this session, early release will become history by July of 1992.

I further requested, and the Board has agreed, to broaden the definition of what are referred to as violent offenders, and lengthen the amount of time they serve before becoming eligible for parole. My message is clear: if you kill someone while driving drunk, if you molest or abuse a child, if you knock over an old lady on a street corner and steal her purse, or if you want to be a big-time drug dealer, you're going to serve a big-time sentence.

But the violent crime we are most exposed to—and most vulnerable to—is drunk driving. If you are out on a Friday or Saturday night, as many as one out of every ten drivers on the road with you is drunk. That is why I am proposing the toughest new DUI laws in Georgia's history.

Other parts of our anti-crime package include forcing drug pushers to forfeit their mansions and using the money to pay for drug rehabilitation and treatment for the people they addict, and a state Hobbs Act to attack public corruption.

I also want to reorganize the state's law enforcement and training agencies. Let me make this clear: The reorganization of the Department of Public Safety will not cost one red cent more than we now spend in the criminal justice area. As you will see in my budget on Friday, it will be paid for by paring back on the existing bureaucracy. The war on crime is too important for our forces to be fragmented. I want all our people fighting crime, not fighting turf battles.

We also have to work harder to protect our environment. Piece by piece our state's natural beauty is being graded under or paved over. Of Georgia's entire land area, only eight percent is in public parks or forests, which ranks us seventh of the 11 southeastern states. In the Piedmont, where more than half of the state's population lives, only two percent of our land is in parks and forests. That's a disgrace for a state that calls itself the Empire State of the South.

It is my goal to protect another 100,000 acres of parkland through public-private partnerships by the end of the 90s. In addition, I will ask you to pass new legislation protecting our mountains and river corridors.

I also want to restructure the Hazardous Waste Authority, not only its membership but also its mission. I have appointed a nationally recognized conservationist, Bob Kerr, as its director, and will ask you to change the membership of the Authority by taking the politicians off and putting professionals on—more scientists, more engineers, more environmentalists.

With Bob Kerr, we will completely refocus the Authority's mission, broadening it from merely selecting a place to dispose of our waste to attacking the problem at its source: reducing the amount of waste we generate here in Georgia, which right now, I am sorry to say, is one of the highest in the nation.

I know of no area in which our investment over the years has paid a more handsome reward than higher education. Although this year's budget allows precious little new money for higher education, as a former teacher I will immediately begin to give it more hands-on support than it's received in many years. I will create a Higher Education Roundtable—to be composed of the Governor, Speaker, the Lieutenant Governor, the Chancellor, and the presidents of the five universities. We will meet at the Mansion for breakfast every quarter to discuss the needs and goals of the University System.

I also intend to promote our research with as much pride as we currently promote our fine athletic teams. Georgia Tech, The University of Georgia and Emory combined perform more research than the three universities of North Carolina's famous Research Triangle. Few people around the nation know that, but they will before we are through.

I am also calling for a permanent fund to meet capital and equipment needs throughout the University System, from libraries to laboratories. We must do this because the most important resource of the Georgia that can be is the educated minds of our sons and our daughters.

Health care is another area in which we face the choice posed to us by the auto mechanic in the TV commercial who said, "You can pay me now, or pay me later." If we invest in a small amount of preventive care, especially for pregnant women and infants, we can save millions down the road. That is why I will offer new initiatives such as expanded early intervention services for infants and toddlers who have developmental disabilities, and perinatal care for pregnant women.

As I promised in my campaign, I will also begin a new program that will give immediate treatment to pregnant females who are abusing drugs. Because I knew poverty, I understand the cruelty of an innocent baby suffering only because her Mama is poor or addicted. And because I know state government, I understand the foolishness of ignoring the problems of impoverished babies in a misguided effort to save money. The end result of neglecting babies to save a pittance is millions spent in welfare and incarceration for the rest of their lives. As Governor, I will do my best to alleviate the cruelty and eliminate the foolishness.

Another goal of my administration is to reform auto insurance in Georgia. With your help, I intend to roll back insurance rates in Georgia right away—and that's just the beginning.

That family that works and saves and sometimes comes up a little short at the end of the month, deserves a break—not only when they pay their car insurance premium, but also every time they buy a bag of groceries. That is why I have introduced a constitutional amendment to give the people of Georgia a chance to repeal the sales tax off all food for all time.

The repeal will be gradual and predictable—a penny a year until it's gone for good. I'd like to repeal the current hodgepodge of a food tax, which exempts peanuts but taxes peanut butter. But please understand this: I will not sign a bill repealing the partial food tax exemption if it comes to my desk without the constitutional amendment. The two are inseparable in my mind, because, to me, flawed as it is, the present law that cuts taxes on some food is better than no cut in the food tax at all.

These priorities are not the end of the Miller Administration's goals. They are just the beginning. If they seem to be ambitious, it's because they are. I believe we can only succeed greatly by daring greatly.

In 1934 a French zoologist applied the theory of aerodynamics to the bumblebee. He found that, because of its inordinate weight and its inadequate wingspan, the flight of a bumblebee is physically impossible. Fortunately, the bumblebee was not made aware of this study, and so it keeps on flying.

There are those who look at the Georgia that is, see our temporary budget problems, and the multitude of other challenges, and say that the Georgia that can be will never fly. They say that a proud and prosperous Georgia, an educated and enlightened Georgia—they say that Georgia will never be. My friends, let us tell the fainthearted to stand back—and watch us fly.

With your help—and God's—I know we shall succeed.

# Budget Address, Fiscal Year 1992

*January 18, 1991*

In my Inaugural Address on Monday, I laid before you the philosophy of the Miller Administration. In my State of the State Address on Wednesday, I set forth the agenda for the Miller Administration. The same promises that I reiterated throughout my campaign, the same philosophy I presented in my Inaugural Address, the same priorities I spelled out in my State of the State address, are now right here before you in this budget.

It is time for a new approach to managing our resources in Georgia. We need creative and innovative solutions to the problems we face. We need a bureaucracy that is lean, and focuses its resources not on sustaining and enlarging itself, but on the delivery of services to the citizens of this state.

Times are tough and they are going to stay tough for a while. But I view this time of tight resources as an opportunity for change, and I hope you do too. Despite the slumping economy, despite a federal government that addresses its deficit by shifting costs to the states, despite our longer-term slowing of revenue growth—despite, or perhaps *because* of all of these things, we will work to meet the needs of Georgia's people through more efficient and through more effective use of our resources. We will do more, but we will do more with less.

Let this be understood, I am not cutting simply because times are tough. I am shifting funds away from an overweight bureaucracy and into programs that provide important services to Georgia's citizens. And as new resources become available, they will be used in new and creative ways, not to restore the old cuts!

Before he got rich and famous, Lewis Grizzard and I used to go to Nashville at least once a year. We'd go to the Opry, see the sights, and hang out around the old Ryman Auditorium. Once we were there, and down the street a little from Tootsie's Orchid Lounge was a western wear place called The Alamo. It was where all the stars bought their rhinestone suits and western wear.

We went in there, killing time and looking around, and stayed about an hour. Lewis tried on a Stetson and a fringed suede coat that cost a thousand dollars. I tried on a pair of boots that cost fifteen hundred. When we were finally ready to leave, Lewis did not buy anything. I bought a pair of socks and a can of black shoe polish.

The cashier looked at us a little funny, like we were a pair of cheapskates. So I said to her, "You have got to understand. I'm from Georgia government and down there we look at what we'd like to have, then we buy what we can afford."

Lewis sent that story off to *Reader's Digest* and made $200. I never saw a cent. But the story makes my point. We buy what we can afford.

Today I recommend to you a budget for Fiscal Year 1992 that totals $7.9 billion and is based on anticipated revenues of the same amount. This figure represents an increase of just about one percent over the original budget we adopted a year ago for FY 91. That is negative growth—it is not even enough to cover inflation.

There is a net spending increase of only $235 million in this FY92 budget compared to my amended FY 91 budget. Add in $49 million in even more spending reductions, and you get $284 million in new money available for expenditure next year.

Now listen carefully, because this is important. I am talking about $284 million *total*. Cost increases resulting from inflation, increases in the state's utility bills—every increase of any sort—has got to come from that $284 million.

For you to understand the magnitude of the task I faced in putting this budget together, let me point out that our state agencies requested almost $2.2 billion in increased spending for next year—$2.2 billion compared to the $284 million we have available.

Ten days ago, I announced cuts of $247 million in the budget for the present fiscal year. That money does not reappear in my budget for FY92, and it will not appear, as I've said before, in any of my future budgets.

Ten days ago, I announced that I would abolish 2,000 positions that were vacant on December 15. Money for those positions does not appear in this budget, and will not appear in any of my future budgets.

Many state agencies will find that their major budget categories for FY92 are even less than they were in the original budget for 1991. Personal services will remain at the same level as my amended FY 91 budget, except for critical service areas like law enforcement, hospitals, and prisons.

Let me make it clear: I am not just injecting a few new dollars into the same old budget pattern. I am rearranging priorities, I am shifting funds around, and I am focusing them on direct services in important program initiatives.

The numbers by agency and line item are in front of you in black and white, so I am not going to spend my time reiterating them. Instead, I want to talk about four program thrusts that are the focus of this budget.

First, you have heard me say countless times that education will be the cornerstone of my administration, and you can see it in the numbers today. Georgia's public schools get by far the largest portion of the new money in next year's budget—some $103 million in new money going into Quality Basic Education  and programs that directly affect students.

In line with my goal of downsizing state government while emphasizing direct services, we have made cuts in administrative overhead and in non-student-related areas. But we have made great positive strides in providing instruction to students.

Throughout my campaign I spoke of the importance of educational opportunities for very young children, especially those who are at risk. This priority is reflected in several programs I am recommending: First, almost $3 million will initiate a pilot prekindergarten program for four-year-olds in 60 classrooms around the state.

During my campaign, I promised to start this program with proceeds from the lottery. But we can't wait; it is so important to Georgia's future, that I wanted to get a pilot program going before the lottery is in place, so that we have tested and refined it and are ready to move with it as soon as lottery revenues become available. Other educational programs for young children that I recommend for expansion include the Special Instructional Assistance program for children in the early grades who are at risk developmentally, and our program for handicapped three and four-year olds.

Anyone who paid any attention at all to my campaign will remember my emphasis on sex education in our schools. And anyone who has looked at the growth rates for either teenage pregnancy or sexually transmitted disease knows how critical it is. I am recommending $754,000 to develop and implement a training program for high school teachers on how to teach sex education. As you know, sex education is already a part of the school curriculum. But these existing teachers want and need high-quality instruction in both the subject matter and in the techniques of teaching this important and sensitive subject. I want them to be able to explain clearly to our children the perils and consequences of irresponsible sexual behavior in a way that they understand and take to heart.

I also talked about drug education during the campaign and in my State of the State address. And this budget includes funds to double DARE, the Drug Awareness and Resistance Education program that we have begun in 42 of our schools.

Another campaign promise you will find here is my commitment to making sure Georgia's brightest high school students have the opportunity to attend college. One million dollars goes to expand our scholarship program to include every high school valedictorian, salutatorian, and STAR student in the state, and another $400,000 to expand the Governor's Honors Program by 400 of our brightest, our gifted students for whom this is the only summer enrichment program we provide.

My education funding recommendations are also designed to move Quality Basic Education forward. In the FY 92 budget, we have boosted QBE formula funding by more than $3 million to expand services. The bulk of this new money—$34.4 million—is the second-year portion of the QBE Weights Task Force formula. The point of this formula is to get the funds we send to our local schools to more accurately reflect the actual cost of educating our youngsters.

In addition, I recommend that $8.9 million total be appropriated for middle-school counselors. This money will fully fund the program we began last year at the level of one counselor for every base-sized middle school.

Other QBE programs that will share in the new funding next year include incentive grants for 35 additional schools to implement middle grades programs; the continued implementation of the In-School Suspension program, which isolates disruptive students without suspending them from school, and special assistance to students for whom English is their second language.

In addition, I am recommending funds to purchase vocational equipment for 21 new high schools slated to open next fall.

To provide for new public school construction, I am recommending bond funding totaling $83.4 million for regular entitlements, with an additional $2.5 million in advanced incentive planning grants. Sixteen public libraries have raised local funds for new facilities, earning state matching grants. I am recommending $9.8 million in bonds for these projects.

I used to be a college teacher before I got in this business. I've taught at one of this state's smallest colleges, and I've taught at this state's largest university. I know from firsthand experience that a strong University System is critical to Georgia's future growth and prosperity.

My FY 92 budget adds $58.4 million to the University System's funding formula.

The bulk of these funds—$33.8 million—addresses increased enrollment around the system. The remainder restores cuts to the formula, with $8.2 million going to restore to full funding the part of the formula that addresses academic programs in the system's classrooms.

The University System formula calls for major maintenance and repair funds of $24 million for the system's 2,500 buildings. The system has a lot of older buildings, so I am recommending that we meet this need in FY 92 by issuing five-year bonds.

In addition to major maintenance and repair, I am recommending five University System capital projects for bonding. I propose that we move ahead with the student physical activities center and a parking facility at The University of Georgia, a residence hall project at Georgia Tech, and a parking facility and a bookstore at Kennesaw State College. The Georgia Education Authority (University) would be reactivated to manage this bond program using receipts generated from the facilities themselves. Special consideration must be given to capital projects like these that generate revenue which, in turn, would then be used to pay off the bonds.

I am aware that the Board of Regents recently adopted a major revision of the funding formula which they would like us to use in the future to determine their appropriation. I appreciate their desire to have a funding mechanism that looks forward to the 21st century rather than back to the needs of a decade ago, and after the session, my budget advisors and I will give careful study and consideration to these proposed revisions.

Georgia has many adults at the other end of the educational spectrum, too—adults who never really learned to read. I spoke to you of adult literacy from this rostrum on Wednesday, and you will see it in my budget here today.

Finally in the area of education, I am recommending $3.2 million for major repairs and renovations at our technical institutes, and $1.7 million to purchase instructional equipment for these institutes.

Let me turn now from education to a second priority you heard me emphasize during my campaign and reiterate during the past ten days—the protection of decent, law-abiding citizens. This is the second major program thrust in my budget for next year, and again you can see that we are going to change the way we've been doing things.

First, I intend to lose no time in implementing the boot camp program I promised during my campaign. My concept of a boot camp is based on my experience as a Marine recruit at Parris Island—shaved heads, bunk beds, a quonset hut with 60-watt light bulbs, and an unrelenting regimen of discipline. My concept also comes from being the only elected official in Georgia to have worked in all three aspects of offender rehabilitation—probation, incarceration, and parole.

The boot camp I propose to you is a barebones, no TV, spartan facility that houses inmates for three months. While they are there, inmates will experience strict discipline, physical training, and hard work—in other words, a military-style basic training regimen. Boot camp will also include compulsory programs that address substance abuse, since this is where offenders who have violated the DUI/Habitual Traffic Violators law will be. Third, and this should not go unnoticed, boot camp inmates will be subject to strict probation and parole supervision after they are released. If they violate probation, they will go to the "big house."

I am recommending $11.25 million in bonds to construct and equip nine boot camp facilities—three as stand-alone units and six adjacent to three existing correctional institutions. The stand-alone camps will be built in Mitchell, Lanier and Emanuel counties at a cost of 2 million dollars each. Two camps will be built adjacent to each of the existing institutions in Hancock, Washington and Chattooga Counties, and will use their support facilities. The reason we are locating six boot camps adjacent to existing facilities is to achieve a more efficient level of staffing and support. They can also be built using inmate labor.

Each of these nine boot camps will accommodate 224 inmates, giving us 2,016 new beds at about one-sixth of the cost of the new prison beds now being built in Georgia. They won't be "Cadillacs," but people who break the law don't deserve "Cadillacs."

In addition, two existing facilities—the Stone Mountain and Putnam Correctional Institutions—will be converted to boot camps, giving us a total of 2,344 new boot camp beds. When fully operational, these 11 boot camps will accommodate nearly 9,400 offenders a year on a 90-day rotation basis.

Although I emphasized boot camps in my campaign, I am fully aware of the need for conventional prison beds. It will take the combination of new boot camps and new prison beds to end the Early Release Program that the Board of Pardons and Paroles has been using to control prison overcrowding. Conventional correctional institutions are another area where we can and must be more cost-effective. I don't like frills anywhere, and I am not certainly not going to tolerate them in our prison system. Any type of prison authorized during this administration will be inexpensive to construct and cost-efficient to operate. You can count on that!

Along those lines, I am authorizing $300,000 to develop plans and specifications for a prototype facility of low-to-medium security that will be cost-effective to duplicate around the state. Another $700,000 is requested to acquire sites for later construction of these facilities.

I also recommend one million dollars in bond funds to expand the wastewater treatment plant at the Georgia Public Safety Training Center. In addition to allowing larger training classes at the Center, this expansion will also allow us to double the inmate capacity at the adjacent Burruss Correctional Institution from 400 to 800 beds.

Once we build prisons, we have to staff them, and that is where the ongoing cost comes in. My recommendations provide operating funds for five new prisons with 4,400 beds. Three of them—the Hancock, Telfair and Washington Correctional Institutions—will be in operation for the full fiscal year, while the Johnson and Mitchell Correctional Institutions will open near the end of the fiscal year. I also recommend full funding for the new 200-bed Treutlen Special Alternative Incarceration Institution.

I have allocated operating funds for the Stone Mountain Detention Center in Rockdale County, which will open in April, and for two additional centers with 150 beds each, which will open in Fulton and Evans Counties near the end of the fiscal year.

Before I leave law enforcement and corrections, let me make one more point. Highway safety is of enormous concern to me, and I want to get more state troopers out on the road during my administration. In the supplemental budget, I recommended funding to start up a new state trooper school of 50 recruits. In 1992, I am recommending $1.5 million to put those 50 on the road.

The third program area that I focus on in this budget is economic development. And with the present state of our economy, I don't expect to find anyone who will argue against making this a priority.

Georgia's ports are a major economic benefit for all of our citizens, whether they live in Dalton or LaGrange or Gainesville. To keep our ports operating smoothly, I am recommending $2.5 million in bonds to construct dikes and expand the spoilage area in the Savannah Harbor.

The Georgia Ports Authority also requested $25.6 million in full state funding to deepen the Savannah Harbor channel to 42 feet. I understand the need to do this and I support it, but there is potential to leverage substantial federal funding for this project. Therefore, I am recommending that the Authority proceed with the design, engineering, and environmental review of the project using $1.2 million in Authority funds, while at the same time pursuing federal participation.

Even though the budget is tight, I want to maintain state funding assistance to local governments, who are also experiencing revenue problems and who are on the front lines of providing the infrastructure industry needs. But I want to make some changes in the way we provide this help.

We have a number of small grant programs, and I am not convinced that the funds are addressing the most serious needs of our counties and cities. I propose that we abolish four and downsize two grant programs that totaled $28.4 million in the original FY 91 budget, and develop instead a $50 million loan program for water, sewer, water supply, and wastewater treatment projects. The new loan program would be financed with revenue bonds sold by the Georgia Environmental Facilities Authority. These bonds would be repaid as local governments repay their loans.

Highways are also an important part of economic development, and I recommend that funding for the Local Road Assistance Program (LARP) continue at a level of $38.6 million, just slightly below the current level of $40 million. These funds complement my recommendation in the 1991 amended budget that the Governor's Road Improvement Program be continued with $76.9 million in bond funds.

Highway construction is another area in which I want to do things differently, and I have discussed this at length with Commissioner Hal Rives. I want to move funds around to take maximum advantage of a rare opportunity.

The federal government has indicated its intention to put a significant level of its new motor fuel tax revenues into a program called the Highway System of National Significance. States would be able to draw this federal money down to match state motor fuel tax funds to enhance particular highways.

Now, you need to understand that many of the Georgia highways that will be identified as part of this new national system are already part of GRIP, the Governor's Road Improvement Program. By rearranging the way we spend our Georgia motor fuel tax revenues, we will be able to leverage some significant federal funds to help us pay for our economic development highways. The bottom line is that in FY 92 we will spend nearly $155 million more in state and federal funds than we spent in FY 90, for roads that will be part of this Highway System of National Significance.

Sometimes overlooked, the quality of life is an important consideration in attracting business and industry to Georgia, and in that sense, our wildlife management and public fishing areas are part of our economic development infrastructure. I am recommending

$150,000 to improve and operate newly acquired wildlife management areas and public fishing areas. These funds are in addition to the $1.45 million in bonds in my supplemental budget recommendations for equipment and capital construction on these lands.

While I am on this subject, let me address the question some have raised regarding the use of funds from that increase a few years ago in hunting and fishing license fees. Back when I was Lieutenant Governor, I was on top of that, and I'm making sure we are putting *all* of the income from those fees directly into game and fish needs. In fact, the state funds going for this purpose have increased. Fee income now makes up only 42 percent of the budget for game and fish compared to 58 percent back when the fees were last increased.

The fourth program area to receive a significant block of new funds is health and social services. Almost a third of our available funds will go to help Georgians in need of these services, with $47.6 million allocated to Medicaid and $33.4 million to the Department of Human Resources.

The combination of rising health care costs and an increase in services and users has sent the Medicaid budget spiraling upward. Of the new Medicaid funds, $32.5 million will be used to fund expanded coverage mandated by the federal government (some of that New Federalism I talked about on Wednesday). Other Medicaid increases will fund reimbursement rate adjustments that were approved in FY 91 and annualize other improvements that went into effect in FY 91.

Growing like kudzu, Medicaid costs are now 10 percent of our total budget. The national average is 12 percent—up from 3 percent before New Federalism. So, in an effort to contain the cost of Medicaid programs, I am recommending that in 1992 we begin requiring Medicaid participants to make a small contribution toward the cost of the health care they receive. These co-payments would range from one to three dollars for certain recipients and services. The total savings to the program for the first year would be $7.8 million, of which $3 million would be state funds.

We do not want to deprive any Georgian of needed health care. However, I believe a small co-payment from Medicaid recipients will help to offset the rapidly rising costs we are experiencing. Twenty-four states already require similar co-payments. We will just be doing what half the states are already doing.

Of course, it is evident that there is no salary increase for teachers or state employees. But I have asked the Merit System Board to preserve the same level of health insurance coverage with no increase in the premium taken out of employees' paychecks, so at least they are spared that increased cost which most workers in private enterprise are having to bear.

The bulk of the new funds I am recommending for the Department of Human Resources will go into Aid to Families with Dependent Children. When the economy slumps, the AFDC rolls rise, and almost $20 million in new money will be needed in FY 92 to accommodate this growth.

Another $4.6 million must be allocated to fund the increased number of children in foster care, which has come as a result of our concerted effort in addressing child abuse. And I propose $2.5 million to expand case management services for developmentally delayed infants and toddlers during their first two years of life. I referred to this in my

State of the State speech, and it is the initial stage of the program for developmentally delayed three and four-year-olds that I mentioned a bit ago when I was talking about education. Similar to what I suggested with DOT, the money will leverage more federal funds. This will allow us to provide a higher level of services for these children from birth until kindergarten age.

Finally in the area of human services, let me point out that amid all of these cuts, one item that has remained unscathed is the State Housing Trust Fund, which provides assistance to the homeless. I am recommending that this fund continue at the same $5 million level in FY 92 as in the original FY 91 budget.

Education, law enforcement, economic development, and human services—these are the program areas through which direct state services flow to the citizens of Georgia, and they are the focus of the budget I present to you today.

Here it is—a pay-as-you-go budget with no fiscal sleights of hand and no cost-shifting to future years.

Here it is—a budget that downsizes administrative overhead and concentrates on getting the maximum level of service per dollar.

Here it is—a budget that sets us on the course that I intend to stay during my administration as your Governor.

# Swearing In the Williams Commission

*January 25, 1991*

With these commissioning ceremonies for the Governor's Commission on Effectiveness and Economy in Government, we launch what I hope will be one of the most significant contributions of the Miller Administration to state government.

Let me begin by saying a sincere and heart-felt thank you to each and every member who has agreed to serve on this Commission. You are a special group of business leaders, men and women of high intellect, determination, and proven accomplishment.

I have asked Virgil Williams, my chief of staff, to assume the chairmanship of this group, and he has agreed to make the work of the Governor's Commission on Effectiveness and Economy in Government his top priority.

Throughout my campaign, I talked about a state-level commission to help me ferret out waste in state government. That was not simply rhetoric designed to get me elected. Nor am I commissioning you here today simply because I feel obliged to honor my campaign promises. You and I are here today because I need your advice and I need your help. I am dead serious about downsizing and streamlining state government. It is long overdue. And I am counting on your advice and assistance to do the job.

In the weeks between the General Election and my budget presentation to the General Assembly last week, I spent countless hours in daily conferences with my budget advisors. During those weeks, we took the initial steps in downsizing and streamlining state government. I tell you this simply to let you know that the easy and obvious cuts have already been made—and a few of the not-so-easy ones as well.

We are now faced with sorting out the hard ones, and this is where I really need your help. Please do not be afraid to ask the hard questions—to go beyond asking, "How can we make this particular operation more efficient?" to asking, "What would happen if we stopped doing this entirely?" I do not want to waste a lot of effort making something more efficient if it does not need to exist.

However, having said that about budget cuts, I hasten to point out that the task with which you are charged has dimensions that go beyond eliminating waste in state government. About two weeks ago, Peter Drucker wrote in a *Wall Street Journal* column that "cutting staffs to cut costs is putting the cart before the horse. The only way to bring costs down is to restructure the work."

Again, we have started some of the necessary restructuring, but we need your help and advice to carry it further. The whole purpose of streamlining and restructuring our administrative overhead is to shift our focus to service delivery. The end result must be not just a slimmed-down state bureaucracy, but one the is more productive and effective in providing high-quality services to the people of Georgia.

This is where I am convinced that you as private sector business leaders can give us a hand. To be successful, to turn a profit, your products and services must compete in a free market. You are in an endless search for ways to deliver a quality product in the most efficient way possible. That is the approach I want you to take to state government. I do not want to diminish the services we provide to our citizens. I want to enhance the quality of those services, and I want Georgia to be a model of excellence in this regard.

The third dimension of your task is cost prevention. We all know what happens when someone goes on a crash diet, but doesn't change their lifestyle and their eating habits. Pretty soon they have gained back most if not all of the weight they lost. And it is always harder to diet to get rid of excess fat than to avoid putting it on in the first place.

Costs work the same way. Left to their own devices, costs always sneak up; they never sneak down. Just as a healthy lifestyle and good eating habits are necessary for a person to hold a constant weight, so do we in state government need cost prevention measures in place to prevent us from ending up right back where we were.

These two additional dimensions to your task—restructuring for excellence and preventing cost increases—are important from the perspective of state employees, and are areas in which our employees can help. There are thousands of fine men and women working for the State of Georgia, and cost cutting by itself worries them. They already know that we can't afford pay raises this year, and they are worried that budget cuts may cost them their jobs.

Cost prevention is another matter, however. Employees not only know and can tell us where the fat is, but they will help us eliminate it, because they know that controlling cost increases and improving productivity will make their own jobs more secure.

In my Inaugural Address, I stated that the over-riding goal of my administration will be to prepare Georgia for the 21st century. It is not so much that I expect the act of flipping over a calendar page a decade from now will bring sudden change crashing down upon us, as it is that the new century is a ready symbol for the dramatic changes that increasingly surround us—changes to which we must open our eyes and on which we must act.

Human beings tend to resist change; we are creatures of habit. Bureaucracies are even more so. Last week I met with my department heads and asked them to give you their full cooperation. They and I view you as a valuable resource to help us with this critical task. Together—you as members of the Williams Commission, I as Governor, and the department heads of my administration—together we will make state government into an operation that is clean and lean, and focuses on the efficient delivery of services to the citizens of this state.

# Georgia Council on Economic Education

*May 8, 1991*

A small boy went into one of these fast-food restaurants with his mother to get some lunch. As his mother waited to order, the boy looked back and forth along the waist-high counter that stretched from one wall to the other without any opening. "How do they get out of there, Mom?" he asked. His mother replied, "They go to college, son."

One of the toughest challenges facing Georgia as we move toward the 21st century is to maintain and improve on a climate that attracts new businesses and helps the ones we already have to grow. That used to be pretty straight-forward. We built roads and rail sidings, and we advertised our low-wage workforce to labor-intensive industries. And it worked in the days when cutting-edge technology meant using machines to leverage the physical motion of the body.

Today, however, we have moved beyond leveraging the body with machinery. We now use computers to leverage the mind.

When I was a boy in high school up in the North Georgia mountains, I could look around my classroom and see who I would have to compete against for that first job after graduation. By the time my sons graduated from high school, their competition was kids in other cities and other states. My grandson, who will graduate in the year 2000, will compete for jobs not only with his peers around the nation, but also with those in Germany and Japan.

It was not long ago—a decade or two—that manufacturing jobs started to move around the globe to places where labor was cheap. In 1970, almost 30 percent of Georgia's jobs were in manufacturing plants. Today manufacturing accounts for less than 20 percent of our jobs.

Today capital and jobs flow easily around the world to the best opportunities with little respect for national boundaries, and white collar jobs have also joined in the migration to the world's best business sites. If insurance claim-processing or accounting is more efficient in Dublin, Ireland, than in Dublin, Georgia, a Georgia business can have it done in Ireland. Satellites and optical fibers will shoot the computerized data back and forth across the Atlantic at the speed of light.

States and nations that want to provide adequate jobs and a good life for their people must make themselves attractive in a worldwide context. Building a rail siding was a much easier task by comparison.

Let's look at a case study of what I'm talking about—the textile manufacturing industry. Back when Georgia was building rail sidings and luring labor-intensive industries with low-wage, low-skill workers, textile mills that looked like the movie "Norma Rae" were going great guns. In 1970 when 30 percent of Georgia's workforce was in manufacturing, the textile manufacturing industry had 116,000 jobs.

When kids got to the eighth grade, they dropped out of school and went to work in the mill. It didn't matter that they were only marginally literate. It was their hands and backs that were important, not their minds. Somebody showed them how to operate a particular piece of machinery, and they just kept doing that same job with the same machinery year after year.

Then came the imports. Cheap as labor was in Georgia, it was even cheaper in other parts of the world where both the standard and the cost of living were lower, and the difference in production cost was more than enough to offset the cost of shipping in textile products from overseas.

During the late 70s and early 80s, textile manufacturing was hit hard. Workers were laid off; mills shut down. Observers began to draft that industry's obituary. Then textile manufacturers turned to advanced technology. Out went the old looms and in came the computers.

A computer monitors the dye vats, constantly turning the heat up or down, and adding chemicals at the slightest variance. A computer-controlled robot glides along a long line of spinning frames, finding the completed spools, snipping the yarn and nudging them onto a conveyor belt, then starting new ones. Automated guided vehicles—high-tech lingo for what Star Wars movie fans would call "robots"—carry two-ton bolts of fabric from one mill station to the next. A computer knows exactly where in the warehouse each completed bolt is stored and how much fabric it contains.

With the improved efficiency and productivity of such high-tech operations, textile manufacturers began to compete with the imports in terms of production costs. The improved speed of production, combined with geographic proximity, gave them the edge over imports in responding quickly to changing market demands. Are the "in" colors for sheets and towels changing from teal and plum, to rust and gold? Have Victorian flowers replaced geometric designs? No problem. Georgia's automated mills can change gears quickly and smoothly.

Automation of labor-intensive industries is often accused of eliminating jobs, and it is true that you will find fewer employees in an automated plant than a labor-intensive one. Mill operations once done by a small army of workers now require only periodic checking by a white-shirted engineer. Despite the textile manufacturing industry's recovery from its deathbed, employment levels remain well below peak times in the early 70s. Georgia had just over 106,000 textile manufacturing jobs this March—10,000 fewer than two decades ago.

But the choice is not between a high-tech or a low-tech operation. The choice is a high-tech operation or nothing. Although the jobs may be fewer in number, nevertheless a healthy, high-tech plant running at full speed offers a lot more to its local economy than a low-tech mill that had to shut down because it could not compete.

And who is operating these high-tech wonder-mills? Certainly not the low-skilled workers of the previous era. No, these new mills require engineers and technicians, chemists and industrial managers who understand computer-integrated manufacturing systems. So textile manufacturers are struggling to bring the skills of their workforce up to the demands of their new technology. They are offering scholarships to Georgia Tech and Southern Tech, and snapping up the graduates before the ink is dry on their diplomas.

So, how do you get out from behind that counter of an economy whose traditional focus was on low-skill, low-wage jobs? You go to college, son. Or to a post-secondary technical institute. The level of literacy required by the job market is on the rise. In 1989, the average job required 12.8 years of education. By the year 2000, 13.5 years will be needed—14 years is projected for jobs here in Atlanta.

By contrast, Georgia has more than a million adults, out of a total population of 6 million, who are functionally illiterate. The Atlanta Chamber estimates that the cost of functionally illiterate adults just here in the metro area is $2.6 billion a year in lost productivity, unrealized tax revenues, lowered purchasing power, welfare, crime and the like.

A group of southern U.S. Senators and Representatives created the Sunbelt Institute, which put out a report on literacy in 1988. It concluded that "the South is at risk of creating a permanent pool of under-educated citizens unable to support themselves. Meanwhile, shortages of educated and skilled workers will become an increasing barrier to the competitiveness of southern business and industry. In plain English, this means that unless we improve the level of literacy in our workforce, we will have too many people on welfare and not enough tax dollars to support them.

We cannot afford to leave more than a million Georgia adults languishing in second-class citizenship, as the rest of us head for the 21st century. We need them in our workforce. Population demographics indicate that 85 percent of the job force for the year 2000 is already at work today. But the bulk of the technology we will be using in the year 2000 either is not yet available commercially or has yet to be invented.

It is critical that we educate not only the next generation coming along, but the workers who are already on the job. And by making education important to the workers we already have, we will at the same time make education important to their children. That is why I introduced a business tax credit for employee literacy programs in this year's General Assembly. And I am pleased to report that its passage made Georgia the first state in the nation to offer such a credit.

We once measured our wealth in gold, silver, precious stones, and land. Increasingly, however, wealth is to be measured in education and information. We can compete on the world market. We can sustain and improve our level of prosperity as we head into the 21st century. We can do it, *if* we have a literate and educated workforce. That is the biggest challenge facing us in the decade ahead.

# Southern Democratic Caucus

*Raleigh, June 22, 1991*

I'd like to speak to you tonight—honestly and urgently—about the present condition of our party, about why we have lost so often in presidential elections, and about the dangers and opportunities of 1992.

Let me begin by stating my blunt belief: The national Democratic problem now threatens to become state and local Democratic defeat, because, for too many Democratic candidates, we are losing younger voters, and with them our future. We are seeing Southern Democrats vote for Republicans in increasing numbers. We are seeing Democratic governors and senators—good and effective leaders, in touch with their people—in electoral trouble simply because of the party label they carry.

We can no longer console ourselves that while we lose the White House again and again and again, well at least we keep the statehouse and the courthouse. If we do not change in fundamental ways, the risk is—no, not the risk, the reality is—that our party will lose cities and states and seats that we have held for generations.

And no, we cannot just wait until 1996, because by then the South may be gone and with it any realistic chance for a presidential victory. We cannot cling to the unworthy hope that a worsening recession will drive the President out of office—that the working people will suffer enough to vote for us out of sheer desperation.

Nor can we delude ourselves that the problem is not us, but the process; that the problem is that we don't have enough computers or phone banks or targeting; or that changing the dates of the primaries or reshuffling the deck will somehow bring about a new deal. What our presidential nominee says is and always will be more important than what our telemarketing says.

We can no longer escape the facts. If we ignore them, the facts will become our fate and the Democratic Party will have no future.

So, what can we do?

I believe the answer is not to abandon our central principles, but to revive them; to return to the Democratic Party's defining purpose. You see, for too many presidential elections, we have had things backwards. We have chosen to fight on social issues rather than to run on the economic issues that shape the daily lives of American families.

When the average American family stays up late into the night, they are not worrying about whether school prayer should be voluntary or mandatory. They are worrying about how to balance the checkbook or where they will find the money for junior's college tuition.

Our party grew up around the economic issues that concern working Americans most deeply, and that is the common bond that unites us. But instead of rallying around those basic, unifying economic issues, we have allowed ourselves to be distracted by social issues that not only divide us but also defeat us. And because we failed to give people good reasons to vote for our nominee, the opposition was able to give them bad reasons to vote against him.

Dukakis and Mondale suffered similar fates, because, in the end, they conducted similar campaigns. Why weren't they focusing on the sky-rocketing cost of health care and demanding change? Why weren't they questioning a tax system that favors the rich at the expense of the average American? Why weren't they focusing on the loss of jobs to unfair foreign trade and demanding reciprocity?

Incredibly, our national party has replaced the cornerstone of our strength—economic populism—with out Achilles heel—social liberalism.

We also have a series of very active special interest groups, organized around liberal causes, that have imposed a filter through which only the purest of the politically pure can pass. To some, it is not enough to be pro-choice; it is demanded that the candidates favor taxpayer funding, even for abortion on demand. To others, it is not enough to endorse government support for the arts; it is demanded that candidates oppose any restrictions on the uses of arts funding, even if they are obscene. To still others, it is not enough to stand up for education; it is also demanded that candidates stand against every innovative idea that in any way infringes on the status quo—from teacher testing to merit pay.

Don't get me wrong. I believe in a lot of the social issues which so many want our party to profess. But I also believe they cannot be the centerpiece of our presidential campaigns. And to the extent that they are, we will not only continue to lose elections; ironically, we will also lose the very social goals that these Democratic elites regard as so important.

As a candidate for Governor of Georgia, I was open about where I stood on social issues. I said I was for sex education, and now we are implementing it. I endorsed a hate crimes bill, and I have said that I would sign legislation repealing Georgia's anti-sodomy law. I am completely committed to a woman's right to choose, and I have never equivocated in my support of the E.R.A. I believe Georgia has the strongest arts council in the South—and as long as I am Governor, that will continue to be the case.

But, you see, those issues were not the sole message of my campaign. Most of all, I stood for economic empowerment—for education, for efficiency, and, instead of higher taxes, for a lottery. You see, I did not become a Democrat to be a social liberal while ignoring fundamental economic choices.

We have to appeal again to working families and the middle class. We have to advance an economic agenda again. We have to define it. We have to run on it. Because, my friends, that is the only way we will ever win.

And by economic issues, I do not mean just marginal criticism of the other side's competence—or just marginal differences with the other side's priorities. I mean a major commitment to address larger questions, like a tax code that robs from the middle class and enriches the upper class; a trade policy that robs our workers while letting our corporations export jobs instead of exporting products; a silly education policy that threatens to take student aid away from anyone whose family earns over $10,000 a year, so that the best schools in America will be open only to the poorest of the poor and the wealthy.

On all these things, we have to fight—and we also have to offer an alternative. We have to fight for a health care policy that cuts costs, not coverage, a health care policy that does something about the undeniable unfairness of America's medical system. You know, today if you're homeless, you can get at least a minimum of care. And if you're rich, you can go to the best private hospital. But if you're middle class, and you or someone in your family gets very sick, you can go very broke.

So next year, I don't care how long the Democratic Party platform is. I just care that it speaks to economic choices—that it speaks to real people and not to a narrow elite.

You see, I don't want our platform to be politically correct as much as I want it to politically connect with working Americans. And to any of my fellow Democrats who may be distressed to hear me say all this, let me reply—that for us and for all our ideals, nothing would be more distressing than losing again in 1992.

Let me suggest that unless we talk about education and jobs, trade and economic development, we won't be able to fill positions on the Supreme Court—because we won't win.

Unless we address the increasing tax burden of the middle class, we won't be able to stop the Republican effort to exploit racial divisions—because we won't win. Unless we deal with what is the first drop in middle class home ownership in 30 years, we won't be able to help the homeless—because we won't win.

Unless we can build a Democratic economic case, we will never be able to rebuild a Democratic electoral majority. And unless we do that, our social policy will become mere social posturing. We will not have the power to pass the Equal Rights Amendment, we will not have the power to protect civil liberties or to end discrimination, and, most of all, we will not have the power to protect the people who do the work, pay the taxes, raise the children, fight the wars and build the nation, the people who work hard every day and still come up a little short at the end of the month, the people who are the heart and soul of the Democratic Party.

But this is not just important to our party. It is also vital to our country. For under the Republicans, our standard of living has slipped to ninth in the world and is still dropping. Our students are last in the industrial nations in math and science—not because they are not good enough, but because the people who are running America today don't care enough. If the Democratic Party doesn't fight to change these things, then no one will.

It's time for the Democratic Party to say again to the working men and women of this country: We will fight your fight, we will ease your burden, we will carry your cause. We will raise Cain, raise Cain against a status quo that far too many Democrats are far too comfortable with, a status quo that is paradoxically sending working people to the poorhouse and to the Republican Party at the same time.

We must stand for a strong America. Not only in force of arms—although we must never be too timid to do that—but also strong in economic might. We must recognize the obvious: that even as the ticker-tape from our military victory was falling from the sky, so was our position falling as the strongest nation on earth. In the economic wars that will determine who leads the world in the next century, Japan and Europe are kicking our butts. It's time that we Democrats kicked back. We should tell the Japanese to let Louisiana farmers sell their rice in Osaka and Tokyo; and we should tell the Europeans to accept beef from Kansas and Texas.

Americans fought for their freedom; we spilled our blood for their liberty; the least they can do is give us a level playing field in return. The administration that brags about the "Smart Bombs" has the dumbest trade policy the world has ever seen.

We must ask why CEO's make 90 times what their shopworkers can earn; why big executives have golden parachutes while working people have no health insurance; why a family that makes $10,000 a year is too rich to get a college grant, but a corporate raider that makes $10 million a year is so poor that he needs a capital gains tax cut.

We must ask why George Bush rushes to bail out S&L bandits, but turns a blind eye to honest, decent family farmers who've lost their land to predatory banks. Why he moves heaven and earth, and rightly so, to oppose aggression, but won't lift a finger to stop a recession.

These issues are the bottom line for the pocket book of working Americans, and they are the issues that made us the party of the middle class. From Franklin Roosevelt on, the economic issue was the engine that pulled the Democratic train up the hill. Social issues were the caboose.

In recent presidential elections, we have too often attempted to turn the caboose into the engine. It is no wonder that the train keeps sliding down the hill.

We have a proud history that is powerfully relevant to a changing nation in a changing world. Working men and women look to us for leadership, but too often we seem to look away. Too often, we seem enthralled with other voices, and there is no one to speak for the middle class.

We must become that voice—for that is the best reason I can think of for being a Democrat. We must make the Democratic Party true again to its overriding economic purposes—so that we can be relevant again, alive again, proud again and yes, victorious again—for ourselves, and for our country.

# National Conference of Lieutenant Governors

*August 7, 1991*

I am happy to be back among the Lieutenant Governors of this nation. I was one of you for 16 years—not long enough to set the record, but long enough to be invited back, and I thank you.

Although each of your jobs differs to a degree, you all have one thing in common: Your concern for the good health of your constituents, and especially the good health of the Chief Executive of your state.

In case you don't know how a Lt. Governor shakes hands with his Governor, let an old-timer show you how to do it. Each day, greet your Governor with hand outstretched and a smile on your face. As you shake hands, extend two fingers up under his sleeve until you can feel his pulse. That's the way a Lt. Governor shakes hands with his Governor.

My Governors always had a strong pulse. They were healthy as horses. So I stayed Lieutenant Governor through four terms. But that period was only half of my political career. I've been in an elective office now in five different decades.

Before and during much of that time, I was a history professor at four of Georgia's colleges and universities. So I've taught history and I've lived history, and now in the autumn of my career let me tell you a little of what that combination of teacher and realistic practitioner has taught me. Let me begin with a little history lesson.

All of you know that in the summer of 1787, a group of political leaders met in Philadelphia's Independence Hall. They were a diverse group—just as diverse in their time as this nation's Governors and Lieutenant Governors are today.

They represented 13 independent colonies—not only newly independent of England, but also independent of each other. Many thought they had gathered simply to rewrite the Articles of Confederation. The idea that they might actually join together in one nation under one central government was a radical shock to many, sprung on them by the leadership after they arrived.

Debate raged throughout the summer. Some threw up their hands and left before it was over. Others hung around to see the final document, but then refused to sign it. In the end, it contained only 39 signatures of more than 100 original delegates. But over the past 200 years, the Constitution of the United States has proved to be one of the most remarkable political documents the world has ever seen.

Its precepts have proven so fundamental, so very true, that it has continued to be viable with only 22 changes through a Civil War, two World Wars, presidential assassinations and even one presidential resignation—viable through the growth of 13 little, isolated states into a 50-state, highly industrialized world power.

You see, what is so remarkable about the Constitution is not that it espouses a particular political ideology, but that it crafts a delicate balance among several ideologies that on the surface seem incompatible. Somehow, in the midst of the uproar and disgruntlement that surrounded its birth, its framers came to the realization that democracy is a healthy tension among several things—some of which today we would label liberal, and others of which we would call conservative.

The central balance in the Constitution reflects the central struggle of the convention: The 13 colonies wanted to maintain their independence on the one hand, while on the other hand they wanted to gain the benefits of community. The compromise they finally reached on this issue permeates the entire document, and our nation has grown up around this delicate balance.

As a people, we have a split personality—glorifying individual freedom while at the same time demanding allegiance to community. And it has worked. It has worked because it is practical and realistic. It recognizes that our daily lives are a constant collision of various forces and beliefs that have to be reconciled. As we in politics know all too well, pure ideologies exist only in the abstract.

In real life, most Americans are in the middle, and they mix both conservative and liberal ideologies in their practical political beliefs. On the liberal side, we Americans believe in helping those who have fallen on hard times, in fostering equal opportunity and equal rights, in providing broad access to housing, education and health care.

But we also believe that traditional families do the best job of raising children, that hard work and self-reliance should be encouraged and rewarded, that destructive behavior should be punished, and that institutions do a better job when they are small and close to home rather than large and run from afar. These ideas are a page from conservative ideology.

We believe in balancing welfare with personal initiative, in balancing rights against obligations. We don't like either permissiveness or selfishness in their extremes. We are a nation of moderates. The political institutions and processes set up by that same Constitution are full of checks and balances that aim for a moderate, middle-ground result.

But the past 30 years of American politics have left middle Americans disillusioned and disengaged. They are skeptical. When political debates are aired, they change the channel. When the polls open, they do not bother to vote. The reason is that instead of using the political process as intended, to move toward the middle in reconciling the issues, American politicians, forced by vocal and well-financed special interests, have moved outward toward the edges and become entrenched in ideological extremes.

Take abortion, for example. Many would have us believe it is a hard, yes/no question, and for the individual woman it is—there is no such thing as being halfway pregnant. But taken as a question of public policy, our split personality exerts itself. Our commitment to individual liberty balks at the idea of government stepping in to make such a private decision. But our shared moral values cry out against large numbers of abortions and their use as a means of birth control.

As a result, middle Americans long ago compromised on the middle ground. They support some government restrictions such as parental permission for minors, while preferring to leave the actual, bottom-line decision to the individual. But many politicians ignore the middle-ground compromise on which the majority of Americans have already settled. They continue to argue the issue over and over in its extremes.

Or take the issue of women. In their everyday lives, most Americans are both feminists and traditionalists—simultaneously. They recognize that a family of father, mother, and children under one roof is the best way to raise children, and they worry about what is happening to our children with so many one-parent families and two-career families. At the same time, however, they know that many women are finding fulfillment in their careers. Even more basic: Working mothers are an economic necessity. They are needed in our workforce, and they provide critical income to their families. Fully half of America's two-career families would slip below the poverty level if the mother quit her job and stayed home.

Or, look at economic issues. Hard-line conservatives want a free market with no government intervention. Hard-line liberals expect government to force the market to behave in a fashion that offsets injustice and demands compassion. Well, middle America sees the former as benefitting the rich and the latter as benefitting the poor. And either way, they see nothing in it for themselves.

Middle America is tired of liberal-conservative confrontations that prolong, seemingly forever, fruitless arguments between two extremes, both of which have their points, but neither of which is acceptable in its entirety. One way middle America has tried to regain an ideological balance at the polls is by electing a Republican President and a Democratic Congress... but the stalemate remains.

And I'm here to tell you that middle Americans are sick and tired of it. Liberal extremists have spit on their values. Conservative extremists have given lip-service to their work ethic, but then glorified those who grabbed instant wealth in questionable ways.

Middle America is ready to move on. And what does middle America want?

Middle Americans want to do the best for their children, but they also need two incomes to maintain their standard of living. They want help in reconciling their jobs with their family responsibilities.

Middle Americans are willing to pay their fair share of taxes, but they are worried about maintaining their standard of living in the face of an uncertain economy and sky-rocketing costs in areas like health care and college tuition.

Middle Americans want a balance between welfare and self-reliance. They want a little encouragement in pulling themselves up by their own bootstraps. They want a few incentives to invest in themselves. And they want their own hard work recognized in the form of tax structures that treat them equitably with the rich . . . and health care benefits that treat them equitably with the poor.

They do not want government to do everything for—or to—them, as die-hard liberals suppose. Nor do they want significantly less government, as die-hard conservatives believe. What they want is simply for government to work. For them.

Middle Americans look at the new world order and see the dangerously shifting sands of the Middle East, the changing face of the Soviet Union and Eastern Europe, the growing economic superiority of Japan. They worry that the world's number one nation is doomed to become a waning and diminishing power in this reconfigured world, and they want an economic policy that addresses the fact that we now live in a global economy in which our standard of living is inextricably linked with that of other countries.

The bottom line, as far as middle Americans are concerned, is that this country is in desperate need of a new approach to politics by both parties. We must recapture a political process that preserves the delicate balances upon which democracy rests, rather than fixating, then stagnating on opposite, 180-degree, polar ideological extremes. Both parties must make politics a process that moves us forward by resolving the problems, rather than continuing endlessly, ad nauseam, to rehash them. We must use the political process to help us find the practical, day-to-day, middle ground on the substantive issues we face, rather than to fight over the trivialized issues that middle America left behind long ago.

Middle Americans want political parties that look ahead and move forward on the important issues we all agree must be addressed—issues like maintaining our standard of living, reducing the pressure on the middle class, restoring hope for the poor, defining our role in a new world.

That process also demands political leaders who will spend their time solving the problems that matter, instead of spending millions of dollars on personal attacks in an effort to recast each other into the same old irrelevant, extremist liberal or conservative molds.

If you, as political leaders from around this nation, can help to restore the political process to its best tradition, then another vision of the framers of our Constitution will also come true. Middle Americans will once again consider those of us engaged in politics to be in an honorable and respected calling. And for themselves, their active participation can then become an expression of enlightened self-interest to be treasured, rather than an irrelevancy to be either endured or completely avoided.

# Special Session to Cut the Budget

*Televised Address*
*August 18, 1991*

Tomorrow morning the Georgia General Assembly will convene in a special session I have called to cut the state budget. It is a task none of us wanted, but which none of us can escape. And I appreciate this opportunity to talk with you about why we need to act—and how we propose to get the job done.

But even before the General Assembly convenes tomorrow, one very important decision has already been made. We are coming together to make cuts, not to raise taxes. From the first day of this administration, I have said I would not use the recession as an excuse to raise your taxes. That decision has surprised some. They note—accurately—that I am a progressive Governor with a long agenda for action: better schools, safer streets, a cleaner environment.

But the working people of this state—the very people I pledged to help—are already facing enough economic pain. I cannot do enough to relieve that pain, but I certainly am not going to add to it.

I consider the members of the General Assembly to be partners in this process. I have consulted closely with the Speaker of the House, the Lieutenant Governor, and other legislative leaders in preparing these budget revisions, and I thank them for their efforts and their cooperation.

You, the people of Georgia, are also partners in this process. None of us should ever forget that budgets are not just written on paper, but in people's lives.

The entire country is in a prolonged recession that has caused state tax revenues to drop sharply all across the United States. Many economists did not recognize the recession's true depth and length, and many states based their budgets on economic projections that were more optimistic than has proven to be the case. As the recession has dragged on, the number eligible for federally mandated welfare and Medicaid has steadily risen, placing a further demand on state resources.

We at the state level are now feeling the severe effects of the federal government's decision over the past decade to deal with its own deficit by shifting increased costs onto the shoulders of the states. In Georgia, federal Medicaid mandates now take ten percent of our total state budget.

As if that were not enough, the state also carries another heavy burden for which the fault rests not in Washington but in Atlanta. For too long, state government used—and misused—the strong revenue growth of the heady 1980s to bloat the state payroll.

The number of state jobs increased by 21,000 in just the past five years. Put another way, that means more than one in five state employees holds a job that did not exist five years ago.

The year before I became Governor, with a hiring freeze supposedly in effect for much of the time, the state payroll still grew by 4,000 employees. The number of state employees has grown more than twice as fast as Georgia's population in the past five years, and in so doing, it has outgrown the taxpayers' ability to support it.

This growth in government has to stop—and it will. Some of it has to be rolled back—and it will be.

The decisions won't all be politically popular. None of them will be easy—and many of them will hurt. But we have to do what's right. We have to streamline, reorganize and downsize Georgia's government now. And we have to strengthen Georgia's economy for the future.

We do begin in a better place than most of the other 35 or so states that are in the midst of a budget shortfall. Our next-door neighbor, North Carolina, which has a budget about our size, had a $1.2 billion shortfall—a deficit more than double the size of ours.

Our six percent deficit may be less, but we take it no less seriously. Georgia may be in better shape than other states, but it will not stay that way if we do not take decisive action. In planning that action, one priority has been uppermost in my mind.

Seven months ago, when I became Governor, I talked about those to whom I wanted to dedicate this administration: the family farmer who plants his own crops and bales his own hay; the small businesswoman who stays open late and calls her customers by their first names; the senior citizen who opens her utility bill with trembling hands, afraid that enjoying heat will mean enduring hunger.

I dedicated this administration to the young family, struggling to pay for day care and save for college at the same time. I dedicated it to every household that works and saves and sometimes comes up a little short at the end of the month.

And I mean to keep my word to all of them—to all of you.

I have stayed up late many an evening, just as you have, worrying over how to make ends meet in our state, searching for ways to scrimp and save so that we can balance the state's checkbook, just as you have to balance your own. The budget I deal with is bigger, but so is the gap between what we spend and what we can afford.

Tomorrow morning, in the halls of the State Capitol, you, the taxpaying citizens of Georgia, will have no paid lobbyist to button-hole legislators on your behalf. But you are the heart and soul of Georgia. You, not government, are what makes this state great.

The Chinese character that stands for the word crisis is a combination of two symbols. One means danger. The other, opportunity. And beyond the obvious dangers of the moment, there are great opportunities.

Georgia is entering a time of profound change, and I want my administration as Governor to be a catalyst in anticipating that change and meeting it with foresight and imagination.

I got into government because I've always believed that government can be an agent of change to accomplish positive good for the benefit of the public. But that doesn't mean we have to have big government. The issue is not whether we have more government or less government. We need wise government that provides fundamental services to its citizens in the most efficient way possible and not in an indifferent, wasteful fashion.

I look at our current situation as an opportunity to improve state government, to make it leaner and more efficient. We must set a new course for Georgia. We should be asking not only how much we spend, but also how sound are the purposes we are spending it for. This is a time to reduce the budget... and to rethink it.

Georgia saw unprecedented growth in state revenues during the 1980s. And state government ate the whole thing. It was a time, as Merle Haggard sang, of "drinking that free bubble-up and eating that rainbow stew."

Now we are faced with a crash diet. But we are going to do more than shed just enough excess government to get us through the present fiscal year. Instead, we are going to go on a serious, long-term diet that will change the habits and patterns of government on a permanent basis. We are going to embark on a ongoing program of fiscal fitness.

We are going to set the stage for a healthier, more stable economy, and pave the way for economic recovery and growth. State revenues will improve, not because we have raised taxes to get us through, but because we are taking strong medicine, swallowing hard when times are tough.

There is an easy way to cut a budget, and a hard way. A right way, and a wrong way. And keeping the same old spending patterns but just at a lower level is the easy, and the wrong way. I do not want to make just simple percentage cuts in the broad categories that appear in the state budget document.

My Commission on Effectiveness and Economy in Government has spend six months looking closely at every agency in state government, scrutinizing the operations within departments. I have placed a high priority on reorganizing and streamlining administration. More than half of the positions that have been cut are administrative.

For instance, improvements in office technology over the past decade have streamlined paper pushing tremendously. Yet we have continued to fund administration as if we were still taking shorthand on note pads and typing letters with carbon paper on manual typewriters. The positions have been continued routinely, year after year, simply because they were there.

We can dismantle the auditing unit in the Public Service Commission that reviewed construction costs for Plants Vogtle, Scherer and Hatch, because its mission has been completed.

We do not need an office to review architectural plans and oversee construction of prisons in the Department of Corrections, because the Georgia State Financing and Investment Commission is doing the very same thing in the process of managing the bond financing for those facilities.

Clearly jobs we do not need are jobs we cannot afford.

I've also made deep cuts in luxuries we cannot afford, like personal cars for employees—I have cut 235. Workers in private enterprise do not have these perks. Why should state government employees have them at taxpayers' expense?

We are also going to sell two of the eight state aircraft and cut back on pilots. We will restrict travel, and we will save an additional half-million dollars on necessary travel by using point-to-point contracts with several airlines.

We have to cut some things so we can keep the others that Georgia must have to grow and improve and more forward. Plainly, education is at the top of the list. Georgia's future well-being depends on a skilled and literate workforce.

We live in a global economy. Money and jobs flow easily across national boundaries, and our workforce must compete not only with Alabama and North Carolina, but with Germany and Japan. Short-changing education today mortgages our economy tomorrow.

In reworking the budget, I have insisted on preserving as much as possible the funds we send to the classrooms of this state. We will not cut teacher salaries, and my recommendations cut the Quality Basic Education formula by about two percent in non-instructional areas. In this revised budget, a higher percentage goes into funding kindergarten through twelfth grade, than in the original budget passed last session.

But I am equally insistent that we will not be content with the same old ways of doing business in the education bureaucracy. Excess layers of middle management will be reduced.

We are going to become clearer about the outcomes we want from our education programs and more rigorous about measuring and evaluating the results. But at the same time, we must and will give local educators more flexibility to find the best way to do the job, and will encourage innovation and creativity by rewarding excellence.

Our University System, too, deserves nothing less than a new commitment to excellence. I am proud of the level of distinction it has achieved, and I am making every effort to guard the quality of our college classrooms by giving the Board of Regents great flexibility in targeting cuts toward non-essential areas.

But in other places in the University System, bureaucracy is at its worst and the winds of efficiency need to blow. For example, my budget reorganizes the Cooperative Extension Service, returning it to its original mission of serving farmers and streamlining it to fulfill that mission with a new level of efficiency.

Another critical area is our prison system. I am proposing some deep cuts in the Department of Corrections, but they are targeted at reorganizing management. The positions that will be eliminated are deputy commissioners, assistant commissioners, deputy assistant commissioners and assistant executive deputy commissioners.

Let me reassure you right now that we are not going to close the budget gap by putting criminals back on the streets. And we are not going to increase the backlog of state prisoners waiting in local jails to move into the state system.

We are going to proceed in an orderly fashion with construction, and by next summer we will be ready with six new boot camps and five new prisons. That means we will be able to end the early release of prisoners on schedule next summer.

We will put new technology into place to secure the walls around 13 prison compounds, reducing the need for tower guards. And we will use those 175 displaced tower guards to help staff other prisons. We are going to make wider use of inmate labor in places where we have other state institutions nearby. In the Miller Administration, every able-bodied inmate who can work is going to work. We will cut operating costs at Central State Hospital, for example, by using inmate labor to do the laundry.

And, speaking of mental health hospitals, let me reassure you that we are not closing any state health institutions.

The thrust of the budget cuts in the huge Department of Human Resources is to reorganize administration for efficiency, while preserving direct services. For example, we are saving millions of dollars by reorganizing and consolidating office functions on Capitol Hill and in the county offices, while at the same time preserving $9.3 million for a new program for handicapped infants, toddlers, and preschoolers.

It is clearly time to reorganize and eliminate projects that are not cost-effective, not generating results or whose time is past. But I am also mindful of the human costs of change. Eight hundred of the 3,000 jobs we have eliminated are vacant as a result of the hiring freeze I put into effect. But there are still nearly 2,200 state employees whose jobs will be ended. Some of them work in my office.

I know it is a difficult time to be looking for a new job, and I am going to be working closely with our State Merit System and Department of Labor to provide as much assistance as we can to the state employees who are displaced by these cuts. They are victims of a state government that too long failed to cast a critical eye at its own operations.

I am confident that state government will be stronger and that as the economy improves, we will be poised to take advantage of it.

This is a great state with a great people, and you deserve a state government that spends your tax money wisely.

It may well be that my destiny in the ongoing history of this great state is to grapple with a difficult time, and so to set the stage for another Governor to live and lead in a future time of economic growth that comes as the fruit of our present sacrifice and labor. So be it.

I hope and believe that in the years that follow, when our children inherit this great state and this responsibility, they will look back and say that our day was not a period of retrenchment and back-pedaling, but that it was the beginning of a new era in Georgia.

Let it be said that in a moment of testing and trial, we gave new meaning to the ideal that government exists to serve the people, and not just to tax them; that it exists to achieve purposes, and not simply to perpetuate itself.

Thank you. God bless you. And good night.

# Georgia Chamber of Commerce
# Prelegislative Forum

*November 14, 1991*

In another month, my first year as Governor will be over. To use a phrase that Thomas Jefferson used to describe the Presidency, it has been "splendid misery."

I've done what I thought was necessary. I've used the time to prune carefully before I would even allow myself to think of any kind of revenue enhancement, understanding that during a recession is the worst possible time to put a new burden on the taxpayer.

So I cut, then cut some more and then cut some more. We cut chefs at the Mansion, personal cars, and assistant executive deputy commissioners. We scrutinized the internal operations of state government in detail, evaluating and putting cost control measures into place, going back to point zero.

I did not take a meat axe to the budget. I took a scalpel. In the budget document I presented to the legislature, and which they passed, there were over 200 individual items to eliminate, abolish, discontinue, or cease. Over 200 more items began with the word reduce. More than a dozen called for us to reorganize, convert or combine.

Sound management is important, and the state did need to get its house in order. But that is only half of the job. In Proverbs it says "Where there is no vision, the people perish." History is full of examples of people who acted with foresight to prepare for the future rather than simply reacting to the immediate circumstances.

When Jerusalem was overrun by Babylon, it seemed like the end of civilization. The prophet Jeremiah was thrown into prison. But Jeremiah bought land from prison, because he knew that the problem with Babylon would run its course, and he needed to get ready for the future.

At one time during the Civil War, Abraham Lincoln could look out of his window in Washington and see the Confederate troops and flags in the distance. Everyone was in a panic. Yet Lincoln ordered construction on the Capitol to continue, because he knew this great country would move beyond the difficulties of those days to peace and progress.

Here in Georgia, we have to adjust for the declining revenues of the moment. This year's budget has got to balance. But we cannot lose sight of where we need to go and what we need to do to prepare for the future. At the same time we are in the short-term prison of this recession, we need to be buying land for the future. At the same time we are embattled by slow revenue growth, we need to be continuing to build.

We have a critical choice to make: We can either fritter away the small amount of new revenue we will have next year by spreading it across the breadth of state government and not making much of an impact anywhere. Or, keep our belt tightened in most places, while we target our limited resources specifically at some critical needs, essential to prepare for future growth, like education and infrastructure.

Most experts believe that the southeastern states may once again outpace the nation in economic growth. They all agree that potential is there, but only, *only* if a state makes two things happen: First, bridge some of the gap between prosperous metropolitan areas and the small, rural towns, many of them desperately poor, that have been left behind. Each time a recession hits, that part of our state's economy is slower to recover and comes back to a lower level than before. Second, upgrade our education programs to insure that the workforce has the skills employers will be looking for.

There are unmet needs in this state, unmet needs that absolutely must be addressed if we are to regain economic strength, if we are to realize our potential for growth. A key is transportation. A network of highways is as important to economic growth as a network of veins and arteries is to a human body.

But the most critical long-term need Georgia faces is an educated workforce. Our traditional, low skill, low wage, labor intensive industries are either undergoing major technological conversion, requiring skilled and literate workers, or they are dying off. In the coming years, we will either move ahead to become a high skill, high wage economy, or we will be left behind in a low skill, low wage economy. That is our choice.

It is not enough for our kids to be educated to the level of their parents. It is no longer possible to drop out in the eighth grade and spend the rest of your life working in a textile mill. The textile mills that have survived are full of computers, robots and engineers.

We live in a global economy where money and jobs flow easily across national boundaries. Our kids must be able to compete not only with kids in Tallahassee and Tennessee, but also with the kids in Tokyo and Taiwan.

Increasingly, education brainpower—along with the roads, airports, computers and fiber optic cables that connect it up—determines a region's standard of living. And education is the first and primary place where I propose to target our limited resources.

As society has changed, the demands we place on our teachers have grown, but their compensation has not. Our teachers are dramatically underpaid compared to other professions that require a college education. Starting salaries for a bachelor's degree in engineering are equal to what the state salary schedule pays for 15 years of experience and a master's degree. Over the past few years, our teacher salaries have slipped out of first place in the Southeast and slid down in the national rankings.

The story is similar for faculty in our University System. Their salaries dropped from first in the southeast in 1982 to sixth for last school year.

If we want to recruit good teachers at all levels, our salaries must be more competitive. Even though revenues are tight for Fiscal Year 1993, it is critical that we scrape together enough money for a 3 percent cost-of-living increase. That is not unreasonable if the economy comes back to any degree at all. And as revenues improve over the remainder of my administration, we are going to do even more.

We must also address the problem of space at our colleges and universities. Enrollment increased by 45 percent during the 80s, and our future prosperity depends on even more of our kids going to college. Yet we have been funding construction at a rate of only 1.3 percent of replacement for the existing facilities, which does not even begin to address increased enrollment.

The national recession presents us with a very favorable bond market, and our current level of bonded indebtedness is only half of our constitutional capacity. With a small investment of $14 million in debt service, we can launch 15 major construction projects in the University System—projects that the Board of Regents have had on the critical list for years.

Third, we need to move ahead with our efforts to provide rigorous sentencing alternatives in the form of boot camps, and to end the early release of inmates from our prisons. We have several prisons and boot camps under construction that will be completed during the course of Fiscal Year 1993. I am committed to opening them, so that violent criminals who need to be in prison stay there.

To meet these demands we will continue to strive for efficiency in state government. My Commission on Effectiveness and Efficiency in Government is looking closely our user fees.

Many of them have not been increased in Georgia in decades, while in other neighboring states they have. We can no longer afford to offer them at a loss.

For example, we lose $1.5million a year on vital records like birth certificates that are issued by the Department of Human Resources. If we make these routine state-provided services pay for themselves, substantial amounts of money will be freed up to meet my goals in education, economic development, law enforcement, and other areas.

In addition, I will recommend an impact fee used by other states such as Florida for out-of-state motor vehicle transfers. In-migration brings more than 125,000 vehicles to Georgia each year. They use our highways, they pollute our air, they affect our daily lives. A $200 impact fee—it's $300 in Florida—will generate $25 million or more, without affecting any present Georgia citizen.

I will also propose a change in our sales tax vendor's compensation. Presently, businesses keep three percent of the sales tax they collect to cover processing costs, no matter what their volume of business. It is one of the very highest rates in the nation. That rate was set long before computers, which have made processing much easier, especially for larger businesses. Why continue to pay huge sums to large businesses when modern technology now holds down the processing cost?

Many states offer no vendor's compensation at all, including our neighbor, North Carolina. However, I do not want to take vendor's compensation away from small retail businesses when times are hard. The remaining states either use lower rates than ours or cap the maximum amount of vendor's compensation. Mississippi has a $600 cap. I propose capping Georgia's at $4,000.

Small retailers would continue to receive the same level of compensation. Businesses with over $3 million in annual sales would get $4,000 for their processing trouble, but no more. This would bring an additional $50 million into the state treasury, while not affecting the compensation level for 9 out of 10 businesses. And local governments, many of which are also struggling with revenues, would receive a $10 million windfall from the vendor's compensation for processing the local option sales tax.

By updating our users fees, scaling back our vendor's compensation, and adding an impact fee on incoming motor vehicles, we can generate a modest amount of revenue that will enable us to make some progress in these specific areas, despite the tough times we are in.

# 1992

# Supplemental Budget Address

*January 7, 1992*

In a few days, I will have completed my first year as Governor. To use a phrase that Thomas Jefferson used to describe the Presidency, it has been "splendid misery." The splendid part of an otherwise difficult year was the unprecedented level of cooperation between the executive and legislative branches. As strongly as I know how I want to thank you for that, and I want you to know that I enter this 1992 session with the same resolve to work together with you that has characterized my administration thus far. Working with you has been the splendid part.

On the "misery" side of things, we've done what we thought was necessary. And the total impact of our reductions, conversions, eliminations, and reorganizations was to reduce state spending in a way the likes of which had never before been seen in this state.

Last August, most all the economists, including our own Dr. Thomassen, projected flat revenue growth during the first half of Fiscal Year 1992, with modest growth during the second half of the year. Well now, the first part of that projection has proved true. So far, revenues for FY 92 are running 1.3 percent behind last year. The forecast for modest growth in the latter half of FY 92 still holds, as you'll be hearing from the good doctor, but I am ever mindful that we have no reserves should it not materialize, and we must be very, very careful.

Therefore, we're going to whittle on this old budget a little bit more. I will reduce my revenue estimate for FY 92 by another $50 million to $7,465 million, which would require revenue growth of 2.8 percent. This move will give us a hedge should revenues not increase as expected during the latter half of the year. And if modest growth is realized, then we can begin the critical process of rebuilding the state's reserves.

Let me emphasize that this $50 million reduction will be achieved without laying off any state employees or reducing any program. It will be offset largely through several revenue sources. First, the benefit of the spending controls put on the departments last fiscal year can now be seen. Careful management has resulted in a lapse of $33 million, which is much, much larger than normal. Another $6.6 million is coming into the treasury from the Georgia Environmental Facilities Authority and the Georgia Building Authority (Penal). And we have over $19 million in surplus debt service appropriations which are available.

Last August we canceled several bonded projects after the bonds had been sold. We repurchased bonds with the revenues from the sale, freeing up debt service funds. And interest rates dropped between August and October when we took our bonds to market, enabling us to save several million dollars in debt service payments.

Finally, those hundreds of downsizing and reorganizing items you enacted in August have already resulted in savings that exceed our projections by $6.65 million. I want to take this opportunity to commend our department heads for their cooperation and their swift and timely action in responding to those budget revisions.

These various fund sources enable us to reduce the size of the budget. At the same time, we will be able to increase funding for several existing programs where the growth in the number of eligible recipients must be addressed.

First, of course, is our mid-year obligation to adjust the Quality Basic Education formula for increased school enrollments. And now that our new program for handicapped preschoolers is underway, we need an increase to accommodate the actual number of children it serves. Our AFDC rolls are also growing and that must be dealt with.

The Indigent Care Trust Fund has grown, with more hospitals voluntarily contributing a total of $95.6 million. These funds will draw down more than $154 million in federal Medicaid funds for a total impact of $250 million. Although new federal Medicaid regulations will end this trust fund next October, I want to thank Medical Assistance Commissioner Russ Toal for his efforts in fighting for the fund and stretching out its life. That's really helped.

Public safety is an area that cannot be short-changed. I recommend that we restore the August cut in state trooper positions and authorize the Public Safety Department to use existing funds to begin a new trooper school before the fiscal year ends. I recommend that the Department of Corrections use existing funds to proceed with opening three new prisons in Hancock, Telfair and Washington Counties.

I am also proposing another $50 million in bonds for local water, sewer, and wastewater treatment programs, to help our cities and counties take advantage of a very favorable bond market.

This supplemental budget is lean and it's fiscally responsible. Its goal is to give our economy the remainder of this fiscal year to begin recovery, and be able to use any substantive growth in revenues during the second half of the year for our depleted reserves. In this year of downsizing, I have downsized the supplemental budget. I wanted to get it to the point of what in my opinion, a supplemental budget should really be. In the past we have always spent our surplus. This year we will bank any surplus we may realize as a result of my reduced revenue estimate.

With a timely passage of these final adjustments to this year's budget, we can then turn our attention to the FY 93 budget, where you will find many new, ambitious, and progressive programs.

Our state did need to get its house in order. But, as I see it, that is only half of our job. With the FY 93 budget, I want to begin the other half. Most experts believe that the southeastern states may once again outpace the nation in economic growth. The potential is there, they say, but only, only if a state can make two things happen:

First, bridge some of the gap between the prosperous metropolitan areas and the small, rural towns, many of them desperately poor, that have been left behind. Each time a recession hits, that part of our state's economy is slower to recover and comes back to a lower level than before. Second, upgrade our school systems to insure that the workforce has the skills employers will be looking for.

There are many unmet needs in this state, unmet needs that absolutely must be addressed if we are to regain economic strength, if we are to realize our potential for growth. A key is transportation. A network of highways is as important to economic growth as a network of veins and arteries is to a human body. But the most critical long-term need Georgia faces is an educated workforce.

In this 1992 session, I will lay before you a four-point program that I call "Georgia Rebound." Georgia Rebound is designed to ensure that Georgia will set the pace in the Southeast in the 1990s. Its four goals are a better education for our children, the preservation of our environment, the promotion of economic activity all across the state, and the protection of our citizens.

I want to take a little time this morning to give you a sneak preview of its budgetary side. You will hear much more about it from me next week in my State of the State and budget addresses.

First, I am proposing a three percent cost-of-living increase for teachers, University System personnel and state employees. I wish we could do more, I wish we could do within-grade pay increases for our state employees. But at this particular time—with Georgia Power laying off hundreds, GM possibly having to close, my friends, this is pretty good. In these times, it's the best I could do.

The pay increase is modest, but I am proposing the most ambitious education construction program ever presented a legislature—$140 million in 92 school systems; $142.8 million on 16 campuses around the University System, and $34.2 million at our Technical and Adult Education institutions.

I propose to restore the 2.5 percent funding cut made to the QBE formula last August, the 60 prekindergarten and 15 foreign language pilot programs, the duty-free lunch periods for teachers, and the expansion of the Governor's Honors Program.

I want to start a Governor's School Leadership Institute to teach school administrators better management skills. I want us to better use satellite technology to dramatically expand Distance Learning, beaming math, science, and foreign language courses to schools in areas where these courses are not available. For our students going to private colleges, I propose increasing our tuition equalization grants to $1,000 per student. And I want to provide matching state funds for constructing public libraries in Bartow, Chattooga, Columbia, Meriwether, Taylor, and Thomas Counties.

The second point of Georgia Rebound is preserving our environment. Among the twelve southeastern states, Georgia ranks seventh in its state-owned natural acreage and ninth in its wildlife acreage. That's pretty bad for the state that calls itself the Empire State of the South.

Most of you are aware of my efforts with Preservation 2000, a public-private partnership whose goal is to acquire 100,000 acres of land for hunting, fishing, wilderness preservation and recreation during my administration. I propose that the state funds going toward this effort be generated through $20 million in bonds and an increase in the cost of hunting and fishing licenses. But we will still keep the license cost below the regional average.

With regards to economic development, I have already mentioned the importance of a good network of highways. And I propose that we sell $100 million in bonds for the Governor's Road Improvement Program, not solely dedicated to, but emphasizing acceleration of the Fall Line Freeway from Columbus to Augusta and U.S. 27 from Bainbridge to Chattanooga. Another $3 million will improve access to the World Congress Center. And of course, we must once again provide $38.6 million to the Local Assistance Road Program, known as LARP.

But I want to say this: Roads are not the only mode of transportation. When you helped me with the selection of Wayne Shackelford as DOT Commissioner, it was understood that we would have a transportation commissioner, not just a highway commissioner. I want the state to purchase a 36.8-mile abandoned rail line between southeast Cobb County and Rockmart. It is a ready-made rail corridor that will be critical to metro Atlanta's commuter needs in the future.

We also must make a comprehensive study of our air transportation needs statewide. It should include helping local governments with matching funds for airport improvements, but it should go far beyond that. The discussions about a second airport in the Atlanta area have indicated to me that we do not have either a sense of our statewide air transport needs or a plan to realize them in any coordinated way.

Expanding Georgia's deepwater ports is critical to boosting our exports. We must deepen the Savannah Harbor Channel and expand our capacity to handle the new and larger container ships.

On the tourism front, we must move ahead with our efforts to make Georgia a destination for tourists, rather than a pit-stop on the way to somewhere else. I propose planning money to replace the welcome center at Ringgold where I-75 comes in from Tennessee. This facility was designed for 175,000 visitors a year. Last year more than 2 million people stopped to use it.

I also propose funding for phase one of the mountain park, a recreational facility first recommended by Governor Harris in 1988 to foster tourism in the North Georgia mountains.

To lay some longer-term economic development groundwork, I propose that we provide more than $15 million in bonds and cash to complement nearly $4 million in private funds already raised by the Georgia Research Alliance.

The Research Alliance is a unique partnership, a partnership among Georgia's six research universities—four of which are units of our University System—and private industry. It will conduct practical, applied research that will boost industry in the areas of telecommunications, environmental science, and genetics. I want it to be the catalyst that will put Georgia, without question, into the forefront of research and development in the Southeast, perhaps even the nation.

Last but not least, the fourth point of Georgia Rebound is the safety of our citizens. My budget for FY 93 provides 6,090 new beds in correction facilities. Five new prisons, six new boot camps, a youth detention center and a parole center will be ready to open during FY 93, and operating funds must be provided. Also, you may recall, we put three boot camps on hold in August so that they could be built with inmate labor. With the completion of the first six, we will be able to put inmates to work on these three, building them for $3.6 million in bonds, compared to the $6 million originally projected.

The second focus of my public safety package is safer streets by cracking down on DUI and drugs. And I will be talking with you about that next week.

Georgia Rebound is an ambitious, far-reaching legislative/budgetary agenda for FY 93, And I thank you for allowing me to begin to lay out some of its most important parts at this meeting today. If it is implemented, without question Georgia will set the pace in the Southeast in education, environmental preservation, economic development, and public safety.

But now, it will mean targeting our limited resources in these specific areas. It will mean making hard choices, setting priorities. And of course, it will cost money. There's an old country song that goes, "Everyone wants to go to heaven, but nobody wants to die." The songwriter was saying what you on these committees know so well—there's a price on everything. Although I've already talked longer than usual for this meeting, it would be irresponsible of me to lay out the basics of Georgia Rebound without also giving you an indication of how I propose we pay for it.

We are not expecting much in the way of new revenues next year. That's one of the cold, hard facts of life. Dr. Thomassen's revenue estimate—his lowest—was 6.2 percent. I cut his lowest and made it even lower. 5.8 percent. So, to finance Georgia Rebound—to fund this ambitious package for Georgia to set the pace in the Southeast—my proposal calls for updating Georgia's outdated, antiquated fee structure, and using funds that for decades have been subsidizing some state services that should have been paying for themselves.

It is now time—it is past time—for Georgia to bring its fee structure into the present and return these services to their once self-supporting status. The total I propose for Georgia Rebound is $209 million. First, I propose raising the cost of a driver's license to $15 for a four-year license. The cost for an individual's license has not increased since Eisenhower was President. It was set in 1955 at $1 a year for a five-year license. If that fee had just simply increased at the same rate as the consumer price index to account for inflation over the years, a Georgia driver's license would now cost $22.50.

The proposed fee increase would cover the cost of obtaining a license, which is over $14, if we did not make any change in the process. However, I recommend that we use $3 million of this money for a much overdue upgrading of the driver's license process. I propose building 15 new satellite facilities in high volume areas around the state, and expanding 10 existing facilities. This will enable us to provide better, faster and more convenient service.

Presently a learner's permit costs $1.50. This, of course, is not nearly sufficient to cover the cost of processing. I propose that we increase the fee for a learner's permit to $10, which covers the processing cost.

The largest fee increase I propose in the area of driver's licenses comes in reinstating licenses suspended for traffic violations. Right now the fee for reinstating a driver's license is $25, no matter why it was suspended. I propose that habitual offenders and those who have been convicted of DUI or a drug-related offense pay a $200 fee to get their license reinstated. Fees for reinstating driver's licenses suspended for other violations would be raised to $50.

I also propose an increase in the cost of a motor vehicle title to $18, which is still less than the regional average. Right now, Georgia has the lowest title fee in the Southeast, and it is substantially below the cost of processing the application. Titles are a one-time charge that is done only when the ownership of the vehicle changes. It is not a recurring expense.

Eugene Talmadge got elected Governor during the Depression by promising a $3 vehicle tag. That was 60 years ago. That same $3 tag today, adjusted for inflation, would cost $37. I propose a $20 tag. That would have been about $1.70 in Gene Talmadge's day. It would put us almost exactly at the Southeast average and significantly below the highest fee in the region of $100. As we increase this fee, I also propose doubling the amount which counties may retain from 50 cents to $1 per tag. Local governments will gain approximately $3 million in new revenue.

Special prestige license tags cost substantially more to produce than regular license plates. And for many years we have made these tags available at considerably less than the cost of producing them. Georgia is also one of only a very few states which do not charge an annual fee for a prestige tag. We charge a one-time $25 amount. Prestige tags are not a necessity—no one has to have one. I propose an annual fee of $25, which would raise almost $2 million a year. And we would still be well below the average annual fee in the Southeast, which is more than $27.

Public ID cards for those who do not drive, but need photo identification, would cost $10 rather than the current $5 to cover the cost of issuing them.

In addition to these fee increases, I am proposing a new $200 impact fee to be assessed on out-of-state vehicles. Incoming vehicles increase traffic congestion and put pressure on existing highways. To help defray the cost, several states have imposed additional charges on these vehicles when registration is transferred.

Every year almost 125,000 vehicles are brought into Georgia from other states. Their owners do not pay any ad valorem taxes whatsoever for the year in which they enter the state. But Georgia residents—your constituents—pay an ad valorem tax on each vehicle at the beginning of the year. This tax can amount to several hundred dollars on an average-priced late-model car. But again, because the car must be in Georgia on January 1, new residents moving in during the year pay absolutely no tax for that year. They get off scott free. The impact fee is about what they'd otherwise pay in taxes. It would correct this unfairness in our tax structure and raise $25 million. It will not affect a single constituent living in your legislative district right now.

Georgia is one of only a very few states in which the cost of regulating utilities is borne largely by the taxpayer rather than by the industry being regulated. The Public Service Commission is a state regulatory body that oversees an industry, just like the Department of Banking and Finance, the Board of Workers Compensation and the licensing boards under the Secretary of State. These other state regulatory bodies operate on the basis of cost recovery, but the PSC's operation is heavily subsidized from the state treasury, the state taxpayer. The PSC's current fee income of $1 million only covers a fraction of the cost of regulation. To cover costs, I propose that fee income be raised by $3,500,000 annually.

And, as you know, I am proposing a change to the current law allowing vendors to keep 3 percent of their sales tax collections to cover the cost of processing the tax. This vendors' compensation fee was established 40 years ago in 1951 when the sales tax was enacted, because back then it was time-consuming to calculate the amount of money owed the state. Since then technological advances have made calculations much easier. Computers can do the work in a fraction of the time it used to take to do it by hand.

Nineteen of the 50 states, including our neighbor North Carolina, don't even have vendors' compensation at all. Other states pay a much smaller percentage than Georgia. Some set caps. I propose to cap vendors' compensation at $4,000, which would not affect 97.5 percent of Georgia's vendors. The 2.5 percent that would see their compensation reduced are the largest stores and retail chains, along with public utilities. Many of them keep substantially more in revenue than it costs them to collect the sales tax.

The revenue gain to Georgia from this change will be $50 million a year. Local governments would also receive a tax windfall of at least $10 million a year—money desperately needed by local governments in these tough financial times.

As I outlined Georgia Rebound, I spoke about a number of capital outlay projects involving bonds. And some of you probably began adding them up in your heads. Let me assure you that we came through the August budget cutting process with our top bond ratings intact.

After reviewing our finances in October 1991, Standard & Poor's commended us for our low debt burden and conservative fiscal management, and indicated their faith that our economy will continue to outperform the nation.

More specifically, let me emphasize to you that we can sell all the bonds I propose in my FY 93 budget with only a very small increase in our debt level—three-tenths of one percent, to be exact. Our debt is at one of its lowest levels in three decades—5.4 percent of the prior year's revenue collections, compared to the constitutional limit of 10 percent.

The combination of retirement of old debt, low interest rates and modest revenue growth presents us with a unique opportunity to build for the future while raising our debt level only three-tenths of one percent—to 5.7 percent from 5.4 percent. Only six times in the past 28 years has the debt level been lower than what I propose for FY 93. We would be foolish not to take advantage of the lowest interest rates in 20 years.

For the past two months, on the Prelegislative Forum and elsewhere, I've been talking about targeting our limited resources, about investing them in areas that will better position Georgia for the future. Georgia Rebound is a coordinated, comprehensive package of legislation and appropriations designed to do just that.

Also, it creates jobs—thousands of them in the private sector all across this state. Jobs now, jobs in the future. Jobs in South Georgia and in North Georgia. Jobs in West Georgia and in East Georgia. Jobs—good jobs. That's what Georgia Rebound is about.

I appreciate this opportunity to give you a preview of my program for the 1992 General Assembly, and I look forward to elaborating on it as we move into the legislative session. I also look forward to working with you and having you visit my office with your constituents.

# Georgia Rebound

*Televised Address*
*January 12, 1992*

My text for this Sunday message is from Proverbs: "Where there is no vision, the people perish."

I am a student and a teacher of history, and history is full of examples where, despite difficult times, leaders still prepared for the future, rather than simply reacting to the immediate circumstances.

At one time during the Civil War, Abraham Lincoln could look out of his window and see Confederate flags and troops in the distance, right outside Washington. Many were in a panic, but Lincoln ordered the construction on the Capitol Dome to continue, because he knew this great country would move beyond the difficulties of the moment to peace and progress.

Here in Georgia, for the moment, we have had to adjust for a recession and declining revenues. We downsized state government. We cut and reorganized. We achieved new levels of efficiency. The state needed to get its house in order. And we will continue that effort.

But at the same time we are embattled by slow revenue growth, we still need to continue to plan and build. Even in difficult times, we cannot allow ourselves to lose sight of where we need to go and what we need to do to prepare for the future. We're talking about our children and their children.

As we look ahead in 1992, we have a critical choice to make: We can either spread our limited resources across the length and breadth of state government and not really make much of an impact anywhere. Or, we can keep our belt tightened in most places, while we target those resources specifically at some critical needs, that are essential to prepare for future growth.

Most experts believe that the southeastern states have the potential to once again outpace the nation in economic growth. But it will happen, they say, only, *only* if a state does two things: First, bridge some of the gap between the prosperous metropolitan areas that have raced ahead, and the small, rural towns, many of them desperately poor, that have been left behind. Second, upgrade our school systems to insure that the workforce has the skills employers will be looking for.

There are many unmet needs in this state, unmet needs that absolutely must be addressed if we are to regain economic strength, if we are to realize our potential for growth. Now is the time of opportunity—the time to move ahead on the unmet needs we face, the time to move Georgia to the forefront in the Southeast.

Beginning this week I will bring to the Georgia General Assembly a budget and package of legislation that all fits together into an ambitious and far-reaching program that I call Georgia Rebound.

Georgia Rebound is designed to use our limited resources wisely in ways that will ensure that Georgia sets the pace in the Southeast in the 1990s and into the 21st century. If we want industry to expand or move to Georgia, we must have a skilled and literate workforce. If we want more jobs, we must offer a high quality of life and a safe place to live. If we want economic growth, we must have the highways, rail lines, ports, and research programs to support it.

These are the four goals of Georgia Rebound—improve education, preserve our environment, make our streets safer, and build our economy all across the state.

Let me tell you more about how we plan to make the Georgia Rebound a reality.

First and most important, education. The days when a young person in Georgia could drop out of school and earn a living with sweat and strain and strength—those days are gone with the wind. And frankly, my dear, I do give a damn. During this session of the General Assembly, we face an urgent choice: We can either move ahead to become a high-wage, high-skill, high-growth economy, or we will be left behind with a dwindling standard of living.

When I think back over my own education, dedicated teachers were the decisive factor. They inspired my achievements and guided my decisions. We are losing our ability to attract and hold talented teachers, because we have allowed salaries, from kindergarten right through college, to slip compared to other states in both the region and the nation. Salaries for college faculty slipped from first to sixth in the Southeast during the 80s. Right now, a high school math teacher with 15 years of experience and a master's degree makes less than a brand new graduate with a bachelor's degree in engineering in private enterprise.

So I propose a modest, three percent cost-of-living increase for the teachers in our schools and colleges. I wish we could afford more.

I want to restore all the cuts in the Quality Basic Education formula that sends state funding to our local schools. That is critical.

Although we have a limited amount of money, I do not want Georgia to continue—as we are now—last in the nation in programs for our children. We must have prekindergarten programs for our four-year-olds, and I want to increase the assistance to college students who receive Tuition Equalization Grants.

Georgia Rebound proposes the most massive education construction program in the history of Georgia—desperately needed buildings in 92 school systems, K through 12; at 16 institutions of higher education; and at 11 of our institutes of technical and adult education.

Our University System has 400 buildings that are over half a century old. Another 1,000 are between 25 and 50 years old, when it's time for a new roof and some renovation.

But over the past decade construction funds have averaged only one percent of the replacement cost of our buildings. I hate to say it, but the collective roof of the University System is leaking.

On top of that, our college enrollments have increased by 45 percent over the past decade. In one way, this is great, because we have got to get more of our kids into college. But right now we don't have anywhere to put them.

Public school enrollment has also increased—by 100,000 students since the fall of 1984—that's 4,000 new classrooms full of kids. Now, thousands of them are not really in classrooms; they are in make-shift mobile homes.

Georgia's industries, competing now in a global economy, are bringing advanced technology into their plants. That demands a higher level of training in their workforce. So, to meet their needs, we must update and expand our training programs and provide for greater student capacity at our technical institutes.

We must address these critical needs in our education infrastructure, and in the process—at the same time—we will create thousands of private-sector construction jobs this very year all across the state.

The second part of Georgia Rebound is environmental preservation, and that has two goals: preserving natural areas and tackling our waste problems. I have created Preservation 2000, a public-private partnership that will help us acquire an additional 100,000 acres of land for hunting, fishing, wilderness preservation, and recreation.

Among the 12 southeastern states, Georgia ranks seventh in its state-owned natural acreage and ninth in its wildlife acreage. That's not too good for the state that calls itself the Empire State of the South and prides itself on its beautiful geography.

I also want to expand the revolving loan fund that helps local governments with sewer, water, and wastewater, and begin the process of assisting them with loans for solid waste disposal. We live in a throw-away society, and we're running out of places to throw it.

The third focus of Georgia Rebound is economic growth. As political barriers break down all around the world, international trade opportunities are picking up. And we must get ready by deepening the channel in the Savannah harbor and by expanding the capacity of our ports to handle the new, larger container ships, so that trade won't go to Charleston or Norfolk.

I also want to expand our developmental highway system all across the state, accelerating construction on the east-west Fall Line Freeway from Columbus to Augusta, and north-south on U.S. Highway 27 from Bainbridge to Chattanooga.

I want Georgia to lead the Southeast in industrial research and development, and then I want Georgia to lead the nation. Georgia's six research universities and the corporate sector have joined forces to form the Georgia Research Alliance—a unique partnership to conduct practical, applied research that will attract industries and spin off new firms. If we can coordinate and expand the research programs of our universities, we will have a most impressive catalyst for economic growth.

Finally, we must make our streets safer for Georgia's citizens. Georgia Rebound proposes funding to open five new prisons, six new boot camps, a youth detention center and a parole center—room to get more than 6,000 criminals off the street.

I am proposing new laws to crack down on DUI and habitual traffic offenders and make it tougher and costlier for them to get their driver's licenses back after they've been suspended. I propose stiffer penalties for drug dealers, who recruit children to help with drug sales and prey upon those in public housing and at parks and playgrounds.

Implementing Georgia Rebound means targeting our limited resources in these specific areas. It means setting priorities and making hard choices, and of course, it will cost some money.

When I was growing up in the mountains of North Georgia during the depths of the Great Depression, isolated and in poverty, my mother used to say to us, "Take what you want, sayeth the Lord. Take it—and pay for it." At the time, I thought that was a quotation from the Bible. It isn't, but it was my mother's philosophy. She was saying, you can do what you want to do. You can be what you want to be. But you must be willing to pay the price.

I think we all want a Georgia that will be better for our children than it was for us. We want a Georgia that has better jobs all across the state, now and in the future. We want our children to have the advantage of an educational system, prekindergarten through graduate school and technical school, that is the best in the Southeast, and just as good as any in the nation. We want a Georgia whose air and water are clean and whose natural beauty is preserved for future generations, a Georgia where the streets are safe for young and old.

We all want these things that I have talked about tonight. But in order to take the things that we want, we have to be prepared to pay for them—with some money, yes, but even more so with commitment.

To pay for this far-reaching program that I have briefly outlined for Georgia to set the pace in the Southeast, I propose that we update Georgia's outdated, antiquated user fees. Like all states, Georgia provides some services for a fee to the citizens who want them. These services were originally—years ago—established on a pay-as-you-go basis.

However, many have not been changed for years—for decades. Some have not changed since Eisenhower was President in the 1950s. These programs, which were designed to be self-supporting in the first place, have now come to be heavily subsidized from our state treasury. And you know who puts the money there—all the taxpayers, whether they use the service or not. Our fee structure is so antiquated, that we have room to adjust fees and still keep the cost below the states around us in the Southeast.

The impact of all these fee adjustments combined will amount to less than $20 a year for most folks—about what it costs for a couple to go see a first-run movie and have popcorn and a Coke each.

This will have the added benefit of removing the taxpayer subsidy from user fees and putting our money where we need it most: making our streets safer, our kids smarter, our water cleaner and our economy stronger.

We will also use this opportunity of revising our fees to crack down on DUI and habitual traffic violators, by charging a hefty fee to reinstate their driver's licenses after they've been suspended.

And we are going to make some things fairer, too. You pay ad valorem taxes each year on every vehicle you own, but new residents don't. They bring their cars from out-of-state after January 1st, and pay absolutely no tax in Georgia on that vehicle for the year. You people who are living here pay, but they don't. I want to correct this unfair provision in our tax structure.

The construction projects and new jobs in Georgia Rebound will be financed with bonds, which work pretty much like the mortgage on your home. So let me tell you briefly, in plain English, about the state's debt.

The Georgia Constitution allows us spend a maximum of 10 percent of our income for debt payments. That is far less than what most of you pay from your personal income for your debt. Our present debt payments total only 5.4 percent of our income. This is one of the lowest debt levels that we've had in this state in three decades. And interest rates are now at their lowest point in 20 years.

We can finance *all* of the construction projects in Georgia Rebound with an increase of only three-tenths of one percent in our debt level. Our debt will remain at a lower level than the last five Georgia governors carried over the course of their administrations. It would be foolish not to take advantage of this opportunity to build, when our kids need new classrooms, our drivers need new roads, and yes, when our working people need new jobs, now.

Georgia Rebound gathers together our limited resources, and makes them count in critical areas. It is bold and ambitious, and even a little risky. But its risks are prudent and have been carefully calculated.

Someone once said that the ultimate act of creativity is to take what you have and make it do something more. The key to our success will be in the creativity with which we relieve the state's economic distress and provide sustained economic growth under drastically new circumstances.

We live in a new economic world, and the old patchwork responses of the past will no longer work. But rather than waste our time cursing the darkness, let us light a candle, and by its light, stride out to meet the future.

I am grateful for this opportunity to explain Georgia Rebound to you, the citizens of this great state. I thank you for your attention. And if you'd like more details about Georgia Rebound, write or call my office at the State Capitol with your address, and I will immediately send you a copy of it.

I also want to thank the participating television stations for their time this evening.

Good night. God bless you and God bless Georgia.

# State of the State Address

*January 14, 1992*

The ancient Chinese had a saying that went, "May you live in interesting times." The Chinese considered it a curse. I prefer to think of it as a blessing.

But whether blessed or cursed, these are interesting times to be in state government. From New Hampshire to New Mexico, from California to Connecticut, state governments are bearing the burden of Washington's abdication of responsibility. Today, in state capitols from Albany to Atlanta, Governors and legislators are living by Harry Truman's motto: "The buck stops here." Nowadays in Washington, the buck hardly even slows down.

All across the country, it seemed like each day of 1991 brought more news of economic gloom, lay-offs, plant closings and declining retail sales. And some of us came to believe the old axiom that no news would be good news.

But I am here to tell you this morning that Georgia is on the move. The name of Georgia is on the lips of more and more people across the nation and around the world. Good things, exciting things have been happening all around us.

We used to be known for naming things after peach trees and for the southern charm that still clung to us from the days of *Gone with the Wind*. But Georgia's building a new reputation across the nation and around the world.

Last February the 24th Infantry Division from Georgia's Fort Stewart became the "gee whiz kids" of the free world for their dash across the Persian sands to block the retreat of Saddam Hussein's Republican Guard.

Georgia's own CNN, long snubbed as the Rodney Dangerfield of broadcasting, came into its own as an unsurpassed international news force. And *Time* magazine named Georgia's Ted Turner "Man of the Year."

*Fortune* magazine named Atlanta the best city in the nation to do business. A study by Louis Harris & Associates concluded it was the best city to locate a business. UPS, Days Inns and NCR pulled up stakes and headed for Georgia.

The World Series was a baseball spectacular in which our Atlanta Braves kept the entire nation on the edge of its seat. Jerry took the Falcons to the playoffs in his second year here. And that was just a taste of what is ahead for us, with the Super Bowl coming in 1994 and the Summer Olympic Games in 1996.

On a more scholarly note, the larger units of our University System continue their rise in the national rankings done by *U.S. News & World Report*, and the Georgia Research Alliance is becoming a promising catalyst in industrial and medical research and development.

For us in state government, 1991 was a time of declining revenues and budget cuts. And some of those cuts were painful. But, as Ben Franklin used to say, "Necessity is the mother of invention." In that respect, this national recession has been quite a "mother."

We used this opportunity to streamline state government, eliminating almost 3,000 bureaucratic positions, calling on our remaining corps of state employees to be leaner, and rewarding innovation, imagination and ingenuity. Our departments and agencies rose to the occasion, doing a remarkable job of carrying out your directives of last August without disrupting services. A headline in the Atlanta papers a week ago read, "Few feeling cuts in state services; agencies lessen impact on taxpayers."

And, despite the cuts, a number of exciting things got underway in state government. Preservation 2000 acquired more than 8,000 acres of natural, ecologically sensitive land. And its advisory council developed the criteria and process for future site selection.

Georgia became the first state in the South to receive a $22 million federal grant to develop child care programs.

The Georgia No-Tillage Assistance Program won a $100,000 award from the Ford Foundation as one of the nation's top ten innovations in state and local government.

We are receiving national attention for The Family Connection, an innovative program that brings together schools, social services, and health services to coordinate community-based assistance for families who are at risk. It is a public-private effort, with the seed funding coming from the Woodruff Foundation.

In another public-private effort, advanced communications technology is bringing medical expertise into rural hospitals and doctor's offices, and beaming math, science, and foreign language courses to schools who otherwise could not offer them.

We have a lot of things to be proud of, but we must do even more.

When the eyes of the world are on us in 1996, I want them to see a Georgia that is thriving and growing toward greater prosperity—a Georgia whose young people are being educated and trained for the jobs of the future—a Georgia whose air and water are clean and whose natural beauty is preserved for future generations—a Georgia whose streets are safe for young and old. And I know that's what most of you want, too.

But it will not happen of its own accord. It will come only as the result of the deliberate action of the men and women in this chamber to make it happen.

We have a critical choice to make: We can either spread our limited resources across the length and breadth of state government and not really make much of an impact anywhere. Or, we can keep our belt tightened in most places, while we target those resources specifically at some critical needs that are essential to prepare for future growth.

I want to target our resources. Beginning this week, I will lay before you a budget and package of legislation that all fits together into an ambitious and far-reaching program I call Georgia Rebound. Its priorities reflect the cares and concerns of the working families who pay our salaries: Making our children's education better, our streets and neighborhoods safer, our environment cleaner, and our economy stronger.

This morning I want to talk about the legislative side of those four points. Only the highlights. The package includes over 40 bills and we'd be here all day if I tried to cover them all.

On Thursday, we will look at programs and projects that require funding.

The primary bill in the education portion of Georgia Rebound is the enabling legislation for the lottery. I have worked closely with Representative Sonny Watson as this legislation was formulated, and I am grateful for his help and advice.

I propose a lottery that is run strictly as a business by a board of proven business leaders, not state bureaucrats. We are not going to take the first cent of state tax revenues away from other programs to operate it. Business will be conducted on a bid basis, and minority and small businesses will be encouraged to participate.

Even though the lottery will be operated as a business independent of state revenues and officials, we are going to provide for legislative oversight to ensure its sensitivity to the citizens of Georgia. And I want a portion of the proceeds to be used for education and treatment programs on compulsive gambling.

I propose that we divide the net proceeds evenly among three critical education needs:

First, voluntary programs for our four-year-olds, where learning is so important. Last month the Carnegie Foundation for the Advancement of Teaching released an extensive study on the readiness of our children to begin kindergarten. It found that here in Georgia, 40 percent of our kindergarten kids are struggling. They came to kindergarten not prepared to learn.

Five-year-olds who do not know their numbers, colors, and letters, and who have not developed social skills, are already far behind when they walk in the classroom door on the first day of kindergarten. Most never catch up. Many will drop out.

Extensive studies document that at-risk children who attend preschool are more likely to complete high school, more likely to find stable employment, more likely to continue their education, less likely to become pregnant as teens, less likely to be on welfare, and less likely to be arrested. Those are facts.

I don't want Georgia to continue to be last in the nation in its programs for children as we are now. Thirty other states already have preschool programs, and we absolutely must start one in Georgia targeted at the 40 percent of four-year-olds who are at risk. But it will be voluntary, because some parents choose to teach their preschoolers at home. And we will provide learning materials for at-home mothers to use and help them every way we can.

Second, equipment and special capital outlay needs in K-12 and in higher education. Computers are very effective, cost-efficient teachers. They never forget a key point, never leave a slow child behind, and a small school can offer an advanced course to one student for the cost of the software. The lottery proceeds can fill our classrooms with these superior learning tools.

The equipment and capital outlay money will also help to update labs in our high schools and institutions of higher learning. This is important, because industry, as you can imagine, is not very impressed with students who are trained on old equipment that is not in use anywhere in the private sector anymore.

Of course, we must not overlook our physical facilities. We have thousands of kids in make-shift mobile homes instead of classrooms. And the roof of the University System is leaking, because we have a lot of older buildings that have not been given the needed renovation and repair.

The third program proposed for funding will be the most all-inclusive scholarship program to be found in any of the 50 states for bright students who otherwise would find it difficult to go to college. Right now only 15 percent of our kids are graduating from college. South of Macon, it is only 8 percent. The national average is 25 percent. Georgia can do better. Georgia must do better.

The most critical long-term need Georgia faces is a better-educated workforce. And just when it is essential to increase the number of youngsters who go into college or technical training, the cost of tuition is soaring out of reach for most of our citizens.

Other than health care, which largely must be answered on the national level by Congress, this is the single best way to help our middle-income families. For them, it is a pocketbook issue of major proportions. With the lottery proceeds, Georgia can provide scholarships by the thousands to deserving students who want to go to college or a technical school.

This is Georgia's opportunity to pioneer the most far-reaching scholarship program in the nation—and not only for those who are minorities or who come from lower income families, but also those middle-income families who are devastated with the cost of education and training beyond high school. If you want to invest in the economic future of this state and at the same time do something to help the forgotten, average working family—this is it.

Finally, a reserve fund. As we all know, the course of the economy never runs smooth—but neither does true love. Economic growth ebbs and flows, and so will lottery proceeds. So we need to assure a constant level of funding for these programs that carries across the dips and swells in the lottery proceeds. To do that, I propose a reserve fund. Each year for the first few years the lottery is in operation, we are going to put 10 percent of the proceeds into a reserve fund until it is built up to a certain level, and then we will keep it there.

That, in a nutshell, is my lottery proposal—a business-like operation, free from political influence, and fair to all who want to be involved; its proceeds used not to supplant current education funds, but to enhance them through prekindergarten programs, equipment and capital outlay, and scholarships for deserving kids from low and middle income families; and a reserve fund so that we can hold a steady course.

While we are on the education portion of Georgia Rebound, let me say a word about pay -for-performance for our teachers. I have had a special commission working most of last year to formulate a plan, and I told them right from the start that I had no preconceived notions as to what form it ought to take. They have recommended that we begin by rewarding schools and giving the school discretion in the use of the funds it receives. Then move on to pay-for-performance for individual teachers.

That is a good way to start, because one of the key messages that has developed over the year as we started The Family Connection, held the Governor's Conference on Education, and launched Georgia 2000 is the importance of local initiative, creativity and freedom to tailor programs to the community's needs. Structuring a pay-for-performance program as my commission has proposed, provides yet another incentive for teamwork at the local level, so that teachers help each other rather than compete against each other.

In the beginning of my remarks, I mentioned several public-private partnerships that got underway during the first year of my administration. Another important education part of Georgia Rebound is the Governor's Institute for School Leadership. Many of our school principals and administrators are former teachers who were promoted out of the classroom. While their teaching experience is very helpful in their new jobs, they often lack comprehensive administrative skills. I want to give them some assistance and instruction in that regard.

There are many other far-reaching education programs in Georgia Rebound, and I will touch on some more on Thursday. But for now let me move on to economic development.

In my televised remarks on Sunday night, I said that we must bridge the gap between the prosperous metropolitan areas that have run on ahead and the small, rural towns, many of them desperately poor, that have been left behind.

I believe that with all my heart, and that is why I want expand the Job Tax Credit. As some of you will recall, we originally enacted the Job Tax Credit in 1989. In retrospect, it has proved to be one of the more insightful things we've done. For every dollar the state loses in the form of this tax credit, we gain three dollars from the new jobs that made the credit applicable.

In the process of putting Georgia Rebound together, I have been working closely with Senator Jack Hill and his Rural Policy Study Committee, and with Representative Ray Holland, whose district includes some of this state's most distressed counties and who has been a prime mover in the House on this issue.

The Job Tax Credit now applies only to manufacturing and distribution businesses in the 40 most economically distressed rural counties. I want to double the number of eligible counties, with the 40 most severely depressed counties having a $1,000 tax credit, and the second 40 to be added at a $750 credit for every job created. I also want to broaden the range of businesses that will be eligible. If we don't do this, South Carolina, with the incentives they can offer, will eat our lunch.

Georgia Rebound also contains a major package of improvements to our economic development infrastructure, and I will get into that more on Thursday.

In the area of the environment, Georgia Rebound focuses on two things: the acquisition of more land for wilderness preservation, hunting, fishing and recreation, and the whole issue of waste. I mentioned the work of Preservation 2000 at the beginning of my remarks, and I will tell you more about it and about my proposals to assist local governments in dealing with water sewer and wastewater facilities on Thursday.

What I want to talk about briefly today is the longer-term focus, which is embodied in the Georgia Research Alliance. For several years, many of us have been going around saying that the University of Georgia, Georgia Techs, and Emory combined conduct more research than the three institutions that anchor Research Triangle in North Carolina. And that's true. But what North Carolina has that we don't is coordination. They gathered their research programs into a package and promoted it.

Well, look out North Carolina, here comes the Georgia Research Alliance. The Research Alliance includes not just three, but all six of this state's major research universities—public and private—in a unique partnership with each other and with the private sector as well.

The Research Alliance has identified three areas in which we already have research going on independently at several universities and which show great promise in private sector applications. They are telecommunications, genetics, and environmental technology.

At the beginning of my remarks, I mentioned the tremendous potential of telecommunications in bringing medical expertise and education enrichment to rural areas of the state, and that is just one application of this cutting-edge technology.

A second emphasis of the Research Alliance is on environmental technology, and that is going to be of tremendous benefit to Georgia because we are a manufacturing state.

Through the Research Alliance, Georgia will launch a major effort to become a center of expertise and move to the forefront in technology that controls air and water pollution and is effective in controlling the environmental problems we have.

The point of the Research Alliance is to coordinate and expand the research programs at its member institutions, which will not only attract eminent scholars and make us a center of expertise, but will also attract businesses and spin off new firms—5,000 high-tech, high-wage jobs projected over the next ten years.

What I hope you are seeing as I speak is the way that all the pieces of Georgia Rebound connect to each other. The Georgia Research Alliance, for example, is made up of educational institutions, but it will be attacking the problems of pollution and environmental preservation, and in the process it will be creating jobs and stimulating economic growth.

The fourth part of Georgia Rebound is public safety. If we want jobs to come to our communities, we must offer not just a good education and high quality of life, we must also have safer streets. On Thursday, I will talk more about correction institutions. Today, I want to highlight briefly my legislation relating to DUI and habitual traffic offenders.

We were all stunned by a feature a few months ago in the Atlanta newspapers that graphically demonstrated the ease with which a drunk driver or habitual offender returns to the road and commits the same offense all over again. We have loopholes to close, and we must close them.

I will propose legislation to expedite significantly the license suspension process for anyone who fails or refuses to take a breath test. And I want us to require some tangible evidence of changed habits before we reinstate the driver's license of a DUI offender at the end of the suspension period.

There is always a human side to everything, and tight economic times play themselves out in people's lives. So there is a human services side of my legislative package as well. I'll tell you more about that on Thursday, but let me mention two pieces of legislation I am coming with. I want to do something about "deadbeat dads."

We have an increasing number of mothers who are desperately trying to get help from absentee fathers to support the children they fathered. To help these mothers, I propose that we strengthen proof of paternity right from the start by recording the name and social security number of the father on birth certificates, and then allow this information to be introduced in court. I also propose that we allow the cost of health insurance premiums to be included as part of a child support order for income withholding.

Of course, Georgia Rebound will cost money. I reminded the Appropriations Committees last week of the Loretta Lynn song that goes, "Everyone wants to go to heaven, but nobody wants to die." She was saying in that colorful way of hers that everything has a price.

So, in addition to legislation in these four areas, Georgia Rebound includes a package of bills updating our user fees to generate the necessary revenue. I'll get into the details on Thursday when we talk dollars and cents. But let me say this here by way of explanation. Like every other state, Georgia provides user services to citizens that want them. And, like every other state, we originally designed those services on a pay-as-you go basis. But while other states around us have been increasing their fees over the years as costs have risen, we have held onto our old, outdated, antiquated fee structure and paid ever larger subsidies out of the state treasury to keep these services operating.

Our user fees have not been increased in years, in decades—some of them not since Eisenhower was President in the 50s. To give you an example of how out-of-whack our fee structure has gotten, Eugene Talmadge got elected Governor during the Great Depression in the 1930s by proposing a $3 fee for car tags. I am proposing a fee that is the equivalent of $1.70 in Gene Talmadge's day. We have ample room to adjust our fees and still keep them below average for the Southeast. I don't want to get out of sync with our neighbors, and under my proposal we don't.

Georgia Rebound is an ambitious, far-reaching legislative/budgetary agenda for FY 93.

If it is implemented, without question Georgia will set the pace in the Southeast in education, environmental preservation, economic development, and public safety. But it will mean targeting our limited resources in these specific areas. It will mean making hard choices, setting priorities, and paying a price.

I'd like to conclude this morning with something Aristotle said. He was once asked to define the difference between a barbaric culture and a civilization. He said that in a barbaric culture, people live from day to day or week to week. They go out and plunder, then they consume what they plundered, and they go out and plunder again. But in a civilization, people go out and they plan and they work for the next generation. They want to pay back what their parents have done for them by doing more for their children. That is how civilization progresses.

There have been ten generations of Georgians since this state was founded, and each one has fulfilled Aristotle's requirement of a civilization. Each left this state in a little better condition than they had inherited it from their parents.

We are the first generation at risk of doing the opposite. Presently, we are not giving our children the education and skills they are going to need to make their own way and earn their own way in the 21st century.

You and I do not want to be part of a generation that leaves that as its legacy. You and I do not want to have had the chance to make a difference and let it pass us by. For the sake of our children—and their children—please give me your help, and let us, together, head this state in the right direction.

# Budget Address, Fiscal Year 1993

*January 16, 1992*

When Franklin D. Roosevelt was struck down by a cerebral hemorrhage in 1945, he was at the Little White House in Warm Springs, posing for a portrait while he jotted down notes for a speech he was to have made. A fragment from that unfinished speech reads, "The only limit to our realization of tomorrow is our doubts of today."

We've got uncertainties these days, with the national recession dragging on. And we are going to deal with those uncertainties in the supplemental budget. But we cannot allow our doubts of today to stand in the way of our realization of tomorrow.

Let me begin by talking first about the immediate situation we face over the remainder of Fiscal Year 1992. Last August, most all the economists, including our own Dr. Thomassen, projected flat revenue growth during the first half of FY 92, with modest growth during the second half of the year. Well now, the first part of that projection has proved true. So far, revenues for FY 92 are running 1.5 percent behind last year. The forecast for modest growth toward the end of FY 92 still holds, but I am ever mindful that we have no reserves should it not materialize, and we must be very, very careful.

Therefore, I whittled on this old budget a little bit more. I have reduced my revenue estimate for FY 92 by another $50 million to $7,465 million, which would require revenue growth of 2.8 percent. This move will give us a hedge should revenues not increase as expected during the latter half of the year. And if some growth is realized, then we can begin the critical process of rebuilding the state's reserves.

Let me emphasize that this $50 million reduction will be achieved without laying off any state employees or reducing any program. It will be offset largely through several revenue sources. We had an unusually large lapse as a result of spending controls, and the August cuts saved more than we projected. We have surplus debt service appropriations from the cancellation of several bonded projects and the drop in interest rates.

I have downsized the supplemental budget. It is lean and it's fiscally responsible. Its goal is to give our economy the remainder of this fiscal year to begin recovery, and use any growth in revenues toward the end of the year for our depleted reserves. We are expecting the January revenue numbers on February 10th, and if we have to, we will whittle even more on the supplemental budget.

Those are the uncertainties of the moment. Let me now turn my attention to the realization of tomorrow—to the budget for FY 93, which—and let me emphasize this—does not begin until next July. And its end is 17 months away, by which time all economists agree that we will be well on our way out of this recession.

On Tuesday, I talked some common sense. Today I want to talk some dollars and cents. As you have been learning from Georgia Rebound 101, the four goals are improve education, preserve our environment, boost economic activity all across the state, and promote public safety.

I begin with the first and most important point of Georgia Rebound—education. My

FY 93 budget includes full restoration of the August cut to the Quality Basic Education formula that sends state funds to local school systems. And for our teachers, I recommend a 3 percent cost-of-living increase. These two combined cost more than $127 million. In addition, we must accommodate a projected enrollment growth of 28,000 new students next school year in the funds for the QBE formula.

I propose that we restore the 60 pilot prekindergarten programs, the 15 foreign language pilots, the expansion of the Governor's Honors Program and the funding for duty-free lunch periods for teachers, which were cut from the FY 92 budget in August. My budget includes stipends for 750 mentor teachers, and funds to begin the Governor's School Leadership Institute, which I explained on Tuesday. It also includes funds to use a satellite transponder for distance learning, enabling us to send a high-quality signal around the state on several channels. Its purpose is to enable small, rural schools to offer enrichment courses in math, science, and foreign languages.

Most significantly, I am proposing the most ambitious K-12 education construction program ever—$140 million for school construction in 92 systems. Another $4 million will purchase vocational education equipment, and $3.5 million will provide matching funds for public library construction in Bartow, Chattooga, Columbia, Meriwether, Taylor, and Thomas Counties.

The biggest complaint from teachers and administrators is the tremendous volume of paperwork. I'm proposing almost $5 million in bonds and cash for the Student Information System to put administrative computer equipment in 100 additional schools. Time-consuming paperwork like class schedules, attendance records, and grade reporting will be turned over to a computer, freeing teachers to devote their time to our children.

For the 34 colleges and universities in our University System and our Technical and Adult Education institutes, I am also recommending a 3 percent cost-of-living increase. And because of increased enrollment, we need to add more than $61 million to the funding formula for the University System.

Just as for our public schools, I propose the largest construction initiative in the state's history for the University System, using bonds totaling almost $185 million. The bulk of these bonds—$142.8 million—will construct sixteen buildings which have been identified by the Board of Regents as the system's most urgent facility needs. They are located on the campuses of: The University of Georgia, Georgia Tech, Georgia State University, Georgia Southern University in Statesboro, Valdosta State College, North Georgia College in Dahlonega, West Georgia College in Carrollton, Georgia College in Milledgeville, Armstrong State College in Savannah, Gordon College in Barnesville, South Georgia College in Douglas, Kennesaw State College in Cobb County, Macon College, Gainesville College, Darton College in Albany, and Fort Valley College.

Another $25.2 million is proposed for major renovation and maintenance. More than 400 of our University System buildings are over a half-century old. Another 1,000 are between 25 and 50 years old, when it's time for a new roof and new systems. Yet over the past decade, we have appropriated construction funds equal to only one percent of the replacement cost of our physical plant.

In my State of the State Address on Tuesday, I spoke of the importance of the Georgia Research Alliance in coordinating and expanding major university research programs to spur high-quality economic growth. I am proposing $15 million in bonds and cash for construction and equipment related to this far-reaching effort.

And in recognition of the increasing cost of going to college, I want to increase tuition equalization grants for students at our independent colleges to $1,000 per student.

Our third educational component is our very fine network of Technical and Adult Educational institutions. Here also I propose the most massive construction program in our history—$32.6 million in bonds for eleven technical institutes, including Douglasville, Warner Robins, Dublin, LaGrange, Sandersville, Augusta, Marietta, Fitzgerald, Rome, Thomaston and Macon.

Georgia businesses must be competitive in a global economy, and they are bringing advanced technology into their plants to do that. But they need a skilled workforce to operate it. For example, the aerospace industries in Middle Georgia are technologically advanced, high-wage industries that we want to keep. But they are having trouble finding enough qualified employees. To meet needs like this, we must upgrade and expand our technical education programs and expand our student capacity at our post-secondary technical institutions. So almost $7 million of the new funds for Technical and Adult Education is earmarked for aerospace training.

I also recommend more than $1 million to expand Georgia's adult literacy programs and provide assistance to the Literate Community Program, which helps local communities begin a comprehensive literacy initiative.

All the education parts of Georgia Rebound are closely related to economic growth, and another key ingredient in economic growth is highways, which are to a state like a network of arteries is to the human body. I propose $100 million in bonds for our road improvement program.

In the past, we expedited construction on Corridor Z across South Georgia and the Appalachian Highway in North Georgia. I now want us to expedite the Fall Line freeway from Columbus to Augusta and U.S. Highway 27 between Chattanooga and Bainbridge, that will take up to 30 percent of the pressure off of I-75. I want to again provide $38.6 million to LARP, and $3 million to improve access to the World Congress Center.

But I want to say this: Roads are not the only mode of transportation. When you helped me with the selection of Wayne Shackelford as DOT Commissioner, it was understood that we would have a transportation commissioner, not just a highway commissioner. I want the state to purchase a 36.8-mile abandoned rail line between southeast Cobb County and Rockmart. It is a ready-made rail corridor that will be critical to metro Atlanta's commuter needs in the future. We also must make a comprehensive study of our air transportation needs statewide.

As political barriers break down around the world, international trade opportunities are going to increase by leaps and bounds. And we must position ourselves to take advantage of them. If we can establish Georgia as an international trade center, we could generate as much as $3 billion in economic activity and 25,000 new jobs by the year 2000.

Expanding Georgia's deepwater ports is critical to boosting our exports. My budget proposes a major expansion program totaling $63 million. And the Ports Authority will be contributing another $14.3 million from its resources. We must deepen the Savannah Harbor Channel, and expand our capacity to handle the new and larger container ships. We will actively seek federal participation to help pay much of the cost of the harbor deepening.

The Ports Authority has enough money to upgrade two existing container cranes to handle the new, larger container ships. And I propose state bonds to upgrade another two, which is a much cheaper alternative than buying new ones, and to complete Container Berth 6. Debt service for these improvements will be repaid by the Authority from its revenues.

In addition, we will establish a Trade Division in the Department of Industry, Trade and Tourism, and create the Governor's Council on International Trade and Business to better coordinate our various trade programs. We will take advantage of the new U.S.-Canada trade agreement by pursing export leads with Canadian importers, and initiate an Agricultural Machinery Export Program.

On the tourism front, we must move ahead with our efforts to make Georgia a destination for tourists, rather than a pit-stop on the way to somewhere else. I propose planning money to replace the welcome center at Ringgold where I-75 comes in from Tennessee. This facility was designed for 175,000 visitors a year. Last year more than 2 million people stopped to use it.

I also propose funding to move forward with the next phase of the mountain park, designed to foster tourism in the North Georgia mountains. This recreational facility was recommended by Governor Harris in 1987 and $3 million was spent during the Harris administration to begin the project. We are moving forward according to the goals established at that time.

My bond program includes funds to renovate and repair our farmers' markets in Atlanta, Cairo, Cordele, Glennville, Moultrie and Pelham.

The third point of Georgia Rebound is preserving our environment. Among the twelve southeastern states, Georgia ranks seventh in its state-owned natural acreage and ninth in its wildlife acreage. That's pretty bad for the state that calls itself the Empire State of the South.

Most of you are aware of my efforts with Preservation 2000, whose goal is to acquire 100,000 acres of land for hunting, fishing, wilderness preservation, and recreation during my administration. Preservation 2000 is a public-private partnership, and we have already acquired more than 8,000 acres of environmentally sensitive land, largely with private funds. I propose that the state funds going toward this effort be generated through $20 million in bonds, and we will use these funds to continue to leverage private contributions.

We are following through on our 1987 pledge to use revenues from hunting and fishing licenses to make improvements to game and fish activities. I am proposing $1 million for a new public fishing lake and management for newly acquired wildlife areas.

The second issue in this part of Georgia Rebound has to do with processing waste and ensuring clean air and water supplies. I recommend that we issue $5.5 million bonds to acquire land for the West Georgia Reservoir. We previously authorized funds for the environmental impact studies needed prior to acquiring the land and designing the reservoir, and I want to move forward with this badly needed water resource in West Georgia.

My budget also includes $1.6 million to hire 21 new employees to handle the increased workload and responsibilities mandated by the Federal Clean Air Act. However, we propose to recover these costs through an increase in the air quality permit fees—

keeping this program on a cost-recovery basis, which we have failed to do with user fees so often in the past.

Last but not least, the fourth point of Georgia Rebound is the safety of our citizens. My budget for FY 93 provides operating funds for 6,090 new beds in five new prisons in Telfair, Hancock, Washington, Johnson, and Mitchell Counties; as well as six new boot camps in Chattooga, Gwinnett, Telfair, Hancock, and Washington Counties, a youth detention center in Dodge County, and a parole center in Clinch County.

Also, you may recall we put three boot camps in Mitchell, Lanier, and Emanuel Counties on hold in August so that they could be built with inmate labor. With the completion of the first six, we will be able to put inmates to work on these three, building them for $3.6 million in bonds, compared to the $6 million originally projected.

Although we did not lay off any troopers last August, we did cut positions that were vacant as the result of the hiring freeze. I recommended that we restore those cuts and begin training troopers in FY 92. And my FY 93 budget includes funds to finish this job.

Just as our fees for driver's licenses have not kept pace with the cost, neither have our facilities kept pace with the demand. I propose a $3 million expansion to our network of driver's license facilities, establishing 15 new locations in high volume areas around the state, expanding ten existing facilities, and adding 60 new examination staff. This will enable us to provide better, faster, and more convenient service in exchange for our higher fee.

Before I leave law enforcement, let me say a word about indigent defense. Government has a constitutional obligation to provide legal defense for poor people charged with crimes. This burden has fallen largely on county governments, who picked up 95 percent of the cost last year. I propose we increase the state appropriation to $2 million. The legal profession will also help with this effort by handling more cases pro bono and making contributions from the Georgia Bar Foundation.

As I indicated Tuesday, I am very aware of the human cost of a recession, and my proposed budget addresses this concern. The largest expenditure we make for human services is Medicaid. The explosive combination of soaring medical costs and a shifting of the burden from Washington to the states means that we must now spend one out of every 10 dollars in our budget for Medicaid. So this was a major area of scrutiny for the Williams Commission, in its search for ways to improve efficiency.

It has recommended a plan that Kentucky uses, in which a local physician is designated to manage health care services for Medicaid recipients, reducing unnecessary and inappropriate care. I propose trying it out with pilot projects in six counties. The net increase in Medicaid funds in my budget proposal is $77.6 million, which will have a total impact of $150.6 million in new spending. Almost $30 million of these funds would be used to expand services to pregnant women and infants.

Many states around this country have cut welfare benefits during this recession, but we have maintained the same level of payments here in Georgia. And the largest new expenditure I recommend for the Department of Human Resources is more than $27 million to address the anticipated increase in our AFDC rolls.

I also want to expand PEACH, our job training and employment program for welfare recipients, to cover 75 percent of the eligible AFDC recipients statewide, and connect these people to our expanded efforts in adult literacy.

Last year we started a new program for disabled infants, toddlers, and preschoolers—an age when intervention is critical to make their lives as normal and productive as possible. We began this program on a phase-in basis, and we need to have it fully operational by 1995 to meet federal funding requirements. I propose an additional $2 million for FY 93 to begin phase two.

I spoke in my State of the State address of The Family Connection, a community-level partnership of education, social service, and health services to assist at-risk families. I propose $500,000 to enable the 14 pilot communities to incorporate a juvenile delinquency prevention program into The Family Connection.

I want to begin family-oriented community mental health services for severely emotionally disturbed children in the 28 counties in the service areas of DeKalb, Glynn, Hall and Muscogee. Right now we are simply allowing emotionally disturbed children to worsen to the point of needing institutional care. If we provide family-based care earlier on, we can prevent hospitalization.

Other human resources increases provide home-delivered meals for 315 elderly at a time, expand residential and day care services for the mentally retarded, and address the increased cost and usage of vaccines by county health departments.

And we've got some capital improvements here, too—$10 million in renovation and repair for fire alarms, heating/air conditioning systems, roofs, and mechanical and utility systems at our hospitals and institutions.

On Tuesday, I spoke to you about what I call "deadbeat dads," so let me mention that my budget proposal includes an expansion of our child support recovery efforts. But the cost will be covered through fees rather than state revenues.

That is a summary—a long one, I know, but there's much in it—of the budgetary highlights of Georgia Rebound. If you add all of them up and put them together with the ongoing costs of operating state government, you get a budget for FY 93 that totals $8.134 billion. Of that total, $7.9 billion comes from existing revenue sources, which I have projected to grow at a rate of 5.8 percent. This projection is significantly below Dr. Henry Thomassen's most conservative estimate of 6.2 percent. I took his most conservative estimate and made it even more conservative.

The budget I've explained to you has $233 million built into it from fee adjustments and other revenue sources. Of that, $207 million will come from the fee adjustments in Georgia Rebound. The remainder comes from legislation that others propose and fees that can be adjusted by administrative action.

In addition, the Williams Commission has recommended several improvements in the collection and management of revenues. Some will take legislation, which I will present to you. Others can be done administratively. The Commission projects increased revenues of $85 million. However, I chose not to include this $85 million in my revenue estimate, because I wanted it to serve as a hedge against any potential shortfall. But you should know and have some comfort that it is there. If our revenue projections are on target—and I think they are—it will go toward replenishing our reserves.

A significant part of this revenue would come from two sources, so let me mention them briefly, because some of them you haven't heard before. First, tax amnesty, which has been used to good advantage by more 30 states over the past decade. The idea is to provide a window of opportunity for delinquent taxpayers to pay their overdue taxes without penalty, then crack down with tougher enforcement and bigger penalties. In conjunction with this effort, we will implement a central taxpayer accounting system in the Department of Revenue to increase our ability to identify and track down delinquent taxpayers.

Second, unclaimed property. The state is responsible for finding the owners of unclaimed property, and if they cannot be located within a certain number of years, the property transfers to the state. At the recommendation of the Williams Commission, I will introduce legislation to strengthen the unclaimed property program and reduce the amount of time unclaimed property is held prior to transfer to the state.

On Tuesday I explained just how far out of line our fee structure had become through our failure to adjust it along the way. Programs that were designed to be self-supporting in the first place, have now come to be heavily subsidized from our state treasury. My friends, there is a connection between the fact that we have the lowest fees in the Southeast and at the same time lag behind other states in programs for our children. We have been taking money away from our schools and other important programs and spending it to subsidize our user fees.

First, I propose raising the cost of a driver's license to $15 for four years. The present cost for an driver's license was set when Eisenhower was President. If that fee had just been increased at the same rate as the consumer price index over the years, a Georgia driver's license would now cost $22.50. And we will use some of the funds from this fee increase to upgrade and improve the process of obtaining a license, as I explained a few minutes ago.

Presently a learner's permit costs $1.50. Obviously, this is not even close to covering the cost of processing. I propose that we increase this fee to $10, which covers the processing cost.

The largest fee increase I propose in the area of driver's licenses—and one that goes beyond recovering the cost—comes in reinstating licenses suspended for traffic violations. Right now the fee for reinstating a driver's license is $25, no matter why it was suspended. I propose that habitual offenders and those who have been convicted of DUI or a drug-related offense pay a $200 fee to get their license reinstated. Fees for reinstating driver's licenses suspended for other violations would be raised to $50.

I also propose an increase in the cost of a motor vehicle title to $18, again recovering the cost, but remaining below the regional average. In fact, right now, Georgia has the lowest title fee in the Southeast. Titles are a one-time charge that occurs only when the ownership of a vehicle changes. It is not a recurring expense.

I propose a $20 tag. It would put us almost exactly at the Southeast average and significantly below the highest fee in the region of $100. As we increase this fee, I also propose doubling the amount which counties may retain from 50 cents to $1 per tag. This is a good way to help local governments. They will gain approximately $3 million in new revenue.

Prestige tags—these are vanity plates—are not a necessity. No one has to have one. I propose an annual fee of $25, which would raise almost $2 million a year. And we would still be well below the average annual fee in the Southeast, which is more than $27.

Public ID cards for those who do not drive, but need photo identification, would cost $10 rather than the current $5 to cover the cost of issuing them.

In addition to these fee increases, I am proposing a new $200 impact fee to be assessed on out-of-state vehicles when the registration is transferred. In Florida, it's $300. Every year 125,000 vehicles are brought into Georgia from other states. Their owners do not pay any ad valorem taxes whatsoever for the year in which they enter the state. But Georgia residents—your constituents—pay an ad valorem tax on each vehicle at the beginning of the year. This tax can amount to several hundred dollars on a late-model car. This fee is about what they'd otherwise pay in taxes. It would correct this unfairness in our tax structure and raise $25 million. It will not affect a single constituent living in your legislative district right now.

To help acquire new wildlife acreage through Preservation 2000 and manage new wildlife areas, I propose an increase of $1.50 in the cost of hunting and fishing licenses. But even with these increases, the cost of the license remains below the regional average.

Georgia is one of only a very few states in which the cost of regulating utilities is borne largely by the taxpayer rather than by the industry being regulated. The Public Service Commission is a state regulatory body that oversees an industry, just like the Department of Banking and Finance, the Board of Workers Compensation, and the licensing boards under the Secretary of State. These other state regulatory bodies operate on the basis of cost recovery, but the PSC's operation is heavily subsidized from the state treasury, the state taxpayer. The PSC's current fee income only covers a fraction of the cost of regulation. I propose that the fee be adjusted to cover costs.

What's called vendors' compensation is another area where we've gotten way out of line because we haven't made any changes for decades. We currently allow retail businesses to keep three percent of what they collect in sales tax. This was set 40 years ago in 1951—before computers, before calculators—back when the sales tax was figured by hand. While it may still take our smaller retailers some time and effort to process the sales tax, our very large businesses simply call up a number on their computer and write a check. And then they keep literally millions of sales tax dollars for doing that.

They have been doing it for a long time, and they've kept a lot of money. But now that tax money is needed for programs that benefit the taxpayers who paid it. Nineteen of the 50 states, including our neighbor North Carolina, don't have any vendors' compensation at all. Other states pay a much smaller percentage than we do, or they set caps.

I propose to cap vendors' compensation at $4,000, which would not affect 97 percent of Georgia's vendors. The revenue gain to Georgia from this change will be $50 million a year. And local governments would receive at least $10 million a year—money they desperately need in these tough financial times.

As I outlined Georgia Rebound, I spoke about several large capital outlay programs to be funded with bonds. And I want to assure you that we came through the August budget cutting process with our top bond ratings intact.

More specifically, let me emphasize to you that we can sell all the bonds I propose in my FY 93 budget with only a very small increase in our debt level—three-tenths of one percent, to be exact. Our debt is at one of its lowest levels in three decades—5.4 percent, compared to the constitutional limit of 10 percent of our income. We can build for the future while only raising our debt level from 5.4 percent to 5.7 percent. Only six times in the past 28 years has the debt level been lower than what I propose for FY 93. With that in mind, we would be foolish not to take advantage of the lowest interest rates in 20 years.

The appropriations for Georgia Rebound target our limited resources, investing them in areas that will better position Georgia for the future.

In addition, Georgia Rebound creates jobs. Over the next two years, it will provide jobs for 15,000 people all across the state, largely in construction. In fact, that's what it's all about—jobs, thousands of jobs in the private sector all across this state. Jobs now, jobs in the future. Construction jobs, high-tech jobs.

My friends, I'm finally bringing these remarks to an end. Let me appeal to the better angel of your nature as you consider this budget. We're in this boat called Georgia together. We can sail together or sink together. We can either move this state ahead or settle for the way it's always been.

I've made my choice. I intend to see Georgia Rebound through to its successful conclusion—using every talent and every tool I have at my disposal—or exhaust myself in the effort. Because, I do not want my grandchildren to sit in an outdated classroom and receive a third-rate education. I do not want to be part of a generation that condemns Georgia to mediocrity and second-best.

I want my grandchildren to sit in state-of-the-art learning centers, and be able to call up the history of these times on computer-generated, laser-projected, three-dimensional holographic images. And I want them to learn that in the last decade of the 20th century, Georgia turned the corner, put aside differences of political party, put aside differences of region, and sector and joined together to give a new birth to the Empire State of the South.

# Georgia Conservancy

*Callaway Gardens, February 29, 1992*

It is a great pleasure for me to join the Georgia Conservancy for your 25th anniversary conference, and be a part of this environmental odyssey, that takes us both back through history and ahead into the future.

When the early explorers arrived in what was to become Georgia, they found vast and majestic forests, weathered mountains, and clear flowing streams that joined into mighty, rolling rivers. The vast horizon of this new world seemed to go on forever, and in the true pioneer spirit, they set out to conquer it—to turn its splendor for their own use and enjoyment.

As this state, together with the rest of the eastern seaboard, became increasingly urbanized and industrialized, that spectacular wilderness began to vanish. The forests were logged, and the naked top soil was washed away by the rain. The brush and tree cover that grew back was a poor substitute for the original.

We have gradually come to understand that the world that once seemed so vast and endless is actually quite finite, and we who care deeply about the environment have come to a special understanding of the words of H. G. Wells when he said, "History becomes more and more a race between education and catastrophe."

Carolyn Boyd Hatcher sent me a list of 50 accomplishments over the course of the Conservancy's 25-year history. As I read it, I had a sense of personal involvement with you, as I saw on that list numerous efforts in which I played a part. But I was also struck by the extent to which the list illustrated the words of H.G. Wells. It is a list of educational efforts and of the prevention of environmental catastrophes, both great and small.

Twenty-five years ago, our pollution problems were obvious to everyone. Factory smokestacks belched black smoke; streams below our industries and cities were clogged with untreated or poorly treated sewage; hundreds of landfills were little more than open, burning dumps. It is in no small part due to your efforts that the past 25 years of environmental history in Georgia are ones of increasing understanding and sensitivity to the importance of preserving our natural resources.

We have adopted major and far-reaching legislation to protect important natural areas and control the production and disposal of waste. We have gone from 196 communities with inadequate sewage treatment to one: from treating less than half of our industrial wastewater to treating 99 percent of it—from 1,500 industrial facilities with inadequate air pollution controls, to none; from 400 open, burning dumps to 185 permitted landfills. Today we require significant water users to be permitted, and we test public drinking water for 87 toxic chemicals. We control the release of more than 400 industrial toxins into the air—far more than mandated by the federal government. And smelly paper mills must now control their release of sulphur.

Twenty-five years ago, chemical wastes went to the local dump or were disposed of on the property of the companies that generated them. Today we hold the distinction of being the first state to get all hazardous waste disposal facilities closed and under clean-up mandates. But even more important, we have experienced a tremendous change in attitudes. Once seen as hampering economic development, environmental protection is now viewed as an essential to health, well-being, and the quality of life—factors viewed as assets to economic growth.

My own sphere of influence, of course, is state government. The environment has always been of great concern to me. The first legislative resolution I sponsored 30 years ago was inspired by my friend, Dr. Charles Wharton. And it set up a committee to study the feasibility of setting aside, of preserving certain natural areas. Sound familiar?

The environment is now one of my top priorities as Governor. And I intend to make major strides forward in this area during my administration. There are two thrusts to my efforts—preservation and prevention. I begin with preservation.

Georgia has one of the richest, most diverse environments in the nation, from barrier islands where rare sea turtles lay their eggs, to one of the most unique swamps on earth, to a mountain terrain that has more varieties of trees and shrubs in a few counties than the entire continent of Europe. Yet we have preserved only seven percent of our land. Among the southeastern states, we rank seventh in our state-owned natural acreage, ninth in our wildlife acreage. That's not so good for the state that calls itself the Empire State of the South and prides itself on its beautiful geography.

One of the first things I did after becoming Governor was to create Preservation 2000, a public-private partnership whose goal is to acquire an additional 100,000 acres of natural lands during my administration. We spent much of 1991 laying groundwork for Preservation 2000. The Advisory Council met and set the criteria and process for choosing which sites to purchase.

I included $20 million in bonds for land purchase in the budget I put together at the end of the year to propose to the General Assembly. As a revenue source to help pay for these bonds, I proposed an increase in the cost of hunting and fishing licenses, which has passed the House and come out of committee in the Senate, and is now waiting to be put on the Senate calendar.

Even though Preservation 2000 is just now coming out of its organizational stage, we have already reached almost 10 percent of our goal. We have acquired Little Tybee and Cabbage Islands near Savannah and the Lighthouse Tract on Sapelo Island. We also acquired additional acreage for Panola Mountain State Park, which I mention because the creation of this park to preserve one of the very few natural tracts of land in metro Atlanta was one of your early advocacy efforts. I remember working with Jim Mackey on it way back then.

These purchases were made possible largely through donations to Preservation 2000 from sources outside state government, and through the Non-Game Wildlife Fund, whose money comes from a state income-tax check-off. So, as you do your income taxes over the next six weeks, please remember to check the Non-Game Wildlife Fund and contribute to this worthwhile effort.

This year, with the site selection process in place and substantial state funds coming, which will help us leverage more private contributions, we will aggressively move forward toward our goal of 100,000 acres.

In addition to acquiring natural acreage, my efforts in preservation include providing greater protection for our natural resources. Last year the cornerstone of my package of environmental legislation was the Mountain and River Corridor Protection Act. This year, I want to change the law on easements to make it easier to protect the natural, scenic and open-space values of real property. My bill has passed the House and is out of committee in the Senate, waiting to come to the floor for a vote.

The prevention thrust of my efforts focuses on waste and pollution. I began this effort last year by restructuring the Georgia Hazardous Waste Authority to include more scientists and engineers and fewer politicians, and by appointing a respected conservationist by the name of Bob Kerr to head it up. Last year we also restructured and strengthened our Environmental Protection Division and made it clear that the doors and ears of the EPD and the Department of Natural Resources are open to you.

This year we are moving forward in several key areas. First, I am proposing a state SuperFund. During the past decade, we've put tough standards into place controlling the generation and disposal of hazardous waste. But we are still carrying a lot of dangerous baggage with us in the form of old disposal sites, dumps, and chemical spills from before the days of regulation. The Basket Creek drum site in Douglas County is a painful example.

We have identified some 800 sites, and EPD continues to find 20 to 30 new sites each year, often in communities where innocent citizens suddenly find that their homes are sitting on an old dump site. Their property is, of course, devalued and their health threatened. At present, only five percent of these sites have been placed on the national priority list for clean-up by the federal SuperFund. We are left holding the bag on the other 95 percent—hundreds and hundreds of sites.

A structure of fees levied on off-site shipment of hazardous waste and on solid waste will create a funding mechanism for a state SuperFund to clean up these sites, and also, importantly, an incentive to reduce solid and hazardous waste generation. In addition, remember that industry, banks, and real estate companies often request the EPD's assistance and oversight in voluntary clean-up efforts, which we have neither the resources nor the regulatory powers to do. My state SuperFund bill also addresses this need. This bill has come out of committee in the House and is waiting to go on the calendar for a floor vote.

Of course, not all dumps and landfills contain hazardous waste, but they still pose a problem nonetheless. We have increasingly become a throw-away society, and we are running out of places to throw it. Another part of the effort to deal more effectively with solid waste is assisting local governments with improvements to their solid waste disposal facilities. My legislative package for this year includes a constitutional amendment to allow the Georgia Environmental Facilities Authority to issue state-guaranteed bonds for loans to local governments to build solid waste disposal facilities. This constitutional amendment and its enabling legislation were voted out of committee in the House yesterday afternoon.

We have also taken on a new group of polluters this year, and it has not been easy. Some call them houseboats, others call them boathouses. By either name they are residences, permanently tied up to the banks or anchored to the river bottom on that grandfather of rivers, the Altamaha. Because they have no engines, they do not come under the laws governing watercraft, but because they do not sit on private land, they are not governed by building and zoning regulations either. Not only are they often an eyesore, but they have taken over public waterways for their own private use. Very few of them have sanitation facilities, but instead dump untreated garbage and raw sewage into the river.

This is an intolerable situation that had to be addressed. I proposed a bill which has been passed by both the House and the Senate and should soon be on my desk. It prohibits any more such structures on tidewaters and other navigable waters. The 200 existing residences will have until July 1st to comply with standards set by DNR for sanitation, structural safety, and personal safety. Then, all live-aboard boats would become illegal on June 30, 1997.

I also have a coastal marshlands bill. I was involved in the original passage of the Coastal Marshlands Act, and we are now doing the first major revision of it since its enactment. In addition to updating its bureaucratic procedures, we are strengthening it and expanding its coverage. The bill expands the jurisdiction of the Coastal Marshlands to clearly include all water bottoms and non-vegetated areas as well as vegetated marshlands. We are also expanding the criteria for deciding what is not in the public interest and therefore is not permissible within this area. And although we have not issued any permits for live-aboard boats in our coastal waters for five years now, we are using this opportunity to make that policy clear in state law as well.

Another focus in this legislative session is major improvements to Georgia's Air Quality Act and the expansion of our vehicle emission inspection law in light of the 1990 Federal Clean Air Act. The bill on the vehicle emission inspection has passed the House and came out of committee in the Senate on Thursday. And the changes to the Air Quality Act came out of committee in the House, also on Thursday.

I've talked about the past and the present. As we look to the future on this environmental odyssey, I want to mention two efforts. First, one which you share as your mission—education. I consider early education on the care of our environment to be critical to the ongoing protection and preservation of our natural resources. So I have another bill before the General Assembly requiring the Department of Education to develop curriculum materials for K through 12 on environmental education and recycling programs. This bill is through the House and out of committee in the Senate, and it is waiting to go on the Senate calendar for a floor vote.

Second, along the educational line, I want to mention the Georgia Research Alliance. You know, everyone has heard of North Carolina's famous Research Triangle. But few know that Georgia Tech, Emory University, and the University of Georgia do more research than their three counterparts that anchor Research Triangle. What North Carolina has that we don't is promotion and coordination. But look out, North Carolina, here comes the Georgia Research Alliance.

It includes not three but all six of Georgia's major universities, public and private, in a unique partnership not only with each other, but with private industry as well, and it will focus on research with private sector applications—research that will attract firms, spin off new businesses, and create jobs. The Research Alliance has already raised nearly $4 million from private sources, and I proposed a state funding package of cash and bonds totally nearly $14 million, which was funded in the supplemental budget that has been passed.

I tell you all this simply because one of the three major research ventures of the Research Alliance is environmental technology. Through the Research Alliance, we are launching a major effort to become a center of expertise, on the cutting edge of technology to control pollution and address environmental problems like clean-up in effective ways.

These environmental efforts, together with a group of other proposals in education, public safety and economic development, form my Georgia Rebound program. In Georgia Rebound I have identified those things I feel are most important for us to invest in today, if we are to move forward to a new level of well-being and prosperity in the future.

Clean air and water, soil that is toxin-free, adequate wilderness areas, the preservation of Georgia's natural beauty—these are among the things we must achieve and safe-guard if we are to bequeath to future generations a state that is in better shape than the one we inherited from our parents. And I hope you will give Georgia Rebound, as a comprehensive program, your active and vocal support as we continue through the 1992 legislative session.

As the 40 days of the General Assembly wear on and we get caught up in all kinds of maneuvering and negotiations, we sometimes allow ourselves to lapse into thinking that the Capitol is a little universe, and what we're doing constitutes the exercise of real power. But then a time comes along when I get away to somewhere like Sapelo, where I was a few weeks ago with some of you, or here at Callaway Gardens, or home in Young Harris. Especially those mountains. By the way, thanks Nell, for the new second edition of the *Guide to the North Georgia Mountains*. I had one, but my sons, who are avid outdoors men, had claimed it as their own.

But anyway, I go back to Young Harris. And I remember that the roots of the Blue Ridge were laid more than a billion years ago. And the mountains themselves are some 300 million years old. By comparison, our power and even our lives as individual humans are measly of scale and brief in duration. As the psalmist wrote, you and I are like the flowers of the field that flourish for a moment. Then the wind blows and we are gone. But we get so caught up in the minutia of day-to-day living, that we get it backwards. We begin to see our brief little lives as the big picture, and the Earth as existing for our benefit and use during our lifetime.

The most graphic thing I carry with me from having read Al Gore's excellent new book, *Earth in the Balance*, is a little anecdote. Gore tells of traveling to the Trans-Antarctic Mountains to visit a scientist, who had removed a core sample of ice from a glacier that was many, many years in the making. The scientist pointed to a place on the ice core that had been laid down two decades before, and said, "See that change in the ice. That's the effect of passing the Federal Clean Air Act." So many of us have no sense of the importance of that law, because its changes had a bigger impact on the grand sweep of nature than they did on the microcosm of our daily lives. And I wonder if the changes we are now making in the General Assembly in tandem with the 1990 Clean Air Act will be read in the arctic ice decades from now.

The vast ecosystems of the Earth move across the centuries with a tremendous power that is far beyond our control. But at the same time, what we do during our brief tenure on earth can and does alter them in remarkable ways. For the moment in which we are here, we are the stewards of those systems. We hold the Earth in our hands. The stewardship of the earth is a much heavier and more far-reaching responsibility than simply exploiting natural resources for our needs and desires of the moment. And once we realize that, then we begin to understand the purpose of the great law of the six nations of the Iroquois Confederacy, which required that in every deliberation, consideration be given to its impact on the next seven generations.

Thank you for your support of my environmental efforts. Thank you for allowing me to join you in the celebration of your 25th anniversary. And thank you for the substantial contribution you have made to environmental preservation in Georgia during the past 25 years, and will continue to make in the future. Together, we will do even more.

# University of Georgia Commencement

*June 13, 1992*

A few weeks ago, events in southern California rocked this nation back on its heels. Both the Rodney King trial and the riots that followed demonstrated the terrible tendency of many Americans—white and black—to see skin color first and foremost—to look at everything through skin-colored glasses.

That shocking videotape raised the question of whether those four policemen were able to see beyond the color of Rodney King's skin. And then we wondered whether it was the color of the skin that took precedence in the mind of that jury, when it failed to convict those officers of excessive force.

But then, in the violence that followed, we saw the same thing in the other direction. People were attacked and injured, simply because they were white. Some of those protestors, like the policemen, like that jury, did not look beyond the color of skin.

When that happens in either direction, we deny the other person's humanity. We deny the fact that there is a fellow human being underneath that skin. We deny the fact that we all feel the same emotions, that the tears we all cry know no color.

Far too often race has been used to distract our attention away from the fact that the rich are getting richer and the poor are getting poorer. The fact is that during the 1980s, a new economic order has been emerging in this nation that is more unequal, more divided than ever before.

During the 1980s, the richest one percent of our population got 75 percent of the growth in wealth. At the same time, the average American increased the amount of time on the job by 158 hours a year—the equivalent of another full month—just to maintain the same income. And the working poor—those who work full-time but earn less than the poverty level—the working poor increased in the 80s by a third.

This is the exact opposite of what should be happening. But racism was used to cover it over; to make working white people think they have more in common with the rich than they do with the African-American person who may work beside them on the job.

I grew up poor. I grew up without a father, without indoor plumbing, for years without electricity, without a car in the family. But I also grew up with hope. I grew up believing that if you worked hard and played by the rules, you could get somewhere; you could become somebody.

But today, many Americans have no hope. They have no hope of escaping poverty, no hope of taking control of their own destiny, no hope of becoming somebody. Kids are not going to study and say no to drugs if the only possibility they can see ahead of them is unemployment and death from a gunshot on the streets of a housing project. The young Leah Sears-Collinses of Georgia need to grow up knowing that it really is possible for an African-American woman to become a justice on the Supreme Court of Georgia.

When violence marred what could have been meaningful, peaceful protests in Atlanta, it distracted attention away from the deeper issues the students were raising. One of the points made by the Atlanta University students was that this is not the 1960s. They are right. It isn't. In the struggle during that time, the aim was to achieve civil rights. That was the right place to begin. And we must continue to guard against those injustices, and not preserve the symbol of those times on our state flag.

But on the opposite side of the same coin from civil rights is economic rights. And that—economic rights—is what our challenge is today. For example, as a result of the civil rights movement, African Americans can now sit wherever they want on the bus, but 43 percent of their children are born in poverty.

For example, as a result of the civil rights movement, African Americans can now use whatever drinking fountain or restroom is most convenient, but their rates of unemployment are double those of whites. For example, as a result of the civil rights movement, African Americans can now eat at the restaurant of their choice, but their infants die at a rate twice that of whites.

You see, America has not yet addressed the economic side of that coin. The social programs created in the 60s were designed to compensate the victims of poverty rather than solve the problems that cause it. They give poor people just enough in the way of Medicaid and welfare and food stamps and housing subsidies to keep and sustain them in their poverty, rather than giving them the skills and opportunities they needed to break out of their poverty.

The world has undergone tremendous change since the 1960s. The industrial age, on which those old social programs were modeled, has given way to a new era of microelectronics, satellites, and fiber optic cables—a world of modern technology. Today the critical infrastructure required to generate economic growth is intellectual. It is a better educated, more highly skilled workforce.

We must change from spending money to sustain people in their poverty, to investing money in training and educating them and providing them with economic opportunity. Theodore Roosevelt once said that "this country will not be a good place for *any* of us to live in unless we make it a good place for *all* of us to live in." Little did he know how very true those words would become.

What all of us have got to realize, and realize pretty quickly, is that, regardless of skin color, we are all Americans. The greater the social and economic equity among us, the more successful we all are going to be.

By the year 2000, half of those who enter the workforce will be African American, Asian, Hispanic, or of Middle Eastern descent. And if all of our children are not equally well trained, well educated, and able to move into the mainstream of a forward-looking economy, we are all in big, big trouble. You who graduate here today, I believe, understand that. You have sought out and acquired an education, and you are the leaders of your generation. You are the trail blazers. You will become the role models for the next generation.

With your help we must turn our backs on an era where one race is pitted against another while the rich get richer and the poor get poorer. And we must turn our faces toward an era in which the barriers to economic opportunity are finally removed. Because, my young friends, if all of us do not advance together, then, surely, all of us will diminish together.

# Keynote Address:

# Democratic National Convention

*July 13, 1992*

Listen to this voice.

It's a voice flavored by the Blue Ridge; a voice straight out of a remote valley hidden among the peaks and hollows of the Appalachian Mountains; a voice that's been described as more barbed wire than honeysuckle.

That this kind of voice could travel from a forgotten corner of Appalachia is a testament to the grace of God and the greatness of the Democratic Party.

This week we are gathered here to nominate a man from a remote, rural corner of Arkansas to be President of the United States of America. That is powerful proof that the American Dream still lives—at least in the Democratic Party.

Bill Clinton is the only candidate for President who feels our pain, shares our hopes and will work his heart out to fulfill our dreams.

You see, I understand why Bill Clinton is so eager to see the American Dream kept alive for a new generation. Because I, too, was a product of that dream.

I was born during the worst of the Depression on a cold winter's day in the drafty bedroom of a rented house, and I was my parents' hope for the future. Franklin Roosevelt was elected that year, and would soon replace generations of neglect with a whirlwind of activity, bringing to our little valley a very welcome supply of God's most precious commodity: hope.

My father—a teacher—died when I was two weeks old, leaving a young widow with two small children. But with my mother's faith in God—and Mister Roosevelt's voice on the radio—we kept going.

After my father's death, my mother with her own hands cleared a small piece of rugged land. Every day she waded into a neighbor's cold mountain creek, carrying out thousands of smooth stones to build a house. I grew up watching my mother complete that house, from the rocks she'd lifted from the creek and cement she mixed in a wheelbarrow—cement that today still bears her handprints.

Her son bears her handprints, too. She pressed her pride and her hopes and her dreams deep into my soul. So, you see, I know what Dan Quayle means when he says it's best for children to have two parents. You bet it is! And it would be nice for them to have trust funds, too.

But we can't all be born handsome, rich, and lucky. That's why we have a Democratic Party.

My family would still be isolated and destitute if we had not had FDR's Democratic brand of government. I made it because Franklin Delano Roosevelt energized this nation. I made it because Harry Truman fought for working families like mine. I made it because

John Kennedy's rising tide lifted even our tiny boat.

I made it because Lyndon Johnson showed America that people who were born poor didn't have to die poor. And I made it because a man with whom I served in the Georgia Senate—a man named Jimmy Carter—brought honesty and decency and integrity to public service.

But what of the kids of today? Who fights for the child of a single mother today? Because without a government that is on their side, those children have no hope. And when a child has no hope, a nation has no future.

I am a Democrat because we are the party of hope. For twelve dark years the Republicans have dealt in cynicism and skepticism. They've mastered the art of division and diversion, and they have robbed us of our hope.

Too many mothers today cannot tell their children what my mother told me—that working hard and playing by the rules can make your dreams come true. For millions, the American dream has become what the poet called "a dream deferred." And if you recall the words of that poet-prophet, he warned us that a dream deferred can explode.

Robbed of hope, the voices of anger rise up from working Americans, who are tired of paying more in taxes and getting less in services. And George Bush doesn't get it?

Americans cannot understand why some can buy the best health care in the world, but all the rest of us get is rising cost and cuts in coverage—or no health insurance at all. And George Bush doesn't get it?

Americans cannot walk our streets in safety, because our "tough-on-crime" President has waged a phony photo-op war on drugs, posing for pictures while cutting police, prosecutors and prisons. And George Bush doesn't get it?

Americans have seen plants closed down, jobs shipped overseas, and our hopes fade away as our economic position collapses right before our very eyes. And George Bush doesn't get it!

Four years ago, Mr. Bush told us he was a quiet man, who hears the voices of quiet people. Today, we know the truth: George Bush is a timid man who hears only the voices of caution and the status quo.

Let's face facts: George Bush just doesn't get it. He doesn't see it; he doesn't feel it; and he's done nothing about it.

That's why we cannot afford four more years.

If the "education president" gets another term, even our kids won't be able to spell potato.

If the "law and order president" gets another term, the criminals will run wild, because our commander-in-chief talks like Dirty Harry, but acts like Barney Fife.

If the "environmental president" gets another term, the fish he catches off Kennebunkport will have three eyes.

So much for the millionaire. But we've still got ourselves a billionaire. A billionaire!

He *says* he's an outsider, who will shake up the system in Washington. But as far back as 1974 he was lobbying Congress for tax breaks. He tried to turn $55,000 in contributions into a special $15 million tax loophole that was tailor-made for him. Sounds to me like instead of shaking the system up, Mr. Perot's been shaking it down.

Ross says he'll clean out the barn, but he's been knee deep in it for years.

If Ross Perot's an outsider, folks, I'm from Brooklyn. Mr. Perot's giving us salesmanship, not leadership. And we're not buying it.

I know who I'm for. I'm for Bill Clinton because he is a Democrat who does not have to read a book or be briefed about the struggles of single-parent families, or what it means to work hard for everything he's ever received in life.

There was no silver spoon in sight when he was born, three months after his father died. No one ever gave Bill Clinton a free ride as he worked his way through college and law school. And the people at Yale couldn't believe it when he turned down a good job in Washington to return to Arkansas and teach.

Bill Clinton is a Democrat who has the courage to tell some of those liberals who think welfare should continue forever, and some of those conservatives who think there should be no welfare at all, that they're both wrong. He's a Democrat who will move people off the welfare rolls and onto the job rolls.

Bill Clinton is a Democrat who has the courage to lead a real war on crime here at home. And around the world he will be the kind of commander-in-chief this old Marine sergeant would be proud to follow.

That either one of us was able, one growing up in an Appalachian valley and the other in rural Arkansas, to eventually become governors of our states is a tribute to the American dream and yes, the Democratic Party that makes it a reality.

When I was growing up back in the mountains, whenever I felt like one of life's losers, my mother used to point to the one and only paved road in our valley—a narrow little strip that disappeared winding its way through a distant gap—and she'd say, "You know what's so great about this place? You can get anywhere in the world from here."

Thanks to her and to God, the United States Marine Corps and the Democratic Party, I did go somewhere. But I've never really left that mountain valley, either. Shirley and I, our children and their children still live in the Appalachian town of Young Harris, Georgia, and tonight, one of my sons is sitting in front of the television set in the living room of that same rock house my mother and her neighbors built so many years ago.

Tonight, let our message be heard in every living room in every home in America. Wherever families and friends are gathered, let them know this:

We have a leader and a party and a platform that says to the everyday working people of this country: we will fight your fight; we will ease your burden; we will carry your cause.

We will hear *all* the voices of America—from the silky harmonies of the Gospel choirs to the rough-edged rhythms of a hot country band; from the razor's edge rap of the inner city to the soaring beauty of the finest soprano.

We hear your voice, America.

We hear your voice. We will answer your call. We will keep the faith. And we will restore your hope.

Thank you. God bless you. And God bless America.

# Legislative Biennial Institute

*The University of Georgia, December 8, 1992*

Let me first extend an official welcome to the many new faces around these tables . . . and also to those others of you who, like I, have been around the Horn a few times. Being a legislator is not easy. I know. It's kind of like Alice in Wonderland, when she was running to keep up with the Queen of Hearts, and she said to the Queen, "In our country, you'd generally get somewhere else if you ran very fast for a long time, as we have been doing." To which the Queen replied, "A slow sort of country. Now here, you see, it takes all the running you can do to keep in the same place. If you want to get somewhere else, you must run at least twice as fast as that."

Like Alice, being in politics in Georgia takes a lot of running just to keep up with what's going on. And if we want to actually do something, then we have to run even faster. For we govern in a difficult, mean, and challenging time. Not only are the problems thorny and complex, but we also have very limited resources with which to address them.

But this is an administration that believes in meeting complex and thorny problems head on. And the purpose of the legislative process is to thrash out our differences on those issues—to find the path on common ground upon which we can move forward together.

On this occasion two years ago, we were in a recession and had not seen the worst yet. And I talked about the importance of some very careful cutting to maintain our fiscal integrity. Today I can say that we have now seen the worst—that during the past two years the drop in revenues bottomed out, and things are beginning to improve.

November's revenue increase was 10.7 percent, breaking into double-digits for the first time in two and a-half years. That reflects October's retail sales—we haven't gotten to the Christmas rush yet, which is looking quite strong. The individual and corporate income taxes both rose together, which is another good sign.

With the crucial help of many of you in this room, we also made the cuts I spoke of back in 1990—not across-the-board cuts with a meat ax, but careful cuts with a scalpel to downsize and streamline state government. We must continue to do that. Even as revenues improve, we must continue to carefully prune and trim away any excess we can find in state government. And I'm not just talking. When I present my supplemental budget to you about this time next month, you will see some $45 million in cuts we made early in the fiscal year, plus some additional places we've found we can trim back even more. You will also see some surplus and lapsed funds from last fiscal year that resulted from the austerity measures we took at that time.

Some of these funds will be used to bring the Quality Basic Education funding formula up to the level that actual fall enrollments indicate. Some will be used to address our growing Medicaid rolls. But the rest of it I will use to lower the revenue estimate by $75 million.

Let me make it very clear: I truly believe we are on track to meet our revenue projections for this fiscal year. But I prefer to err on the side of caution, especially since our reserve fund was completely depleted in June of 1990—six months before I took office. And we've been operating without one red cent in it since then. If revenues should fall short, we will be prepared. If they come in as projected—as I believe they will—then we will have a jump on our mid-term education adjustment for next year and maybe even on rebuilding our reserves.

For most of our lifetime, the 21st century has seemed to be a time far, far away—a remote, futuristic time inhabited by science fiction stories. And it's kind of shocking to now realize that the 21st century will be upon us in only seven years. In many, many ways, it will be much, much different than the 20th century has been, and we absolutely must be planning for it and prepared for it. On the horizon are the 1994 Super Bowl—just two years away—and the 1996 Summer Olympics—just four years away.

We have started moving forward in several important areas—areas that are critical and should not be interrupted or stymied if we are to present Georgia to the world as a healthy, progressive, thriving state with a high quality of life.

The Governor's Development Council was reconstituted last session into a strong public-private initiative. This Council is going to coordinate and broaden out our economic development initiatives far beyond our traditional approach of simply recruiting businesses. It will also strengthen support for our existing traditional businesses, expand our exports, encourage new technology companies and strategically develop the broader infrastructure that modern industry must have.

Preservation 2000 is another public-private initiative to preserve an additional 100,000 acres of natural recreational and wilderness area. I'm very proud of this program. It's one of my pets, and I thank all of you who have worked to make it a success. We have already preserved scenic wilderness from Tallulah Gorge to Little Tybee and Cabbage Islands, from Buffalo Swamp on the Altamaha River to Sprewell Bluff on the Flint. If you add in the acreage that is now under negotiation, we are more than half of the way to our goal of 100,000 acres. I'd like to exceed that goal, and I think we can.

In the area of public safety, in the past two years we have created 2,172 boot camp beds. And even as the naysayers and skeptics were shaking their heads, Georgia's boot camps were becoming the model for other states. They separate young drug offenders from the influence of harder criminals in prisons, and put them through a stark, highly disciplined, basic training regimen combined with drug treatment and education to prepare them for a successful time of supervised probation.

Not only are these boot camps effective, but they are also much cheaper than prisons. It costs $2,500 a bed to build a boot camp using inmate labor, compared to $27,000 a bed for a prison. It costs $42 a day for each prison inmate, but only $25 a day for an offender in a boot camp.

But the most critical effort we must make to prepare for the future must be to improve education. In the climate we live in today, the only way to make some new, major improvements in education, which we simply have got to make, is to seek out alternative revenue sources like the lottery.

Last year Representative Sonny Watson and many other legislators spent long hours crafting our lottery legislation based not only on what we want for Georgia, but on the legislation and experience of 34 other states. Presently, we have a good and very sound lottery law in place, and I hope we will give it a chance to operate as the General Assembly in its wisdom decided in 1991 that it should operate. Let's not start "fixing it" until we find out whether it's broke. Let's give it a chance to work.

Many of you heard me explain the lottery when you were out to the Mansion for lunch last month. But allow me please to tell you again, because I want to be double-sure you understand how I envision it. Contrary to what you may have heard, Georgia's lottery is not like Florida's lottery. Not only does our constitutional amendment put the proceeds into a special trust fund rather than in the general treasury, but last session we dedicated that money by law for three new education initiatives.

First, prekindergarten on a voluntary basis for four-year-olds—voluntary by the parent, voluntary by the school system. An extensive study by the Carnegie Institute for the Advancement of Teaching shows that 40 percent of Georgia's five-year-olds are already struggling in kindergarten. Another study in a state with prekindergarten tracked four-year-olds for 20 years. It found that kids who went to preschool had fewer absences, higher grades and better test scores. They had fewer teen pregnancies and arrests. More of them went to college, and they entered the workforce at higher salaries.

Let me emphasize again that what I am proposing is not an expansion of the Quality Basic Education program with a class of four-year-olds at each elementary school. In some communities, it may very well be part of the school system. But it could also be an expanded Head Start program, or a new or expanded private, non-profit program. Each school system and community can look at its own needs and its own resources, and voluntarily propose a plan to the state that would be most efficient and effective for them.

We will first target at-risk kids, as our pilot projects have already started to do. They will be our first priority. And then we will continue to expand the program as communities are ready and lottery proceeds are available. Once more, it's voluntary, and it's not a program that runs on the school year or has to start all together, or all be just alike, or all start at a certain given time.

Second, the Georgia lottery will fund a unique scholarship program that I call HOPE, Helping Outstanding Pupils Educationally. Today, just seven years before the dawn of the 21st century, we are at a critical juncture in our state's history—truly a cross-roads. It has never been more important for our students to get a college education, but at the same time, it has never been more difficult for their families to pay for it.

HOPE has the potential to touch the lives of 90,000 students in Georgia beginning in the fall of 1993, so let me tell you how it would work. Any high school student with a B average—a 3.0 grade point average—when that student walks across the stage at graduation, they will get a HOPE certificate good for tuition at any institution in the University System of Georgia where they are accepted, if their family income is less than $66,000 a year. If I were a high school student, I can just hear my Mama saying, "Son, I can't afford to send you to college, so you'd better study hard and make sure you have a B average so you can get free tuition."

The second part of HOPE is that if the student, has a B average in their freshman year, they can get a loan for tuition for their sophomore year. And if they keep a B average for their sophomore year, the loan is forgiven. In other words, it would be possible for a student who holds a steady B average to get free tuition for their first two years of college.

There will be nothing else like it in the United States of America.

Now, of course, not everybody wants to go to college and not every job takes a college degree. So the third part of HOPE is free tuition for diploma-granting programs at our state technical institutes.

The fourth part of HOPE is for those Georgians who drop out of school, then realize the importance of education and go back to get their GED. There were 16,000 in Georgia last year. I propose that we give our GED graduates a $500 certificate to use for books, materials, or fees at a public college or technical institute.

Finally, we've got a number of independent, private institutions in this state that educate a lot of students—saving us the cost of providing state funds for those students at our university system institutions. As you veteran legislators know, since the early 1970s, we have given what we call tuition equalization grants to private, independent colleges for Georgia students, helping to offset the higher tuition they must charge. Last year we brought them up to $1,000 per student per year. As the fifth component of HOPE, I propose using lottery proceeds to bring tuition equalization grants up to $1,500 for freshmen and sophomores at our independent colleges.

The third program is capital outlay for special equipment and construction needs. The labs in Georgia's high schools, colleges, and technical schools are woefully out of date. And I don't think I have to tell any of you that all of our schools need more computers. We have thousands of kids in make-shift mobile-home classrooms because school construction has not kept up with population growth. And the roof of the University System is leaking, because we have hundreds of older buildings that have not been given the needed renovation and repair. We've got to deal with this.

This third program is also a safety valve, because it involves one-time expenditures. It can expand and contract as lottery proceeds ebb and flow and the needs of the other two programs change. The second built-in safety valve to hold these important education programs steady across the dips and swells in the lottery proceeds is a 10 percent reserve fund.

I will be spelling out the details of these programs in the course of making budget recommendations to you, within the context of the special budget category and the legal parameters already in place.

I've taken a lot of time explaining the HOPE program, because never before has higher education been so critically important. The average job in the Atlanta area requires 14 years of education, and the rest of the state is not far behind. And while we are on the campus of this university that means so very much to our state's future, let me tell you a little of what is going on in higher education in Georgia.

In just the past five years, the number of students enrolled in Georgia's public and private colleges and universities increased by 28 percent—that is more than double the national increase which was only 12 percent. If you separate public and private colleges, you find that during the last half of the 80s, our University System enrollment grew by a phenomenal 31 percent. That's more kids piled into our University System in five years than we'd have if we had duplicated every single one of our 15 two-year colleges. It's more students in five years than if we had created another University of Georgia *and* another Georgia Tech *and* another Medical College of Georgia, all combined. That's a lot of young warm bodies, a lot of inquisitive young minds. It's the future of Georgia.

But the amount of money we have been putting into higher education has not kept pace with that dramatic and unanticipated growth in enrollment. It didn't even keep pace with the growth in revenues. In FY 85, we put 7.9 percent of the budget into higher education. In FY 90, it was down to 6.6 percent.

Our failure to keep up the pace in funding for higher education has shifted a greater portion of the cost onto the shoulders of Georgia families, and they are assuming unprecedented levels of debt to handle it. Over the past 20 years, the cost of higher education has been rising faster than the median family income. And if present trends continue, by the year 2000—that significant time I've been talking about just seven years from now—the cost of one year at a state college or university will equal 20 percent of median family income. And the cost of one year at a private college will be half of median family income.

I hope this data helps you to appreciate the significance of the HOPE Scholarship Program, and why it is so very important to your constituents that it be enacted. And I also hope it helps you understand why last session's Georgia Rebound contained the most massive construction program for higher education in Georgia history, and why we've got to do some more.

Over 400 of our University System buildings are more than 50 years old. Another 1,000 buildings are between 25 and 50 years old—the time framework when roofs and major systems have to be replaced. Yet—despite these renovation needs and despite a phenomenal enrollment increase—during the 80s our annual appropriation for construction equaled only one percent of the existing physical plant of our University System. I've said it before: The collective roof of the University System is leaking, and broom closets are being pressed into service as faculty offices.

University System buildings are not cheap; some are quite expensive. State-of-the-art research means computer labs with massive electrical cables running under the floor; it means vibration-free construction for delicate instruments that can be thrown off by the rumbling of a dump truck out in the street.

In the weeks ahead I will be recommending to you two large and costly, but needed projects right here on this campus. They are the Comprehensive Agricultural Livestock and Poultry Complex and the Biocontainment Research Center. These buildings will catapult us to the forefront in the nation, especially the Biocontainment Research Center. There are very few adequate biocontainment facilities in the nation, and if we build this one, national research on animal diseases is going to focus right here in Athens.

In the two years since we met for the last Biennial Institute, I have had open lines of communication and a very active, intense working relationship with the General Assembly.

I want to thank you for that, and I intend to continue it. During the session, you will need no appointment to see me. My office door will be open from dawn to dusk, and sometimes beyond. Walk in—let's dream and reason together. Because that close working relationship is what has enabled Georgia to make tremendous progress in economic development, in environmental protection, in public safety, and in education, despite our limited resources.

When teacher Christa McAuliffe was killed in the tragic explosion of the space shuttle Challenger, another woman named Barbara Morgan stepped right up to become NASA's first teacher in space. When people asked her why she was so ready and willing when the terrible risks had just been so graphically demonstrated, she said she wanted to show kids what you do in difficult situations. She said, "You don't quit, you don't back up, you go on" and become "a leader who shows all of us the way by literally reaching for the stars."

Today we are standing at the threshold of the 1993 General Assembly. But we are also standing at the threshold of the 21st century. And our sights must be set beyond the next three months; our sights must be set even beyond the next two years. Of course, we have complex problems and we have limited resources. The future has never been easy. It's not the business of the future to be easy. But this is no time to stand around in the corners of this state wringing our hands and saying, "What shall we do?"

On this, the eve of the 21st century, now is time to exert strong, progressive, and courageous leadership. Now is the time to suck it up and march boldly forward to make the most of the opportunity before us. And I look forward to working with you to do just that.

# 1993

# Supplemental Budget Address

*January 5, 1993*

This afternoon, I present to you an amended budget for Fiscal Year 1993 that does what a supplemental budget is intended to do and nothing more. It does not undertake any major new expenditures, but simply fine-tunes the budget you enacted early last year.

It has two prominent features: First, it is based on a revenue estimate that I have reduced by $75 million—from 8 billion 174 million dollars to 8 billion and 99 million dollars. Second, it fulfills our legal obligations to provide mid-year adjustments, primarily for our schools and for Medicaid.

Right now I want to explain the fund sources that have allowed us both to accommodate our mid-year adjustment requirements and to reduce the revenue estimate at the same time. And I'm very pleased that we could do both.

First, we have kept a very tight control on expenditures all through last year. Because of that careful management, we ended the year with a $61.6 million surplus, mostly in funds that had been appropriated but we did not spend.

Second, last August, right in the beginning of this fiscal year, my budget advisors and department heads made nearly $47 million in cuts, because we wanted to continue our efforts to be as tight-fisted, as prudent as possible. We knew that it is easier to tighten up at the beginning of the fiscal year rather than on up into the year.

These cuts are reflected in this amended budget. And I want to emphasize to you that Quality Basic Education funding and essential health services were not subject to any cuts last August. The cuts in higher education and technical and adult education were held to one percent. And no agency took a cut of greater than two percent.

Since making these prudency cuts, we have continued to go through the budget with a fine-toothed comb, making adjustments and culling out any extra funds as new data gave us a better sense of our needs. The best example is what we have done with AFDC. Our welfare rolls had been growing at an average rate of 15 percent a year for the past several years, and that was the projection last January. But as Georgia's economy improved over the past year, growth in rolls slowed to about half of that: 8.7 percent. This means we can trim $14.2 million from the AFDC budget and still provide for all new eligible recipients.

Let me emphasize that this is not a cut, but an adjustment in the amount of new money going into AFDC. This budget still increases state funds for AFDC by $15 million over last year for a total increase of $39 million.

We were also able to sell bonds at even lower interest rates than were anticipated as well as retire some bonds early, which freed up $5.4 million that had been allocated for debt service.

You also will remember an appropriation of $1.8 million for a hazardous waste incinerator. The restructured Hazardous Waste Authority has since decided that it does not need to be built. So that money is now available for other purposes.

As you can see, these are not cuts in programs. These are not cuts in services. It is the ongoing effort of this administration to carefully adjust our expenditures to our needs, and cut—not spend—any excess funds. So, with these funds, we then set about fulfilling our mid-year obligations.

As those of you know, who are familiar with the Quality Basic Education law, we update funding for our public schools each January based on actual enrollments for the current school year. This is the over-riding reason why a supplemental budget is needed, and will be needed as long as we continue to be one of the fastest growing states in the nation. Each fall our school enrollments increase dramatically, requiring more funds to be added to the QBE formula at mid-year. This fall's enrollment increase requires $60 million in additional funding.

You may recall, last winter we put an extra $25 million into the original 1993 budget in anticipation of the need for additional QBE funds at mid-year. The budget before you contains the remaining $35 million required to accommodate enrollment growth. It also includes another million dollars to provide textbooks for all of these new students.

We also have another obligation under QBE which must be met—incentive grants to school systems who convert to a middle school arrangement. Therefore, I am proposing $3 million for the 13 systems who converted to middle schools this school year. Then there is another education appropriation: $650,000 for advanced placement examination fees, in accordance with Senate Bill 417.

The second major area of expenditure is $15 million for Medicaid, which will be matched by federal funds for a total of just over $39 million. While AFDC growth slowed, Medicaid rolls grew. And we are now experiencing a shortfall as claims come in for services provided toward the end of last year.

In addition, you will find a deferral of $8.3 million in Medicaid funds from this budget into the FY 94 budget that I will present to you next week. This kind of transfer of Medicaid funds across fiscal years, as most of you know, is routine and adjusts to time lags in the process. There's an indefinite amount of time between when a person qualifies for Medicaid and when they actually receive an eligible service. Then the claim for that service might not be filed until up to six months after the service is provided. In the meantime one fiscal year has ended and the next has begun. So we are continually adjusting funding across fiscal years.

You will also see a $90.6 million dollar item in the Medicaid budget. This significant sum represents voluntary contributions from 74 hospitals to the Indigent Care Trust Fund. It will be matched by federal funds for a total of $239 million. But unfortunately, because some foolish federal regulations shut the door on this program, we are now considering the alternatives which have been made possible under the constitutional amendment passed in November. I will be making a recommendation later on, restructuring the Indigent Care Trust Fund.

I am proposing several other health-related adjustments in the budget for the Department of Human Resources. First, an increase of $5.4 million to pay for court-ordered placements of troubled children. When severely troubled children come under the care of the courts, and the courts assign them to intensive care facilities, the state must pay the cost. We have no choice. Because the number of children placed is growing rapidly and the rates for their care are going up, we are obligated to increase our funding appropriation.

I am also recommending an appropriation of almost $2 million for mental health, mental retardation, and substance abuse hospitals. Now that we have had a chance to see how the budget cuts actually played out for these facilities, we need to come back and make some adjustments to assure client safety and make sure federal certification is maintained.

Finally, I an recommending nearly $518,000 for the AZT drug, to carry existing AIDS patients through several months when federal funds will not be available, and to add 325 recipients over the course of five months. I earlier allocated $158,000 from my emergency funds until we could address this critical need in the supplemental budget.

Now, the budget for the Department of Transportation. Because motor fuel tax revenues are dedicated by the Constitution for road and bridge construction, they are not subject to normal appropriation. Last year, we took in $2.8 million less than anticipated, so you will see a reduction in the budget of that amount.

Also, last winter, we transferred motor fuel tax revenues into the bond section of the budget to assure coverage of debt service on bonds for Georgia 400. This money has earned $513,658 in interest, which is being returned to DOT.

There is also language to use $5 million in existing motor fuel tax revenues to plan and design a replacement for the Sidney Lanier Bridge in Brunswick. Brunswick is a growing port which handled nearly 2 million tons of cargo in 1992. However, the narrow opening of the Sidney Lanier Bridge, combined with the channel currents, presents a problem for larger ships. The bridge has been struck twice, including an accident that killed ten people. Congress has declared this bridge an unreasonable obstruction to navigation, making its replacement eligible for federal funds. I want to take advantage of this opportunity, so that larger ships will continue to call at Brunswick, rather than at the competing ports of Charleston and Jacksonville.

There is another $100,000 to begin planning and design work on a multi-modal transportation hub in Atlanta, and let me say a brief word about that. Atlanta is a major hub for air, rail and highway transportation in the Southeast. But it is far from achieving its potential, because there has been little coordination and planning among various modes of transportation.

Another consideration is air quality. The Atlanta region is having problems meeting current federal air standards because of motor vehicle emissions, and the standards are going to get even tougher in the future.

We have an opportunity to address these needs with a multi-modal transportation station in that large open space between the old Rich's store and the CNN Center. This project would be paid for in large part with federal funds.

The final expenditure I would note is $160,000 to cover a postage increase for the *Market Bulletin* in the Department of Agriculture.

These mid-term requirements and other adjustments, combined with the reductions I described, bring the total amended budget to $8,251,716,454.

You will notice that I have not mentioned the $44.2 million we collected through our very successful tax amnesty program last month. When I proposed the amnesty program a year ago at the recommendation of the Williams Commission, with a projected income of

$30 million, there were many who thought it would be a wild goose chase. And I deliberately did not include it in my revenue estimate, because I wanted it to be that cushion we are always needing. This money still is not included in my revenue estimate, nor am I recommending that we spend any of it in this budget.

Right now revenues are on target as we projected for this year. November's revenue increase was 10.7 percent, breaking into double-digits for the first time in two and a-half years. The totals for December will not be final until later this week, but indicators point toward another strong month. Even with the tax amnesty revenues set aside, we are anticipating double-digit growth again for December, possibly exceeding November. So at this point we are on track to meet the revenue estimate for this year. But I prefer to err on the side of caution, especially since our reserve fund was completely depleted in June of 1990—six months before I even came into office. And we've had to operate without one red cent of reserves since then.

Now I have heard the talk that some seem to think we won't meet our revenue estimate. I think we will. I'm confident we will and so are some of our state's leading economists. But, let's say I'm wrong and these nationally known economists are wrong. Then let me say this: The combination of the reduction in the revenue estimate plus the amnesty income will give us an extra $120 million cushion to meet any shortfall. It's a fail-safe situation. But if I'm right and revenues come in as we expect, then we will have an extra $120 million for next year's mid-year adjustment and to begin to rebuild our reserves.

These, basically, are the supplemental budget changes and recommendations. And I'd like to thank you for giving me this time to outline them to you.

I would also like to take a few more minutes to lay the groundwork for a major new section that will appear for the first time in the FY 94 budget—the expenditure of anticipated lottery proceeds. We expect the lottery to be up and running before next fiscal year begins, but the various types of games will be phased in gradually.

We are projecting $139 million dollars in lottery proceeds for FY 94, based on the experience of other states with lotteries. However, I will propose that we appropriate only $125 million, holding the remaining $14 million—10 percent—as a reserve. I think that is responsible and necessary, at least until we get a better feel for how it will go.

As you know, the lottery law stipulates expenditures in three areas: prekindergarten, college loans or scholarships, and special equipment and capital needs. Allow me to very briefly preview each of these.

First, prekindergarten. Let me emphasize once more that it will be voluntary by the parent and voluntary by the school system. Each community can look at its own needs and its own resources, and then propose a plan to the state that would be efficient and effective for that particular community. In some communities, it may very well be a traditional part of the school system. But it could also be an expanded Head Start program, or a new or expanded private, non-profit program.

It will be phased in with the first priority being kids who are at risk. As you know, we have already begun to target them in pilot projects. Then we will continue to expand the program as communities are ready and lottery proceeds are available. I will propose $40 million for prekindergarten, based on the Department of Education's estimate of the number of at-risk four-year-olds to be targeted and the number of programs that can realistically be up and running during this first year.

The second program legally designated to be funded by the lottery is loans and scholarships for college and technical education. I propose a program that I call HOPE, Helping Outstanding Pupils Educationally. Any high school student with a B average—a 3.0 grade point average—that student would get a HOPE certificate good for tuition at any institution in the University System of Georgia where they are accepted, if their family income is less than $66,000 a year. If I were a high school student, I can just hear my Mama saying, "Son, I can't afford to send you to college, so you'd better study hard and make sure you have a B average so you can get free tuition."

In HOPE's second part, students with a B average in their freshman year, can get a loan for tuition for their sophomore year. And if they keep a B average for their sophomore year, the loan is forgiven. In other words, a student who holds a steady B average can get free tuition for their first two years of college. There will be nothing else like it in the United States of America.

Now, of course, not everybody wants to go to college and not every job takes a college degree. But the average job today requires two years of training after high school. So the third part of HOPE is free tuition for diploma-granting programs at our 32 technical institutes, ranging from licensed practical nursing to electro-mechanical engineering technology.

The fourth part of HOPE is for those Georgians who dropped out of school, then go back to get their GED. There were 16,000 in Georgia last year. I propose that we give our GED graduates a $500 certificate to use for books, materials, or fees at a public college or technical Institute.

Finally, Georgia's many independent, private institutions, that save us the cost of providing state funds for their Georgia students in the University System. Since the early 1970s, we have given what we call tuition equalization grants to these colleges for Georgia students, helping to offset the higher tuition they must charge. So, as the fifth component of HOPE, I propose increasing tuition equalization grants from $1,000 to $1,500 for freshmen and sophomores at our independent colleges.

I will propose that we appropriate $39.7 million for the HOPE program. This figure is based on the actual number of high school graduates last spring whose grades would have qualified them for this program and who went on to Georgia colleges or technical institutes.

Both prekindergarten and HOPE are programs that I have been proposing and promoting for a long time. They were the reason that a majority of Georgia voters supported the lottery last November.

The third program to be funded with lottery proceeds is special equipment and capital needs. I have not detailed this before, because it will change from year to year. It is also a safety valve, because it involves one-time expenditures. It can expand and contract as lottery proceeds ebb and flow and the needs of the other two programs change.

After funding the first two programs, we will have about $45.3 million for this category. I am proposing that we use this money to bring technology into Georgia's schools and move them toward the 21st century.

Last year I proposed and you passed legislation creating a state telecommunications program to bring world-class educational resources into every Georgia school, no matter how rural, no matter how small. We now have distance learning pilot programs serving some 1,000 Georgia students. And we have also surveyed all of our school systems to learn what technology they need to take advantage of distance learning.

Based on that survey, I propose we appropriate nearly $15 million for more than 1,700 satellite dishes, so that every school—every school, literally from Rabun Gap to Tybee Light, from Flintstone to Attapulgus—every University System college and every technical institute in Georgia has a dish and can tap into the rich educational resources available through telecommunications.

Second, computers. I propose $10.3 million to set up an early learning computer lab at every one of our 1,031 schools with elementary grades. Each school would receive four computers, a printer and innovative software designed to stimulate young students. In addition, I propose $3 million to equip four regional computer centers to train our teachers in how to make the best use of technology in their classrooms.

And while we're talking about computers, I recommend $2.5 million for a computer lab at each one of our 32 technical institutes to train students in computer skills for word processing, business software, computer-assisted design, and computer programming.

Finally on computers—and this is also very important—I propose we allocate about $1.6 million for technology in adult literacy. It will connect literacy providers around the state, provide computers to help handicapped persons who are seeking literacy skills, assist the Satellite Literacy Training Project, and give small businesses access to literacy training for their employees. You see, 85 percent of the workforce for the year 2000 is already on the job, and in Georgia more than half of them are either illiterate or have only marginal skills. We have got to pay more attention to workforce education.

Then for our University System, I will recommend $7.5 million to begin an equipment, technology, and construction trust fund. This fund would provide a one-for-one match for private dollars contributed to our University System institutions for construction and advanced equipment for instruction and research. So the total impact would be $15 million. And I want to double or triple this fund once the lottery is fully up and running.

The facilities for our educational TV network, operated by the Public Telecommunications Commission, need to be updated and expanded. A private source has offered us land. So I will propose about $2 million to begin facility design. The new facility will produce Georgia-grown instructional programs for broadcast to our schools through their satellite receivers, as well as high-quality programs showcasing Georgia for national distribution.

Finally, I suggest that we provide $3.6 million to expand the Carroll Tech satellite center in Douglas County. One of the major focal points of my administration is to get state agencies to work together at the local level. This expansion has been well thought out and is ready to go. It offers us a chance to coordinate technical education, adult literacy, the Job Training Partnership program, PEACH (which gives job training to AFDC recipients) and the Department of Labor at the community level. If it works as well as we expect, it will be the first of several centers around the state.

That, in a nutshell, is what I will propose in FY 94 relative to expenditure of lottery proceeds. I will elaborate more on it in my budget address next week. As was promised all along, this money does not supplant one single red cent of existing educational funds, but provides a whole range of new and exciting educational improvements. Not only are these programs designed to meet critical needs in education, but every single school system, technical institute, and college in the entire State of Georgia will benefit from the lottery proceeds. In this way, every school system in your district can see some tangible results, and see them soon.

Thanks for your patience in listening to this fairly long discourse. I know that you have much work to do and many other people to hear from.

Thirty years ago I was first on the appropriations committee. I've been involved in this process, I think in this very room now, for 19 straight years as Lieutenant Governor or Governor of this state. As Vern Gosdin sings, "This ain't my first rodeo." Sometimes I've held on for dear life until the sine die buzzer sounded. And, yes, I've been thrown a few times, too. But I've always gotten up, dusted myself off, and gone back to the chute to try again.

I look forward to this session with more enthusiasm and anticipation than any I have been a part of since I came here in 1961. And I look forward to working with you. Because I respect you, and I appreciate and value your contribution to this time-honored process. I have sat where you sit, and I understand the perspective of where you will come from.

Thank you for your consideration. Thank you for what you mean to me. Together we are going to do some great things.

# State of the State Address

*January 12, 1993*

Lieutenant Governor Howard, Speaker Murphy, members of the General Assembly, members of the Consular Corps, members of the Judiciary, ladies, and gentlemen.

I thank you for this opportunity to once again come before you and report on the state of this great State of Georgia.

And I will tell you this up-front: State government is serving more people and is leaner and more streamlined than at any time in our history. As Dizzy Dean used to say, you can look it up. In the past two years, state spending rose much faster around the South than in Georgia. And nationally, the average growth rate for state spending was five times higher than it has been in Georgia.

The revenue estimate I gave you last week for Fiscal Year 1993 is only four percent higher than the revenue estimate I inherited for FY 91 two years ago. Four percent! Yet during the same two years, our public school enrollment grew by 5 percent; our University System enrollment grew by more than 10 percent; our AFDC cases grew by 26 percent; and our Medicaid recipients grew by 30 percent. Careful management and improved efficiency has enabled us to offer a consistent level of state services in spite of these dramatic increases in the number of our citizens being served.

Two years ago, I pointed out that the state payroll had grown by 12,000 jobs between 1987 and 1991. And we cut 5,000 positions from the state budget during my first year in office.

We have continued to prune the state payroll, with a net decrease of nearly 1,500 employees during FY92—an exception to the rule around the South, where most states increased, not decreased state employment.

Georgia also has one of the lowest debt levels among the 50 states—ranking 46th in debt per capita and 45th in debt relative to budget size. Needless to say, we continue to maintain top-level bond ratings.

November's revenue increase broke into double-digits for the first time in two and a-half years. December was another record month, even without the tax amnesty income. And now, even as revenues improve, we are continuing to carefully prune and trim away any excess we can find in state government.

Because of this careful financial management, we have saved enough money to allow us now to meet our mid-year funding needs for our schools and Medicaid, *and* at the same time to reduce this year's revenue estimate by $75 million, which, added to the $44 million from the tax amnesty program, gives us a cushion of $120 million.

Last year on this occasion I outlined a comprehensive legislative package called Georgia Rebound, and I thank you for adopting it. It addressed the education, economic development, public safety, and environmental needs of this state. Georgia Rebound contained a number of economic development initiatives, like the tax credit for new jobs, which brought a major Cargill poultry processing operation to the Dooly-Macon County area almost immediately.

But the Georgia Rebound initiative that may mean the most in the long run is one that got little attention—the reconstitution of the Governor's Development Council into a working public-private partnership. This Council, made up of some of Georgia's most able business leaders, has begun the task of reforging Georgia's economic development strategy to meet the needs of the 21st century.

We are expanding beyond our traditional approach of just recruiting businesses from other places, to supporting existing industry, expanding our exports, encouraging new technology companies, promoting unique regional strengths within the state and developing the broader infrastructure that modern industry must have.

Preservation 2000 is another public-private initiative of this administration to preserve an additional 100,000 acres of natural recreational and wilderness area. We have already preserved scenic wilderness from Tallulah Gorge to Little Tybee and Cabbage Islands, from Buffalo Swamp on the Altamaha River to Sprewell Bluff on the Flint. The total acreage identified for protection is nearing our goal of 100,000 acres. And more than half of it is either already preserved or presently under negotiation.

In the area of public safety, we have created 2,172 boot camp beds in the past two years. And even as the skeptics were shaking their heads, Georgia's boot camps were becoming the model for the rest of nation. They separate young drug offenders from the influence of harder criminals in prisons, and put them through a highly disciplined, basic training regimen combined with drug treatment and education to prepare them for a successful time of supervised probation.

Not only are these boot camps effective, but they are also much cheaper than prisons. It costs $2,500 a bed to build a boot camp using inmate labor, compared to $27,000 a bed for a prison. It costs $42 a day for each prison inmate, but only $25 a day for an offender in a boot camp.

Our goal is to make sure that our prison beds are used for criminals who really need to be behind bars and stay behind bars. During the past two years we have brought 4,300 prison beds on line and ended the practice of early release of inmates.

This session, I will propose giving our courts the option of imposing a sentence of life without parole if aggravating circumstances warrant it. Right now, as all of you know, our so-called "life" sentences are one of the greatest frauds ever perpetuated on the public. I think it's time we had a sentence that means what it says—*life* in prison.

I am also proposing a bill to allow victim impact statements in court in cases involving capital felonies. We already allow victim impact statements in all but capital felonies, and this bill simply fills in that missing piece. Georgia is the only one of the 50 states that does not have such a provision.

For the third straight year, I am continuing my efforts to crack down on drunk driving. Some of you have seen the portrait of a lovely and intelligent young woman on the table beside my desk. She is not my daughter or granddaughter. In fact, I never met her; I never had the chance. She was killed a year ago by a drunk driver, snuffed out on the threshold of becoming a leader among the next generation of Georgians. After her death, her father asked me to put her picture in my office. And it reminds me daily of the devastating cost we pay by allowing drunk driving on our highways.

So here I come again—I'm back with a bill to require immediate driver's license suspension for first-time offenders. I also want to give judges the option of requiring ignition interlock devices that lock a car's ignition until the driver passes a breath test, because the best way to stop drunk driving is to stop drunks from driving.

There is nothing more important in my administration, nothing more critical to Georgia's future, than education. During the past two years, we have made some significant strides:

* We have moved to elected school boards and appointed superintendents.

* We have begun a new program of fewer but tougher student tests.

* We have created Georgia 2000 to support local community partnerships as they work toward the six national education goals.

* We have streamlined teacher certification procedures.

* We have undertaken the largest construction program in Georgia history for our schools.

* We have provided computers to begin to ease the paperwork for teachers and administrators.

* We have expanded the Governor's Scholarship Program.

* We have placed counselors in all middle schools.

* We have established the School Leadership Institute to teach school leaders how to bring about innovation and positive change in their own schools.

* We have piloted The Family Connection to coordinate family social services for at-risk kids, so that students and teachers can focus on learning in the classroom. The initial funding for this innovative program came from a private foundation, and Georgia is now a finalist in a nationwide competition for a prestigious Pew Grant.

Last year we also began a telecommunications initiative that included distance Learning to bring world-class educational resources into every school, no matter how small. Two thousand Georgia students are now taking courses by interactive satellite or fiber optic networks, and I am proposing that we use lottery proceeds to make sure every single school, technical institute, and University System college has a satellite dish.

While I'm talking about telecommunications, let me mention our telemedicine program, which is so sophisticated that a medical specialist in Augusta can look inside the ear of a patient in Eastman. The *New York Times* reports that it is the most sophisticated program of its kind in the nation. It has the potential to revolutionize health care in rural Georgia.

The lottery is going to make some significant new things possible for our schools. The law provides that we use the lottery proceeds for prekindergarten, tuition scholarships and loans, and special equipment and capital needs. Let me tell you briefly why these three programs are so important.

First, prekindergarten, because that is where it all starts. A recent study by the Carnegie Institute shows that 40 percent of Georgia's five-year-olds are struggling in kindergarten. Our first priority will be these at-risk kids, and we have already begun to target them with pilots. Then we will expand prekindergarten as communities are ready and lottery proceeds are available.

I want to emphasize that prekindergarten will be voluntary—voluntary by the parent and voluntary by the school system. We will invite individual communities to develop a plan that would be efficient and effective for them. It could be part of the traditional school system. But it could also be an expanded Head Start program, or even a new or expanded private, non-profit program.

Second, I propose a unique and far-reaching scholarship program called HOPE— Helping Outstanding Pupils Educationally. There will be nothing else like it in the United States. It has never been more important for our students to go to college, but it has never been harder for their families to pay for it.

HOPE would give any high school student with a B average a certificate good for tuition at any University System college where they are accepted, if their family income is less than $66,000 a year. If they have a B average in their freshman year, then they could get a tuition loan for their sophomore year. And if they keep a B average for their sophomore year, the loan is forgiven.

HOPE would also provide free tuition for all the diploma-granting programs at our state technical institutes. And for those Georgians who go back to get their GED—there were 16,000 last year—I propose a $500 certificate for books, materials or fees at a public college or technical institute.

Finally, our private, independent colleges save us the cost of University System funding for their Georgia students. For 20 years now, we have given tuition equalization grants to these colleges for Georgia students, helping to offset the higher tuition they must charge. I propose increasing these grants from $1,000 to $1,500 for freshmen and sophomores at our independent colleges.

The third lottery program for special equipment and construction gives us the chance of a lifetime to bring technology into our schools. Our classrooms should be in the forefront of technology—the place where our children encounter technology and learn to really use it. Unfortunately, the exact opposite is true. Of all the places in our children's lives, our classrooms offer the least technology. There is more technology in a supermarket check-out line than in the average classroom. There are ten times more Nintendos in our homes than computers in our classrooms. Banks have automatic teller machines, but classroom math is stuck in the days when human tellers wrote in passbooks by hand.

I propose an early learning computer lab for every single elementary school. And regional computer centers to train our teachers in how to use technology in their classrooms. I propose a computer lab at each one of our 32 technical institutes to train students in job-related computer skills. I propose more computers for adult literacy programs, because more than half of Georgia's workforce is either illiterate or has only marginal skills. And for our University System—a trust fund for equipment and construction that would provide a one-for-one match for private contributions.

I'll elaborate on these programs a little more in my budget message on Thursday. Right now I want to simply emphasize that this money does not supplant—let me repeat, does not supplant—one single red cent of existing educational funds. But it provides a whole range of new and exciting enhancements and improvements that address critical needs in education. Improvements for our children that go into every single school system, college and technical institute in the entire State of Georgia.

Too many of our schools are caught in a time warp. That's why I want to create an environment that allows for experimentation and dramatic change in how we educate our children. I am proposing a program, that will allow local schools more freedom than they've ever had before to create better, more up-to-date learning environments for children.

These schools will operate under a charter agreement with their local system and the State Board of Education to work toward the six national goals in education. They will be free from state regulations, restrictions, and limitations, and instead will be held accountable to performance-based evaluations and measures.

To provide their funding, I propose a unique public and private partnership that includes some of this state's top business leaders. We call it the Next Generation Schools Project, it will pool private, state and local education funds in a one-third/one-third/one-third match.

All these new educational initiatives are geared toward keeping children in school so they are better prepared to enter the workforce. That is why I believe we should increase the compulsory school age from 16 to 17 next school year, and then from 17 to 18 the following school year. Six other southern states have already raised their compulsory age to 17 or 18. We cannot allow Georgia to continue to drag along at the tailend.

Georgia has some of the best teachers to be found anywhere in this country, but we still need to recruit even more highly qualified teachers. To help that situation, I will soon execute an agreement with the U.S. Department of Defense to allow Georgia to fast-track military personnel who have the necessary skills to make the transition into teaching careers. Senator Nunn has been the leading proponent of this idea on the national level, and I am proud that Georgia will be one of the first states to put it to work.

I also propose we create a Georgia Council for School Performance, a neutral voice made of business and professional leaders, to offer an annual, impartial evaluation of the progress we are making in our schools.

Georgians have always valued family, individual responsibility, and hard work. Our present welfare system undermines every one of those values. It promotes single-parenthood; it promotes dependence. While AFDC may be a hand up for some, for far too many it has become just a hand-out. A full 25 percent of the Americans on welfare remain there for more than 10 years.

I believe that welfare recipients should not be immune from the realities and the personal obligations that face hard-working Georgians every day. We must offer opportunity and incentives for people to take responsibility for their own lives, not encourage them to surrender their lives to a faceless bureaucracy, where the check just shows up automatically in the mailbox each month.

Congress has recently changed the requirements governing AFDC to allow for some state-level reforms. And I believe that we must take advantage of this opportunity, as other states are doing, to create a welfare system in Georgia that is both more effective in achieving its goals and more efficient in using the tax dollars that support it. The money for AFDC comes from the pocketbooks of hard-working Georgians, and I cannot recommend simply taking more of their money. We must try to make the system more efficient, more effective and free from abuse.

First, I propose we expand the PEACH program to give welfare recipients education, job skills, and help in finding jobs. I propose that we bring the Georgia Labor Department into AFDC and Food Stamp offices to assist able-bodied persons in finding work and identify those who refuse to work.

We've had an all-out effort going to crack down on absentee parents who fail to pay child support. And as a result, the Office of Child Support Enforcement last year increased its collections from absent parents by 22 percent. But we can do even better. I will propose a new reporting system that will give the Office of Child Support Enforcement better and more up-to-date information.

And, yes, I will propose that we *not* increase benefits for a recipient who has another child *while* on the AFDC rolls. Welfare families should assume the same sort of decision-making responsibility that everybody else faces in deciding whether or not to have a child. I will propose that unwed teen mothers continue to live with a parent or guardian to receive AFDC benefits, encouraging families to stay together and teenage mothers to stay in school.

But while we are shifting the focus to a second chance for parents, I do not want their children to suffer. And that is why I will propose an expansion of Medicaid benefits for dependent children.

We all know the growing problems with our health-care system. Roughly 1.5 million Georgians have no health insurance, and millions more fear they may lose theirs. This is not just a problem for our people; it's a problem for our economy. Georgia employers are paying an average of $3,600 per employee for health insurance. It's also a problem for every single Georgia taxpayer. Because the state buys health care for more than one million Medicaid recipients and insurance for state employees and their families. The state is being hit just as hard as every private sector employer.

Some might argue that 1993 is not the right time to take strong action on health care at the state level, with a new administration taking office in Washington. I think they're wrong. Every signal coming out of Washington since election day indicates that the states will be given a key role in managing health costs and expanding coverage, no matter what specific plan is adopted.

There are six elements to my package of health-care proposals. The first two build on the hard work of Insurance Commissioner Tim Ryles in promoting both greater access and lower costs for private health insurance. Most of you are familiar with this plan already. It authorizes the state to work with health insurers to develop three voluntary statewide plans, aimed at making affordable health insurance available to all Georgians regardless of age, medical condition, place of residence, or job status.

It would enable Georgians to retain their health coverage while changing jobs. It would help control costs. It would encourage preventive health measures. And, very importantly, it would not require any new taxes.

Second, I will propose legislation to enable the Insurance Commissioner to develop a variation of the low-cost, no-frills Basic Health Plan he has already worked out with insurers. This variation will be aimed at the specific health needs of children. We are targeting families with children between the ages of one and six and incomes between 100 and 185 percent of the federal poverty level. These children are not now eligible for Medicaid coverage. I intend to seek a waiver from the federal government to permit us to use dollars from the Indigent Care Trust Fund—plus federal Medicaid matching money— to purchase the new basic coverage for these children.

Third, I am proposing an immediate step to make health insurance available to about 108,000 Georgians, most of them children, through Medicaid. Beginning in July, we would make Medicaid available to pregnant women and infants in families with incomes up to 185 percent of the federal poverty level—the maximum allowable under federal law. At the same time, we would cover under Medicaid kids up to age 19 from families with incomes up to 100 percent of the poverty level. Now we cover them only to age nine.

This initiative means more healthy babies and more healthy children ready to learn. We cannot continue to bear the human and financial costs associated with lack of access to prenatal and preventive care for children. It will be financed through payments into the Indigent Care Trust Fund by disproportionate-share hospitals, through a system that we believe the federal government will approve.

Fourth, I propose that Georgia begin a pilot Primary Care Case Management program, based on a successful system pioneered in Kentucky. This initiative, recommended by the Williams Commission, would place doctors in charge of decisions on procedures and referrals for Medicaid patients. By avoiding unnecessary referrals and high-cost visits to emergency rooms, these physicians can help make sure Medicaid patients get the care they need, while significantly cutting costs.

Fifth, I will propose funding for our Office of Health Data Collection to make its comparative data on medical charges more broadly available to the public. This will help individuals and employers to choose the most cost-effective providers, ultimately reducing costs.

Sixth and finally, I will create by executive order a Governor's Commission on Health Care. It will develop a broad plan for reforming health care financing in Georgia, with special emphasis on preparing our state for the new responsibilities we will inherit under a national health care reform effort.

The commission will be composed of representatives of all state agencies involved with health care; our cities and counties, and the business community. It will be served by a panel of distinguished health care experts, and will be charged with soliciting advice from consumers, providers, and insurers. I am pleased and proud to announce that former Congressman Ed Jenkins has agreed to serve as the commission's chairman. I cannot imagine a more qualified individual to head this effort.

These are just a few of the legislative recommendations I will be making to you during these busy 40 days. They continue the central priority of this administration—to prepare Georgia for the 21st century.

But in addition to the primary task of preparing our infrastructure and our programs for a new century, we should also be preparing our hearts and our attitudes for a new South.

Next week, Bill Clinton will become the third consecutive Democratic president from the South. And for the first time since 1828, when Andrew Jackson and John C. Calhoun took office, two sons of the South will assume the top two positions in the United States government.

The South is the fastest growing area of the country. And our growing dominance in national leadership reflects our growing prominence in the world economy. Yet at the very time when all southerners may rightly take pride in this region's current success, some Georgians persist in believing that the pride of the South is better defined by a symbol of defiance and intolerance—the Confederate Battle Flag, which was imposed on our state flag in 1956.

Of all the arguments that have been made for keeping this flag, the most infuriating to me is the contention that if we don't, we will somehow forget the sacrifices made by those who fought for the Confederacy. We will not forget. We cannot forget. Our graveyards, our literature, and many of our own family histories will forever keep alive the memory of those who died for the Confederacy—and the memory of those whose freedom from slavery depended on the Confederacy's defeat.

I certainly cannot forget my own Confederate ancestors. I will never forget my great-grandfather, Brantley Bryan, who was wounded while fighting with Stonewall Jackson at Chancellorsville, then wounded again and more severely at Gettysburg in the same battle that took his brother's life.

But I also cannot forget the many millions of Georgians, my ancestors and yours, who also made sacrifices in other wars both before and after the War Between the States. And in reverence to their memory, I cannot accept the idea that the brief, violent, and tragic period of the Confederacy is the only part—the only part—of our long history that defines our identity and our traditions.

Georgia will be 260 years old next month. For 43 of those years, we were a British colony; for 11 years a sovereign state under the Articles of Confederation; and for more than 200 years a member of the United States.

For four brief years—that's 1.5 percent of our state's entire history—Georgia was a member of the Confederate States of America. Yet it is the Confederacy's most inflammatory symbol that dominates our flag today. We all know why. And it has nothing to do with the bravery of the Confederate troops.

You may quibble all you want about who said what in 1956. It is clear the flag was changed in 1956 to identify Georgia with the dark side of the Confederacy—that desire to deprive some Americans of the equal rights that are the birthright of all Americans, and yes, the determination to destroy the United States if necessary to achieve that goal.

The legislators who voted to change the flag in 1956 were prepared to defy the Supremacy Clause of the U.S. Constitution. They were prepared to eliminate our public schools and even prohibit our college football teams from competing in bowl games—in order to maintain segregated schools, public transportation, drinking fountains, and recreational facilities.

We have long since repudiated every element of those shameful 1956 days of defiance—except for the flag they created. We now proudly send our sons and even our daughters abroad to defend the United States of America. Yet we maintain as a symbol of our state a flag that challenges the very existence of the United States of America. And a flag that exhibits pride in the enslavement of many of our ancestors.

There is one, and only one, argument for maintaining the current flag: the polls,. The polls say it is popular. I submit to you that this one issue, by its very nature, transcends this particular session and this particular climate of opinion. It goes to our identity as a state, and it goes to our legitimacy as public officials.

Very probably this one vote will be the only one for which this General Assembly is ever remembered, and the one vote for which each and every one of you will be held accountable, not just by your constituents, but by posterity and history. You will have to live with this one decision far beyond the next election—10 years from now, 30 years from now, to the end of your public career, to the end of your life. If you don't believe me, think about those Congressmen who followed the polls of their day and voted against the Civil Rights Act of 1964. Some were ruined, and the rest forever regretted it.

I submit to you that you cannot escape this individual decision. You cannot hide in the crowd. This issue will not go away, and I do not believe a single one of you in this chamber really believes that the present flag will survive for very long into the future.

So, that brings it down to a matter of sheer guts. Will you do the easy thing, or the right thing? When your grandchildren read about this in school and ask you how you voted, will you be able to answer in a forthright manner, or will you say, "Well, you see, the polls looked bad back then." Or, "I wanted a referendum first."

Will you proudly act as an individual, or will you just go along with the crowd?

My all-time favorite movie is "To Kill a Mockingbird"—the Academy Award winner based on Harper Lee's story about life in the South in the 1920s, with Gregory Peck as Atticus Finch, a lawyer raising two small children. In that movie's key scene, Atticus is defending a black man unjustly accused of rape, and a lynch mob tries to take justice into its own hands.

As Atticus confronts the mob at the jailhouse door, his daughter "Scout" joins him and sees that the leader is someone she knows. And she calls him by name. "Hey, Mr. Cunningham—remember me? You're Walter's daddy. Walter's a good boy. Tell him I said hello." After a dramatic pause, Mr. Cunningham turns and says to the mob, "Let's go, boys." A group bent on injustice, turned aside by one small girl who appealed to them as individuals.

Well, my friends in this chamber, I know you. And I appeal to each of you as individuals—as fathers and mothers, as neighbors and friends, most of whom were taught in Sunday schools to "do unto others as you would have them do unto you."

Leaders of this General Assembly—I know you. I know the love and dedication you have exhibited over the years to your children and grandchildren—and so often to the underdog in a fight. Let that love manifest itself now in a way that will crown your proud careers with the glory you deserve—not with the scorn of posterity that will obscure forever your proper respect.

Veteran legislators—those who remember the segregationist frenzy that changed the flag before—I know you. Rarely does one have a chance to rewrite one's own personal history and erase one great blot. You do. Take it before it is too late.

Rising stars who aspire to future leadership—I know you. I know you are doubly tempted to hedge on an issue where both popular opinion and the powers that be blow harsh against your principles. But, my friends, you cannot lead with a finger raised to the wind and an ear to the ground—it's an undignified position. Lead now, or you find it very difficult to lead in the future.

Republicans, believe it or not, I know you. I respect your traditions, and the rebel yell of the Lost Cause sounds especially harsh and awkward in your throats. Your vote on this issue will say much about where you aim to take the Party of Lincoln in a changing state.

Freshman legislators—I don't know you yet, but I do understand the desire for change that brought you here and the unlimited horizons you face. If you vote against changing the flag, then, no matter what other innovations you may promote, you will forever be cast as a member of rearguard faction that refused to hear change knocking on the door.

Oh yes, you can be re-elected, not just in 1994 but, perhaps, again and again. But in your quest for change, you will never overcome this one retrograde vote.

I know you, members of the General Assembly. And I hope you know me well enough to know that I am dead serious about this issue. And, to paraphrase Rhett Butler, frankly, my dear friends, I do give a damn.

Since 1789, Georgia's motto has been: "Wisdom, Justice, Moderation." There is nothing wise, just or moderate in a flag that reopens old wounds and perpetuates old hatreds. Our battlefields, our graveyards, our monuments are important reminders of our history, both the proud and the painful. They will and always should be there. That's history. But our flag is a symbol—a symbol of what we stand for as a state.

I want to see this state live by the words of George Washington to the sexton of the Rhode Island synagogue: "Ours is a government which gives to bigotry no sanction, to persecution no assistance."

If you're truly proud of the South, if you're truly proud of this state, of *all* its 260 years. If you look forward and want to play a significant part in what Georgia can become, then help me now to give bigotry no sanction, and persecution no assistance.

# Budget Address, Fiscal Year 1994

*January 14, 1993*

More than 200 years ago, Thomas Paine, that champion of democracy who helped to spur the American Revolution, wrote these words: "Public money ought to be touched with the most scrupulous conscientiousness of honor. It is not the produce of riches only, but of hard earnings of labor."

When I launched this administration two years ago, I promised to be bold and creative with ideas, but frugal and prudent with tax dollars. And two days ago in my State of the State Address, I reported to you that our careful and conservative money management has made Georgia one of the healthiest states in the nation, even while we maintained a consistent level of services to one of the fastest growing state populations in the nation.

At the same time, we have made tremendous strides forward in education, economic development, public safety, environmental protection, and human services. Today, I lay before you a budget for Fiscal Year 1994 that continues this pattern of using our resources creatively but with fiscal discipline to bring about progress.

Although growth in state revenues has improved steadily since last February, and registered in double digits for November and December—nevertheless, I am projecting modest revenue growth for FY 94 of 7.5 percent above my reduced revenue estimate for FY 93. If we meet the original revenue estimate for FY 93 as we expect, then we will need revenue growth of only 6.5 percent next year to meet this budget.

Economists agree that the national recovery is likely to be slow. And I am committed to rebuilding our reserve fund, which was depleted six months before I ever took office. So I intend to continue the pattern of caution and tight-fisted management even as revenue growth picks up again.

The bottom line for the budget before you is 8 billion 948 million 692 thousand 764 dollars. And you're going to quickly deduct that this is more than a 7.5 percent increase over FY 93. The reason is because this budget includes funds from two new sources: first, the Indigent Care Trust Fund, which under prior federal regulations was injected into the budget at mid-year. And second, the proceeds from the Georgia Lottery for Education. And I'd like to begin my presentation of budget items with the Lottery for Education.

It will be up and running by the time FY 94 begins next July 1st. However, the various types of games will be carefully phased in over several years. We are projecting $139 million dollars in lottery proceeds for FY 94, based on the experience of other states with lotteries. But I propose that we appropriate only $125 million, holding the remaining $14 million—10 percent—as a reserve. I think that is necessary, at least until we get a better feel for how it will go. Folks, it will be very tempting for you to spend this reserve, but you and I know that it would not be very fiscally responsible for you to do so.

As you know, the lottery law stipulates expenditures in three areas: prekindergarten, college loans or scholarships, and special equipment and capital needs. In the budget document, these expenditures appear as special designations under the budgets of each of the appropriate education agencies. But I want to talk about them as a group.

First, prekindergarten. Let me emphasize once more that it will be voluntary by the parent and voluntary by the school system. Each community can develop its own plan— whether part of the school system, an expanded Head Start program, or even a new or expanded private, non-profit program. It will be phased in with the first priority being children who are at risk. I propose $40 million for prekindergarten, based on the Department of Education's estimate of the number of at-risk four-year-olds to be targeted and the number of programs that can realistically be up and running during this first year.

The second legal use of lottery proceeds is loans and scholarships for college and technical education. As you may have heard—more than once—I propose a program called HOPE, Helping Outstanding Pupils Educationally. Any high school student with a B average—a 3.0 grade point average—would get a HOPE certificate for free tuition at any University System college where they are accepted, if their family income is less than $66,000 a year. Second, students with a B average in their freshman year, can get a loan for tuition for their sophomore year. And if they keep a B average for their sophomore year, the loan is forgiven.

Third, HOPE would provide free tuition for diploma-granting programs at our 32 technical institutes. Fourth, for those Georgians who dropped out of school, then go back to get their GED—a $500 certificate for books, materials or fees at a public college or technical institute. Fifth, I propose increasing tuition equalization grants from $1,000 to $1,500 for freshmen and sophomores at our independent colleges.

I recommend $39.7 million for the HOPE program, based on the actual number of students who would have qualified last spring.

The third program to be funded with lottery proceeds is one-time special equipment and capital needs that will change from year to year. It will be a safety valve in addition to the reserve, expanding and contracting as lottery proceeds ebb and flow and the needs of the other two programs change. After funding the first two programs, we will have about $45.3 million for this category. As I indicated on Tuesday, I believe that we must use this money to bring technology into Georgia's schools.

Last year we created a state telecommunications program to bring world-class educational resources into every Georgia school, no matter how small. Since then, we did a survey of our school systems to learn what technology they need to take advantage of distance learning. Based on that survey, I propose we appropriate nearly $15 million for more than 1,700 satellite dishes, so that every school, every University System college and technical institute in Georgia has a dish and can tap into the rich educational resources available through telecommunications.

Second, computers. I propose $10.3 million to set up an early learning computer lab at every one of our 1,031 schools with elementary grades. Each school would receive a minimum of four computers, a printer and innovative software designed to stimulate young students. Another $3 million would equip four regional computer centers to train our teachers in how to make the best use of technology in their classrooms.

I also recommend $2.5 million for a computer lab at each one of our 32 technical institutes, to train students in computer skills for word processing, business software, computer-assisted design, and computer programming.

Finally on computers—and this is also very important—I propose we allocate about $1.6 million for technology in adult literacy. These funds will connect literacy providers around the state on a network, address the literacy needs of handicapped persons, assist the Satellite Literacy Training Project, and give small businesses access to literacy training for their employees.

And then for our University System, I recommend $7.5 million to begin an equipment, technology, and construction trust fund. It would provide a one-on-one match for private dollars contributed to our University System institutions, so the total impact would be $15 million next year. And I want to expand this fund as lottery proceeds increase.

The facilities for our educational TV network, operated by the Public Telecommunications Commission, need to be updated and expanded. I want it to produce instructional programs for broadcast to our schools through their satellite receivers, as well as high-quality programs showcasing Georgia for national distribution. A private source has offered us an excellent site. So I propose about $2 million to begin the new facility's design.

Finally, I suggest a $3.6 million expansion of the Carroll Tech satellite center in Douglas County to coordinate technical education, adult literacy, the Job Training Partnership program, the PEACH program, and the Department of Labor at the community level. If it works as well as we expect, it will be the first of several centers around the state.

Every single school system, technical institute and college in the entire State of Georgia will benefit from the lottery proceeds. Every school system in your district will benefit. As I promised all along, this money does not supplant one single red cent of existing educational funds. Your constituents are going to be very interested in that fact.

In addition to the lottery money, I am recommending about $157 million in new state funds for our schools and for teacher pay raises. Of course, $108 million of it accommodates enrollment growth under the Quality Basic Education formula. But there are also new proposals.

There's $2 million for the Next Generation Schools Project, which is a public private partnership that will bring together $2 million in state funds, $2 million in private funds and $2 million in local education money to provide funds for charter schools.

Last year you began an administrative computer system for schools, helping reduce cumbersome paperwork for teachers. I recommend $7 million for equipment and $2.76 million for installation and project management, to expand this system to every high school in the state.

The Family Connection is an innovative pilot program that provides local coordination of social services for the families of children who are at risk. It has been so successful that Georgia is under consideration for a prestigious Pew Grant. I recommend providing about $2 million to keep our 14 pilot sites operating after the private grant that started them expires, and to fund 16 new Family Connection sites.

One of the problems in retaining teachers in the profession is salaries, and that is especially true for more than a third of our teachers whose salaries have reached the ceiling on the salary schedule. This has bothered me for a long time. So this year I propose we do something about it. Rather than a flat percentage-based pay raise, I propose that we adjust our teacher salary schedule, which is based on experience and ongoing professional training.

I want to increase what teachers can expect to earn if they stay in the profession, by making improvements throughout the salary schedule for teachers in our schools and technical institutes. And I recommend that we add a fifth tier to the end—that L-5 step you've heard so much about. The total cost of these salary adjustments will be $42.4 million, and I wish it could be more. An individual teacher's pay raise would depend on where they are on the salary schedule, but teachers who are moving a step could receive 3 percent or more, and the third of our teachers who will go into the new fifth step could receive as much as 4.2 percent.

On capital outlay for public schools, I am recommending $148 million for construction in 60 different schools systems, in compliance with the current QBE construction law. The bond section of the budget also includes $6.9 million for vocational education equipment in high schools and middle schools.

As more and more Georgians realize the importance of education in today's workplace, enrollments are soaring at our 34 University System institutions. Last school year, University System enrollment grew by 6.5 percent—which is more students than the total enrollments of Augusta and Columbus Colleges combined. So, if you compare your two budget documents for this year and next—you will see more than $100 million in new funds for the State Board of Regents. The bulk of it is for the funding formula, providing for increased enrollment, health insurance costs, and pay raises.

I am recommending not only the 1.5 percent that is called for in the funding formula for pay increases, but also another half percent to be added to that, to give the Regents more flexibility in adjusting salaries to attract and retain high-quality personnel.

I also propose that we fund the first three projects on the Regents' capital outlay priority list: a $31 million Comprehensive Agricultural Livestock and Poultry Facility at The University of Georgia to provide classrooms and modern animal research labs; a $41 million Children's Medical Center at the Medical College of Georgia, which will not only make MCG a leader in pediatrics research and training, but will also serve children from all over Georgia; and a Biocontainment Research Center at The University of Georgia, to be built with a 50-50 match of state and federal funds, our share being $8 million. There are very few adequate biocontainment facilities anywhere in this country, and this center will make Georgia a national leader in animal disease research.

I also propose $27.8 million for renovation and repairs throughout the System, which has over 400 buildings that are more than 50 years old and another 1,000 buildings that are 25-50 years old. And I recommend four University System projects that will pay back the cost of the bonds from the revenues they generate. They include dormitories at Georgia Tech for $113 million and at Gordon College for $2.4 million, and parking decks at Georgia Tech and Georgia State University totaling $11.6 million. So, when you see that total of $250 million in University System bonds, remember that more than half of it will be paid back by revenues generated by the projects themselves, and not out of the general treasury.

As the education and training demanded by the average job approaches 14 years, technical and adult education is becoming more and more essential. In addition to the lottery funds that go into technical and adult education, I am proposing $3.8 million in new money for technical training, including funds to begin the second year of the two-year programs at Georgia's four newest technical institutes at Jesup, Vidalia, Statesboro, and north metro Atlanta.

I also propose funds for faculty and operations at the expansions authorized last year at eleven institutes. And then I propose that we expand programs like electronics, technology and health occupations, that are in demand both by entering students and employers.

More than half of Georgia's workforce is either illiterate or has limited skills, and this state has a growing population of chronically unemployed adults who lack basic job skills. That is why I am proposing a goal of at least one full-time adult literacy teacher in each county, to be achieved over the next two years. The first year's cost will be $2.7 million for 68 teachers. And, as I mentioned above, we would use lottery proceeds to provide some computer equipment.

Last year my capital outlay recommendation was $32.6 million for 11 technical institutes. This year I propose another $31 million for seven construction projects at Americus, Clarkesville, Jasper, Gainesville, Sandersville, Swainsboro and Thomasville. I also propose funds to plan the new Middle Georgia campus, because the old one now is land-locked, and the training needs of our growing aerospace industry demand a program expansion. And planning funds for the Forsyth County satellite of Lanier Tech, which will focus on high tech and health occupation programs.

I also recommend $3.5 million to upgrade our training equipment, and $2.5 million for renovation and repair. More funding has gone into our technical institutes in the past two years than at any comparable time in our history. But never has it been needed more.

I want to build public libraries in Charlton, Crawford, Effingham, Gwinnett, Madison, Meriwether, and Oglethorpe Counties and two in Fayette County, that have qualified for $7.6 million in construction assistance.

Last year, we reconstituted the Governor's Development Council into a public-private partnership to direct the expansion of Georgia's economic development efforts. I chair that Council, and my legislative and budget recommendations for economic development have been formulated by the Council.

The centerpiece is $22 million for the Georgia Research Alliance—our answer to the Research Triangle of North Carolina. It is a public-private partnership of our six major universities, industry and state government. It is coordinating and expanding our research capability in telecommunications, genetics and environmental sciences—three areas of emerging technology with great potential for future economic and industrial growth.

You will be interested to know that the $15 million we put into the Research Alliance last year has already attracted $32 million in federal and private research funds. This year's recommendation is expected to bring in $61 million in federal and private funds. So, in the course of making a long-term investment of $37 million in state funds, we are seeing an immediate economic impact of $130 million. Not a bad return!

This year's investment includes $13.6 million to construct or renovate facilities and purchase equipment. The remaining $8.4 million would help endow nine new eminent research scholars at the four largest universities, and fund a center at the Tifton Agricultural Experiment Station to develop and promote environmentally sound agricultural practices.

The second initiative of the Development Council is $7 million to provide technology assistance to the pulp and paper, textile and apparel, and food processing industries that are the bedrock of our economy. Georgia is the national leader in wood pulp and paperboard, and for our pulp and paper industry I propose $2.5 million in state funds to be matched one-on-one by private funds for research and technology transfer. Another $3.2 million will update and expand the prestigious Herty Foundation lab.

For our textile and apparel industry—the largest manufacturing employer in the state—half-a-million dollars will be matched by $2 million in federal funds to bring Georgia Tech into the National Textile Center. Another half-million dollars will again be matched by $2 million in federal funds for the Apparel Manufacturing Center, which is a joint project of Southern Tech and Georgia Tech.

Our food processing industry has tremendous potential for South Georgia, and we just launched a new export initiative to help it. For both the food processing and the textile and apparel industries, I propose funds to develop public-private initiatives to achieve greater competitiveness for these industries.

Of course, our transportation infrastructure continues to be important to economic development. I am recommending $125 million in bonds for our economic development highways, more money than last year, but with the same continuing emphasis on accelerating the Fall Line Freeway from Columbus to Augusta, and U.S. 27 through West Georgia from the Tennessee to the Florida state lines.

At our ports facilities, we must continue last year's progress on the long-term "Focus 2000" expansion plan. I recommend we authorize nearly $24.7 million in bonds, to be paid for out of Ports Authority revenues. These funds would purchase two new container cranes and begin Phase I development at Container Berth 7 in Garden City. An additional $13.5 million is required as the state's final payment on the Savannah Harbor deepening project which will soon be underway.

Atlanta is an important hub for many modes of transportation, but its great potential has yet to be fully realized because of a lack of coordination among various types of transportation.

The amended budget for FY 93 includes planning funds for a multi-modal transfer facility in downtown, and this budget includes $13.2 million for the first phase of construction. Again, I would like to point out that the bulk of the funding for this facility would come from the federal government.

I also recommend $1.7 million in bonds to acquire and rehabilitate various rail lines, preserving existing rail corridors. It will leverage $3.1 million in federal dollars.

I also propose $2 million in state matching funds to leverage $12 million in federal funds for low-income housing assistance.

With regards to tourism, the visitors center on I-75 at Ringgold is old, too close to the highway for safety, and is trying to serve more than ten times the volume of visitors that it was designed for. A new center will cost $4.8 million, with $4 million in federal funds, and the remaining $800,000 state match recommended in this budget.

I am also recommending the $6.5 million needed to build and equip the Georgia Music Hall of Fame in Macon. But this money will be contingent on local funds being raised to renovate the Douglass Theater and develop a music park, giving this facility the substance it needs to become a major tourist attraction.

In addition to education and economic development, a third priority for this budget, my administration, and many of you, is healthy children. We must do a better job than we are doing, and we will with the revised Indigent Care Trust Fund. I am recommending that $10.3 million from this fund be used to expand coverage for pregnant women and their infants up to an income level of 185 percent of the federal poverty level. All southeastern states except Alabama and Georgia have already taken this step to help combat infant mortality. Georgia has a higher infant mortality rate than anywhere in the nation except Washington, D.C. Let's not be dead last in the whole country to address this problem.

Another $19 million would extend Medicaid coverage to children under age 19 in families with income up to 100 percent of the federal poverty level. Right now we go to age nine. These are school kids who are at risk, because they have trouble learning when unaddressed health problems get in the way.

New federal regulations require a revision of the Indigent Care Trust Fund, and a recent constitutional amendment has paved the way for us to do that. Briefly and without losing you in that dark and dense forest of Medicaid terminology—money can be transferred into the Trust Fund from public entities, hospital authorities, the Department of Human Resources, and the Hospital Equipment Financing Authority, and then used to draw down federal Medicaid funds. The $120.7 million coming into the Trust Fund in FY 94 will leverage federal Medicaid funds for a total of more than $321 million.

In addition to the statewide programs I've just described, this fund will continue to assist hospitals that have disproportionate indigent caseloads with additional Medicaid payments.

Medicaid is the fastest growing program in all of state government, and the second biggest budget category, exceeded only by our public schools. Counting all state, federal and trust fund money, the FY 94 total for Medicaid surpasses $3 billion. Not only are medical costs soaring, but, as I told you Tuesday, the number of Medicaid recipients has increased dramatically. In FY 94, Medicaid is projected to serve slightly over one million Georgians—think about that—one of every six citizens in this state. This number has doubled in the last six years. And the number of claims we expect this year is double that of just four years ago.

Medicaid presently absorbs one of every three new dollars we take in in revenue. Its growth takes money away from education and other important programs. So a major reason for the changes I outlined on Tuesday is to stretch our dollars as far as we can. More than half of the states require a small co-payment from Medicaid recipients, including Alabama, North Carolina, South Carolina, and Florida, all right around us. They have found that it reduces unnecessary services. I am recommending that Georgia require co-payments of one dollar on any non-emergency physician, drug, home health, or hospital out-patient service. We would exempt pregnant women, children, and nursing home residents.

Tuesday I said I want to pilot a primary-care case management initiative that has saved money in Kentucky. And to encourage its use, I propose that we exempt its participants from the copayment.

In addition to Medicaid, I am recommending an increase of nearly $51 million for other health and social service programs in the Department of Human Resources. In last year's budget, we began family-oriented community-based services for severely emotionally disturbed children in the DeKalb, Glynn, Hall, and Muscogee service areas. My first priority this year is to expand these services into five more service areas based in Ware, Chatham, Floyd, Houston, and Troup Counties.

As I mentioned Tuesday, I want to expand the PEACH program, which provides job training to welfare recipients. With this $2.5 million recommendation, we will have doubled the number of clients in the PEACH program since FY 91.

Some other recommendations include: $300,000 to purchase AZT for AIDS patients; $2 million to add 1,524 more youngsters to our early-intervention family support services for developmentally delayed preschoolers; and $279,000 to match a HUD grant which supports two 75-bed residences for the homeless mentally ill in metro Atlanta.

Finally, $10 million in bonds will enable 14 DHR facilities to undertake 32 badly needed, major renovation and repair projects.

For Natural Resources, my budget includes $20 million in bonds for land acquisition for Preservation 2000, $2.5 million for renovation and repairs at Sapelo and Ossabaw Islands and various state parks. I recommend start-up funds for the new state park at Tallulah Gorge, funds for a development plan at Sprewell Bluff and $18.5 million in bonds for the Mountain Park to be paid by revenues from the park.

For local governments, who bear the brunt of increasing demands for water, sewer, and waste water treatment, I recommend $30 million in bonds to continue our low-interest loan program. In the past decade, this program has provided almost a quarter of a billion dollars in loans to local governments. Another $1 million will start the parallel program of local government loans for solid waste and recycling facilities, augmented by $4 million from the Georgia Environmental Facilities Authority. I also propose $400,000 for matching grants to local governments to encourage the planning of regional solid waste facilities.

And I recommend $1 million in state matching money for a revolving loan fund through the Georgia Housing and Finance Authority to assist manufacturers and businesses who must build wastewater facilities.

For the Department of Corrections, I recommend $19.4 million to open new prison beds, and $27.2 million to annualize the operating cost of the prisons we're opening during FY 93 and to provide for increased inmate health costs.

I want to take a minute to talk more broadly about corrections in Georgia, and how it is changing. We used to have only two options—prison, and probation or parole. However, as I pointed out to you on Tuesday, prisons are very expensive to build and operate. Alternatives like boot camp are not only much cheaper, but for certain offenders they are also much more effective.

So more recently we have developed a wider range of alternative programs like intensive probation, diversion centers, and boot camps.

We are now in the process of sorting out who belongs where by adjusting sentencing guidelines, fine-tuning our parole grid, and modifying boot camp regulations. And House Bill 1607—a landmark piece of legislation—has had a major impact on our prison population by allowing the use of alternatives to incarceration to penalize technical violations of probation.

At the same time that our alternative programs are reaching full stride, a major prison construction program begun several years ago has resulted in 5,400 new prison beds, all ready to come on line simultaneously. So we have enough prison beds to end early release and keep violent criminals behind bars, where they belong, for a long time. And we will do that.

However, I see no reason to waste valuable state resources by staffing empty prison beds. We anticipate that we will need 2,322 new prison beds in FY 94, and this budget includes funds to open them in the most efficient way possible. We will then bring the remaining beds on line as we need them. And you will find no additional prison construction in this budget—only $10.8 million in equipment for the new prisons and diversion centers we will open, $3.3 million for redevelopment at the Georgia Women's Correctional Institution, and $2.6 million for Phase II support construction at the Calhoun, Wilcox, Tattnall, Pulaski, and Macon County institutions.

For troubled children served by the new Department of Children and Youth Services, the critical need is increased placement services, especially for youth with special needs. I recommend expanding six intensive supervision programs and two short-term residential programs to care for 140 more children.

I also propose that we increase our electronic monitoring capacity by 100 children and our aftercare program by 50 children, as well as provide additional funds for alcohol and drug testing and to increase the assessment staff.

I recommend $5.7 million in capital outlay at eight Youth Development Centers, including constructing replacement cottages at Augusta and Milledgeville; designing new centers in Fulton, Chatham, and Cobb Counties; and repairing the centers in Milledgeville, Albany, Augusta, and Gainesville.

Another area of special interest in this budget is the bonded capital outlay projects that relate to the 1996 Olympics. The Olympics will have a $5 billion dollar economic impact that will be felt all across this state. But the real reason why the state needs to be involved is that two-thirds of the Olympic venues are on state property. Stone Mountain Park, the Georgia Dome, and the World Congress Center are among this state's biggest and best tourism and convention facilities. They support themselves with their own revenues, they bring money into the state, they create jobs, and they generate millions of dollars in tax revenues that benefit all of your legislative districts.

I am proposing projects taken from the long-term plans for these facilities, that we would build whether the Olympics were coming or not. They will generate revenues which will pay off the bonds issued for their construction, which is our normal budget procedure for these facilities.

Even the Olympic Village housing at Georgia Tech is designed to pay off its own bonds by providing desperately needed dormitories for students after 1996.

Let me make this very clear: We are not building anything for the Olympics! We are using the state's bonding capability to make improvements that we planned to make anyway and that for the most part will generate the revenues to pay off the bonds.

The final topic I want to address is state government itself. For our state employees I recommend a pay raise that takes a first step toward a performance-based plan. I propose that state agencies evaluate their employees on the anniversary of their employment date, and reward good performance with a 2.5 percent pay increase at that time.

I also recommend $15 million in bonds to renovate the Atlanta Bank Tower, which was recently purchased by the Woodruff Foundation and donated to the state; $2.2 million in bonds to continue fire code renovations at the Capitol; and $1.8 million to replace plumbing, heating and electrical systems at the Department of Public Safety headquarters building.

Now, I've mentioned bonds for a variety of projects, and you are probably adding them up in your head and wondering if you ought to get worried. So in conclusion, let me say this about Georgia's bonded indebtedness.

Georgia has very conservative constitutional restrictions not only on the volume of state debt, but also on the control of it. We mostly require general obligation bonds, while other states use a much broader array of debt vehicles. And we have been so conservative within those restrictions, that the bonds in this budget still do not put us anywhere close to our constitutional debt ceiling.

The Constitution limits us to spending 10 percent of our income for debt payments. The bonds I am recommending for FY 94 would put our payments right at 6 percent of our income. And I want to emphasize this: That's actually a slight reduction in our debt level from the prior year, and it does not change the same basic level we've held during the past two decades.

Since I've been Governor, I've had lengthy and in-depth discussions with staff from the major bond rating services—Moody's and Standard & Poor's, both of which give Georgia top ratings. And I have learned that they do not simply look at your outstanding debt in evaluating your state's financial health. These professional analysts are also looking for initiatives that will improve state services and create a climate that stimulates future economic growth and prosperity.

It is not enough to be fiscally conservative. We must also demonstrate an appropriate balance of assertive fiscal management and progress. That's what we've done in the past, and that is what this budget is designed to do.

I thank you for your patience as I've gone through this long, complicated, but very necessary process. And I look forward to working with you as you now take your turn in the time honored process of helping to shape this budget.

# B'nai B'rith Klutznick Museum

*Washington, D.C., May 18, 1993*

I want to thank you for that gracious introduction. For a guy like me to come to a place like this and speak to a group like y'all is proof positive that the American Dream can come true. Over the years I've attended many B'nai B'rith events, mostly sitting in the audience paying a silent personal tribute to an organization I've always admired greatly. So it is with a deep and touching honor to be part of your program tonight.

Back during the Second World War, when the Nazi bombs were raining over London, Winston Churchill was speaking to a group of society ladies. A small, older woman in the back of the room stood up to chastise Churchill for drinking during the war. "Sir, if we poured all the brandy, all the whisky, all the wine you've drunk during this war into this room, it would fill it up to here,"—and she held her hand at the top of her head. Churchill looked at the top of the woman's head. Then he looked way up to the magnificent vaulted ceiling of the ballroom they were meeting in, and he said: "My dear little lady. How much we have done. How much we still have to do."

So it is with issues of unity and community here in America. Gone are the days when African-Americans in my state of Georgia were denied access to lunch counters. Gone are the days when Japanese-Americans were herded into camps because we were at war with Japan. But how much we still have to do.

When far-right hate groups are lining up to buy copies of David Duke's list of campaign donors, we still have much to do. When sexual harassment is still a part of the standard operating procedure in too many workplaces in America, we still have much to do. When our radio airwaves and our college campuses are assaulted with the hate-filled message of fanatical fringe groups, we still have much to do. When a black baby born in America today has a greater chance of being killed by gunfire than an American GI in World War II, we still have much to do. When the owner of the oldest professional baseball team in America, the Cincinnati Reds, praises Hitler and slurs African-Americans, we still have much to do. When the flag that flies over a state capitol perpetrates old hatreds and keeps old wounds from healing, we still have much to do.

But we take heart from the words of the ancient Hebrew text: "The day is short, the work is great. It is not thy duty to complete the work, but neither art thou free to desist from it." You have been carrying on that work for many a long day. And I am proud to salute you for it.

The thing that has always impressed me most about B'nai B'rith is your "outward" vision. So many organizations that embrace an ethnic or a cultural or a religious tradition look inward. They are concerned only about preserving the traditions and rights and well-being of their own people. That's fine... as far as it goes, but I want to salute you for going the extra mile and caring about the larger world in which we all must live.

Two centuries ago, Moses Sexius, warden of the Hebrew Congregation of Newport, Rhode Island, wrote to the President of this new nation of his delight at the birth of "a government which to bigotry gives no sanction, to persecution no assistance, but generously affords to all, liberty of conscience." Today, we dedicate the historic letter that George Washington wrote back, affirming that the government of the United States would "give to bigotry no sanction, to persecution no assistance."

But, oh how hard it sometimes is to actually live our lives by those words. I guess it's a natural human tendency to feel that your own way of thinking, believing and doing things is best. That's why we tend to gravitate toward people who are like us. I suspect it gives us a sense of security to be with people who are likely to say or do things that same way we would. So we gather by racial groups, by religious or ethnic groups, by age groups, by socio-economic status.

Next thing you know, we're all living in neighborhoods or subdivisions or communities that are full of people just like us, and we begin to devote ourselves to being more like the Joneses than the Joneses are, without realizing how that approach constricts us and narrows our horizons. We become prisoners—with no freedom not to keep up with the Joneses, no freedom to do anything differently from any of our neighbors. Suspicion grows toward anything outside of life according to the Joneses, and we begin to think we need to be protected from it. As time goes by, suspicion turns into fear, and fear turns into hatred, and those combustible ingredients explode into bigotry.

It's true for all of us. It may be hard for you to imagine, but there is a place where everybody sounds just like me. In the remote Appalachian village where I grew up, they wouldn't believe that there are places where people actually pay to eat raw fish. And y'all probably didn't know there was a place where people pay to eat peanuts that are boiled.

Without realizing it, we all tend to look inward rather than outward. It's so easy to slide into an "Us versus Them" mentality. A generation ago, this city burst into flames when it heard the news of the murder of Dr. Martin Luther King, Jr. A young student at Georgetown University—a Baptist boy from a small Southern town, studying at a Catholic school in a large Northern city—had been so impressed by Dr. King's message that he committed every word of the "I Have A Dream" speech to memory. When the riots broke out, he painted a big red cross on his old, white Buick and sped into the heart of the riot zone, bringing blankets and food to the cold and hungry huddled in church basements.

That young man became our President last January, and one of the things he likes to say is, "there is no them. There is only us. And we're going up or down together." As our nation moves into its third century, our population is growing more and more diverse. Nearly one-fourth of our people are now minority. Nearly a third of our school-age children are minority. By 1995, more than half of California's high school graduates will be minority—the minority will have become the majority. Other states will gradually follow as we move on into the 21st century.

One of every seven Americans speaks some other language than English in their homes, an increase of a third since 1980. In my home state of Georgia, those with some language other than English as their primary tongue have more than doubled in the past decade—the largest increase of any state in the nation.

Here in Washington, and back in the red clay hills of Georgia, all of us are struggling to answer the simple question—and the daunting challenge—posed to us a year ago by Rodney King: "Can't we all get along here?" Can't we all try to live our lives by what we know deep in our hearts: That all men—*and* women—are created equal? All of us: We eat; we sleep. We have strengths and weaknesses; we have dreams and anxieties. A tear knows no race, no religion, no color.

We all cry in the same language. But freedom from prejudice and discrimination is more than simple tolerance or overlooking of differences. It goes beyond merely trying to ignore our differences—and instead it celebrates our differences. You understand better than anyone that our diversity must become our greatest strength. Or our prejudice will become our crippling weakness.

Many years ago, the Rabbis were asked why was it that in the beginning God created just one man, Adam, and just one woman, Sa-ba, or Eve. Surely God could have created multitudes.

The Rabbis said that only one man and one woman were created to help us all remember that we all come from the same mother and father. No one should ever say, "I'm better than you," and no one should ever feel, "I'm less than you."

The only son of Georgia ever to win the Nobel Peace Prize, Dr. Martin Luther King, Jr., wrote to us from his jail cell in Birmingham: "We must come to see that human progress never rolls in on wheels of inevitability. It comes through the tireless efforts and persistent work of people willing to be co-workers with God... Now is the time to make real the promise of democracy...Now is the time to lift our national policy from the quicksand of racial injuries to the solid rock of human dignity."

Now is the time. This is the place. And you are the people whose tireless efforts and persistent work will truly make you co-workers with God in the great project of building the kind of country we want to leave to our children and grandchildren.

# Darton College Commencement

*June 11, 1993*

Today, you are graduating from a growing, thriving institution that has experienced a steady rise in enrollment that has increased your student body by nearly 40 percent over the past seven years. We've appropriated state funds for a new building for allied health, community service, and classrooms in response to that growth. And I look forward to seeing it become a reality.

Today, on the threshold of your careers, you live in a world that seems uncertain, a world that seems to be dominated by problems and unrest. The jubilation over the end of the Cold War, the destruction of the Berlin wall, the demise of Communism, and the emergence of free market systems in Eastern Europe is being replaced by a uneasiness about other parts of the world. Somalia, Yugoslavia, and Iraq are just three countries at the top of the list.

Here at home, some recite a litany of woes casting shadows on the future. There is recession, inflation, depression, the coming ice age, the greenhouse effect, the warming of the oceans, smog in our cities, the energy crunch, the population explosion, and wildlife extinction. Some turtle somewhere is becoming extinct while we're having this graduation.

There are holes in the atmosphere, radon in our basements, mercury in our oysters. The snail darters have disappeared—and the killer bee is making its way to Georgia just as the boll weevil did decades ago.

My point is not to make light of the real problems of our civilization, but to suggest that every now and then we—we all—need to put things into perspective and celebrate our progress.

A few years ago, my mother died at the age of 93. She was born when Victoria was still Queen of England. And as we laid that dear lady to rest, I thought of all she had lived through—all she had seen—all she had dealt with in the course of just one lifetime.

She witnessed the greatest wars in all of history, financial panics, killing strikes, crippling blizzards and tornadoes, and terrible epidemics of influenza, polio and diphtheria, diseases that killed loved ones and wiped out whole families that she knew. She went through so many chilling adversities and coped with so many tough situations that most of today's problems and predicaments look positively idyllic by comparison.

Yet she always maintained this unfailing optimism. She found absolute delight in so many little pleasures, so many day-to-day things. She believed in the present—she looked forward to the future.

She saw the invention of so many things that are so commonplace to you today, that it is almost foolish to name them. But when she first encountered them, they were small miracles. Like radio. To her it was a wonder to hear the voice of the President of the United States in your own home.

Central heat! Airplanes! Electricity! Paper Ttowels! Frozen strawberries! Restaurants that serve you in minutes, or sell dinners to take home! All the wealth of 20th century wonders and blessings. She loved it all—all this *progress* that we now take for granted.

So, young ladies and gentlemen, I am here to tell you what you essentially already know. Every age always has its woes and miseries. It is the business of the future to be dangerous.

But the plain fact is that human beings have never been in a better position to reach that goal of a better life—for more people—than right now in 1993.

I am often asked about my advice for the future. It is simple. Challenge the self-appointed experts and take the long view. Be willing to go against the grain, even if it means a few splinters.

There will always be doom and gloom, anti-growth folks, trying to influence and, if possible, regulate your life. But let's look at their records. One of the biggest best sellers of the late 60s was *The Population Bomb* by a man named Paul Erhlich. In 1968 he wrote that "in the 1970's the world will undergo famines—hundreds of millions of people in America are going to starve to death." And he predicted the world would end by 1983.

It simply did not happen. Now, of course, in isolated places of the world like Somalia, famine exists. But it is because of conflict and distribution issues, not food supply. In fact, over the past two decades world food production has dramatically outpaced demand.

Another shattering report of a few decades ago called *The Limits To Growth* predicted that the world's oil supply would be exhausted by 1992, and all the gold, mercury, tin, and zinc were also to be gone by now. Well, that has not happened, either.

What makes these kinds of dire warnings so silly and so unrealistic is that they all take a static view of society. They treat human beings, you and me, as if we were a herd of deer who will simply eat what is in front of us until it runs out, and then starve to death. They ignore our ability to invent new technologies, solve problems, and fundamentally reshape our world, our nation, our beloved State.

Applying our talents in new ways! That is what we have always been able to do. Humans are uniquely productive creatures, and unlike other species, we can and will increase the supply of resources available to us. We do it every day.

The simple fact is that since the middle of the 18th century, the gross work product has multiplied more than 1700 fold, while the world's population has risen only sixfold. That is an incredible accomplishment and one that clearly indicates how creative and productive we can be.

No one wants an economic downturn, but when they have come, resourceful entrepreneurs have always used today's hard times to lay the groundwork for tomorrow's prosperity. My mother was born during the panic of 1893, and it ran for a number of years. Hundreds of banks went under. Seventy-four railroads went into receivership. Yet that decade was called the "Gay Nineties," and as it drew to a close, Americans approached the 20th century with incredible, boundless optimism.

Today, Georgians should be approaching the next century with similar optimism. Over the past decade or so, Georgia has had a lot to be proud of. Between 1980 and 1991, personal income rose 108 percent. Three-quarters of a million more workers are on the job rolls than a decade ago. We now have over 1,400 international firms operating in Georgia, employing more than 100,000 people, and more coming.

Financially, our indebtedness, relative to budget, is a healthy 45th among the 50 states. In education, we have undertaken the largest construction program in the history of our schools, and taken real steps to improve what happens inside those classrooms.

And of course, the best single indicator of health and welfare is life expectancy. At the beginning of this century, the average life expectancy of a newborn Georgian was only 47 years. By 1940, it had improved 36 percent to 64 years. Today a newborn Georgian can expect to live over 75 years. An improvement of almost 60 percent from 1900.

Political humorist Art Buchwald once told a graduating class, "We are giving you a perfect world. Now don't mess it up." But I'm not ready to go quite that far. Certainly, there are major issues in Georgia that still need to be resolved. No, everything is not perfect. We are not perfect. We are fragile human beings. Perfection exists only in heaven.

But I am convinced that as we move through this decade and into the next century we will be participants in the greatest period of advancement and improved living standards in the history of mankind. Why should it be otherwise?

We live in a great state in the greatest nation on earth, with the most dynamic economic system ever invented, with a wonderfully diverse and creative population of all races, creeds, and colors. The facts are we are the most fortunate people who ever lived. And I believe we should have the good sense to say that to ourselves every now and again.

You know, every one of you sitting out there right now has a story. Every person here is a book. Every one of you graduates has had your trials, defeats, and disappointments, but every one of you was also able to see through difficulty, to make it to this important day in your lives and now to see promise, hope, joy, and success.

You are all treasures of this State and it has been a privilege to share a few moments with you. Congratulations. And God bless you.

# Cherry Learning Resources
# Center Dedication

*DeKalb College, October 10, 1993*

I'm glad to be with you this afternoon and be part of this dedication program for the Jim Cherry Learning Resources Center. I'm proud to have had a bit of a hand in this project, beginning in early 1990 when, as Lieutenant Governor, I helped to hold the construction funds in the state budget as it moved through the General Assembly. Then in late 1990, as Governor-elect, I was faced with cutting $200 million from that same budget, and again I preserved the funds for this facility. I had the honor of speaking at the ground-breaking here two years ago, and I am delighted to be back with you to help dedicate it. What this facility says is that in the midst of tight revenues and budget cuts, we have held fast to the things that are most important and count most in the long run—the needs and the educational experience of our students.

I cannot tell you how pleased I am that this fine facility is to be named for Jim Cherry, who was truly one of Georgia's great educators and visionaries. Jim Cherry was a farm boy who was born in Calhoun County and began his career teaching in rural South Georgia, before eventually finding his way to the big city.

His critics may have thought that he ruled the schools of DeKalb County with an iron hand, but the fact is that it took a person with his determination and strength of will to do the formidable task that faced him. He became superintendent of DeKalb County Schools in 1949—a time, as he later recounted, when the county's white schools were bad and its black schools even worse.

During his 24 years as superintendent, school enrollment in DeKalb County soared from 9,000 students to 129,000. Jim Cherry campaigned successfully for more than 20 bond issues. Just imagine—a bond issue for every year he was superintendent! Those bonds built 53 new schools to accommodate enrollment growth. At one point he dedicated 14 new schools in one year.

But in the midst of the demands placed on him by seemingly endless enrollment growth, bond crusades, and new schools, Jim Cherry still found time to dream—dreams like this college and DeKalb Technical Institute and Fernbank Science Center—all unique resources for a public school system to own and operate. Not only that, but he also had the practical skills and political savvy to make his dreams come true. It was a rare combination.

Today we see the fruits of his vision and his labors. Fernbank now includes a magnificent museum of natural history, and DeKalb College is a multi-campus institution that enrolls more than 16,000 students.

I was a young State Senator in the early 60s when Jim Cherry went about the creation of this college, and the idea of a public school system starting a college was so unique that it took a special state law to allow it. I got to know Jim Cherry personally in the anteroom of the Senate Chamber as he lobbied for the votes to pass that law. It only stayed on the books for a few years. It was enacted specifically for Jim Cherry to start DeKalb College, and this is the only college ever to result from it.

Jim Cherry directed the purchase of the campus site, personally oversaw the construction of the first four buildings here on what has become the central campus, and hired the faculty, which included me. He was my boss when I taught here during the late 60s. So for me, like many of you, this celebration brings back many fond memories of a man I knew and worked for and admired.

Just as Jim Cherry made such a tremendous difference in the life of DeKalb County, so this facility, named in his honor, is going to make a tremendous difference in the life of DeKalb College. With its striking four-story glass rotunda, it has already become the visual focal point for the campus. And it is destined to become the heart of the educational experience of DeKalb College. With this ceremony, that heart begins to beat.

There's a verse in the Book of Proverbs that says that instruction is better than silver, and knowledge is better than gold. But wisdom is even better than rubies and there's nothing else that can compare with it. There is instruction in the classrooms of DeKalb College. There is knowledge in its faculty and student body. But the wisdom of the ages is to be found here in the Jim Cherry Learning Resources Center.

If this were back when I was on the faculty here, we'd be calling this building the Jim Cherry "Library," because what we would have had to put inside it would have been pretty much just books, periodicals, and documents. Things like on-line computerized catalogues with 185,000 computerized documents and numerous databases... things like computer labs and media services were simply unheard of in those days. But they are an important part of the Jim Cherry Learning Resources Center, and will add a wonderful richness to the educational experience at DeKalb College.

Nevertheless, I'm glad that this learning resources center also has shelf space for 300,000 volumes. Because in this age of electronic media, there is something solid about a book that I find reassuring. You can carry it around in your hand and you don't have to find a power source to make it work. You can read as quickly or slowly as you like, stopping to think or dream, going back to reread and savor a well-written passage, and the rest of the book waits patiently until you get to it in your own good time.

No, the mystery of a book is not in a maze of wires or microchips that makes it work, but in the ideas it contains. And there is a quiet air, a sense of calm, among the stacks of a library that I've never found in a video rental store—a sense of roots and history. Michelangelo is up there on that shelf. Sir Isaac Newton is here; Shakespeare right over there. They are ready and waiting to share their knowledge at our convenience.

Even though the Jim Cherry Learning Resources Center is shiny and new, and its systems are high-tech, it is the wisdom of the ages that is stored inside its quiet nooks and crannies. It is here that the members of the DeKalb College community—its faculty and students—will find treasures whose value is above rubies, waiting to be discovered.

# 1994

# Supplemental Budget Address

*January 4, 1994*

It has been my custom to come before this joint assembly of Appropriations Committees with a very lean amended budget. The first three times I've done it, we were in a recession and this document was a tool to make cuts in state government as we reorganized, downsized, and streamlined. But now that this state is in the best shape it's been in for several years—now that our economy is growing again and a solid economic expansion is underway in Georgia—still, even with that, I am once again, as is my custom, bringing you an amended budget document that is straight-forward and short, because that is what I have always believed the supplemental budget should be.

To my way of thinking, the purpose of the supplemental budget is to fine-tune the budget we agreed upon last session. After that, we then put all the programs and needs on the table together in the big budget so that we can properly establish our spending priorities.

After allocating $83.5 million to the Midyear Adjustment Reserve as called for by law, we still have $122.6 million in surplus, lapsed funds and tax amnesty funds to put into the Revenue Shortfall Reserve. It should be noted, this is the first we have been able to add money to it since 1989. When I became Governor in January 1991, you will remember the reserve fund of this state did not have one single red cent in it. And I can promise you right now that in January 1995, whoever the governor might be, that governor will have one of the largest shortfall reserve funds any administration has ever left for the next.

Outside of a few items, the budget on the desk before you is an education budget that invests in Georgia's children. It contains the most money for K-through-12 education of any amended budget in the history of this state. Both of its fund sources—the mid-year adjustment funds and the additional lottery funds above what we projected—are being used almost entirely for Georgia's schools.

As always, in this growing state, the biggest and most important mid-year adjustment of any supplemental budget updates school funding at mid-year to reflect actual school enrollments. That is the primary purpose for having a supplemental budget. Georgia's schools have experienced strong enrollment growth, and the budget before you includes $68.8 million to accommodate that growth.

The education budget also includes $9 million to replenish the pupil transportation fund, replacing money the Fiscal Affairs Subcommittee transferred from it to help schools deal with their enrollment increases during the early months of the school year until we could adjust the budget. In addition, there is nearly $5 million in middle school incentive grants, and $2.2 million to help high school students take advantage of post-secondary options.

Another $7 million for our children will be spent in other ways: $3.3 million to provide day-care for 5,700 children whose mothers are in the PEACH program—either training for a job or in their first year of employment, and another $3.6 million to serve troubled children who are wards of the court.

There are just a few other mid-year adjustment items I want to mention before I get into the lottery, which is the focus of today's remarks. First, I know that you have received letters and phone calls from constituents, just as I have, about the length of time it takes to process vehicle tags and titles. I agree with them. The present method is completely unacceptable. It takes much too long, and we must change that.

I know there's a legislative committee working on a long-term solution to this problem, and I welcome their recommendations. But in the meantime, this budget includes $1.7 million in additional funding for some urgently needed reforms to improve this process. Right now the Department of Revenue gets almost twice as many telephone calls a day as it is capable of answering. So the first thing I propose we do is expand their phone capacity with two automated systems. An additional $580,000 will get all 159 county tag offices on-line with the state's master computer file. That will enable county offices to check on the status of any tag or title application without having to go through the staff at the Revenue Department. It will be a time-saver on both ends of the process.

Second, it's not reflected in a budget number, but we are also expanding an interactive voice response system for vehicle dealers and banks. With a touch-tone phone and a special identification code, they will be able to get tag and title information from an automated system without needing to talk to the Revenue staff. And the only cost to them will be what the phone company charges for the call.

Then just over a million dollars will be used to speed up the existing process for applications that are mailed in, to provide a 10-day turn-around for processing title applications and a five-day turn-around for replacing lost titles. And finally, as I promised, our efforts to make state government more cost-effective were not just in response to the recession, but are still underway.

This budget includes the privatization of several functions in the Departments of Administrative Services and Medical Assistance. And I want to assure you that as these functions are phased out of state government, we will make every effort to place their employees in other jobs.

As I mentioned at the start, this is an education budget. Not only is the bulk of the mid-year adjustment devoted to our schools, but the Georgia lottery has raised more money for education than was initially projected, and I want to spend the rest of my time on the programs funded by the lottery.

You will find the lottery items in the education sections of your budget document, but please note that they run on a completely separate track and are never mixed in with general funds. Last year, before the lottery began, we examined the performance patterns of other state lotteries, and we formulated a conservative revenue estimate for the Georgia lottery. That projection was $139 million, of which we held $14 million in reserve and appropriated $125 million for the three education programs designated by law: the HOPE scholarship program, prekindergarten for four-year-olds, and equipment and special construction for our schools, colleges and technical institutes.

Now that the lottery has been underway for six months, the Lottery Corporation is projecting $280 million in proceeds for education this year. I think this says two things:

One, the lottery is being professionally run as a business, a corporation, as I envisioned. The second thing it says to me is that the people of Georgia not only accept the lottery, but enjoy playing it.

I am proposing that we use almost all of this additional $141 million for one-shot, non-continuing items, largely for equipment purchases, and that we defer expansions to the ongoing and highly successful HOPE scholarship and prekindergarten programs to the FY 95 budget. That way, we can look at all three programs together in light of a full-year's projected income from the lottery.

Of course, the first thing I think we should do with the additional proceeds in this fiscal year is to put another $14.5 million into reserve, always being careful, always being cautious. That would bring our lottery reserve up above $28 million—which is 10 percent of our anticipated revenue for this year.

Now, before I outline all my proposed lottery expenditures for Fiscal Year 1994 and also, by the way, for FY 95, let me emphasize one thing to you. The Georgia lottery is designed to provide opportunities to students and to local school systems to do things they want to do in their schools. The lottery funds that have already gone out for prekindergarten and technology are being spent according to proposals that were developed at the local level.

The additional expenditures I lay before you today, I believe, should be done the same way. You will notice that I will propose general types of equipment and program guidelines. The actual decisions will be made and proposals developed at the local level based on the needs and desires of individual schools.

This year, FY 94, we will realize $280 million from the lottery for education. For FY 95, beginning in July, we are basing the lottery budget on a projection of $240 million. That is about 15 percent less, allowing for the possibility that lottery revenues may taper off as they sometimes do the second year.

The lottery proceeds, as you know, are designated by law for three very specific purposes:

Prekindergarten for four-year-olds who are at risk, scholarships at Georgia's colleges and technical institutes, and equipment and special construction needs throughout our public educational system. As I have said, this afternoon I'm going to give you an outline of what I am proposing to this General Assembly for those three programs—both in the supplemental budget and the budget for FY 95. I'm doing it that way because I want you to be able to see the whole picture on lottery expenditures, not just what I propose in supplemental.

First, the voluntary prekindergarten program for four-year-olds who are at risk, which is now serving nearly 6,500 children in 127 locations around the state. We are now in the process of expanding this program, and by the end of FY 94, we expect to be serving 10,000 children. I am recommending $80 million for this program in FY 95, to enable us to double the number of children served to 20,000 and to offer at least one program in every county of the state. I believe that is a realistic goal based on the number of communities that are now preparing their proposals to either expand existing programs or begin new ones.

Long-term studies that have followed prekindergarten pupils in other states document clear-cut advantages that continue into adulthood—from higher education levels and better jobs to lower incidence of arrests and welfare. Never forget that the bottom line is that every dollar spent for early childhood intervention saves about five dollars along the way in education, criminal justice, and welfare.

The second lottery program is HOPE—Helping Outstanding Pupils Educationally. If you do not already know this you should: We have created in Georgia the largest and most far-reaching state scholarship program in the nation. It astounds people from other states when you tell them that in Georgia if a high school student graduates with a B average they can go to a public college tuition-free.

The supplemental budget before you includes a $15 million increase for HOPE. And let me explain why it's there. We moved very rapidly to put HOPE into place, because we wanted to offer tuition scholarships to students at colleges and technical institutes when the current school year began last September. For some of our colleges, the application deadline for fall quarter was already past before HOPE became a reality. In other cases, students did not learn about HOPE in time to apply for fall quarter.

But as HOPE gets underway, many students, parents, high school counselors, and college financial aid offices are coming to realize what a tremendous opportunity this unique program offers. So the number of HOPE scholars continues to be in flux and continues to grow, and we are expecting a surge in HOPE scholars in winter quarter.

We are finding more and more students like Michael Hair, a freshman at Georgia Southern University, who calls HOPE a "dream come true," because he never could have gone to college without HOPE. Or LaSonda Cook, a young woman now attending Albany Tech who is there because her tuition is free, and, as she said, she no longer had a reason not to go to school and get the job training she needs.

We have launched a broad information campaign, and we are seeking out eligible students to make sure they know about this unique educational opportunity. The Student Finance Commission is presently receiving about a thousand calls a week from parents and students, asking about HOPE. That is great news for a state that has always been at the bottom when it comes to our young people going on to college.

That is why I've included an extra $15 million for HOPE in this budget as a safeguard. I do not want to turn a one, not a single one of those bright, young, eligible students away. And I don't think you do either, because they might be living in your district.

Then in FY 95, I am recommending about $87 million for the HOPE program, enabling us to expand it in several significant ways. As we implemented the HOPE program this summer, we realized that we were not reaching some of the students we ought to reach—for example, a family in which both parents are public school teachers and understand the critical importance of college—together they come in above the $66,000 family income cap. Do you want to keep Georgia public school teachers from having their children eligible for HOPE? I certainly do not.

There are those who on one hand complain about our teacher's salaries being too low, which they are, and then on the other hand argue that these same teachers make too much to be eligible for HOPE scholarships for their kids. So I want to raise the income cap from $66,000 to $100,000 to include the full range of Georgia's middle-income families. And I can tell you right now that we're already getting call upon call about it from students and parents who are planning for next year. I want to make this scholarship as universal as possible. I want families with both parents working to be able to have their children go to college.

Over half a century ago, it was heralded as a great progressive move when the Georgia legislature decided to provide free books and a nine month school year. No one said then that it should be limited to a certain group. Today, on the eve of the 21st century, a college education has become even more important than a high school education was back then. Let us at least be as progressive in 1994 as the legislature was back in 1937.

I also do want to expand HOPE to cover juniors and seniors who continue to maintain that 3.0 grade point average, and pay for mandatory student fees and even a book allotment for HOPE scholars at our public colleges and technical institutes. Folks, that would mean that any student who graduates from high school with a B average and then keeps a B average each and every year of college could go all the way through four years of college and get a college degree without paying any tuition at all. Think of it, there will be nothing else like it in the United States of America. This State of Georgia would instantly become number one in providing opportunity to receive a college education.

Of course, we want to maintain Georgia's strong contingent of private, independent colleges who also help to educate our workforce. During the past decade, an enrollment decline was projected nationwide for private colleges, and many did experience it. But not in Georgia; our private college enrollments increased by 45 percent from 1984 through 1992. Then last year they led the nation with a 5.5 percent increase—largely because TEGs kept them competitive.

So to keep a healthy balance, I am proposing that we increase the HOPE program's second-tier tuition equalization grants for Georgia students at Georgia private colleges from $500 to $1,000 a student, for a total TEG of $2,000. This will bring Georgia's Tuition Equalization Grants to the highest in the nation. No other state would be doing as much for its private independent colleges.

Finally, I am proposing a full scholarship program, one that covers everything: tuition, room, board, books, and fees for the dependent children of all public safety officers killed or permanently disabled in the line of duty in Georgia since 1978. As crime becomes more violent, our public safety officers increasingly risk their lives on our behalf every day. I believe we owe them the assurance that we will provide this educational opportunity for their children if something happens to them.

Last year, Lee DeLoach, a GBI agent from Claxton, was killed in a helicopter crash as he was searching for drugs along the Altamaha River. I attended his funeral, and I am still haunted that he left behind a two-year-old daughter. It's not easy to grow up without a father. I know. The very least we can do is to make sure that orphaned daughter has the opportunity to go to college if she wishes.

The men and women who serve us in law enforcement, as EMTs, and firemen put their lives on the line every day, and in the past 15 years, 78 of these courageous individuals have made the supreme sacrifice. Enabling their children to go to college is the least we can do for these survivors.

The third purpose of the lottery is to fund educational equipment and special construction. And as I noted earlier, these expenditures are contained largely in the supplemental budget that is before you. Most of you already know that as part of my plan for addressing youth violence and school safety, I have been urging schools at the local level to get together with law enforcement officials and parents and develop a local, safe school plan.

At the Governor's Conference on Education in September, I proposed that we devote $10 million in lottery proceeds to help those schools that decide they need security equipment of some type to implement the safe school plan they have developed. Again, it the local school system that decides whether they need security equipment, and what type of equipment it should be. We require only that they involve parents and law enforcement officers in developing their safe school plan, and then show us how they would use the equipment in the context of their own individual safe school plan.

The response to this proposal has been overwhelming. We now have solid proposals in hand from 165 of our 181 local systems, representing 610 middle and high schools, for $20 million, not $10 million, worth of equipment. I do not want to shortchange any school in this state on this important program, so today I propose we fund the entire $20 million that they need, not just the $10 million I had originally proposed. We cannot turn schools away and refuse to help them with this critical problem.

My school safety proposal also encourages local school systems to create alternative schools for students who regularly disrupt class, but haven't done enough to be sent away. A principal of a South Georgia high school that has more than 1,000 students, has said that if he could just get 27 of those students into another area, he would have a completely different atmosphere in which the other children could learn and the teachers could teach.

While lottery funds are restricted to equipment and cannot be used for salaries or other operating expenses, I am proposing in the FY 95 budget that we make $8.5 million available to help local systems equip alternative schools. And, I am also designating $7.5 million from general funds in next year's budget for a total of $16 million just for alternative schools.

To recap: $20 million for safe schools, $16 million for alternative schools—$36 million for school safety! If you will help me we are going to keep order in our classrooms in this state.

Last year in my State of the State I said that classrooms ought to be where our students encounter technology and learn to use it. But in reality, there is more technology in the average supermarket check-out line than in many of our classrooms.

Computers are wonderful tools to help children learn. They expand a teacher's capacity for one-on-one instruction; they are interactive and challenging; and they never forget a key point or get tired of repeating the same thing over and over. In the initial version of this year's budget, I proposed and you accepted an appropriation of $10.3 million for computer equipment at all 1,158 of our schools with elementary grades. Each school was allocated an equal amount of funding, and each school made its own proposal as to how it wanted to use that money. We have already distributed that $10.3 million, and even as I am speaking to you right now, thousands of children are busy learning with that computer equipment.

I now propose another $10.6 million to be used the same way, allowing every one of Georgia's elementary schools to do another expansion of their computer equipment this spring, for a total of almost $21 million. In addition, this supplemental budget also includes $10.6 million for computer equipment at each and every middle and high school in the state. Each school would get $17,500, and, again, each school would decide the details on how to spend it just as long as it went for computer technology in the classroom.

But a quality education requires more than just the presence of technology in our schools. Educators need to know how to incorporate that technology into their teaching methods and curriculum. So we identified schools all around the state that are already making creative and innovative use of technology, and we are going to use $10 million in lottery proceeds to build on that base and develop 38 model technology projects. These projects involve 42 schools at all levels, and they will pilot the use of educational software, programming, networking, and distance learning, and then share what works with all of our schools.

Last year I visited more than three dozen of Georgia's best schools—schools of excellence and schools that had produced STAR students. I wanted to see what they were doing right and to learn firsthand about some of their most urgent needs. One of the things I learned was that the media center—what was the library when I was a student—is the heartbeat of any good school.

So I propose in this amended budget that we provide $17,500 for technology in the media center of every single public school in Georgia—elementary, middle, and high school. All 1,759 of our school media centers would be given this opportunity to upgrade their equipment.

It's exciting for me to think what $17,500 could do for the media center of the middle school I visited in rural Long County. They might choose to buy a CD-ROM tower, for example, to get access to an endless supply of newspapers, magazines, books, and encyclopedias. Not only are computerized encyclopedias now cheaper than bound volumes, but when you look up an entry in a CD-ROM encyclopedia, you don't just get the printed text; you can also see a film or video clip. Look up Charles Lindbergh, for example, and you can watch his airplane landing in Paris and all the people cheering. Look up the blue whale and you can see it swimming around in the ocean.

I also propose that Georgia's 54 regional libraries have the same opportunity to purchase $17,500 worth of technology apiece. And in addition to the regional libraries, I propose that we provide technology grants to our other 316 public libraries around the state, giving each library a grant of $17,500.

This media center proposal would cost $37.5 million but I can tell you, it will be of tremendous significance in preparing our students and our citizens for the 21st century. I can think of no better way to reach every student in every school in this state than with this one shot item.

Our 32 technical and adult institutes play a key roll in preparing our future workforce in this state. All have growing enrollments, some have enrollment growth of over 50 percent from last year. The average growth is 12 percent, and all have waiting lists.

Last year from the lottery we funded the Douglasville Satellite Center. In FY 95 I want to start that same process on eight others by recommending planning and design money for the following: a Lanier Tech satellite in Forsyth County, a Macon Tech satellite in Milledgeville, a Chattahoochee Tech satellite in Paulding County, a Moultrie Tech satellite in Tift County, an Athens Tech satellite in Elbert County, a Coosa Valley Tech satellite in Gordon County, a Ben Hill-Irwin Tech satellite in Coffee County, and a

Thomson Tech satellite in McDuffie County.

I have visited many of our technical schools recently, and I have not been in one yet that did not need, and need desperately now, more modern equipment. So, I propose that we allot $500,000—half a million dollars—to each and every post-secondary technical institute to buy some urgently needed equipment immediately.

The list is long. It ranges from EKG machines in health occupations, to computerized numerical-control lathes in the machine shop, to the fiber-optic fusion splicers needed to train technicians to install and repair the equipment for distance learning and Telemedicine. And I don't know of a single technical institute that doesn't need to upgrade its hardware and software to keep up with the rapidly changing world of computers. So, I propose our technical institutes receive this $16 million shot in the arm to improve and update their equipment. It's needed and needed badly. Let's do it.

The many equipment expenditures in the amended budget are targeted at our public schools, technical institutes, and libraries. And the equipment and construction items in the big budget for FY 95 will complement that by focusing more on our public colleges.

I will propose that we double the Equipment, Technology, and Construction Trust Fund for the University System from $7.5 million to $15 million in FY 95. This fund matches private contributions to our University System institutions for lab equipment, technology and related construction. It's a leveraging tool to help our colleges and universities expand their private fund-raising. For example, at Georgia Southern in Statesboro, $55,000 from the trust fund attracted $110,000 from the printing industry for new printing equipment in the University's Industrial Management program.

At Valdosta State University $145,000 from the trust fund attracted a $145,000 match from McDonald's Inc. to fund a mobile learning lab which will travel among the school districts in Valdosta State's region, educating teachers on how to integrate technology into their classroom curriculum. At Columbus College, $31,000 from the trust fund matched $31,000 in private contributions to equip a multi-media technology instruction center for the faculty to develop multi-media presentations to use in their teaching. At Albany State, $40,000 from the trust fund is being matched by $60,000 in private contributions, to develop a $100,000 state-of-the-art demonstration and research lab for the School of Nursing.

These are just a few examples of the exciting improvements the trust fund is helping to provide on the campuses of our University System institutions. The University System now has in-hand, requests for more than $15 million from this trust fund, that will be matched at least one-to-one by private contributions. And that is the basis for my recommendation that the fund be doubled.

I will also recommend $10 million for research equipment for the Georgia Research Alliance, which brings Georgia's six research universities together with private industry to promote research that will stimulate economic development. Again, these state funds are seed money that helps to leverage investments from other sources. In the last two fiscal years, I have recommended and you have enacted funding for the Research Alliance totaling $32 million, which has attracted another $100 million from other sources.

The third major item in the FY 95 budget is $19.6 million to construct the new production center for Georgia Public Television. Let me emphasize to you the importance of this building. It is telecommunications more than any other factor that will enable rural Georgia to thrive in the 21st century.

We have made and are making major investments in this state in distance learning technology—in fiber-optic networks, in satellite dishes and transponders—to enable every school in this state, no matter how small, no matter how remote, to offer unlimited educational resources and opportunities to its students. But it is not enough to have the technology in place. You must also have the high-quality educational programming to send out on that technology. The technology is pointless if you don't also have the content. And that is why this building is important to the schools in every single one of your districts.

Finally, I am recommending that we use just over $1 million to purchase and prepare the land and complete architectural studies for a telecommunications research facility. Telecommunications is an area of emphasis for the Georgia Research Alliance, because Georgia is strong in all five technologies that are coming together at the cutting edge of telecommunications. We have the potential to become a world center of telecommunications expertise, and realize tremendous economic growth from it. I don't want to miss this great opportunity.

The Georgia Center for Advanced Telecommunications Technology, which is part of the Research Alliance, already has four eminent research scholars and is conducting 24 research projects in partnership with the telecommunications industry. They are spread among Georgia Tech, the University of Georgia, the Medical College of Georgia, Emory University and Clark-Atlanta University. They are like a new church that has been meeting in a school or community center, but has grown and thrived, and is now in need of its own facility if it is to really take off.

In FY 93 we appropriated $750,000 to begin planning for this facility. The GCATT Board is now actively seeking a private developer to actually finance and build it, and I propose that we move ahead with preparations.

When you look at all of these lottery proposals in the amended budget for this year and in the big budget for FY 95, you are looking at hundreds of millions of dollars that have been generated for education that would never have even existed except for the lottery.

I have always been very careful to say that the lottery is not the panacea for education. It isn't. But it allows us to fund some very needed programs we could otherwise not fund. You have heard some of them the last half hour.

In these times, when an educated workforce is what will increasingly drive our economy, we are giving our children and our schools opportunities far beyond what we could ever provide for them with general funds. We are taking this state from among the bottom in some areas of education and putting Georgia among the leaders. I don't know about you, but for me that makes it all worthwhile.

# State of the State Address

*January 11, 1994*

Lieutenant Governor Howard, Mrs. Howard, Speaker Murphy, Senators and Representatives, members of the Judiciary, Members of the Consular Corps, other honored guests, my fellow Georgians.

When I stood here for the first time as your Governor in January of 1991, I spoke of two Georgias. Today it's more accurate to speak of three Georgias —the Georgia that was, the Georgia that is, and the Georgia that can be.

The Georgia that we inherited in 1991—the Georgia that was—was mired in a national recession. The Revenue Shortfall Reserve was empty, and the state budget was on a collision course with red ink. It was a time of freeze and squeeze. We cut the budget, and then I called you back and we cut it some more. We put stringent hiring and spending guidelines in place. We worked together.

Because we made those tough management choices at that time, I am pleased to report to you at this time our ship of state has a full head of steam, is on course and is moving in the right direction. Now, the Georgia that is—has a state government that is leaner and more efficient. Our budget is balanced. Our top bond ratings are intact, and we have saved enough to put $122.6 million into the rainy-day reserve.

Throughout the recovery, Georgia's job growth has been steady and has outpaced the nation. That pattern is expected to continue. We have now replaced all of the private sector jobs that were lost in Georgia during the recession and added 100,000 more. In 1993, one out of every nine new jobs created in America was in Georgia, and the Selig Center at the University of Georgia predicts we will create another 90,000 jobs in Georgia in 1994.

So, the Georgia that is is getting stronger every day. Housing starts and retail sales are up sharply above the national average. Personal income is up. Unemployment is down. Georgia has become a magnet for people seeking opportunity. Between July 1992 and July 1993, we were second in the nation in attracting population from other states.

Our prosperity in the 21st century—the strength and security of the Georgia that *can* be—will depend more on strong minds than on strong backs. As we look to that future— as we build the Georgia that can be—we gather the strength and courage we need to change and prosper by remembering our heritage and the values that have made this nation great.

The fundamental premise upon which this state and this nation have been built is found in the first three words of the United States Constitution: "We, the People." In that remarkable document, crafted more than 200 years ago, our forebears struck a delicate balance between opportunity and responsibility.

They created a nation where no one was guaranteed happiness, but where everyone was given a chance to pursue it. It was up to each individual to exert some personal initiative, to show some personal responsibility, and to be creative and resourceful with their opportunities.

This nation did not become great because of the efforts of a governmental bureaucracy. This nation became great because "we, the people" worked to build it up, together in our communities and individually in our own lives.

My mother used to quote what I thought was from the Bible. She would say, "Take what you want sayeth the Lord, take it and pay for it." I was a grown man before I realized that is not in the Bible. But it was my mother's philosophy, a philosophy about opportunity: "take what you want;" and about responsibility: "and pay for it."

Those are the values that we must now renew and strengthen as we look toward the 21st century and the changes that are even now swirling around us. They are also the values that underlie my goals for Georgia—on the one hand, providing opportunity, but on the other, requiring responsibility.

So today, at the start of the 1994 Georgia General Assembly, I want to look with you at those goals and at the progress we are making toward providing opportunity and requiring responsibility: those values that define the Georgia that can be.

The Georgia that can be is a state where it's safe for adults to sit on the front porch and for children to ride their tricycles on the sidewalk, instead of having to live behind burglar bars and double locked doors while thugs take charge of the streets.

And we're on the way—Georgia is moving in the right direction to becoming a safer state and protecting our citizens from those who would destroy their opportunities. This administration has opened more prison beds than any administration in history. This administration has opened more boot camps than any other state in the United States. And today in Georgia, violent criminals are spending more time behind bars than ever before. For the first time, judges and juries can now give depraved murderers life sentences that mean what they say—life in prison, with no chance for parole.

But, this is not enough. It is only a start in the right direction of truth in sentencing. Over and over again, our constituents ask, "Why can't violent criminals get tougher sentences? And why can't they actually serve the time the judge gives them?"

Well, I'm here today to tell you—they should, they can and they will! In Georgia, I want it to be where if you do the crime, you're going to do the time. I will propose to you that for certain violent crimes, offenders get a mandatory minimum prison sentence of ten years—the judge can give more—and they will serve the full length of whatever their given sentence is. No parole. No loopholes. No exceptions.

I want criminals who have been given a life sentence to spend 14 years in prison before they are even considered for parole—double the current seven years. And once a criminal has committed a second violent felony—that's right: second—I want him gone from society. I want to see him spend the rest of his life behind bars. We will give them a second chance to be responsible citizens, but that's all they get. Some talk about three strikes and you're out. That's in baseball. Violent crime is not a game. In Georgia, I want the rule to be two strikes, and you're gone—gone forever.

The Georgia that can be is a state where our citizens have the opportunity to be safe from drunk drivers as they travel our streets and highways. Every legislative session since I have been Governor, I have pushed for tougher DUI laws, and every year we have made a little more progress.

And, we're on the way... Georgia is moving in the right direction. Deaths caused by drunk drivers have declined by 24 percent during this administration.

But we can do better. I believe we must do better. So once again, I'll be coming with tougher DUI proposals. Last year I sponsored Senate Bill 27 to administratively suspend the driver's license of a first-time DUI offender. It passed the Senate and I will continue my efforts to get this crucial piece of legislation through the House of Representatives.

But I will also propose a new, comprehensive DUI bill. In Georgia, if you drink and drive, and get caught, even for the first time, I want you to spend at least 24 hours in jail, sobering up in more ways than one. And, I want to see it where nobody—not first-time offenders, not repeat offenders who've had at least five years pass since their last conviction—nobody will be able to use the "nolo" plea to get out of having their license suspended.

The Georgia that can be is a state where children have the opportunity to concentrate and learn at school, because they are safe and free from the fear that somebody will pull a gun on them.

And this week I will bring you legislation and funding proposals for a comprehensive plan to make our schools safe, ban the possession of handguns for those under 18 with certain appropriate exceptions and make it a felony for anyone to sell or furnish someone under 18 a handgun.

My budget contains badly needed aid to help schools with security equipment to implement their safe school plans—plans that have already been developed on the local level with parents and law enforcement officials.

I also propose that we help local systems—and I mean help in a really meaningful way—to create alternative schools for those students who continually disrupt classes.

And I want to modernize our juvenile justice system to crack down on those young punks who commit violent crimes. We must understand that our present system did not envision the level of violence and viciousness among young offenders today. These are not the Cleaver kids soaping up some windows. These are middle school kids conspiring to hurt their teacher, teenagers shooting people and committing rapes, young thugs running gangs and terrorizing neighborhoods... and showing no remorse when they get caught.

That is why I will introduce legislation to require that those between the ages of 13 and 17 who commit certain violent crimes such as rape, murder and aggravated battery, be tried and prosecuted as adults in superior court. And if they are convicted, they should be given an adult sentence, to be served in a separate youth facility run by the Department of Corrections.

Please do not fail to note that this will also enable us to devote more time and more space for those young offenders who can be reclaimed, those young offenders who can be rehabilitated, and in my budget I am recommending more alternatives for that type of young offender.

The Georgia that can be is a state where four-year-olds who are at risk have an opportunity to get the readiness skills they need in pre-kindergarten, because every dollar you spend for early childhood intervention saves five dollars along the way in education, criminal justice, and welfare.

And we're on the way—nearly 6,500 children right now are in voluntary prekindergarten programs funded by the lottery. Within the next six months, we will have expanded to 10,000 children. And then, during Fiscal Year 95, as you will see, I propose to double that number to 20,000 children and have at least one program in every county in the state.

The Georgia that can be is a state where we do all we can to open the doors of opportunity to Georgia's children—and in return, we'll look for parents, teachers, children, and their communities to shoulder the responsibility that's theirs.

And we're on our way. This year I'm proposing we expand the HOPE Scholarship Program by raising the income cap to $100,000 to include more Georgia families. And cover mandatory fees and provide a book allowance. And we are also proposing that we expand the HOPE program right through the senior year of college for students who maintain a B average every year.

In other states, the doors of college opportunity are being closed. The cost of college has increased so much that a college degree is out of reach for the families of many middle class students. But not in Georgia. Any child, regardless of means, would be able to go from kindergarten to a completed college degree tuition free.

HOPE is also opening wide the doors of opportunity for students at our technical institutes. That's giving these students the chance to get the skills they need to compete for tomorrow's jobs, not yesterday's—jobs that you can build a future and a family on.

The Georgia that can be is a state where parents, teachers and communities have the opportunity to make decisions about their schools that are right for them. And we're on the way. Our charter schools, Georgia 2000, The Family Connection, and Next Generation Schools are all programs that encourage local participation, programs that challenge local communities to reinvent education from the bottom up.

The Georgia that can be is a state where we give our children the tools they need for today's world. That means computers in the classrooms, satellite dishes at the schools and training equipment in our technical schools that matches what's used in today's workplace.

We're on the way. Using lottery proceeds, we're modernizing Georgia's schools and classrooms. And as I outlined last week in my presentation of the amended budget for FY 94, we're about to put even more technology into our classrooms, media centers and technical schools.

Let me say one other thing about education: For everything that we just talked about to really work, we need to rededicate ourselves to some old values. Discipline in the classroom. Stronger parental involvement. A reinvigorated commitment on the part of teachers. I come from the old school that says, when it comes to education, children have to work hard, parents have to care, and teachers have to inspire. There's no government program that can force all that to happen. But as an old school teacher, I can tell you there's no stopping a child when it does.

I grew up in a single-parent household. My father died two weeks after I was born. My mother worked as a substitute school teacher and part-time at the post office, sold magazines and wooden plaques she made and painted mountain scenes on—whatever it took to put food on the table. And she raised me to work. I got my first real job when I was twelve. My mother had moved us to Atlanta during World War II, and I wore a big plastic peanut costume and stood in front of a Planter's peanut store on Peachtree Street handing out teaspoons of peanuts. I also delivered *The Atlanta Journal.*

When we went back to Young Harris after the war, I worked summers on a timber cutting crew for $3 a day. I washed pans in the dining hall at Young Harris College, and waited tables and cooked hamburgers for $1 an hour when I was at the University.

What does that have to do with being Governor? Not a darn thing. But it has something to do, I submit, with a person and his values. That's why I have no patience with those who have made welfare a way of life, sometimes through four generations. For many it has become a snare, not a safety net.

But we're on the way. Georgia is moving in the right direction toward requiring more personal responsibility with welfare reforms that demand more personal accountability on the part of recipients, compelling able-bodied adults without small children to work, requiring unmarried teenage moms to stay with their families, encouraging welfare recipients to delay having another child until they can take personal responsibility for bringing that new child into the world.

As divorce and out-of-wedlock births have become more prevalent in our society, more and more parents have taken to weaseling out of the responsibility for raising their children. It takes two to create a child, and I believe that two ought to be held accountable for raising that child. So we've made it easier for mothers to prove the paternity of their child, and tougher for "deadbeat dads" to avoid paying child support.

This year I will bring you another welfare reform proposal. I want to take another step requiring more personal responsibility from welfare recipients. It will provide up to 10 pilot programs which require any welfare recipient who does not have pre-school children at home and who has been on welfare for more than 24 months to simply start doing a little work in exchange for those benefits by putting in 20 hours of community service every month.

Many of today's welfare recipients are on the rolls because they have never learned the personal responsibility of carrying out certain tasks that a job requires. The best way—the only way—to learn that is through work experience. I hope you can help me with this, because I think it is very important that Georgia be one of the first states in the nation to have such a program. And if it works as we expect it to, I want to see it expanded statewide.

Then, for those families not on welfare, those families who do work and save and sometimes come up a little short at the end of the month—the families to whom I dedicated this administration—I want to provide opportunity to this responsible group in the form of the biggest tax cut in Georgia history.

Now that the economy has turned around, we are not going to return to business as usual in this state government. We have steered the ship of state onto a new course and we are going to hold to it. We are going to do whatever is necessary to remove crime from our communities. We are going to do whatever is necessary to improve education for our children. We are going to fulfill our responsibilities. But beyond that, I am proposing that we return the remaining tax revenues to the citizens of Georgia.

I want to put money into the pockets of our working families with children by increasing the income tax allowance for each dependent from $1,500 to $2,500. And into the pockets of our senior citizens by increasing the ceiling on the retirement income that is excluded from taxation from $10,000 to $12,000. This is another kind of investment, an investment in our people—a $100 million investment that will tell our hard-working families and senior citizens that here in Georgia, we really are changing the way government does business.

Finally, the Georgia that can be is a state where parents teach their children the lessons of personal responsibility and good conduct, of self-control and self-reliance.

State government can provide the external constraints. We can help schools purchase the security equipment they decide they need. We can ban the possession of handguns by youngsters. We can provide tough penalties for violent crimes. And we can lock up repeat violent offenders. These are things that government can do, and I believe we have come to the point in time when we must do them.

But they will never, ever take the place of parents doing what they ought to be doing at home. Nothing can take the place of that. Certainly not government. We must give our children more than just the tools. We must give them our time. Parents must read to them. Parents must demand that they do their homework. Parents must shut off the Game Boy and teach them the rules in the game of life: work, study, obey the law, respect your elders and your fellow citizens, get ahead, raise a family, live the Ten Commandments. We can not expect the schools to raise our children. In fact, it is the parent's duty to help the teachers teach our children.

I am a teacher by profession. I am a parent whose sons graduated from our public schools, and now I am a grandparent with grandchildren attending our public schools. And I see things and feel things from that perspective.

Providing opportunity by improving education and reducing taxes for working families—demanding personal responsibility by getting tougher on crime and reforming our welfare system—that is what my mother meant by "taking what you want, and paying for it."

That is the goal of this administration. That is what I will continue to work with you on as we enter this 94 session—and as this generation of Georgians looks ahead to our rendezvous with the 21st century and the Georgia that can be.

God bless you. God bless Georgia.

# BUDGET ADDRESS, FISCAL YEAR 1995

*January 13, 1994*

In my State of the State Address on Tuesday, I outlined my proposals to continue our progress in providing opportunity and requiring responsibility. Today, I bring you a financial blueprint to carry us forward toward our goals of improving education, getting tough on crime, reforming welfare, and stimulating our economy.

In a couple of weeks we will host the 1994 Super Bowl. In a couple of years, we will host the 1996 Olympics. Sports events like these attract attention to Georgia. And now that the eyes of the world are on us, what do they see?

They see a Georgia that created 90,000 jobs last year—third highest in the nation—and is expected to do it again this year. They see a Georgia whose retail sales are outpacing the nation, and whose new car sales are 25 percent higher than a year ago. They see a Georgia whose housing starts increased by more than 14 percent last year. Metro Atlanta is projected to lead the nation's cities in housing starts for 1994. They see a Georgia that is the fastest-growing state east of the Mississippi for the second year in a row, the only state in the nation to rank near the top both by numerical increase in population and by percentage of population growth.

They see a state where the economy is sound and growing, a state where people and businesses want to be.

These strong economic indicators, these leading national rankings, did not just happen. They did not come about by accident. They happened because we had the vision, and together we laid the groundwork for Georgia to run out on the leading edge of the recovery and to rebound to renewed economic growth and expansion. They happened because together we paid the price and made the tough and timely decisions that were required.

The way I see it, government cannot provide all and government should not take all. So we made cuts that caused a net reduction in state spending of nearly $700 million and conducted the largest downsizing of state government in our history. Last Friday's *Wall Street Journal* cited Georgia as the only state in the South where the growth in public employees was far less than growth in population. It pointed out that from 1990 to 1993 Georgia "restrained tax-paid employee growth to one percent, while the state grew by 6.8 percent," and contrasted Georgia to other southern states where public employment increased faster than population.

Just like mid-winter pruning, our decisions prepared the way for the renewed growth and vibrancy we are now experiencing. Because of the tough management decisions we made and the economic growth that followed, I am able to report to you today that our Revenue Shortfall Reserve, which was completely empty when I took office, now has $122.6 million in it. And I am able to present to you a solid, progressive budget for Fiscal Year 1995 that addresses our needs and fulfills our responsibilities.

But once we have addressed our needs and fulfilled our responsibilities, I believe we ought to return what remains to the taxpayers of Georgia in the form of the largest tax cut in our history. I am proposing that we reduce state income taxes by $100 million, by providing additional deductions to Georgians with dependent children and to retired Georgians—those who need it the most. And I have reduced my revenue estimate by the $100 million it will take to fund this tax cut.

Even then, state revenues will grow by 7.8 percent, and this budget directs those new revenues toward our goals of improving education, getting tough on crime, reforming welfare, and spurring our economy.

This budget contains more than $3.5 billion for Georgia's public schools. This is an increase of more than $1 billion for K-12 education since the year I became Governor. I believe the most important investment we can make in people is to educate them.

But the very first thing that we have got to do is make our schools safe. In this budget and in the supplemental—together, I am proposing more than $46 million for safe schools through four programs.

The first $20 million is in the supplemental budget to address the needs of the 166 of our 181 school systems that, at my urging, have developed local safe school plans together with parents and law enforcement officials. They are now coming to the state for some help in purchasing the security equipment they determined is needed to implement their plan. Surveillence equipment—video cameras and the like—accounts for about half of the funds requested. Metal detectors account for less than $700,000 of the $20 million.

Second, I want to provide $16 million to help local school systems set up alternative schools for students who repeatedly disrupt classes. A South Georgia high school principal with more than 1,400 students has said that if he could get about 27 of those students into an alternative school, he would have a completely different place where students could learn and teachers could teach.

Eight million five hundred thousand dollars of this money comes from lottery funds to help local systems with the equipment they need to set up alternative schools. And then $7.5 million is in general funds to help with operational costs. We're going to do it like we have done most of my education initiatives—with proposals coming from the local level, and not some cookie-cutter model dictated by the state.

Third, the frustrations and fears our kids are experiencing in their homes and neighborhoods are not parked outside the school building each morning. They come right in the front door and get in the way of teaching and learning. We need to give teachers help in dealing with the frustrations and fears of our children. That's why I want to begin putting counselors into the elementary grades for the first time. I am proposing $8.2 million to hire 425 elementary school counselors under the program for grades four and five. They'll be funded based on student count, but every system in the state will get at least one.

And fourth, there's $2 million across both budgets for educational materials on the problems of violence and drugs. We are working with the highly regarded *Scholastic Magazine* to develop an education packet to put into the hands of every student, parent, and teacher next spring using the funds in the supplemental budget. And we'll do it again next school year with the funds in the big budget.

We're also expanding DARE—Drug Abuse Resistance Education—which brings law enforcement officers into our schools to teach kids about the dangers of drugs. With this budget, we will have doubled our training capacity for the local law enforcement officers who participate in DARE. And we are expanding the program from elementary schools to middle schools.

In addition to school safety, this budget also expands opportunities for middle and high school students. I want to begin a Youth Apprenticeship program at the 15 sites that received planning money in the current year's budget. As the jobs of the future become more demanding, our high school students need to be better prepared to enter the workforce.

Our Youth Apprenticeship program is designed to expose high school students to the workplace and help them learn firsthand the skills and responsibilities they need to be effective workers. Students who complete this program will have a high school diploma, and the training and experience they need to make an immediate impact in the workplace.

I also have $3.7 million to create a summer enrichment program for at-risk students in grades four through eight. It would be designed to strengthen their academic skills in math, English, science, and social studies.

Another $2 million in this budget will expand The Family Connection to the 15 sites that have been in the planning process, and start planning at 25 more sites. As I'm sure you recall, The Family Connection is an innovative, community-based program that assists at-risk children by closely coordinating the programs that serve their families at the community level.

Two years ago, you passed a bill paving the way for pay-for-performance for teachers. And I appointed a commission that developed a plan that encourages teamwork initiatives and rewards school-level achievement. So you'll find $1.6 million in the budget for stipends of $2,000 per teacher to reward schools who set high goals to improve their performance and then achieve those goals.

I also want to begin a Teachers Honors Program, similar to our summer program for high school students, to give top-flight teachers the opportunity for summer professional enrichment. In exchange they would share what they learned with their colleagues back at their school. In the budget you'll find a little over $1 million, which would allow 300 teachers to participate in a Teachers Honors Program and give each one of them a $1,500 stipend.

The budget also includes nearly $158 million in bonds for construction in 64 local systems, and $10 million in bonds for high school vocational equipment and administrative computers to free educators from red-tape and give them more time with our children. Another $6.4 million in bonds will build libraries in Fayette, Paulding, Pickens, Terrell, and Troup Counties.

Right now we have a University System that not only is the fourth largest in the nation with more than 200,000 students, but Georgia is the fastest-growing state in the nation in college enrollment. That doesn't just happen. There are reasons.

*The Chronicle of Higher Education* recently ranked Georgia first in the nation in increased state funding over the past two years. And I am recommending a record high of more than $1 billion in state general funds plus more than $50 million in lottery funds for the University System.

My budget includes $20 million in general funds to address enrollment increases, $17 million for other operating costs, and nearly $30 million for major renovation and repairs.

Another $21 million is for the Georgia Research Alliance, which brings together Georgia's six research universities with private industry to pursue research that will generate economic development. In the last two years, we've put $37 million into the Research Alliance, and it has attracted $100 million from other sources.

I am also proposing that we double the Equipment, Technology, and Construction Trust Fund from $7.5 million to $15 million. This is a matching fund to attract private contributions to our state colleges and universities. The FY 94 appropriation of $7.5 million has attracted more than its equivalent in private funds for some very exciting projects on campuses all across the state. We now have requests in hand from our colleges for $15 million from this fund, to be matched at least one-on-one with private money.

The bond section of this budget includes $10.6 million for the University System, much of it in planning and design funds for six new buildings at Albany State College, Augusta College, Kennesaw State College, Georgia Southern University, DeKalb College, and Armstrong State College.

Currently the largest construction program in the history of the University System is underway—33 buildings costing $385 million are under construction on 18 campuses. So while the surge of projects from the past two years moves through the construction process, we are now putting the next round of projects onto the drawing board for planning. That way we can move more directly into the construction phase next year.

We are going to proceed with a major renovation of the underground, hot water distribution system at Abraham Baldwin Agricultural College, which needs immediate attention. At Georgia Military College, I want to match private funds for a new academic building and I want to expand the library.

Our post-secondary technical institutes are literally bursting at the seams and have long waiting lists. This year we will complete funding for an unprecedented, three-year, $100 million, major expansion program at our technical institutes with nearly $34 million in bonds for buildings at Albany Tech, Athens Tech, Augusta Tech, Columbus Tech, Lanier Tech, Okefenokee Tech, Valdosta Tech, and Walker Tech. And then lottery funds to plan for a new concept in expanding our post-secondary technical education programs—satellite centers from existing technical schools in Paulding, Forsyth, Baldwin, Tift, Elbert, Gordon, Coffee, and McDuffie Counties.

As the level of education required by the average job continues to increase, we are likewise continuing to expand our adult literacy and GED programs to give Georgia's workforce the opportunity to keep pace. Shirley's been working very hard in this effort, and this year Georgia awarded a record high 17,800 GEDs—up by 1,700 from last year when we were seventh in the nation.

Last year I told you about my goal of at least one full-time adult literacy teacher in every Georgia county, and we took the first step toward that goal. In this session we take another step, hiring 25 additional teachers and providing computer equipment for adult literacy.

It is telecommunications more than anything that will enable rural Georgia to thrive in the 21st century. But in addition to the technology, you also have to have the content. My recommendation for a production facility for educational television is to provide that content—the quality educational programming—to send out over the distance learning networks we're developing.

For our hard-working teachers, I am proposing a 5 percent increase on the teacher salary schedule as well as for our University System. In addition, I will introduce legislation to allow the Teacher Retirement System Board to reduce the teacher contribution into the system from 6 percent to 5 percent of salary. This can be done without either reducing any retirement benefits or weakening the financial stability of the system. Last month, at my request, the board passed a unanimous motion of intent to make that 1 percent reduction if you pass the enabling legislation. This will put more cash directly into teachers' pockets.

The Georgia Lottery will produce $280 million in new funds for educational improvements this year. We are projecting $240 million for FY 95 to allow for some taper-off. The lottery funds are designated by law for three new programs: voluntary pre-kindergarten for four-year-olds, the HOPE scholarship program, and equipment and special construction for our schools, colleges and technical institutes.

I covered my recommendations for these three programs in great detail in my amended budget message last week. Very briefly, the prekindergarten program began last fall, serving 6,500 four-year olds in locally-developed programs. We are now in the process of expanding to 10,000 children. My recommendation for FY 95 allows us to double that number to 20,000 children and have at least one program in every county next school year.

Today, on the eve of the 21st century, a college education has become even more important than a high school education was when I was young. That's why the HOPE Scholarship Program is so important to Georgia. We've got HOPE scholars like Michael Hair, a freshman at Georgia Southern University, who calls HOPE a "dream come true," because he never could have gone to college without HOPE. Or LaSonda Cook, a young woman now attending Albany Tech, who is there because her tuition is free and, as she said, she no longer had a reason not to go to school and get the job training she needs.

The Student Finance Commission is getting 1,000 calls a week about HOPE from students and parents. The number one question those thousands of students and parents are asking is, "When does the income cap go up to $100,000?" The number two question is: "When are juniors and seniors included?" Both of those are in this budget. I want to expand the program to pay the tuition of our HOPE scholars through their junior and senior years, provided that they keep that 3.0 grade point average every year. I have included the necessary funds in this budget to cover mandatory fees and provide a textbook allowance.

And I do want to raise the income ceiling up to $100,000. Let me tell you why. First and foremost, this scholarship program is not about income levels. It's about performance. It's about responsibility. When we implemented the HOPE program, we realized that we were not reaching some of the students we ought to reach—for example, a family in which both parents are public school teachers and understand the critical importance of college—together they come in above the present family income cap.

Folks, HOPE means that virtually any student who graduates from high school with a B average and then keeps a B average each and every year of college could go all the way through four years of college and get a college degree without paying any tuition at all. Think of it, there will be nothing else like it in the United States of America. This State of Georgia would instantly become number one in providing opportunity to receive a college education. That's more important to me than being number one in football.

Of course, we want to maintain Georgia's strong contingent of private, independent colleges who also help to educate our workforce. If we were educating their students in the University System, it would cost us an additional $173 million in state funds.

During the past decade, an enrollment decline was projected nationwide for private colleges, and many did experience it. But not in Georgia; our private college enrollments increased by 45 percent from 1984 through 1992. Then last year Georgia private colleges led the nation with a 5.5 percent increase—largely because TEGs kept them competitive.

So to keep a healthy balance, I am proposing that we increase the HOPE program's second-tier tuition equalization grants for Georgia students at our private colleges to $2,000, which will be the highest in the nation.

Finally, two special scholarship programs. For dependent children of all public safety officers, including EMTs and fire fighters, killed or permanently disabled in the line of duty in Georgia since 1978, I am proposing a full scholarship program, one that covers tuition, room, board, books, and fees. As crime becomes more violent, our public safety officers increasingly risk their lives on our behalf every day. I believe we owe them the assurance that we will provide this educational opportunity for their children if something happens to them.

And second, we're going to establish 30 scholarships to Georgia Military College, to be repaid through military service.

The third lottery category is equipment and construction. The FY 94 amended budget focuses on the computer and media center needs of our schools and public libraries, and on the training equipment needs of our technical institutes. So the 1995 budget complements the supplemental budget by focusing on special construction projects and on the University System.

Moving now to our second goal—it's about making Georgia safer. On Tuesday I laid out a tough legislative package to crack down on violent criminals, both adults and juveniles. I want offenders who have committed certain violent crimes to receive a mandatory prison sentence of at least 10 years, and to serve the full extent of their sentence behind bars.

I want criminals who have been given a life sentence to spend 14 years in prison before they are even considered for parole—double the current seven years. And if you commit a second violent offense, you're gone—for life—with no chance of ever getting back out of prison.

The reason why I can bring you such a tough and timely proposal on violent crime is that we have been laying the groundwork for it over the past several years. On Tuesday I pointed out that this administration has opened more prison beds than any other in Georgia history, and built more boot camps than any other state in the nation. With this budget we will have opened 11,300 prison beds and about 2,000 boot camp beds since 1991, and our correctional system will be running at full strength.

So the reason I can come to you now, proposing longer, tougher sentences for violent criminals—the reason a lot of states could not do it even if they wanted to—is because in Georgia, we have been working together to expand the capacity of our correctional system in a planned and systematic fashion over the last three years.

On Tuesday I also told you that I want to modernize our juvenile justice system. I want to try juveniles ages 13-17 who commit certain violent crimes as adults in superior court, and send them to a separate youth facility run by the Department of Corrections to serve their time. And then update and expand our other juvenile programs serving youngsters who can be rehabilitated.

Two years ago, you responded to my call for a separate Department of Children and Youth Services to give juvenile justice a new focus and level of attention. And the reason I can come to you now, proposing major and timely changes in our juvenile justice system, is because we have been able to lay the groundwork for it over the past two years.

We are moving forward with a separate facility for violent juvenile offenders the youth boot camp is underway. This budget contains $12.6 million in cash and bonds to make improvements at our state Youth Development Centers and regional Youth Detention Centers, and to expand our other alternatives. We're going to open another group home, open two new wilderness programs, and increase the number of specialized care slots.

The second law enforcement initiative you will find in this budget has to do with our public safety officers. It includes funds to increase the number of state troopers and GBI agents out in the field. Our troopers no longer simply enforce traffic laws and investigate accidents. They also make an important contribution to fighting crime, especially drug traffic, and Georgia troopers have been recognized nationally for their successful tactics.

So, for state troopers and GBI agents who are out on the front lines of protecting our citizens and their property, I want to recognize the added risk and responsibility they face by moving their positions up a pay-grade on July 1st, then also give them the same four percent that state employees get on the anniversary of their employment. And for the third year in a row, I'm asking you to increase the hours of training we provide for local law enforcement officers—this year by 30 percent.

Our law enforcement officers also need better tools. I am proposing that we provide the funds to build a computer database of the DNA prints of known criminals, so that a sample taken at the scene of a crime can be compared against the databank for a possible match, and that we provide two new regional services for South Georgia: a medical examiner in Moultrie and an automated fingerprint system in Albany. This will not only help South Georgia, but also speed up law enforcement investigations statewide.

Our third goal is welfare reform, and once again this budget document gives you a financial blueprint. As I told you on Tuesday, many of those who are on the welfare rolls long-term are there because they never learned the kind of skills and personal responsibility it takes to work. That's why a key part of my welfare initiative is expanding the PEACH program, which teaches AFDC recipients the educational and personal skills they need to hold down a job.

I am proposing that we expand PEACH to serve an additional 4,750 clients. This brings the total served by the PEACH program to nearly 25,000 clients. And 3,420 slots for their children are included in the $5.5 million in new funds for day care. During the course of this administration, we have tripled the PEACH program.

Last year you approved my proposal to begin requiring small Medicaid co-payments as a way to encourage personal responsibility among Medicaid recipients. This year I am recommending an expansion of co-payments to 15 additional services for a savings of nearly $6 million. But we will continue to exempt pregnant women, children, nursing home residents, and emergencies. Even with the expanded co-payment, you will find a net increase of $82.4 million in Medicaid funds in this budget.

While we're on the subject of human services, let me say that I strongly support Lieutenant Governor Howard's timely initiatives in child abuse prevention, and this budget reflects that support. Over the past decade since 1983, we have experienced a 275 percent increase in reports of child abuse and neglect. And in recent years, we have seen the effects of the strain that this overload has placed on our child welfare system. I am proposing more than $10 million to expand child welfare services, including 149 additional child protection staff.

We are also expanding services for severely emotionally disturbed children, with new core services in Cobb, Clayton, and Dougherty County service areas, and for the chronically mentally ill, with new services in the Spalding and Sumter County service areas. And we are implementing the third and final stage of our early intervention program for disabled infants and toddlers, increasing funds for this important effort by five-fold over the course of my administration.

The fourth goal reflected in this budget is the stimulation of economic development. Happy as we are about the positive statistics I cited at the beginning of my remarks, we must remember they are statewide averages that disguise some real disparities within this state. But our efforts to address that are beginning to succeed. Last year seven of the 10 largest new manufacturing industries to come to Georgia, and eight of the 10 largest expansions among existing manufacturing industries were outside of metro Atlanta. Our challenge is to build the current recovery into a solid pattern of economic development all across the state by helping each region of Georgia participate in that growth.

Anticipating this challenge, last year I created a public-private partnership called the Governor's Development Council. Many of you participated this summer, as I personally brought members of the Council to each of Georgia's 11 economic regions. I wanted to learn firsthand about their goals and the barriers they saw to achieving them.

In response, this budget includes a new appropriation of $4 million targeted at those regions—for small business assistance loans, marketing funds, export assistance loans, and industrial projects—depending on their regional priorities and needs.

I'm pleased to report that since the last time we met, the 1996 Olympic Games have broadened out across the state, with rowing in Gainesville, soccer in Athens, softball in Columbus, beach volleyball in Savannah, a training facility for divers in Moultrie—the list goes on. These games are truly becoming the Georgia Olympics, and this budget contains a new $1.5 million commitment to help the 40-plus communities that are seeking commitments for training facilities from teams of various countries, and to use the Olympics to market all of Georgia.

Another $5 million will fund equipment and research for the Council's initiative to assist our traditional textile and apparel, food processing, and pulp and paper industries as they strive to remain competitive. We must never forget what these industries contribute to our state.

For our poultry industry, I am proposing three new diagnostic labs in Carroll, Macon, and Mitchell Counties to serve industry growth in these regions, and for our livestock industry, a testing facility at the Experiment Station in Tifton.

We are also going to continue our traditional economic development measures, with $125 million again devoted to developmental highways with emphasis on the Fall Line Freeway across central Georgia and the U.S. Highway 27 corridor down the western side of the state.

For our ports, we are continuing the upkeep of the dredged areas of the Savannah harbor, and designating motor fuel tax revenues for approaches to the new Sidney Lanier bridge in conjunction with anticipated federal funds. This bridge is needed if Brunswick is to realize its full potential as a great port.

I'm also recommending $8 million for land and site work, planning and design for the Maritime Trade Center in Savannah, and $27 million for parking decks to serve the World Congress Center, Georgia Dome, and Omni.

Another $25 million will provide loans to local governments for water and sewer facilities and for multi-jurisdictional solid waste facilities, and $4 million will help local governments with economic development projects and address the availability of affordable housing. Nearly $3 million for the Georgia Housing and Finance Authority will draw down more than $15 million in federal funds from the HOME Housing Block Grant Program.

Tourism is a big business for Georgia. Tourists spend more than $10 billion a year in Georgia, supporting more than 300,000 jobs with a payroll that exceeds $6 billion. That is why I propose that we continue to improve our state parks and historical sites with a $5.2 million package for five state parks.

Historic Tallulah Gorge—truly one of America's great natural wonders—was recently protected under Preservation 2000 in partnership with the Georgia Power Company. We will develop Tallulah Gorge State Conservation Park, with a visitors' center, a system of trails, and numerous landscaped overlooks.

South Carolina has already developed their side of Lake Richard Russell and proved its tourism potential. Our Lake Richard Russell State Park is presently a day facility only, and I want to take a first step in broadening its use by building a camping area.

Laura Walker State Park is next to Okefenokee Swamp, one of the world's most unique natural areas and the setting for the world-famous Pogo comic strip. I am proposing an 18-hole golf course to expand the recreational opportunities needed to make the Okefenokee Swamp area even more of a tourist attraction. And I want to see a clubhouse and other facilities come later.

You've been hearing about the decay in the pool and springs facilities at Warm Springs that became famous when President Franklin Roosevelt used them, and I'm proposing state funds to help with their renovation.

Finally, to enhance tourism for Georgia's Golden Isles, I have proposed an interpretive center at the Meridian Dock in McIntosh County to educate the public about Sapelo Island and the research being conducted there.

There are two other historic sites that are not owned by the state, but are important tourist attractions and need a little help from us to realize a higher level of activity. Congress has designated the historic cemetery at Andersonville as a National Memorial to All American Prisoners of War and is orchestrating funding for the National Prisoner of War Museum to be built there. Our state contribution of $250,000 to this project is intended as a signal to Congress of the importance that we place on it, so that Congress will proceed with the full funding of the project.

And second, the Aviation Museum in Warner Robins—the only one of its kind in the Southeast—is expanding, and I have proposed a grant of $240,000 to help.

We continue to expand our natural acreage under protection through the Preservation 2000 program. Presently we have protected more than 56,000 acres, with another 36,000-plus under active negotiation. So you can see that we are nearing our goal of 100,000 acres.

This budget provides the third increment of $20 million in bonds to continue the protection of environmentally sensitive land and the acquisition of natural acreage for wildlife and recreational purposes.

Finally, let me mention just a couple of items that relate to state government and its services. For state employees, I have recommended a four percent pay increase to be awarded the same way as last year—on an employee's anniversary date of employment and merit-based on a satisfactory job evaluation.

Two public services that are used by more Georgians than just about any others are procuring and renewing drivers licenses and registering to vote. This budget contains significant improvements for both of them. I want to open 15 new driver's license stations to relieve congestion and make it easier for citizens to renew their driver's licenses. At the same time, I want to begin to offer voter registration services at our driver's license stations, as mandated by the new National Motor Voter Registration Act. The idea is to make voter registration more accessible and to get people in the habit of keeping up with it at the same time they're keeping up with their driver's licenses.

But making life easier for voters can make it harder for those local election officials who must keep up the voter registration lists. So my budget includes $6.6 million to develop a statewide computer network for voter registration and make it easier to implement the national law.

I also continue the interim improvements begun in the supplemental budget for the vehicle tag and title process until we can make some major decisions together about long-term changes.

Those improvements consist first of implementing two automated communication systems that do not require hands-on involvement from the Revenue staff. One will give all county tag offices access to the state's master computer file so they can check on tag or title applications. The second will use an automated touch-tone phone system to provide information to dealers and lending institutions.

And second, we're going to speed up the existing process to provide a ten-day turn-around in processing title applications and a five-day turn-around in processing lost title replacements.

I've been talking a long time, but I've only covered some of the highlights in a document that is 450 pages long. Because the General Assembly has expressed a wish to be more knowledgeable about the budget, I have taken longer today, and we have worked harder this year to make the budget document on your desks more accessible and user-friendly. And I encourage you to study it.

This financial blueprint directs state funding with an emphasis on improving education, reducing crime, reforming welfare, and stimulating our economy. Those are my budget priorities to help us achieve our goals of providing opportunity and requiring responsibility as we build the Georgia that can be for the 21st century.

# Nature Conservancy of Georgia

*April 16, 1994*

I want to take this opportunity today to thank you all from the bottom of my heart for the help you have given me over the past four years. We have made tremendous strides together, and we never could have come nearly this far if you had not given me your active help and strong support.

It means a lot to me personally, because, you see, for me conservation is not just another political issue, but a way of life. I grew up surrounded by the natural beauty of the North Georgia mountains. And since my family never owned a car until I was in college, we did a lot of walking.

I was six when I first walked, with my mother and sister, the eight miles from Young Harris through Track Rock Gap to Choestoe, where my father's family lived. We always stopped to rest beside the spring in Track Rock Gap, among the amazing soapstone boulders that contain what looks like the tracks of ancient giant bear, opossum, raccoon, and birds. Many a time I have climbed the seven or eight mile trail up the back side of Brasstown Bald Mountain—first with my mother, who carried me in her arms until I could walk it myself. Then, as I grew older, with friends or by myself.

Those mountains in North Georgia are about as everlasting as anything we humans will ever experience firsthand. They are among the oldest mountains in the world, with rock formations over 600 million years old. They also contain more kinds of flowering plants than the entire continent of Europe, and while Europe claims 85 native species of trees, our Georgia mountains boast 130. They are also the birthplace of some of our great rivers.

They have a long history of surviving human exploitation. Their wolves and puma have all been exterminated. In the hundred years between the Cherokee Indian Valuations of 1836 and my own birth, one of the finest virgin forests in the world's temperate zone was logged over, burned over, grazed over, or in some other way marred then abandoned.

I was four years old when the Chattahoochee National Forest was dedicated and the process begun of replanting trees, restocking fish and game, and repairing the damage from erosion. Since then, during the course of my lifetime, I have seen the mountains opened to development. To retirees and tourists, who come to hike and hunt in the quiet forests, to fish and boat and swim in the clear streams and lakes, to photograph eagles and wildflowers, to eat mountain trout and sourwood honey. And while I want visitors to come and enjoy the sights and pleasures of the mountains, I also harbor a deep-seated fear that those same visitors will, unwittingly or no, destroy the delicate natural features they came to enjoy.

I grew up living, playing, walking among places with names that described their natural features—names like Frogtown Gap, Track Rock Gap, Wolf Creek and Choestoe, which means "land of the dancing rabbits." It pains me to think that unless everyone who lives in and visits these mountains understands and cares for their fragile environment, those names will eventually be all that remains to remind us of the beautiful natural creatures and features that once characterized these places.

When the early explorers arrived, the majestic forests, the clear streams and rolling rivers, the wide horizons of this new world seemed to go on forever. And in the true pioneer spirit, they set out to conquer it—to turn its splendor for their own use and enjoyment. But as Will Rogers pointed out more than 60 years ago: "We are just now learning that we can rob from nature the same way we can rob from an individual. The pioneer thought he was living off nature, but it was really future generations he was living off of."

The first resolution I ever sponsored in the Georgia Senate more than 30 years ago was inspired by my friend, Dr. Charles Watson, and it set up a committee to study the feasibility of setting aside, of preserving certain natural areas. That was the initial seed that eventually grew into Preservation 2000, which I announced on Earth Day of 1991, just a few months after my inauguration.

Preserving 100,000 acres of natural land in four years was viewed by some as wildly ambitious, even unrealistic, not only because 100,000 acres is a lot of land, but also because it represented such a dramatic increase in the amount of natural land that was being preserved by the State of Georgia. But I believed it could be done, and a primary reason for my great faith was that I knew I could count on your help and support.

You helped us get started with the purchase of Little Tybee and Cabbage Islands near Savannah, to maintain them in their natural state as Heritage Preserves. And from this initial purchase of 7,700 acres three years ago, we have moved rapidly toward our goal of 100,000 acres. As of this week, Preservation 2000 has officially protected 48,906 acres. We have another 7,086 acres under option to buy. And we have 55,514 acres under active negotiation, for a grand total of more than 111,500 acres.

These sites are spread all across the state in 58 different counties, from Dade and Walker in the northwest to McIntosh in the southeast, from Rabun in the far northeast corner to Decatur in the far southwest corner. It is land for hunting, fishing, boating, hiking, camping and bird-watching. It protects cave entrances and wetlands, and wards off encroaching development. It restores and protects the habitats of rare or endangered plants and animals. It preserves scenic views and offers opportunities for environmental education.

The phenomenal success of Preservation 2000 would not have been possible without the strong support of The Nature Conservancy, and I am deeply grateful for your help. The Conservancy was the actual agent of purchase for the Montgomery Bluffs property on the Flint River, which was then signed over to the state. And you are presently serving as the agent for two more tracts that are under negotiation.

But in addition to this official role you have played on behalf of Preservation 2000, I also want to thank you for your ongoing, informal counsel and advice. The Conservancy has a wealth of experience in land preservation and conservation here in Georgia, across the nation, even around the world. You are experts at it.

At the same time you've been helping us with Preservation 2000, you've been buying Broxton Rocks down by Douglas and expanding your Marshall Forest Reserve in Rome. And your two-year study of the Altamaha River system is a significant blueprint for us all. You have shown us sites we weren't aware of. You have helped us sort things out and make decisions about what was appropriate to acquire and by whom. You have worked informally in a close and collegial relationship with the Preservation 2000 Council, and we have come to value and rely on your wisdom and sound advice.

We are also indebted to you for generating public support for Preservation 2000. Even when we were in a recession and money was tight, the General Assembly never questioned the importance of acquiring land for Preservation 2000, because the support from The Conservancy and other environmental organizations was so strong and so solid. It is a wonderful gift for all Georgians to enjoy, and an incredible legacy for their children and their children's children.

But in a very real sense, the cornerstone of conservation is education—raising up a whole generation of children who understand that they hold the future of the earth in their hands and that their daily behavior and habits have a direct impact on the natural environment around them. And I want to thank the Conservancy for your support of the Georgia Environmental Education Council, especially for incorporating the Council into your meeting a year ago in Savannah and connecting them with experts in other states to share ideas.

The Council brought me its report last October, and we have begun implementation with $100,000 for their recommendation that we provide small seed grants to Georgia schools for "outdoor classrooms" on the school grounds. These will be places where students, teachers, and parents can create wildlife habitats for plants and animals, and observe and learn about the natural environment. This is a small beginning to incorporating more environmental education into the lives of our children, and we need to continue it and expand it. Because, as the Council pointed out in its report, the future well-being of our children is tied to their understanding and stewardship of the environment.

I spent the day after Palm Sunday assessing tornado damage in North Georgia. It was a vivid reminder of how incredibly powerful the forces of nature can be. Structures that we as human beings considered to be solid and permanent were completely crushed in an instant by the wind. And I thought of the words of the psalmist, who compared our human lives to the flowers in the field that flourish for a moment. Then the wind blows and we are gone.

The earth and the sky, the mountains, the rivers, the seas and even the trees are so huge compared to human beings. Their vast ecosystems move across the centuries with enormous strength and power beyond our control. Sometimes it's hard for us to grasp the fact that this natural environment that is so powerful and so everlasting, is at the same time also so fragile and so sensitive, that small things that we do or don't do in the course of our daily lives can either spoil it or save it for generations to come. But our understanding of that paradox is the key to the future of the earth and to our own future as inhabitants of it.

You, the members of The Nature Conservancy of Georgia, have undertaken the critical task of teaching us and reminding us of that truth. Thank you.

# Campaign Announcement Speech

*Young Harris, April 24, 1994*

Thank you my friends, my neighbors, students, and faculty for being here. Thanks to my former student and the catcher and cleanup hitter on my baseball teams of 1961-62, Reverend Don Harp. Thank you Dr. Yow and, of course, thanks to one of my great friends, my fellow mountaineer and my hero who has run and won a few races of his own, Bill Elliott.

I grew up in this valley. It is my home where my family lives, where my parents are buried, where my roots are. This chapel has special significance. It is where my father's funeral service was held, where I was baptized, where I joined and attended church as a child, where I went to a movie, or a "show" as we called it, on rare Friday nights. They'd have to turn on the lights to change the reels every 20 minutes.

It was here that I participated in my first debate, where I courted Shirley, where my sister was married, where in 1990 I began the journey that led to the Governor's Mansion.

Whenever I come home to this valley and to this sanctuary, the memories of squirming on these hard pews beside my mother every Sunday morning come back so very vivid and clear. And along with those memories comes the powerful realization that today, on the eve of the 21st century, an amazing thing has happened. As parents and as grandparents we have worked so hard and been so eager to give our children what we didn't have, that we have neglected to give them what we did have.

It's time we gave them what we did have—the basics: reading, writing, 'rithmetic, and the difference between right and wrong.

My mother could not provide a lot of the material things we take for granted today. I never tasted steak until I joined the Marine Corps. My family never had a car until I had graduated from Young Harris. We didn't have indoor plumbing. There was no central heat, only a fire place or wood heater. I often wore hand-me-down clothes from a cousin who was fatter than I was.

I didn't have these material things we now take for granted. But I had a mother who used to tell me "Tell the truth and bear the blame," and that if you cheated in school, "You'll only be cheating yourself."

In fact, she was so afraid she might cheat somebody that she often cheated herself. She sold her paintings dirt cheap; she took only half the commission she was supposed to get on the magazines she sold. I remember her selling home-grown tomatoes for ten cents a basket, and she would heap the baskets high with the biggest and best tomatoes she had, to be sure she hadn't cheated someone. All her dealings with people were that way. Honesty—a virtue to cherish, a value to live by. We must teach honesty to our children.

I had a mother who drilled into me that you did not steal, trespass on or disturb any property that was not your own, and that included public property. I'll bet some of you here today remember my mother walking from our house to the post office picking up trash, "trying to make this town look better." Stewardship/citizenship—a virtue to cherish, a value to live by. We must teach good citizenship to our children.

I had a mother who taught me discipline. "If you get a whipping at school, you'll get another one when you get home." I heard that constantly and I bet some of you did too. And no one can tell me it was not a deterrent to bad conduct. Sometimes I misbehaved, but I'll tell you this: If I did, my sins found me out. I was ashamed and embarrassed, and I felt like I had let my mother down. Discipline—a virtue to cherish, a value to live by. We must teach discipline to our children.

I had a mother who taught me kindness. She was a strong but gentle person. She had great respect for her children. And she took time, lots of time, to read to us and teach us and explain things that came up in our little lives. I am a better person because she taught me to be kind through her own example. Kindness—a virtue to cherish, a value to live by. We must teach kindness to our children.

Critics may ask, what does all this have to do with running for Governor? What do values have to do with it? Does cheating matter? I don't want anyone doing brain surgery on me who cheated his way through med school. Does honesty matter? I don't want the bridge to collapse under me because the contractor used shoddy materials to make a quick buck. Does respect for other people's property matter? Ask someone who's experienced a car-jacking or whose home has been ransacked by a burglar. Does discipline matter? Ask the teachers who have worked hard and prepared themselves with knowledge, who have a great love for children or they never would have gotten into the teaching profession.

Government can never take the place of parents in raising children. Government can never take the place of families and churches and synagogues in teaching values. Government can never take the place of people in our communities working together and looking out for each other. Government programs by themselves can never do the job. But what I believe government must do is provide opportunities and encouragement for families and communities to strengthen and renew the ties that bind. And government programs must be based on and driven by those same values that I learned at my mother's knee.

These values that are captured for me in the memories, the special meaning that this beautiful old structure holds for me—these are the values I have tried to live by, as a husband, a father, a grandfather, and during the last four years as your Governor.

I am proud of what you and I have accomplished together in these four years. We have a solid record of reform and progress. It is a record of real progress based on the values we hold dear, but it has even more potential to be realized. It is not a record to rest on; it is a record to build on.

Because I believe in safety, discipline, and respect for others, I have a record that is tough on crime. Crime is the number one problem in this nation. Crime is the number one problem in this state. The question I'm asked more than any other is why can't criminals serve the sentence they are given.

All over this country politicians talk about "three strikes and you're out." My mother always taught me a person deserved a second chance, and I believe that. Three strikes are okay for the game of baseball, but in real life I don't believe murderers should have a third chance to kill or a rapist three chances to attack—not in Georgia, not while I'm Governor. This November, in the same election you will vote for Governor, you will also have the opportunity to vote for constitutional amendments. Amendment number two will be my "two strikes and you're in." It addresses our most violent crimes and here's how it works:

For rape, armed robbery, kidnaping, and the like, whatever time the judge gives you is what you will actually serve. If the judge gives you 15 years, you serve 15. If the judge gives you 20 years, you serve 20. For murder, we've got capital punishment, life without parole or regular life. If you get regular life, we will double the time you have to serve before you're even eligible to be considered for parole. And if you are convicted a second time for one of these "seven deadly sins," you'll be sent away for life: No parole, no loopholes, no exceptions.

A lot of states would like to be able to do this. Georgia is one of the very few that can. Why? Because even when I was cutting the budget, I was pressing forward with new boot camps and continuing construction on more prisons. I've opened more prison beds than any other Georgia Governor. We've built more boot camps than any state in the nation. Unlike most states, Georgia has paid the price and built the prisons, and so here in Georgia criminals must pay the price and fill the prisons.

When I came in as Governor, an early release system was in effect, not even waiting until they were eligible for parole. I stopped that, and now Georgia's murderers, rapists, and armed robbers are getting the message: If you're going to commit a crime, don't do it in Georgia: We will lock you up. And they are not just lying on their backs or sitting on their butts. Our prisoners work. There is no such thing as doing "easy time" in Georgia. It's hard time, at hard work.

Violence by youthful offenders has become a major problem. So we passed a law which provides that these young punks who commit violent crimes will be tried as adults and sentenced to a separate youth facility run by the Department of Corrections.

Every year I have been Governor, I have fought for tougher penalties for drunk and drugged drivers; I have fought to lower the legal level of blood alcohol. And we are making progress. Deaths caused by drunk or drugged drivers have decreased dramatically since I became Governor. They are lower today than at any time in more than a decade. And I will continue this effort, because there is still more to be done.

You don't have to believe my rhetoric; ask the sheriffs and police officers and district attorneys of this state. Ask them. They will tell you—law enforcement supports Zell Miller because Zell Miller supports law enforcement. So, if you want a governor who will be tough on criminals, you've already got one.

Because I believe in honesty in my dealings with others, my record is also one of fiscal responsibility. The Cato Institute, a conservative think tank, ranked me in the top six governors for being tight-fisted with tax dollars. They said, "[Miller] has not raised any major new taxes and the tax burden actually fell about $150 per family in 1992." That was *before* we cut taxes this year by $100 million for working families and retirees.

When I became Governor in January 1991, this state was mired in a recession, the budget was not in balance and the so-called "rainy day fund" was dry as a bone. Like businesses and families all across this state, we did more with less. We cut nearly $700 million in spending and abolished 5,000 bureaucratic positions—without massive layoffs. It was not easy, but it was necessary. We downsized and streamlined, and as a result Georgia rebounded and ran out ahead on the leading edge of the recovery with a leaner and more efficient government.

Georgia is now one of the most fiscally healthy states in the nation. We have one of the best bond ratings in the nation. Our reserve fund should soon top $200 million. And I gave our families and senior citizens a $100 million income tax cut—the biggest tax cut in Georgia history.

We are the fastest growing state east of Colorado for the second year in a row, and our economy is growing stronger every day. During my administration 243,000 new jobs have been created—third highest in the nation. We have more people working in Georgia than at any time in the history of this state. And the Selig Center for Economic Growth at the University of Georgia says we will create 90,000 more this year of 1994. Permanent, productive, private-sector jobs.

During this administration, we have cut taxes not once but twice. The first time in 1991 by $30 million for the working poor who do not receive food stamps and spend a high percentage of their income on food. As you know, I had wanted to take the sales tax off food—still do—and will the first chance I see how it can be done in a responsible way. Then $100 million this year—the largest tax cut in the history of this state—cut from the taxes of our families and our retired senior citizens.

We've done pretty well these past four years without new taxes. Others may *say* they won't raise taxes. But you don't have to read my lips. You can read my record. So, if you want a Governor who will cut fat and cut taxes, and make government do more with less, you've already got one.

My mother used to say "Take what you want sayeth the Lord, take it and pay for it." I used to think that came from the Bible. It doesn't but it was my mother's philosophy: about opportunity, "take what you want," and about responsibility, "but pay for it."

She worked harder than anyone I've ever known, and she raised me to work. I got my first real job when I was twelve, wearing a big plastic peanut costume, standing in front of a Planter's peanut store on Peachtree Street handing out teaspoons of peanuts. I also delivered papers. I worked summers on a timber cutting crew for three dollars a day. I washed pans in the dining hall here at Young Harris College and waited tables and cooked hamburgers for $1 an hour when I was at the university.

That's why I have a record of welfare reform; I was raised to value work and self-respect, and I have no patience with those who have made welfare a way of life, sometimes through three or more generations. Welfare was designed to help those in need temporarily 'till they could get on their feet. But, today in Georgia almost 40 percent—four out of ten—who go on welfare stay on it more than five years. Our welfare system by any criteria has been a failure with two sets of victims: those caught in its trap and those who have to pay for it, the taxpayers.

Up in Washington, they're still talking about doing something about welfare. Here in Georgia, I didn't just talk, I acted. Today Georgia has one of the most comprehensive welfare reform programs in the nation. We're starting pilot projects in ten counties around the state where if you've been on welfare two years and don't have preschool children at home, you must put in 20 hours a month of community service work. I think that's the least they can do, and if it works like I think it will, we will expand it statewide and we will expand the required hours of work per month.

In Georgia: If you're on welfare and don't have small children, and you are offered a job and don't take it, off you come. If you are a teenager and have an illegitimate child, we make you stay at home with your parent and not move out and have a separate apartment paid for with taxpayer's money. If you've been on welfare over two years and conceive and bear another child, you can't get an extra monthly allowance. The child can get health care from Medicaid; the child won't go hungry because of food stamps. But the mother doesn't get anything extra.

These reforms will help make welfare what it ought to be: a temporary hand *up* not a permanent hand out. So, if you want a Governor who goes beyond talking and actually does something about welfare reform, you've already got one.

Both my parents were teachers. They both taught in that building across the way, Sharp Hall. I am a teacher. I taught in that same building.

This college was started more than a hundred years ago by a Methodist circuit rider to give mountain boys and girls an opportunity to get an education. And today, as I look into the eyes of Georgians all across this state, I see that same desire reflected. I see a desire for the opportunity to achieve, and a willingness to work hard to make their dreams come true.

We have made some impressive strides forward in education in the past three years. I want to do more. We face tremendous challenges, but Georgia has never been so ready to meet them.

I have taken a major first step in dealing with the dropout problem by establishing voluntary prekindergarten programs for Georgia four-year-olds who are at risk. By the end of this year we'll be serving 20,000 children with programs in every county. We started with youngsters who are at risk, because they are the ones who need it the most. But I want to carry it forward another step and provide a statewide voluntary prekindergarten program for all four year olds—at risk or not.

In addition to an expanded system of voluntary prekindergarten for four years olds, I will also fight for and achieve a mentor or shepherd program that will offer one-on-one guidance and support to every at-risk student, K-12. In Georgia today we have 525,000 at-risk students in school. I'm going to find that many volunteers. That will be an enormous undertaking, but my goal will be to link up every at-risk child with a caring, responsible adult who will be become part of a team effort with the child's parents, teachers, and school mentor coordinators.

But having the best teachers and schools is not enough if students are worried that the bully in the hall might be packing a pistol. So we are also making our schools safer. We've banned the possession of handguns by children under 18, and strengthened penalties for handgun crimes against students or teachers. We asked schools to draw up their own school safety plans together with parents and police officers, and we're helping them buy the security equipment they decided they need.

We're also giving older kids lots of good reasons to stay in school. I have begun to pilot a youth apprenticeship program to provide students with hands-on experience on what will be expected of them in the real world of work. They will learn the importance of staying in school, and when they finish, Georgia's industries will get employees who are better prepared. I'm going to refine and expand this pilot program.

We have also created the most comprehensive and far-reaching state scholarship program in the nation to help high school graduates go on to college or technical institute. The HOPE Scholarship Program is already providing financial assistance to nearly 50,000 Georgia students, and we have just expanded it dramatically.

This unique scholarship program is not about income levels—95 percent of the families in Georgia qualify. It's about giving young students an incentive to study and work hard in school, by rewarding their efforts with a chance to get the education and training they need for the jobs of tomorrow—jobs they can build a future on, jobs they can raise a family on. So, if you want a Governor with a record of achievement and creative ideas on how to improve education, you've already got one.

As Governor, I have provided more high-tech, high quality tools for education than any other Governor in our history. Georgia is the only state to put a satellite dish at every single school and own a transponder on a Telstar satellite to send out the programs. We have placed thousands of computers in every single school, media center, and public library in this state, technology in amounts unheard of, unthought of even a few years ago. All of these things are available to all Georgia students.

But if we really want to improve education, we need more than new technology; we also need old values. Disciplined students. Involved parents. Committed teachers. I may be old fashioned, but I believe that when it comes to education, children have to study, parents have to care and teachers have to inspire. There is no government program that can force all that to happen. But as an old school teacher, I can tell you there is no stopping a child when it does. So if you want a Governor who values educational opportunities for Georgia's children and families to build a future for themselves, you've already got one.

Over the past four years, I have built a record of being tough on crime, cutting taxes, reforming welfare, and improving education—a record that is based on the values my mother instilled in me when I was growing up, the values I live by, the values I am striving to pass on to my children and grandchildren.

We have come a long way toward shaping a state government whose programs are rooted in those values and encourage our citizens to live by them. But that task is not complete. And that is why I am here again today—to finish the journey that you and I began four years ago.

And now, after a little picnic I hope many of you will be able to attend, I begin a week-long, 2,000-mile trip with 28 stops in Georgia towns and cities along the way. From the mountains of Rabun Gap to the beaches of Tybee Island. Once again criss-crossing a Georgia I know so well and love so deeply.

And like Tennyson's Ulysses—old in years but still young in ideas and strong in will "to strive, to seek, to find, and not to yield."

# GPTV BASEBALL SPECIAL

*July 30, 1994*

I would like to thank the Atlanta Braves for sponsoring this special preview. We can only imagine what a treat this series is going to be for a team that is part of the story.

My entire life has been built around the rhythms of baseball. From the time that I was ten years old until this morning's sports page, I have followed this sport with fanatical zeal. I sat in the bleachers at the old Ponce de Leon field and watched young Billy Goodman and Eddie Matthews of the Atlanta Crackers, as they made their way to the big leagues, where Goodman was an American League batting champion and Matthews was a Hall of Famer.

Neither one was my favorite Atlanta Cracker, though. Country Brown was. He could fly, and he was the best drag bunter there ever was. But he only got to the big leagues for a few games, and later went home to the textile mills of northwest Georgia.

Talking about the textile mills, they were the source of a very good and exciting brand of baseball. That's where I played—on the old mill teams and town teams of local communities.

I can still remember how my chest swelled with pride when at 16 I made the town team, playing with men much older than I, and got my first real uniform. You see, there were no well-financed Little League teams in those days. That uniform was gray wool and scratchy, and on the back it said "M.C. Hood Gen. Merchandise" with a number 4.

The happiest days of my life were spent on the skinned infields of North Georgia, western North Carolina and eastern Tennessee. Sometimes we would ride in the back of a pick-up truck to the games. When we played at home—in the days before television—huge crowds would turn out on Saturday and Sunday afternoons to cheer the local team. When someone hit a home run, they would pass the hat and present the hero with a pocket full of change and wadded up dollar bills.

I later coached—with winning seasons, by the way—at Young Harris College. Just last year I got Mickey Mantle and Hank Aaron to come to a dinner at the Governor's Mansion, and we raised $60,000 for a new ball field at the college.

Talking about Hank, I went with him a couple of years ago to Cooperstown. I had gone there earlier with my friend and fellow mountaineer Johnny Mize, the Big Cat, when he was inducted. But I went there with Hank to be with the Legends of Negro Baseball. That's when I met Buck O'Neill, who honors us with his presence tonight, and I shouted with glee, Ken, when I saw Buck was going to be part of this project. And I met others— Ted "Double Duty" Radcliffe—ever heard of him? He'd pitch the first game of a doubleheader, then catch the second.

Baseball endures because its myth and statistics endure. It is constant. Winning 20 games or batting .300 is still the same measure of excellence today as it was before I was born.

Someone wiser than I am once wrote that whoever wants to know the heart and mind of America had better learn baseball. How true. I doubt that many football fans can say how many touchdown passes Fran Tarkenton threw, or that many basketball fans can say how many goals Wilt Chamberlain scored. But all real baseball fans know that Ted Williams hit .400, and Hank Aaron broke Babe Ruth's record of 714 home runs.

In many ways, baseball is a simple game than anyone can follow and enjoy. It is also a complex game. I once read that somebody computed 18,000 different situations that players have to react to without thinking.

Another thing to think about with this game: Failure is the norm. Babe Ruth struck out twice in one inning 32 times. Hank Aaron ground into more double-plays than any other player. Nolan Ryan lost more games than all but seven pitchers in major league history. Yet they are all Hall of Famers. That's the essence of baseball, and of life—how you deal with failure.

So you see that is why I, as a historian and a fan, was so thrilled when I learned that the same creative genius who kept us spellbound and touched our souls with his "Civil War" series, had turned his remarkable talents to baseball.

Traditionally filmmakers have approached documentaries as if they were an extended version of a story from the network news. The dates and facts were pieced together and laid out in a straight-forward, cut-and-dried fashion. But Ken Burns has redefined the word "documentary," and given it a deeper and richer meaning. He goes beyond the simple piecing together of well-chosen material and puts us inside the story. To him, a faded black-and-white photo from an old scrapbook is not a historical relic, but a freeze-frame in an ongoing, moving drama. And he looks for a way to bring it to life and catch up the viewer in the motion and emotion of the drama it represents.

He collected more than 150 recordings of "Take Me Out to the Ball Game" in every conceivable musical style, so that he could communicate every emotional nuance of the game.

In a Ken Burns documentary, the facts come alive. We learn how it felt to be there, and we come to a new level of understanding of how things happened and why.

I am looking forward to his "Baseball" series with great anticipation, because I expect to gain a deeper understanding of the game and its development. But also because I expect that his "Baseball" is going to give us a good look at 150 years of American history from a new and interesting angle.

It is my great pleasure to present to you a Red Sox fan who, in the course of working on this exceptional series, took his baseball nickname from the legendary Ted Williams—Ken "The Kid" Burns.

# Legislative Biennial Institute

*December 6, 1994*

The first thing I want to do is extend an official welcome to the many new faces around these tables and also to the rest of you who, like me, have been around the bases a few times.

Thirty-four years ago, in December 1960, as a new legislator, I attended this seminar, and I went on to spend twenty years of my life in the legislative arena. I know that being a legislator is not easy.

It's kind of like Alice in Wonderland, when she was running to keep up with the Queen of Hearts. And she said to the Queen, "In *my* country, you'd generally get somewhere else if you ran very fast for a long time, as we have been doing." To which the Queen replied, "A slow sort of country. Now *here*, you see, it takes all the running you can do to keep in the same place. If you want to get somewhere else, you must run at least twice as fast as that."

Like Alice, we have to do a lot of running just to keep up with everything that's going on in Georgia. And if we actually want to do something, then we have to run twice as fast. But I came here today to tell you that that's what I intend to do. This old man is going to run twice as fast, because I intend to do something. And I invite and encourage you to join me.

Regardless of what branch of government we serve in, regardless of where in the state we come from, regardless of what party we belong to, we all share the same commitment: to make Georgia better. Right now, Georgia is poised on the threshold of national prominence and leadership. Never before in history has this state been better positioned to lead the nation. If we work together, we can seize this opportunity, we can move Georgia forward to a new level of greatness.

If all of us work together... together in a spirit of open discussion of our sincere differences, but with genuine dedication to serving the best interests of this state, we can meet the challenges before us. We can take advantage of this unprecedented opportunity to catapult Georgia to the forefront of the nation.

For the second year in a row, Georgia is the fastest growing state east of the Rocky Mountains. In the past four years, 362,000 new jobs have been created—only two states have created more over that same time.

A big part of what makes Georgia so attractive to businesses is that we are one of the most financially healthy states in the nation. Don't take my word for it—I'm biased. Listen to a senior executive in New York at the investment firm of Dean Witter:

"The state's credit strength and profile is stronger now than at anytime during this decade. Employment gains exceed the region and the nation. Employment growth is the highest for the nation's 12 largest states... The state's depleted rainy-day fund has been restored... A balanced budget is in place for the 1994-95 fiscal year along with $100 million in personal income tax cuts.

"State debt burdens are low. The state can afford more debt but it chooses not to do so. A little more than half of the state's debt will be retired within 10 years—this is a rapid pace of amortization. In fact, Georgia, as a matter of policy, buys its own debt back in the open market and has done so for the past 10 years. During fiscal year 1994, the state bought back $51 million of bonds at a cost of 82 cents on the dollar.

"The Index of Economic Momentum, published by State Policy Reports, compares the performance of each state to the national average with respect to personal income growth, employment and population. Georgia was ranked fifth, surpassed by only Nevada, Idaho, Utah and New Mexico. These are all small states, with a combined population smaller than the State of Georgia. Therefore, percentage gains are exaggerated by the relatively small base. These states have also benefited from the fallout from California.

"It would not be an exaggeration to say today that Georgia is the leading state in the nation."

As he said, that Revenue Shortfall Reserve, the rainy-day fund that was completely empty four years ago when I took office, is now completely full with $267 million—its highest level in state history. Also full is the Midyear Adjustment Reserve at $89 million. That money will be included in the supplemental budget, earmarked for our schools to address enrollment increases in our fast-growing school systems.

For the current fiscal year, FY95, we need revenue growth of 6.8 percent above last year's actual collections if we are to both meet the budget and maintain the Revenue Shortfall and Midyear Adjustment Reserves at their full legal level. That's 6.8 percent. So far, actual revenue growth has exceeded 8 percent for each of the five months of the fiscal year through November.

Georgia's lottery, which in its first year was the most successful lottery in the history of the United States, continues to out-perform our projections. Last fiscal year—the lottery's first year—it provided $360 million for education. That's $80 million above and beyond what we had projected. For the current fiscal year, we had projected $250 million. The Lottery Corporation is now estimating that it will actually be about $380 million, so we will revisit our lottery expenditures for education in the supplemental budget.

Some of you are aware of the court case involving retired federal and military employees, which goes back into the 1980s and has most recently been before the U.S. Supreme Court. I believe the right thing to do is to refund the money owed these people, so I have been working for many months to negotiate a settlement. We reached an agreement to provide tax refunds to these individuals beginning next October, involving $27 million a year for four years at 7 percent interest.

Just this morning, the U.S. Supreme Court ordered the state to provide "meaningful relief" for these retirees. We are now going to take a second look at the agreement to make sure it meets the requirements of the Court ruling, and I will be asking for your help to pass any necessary legislation.

In addition, the supplemental budget will contain funding to cover the state's obligations relative to several other long-pending lawsuits. Two cases involve school desegregation and busing. The Savannah case will require approximately $9 million in this year's supplemental budget. The DeKalb case is still under appeal. Also negotiations with the U.S. Department of Labor suggest that it will take about $6.5 million in this year's supplemental budget and again in next year's budget to satisfy the requirements of the federal Fair Labor Standards Act.

Back in the cloudy days of the 1991 recession, we had to take some difficult steps to cut state spending immediately in order to balance the budget. One of those steps was to suspend within-grade increases for state employees. We were later taken to court, and the cost to the state of the settlement is estimated to be $13 million.

These are all legal obligations that go back a number of years, and I have been working to get them cleared up and out of the way, so we can move forward.

The other unique item you will find in the supplemental budget is a one-time expenditure of $55 million for infrastructure rebuilding and repair required by the flood of last July.

Last month Georgians voted overwhelmingly to pass constitutional amendment number two, giving this state the toughest law in the nation for certain violent criminals. For the seven most violent crimes, whatever number of years the judge gives is what you will actually serve. No parole. You serve every day the judge gives you, and the judge cannot give you less than ten years. Then, if you are convicted a second time for any of these violent felonies, you'll spend the rest of your life behind bars.

We can do that, because in the past four years, Georgia has opened more prison beds than at any other time in our history—more than 13,500 new beds. It has come at a tremendous cost. But that is what enabled us to end the early release program back in 1992. And that is why the Pardons and Parole Board can now keep Georgia's offenders in prison longer than ever before.

Today the Department of Corrections has an inmate population of nearly 32,500, with another 1,500 beds coming on line later in this fiscal year for a total of 34,000 beds. But we're not stopping there. I will ask you for funds to fast-track the construction of another 1,600 beds at four existing facilities in the supplemental budget. And it will not end there.

We are also moving forward with new initiatives for juvenile offenders. And again, it is going to cost a lot of money... Money, quite frankly, I wish we could be putting into education.

In October we opened a 100-bed youth boot-camp at Davisboro, run by the Department of Corrections, which is helping to relieve some of the overcrowding in the Regional Youth Detention Centers.

We are about to open a new YDC at a privately-funded facility in Irwin County, that was originally built to house federal prisoners. It will accommodate more than 300 youth. We are contracting with Irwin County for the use of the facility, with the Irwin County School System for educational programs and with a private contractor, that's right, a private contractor, for the operation of the facility.

We are also starting a new outdoor therapeutic program for non-violent juvenile offenders, located in Polk County. This alternative program is called "Excel," and again, we are contracting with a private provider. We expect to be serving about 130 youth by about May.

But again, the supplemental budget will contain construction funds for 700 more beds, including 300 at the Eastman facility, which houses young violent offenders. As you can see, we are significantly expanding our bed capacity for juvenile offenders, as well as expanding alternative programs.

I will also be coming to you with a number of bills on crime, because more remains to be done, much more. I want mandatory community service for offenders who are convicted, but not sentenced to prison. If you violate the laws of Georgia, you should give something back to Georgia. I want a Bill of Rights for Georgia's crime victims, to give victims and their families the information they need and the voice they deserve.

Once again, just like each and every year I've been Governor, I'm coming with tougher DUI legislation. I want some mandatory jail time for every drunk driver; I want to get rid of the nolo contendere plea completely; and when a habitual violator is convicted of driving on a suspended license, I want to impound the license plate on their vehicle.

For those criminals who have received the death penalty, I want to limit them to one state court appeal, including any habeas petition, so that cases involving the death penalty cannot drag on and on in state court. I also want to tighten Georgia's bail laws to deny bail for certain repeat violent offenders with considerable evidence of violent behavior.

The next thing I want to emphasize to you is that I meant what I said during the past year about the state flag and about state taxes. That was not mere campaign rhetoric. It was and continues to be a very serious commitment on my part. I will take no part in any attempt to change the state flag, this year, next year or any year.

I also remain opposed to any kind of tax increase—*any kind*! Those who were in the legislature during my first term helped me cut the income tax twice: a $30 million tax cut for low-income families in 1991, and a $100 million tax cut for families and senior citizens last year. I thank you again for your help. I want to cut more, and in the first week of the session, I will introduce legislation removing the sales tax from groceries at the rate of one cent a year. And so there will be no misunderstanding, let me say this: I believe a tax cut should be a tax cut. That means I am not interested at all in adjusting for a tax cut at one place by raising taxes at another place.

I am also going to continue my efforts to reorganize state government to achieve both greater efficiency and better service for Georgia citizens. I believe it's time for major restructuring in our public health services, in the way we do economic development, and in the way we give customer service to those needing vehicle tags and titles. I will have more to say about all three at a later date.

But the emphasis for my legislative agenda will continue to be on education. Since I've been Governor, we have downsized the central office of the Department of Education by about 20 percent. I agree with our new school superintendent that it can be further reduced, and I have told her that I want to work with her to do just that. I also told her that I want to work with her to cut the administrative costs in the local school offices and transfer that same amount of money to the classroom to help reduce pupil-teacher ratios in the very early grades.

I want to expand the voluntary prekindergarten program, which now serves about 20,000 at-risk children and has a program in almost every county, to make it available to every four-year-old whose parents want it.

I want to expand the HOPE Scholarship Program in several ways, one being scholarships for 1,000 Georgia teachers each year to do graduate work in areas where we have teacher shortages.

I want to begin a mentoring program called "One at a Time" to provide adult guidance and role models for our children, with local schools having flexibility to develop programs that suit their own particular needs.

I want to expand the Youth Apprenticeship program that we are now piloting at 24 sites. It puts students into the real workplace for several hours a week to better prepare them for the transition into the workforce.

I want to take another look at charter schools, to see if we can make some adjustments that will encourage schools to participate, such as lengthening the term for the charter to five years, providing planning grants, and lowering the present two-thirds vote to a simple majority.

I want to create a guaranteed high school diploma. If a business hires a new graduate, then finds that the student's skills do not live up to their diploma, the state would provide additional courses, at no cost to the student or the employer, to make that new worker job ready.

There's more, a lot more, but that will have to wait until another day.

I said at the beginning that Georgia was poised on the threshold of national prominence and leadership. Here on this great university campus, I want to say that nowhere are we closer to achieving that goal than with the University System of Georgia. The University of Georgia and Georgia Tech are nationally ranked research universities. Georgia State is growing steadily into one of the nation's great urban universities, and breathing new life into downtown Atlanta in the process. The telemedicine program at the Medical College of Georgia has been called the most sophisticated in the nation by the *New York Times* and was recently featured on "Good Morning America." Georgia Southern and Valdosta State Universities are experiencing record enrollment growth in a part of the state where going on to college had not been a strong tradition.

I believe that our new chancellor, Dr. Steve Portch, is truly the right man at the right place at the right time. He combines innovation and vision with a lot of practical, common sense and energy, and a sense of humor thrown in besides. I am enjoying working with this remarkable leader, and you will, too. And I have high hopes for the University System of Georgia under his leadership.

I am proud of our accomplishments. Our state is in great fiscal shape. Our economy is strong. We have the toughest record on violent crime of any state in the nation. Our innovative education programs are attracting national attention.

But there is much more hard work to be done. Now is the time to build on that record by working together. Now is the time to press forward with more improvements in education and crime. Now is the time to generate results on those bread-and-butter issues that Georgians care most about. Now is the time to make a difference in the life of this state that will strengthen and sustain our momentum and carry us forward toward new heights.

Some of us have just come through some really tough campaigns. No one fights harder in a campaign than I do, but now is the time to come together.

I grew up and started my political career in a county that for more than 130 years has been almost exactly half Democrats and half Republicans. I am a lifelong Democrat, but the families on all four sides of the Miller property were lifelong Republicans. They were the Corns, the Ensleys, the Berrys and the Nichols. On election day, not a one voted for me, and I knew better than to ask them to. But on the other 364 days of the year, they were wonderful neighbors and have remained among my best friends all my life.

We borrowed cups of sugar and flour from each other, and shared meat when someone butchered a hog. If there was a birth or a wedding, or sickness or death in one of our families, we were there for each other. We worked together. We played together. We prayed together. Any one of them would have given us the shirt off their back if we needed it, and we would have done the same for them.

I'm going to be living and working down on that second floor of the Capitol for the next four years, and I want to be your good neighbor. I want to work with you. I want to get to know you and I want you to get to know me. I'm going to reach out to you, and I hope you will reach out. Because it will take all of us working together to generate the results we need for Georgia to lead the nation.

I wish all of you a very happy holiday season, and I look forward to working together with you to seize this once-in-a-lifetime opportunity that is now before us.

# 1995

# Supplemental Budget Address

*January 3, 1995*

I want to welcome all of you back from what I hope was a restful, relaxing holiday season, as we join together once again in this important task that we have before us.

This new year Georgia will become the 10th largest state in the nation. We now have 7.1 million people. We grew by 577,000 in the past four years—for three straight years the fastest growing state east of the Rockies—and we'll grow by another 500,000 in the next four years.

We head toward the millennium as one of the leading states in this nation, and I'm honored to be serving as its Governor. I'm also honored to be working with you on behalf of the citizens of Georgia. This state's destiny is in our hands, and I'm not going to accept anything short of excellence. I know you won't either.

This supplemental budget must from necessity go beyond where I like supplemental budgets to go, and where my prior four supplemental budgets have gone. The document before you increases the Fiscal Year 1995 budget by about $440 million, from $9.8 billion to $10.2 billion.

But fully half of that increase—a total of $225 million—comes from the lottery. Part of it is the additional income beyond our projections from last year. And part of it is an increase in our estimated lottery funds for this year based on revised projections from the Lottery Corporation.

A second source of funds is $89 million from the Midyear Adjustment Reserve, which, as I indicated last month in Athens, is full. For those of you who are new to this process, the Midyear Adjustment Reserve is mandated by law to provide for the state's ongoing obligations in the supplemental budget—primarily funding for enrollment growth at local schools.

Another $30 million is available from surplus and lapsed funds from last year. Then the remaining $96 million is from an increase in the revenue estimate. As I indicated in Athens, our actual revenue growth for the first part of the year is running well ahead of the very conservative projection I made last year when I put this budget together. There is ample room for an increase in the revenue estimate while still retaining a conservative posture.

In addition to these new funds, we also have more than $44 million available from the Department of Medical Assistance and more than $10 million from the Department of Human Resources, as a result of our lower utilization of Medicaid and AFDC.

Over and beyond that, circumstances have given this year's supplemental budget several unusual twists, and I want to begin by pointing them out. First, the worst flood in Georgia history, which affected 55 counties and took 31 lives last July. Then more floods along the coast and in South Georgia in October.

In this budget you will find $59 million in flood-related expenditures, and we certainly expect them to be one-time expenditures—I don't think any of us wants to see another flood like the one we saw last summer. Nearly $45 million of this total is consolidated in the budget for the Office of the Governor, because it is matching money that will leverage federal disaster funds totaling roughly $500 million. The remainder is lodged with the appropriate departments.

In addition, Albany State College sustained terrible destruction, with heavy flood damage totaling nearly $100 million. About half of that will be covered by federal and insurance funds, and we must help with the remainder. The Board of Regents moved swiftly to help clean up the campus and provide temporary buildings, and I'm proud to say that fall quarter began on schedule. That in itself was an amazing accomplishment, and I commend the Board, the Chancellor and Albany State.

We must now move forward with the state's share of the rebuilding funds, beginning in the supplemental budget and continuing in the FY 96 budget, so that the rebuilding can take place as quickly as possible. You will find $13.5 million for Albany State in this budget, and nearly $26 million in the FY 96 budget.

A second unique aspect of this budget is reflected in the bond section, which contains nearly $174 million in bonds, yet only increases the state's authorized debt by $34 million dollars. Let me explain that, because this, too, is an unusual, one-time circumstance.

Some of you may recall that two years ago, we placed $140 million in bonds in the budget for a facility in middle Georgia, which we hoped the U.S. Defense Department would lease for administrative purposes. But, while we got all dressed up to go to the dance, the Defense Department did not. They changed their reorganization plans, and it appears that such a facility will not be needed. So I am recommending that the General Assembly reauthorize this $140 million and move forward with some other badly needed projects that have been on the drawing board. I'll be mentioning many of them as I go along.

Then third, as I explained in Athens, I have been working to settle several legal obligations that go back a number of years. I want to get them cleared up and out of the way, so that we can move forward with a clean slate. Therefore, you will find $20 million in the supplemental budget for the Savannah/Chatham County busing case, for the suspension of the within-grade increases for state employees, and to satisfy the requirements of the federal Fair Labor Standards Act. The settlement for federal and military retirees is not a budget item. It will be handled through income tax refunds and its impact will be to reduce revenue collections.

Now, having explained some of its unique features, I'd like to give you a thumbnail overview of the document before you. This budget focuses largely on the two issues I believe that Georgians care about the most: education and law enforcement.

I told you how fast Georgia is growing. Nowhere is that growth more evident than in the enrollment increases many of our school systems are experiencing. So this budget contains nearly $72 million from the Midyear Adjustment Reserve to provide funds to local school systems to accommodate enrollment growth. Another $2.6 million fulfills the Quality Basic Education requirement to provide middle school incentive funds.

For our most rapidly growing systems whose enrollment growth has outstripped the normal construction formula, I have used $50 million in surplus lottery funds for additional construction, fulfilling the law we passed last year.

This budget also fulfills Senate Bill 417, by providing state funds to cover the fees for advanced placement exams. Another $600,000 will cover tuition for the exceptional high school students who are moving ahead and taking advantage of the postsecondary options program to begin college coursework.

I have also proposed an additional $1 million for summer enrichment programs, with more to come. Last summer, when we provided this program for the first time ever, the response from students was phenomenal. I want to expand these enrichment programs this summer to better meet the demand, and because the summer school schedule bridges the change in fiscal years, we need to begin the funding for an expanded program for next summer in the current fiscal year.

As I mentioned earlier, the lottery continues to outperform all expectations and is injecting an additional $225 million into this budget for education. Like last year, I am again proposing that we use these funds largely for one-time technology and construction expenditures, and defer new expenditures for the expanded prekindergarten and HOPE Scholarship programs until the big budget.

Let me outline the lottery expenditures I am recommending for technology. First, $32 million for another round of classroom computers—$17,500 for each one of our 1,845 public schools. Now, some of you have heard from your local school officials that to make full use of this new technology, they need money for wiring upgrades, retrofitting, and other renovations and equipment. They do, and we should bear that cost. So I am recommending $10,000 per school to do this, for a total of another $18.5 million. Another $2 million will go to new schools that are opening this year, to bring them up to par in classroom technology.

We are also adding $2.2 million for education technology models, bringing the total in the current fiscal year up to $10 million. As you may recall, we asked local educators across the state to develop proposals on how to use education technology well. We received nearly 300 proposals, which have now been rated by outside education agencies and technology experts. This $10 million will fund demonstration models of the best ideas, to explore how well they actually work, adapt them, and develop working models that other schools can learn from.

I've also recommended lottery funds for a Zoo Atlanta educational resource center. Zoo Atlanta is one of the unique resources on our state interactive distance learning network, which includes 100 public schools and is growing. The Zoo Center will provide educational programming that will be available to schools all across the state through distance learning.

We have already opened nine regional Education Technology Centers to train our classroom teachers to incorporate computers and distance learning into their teaching methods.

I am now recommending that we expand that effort with $1.7 million for 14 mobile training units. They would be based at Education Technology Centers and RESAs, and will travel out to schools to train teachers on site. When I discuss the FY 96 budget next week, I'll be talking about technology specialists in every school that I want to fund by shifting money from the central office bureaucracy.

In addition, under the Professional Standards Commission, you will find $1.5 million for equipment and software for our colleges of education to use in training prospective teachers in how to incorporate technology into classroom instruction. This supplemental budget also includes $2.5 million for technology to assist students who have disabilities, and $4.6 million for vocational equipment related to new construction.

We are also adding $4 million for school safety equipment under the initiative we began last year. This equipment is working. Last month a gunman hijacked a school bus in Savannah. The whole incident was recorded by a video camera purchased for the bus with a state safe-school grant, and that videotape enabled the police to identify and arrest the gunman.

We have had requests from systems reflecting additional needs including some special cases at elementary schools—the first round of funds focused on middle and high schools. So I want to provide a second round of $4 million for which schools can again submit proposals.

I am a great believer in and strong advocate of our technical schools. We're in the middle of the largest construction program in their history, and their enrollments are increasingly rapidly because of the HOPE Scholarship Program. Last year we gave each one $500,000 in lottery money for new training equipment. But we're not through with what needs to be done.

So I am recommending for the Department of Technical and Adult Education lottery funds for $7 million in equipment for new facilities that are about to open, another $5 million to replace training equipment that is obsolete, and another $7 million to help with renovations to existing facilities.

The lottery expenditures for the University System include a number of pieces that fit into our broader initiative to make Georgia a world center of excellence in telecommunications. Most obvious is the funding for the Georgia Center for Advanced Telecommunications Technology, or GCATT for short, which is part of the Georgia Research Alliance.

The General Assembly approved this building last year. But we did not appropriate the construction funds, because we wanted to pursue the alternative of a lease arrangement with a private developer building the facility. We went on to find that we can build it cheaper and as quickly by doing it ourselves, and I am proposing that we do this with a combination of state funds and private contributions.

Several other items also fit together with GCATT, like the $4 million for FutureNet at Georgia Tech, which will leverage another $10 million from several other sources. This campus-wide telecommunications system will not only make Georgia Tech a national model, but will also enable us to showcase the most technologically advanced Olympic Village the world has ever seen.

A third telecommunications initiative is $8 million to create a systemwide electronic library for the University System of Georgia, because keeping a college library up-to-date is a very expensive proposition. This plan allows us to do it efficiently and effectively with technology that enables our University System units to share library resources with each other. This is a Chancellor Steve Portch initiative, and I like it. I like it very much.

Just like at our public schools, many of our University System buildings need rewiring and retrofitting to accommodate technology. I have recommended $3 million in lottery funds for labs and distance learning classrooms at our state colleges and universities. And the new facility for the Georgia Public Telecommunications Commission is designed to provide the classroom programming that will enable us to use this technology to make a real difference in the educational process.

I am also recommending that we use some of that freed-up bond money to move forward with the new children's medical center facility at the Medical College of Georgia, which has been under design. The Medical College of Georgia in Augusta has developed into a major medical center for children, not only for Georgia but for the entire Southeast. This building will provide badly needed space for an important program that is growing in size and prominence.

Unlike many states, which are reporting declines in college enrollments, Georgia's college enrollments continue to grow, both at our University System units and at our private colleges.

The increasing number of Georgia students attending Georgia's very fine private colleges requires that we add more than $3 million to fund tuition equalization grants.

Finally, I believe we need to extend the provision of educational technology to students outside our regular schools, and I have recommended just over $1 million for computers at juvenile detention facilities and the Georgia Sheriffs' Youth Homes.

Which brings me to the second area that is featured in this budget—law enforcement. The citizens of Georgia are calling loud and clear for stronger law enforcement and longer sentences, and we are going to heed that call.

At the biennial institute, I outlined some of the initiatives we already have underway for juvenile offenders. In this budget you will find nearly 1,500 new juvenile beds in three categories: First, to immediately ease overcrowding, I am recommending funds to contract for the use of 516 beds. As I mentioned at Athens, 100 of them are at the Davisboro boot camp and 316 are at the prison in Irwin County. The remaining hundred are at local facilities in Chatham, Crisp, and Fulton Counties. These are mostly new jails that have just opened, and arrests have not yet caught up with the surge in new beds. So we are going to take advantage of this temporary excess bed capacity and house juvenile offenders in them while we are bringing more juvenile beds on line.

Second, I propose that we add nearly 700 beds at YDCs and RYDCs, through the renovation and expansion of four existing facilities, the design of three new facilities with 400 beds total, and the construction of a new Fulton County Detention Center, to be managed by the state, which will add 44 beds.

Third, I want to add 300 beds in the form of two new units at the Eastman facility. You helped me pass the new law providing that juveniles, ages 13-17, who commit certain violent crimes, are tried as adults and serve their sentences in a separate facility run by the Department of Corrections. We are doing that, but there are still also a lot of tough kids who make trouble at the YDCs and have proven impossible to control in that setting. They are being sent to the Eastman facility, and adding 300 beds at Eastman will help ease overcrowding at our YDCs by getting the worst trouble-makers out of there.

The budget also includes more than $3 million to expand community programs for juvenile offenders, including 132 slots in the Excel program, the alternative program I mentioned in Athens, and 116 slots for specialized services. That's a lot of money for juvenile justice, an unprecedented amount, but we have an unprecedented problem.

For adult offenders, this budget contains funds for 1,600 new beds by expanding four existing institutions—Autry, Dooly, Macon and Washington—by 400 beds each. I am also recommending an additional $3 million for health care to accommodate our growing inmate population, and an additional $3 million for subsidies to county jails to cover their costs in housing state prisoners from arrest through trial and sentencing.

In the budget for the GBI, you will find $183,000 for an aggressive attack on the problem of Medicaid fraud and abuse. There are some vultures out there, and we're going after them, and we're going to put them in jail.

And $3.4 million in bonds will build a regional forensics lab to serve northwest Georgia. This lab is part of our growing network of regional labs, that help to ease the workload at the State Crime Lab and give law enforcement agencies and the courts around the state ready access to lab specialists.

There are some other areas in addition to education and law enforcement that I want to mention briefly. First, we are facing yet another round of evaluations and potential military base closings. This supplemental budget includes $300,000 in the Department of Community Affairs to assist local communities as they prepare to defend their bases against potential closing—that is $50,000 per base for each of six bases.

You will also find language in this budget that refers to planning money that will appear in the big budget for FY 96 for an educational facility in Houston County. This facility will provide specialized training for employees of companies that are connected with Robins Air Force Base. The availability of specialized workforce training, combined with the strong core of local aerospace industries, will be a unique asset that could very well help to prevent Robins from closing.

Other economic development items include an increase of $800,000 for the Quick Start program, which provides job training at new and expanding businesses. It's one of the best of its kind in the country, and we're going to make it broader and better.

The bond section includes funds to renovate our welcome centers before the Olympics. And there is $420,000 for the Department of Industry, Trade and Tourism to publish multi-lingual brochures for the Olympics. During the course of the Olympics, visitors will invariably have off-days when they have no event tickets, and this brochure series will promote one-day excursions out into the state for them to take those days.

Finally, in the area of human resources, I propose adding $2.5 million in state funds to the DHR budget, which will be matched for a total increase of nearly $6 million. These funds will be used to increase placements for troubled children, and to expand the community-based pilot transportation projects we have begun to serve elderly and disabled Georgians.

Those are the highlights of the supplemental budget for FY 95. It's a pretty big one, with a lot of things in it, and with its emphasis on the critical areas of education and law enforcement, as it will continue to be while I'm Governor. I look forward to working with you. I need your help. Together, we can do some great things.

# Second Inaugural Address

*January 9, 1995*

Lt. Governor Howard, Speaker Murphy, Governors Harris, Busbee, and Maddox, Members of the General Assembly, members of the Judiciary, members of the Consular Corps, my fellow Georgians:

I come before you again as your Governor with a deep sense of humility, gratitude and responsibility. Your repeated confidence in me fuels my determination to work on your behalf to the full extent of my energy, capacity, and passion. For you see, I not only remember from where I have come, but I also see the new heights I want Georgia to reach.

About 40 miles from Young Harris, the three states of North Carolina, Georgia, and Tennessee all come together. On the Georgia side is the town of McCaysville, Fannin County. Right across the state line is Copperhill, Polk County, Tennessee.

As a young man, I played a lot of baseball in that area. Back then it was a place unlike anything you'd ever seen. There were no trees. There was no grass. No foliage of any kind, not even kudzu. There was only a huge, vast, ugly scar covering miles and miles of what had once been lush, green, beautiful mountains.

That shameful wasteland was created by human beings in the early 1900s. They cut the trees and fed the fires under simmering copper ore, whose toxic fumes laid bare whatever other vegetation remained. To the traveler spending the night at the Sahara Motel, or even to a young lad mostly interested in baseball, it was a depressing example of human destruction—of putting short term gains ahead of long term benefits.

Fortunately, that land has been largely reclaimed since those days, although you still can see signs of how it once was.

In Copperhill and all across this nation, Americans, somehow, collectively, almost unanimously, arrived at the conclusion that we cannot afford to waste or destroy our soil or our rivers or our woodlands. Protecting our natural environment has come to be part of a common mindset about the legacy we must leave.

Today we face a similar question that requires a similar response: What about the waste of our children? Or as Carl Sandberg called them, "the human reserves that shape history." What about the thousands of children in the inner-cities and the remote rural areas of Georgia, whose lives are dominated by poverty and whose futures are as barren as Copperhill used to be? What about those young Georgians who are not trained to take part in our rapidly changing economic life and are condemned to live on the outer fringes of Georgia's growing prosperity?

Is this waste not also an ugly scar? Is this waste not also a painful indictment of our neglect? Are not our children even more important to our future than our natural environment? Are not our children the "ultimate" legacy that we leave here on this earth? Can we not somehow arrive at the conclusion that we cannot afford to neglect, to waste or to destroy our children? And then move from that conclusion into bold action, so that together we make that human wasteland green and growing?

I am at heart a teacher. Perhaps it's genetic, for I am the son of teachers. Whatever its source, a commitment to education runs deep in my soul, and I want to leave a long-term legacy that outlasts all the short-term political gains. I want the children of Georgia to have better lives, more productive careers and be finer citizens.

This is why as Governor I have chosen to focus on education. For all our other challenges in this state—be it crime or welfare, economic development or environmental responsibility—have at their root the same solution: children who are loved and educated.

Of course, the starting point must be with parents—mothers and fathers who take responsibility for the young lives they have created. The traditional values, the values that have built this nation and made it better for each successive generation—honesty, integrity, hard work, self reliance, respect for others—are not embedded in DNA and somehow passed biologically from one generation to the next. They must be taught at home by parents who devote love, time, and resources to raising their children.

But government also has a role to play in the future of the next generation, and today there's a lot of conversation about what that role should be. Government has indispensable functions... from public safety and prisons to transportation and public health, from environmental protection and water resources to, most certainly, economic development.

Here in Georgia, we are moving on all those fronts. And we are moving with a sense of urgency and a spirit of innovation.

We are aggressive in attacking crime, and Georgia now has the toughest laws in the nation for violent criminals. We have cut income taxes, and I want to take the sales tax off groceries. Georgia is a national model in fiscal responsibility. Our economy is healthy; we are at the national forefront in many economic indicators. All of these are important.

But I believe that those of us who are entrusted to lead are charged with an even more fundamental mission: ensuring that all our citizens have the opportunity to develop fully the talents they were given by God.

The starting point for government must be education—sound and meaningful education. I believe education is everything. A good education provides each person the capacity to add a gift and make a contribution to their generation, thereby becoming part of the progress of humankind.

It is the educated individual who makes this state stronger. It is the educated individual who adds to its wealth, protects it against enemies and carries forward its ideals and faith. H.G. Wells had it right when he said, "Human history becomes more and more a race between education and catastrophe."

If we are to win that race, we must work together, putting aside party and politics, geography and gender, to form a partnership... each trusting the other, all committed to using education as the instrument for the creative development of our human resources.

And if we all make that commitment, keep that commitment and honor that commitment, Georgia will fulfill the fondest dream any Governor or legislator or citizen can dream. Georgia will give our students opportunities that cannot be found anywhere else. Georgia will lead the nation. Georgia will be the best there is.

We have made some truly significant gains in education in the past few years...

landmark achievements. No other state has anything like the HOPE Scholarship Program. It has been called Georgia's G.I. Bill. It is the most far reaching scholarship program in the United States, and we are about to make it even more far reaching.

Our prekindergarten program for four-year-olds is also unique. No other state has reached out to such a high percentage of its at-risk four-year-olds as Georgia has. And no other state provides voluntary prekindergarten for all four-year-olds, as I am recommending.

It will be many years before we reap all the benefits of investing in young children. I will no longer be in the Governor's Office. I'll probably be back up in Young Harris coaching third base for some Little League team. But I know today what the statisticians will tell us tomorrow. Our investment will have its returns in fewer dropouts and higher college participation rates. It will produce happier, smarter children. It will produce adults with higher earnings, lower criminal arrests and a greater commitment to marriage and parenthood.

It is our responsibility to begin, and we must not shirk that responsibility.

The Latin phrase "alma mater" means "nourishing mother," and that is a pretty good description of what our schools should be for our children. Teaching is much more than pouring a certain volume of factual information into young heads like tea into a cup. Teachers are the architects who guide and shape the building of young lives, with a special emphasis on creating a strong foundation for life-long learning. Teachers are the key ingredient to improving education. Teachers are the ones who call forth the best from our children and inspire them to new heights of achievement.

If we are to build a first-class education system in Georgia, we must have at least a fighting chance to attract and hold good teachers. That's why my goal during this administration is to raise Georgia teacher salaries at least to the national average and to attract the best and brightest to become teachers.

I know money alone is not the answer. It is a matter of quality and value. In the classroom, like everywhere else, you get what you pay for. As we raise teachers' salaries at our schools and yes, at our colleges, we will also raise our expectations of excellence in the classroom. And I am confident that our teachers and professors will rise to that challenge.

As our students are called to new levels of achievement, I want them to know, in the words of that old song, "You'll never walk alone." Because I want to create a mentoring program which pairs adults with students who are at risk. I know from experience this can make a difference. It worked on me when I was a wayward young teenager and Edna Herren, my teacher and mentor, helped put me on the right path.

And I want to give those high school students who are not headed for college some real hands-on experience in the work place. The Youth Apprenticeship program I have started and want to expand will build a partnership between business and education that will make training for a job part of the classroom experience.

I believe it's time our schools gave a warranty on their product: the student. A diploma must be more than just a measure of attendance. That is why I will propose a guaranteed high school diploma, where employers can get additional education at no cost for recent graduates whose skills do not live up to their high school diploma.

I want to give our children and their parents more choices. I want to give our schools more flexibility...with fewer top-down regulations and paperwork. I believe in the philosophy of charter schools—free from all state regulations—and I want to make it a lot easier for local schools to set them up and get them going.

We are putting classroom computers, media center technology, satellite dishes, distance learning networks into all our schools—technology in amounts unheard of before in Georgia, and unheard of still in many other states.

But it is not enough to lead the nation in new technology. We must also lead our children to enduring values. Yes, our children must know about gigabytes and CD-ROM. But it's even more important that they know about the Golden Rule, and right and wrong.

Yes, I believe that schools should join with parents and churches as bearers of society's standards. Students should be taught morality as well as math, ethics as well as English. You see, our children are as strong or as weak, as intelligent or as frivolous, as serious or as silly, as disciplined or as wild, as we have taught them to be. And if our children don't have the values that we or our parents cherished, it is because someone has failed to teach them their meaning—and help make those values a part of their young lives.

Stronger schools will allow our technical institutes and our colleges and universities to concentrate on higher learning. The University System of Georgia right now is poised and ready, and I'm going to be the best partner I can be to Chancellor Portch to propel our University System to national preeminence. I believe we must help older students who want to return to college or to a technical institute. For, you see, I want a more highly educated Georgia. These are the new heights I want Georgia to reach. But, my friends, I know we will not finish the job of improving education in the next four years or even in my or your lifetime.

Someone once said that one of the things education does for you is to open your eyes to the vast wealth of knowledge that still remains for you to learn. It's like that with improving education. The further you get into it, the more your eyes are opened to how much there is yet to do. It will always be an on-going, never-ending process.

In the race that H.G. Wells mentioned between education and catastrophe, Georgia is moving fast. But this race is not a hundred-yard dash. It is more like a series of marathons; each generation carries the torch as far as it can, then passes it on to the next. Our job, as the Apostle Paul put it, is to fix our eyes on the prize and run with patience the race that is set before us.

And if we do our job, if we honor our commitment, then the torch we pass will burn brighter, the course our children run will be smoother, and our ultimate goal of giving the sons and daughters of Georgia the boldest dreams and the broadest opportunities will be closer than ever before. That is the Georgia we seek. We shall not see it tomorrow or the next day or the next. But if our children and their children are ever to see it, we must carry on the work we have begun.

After all, the hope of a better future is why young people dream dreams, and old people plant trees. I'm working to turn my dreams into trees. With your help and God's, the trees we plant will grow strong, nourished by virtue and the values we hold dear, and they will bear fruit for generations to come.

Thank you. God bless you. And God bless Georgia.

# State of the State Address

*January 12, 1995*

Lieutenant Governor Howard, Speaker Murphy, members of the General Assembly, members of the Judiciary, members of the Consular Corps, ladies and gentlemen...

I thank you for this opportunity to come before you once again to report on the state of this great State, and lay before you the budget that will set the course I believe we must travel.

I am proud to report that Georgia is striding toward the new century with a strength and confidence that is turning heads across the nation and around the world.

Pick up the *Los Angeles Times*, and there is Georgia's HOPE Scholarship Program. Pick up the *New York Times* or tune in "Good Morning America," and there is Georgia's telemedicine program. Turn on the network news, and there is Georgia's "two strikes" provision that makes us the toughest state in the nation on violent crime.

Not even counting Olympic-related visitors, international travelers to Georgia increased by 34 percent last year. And international trade by Georgia firms rose 23 percent.

Last year alone, 132 new manufacturing plants were announced in Georgia, and the value of their investments represents an increase of 176 percent over 1993.

1994 was the third year in a row that Georgia was the fastest growing state east of the Rocky Mountains—577,000 new Georgians over the past four years, and that will continue for the next four. We have created more new jobs in the past four years than all but two other states.

Together, we set the stage for that growth with a record of fiscal responsibility. We cut state spending by $700 million. We cut income taxes twice by a total of $130 million. Our rainy day savings account, which was completely empty four years ago, is now full at $267 million. That is its highest level in history. And we continue to maintain our top bond ratings.

Without question, Georgia is clearly a progressive, exciting place where people and businesses want to be.

But there is more to do. For if we slack off, if we slow down, our competitors will overtake us. As someone once said, even when you're on the right track, you'll still get run over if you just sit there.

As you already know from my inaugural address, education is and will continue to be the top priority of this administration, because it addresses so many of the other challenges we face, from crime to economic development. And education, of course, is the focus of the legislative and budget proposals I bring to this session of the General Assembly.

Let me underline this, because there's never been anything like it: 73 percent of the money added to the current fiscal year in the supplemental budget is going for education. And 66 percent of the increased funding in the Fiscal Year 1996 budget is dedicated to education.

But let's also understand this: Much of the new funding and many of the exciting and unique initiatives Georgia is now able to undertake in education are the direct result of the lottery, which is injecting more than $400 million dollars into the budget.

The HOPE Scholarship Program is the most far reaching program in the United States. It is Georgia's G.I. Bill. And I am proposing that we make it even more far reaching by expanding it in several ways: First, give college students who lose their B average *one* second chance to earn their way back by getting their grades back up to a 3.0.

Second, remove the income cap to make all Georgia families eligible. This a scholarship program, not an entitlement. I believe it should reward hard work, regardless of income level. Third, give students who could not go to college right out of high school a chance to earn their way on to HOPE by maintaining a "B" average during their first two years of college.

Fourth, give outstanding students at our public *and* private colleges an incentive to become teachers. If they have a 3.6 grade point average or better, HOPE would provide forgivable loans for up to $3,000 a year during their junior and senior years. They would pay off their loans by teaching in Georgia public schools for four years.

I also want to provide 1,000 scholarships each year of up to $10,000 each for teachers to pursue advanced degrees at public or private colleges in demanding areas where we are experiencing teacher shortages. In return, the recipients would teach in Georgia public schools for four more years.

Finally, I am proposing another $500 increase per student in the tuition equalization grant for our private colleges and universities. This makes a TEG total of $2,500 per student, or three times what it was four years ago. It will make Georgia's TEGs the highest in America.

Our prekindergarten program for four-year-olds is also unique. We are serving about 20,000 four-year-olds with at least one program in nearly every county of the state. These programs are locally designed and locally controlled, and they use both public and private providers.

No other state has reached out to such a high percentage of at-risk four-year-olds. We're reaching about 50 percent of ours. And no other state provides voluntary prekindergarten for all four-year-olds, as I am recommending in the FY 96 budget.

I cannot overstate the importance of this program. Not only will prekindergarten save the state up to seven dollars down the road for every one dollar we spend on it. But prekindergarten is also one of the most effective crime prevention programs we could have.

Yes, Georgia is catapulting ahead of the rest of the nation in these areas, and I'm proud of it. I hope you are, too. But there are other areas where we must improve. Something is wrong in education... something is wrong when, as an educator, the further away from the children you get, the more money you make and the more prestige you receive. I want to change that in Georgia.

That's why I am asking for you to help Superintendent Schrenko and me perform radical surgery on the education bureaucracy of this state. This budget cuts $30 million out of the education bureaucracy and puts it into the classroom. Because I believe the closer we can keep the money to the children, the more good it will do our children.

This budget cuts central office administration, both in our local school systems and across the street at the state level. The money would then be used for technology specialists and elementary school counselors. It would free up a teacher for part of the day at every single school in this state to share technology skills with their colleagues—a teacher who has been trained and is skilled in using classroom technology. And we can complete the process we began last year of providing counselors in the elementary grades, so that for the first time ever we will have state-funded counselors for every grade, K-12.

In moving this money to the classroom, I am proposing a fundamental change in the way the state funds central office personnel for school systems. My plan creates six levels based on the size of the school system, beginning with three central office staff for the smallest systems and then ranging up to 12 positions for the largest systems. From three to 12 administrative staff in the central office, paid for by the state. Shouldn't that be enough?

And I emphasize, these cuts are from the local system's central office, and not a single one is at the school level. Under this plan, there are no cuts anywhere in school level staff, and don't let anyone tell you that there is.

As I said in my inaugural address on Monday, our children need and deserve a high quality education. And if we want to require a higher level of performance from our teachers, then we need to be willing to pay quality salaries. But teachers must understand that in return for higher salaries, the citizens of Georgia will expect higher quality in the classroom and higher levels of student achievement.

When you build a house, you hire a skilled electrician, because you don't want to wake up some night and find your house on fire from faulty wiring. You hire a skilled plumber, because you don't want a ceiling to fall in some day from a leaky pipe.

You have to pay more to get good work, but you do it, because quality is important to your future life in that house. And in exchange for paying more, you expect a standard of work that lives up to the additional cost.

It's the same with education. I want a higher level of excellence for Georgia's children, and I'm willing to pay more to get it. Do a little arithmetic with me. Our annual teacher's salary is about $5,000 below the national average. If you will join with me in committing to a 6 percent increase each and every year for the next four years Georgia will reach the national average by the end of this administration. That is my goal, and if you will help me, we can do it, even taking into consideration that the national average is a moving target, as other states also enact increases.

It is the same with our University System. We are making significant progress and gaining national recognition, but our faculty salaries are far from where they need to be to attract and keep the best teachers. We're sixth in the Southeast. That's completely unacceptable for the Empire State of the South, the capital of the Southeast.

Again, if you will join with me in committing to a 6 percent salary increase each and every year for the next four years we can move Georgia up among the top states in the Southeast, again taking into consideration that we're shooting at a moving target. I understand that to do this will not be easy. But it can be done, and I believe it must be done.

To spur teachers on in this quest for classroom excellence and improved student achievement, I want to expand the pay-for-performance initiative we began last school year. It rewards excellence with real bonuses, similar to those in the private sector. Each school that chooses to participate, sets its own goals for improving student performance, and works together to achieve them.

For example, Tritt Elementary School in Cobb County decided last school year that they wanted at least 90 percent of their third and fifth grade students to meet or exceed state performance standards for math. By the end of the year, 99 percent of the students in both grades had met the state standards!

Successful schools like Tritt who meet their goals earn funds equal to $2,000 per teacher. And the faculty of these schools—the ones who achieved the goals—decide how to spend that money at their school.

This school year the program has just about tripled to include 45 schools. And the money you see in the budget is to reward them next summer if they meet the student achievement goals they set for themselves.

Some of you may have noticed that last week 81 gifted teachers in the United States were awarded national teaching certification—the idea being to raise standards for teachers and elevate their status, treating them more like doctors and other professionals. Two of those 81 teachers are Georgians. I'm proud to say that they are here with us this morning in the gallery, and I'd like to ask them to stand: Karen Doty of Marvin Pittman Elementary School in Bulloch County, and Shari Britner of Snapfinger Elementary in DeKalb County.

To encourage Georgia teachers to improve their skills and raise standards, I will propose that the state pay the participation fee for all teachers seeking national certification if they have taught at least three years. And for those who earn national certification, a one-time 5 percent increase in their salaries over and above the annual increase.

Also present in the gallery are Georgia's Teachers of the Year for the past five years, and I'd like to ask them to stand: Cathy Pittman of Glynn County, Valleye Blanton of Lowndes County, Nancy Royal of Coweta County, Sue Ellen Cain of Carrollton City, and Jeff White of Gwinnett County. I'm proud of each of you, and I'm looking forward to having lunch with you after this long speech.

One of the most important programs I want to begin is called "One At a Time." It will create one-on-one mentoring relationships for students in the middle grades. It will pair adults with students who are at risk, to give them positive role models and a special personal relationship which can help them as they make decisions on their future. The funds in the budget are for local grants to schools and communities to help with the cost of planning and coordinating these volunteer programs.

I want to give those high school students who are not headed for college some real, hands-on experience in the work place. The Youth Apprenticeship program I started is now at 24 sites and working well. I want to expand it, and continue to build a partnership between business and education that will make training for a job part of the classroom experience.

On Monday I said that it's time for our schools to give a warranty on their product in the form of a guaranteed diploma. And Tuesday an administration bill was introduced to do just that.

What I am proposing is that high schools issue to their graduates a two-year warranty on a basic standard of academic skills in reading, writing, and math. If an employer discovers that the graduate's skills do not live up to the warranty, then the employer can request additional education for the graduate at a state technical institute at no cost to the graduate or the employer.

I want to give children and their parents more choices—to allow local schools to be creative and innovative, and concentrate on achieving high student performance rather than on meeting state regulations. We passed Georgia's charter school law in 1993 and have offered information and assistance to schools at two statewide conferences since then. But our schools are still hesitant to take advantage of this opportunity.

So another piece of legislation I will propose will make it easier to start charter schools, by requiring only a majority vote rather than two-thirds, by extending the term of the charter from three years to five, and by giving charter schools preference in grant programs for local school improvement. Then the budget includes $50,000 to provide local schools with planning grants to prepare their charter school applications.

For students who want or need more time in the classroom, I want to expand our summer programs. We have the Governor's Honors Program for gifted students. Last summer, for the very first time, we gave local school systems funding for summer programs to help students in grades 4-8 who were falling behind. It was voluntary, and the systems were given extensive flexibility to be creative in developing their own programs. Demand was greater than anyone ever imagined, and I want to open the doors to more students to be part of these creative summer programs.

The budget also continues and expands the Crossroads alternative school program we began last year. It provides grants to local systems for programs they design to meet their own needs for alternative schools. We now have 81 local programs, and with the expansion I am proposing, we will have a statewide alternative school program.

As the demand for a skilled workforce grows, more and more jobs are requiring additional training beyond high school. At the same time, the HOPE Scholarship Program has made technical training affordable for virtually every Georgia citizen. The combination of these two factors has sent enrollments soaring at our technical institutes. They are serving more than 200,000 students, and many of them have waiting lists. So the focus of our efforts in the Department of Technical and Adult Education has been to build, equip, and staff all the facilities we need to meet the demand and train Georgians for the jobs of the future.

Presently the largest construction program in the history of Georgia technical education is underway, with new or expanded buildings on almost every campus. But we are determined to expand technical education in a cost-effective way that focuses on the students with a minimum amount of additional administrative overhead. That is why, instead of creating a lot of new institutions, we are building satellite campuses from our existing institutions. You are going to find that the budget continues the systematic expansion of several of these facilities, equips the new facilities we have coming on line, and provides the teachers they require.

During the past four years, Shirley has devoted a lot of her time to adult literacy, and Georgia has become one of the leading states in the nation in this critical area. Since 1990 the number of Georgians getting their GED has grown more than twice as fast as the national average. Last year we hit an all-time record high, with 21,200 Georgians receiving GEDs.

Although that's one of the highest rates in the nation, we can do even better. It costs $25 to take the GED, and I want to waive that fee so that nothing stands in the way of adults continuing their education. And, you will remember, along with every GED diploma comes a $500 voucher from the HOPE scholarship program toward cost of attending any college or technical institute in Georgia.

During my first term, we began an effort to put a full-time literacy teacher in every Georgia county, and 83 counties are now covered. This budget includes funds to add another 25 counties and provide some computers for their students.

Nowhere is this state closer to achieving national prominence and leadership than with the University System of Georgia. You don't have to take my word for it. Ask Chancellor Portch. Look it up in *US News & World Report* and other periodicals. Our enrollment growth continues to outstrip most of the nation. More and more of our University System units are appearing in the national rankings.

As I noted last week in my supplemental budget address, we want to undertake several exciting new technology initiatives under Dr. Portch's leadership. And that continues to be the theme for the University System in next year's budget. Not only do we need to continue rewiring and retrofitting our older buildings to accommodate high-tech labs and distance learning classrooms, but we also want to use technology to make new connections.

We want to connect all the libraries in the system, enabling them to use technology to share resources for students and faculty in a cost-effective way. We want to connect University System units with their partners in private industry, strengthening a relationship that fosters economic growth. We want to connect students with student services, to serve them faster and better. And we want to connect technology with teachers, by expanding the academic programs that use distance learning.

I also want to forge a stronger connection between minority institutions of higher education and the minority business community. So I am proposing some expansions to the Economic Development Center at Clark Atlanta University, and a match for federal funds at Savannah State College to promote economic ties between Africa and Georgia. And we are going to keep the Georgia Minority Supplier Directory up to date and broadly distributed.

I am also recommending that we continue a significant level of funding for the Georgia Research Alliance. As most of you know, the Research Alliance is Georgia's answer to North Carolina's Research Triangle—a partnership of Georgia's six research universities, private industry, and state government to generate economic development in advanced technology.

The state's role is to provide "seed" money to build and equip labs, and create endowments for the eminent scholars who drive the whole process. It attracts other investments like a light attracts moths. Let me give you an example. We appropriated $1 million toward an endowment for an eminent scholar in designing new faster, cheaper electronic microchips. It was matched with another $1 million in private funds.

This endowment enabled the Research Alliance to recruit one of the top experts in the world. And the presence of this man here in Georgia enabled us to attract a $40 million national research center. This center has 35 major corporate sponsors nationwide, and over the next decade, its work will help to generate some 2 million new jobs in the U.S. electronics industry and another 5 million jobs in support industries. Georgia will be right in the middle of it all. That's one example of the tremendous potential of the seed money we invest in the Research Alliance.

During the past four years, we have invested $58 million in the Research Alliance, and it has leveraged another $177 million from other sources. I will continue to support this significant program in a significant way each and every year I'm Governor.

I've now been talking with you for about 30 minutes about education. And I could go on talking about education—what we're doing, what we still need to do; where I want to go, where we must go. But some of you might want some lunch eventually, so I'm going to move on to another pressing issue that is a top priority for all of us: law enforcement.

Let me begin with the most pressing and distressing aspect of it—juvenile offenders. They have been increasing rapidly, both in numbers and in the seriousness of the crimes they commit. And we are in the midst of a massive effort to respond in an unprecedented manner in this state.

We are not only increasing the number of beds for juveniles, but we are also expanding the types of correctional programs we provide, so that we can respond appropriately to the needs of all kinds of young offenders. That effort is now in the capable hands of Gene Walker, whose sheer size is enough to impress anyone, but who has a heart of gold, a deep commitment to youth, and a lot of expertise and experience to bring to this job. And I want to give Gene Walker the tools he needs to do the job.

It begins with an increase of $17 million for the Department of Children and Youth Services in the supplemental budget. Then the FY 96 budget continues that new funding and adds to it, bringing the increase up $35 million and the department's budget to nearly $125 million. In addition to that, I am recommending $35 million more in bonds for DCYS construction.

Last year you helped me change the law to require that teenagers who commit certain violent crimes be tried and sentenced as adults. We are doing that, and they are serving their sentences in a separate facility run by the Department of Corrections. But we still have a lot of young toughs who are tried as juveniles and sentenced to Youth Detention Centers, where they are disruptive and impossible to control.

I propose to put those offenders in Eastman, and ease overcrowding at the YDCs as well as remove the worst behavior problems. So we're going to expand the Eastman facility.

We're also expanding our YDCs to provide more beds, improving these facilities and upgrading their staff so that they can do a better job of reclaiming the non-violent offenders. Then for certain other juvenile offenders, we've begun a youth boot camp at Davisboro. To supplement our wilderness programs, we've opened the Excel program, operated by a private firm that specializes in alternatives to incarceration for juveniles. And we are expanding the placement slots for youth who are so seriously disturbed that they can't function in any of these programs.

We are also making tremendous progress with adult offenders. On January 1st our "two strikes" provision went into effect, and Georgia now has the toughest law on violent crime of any state in the nation. We are making it clear that here in Georgia, life is precious, and if you damage or destroy it, the consequences will be heavy.

We are going to have the prison beds ready, so that those who do the crime will also do the time. The supplemental budget includes funds for 1,600 new beds in fast-track expansions to four existing prisons. The FY 96 budget does more of the same. It expands the Washington and Hancock Correctional Institutions for a total of nearly 400 new beds, and includes planning funds for two new prisons of 1,000 beds each. And we must expand our substance abuse programs, because three-fourths of our prison inmates and two-thirds of our probationers have significant substance abuse problems.

But there is much more to law enforcement than prisons. I believe that every offender who is convicted but not sent to prison ought to be required to do some community service and give something back to the community they wronged. I'll be bringing you a bill to require that, and you'll find funds in the budget to begin phasing it in.

Once again, my friends, as I have every one of the past four years, I'm going to be coming with tougher proposals for DUI. I want mandatory jail time, even for first-time offenders. I want to eliminate nolo pleas completely. I want to impound the license plates of those convicted of driving when their license has been suspended for habitual DUI.

And finally, for young drivers, I will send you legislation to reduce the legal tolerance for alcohol in the blood of minors under age 21 to zero. I also want to prohibit young drivers under age 18 from driving between one and six in the morning, with appropriate exceptions such as medical emergencies, traveling to or from jobs, or when a parent is with them. And I will push for legislation to require all passengers to wear seatbelts in vehicles driven by teenagers under 18.

Data from the Insurance Institute for Highway Safety indicates that 16-year-olds are eight times more likely to have a vehicle crash than adult drivers. The cause of those crashes is largely inexperience and errors in judgment. Experts say it takes about two years to learn to drive defensively and become fully aware of how quickly you can lose control. So I believe these limits are appropriate.

My package of crime legislation will also include three bills that address the judicial process. First, I want to set a limit of only one state appeal for criminals who have been sentenced to death. Many death row cases drag on for 10 years or more, with one appeal after another. We cannot do anything about federal court appeals. But by restricting state death penalty appeals, I believe we can reduce by two-thirds the time between the imposition and implementation of the death penalty.

Second, I want to make our bail provisions tougher for those violent criminals who have been arrested and charged with their second strike under the "two strikes" provision.

Third and very important, I am proposing that we add an assistant district attorney for each of our 46 judicial circuits. They will be advocates for victims' rights, and help to speed up prosecutions and deal with the increased number of trials the "two-strikes" legislation is expected to cause.

Let me say just a few words about a most important issue—economic development. Last year we created Georgia's BEST—our Business Expansion Support Team. You remember, this program provides tax incentives both to attract new companies to Georgia and to help existing Georgia businesses expand. It's working; it's working well. The value of investments in new manufacturing facilities went up 176 percent last year; expansions increased by ten percent; and the number of new jobs being created by these investments went up 21 percent.

BEST is an important part of our pro-business climate that promotes this kind of growth. I'm going to ask for your help to fine-tune this program a little based on our practical experience, to make BEST even better.

But the main focus of our efforts for the coming year is on making the most of the economic development opportunities presented by the 1996 Olympics. Make no mistake about it, folks, this is it! By the time this big budget before you now reaches its close, the start of the 1996 Olympic Games will literally be only a few days away. It's now or never.

So I am proposing $10 million—you heard me right—$10 million for a statewide marketing campaign called "Georgia Global Now" to advertise and promote a powerful image of Georgia, its products, its tourist locations, and its pro-business climate. We will target influential travelers, who travel the world for business and pleasure and who make or influence business decisions. Granted, we've never done anything like this before, but then we've never had anything like the Olympics before, either.

As I noted at the beginning, Georgia's international trade rose 23 percent last year. But the Olympics give us a great opportunity to do even better. And I want to give Georgia companies the help they need to use this once-in-a-lifetime opportunity to expand their exports.

That's why I want to create a Georgia Export Assistance Center in conjunction with the new Federal Regional Export Assistance Center. It will have a 1-800 phone line, and use the telecommunications network we built for education to also serve businesses all over the state through video conferences and distance learning.

At the other end of the pipeline, I want to expand our trade representation to new parts of the world. As you probably already know, Georgia has trade representatives in Europe, Japan, Canada, Mexico, and Taiwan. I want to expand into the other emerging world markets. And there's $400,000 in the budget for Georgia trade representatives in China, Southeast Asia, India, and South Africa.

We have made $167 million in improvements to our ports in the past four years, which are being paid for from port income. And the deepening of the Savannah River channel has eliminated shipping delays caused by low tides and opened the ports to 98 percent of the world's shipping fleet.

As a result, our state port facilities are now moving more than 9 million tons of cargo a year. Savannah's container cargo has increased by 25 percent just since 1990, and it is becoming one of the premier container ports in the United States. So, to help handle our increasing volume of trade, I am asking you to fund a new container berth at the Garden City port terminal.

And to continue to improve our ability to move those goods through the state, another $125 million increment for economic development highways.

We are also continuing to improve our state parks. I especially want to mention Lake Richard Russell. South Carolina has already developed its side of this lake into a tourist attraction, and we want to take advantage of that on the Georgia side.

You will also notice in the budget that the additional funds generated from hunting and fishing licenses continue to be devoted in their entirety to developing and upgrading public fishing and wildlife management areas.

I am also proposing $5 million in bonds to begin RiverCare 2000. Modeled on Preservation 2000, this program will use public and private funds to protect natural property along our rivers.

The budget has historic preservation funds as well, including the Heritage 2000 program, which provides grants to local communities to help restore historic buildings. Historic sites not only preserve our heritage, but they are also part of our tourism infrastructure. Our Office of Historic Preservation is doing an outstanding job in operating programs and attracting funds to Georgia, and I have upgraded it to a Division to give this important aspect of our life and heritage the attention it deserves.

Important as all these facilities are however, it is people who are, in the words of Carl Sandberg, the "human reserves that shape history." In the area of human resources, we continue our efforts to expand community-based services for emotionally disturbed children, the elderly, the mentally ill, the mentally retarded, and the homeless.

I am also recommending that we continue to expand the well-received and highly successful Family Connection program, which was started with a private grant from the Whitehead Foundation. This program works at the local level to bring together the agencies that serve at-risk families and coordinate their efforts into a seamless web of support. We now have 55 local programs, and our prekindergarten and alternative school programs are tied into them.

I am recommending that we move forward with implementing The Family Connection in the 25 communities that got planning funds last year, and provide 15 new communities with planning funds.

I also want to mention several new health care initiatives. First, the use of advanced computer and communications technology to solve public health emergencies and strengthen public health programs.

The Robert W. Woodruff Foundation has generously given us a grant of more than $5 million to develop an Information Network for Public Health Officials, and I am recommending the additional $1.5 million it requires. This innovative, collaborative network will connect all 19 public health districts with state health officials, and with resources like the Medical College of Georgia, the Centers for Disease Control and Emory University's School of Medicine. It will continue and strengthen Georgia's national leadership in using telecommunications technology to upgrade medical services.

Second, one of the exciting developments in health care has been the formation of the Georgia Coalition for Health—a group of Georgia business people, health care providers, citizens, and government representatives coming together to work out their differences on this important issue. Because the resolution of the different perspectives they represent is critical to health care reform, I have included funds in the budget for the Health Policy Center at Georgia State University to serve as the vehicle for this Coalition.

They have agreed to take up the recommendations of the Health Care Commission in their discussion of how to resolve their differing positions, and I thank them for that. But in the meantime, I want to move forward with two of the Commission's recommendations.

First, insurance reform legislation to make it easier for Georgia workers and their families to obtain health insurance and maintain it when they change jobs, and second, a Department of Public Health, to single out from the massive Department of Human

Resources those functions that relate to physical health and public health issues. And I am proposing that the board for this new department have a majority of health care professionals on it, and that the commissioner be a medical doctor.

We've got some departments in state government that are trying to do several different things all at the same time, and consequently not doing them as well as they could be done. We need some reorganization to allow our agencies to focus all of their attention on doing a particular function efficiently and well.

Making government serve citizens better is the reason for a Department of Public Health, and it is also the reason I am proposing a new Department of Motor Vehicles for processing vehicle titles and tags. I believe that if we take this important function out of the shadow of the Department of Revenue, whose primary responsibility should be the collection of state taxes, we can provide better, faster service the citizens of this state. And if you also adopt the bill that I will offer to stagger the renewal of tags, we can handle this service quickly and efficiently with a minimum of administrative overhead.

I'm getting close to the end. Just a couple more important matters. One of the most important, a 5 percent pay increase for our dedicated state employees—more than the rate of inflation.

Then I have proposed a resolution calling for a constitutional amendment to be voted on by the people in 1996 that will require a referendum on any and all state tax increases.

And yes, I will ask you to pass my bill to remove the sales tax from groceries. It is the fair and right thing to do. If you will pass this bill, next year at this time, I will present to you a budget with $122 million in reduced spending and revenue growth to implement it. I'll do the same in 1997, with another $125 million, and then again in 1998 with $132 million. And the preliminary budget I prepare in 1999 will include the final $141 million to fully implement it. Then there will be no state tax on groceries in Georgia.

It is not going to be easy. But we can do it, and Georgia will continue to grow and prosper.

These are the highlights—I have left out a lot of the details—the highlights of the legislative package I will send you. It includes other items, like the legislation required to settle the court suit regarding federal and military retirees and a tougher littering law to encourage Georgia to present a clean face for the Olympics.

This old professor has now lectured for about the length of one class period, and I've barely scratched the surface of this budget, which is the tool that will enable us to achieve the results I've been describing.

But the focal point of it all is and will continue to be improving the education we give our children. Again, I remind you that two-thirds of the increased spending in this budget goes to education. It also continues cracking down on crime, especially violent crime, reducing taxes for our working families, and making government work better for the citizens it serves.

I know that you, regardless of political party, share those goals, and I look forward to working with you over the course of the next 36 days to make Georgia stronger and better for the years ahead.

Thank you for your patience in listening. God bless you. And God bless Georgia.

# Case Conference

*San Francisco, December 8, 1995*

In William Faulkner's *Intruder in the Dust*, a young Chick Mattison says, "Yesterday won't be over until tomorrow, and tomorrow began ten thousand years ago." I'm no literary scholar, but I think Faulkner is writing here about the age-old struggle in the South between a distinctive past and an elusive future.

Now, I know many believe that Southerners live in the past. But take it from this old southern historian: The future was an obsession for the South's leaders long before the past was.

The colonial South was portrayed time and time again as a Garden of Eden with unlimited potential. Even as the South lay ravaged from the Civil War, Atlanta newspaper editor Henry Grady optimistically described Sherman's burning of Atlanta as a fortuitous "course direction" to set us on the right track. Grady had a disciple named Edward Mims, who in 1927 on the eve of the depression made a speech on "Looking Good and Getting Better."

Never mind that the South soon thereafter was to be called the "Nation's Number One Economic Problem," and that Franklin Delano Roosevelt would be looking straight at us when he said, "I see one-third of a nation ill-housed, ill-clad and ill-nourished." Or that even as late as 1982, six of the ten poorest states in America were located in the South.

Historically, the South has lagged behind the rest of the nation by numerous measures, one of which has been providing resources and opportunities for public education. I came into office determined to change that in Georgia. It has been my passion—my critics would say my obsession. And I proudly plead guilty.

As Chuck Knapp told you, I am at heart a teacher. I came to politics from the classroom and I will return to the classroom when my time as Georgia's Governor is completed. Perhaps it's genetic, for I am the son of two teachers, and it was teachers who have had the most profound impact on my life.

Whatever its source, a commitment to education runs deep in my soul. Education is my top priority as Governor of Georgia. I believe education is the starting point for government. I believe H. G. Wells was right when he said, "Human history becomes more and more a race between education and catastrophe."

In Georgia, we are now running hard and with great determination to win that race. That tomorrow that is "another day," as Scarlett put it, has arrived. So what I'm doing out here today is bragging on what we've been doing in Georgia, although I will remind you that Dizzy Dean once said, "If you've already done it, it ain't braggin'."

I got into politics with high aspirations for Georgia. When I became Governor, I wanted not only to catch up with the rest of the nation—I wanted to move ahead of the rest of the nation into the 21st century. But I knew that although we needed more resources to do that, we could not get them by increasing taxes. Not in this day and time.

Remember Russell Long's lament when he was chairman of the Senate Finance

Committee: "We can't tax you. We can't tax me. Tax that man behind the tree." For me, "that man behind the tree" was a state lottery. Now, a lottery is nothing new—35 states have them.

What is new, however, is the way Georgia uses its lottery. What sets Georgia's lottery apart from every other state lottery in the United States is that I followed what I believe is the cardinal rule of all public finance these days: You've got to show citizens just exactly what their money does and how it benefits real, live people whom they know personally.

By law, Georgia's lottery proceeds cannot be used to *supplant* any existing education funds. They must *supplement* education funding. From what I'm told, Georgia may be the only state to succeed in doing that. I have been absolutely committed to this principle since I began to design the Georgia lottery five years ago, and any effort to dilute the lottery funds brings out the old Marine sergeant in me.

Our lottery proceeds go directly to three specific education initiatives, above and beyond normal state financing—three purposes that are clear and obvious to all Georgians. First, the lottery supports what the *L.A. Times* has called the nation's most far-reaching scholarship program: HOPE, which stands for Helping Outstanding Pupils Educationally. I dreamed it up and named it, and it is the accomplishment of which I am most proud as Governor. Let me tell you how it works. And I think some of you may find it hard to believe.

Every student from every Georgia high school—public and private—who graduates with a B average, can get free tuition and a book allowance at any Georgia public college for their freshman year. If they keep that B average, those scholarship benefits continue through all four years of college. HOPE also helps the Georgia students at our private colleges with their tuition costs.

We understand that many of the jobs of the future will not require a college degree, but *will* require further training beyond high school. So HOPE gives students who don't have a B average or don't want to go to college, the same deal for a diploma program at a post-secondary technical institute—free tuition and a book allowance.

In its first two years, HOPE assisted more than 105,000 students. This year, 98 percent of the Georgia freshmen at Georgia Tech and 97 percent of the Georgia freshmen at The University of Georgia are HOPE scholars. They are not paying one penny of tuition.

HOPE's most profound effect begins long before those students even brighten the doorway of their first college class. All over Georgia, parents are becoming more involved with their children's education. All over Georgia, you can hear them saying to their children: "Keep up that B average. Otherwise we can't afford to send you to college." It's working well.

The second program supported by lottery proceeds is technology for our colleges, technical institutes, and public schools. First, we made sure every single public school, college, and technical institute in the state had a satellite dish. Then we became the first state to own a transponder on a Telstar satellite. Now we are building a $31 million educational telecommunications center to expand our instructional program production.

In fact, Georgia today leads the nation in many distance learning measures. We rank first in the production of educational programming, first in the number of both students and schools served by satellite-based instruction, and first in the number of young children served by "ready-to-learn" programming.

We also have a statewide, hard-wire, interactive network that connects all of our public colleges and technical institutes, and nearly 200 of our public schools. More than 8,000 courses are offered on this network, which allows up to eight sites to be interactive at the same time.

Georgia's University System has seen a 60 percent enrollment increase in the past 15 years. We now have the fourth largest public system in the nation, with 200,000 students in degree programs, and another 325,000 students taking continuing education courses.

To deal with that rapid growth, we've had the largest building construction program in our history. But our distance learning technology has also helped us manage our space needs by enabling us to take courses to where the students are. You can live out in rural Georgia, for example, and get a master's degree from Georgia Tech entirely by satellite. Professors hold telephone office hours, and hand-outs, tests, and assignments are faxed back and forth.

We have also created a massive $10-million electronic library, based at The University of Georgia and operating off a computer platform at Georgia State University. It serves every one of our University System units with more resources than any of them could afford alone. So that little, rural Waycross College, for example, on the edge of Okefenokee Swamp, can have full access to the library holdings at The University of Georgia hundreds of miles away, without ever leaving campus. It is a two-way street, because some of our smaller institutions have unique specialty collections that cannot be matched at our larger universities. Georgia College in Milledgeville, for example, has the world's largest collection on Georgia author Flannery O'Connor.

But it is not enough to buy the computer hardware and software for our classrooms and labs, the CD-ROM towers for media centers, and the satellite dishes and cable connections for our schools, all of which we've done. Our teachers at all levels must know how to make the best possible use of these educational tools. As Churchill used to say during World War II, you can build an airplane in a few weeks, but it takes longer to train a good pilot. And without the pilot, there's little point to the plane.

So we opened eight technology centers around the state to train teachers in using educational technology. The training is tuition-free, and over half of our teachers have already attended at least one session. Four of these centers are located on college campuses and represent a unique partnership between K-12 public education and our University System.

The third program that our lottery supports is a nine-month prekindergarten program that is being funded right now at the rate of $1 million each school day. It is the most comprehensive program in the nation. It reaches a higher proportion of our four-year-olds—those at risk and those not at risk—than any of the other 49 states. And it not only prepares our youngsters for school, but it also requires parental involvement and coordinates community resources to help strengthen families. Right now, Georgia is the only state in the nation that is committed to making prekindergarten available to every four-year-old whose parents want it.

Now, I know that prekindergarten for four-year-olds may seem far away from most of you. But I am firmly convinced that the interests of higher education must begin in prekindergarten with four-year-olds. In the past—let's face it—most students have been able to muddle their way through most of their educational career without giving much thought to preparing for the academic rigors of college. And you have been left to deal with the resulting remedial work. How much better it would be to begin with our four-year-olds, and educate all of them to meet a high level of academic excellence all the way through school, so that every single one of them graduates from high school academically prepared for college if they choose to go. And if not, they have a stronger skills for the demands of a technical institute or today's workplace.

In Georgia we have created what we call the P-16 Council. The "P" stands for prekindergarten and the "16" for four years of college following high school. It could also be called "P to E"—prekindergarten to employment. It brings together our three public education systems—our University System, pre-K through 12 public schools, and technical and adult education—in a concerted effort to do comprehensive, coordinated education reform and lift everyone up together. And our chancellor and the University System are taking the lead, because they know that their freshmen will only be as good as their cumulative educational experience.

When it comes to improving that educational experience, let me say this: I believe the most fundamental reality of education reform is the simple fact that education takes place in the classroom. No one learns to read or write a literate sentence in a governor's office. No one learns how to multiply or divide numbers in the halls of Congress or the 50 state legislatures.

You can get together at conferences and talk all you want... I can make speeches ad nauseam—which I have, and am... but if we do not change what happens between teachers and students in the classroom, then we have accomplished very little.

So another of my education goals is to attract and hold the best possible teachers and faculty members for our classrooms at all levels. I want to be able to demand excellence from Georgia's teachers. And I know that if we want top quality, we have to be willing to pay for it.

So, in addition to a state lottery dedicated exclusively to the three new initiatives I described, I wanted to find more money for teacher salaries at our colleges, technical institutes, and public schools. Last year, Georgia gave its teachers, including our college faculty, a 5 percent increase, and this year a 6 percent raise. It was very hard to find the funds to do that, but we did it because it was my priority.

I am committed to giving Georgia's teachers and faculty another six percent raise next school year, and then another six percent the year after that. That should make Georgia the top state in the Southeast. These raises are going to be tough to do, because like all states we are anticipating cutbacks from federal funding. We also expect our economy to slow after next summer's Olympics.

So, in the atmosphere of no more taxes—cut taxes—we live in today, the only way to get that kind of money is to squeeze it out of other areas of state government. I am doing that. I'm doing it with what I call "budget redirection." Its purpose is to establish clear priorities, like a salary increase for teachers, and then shift our existing resources toward those priorities.

We are taking a very hard look at every single state agency in Georgia, identifying activities that are not as useful as they once were, or are not producing the results we want, or not central to our mission. I am requiring every one of them to cut at least five percent of its budget through reorganizing, privatizing, and reducing or eliminating those least productive activities. Another five percent must be identified next year, and yet another five percent the year after that.

In the budget I present to the legislature in January, most Georgia state agencies will see a flat budget for next year, many of them will see cuts, as I shift money from all across state government toward education. And I am going to be very emphatic about putting those funds into our classrooms.

In Georgia, we don't consider it enough for our institutions of higher education to give our students a first-class education. We ask them to do double duty. They are partners in economic development as well.

Economic growth was another area in which Georgia has lagged behind in the past, as we relied on cheap labor and abundant natural resources for our growth. Those days are now "Gone With the Wind." Today, Georgia has been the fastest-growing state east of the Rocky Mountains three years in a row. Atlanta leads the nation's cities in creating new jobs. Atlanta is the only city in the world to consistently rank among *Fortune* magazine's top ten cities for doing international business every year for the past decade.

But we can't stand still. We know that if we want to keep our economy strong, if we want to remain competitive, we must continually push toward the cutting edge. Not only has technology grown more complex, but the pace at which it changes has increased dramatically. Today, any business that wants to be competitive must continually adapt new technology into its products and operations. At the same time, it must also be lean on the bottom line. So at the very time when corporate research and development is becoming more essential than ever before, it is harder than ever for private industry to find the resources to do it.

That's why we created what we call the Georgia Research Alliance—our answer to the Research Triangle, Silicon Valley or Highway 128 in Boston. It is a partnership of Georgia's six major research universities—public and private—with private industry and state government. Its goal is to drive our economy forward by coordinating and promoting university research—university research that has practical applications for key Georgia industries. All of its research projects have clear economic development objectives.

All of its projects also involve bona fide collaboration between at least two member universities. The university presidents have told me that much of their most productive research goes on between disciplines and between institutions. So we are taking advantage of that synergy.

The state's role is to provide seed capital that helps build and equip sophisticated university research labs, and helps fund endowments to attract and support eminent research scholars, because we believe that the labs and the researchers are the engine that drives the process of building a high-tech economy. In the past three years, we've invested $81 million in state funds for equipping labs and endowing research chairs. It has attracted more than $200 million from private industry and the federal government. That's not a bad immediate return on our investment.

We are beginning to see the long-term return as well, with new companies spinning off and existing high-tech firms looking to locate in Georgia. For example, stories have been popping up in publications from *Business Week* to *Popular Science* about a slimy grass-like substance with outstanding environmental clean-up powers. It was concocted by scientists at Clark-Atlanta University in a Georgia Research Alliance project. This amazing substance has been trademarked, has a patent pending, and arrangements are being made to house a start-up company in our business incubator at Georgia Tech.

In another Research Alliance project, enzymes were developed at The University of Georgia to replace chlorine in bleaching wood pulp for paper, and remove ink in a new and improved way from recycled paper. A new company was spun off this year to manufacture the enzyme, and trials are underway at several large paper mills.

Last summer Rhone Merieux—the global leader in animal vaccines—announced they would relocate an operation to Georgia, because they wanted this expanded operation to be near The University of Georgia. A high-tech poultry genetics firm called Avian Farms chose Georgia for its new international headquarters, research labs, and production facilities over very competitive sites in three other states. Rayonier, a major international timber and pulp supplier, is moving its research center from Washington State to a new, state-of-the-art facility in Georgia.

When six out of every 10 people in the entire world watch the Olympics next summer, they will see the most sophisticated, high-tech Games ever held. Because we are determined to use the Games as an opportunity to showcase our telecommunications expertise.

The Research Alliance already has two dozen major telecommunications projects underway involving five universities. And the state has provided $24 million of the $40 million total cost for a state-of-the-art telecommunications research center that is going up right now next door to Georgia Tech and Turner Broadcasting.

The Alliance uses a statewide state-of-the art hardwire network for a telemedicine program that the *New York Times* has called the most sophisticated in the nation. Sixty hospitals all across the state are connected to the Medical College of Georgia. And the specialists do more than consult. Georgia is the first state to offer actual, reimbursable medical care by telemedicine. Tiny, high-tech video cameras are connected to all sorts of medical equipment; X-rays are enlarged and enhanced by cameras; and we are developing a tactile glove to provide the sensation of actual touch.

These are examples of the kind of long-term, high-tech economic development the Georgia Research Alliance has begun to generate.

But the bedrock of Georgia's economy is in our traditional industries—textiles, pulp and paper, agriculture and food processing. And we know that we must infuse these industries with technology if they are to survive and thrive in the 21st century. So we have a second research initiative that is more broadly spread among our University System institutions and is designed to serve the needs of our traditional Georgia industries.

I want to emphasize that none of these changes could have occurred if I had not been joined in making them by a group of outstanding University System presidents, who have worked together as never before, and not fought over turf as their predecessors had done. And by a new chancellor, a young and dynamic individual named Stephen Portch, whom we recruited from Wisconsin. You may have seen the recent article in the *Chronicle of Higher Education*, headlined "Georgia's Hard-Charging Chancellor Enjoys a Long Honeymoon."

Hard-charging is what we must be. I realize that as Governor, I have only a few more years before I'm history and back to being a history professor. So let me close by speaking not as a professor—I'll have time for that later on—but as a cold-eyed, practical politician, and share a few thoughts on what I've learned from working on education issues. And perhaps we can continue this during the discussion period.

I've learned that collaboration is essential; that all educators have to be concerned about lifelong education. I challenge you to break through the barriers between levels and types of education.

I've learned that creating a positive public environment for change brings greater results than constant criticism. I challenge you to do your part to create a climate that anticipates positive change.

I've learned that the public expects results and accountability—it's really to the point where they are going to demand it. In Georgia, every unit of the University System held an "accountability day" to show their local legislators how they had spent last year's budget. I challenge you to increase your assessment of student learning and to strengthen sensible accountability.

I've learned that technology can be a great equalizer, but it can also be a great divider. I challenge you to use it as an equalizer.

I've learned that the greatest thing you can do for people is raise their educational aspirations and to link those aspirations to their children. I challenge you to do just that.

I've learned that research and development can play key roles in improving lives, creating jobs, and stimulating economies. I challenge you to tell those stories more vividly to your business community and chambers of commerce.

And I've learned that there are no substitutes for high quality and high expectations. I challenge you never to compromise on those principles. Keep raising that bar.

I began with Faulkner's Chick Mattison. Let me end with him also. He says at one point that the rest of the country seemed like a mass of "faces looking down at him, ready to believe anything if it were bizarre enough and strange enough." And that is how many Southerners have felt throughout history, that our short-comings and personality quirks have been magnified to the rest of the nation. I grew up feeling that way.

But today, on the eve of the millennium, my state of Georgia is poised to take its place as a national leader in economic growth and in excellence in higher education. Whatever I have added in any way to that educational legacy, it is just the rent I am paying for what education and teachers have meant to me. You are the educational landlords. I thank you and applaud your efforts for the people of this nation.

# 1996

# Supplemental Budget Address

*January 2, 1996*

Let me begin by wishing all of you a happy New Year and welcoming you back to what I expect will be an exciting and—I trust—productive legislative session.

My top priority for this session, as it has been in the past, is to continue to improve education for our children in the classrooms of Georgia's schools. And you will see that priority reflected more clearly, I believe, than ever before in the budgets that I will submit to you.

You will see a sharply focused, comprehensive effort, using budget redirection, to make state government leaner and more efficient, enabling us to focus more of our resources on education, which we must never forget is the up-front solution to most all our problems: crime, poverty, welfare, job creation.

And yes, as I put this budget and Fiscal Year 1997 budget together, I have prepared in advance for the biggest tax cut in Georgia history. I am grateful for the consensus, the strong consensus, that has developed on this issue. By the end of next week we should have a law that eliminates the sales tax from groceries. The first two cents will come off in October of 1996, the third cent comes off in October of 1997 and the last cent in October of 1998. This is a $500 million tax cut. We are going to do it by being frugal and careful—some might say downright stingy—with the money entrusted to us by Georgia's taxpayers.

Now, let me tell you about the supplemental budget for Fiscal Year 1996, which is before you. The document shows an increase of $289 million in the current fiscal year. But most of that money does not come from general revenue sources. It comes from several special sources: $81 million is lapsed funds, saved from prudent management, from all across state government—as you know, this is one-time money, and I want to use it to pre-pay some debt service—$63 million comes from a surplus in the lottery; $35 million comes from motor fuel tax collections, which are up, and it is constitutionally dedicated to roads and bridges.

Most of that $289 million increase goes to designated sections of the budget: The Midyear Adjustment Reserve accounts for $96 million, which goes mostly to update school funding as a result of our continuing enrollment increases in this, the fastest growing state east of the Rocky Mountains. The $63 million in lottery revenues goes to expand the HOPE Scholarship Program and the prekindergarten program.

The $35 million in motor fuel tax revenues goes for roads and bridges, including a large sum for the Sidney Lanier Bridge replacement. As many of you know, the Sidney Lanier Bridge is too narrow and too low for today's ships, and the Brunswick harbor channel cannot be deepened without undermining the integrity of the bridge piers. During this administration, we have designed the replacement bridge, completed or contracted the approaches to it, and appropriated the most of the state funds for the main span. I am recommending that $20 million of the motor fuel tax funds in this budget be used to complete the main span. I want us to realize the full potential of this port, and that simply cannot be done without this new bridge. We did it in Savannah and it worked. Now we're going to do it in Brunswick.

Because we are preparing the way for the largest tax cut in Georgia history, I am recommending that we use the $81 million in one-time, lapsed funds to pre-pay debt service, thus reducing state debt rather than spending it and increasing the size of state government. This is the kind of responsible fiscal management that has kept our top bond ratings and made Georgia one of the most fiscally sound states in the nation.

If you add up the four items I just mentioned—the lottery funds, the motor fuel tax funds, the adjustment to the Quality Basic Education funds and the early debt payments—they account for $278 million of the $289 million that is added to this budget, leaving only $11 million for general expenditures.

I also want to point out that many of the items in this budget do not involve new funds, but are the early evidence of the budget redirection effort we have begun throughout state government. Especially in the FY 97 budget and beyond, you are going to see a lot of money being shifted around, as departments cull existing funds from lesser priorities and focus them on higher priorities.

For example, in the budget for the Department of Technical and Adult Education, you will find an increase of $2.5 million for Quick Start, which provides employee training for new and expanding industries, and is one of our great tools in industry recruitment. This is not $2.5 million in new funds; it is $2.5 million in existing funds that has been squeezed from other places in the Technical and Adult Education budget and redirected toward Quick Start, because that is a very high priority item.

This is just one example. You will see a lot more of this kind of redirection in the big budget for next year, a lot more.

In addition, we have also experienced declines both in our welfare rolls and in our Medicaid expenditures, which together freed up about $20 million in existing funds to be used for other purposes. You'll see more redirection in FY 97. WorkFirst and welfare reform are working in Georgia.

As you look through this budget, you will also find that some of the new expenditures that were initially proposed for this year are now reflected as cuts. As we downsize government and pave the way for a historic tax cut, I'm continuing those deferrals that I made last fall, although some may be taken care of through redirection in the big budget.

In this budget there is a one-time expenditure of $9.5 million for Olympic security. We need to go ahead and nail down the contracts for housing and food for our security people in advance, and we must do some specialized training. These funds will enable us to move forward with that part of preparing for the Olympics. And in FY 97, there will be $12.2 million more in security expenditures.

The revenue bump we get in those few months next summer will pay for this security. It will be about a wash. I know you're meeting with G. Hogan tomorrow and he will be giving you a detailed breakdown on all this.

There is also some additional one-time funding for our Georgia Welcome Centers, to allow them to be open for longer hours this summer to better serve the millions of Olympic visitors.

And then there are a few other items of significance that I want to point out to you: We are setting aside $2 million and making available some other disaster reserves to form the state-local match for federal disaster assistance in the wake of Hurricane Opal.

The budget for the Judicial Branch includes $6 million for the new positions created by last year's General Assembly. You will remember we added an assistant district attorney to each circuit to speed up prosecutions and be advocates for victims' rights. You also added ten new judgeships.

We also made the decision sometime back to issue new vehicle license plates in 1997, so this budget contains the third installment to cover the cost of manufacturing the plates.

Finally, let me comment on the $2.5 million appropriation for the World Congress Center Authority. As you may recall, one-quarter of each cent of Atlanta's hotel-motel tax has been dedicated to the Authority and used to pay off debt associated with the Georgia Dome. This fund source generates about $1 million each year.

The Dome has been doing well, very well, and only $2.5 million remains on the debt that was being paid by the hotel-motel tax. So I am recommending that we go ahead and pay it all it off, and rededicate the funds from the quarter-cent of hotel-motel tax to the Centennial Olympic Park. This arrangement would establish an ongoing source of revenue to maintain and operate the park, for which the state is responsible. Its cost would be paid by visitors to Atlanta, and no annual appropriation would be required for the park.

At the start of my remarks, I mentioned that this budget includes $63 million in lottery funds for the HOPE Scholarship and prekindergarten programs. And I want to spend the rest of my time with you discussing these programs—not only what is included in this budget, but also what I am proposing for the future.

First, I want to point out that there was a surplus in lottery funds of $138 million. The $63 million in lottery funding that is being injected into this budget represents a little less than half of the surplus, so let me explain what I've done with the other $75 million.

As you may recall, we have a special reserve for the HOPE Scholarship Program that is to be built up to a full 50 percent of the cost of the program, to ensure that this program is never threatened by a funding shortage. This reserve is in addition to another general lottery reserve, which contains an amount equivalent to 10 percent of the lottery proceeds. I believe it is good business to keep these lottery reserves completely full, just as I have the Revenue Shortfall Reserve Fund. I want to leave all these reserves full for my successor, and I want to ensure that HOPE will always be available to Georgia's students. So I have used the first $75 million of last year's lottery surplus to go ahead and completely fill the HOPE scholarship reserve to 50 percent of the cost of the program now. And then the remaining $63 million in surplus lottery funds is split almost equally between the prekindergarten and the HOPE programs.

When we began the prekindergarten program, we knew how many four-year-olds were out there. But because this program is voluntary, we had no way of knowing how many of their parents would want to send them to prekindergarten. We now know that the answer to that question is a lot. But that's not bad news. That's good news. Very good news. It is exciting to see how enthusiastic and determined parents are about getting their children ready for school and giving them a good foundation for their education.

But it has also been a challenge to get enough local programs up and running quickly enough to address the demand—especially because these programs are voluntary at the local level. That is where they originate, as they should. They rely on community initiative to get started. This year—in one year—we have more than doubled the number of children the program serves, from 20,000 to 48,000. And these funds in the supplemental budget enable us to catch up with that very rapid expansion.

Most of what you've heard or read in the local news about Georgia's prekindergarten program has been about the problems that are inevitable any time you start up a massive program as fast as we did. But if you take a step back and look at our prekindergarten from a national perspective, you'll find that Georgia has the most comprehensive program of any of the 50 states. Georgia reaches a higher proportion of our four-year-olds—those at risk and those not at risk—than any other state. I'm very proud, and I hope you are also, that Georgia is the only state in the nation committed to making prekindergarten available to every four-year-old whose parents want it. Think about it! Georgia is leading the nation in this most important educational initiative for our very young.

I urge you to please don't ever change this program. Don't ever short-change its funding. This program's rewards are not short-term political rewards. Its real rewards will not come this year, nor the next, nor the next. I will be 76 years old, if I'm still living, when these four-year-olds reach their 16th birthday and don't drop out. I'll be even older (or deader) when they graduate from high school and a larger percentage of them go on to college. These are our grandchildren and great-grandchildren. This is one of the most significant things you can do for them. Its long-term implications for this state are monumental.

A few short years ago, thousands of young Georgia high school graduates could not afford to go to college. No more! The funds for HOPE in this budget address the growing number of students who are taking advantage—an advantage many never had before—to further their education. It is convincing proof that Georgia's young people and their parents do understand just how important education is to their future success. Georgia parents have always wanted their children to go to college. They just didn't have the means. And it is a dream come true to see more and more Georgia students taking advantage of the opportunity HOPE provides to enroll at our colleges and technical institutes.

As with prekindergarten, we got the HOPE Scholarship Program up and running in a very short period of time. We are still in the process of evaluating it and adjusting it in response to our initial experience and in response to the concerns we are hearing from around the state. One of the most significant concerns that has been raised is this: Students at public colleges must have a B average in high school to get a HOPE scholarship, and then to continue receiving those HOPE benefits through all four years of college, they must keep up that B average as they go along. But students at Georgia's private colleges get HOPE benefits no matter what their grade point average. This concerns a lot of people, who point to its inequity.

I have always maintained that a primary goal of the HOPE program must be to encourage and reward hard work and academic excellence, and I agree that this ought to be the case at both public and private colleges. So, the FY 97 budget will reflect a significant change in the HOPE Scholarship Program as it relates to private colleges. We will, of course, continue the $1,000 regular tuition equalization grant out of general funds for all Georgia students at our private colleges. This is a money-saver for us. If the students in our private colleges were enrolled in our public colleges, it would cost us many times that amount for each one. So our modest TEG will continue.

However, beginning next fall, in order to get the additional assistance in HOPE funds that comes from the lottery money, students at our private colleges will have to have a B average. So, instead of every student getting $1,500 in HOPE funds as they do now, only the B students will get HOPE funds, as they do in public colleges. And, since HOPE covers costs that range up to $3,000 a year for University System students, I am proposing that we treat private school students the same by offering a HOPE scholarship of $3,000 to those Georgia students at our private colleges who maintain a B average. This change will provide parity between public and private colleges—both in the academic requirements of the HOPE program and in the financial assistance it provides.

The second major change for HOPE comes in response to the experience of our colleges and universities with their first two classes of HOPE scholars. This is what they have discovered: Many of the HOPE scholars who now need remedial work or are having a lot of trouble keeping a B average in college, had gotten their B average in high school by doing well in easy, non-academic courses. That is not fair, and it really short-changes that student in the long run.

So in addition to requiring a B average, we are going to set higher standards. We are going to set academic course requirements that high school students must meet to get a HOPE scholarship. And to give all students a fair chance to build the kind of high school record they will need to become a HOPE scholar, we are going to start those requirements with the high school freshmen of next school year—fall of 1996.

To qualify for a HOPE scholarship, the students who begin their freshmen year of high school next fall will have to maintain a B average in what is called the core curriculum. This includes four years of English, three years of math, three years of science, three years of social studies, and two years of foreign language. In these courses, is where the B average must be maintained, not including electives. This way, you see, we can use the HOPE Scholarship Program as a carrot, as an incentive to encourage high school students to work harder and do well in the more difficult courses. And we're giving ample time for it to happen. No one can say, "You didn't tell me that I had to meet these higher standards in the beginning." Make no mistake about it—this is a very important change. But the HOPE scholarship will mean even more; it will be even more prestigious. In the long run we will have better-prepared students entering college, which will reduce both the need for remedial course work and also the number of students who lose their HOPE scholarship after they enter college.

I believe that this legislative session can be a very real opportunity to respond to the concerns of the citizens of Georgia and to show them that we are making government work for them. We get to come here to this historic old building, we have the titles and the perks and the desks. But we can never forget that this government belongs to the people of Georgia. They are the ones who foot the bill to operate it. As their Governor, I am striving to make it do what they want it to do, and I know you want to also. So let us work together to accomplish that goal.

# State of the State Address

*January 10, 1996*

Lieutenant Governor and Mrs. Howard, Speaker Murphy, members of the General Assembly, members of the Supreme Court, members of the Consular Corps, ladies, and gentlemen.

Once again I stand before you to report on the State of the State of Georgia, home of the world champion Atlanta Braves.

Next summer, hundreds of millions of people—six out of every ten human beings on the planet—will be watching Georgia as the 1996 Olympic Games unfold in the biggest sporting event in world history. And I am proud to report that we have a strong and dynamic profile to showcase; we have a great story to tell about a state that is striding toward the millennium.

You and I live in one of the most vibrant states in the nation. During the 90s Georgia has been the fastest growing state east of the Rocky Mountains. Only one other state has had more people moving in from out-of-state. Some moaning Minnies whine and run our state down, but it is clear that Georgia is a state where people and businesses want to be.

Since January of 1991, Georgia's employment level has increased by a half-million jobs. For the first half of this decade, we ranked third in the nation in job creation, behind only Florida and Texas, both of which, of course, have larger populations than we do.

While the United States may have a trade deficit, Georgia has a trade surplus. In the first half of 1995, the value of our exports was $375 million more than the value of the imports coming into Georgia.

State government in Georgia has also become a national leader during this decade, and our most significant strides have been in education. The Georgia Lottery has been a tremendous success, not only as the best start-up of any state lottery in history, but also as a source of supplemental funds for new education programs.

In less than a week from now, we will hit the $1 billion mark in lottery funds for education, and we have kept our word that it has not supplanted one single cent of existing education funds. In fact, the percentage of our general funds devoted to education, has also been increasing, and it reaches 54 percent of the total budget for FY 97.

The lottery funds the most comprehensive prekindergarten program for four-year-olds of any of the 50 states. Georgia is reaching a higher proportion of our four-year-olds—those at risk and those not at risk—than any other state.

In the big budget for next year, I propose that we continue to expand the prekindergarten program from its present level of 48,000 children up to 60,000 children to ensure enough space for every child whose parents want them to be enrolled.

I am very proud, and I hope you are too, that Georgia is the only state in the nation committed to making prekindergarten available to every four-year-old whose parents want it. Think about it! Georgia is leading the nation in this most important educational initiative to get our young children ready for school.

I am also very proud, as I hope you are, of the HOPE Scholarship Program. The *Los Angeles Times* has called it the most far-reaching state scholarship program in the nation. As you know, under HOPE every Georgia student who graduates from high school—public high school or private high school—with a B average, can get their tuition paid and get a book allowance at a state college or university. If they keep up that B average, their HOPE scholarship benefits continue through all four years of college.

As we have implemented HOPE, we have been listening to the concerns of our constituents and learning from experience. As a result, I have proposed that we raise the standards for HOPE in two different ways:

First, require a B average from HOPE scholars at our private as well as our public colleges. Our regular tuition equalization grant of $1,000 per Georgia student at our private colleges will continue as before. But instead of every student getting another $1,500 in HOPE funds as they do now, only the B students will get HOPE funds, just as they do at our public colleges. Since HOPE covers costs that range up to $3,000 a year for University System students, I am proposing that we treat private students the same by offering a HOPE scholarship of $3,000 to the Georgia students at our private colleges who have a B average. This change will provide parity between public and private colleges—both in the academic requirements of the HOPE program and in the financial assistance it provides.

Second, we have learned from experience that many of the HOPE scholars who now need remedial courses or have trouble keeping a B average in college, had gotten their B average in high school by doing well in easy, non-academic courses. That is not fair, and it really short-changes the student in the long run. So in addition to requiring a B average in high school, we are going to set higher academic standards that high school students must meet to get a HOPE scholarship.

To give everyone a fair chance to build a strong high school record, we will begin these new standards with the students who will be freshmen in high school in the fall of 1996. To qualify for a HOPE scholarship four years down the road in the year 2,000, students will have to have maintained a B average in what is called the core curriculum. This includes four years of English, three years of math, three years of science, and two years of foreign language. In these courses is where the B average must be maintained, not in electives.

This change will use the HOPE Scholarship Program as an incentive to encourage high school students to work harder and do well in the more difficult courses. In the long run, we will send our colleges better-prepared students who will be less likely to lose their HOPE scholarships.

We know that 70 percent of the jobs of the future will not require college degrees, but will require post-secondary training. So, for students who don't have a B average or don't want to go to college, HOPE pays their tuition and provides a book allowance for a diploma program at a post-secondary technical institute.

In its first two years, HOPE has assisted more than 105,000 Georgia students. It is convincing proof that Georgia's young people and their parents do understand just how important education is to their future success.

At all levels of education—K-12, our technical institutes, and our University System—my goal is to concentrate our resources on our classrooms, because that is where learning takes place. No child learns to read in the Governor's office or in the chambers of the General Assembly. No child learns to multiply or divide in the offices of the State Department of Education or their local superintendent. If we want to improve education, we must change what happens in the classrooms of Georgia where our children learn.

That is why I want the best teachers for Georgia's children, and I want to demand excellence in the classroom from those teachers. But I also understand that if you want excellence, you have to be willing to pay for it.

Two years ago, we enacted a five percent teacher salary increase. As a result, Georgia moved up from 33rd to 30th in the state rankings for last school year. Last session we enacted a six percent increase for the current school year.

And we are going to keep making progress. Just like I promised, this budget includes $166 million for another six percent raise for teachers in our public schools next school year. If we do it again for two more years after this, Georgia's teacher salaries will reach the national average, and, even more importantly, Georgia will lead this region.

That is the only way we are ever going to be able to attract and hold the best teachers for our children. That is the only way we will be able to demand excellence and improved student performance in the classroom.

To make it easier for public school systems to give that full six percent raise to teachers, I have recommended an increase of $39 million in maintenance and operations funds for local systems and $39 million to pay for Medicare on teacher salaries.

Georgia state government has excelled in other areas as well. Our top-notch bond ratings are intact, with the bond rating agencies specifically citing the replenishing of our state reserves ahead of schedule, our strong economy, and the responsible way in which we are improving education and expanding the infrastructure we need to sustain future growth.

The Revenue Shortfall Reserve, which was completely empty when I took office, has been refilled to its legal limit of $288 million and is the highest it has ever been in history. Our general lottery reserve of 10 percent of the previous year's lottery collections is also full.

In addition, as you may recall, we have a special reserve for the HOPE Scholarship Program that is to contain a full 50 percent of its cost, to ensure that our HOPE scholars are never threatened by a funding shortage. I used the first $75 million of the lottery surplus from last year to go ahead and completely fill the HOPE Scholarship Reserve to 50 percent of the program's cost. And then the remaining $63 million in surplus is in the supplemental budget.

It is my goal as Governor to leave all of Georgia's reserves full for my successor, and I want to ensure that HOPE will always be available to Georgia's students.

I know it was pointed out yesterday, but it bears repeating. Georgia is a low-tax state.

The amount of tax and fee revenue we collect per capita in Georgia is lower than all but two other states.

What is happening this week will improve on that, and I want to say thanks for your support for the biggest tax cut in Georgia history. Of all the necessities of life, food is the most fundamental. So we are going to remove the state sales tax entirely from groceries, giving a tax break to every Georgia household every time they sit down to dinner. It is a $500 million tax cut.

The first two cents of state sales tax will come off of groceries in October of this year. The third cent will come off in October of 1997, and the fourth cent in October of 1998. We can do it by being frugal and careful—some might say downright stingy—with the money entrusted to us by Georgia taxpayers.

Theodore Roosevelt, one of my all time favorite statesman, once described his square deal and I quote, "Exactly as much a square deal for the rich man as the poor man, but no more." That's the philosophy of this tax cut. Everyone is treated exactly alike, the rich man and the poor man.

And speaking of Theodore Roosevelt, you may remember it was the extremists in his party that caused him to leave the Republican Party and form a new, more moderate party. In fact most of his "Square Deal" legislation, he couldn't even get through an extremely conservative Republican Congress.

But you know, the thing I admired most about him was when he was the minority leader in the House of Representatives in his home state of New York. In 1883 this young Republican assisted the Governor, Grover Cleveland, a Democrat from the opposite party, with the Governor's legislation in the House. Working together! A Republican minority leader helping a Democratic Governor because he knew it was right. We need more of that kind of statesmanship today and I'm glad that we're going back and looking at this remarkable Republican leader who throughout his career always put principle before party.

Over 200 years ago, this nation was founded on a belief in limited government. But over the past several generations, government has been increasingly called upon to intervene in more and more social and economic problems. As a result, the size of government has increased dramatically, with too little thought given to the question of just exactly what role government ought to play, or to the long-term costs and consequences of a government that keeps getting bigger and bigger.

So today, many have come to see government as the problem, and not the solution. They often see waste and inefficiency. They see too many of their hard-earned tax dollars being spent with little results for them.

This government is not yours; it is certainly not mine. It belongs to the people of Georgia, who foot the bill and pay its costs. The only reason, the only reason you and I are here, is to make it do what they want it to do.

That is why I have undertaken major government reform through budget redirection, and through a bipartisan, public-private commission that is taking a hard look at exactly what government should be doing, and what should be left to the private sector.

Let me state three facts, three givens: (1) Our citizens want better service from state government on the issues they care about. (2) They are not willing to pay more to get those services, because (3) they are not convinced that they have been getting value for their tax dollars. Many of them stay up late at night, sitting at the kitchen table with their checkbooks, worrying over how to make ends meet. And they ask themselves a critical question about almost every item in that checkbook: Can we afford it?

Can we afford it? That is the same question we must ask in state government. It is at the heart of budget redirection. We are taking the money we already have and making it do more. Every single state agency and department has worked together with me to cut administrative costs and identify programs that are out-of-date, or not producing results. And I want to commend and thank them for their efforts.

We have culled existing funds away from administrative overhead and from programs that are outdated or not working, and we have put that money into the top-priority programs of our citizens and taxpayers like education. This, my friends, is how we have been able to increase funding for education by over one billion new dollars this legislative session, while at the same time enacting the biggest tax cut in Georgia history.

In addition, this bi-partisan privatization commission is examining every area of state government to identify functions and programs that should be privatized, either because they belong in the private sector, or because out-sourcing is a more efficient use of our resources.

I want to emphasize that the commission is giving careful study to the ramifications, and consulting with the Attorney General to make sure that all private contracts protect the interest of the state and the public.

In this budget, I have passed along several privatization initiatives proposed by the commission, including the War Veterans Nursing Home in Milledgeville. The commission's study found that South Carolina operates a similar facility under private management with 169 fewer employees and at 50 percent of the cost of the Milledgeville facility. Can we afford that kind of extravagance? I think not.

Other projects for privatization are the Evergreen Resort and Conference Facility and the Olympic Tennis Center at Stone Mountain Park; the Lake Lanier Islands Resort and Water Park; the lodges and conference facilities at Unicoi, Amicalola Falls, and Red Top Mountain State Parks; the new 500-bed prisons in Coffee, Wheeler, and Charlton Counties; and the collection of delinquent taxes.

The commission is continuing to examine additional functions, including vehicle tags and titles, revenue collection, building maintenance and security, welcome centers, Medicaid and administrative support functions.

Government cannot do everything; it cannot do all the things we used to think it could. We need to identify clearly the important responsibilities that government should rightfully undertake, and then deliver those vital services effectively and efficiently with a minimum burden on our taxpayers. Privatization offers us the opportunity to do that, and I ask for your bi-partisan support of this important bi-partisan initiative.

I will also bring you legislation to revise the State Merit System, which was established more than 50 years ago to create a professional workforce that was free of political cronyism.

At that time, that was a valid and important goal. But too often in government, we pass laws to fix particular problems of the moment, and then we allow half a century to roll by without ever following up to see what the long-term consequences have been.

Folks, the truth of the matter is that a solution in 1943 is a problem in 1996. The problem is governmental paralysis, because despite its name, our present Merit System is not about merit. It offers no reward to good workers. It only provides cover for bad workers. It can take six to eight weeks to fill a critical position in state government. It takes a year to a year and a-half to fire a bad worker, because of a mountain of endless paperwork, hearings, and appeals. Productivity is the name of the game, and we lose it when positions go unfilled.

We also encourage resentment among the many good state employees when they see a few bad workers kept on and given the same pay raises, because managers are discouraged and intimidated by the endless and complicated process of firing or even disciplining them. And yes, do not overlook this important fact: The present Merit System also makes it difficult in many cases to hire qualified minorities.

I have talked at length with Philip Howard, author of the best-selling book, *The Death of Common Sense*. I had department heads read it, and I commend it to all of you. He's right when he says, "Universal requirements that leave no room for judgment are almost never fair, even when the sole point is to assure fairness."

So I am calling on you to join with me in creating an up-to-date, modern, and responsive state personnel system to better serve the taxpayers of Georgia. They are the ones who are now paying for its waste and inefficiency. Please listen closely and underline this: My plan will have absolutely no effect on the job security of a single present state employee. Not the first one. But beginning on July 1, 1996, I am proposing that all *vacant* state positions become unclassified. This will provide for a gradual and orderly transition from the old, antiquated system to the new, streamlined one.

To ensure that our new state compensation plan is fair—and that is very important to me—we will continue to maintain a system of statewide pay ranges which will apply to both classified and unclassified workers. Also, please understand that qualification standards and training programs will continue just as they are, and as an additional safeguard, regular and comprehensive audits will be conducted to ensure that the new state personnel system is not abused.

If you look back over the course of this administration, you can see that we have been laying the ground work for government reform for some time. Growth in state employees since 1991 has been lower than growth in population, and significantly less than the job growth in the private sector.

The only reason we have had any state employment growth to speak of at all, is because we have opened over 14,000 new prison beds—an increase of over 50 percent— since 1991. Our prisoners are serving longer sentences. We have developed a boot camp system that has become a national model. And our "two strikes and you're out" law is the toughest in the nation for violent crime.

Those efforts are paying off. Georgia is becoming a safer place to live. GBI statistics show that Georgia's violent crime rate has declined by 20 percent during the first half of the 90s.

But more needs to be done. The *Augusta Chronicle* recently cited a national survey which found that as many as half of America's teen pregnancies are the result of males age 20 or older taking advantage of young girls. I want it to be clear that in Georgia these predators who prey on our young girls will be put away for a long time. So I will bring you a change to our statutory rape law to require a mandatory sentence of at least 10 years for any adult who has sexual relations with a child who is less than 14 years old. I also want a minimum sentence in cases where the victim is between 14 and 16, and the predator at least 21 years old.

Another area where the citizens of Georgia want government to work for them is making streets and highways safer. Every day somebody's loved ones are hurt or killed by drunk drivers, and we need to send them a strong message: In Georgia, we will not tolerate drunk or drugged drivers on our roads.

So this year, just as I have every year I have been Governor, I will bring legislation to you to close up loopholes and provide tougher penalties for DUI. I want first-time offenders to spend at least 24 hours in jail, which ought to be a sobering experience. I also want zero tolerance for alcohol in the blood of underage drivers, who are not legally supposed to be drinking at all.

And on this provision, I am now coming with the weight of Georgia's federal highway funding behind me. We risk losing some of it if we don't enact a zero tolerance law for underage drivers.

I am also asking you, once again, to close that huge, gaping loophole provided by the nolo plea, which allows far too many drunk drivers to avoid license suspension. To my knowledge, Georgia is the only state in the nation that allows avoidance of license suspension with a "nolo" plea. And to make our efforts to keep habitual offenders off the highways more effective, I want to impound the license plates from their vehicles.

Now, since there's plenty of time left before lunch, and you are getting two for the price of one today, I'd like to look a little more closely with you at the budget for Fiscal Year 1997 which was put on your desk this morning.

First, you should know that this budget reduces the number of state government jobs by a net—a *net* of 902. I have actually eliminated several hundred more positions, but they are offset by new jobs created by the opening of new prisons and the like.

Next, you should know that this budget redirects more than $627 million in existing funds from lower priorities to higher priorities. About two thirds of that redirection happens within agencies, and the remaining third is redirected across agency lines.

Even after you add in the four percent pay raise that this budget provides for state employees, half of our state agencies will still have less money to spend next year than they had this year.

But that does not mean they will be less effective. The Department of Human Resources, for example, is one of those agencies whose budget for next year is slightly less than this year. But a lot of positive things are happening in the DHR budget. A lot. Nearly $74 million has been culled from places like administration, ineffective programs and the closing of 236 institutional beds.

Much of that money has been redirected to prevention, early childhood intervention, education, and community-based services. More than $4 million of it expands core community-based mental health services to severely emotionally disturbed children, making these basic SED services available statewide for the first time. Before this administration, these services were available in only two counties.

We are also expanding core community-based services for the chronically mentally ill so that no area of the state will be without some level of CMI community service. We are again adding more slots to community programs for the elderly—over 800 slots this time. And we are allocating nearly $2 million to continue to expand community-based day and residential services for the mentally retarded.

The DHR budget also reflects the undeniable success of Georgia's welfare reform and Work First initiatives. We are a national leader in welfare fraud investigation. We are third in the nation in getting AFDC recipients off welfare through child support collections.

Speaking of child support, let me remind you of the bill I proposed and the Senate passed last year to suspend the professional licenses of deadbeat parents. I want to make that bill even stronger this year by adding driver's licenses as well. Other states are using this policy with great results. Texas, for example, collected an additional $5 million in the first three months that their license suspension law was in effect. Please, let's amend and pass this bill in the House and give our child support enforcement staff another very important tool in forcing parents to take responsibility for their own children.

Mike Thurmond is running an agency that is putting people to work rather than on welfare. For years, before Michael came along, the old system of welfare denied them that dream.

Today in Georgia, people may go to their local DFACS office intending to go on welfare. But what they find as soon as they walk in the door is a listing of available jobs, and materials on how to apply, write a resume or get job training.

The Macon DFACS office, for example, has steered more than a third of its new welfare applicants into jobs rather than onto the AFDC rolls. I like what *Macon Telegraph* editorial said about that: "Nothing magical here, more like common sense in action."

As a result, our welfare rolls have begun to decline. More than 6,000 have dropped off the rolls since August of 1994, and because they have, we are able to reduce our AFDC appropriation in both the supplemental and the big budgets, and redirect that money to other uses.

We are still waiting for Washington to make up its mind on welfare, but you can see in this budget that Georgia's emphasis is going to be on work. We are moving 140 staff away from the job of determining eligibility to get onto the welfare rolls, and putting them into the WorkFirst program to get people off of the welfare rolls.

And we doing something else that I think is important. We are putting a higher priority on helping low-income families with day care, so that they can stay off of welfare. This budget helps working parents with the cost of daycare for 7,000 children— 3,800 whose parents are in the WorkFirst program, and 3,200 from working poor families who are at risk of going on welfare.

In the Department of Medical Assistance, we did a serious, detailed study of our provider rates. What we found was an eye opener. In many instances our rates in Georgia were much higher and much more generous than the states around us. We found instances in which our rates resulted in some hospitals being paid more than their actual costs. We found instances in which our rates were much higher than the rates paid in the private sector for the very same services.

So we have adjusted our provider rates to put Georgia in line with the rest of the Southeast and with other states of similar size and demographics across the nation. That produced $85 million in savings. In addition, we expect to save $18 million by expanding our managed care initiatives, and $9 million from our initiative to crack down on Medicaid fraud and abuse.

We have taken $60 million of these savings and used it to provide for modest growth in Medicaid recipients. And $10 million will establish community-based programs as alternatives to institutions.

Medicaid is another issue on which we are waiting for Washington to make up its mind. And the Georgia Coalition on Health—which includes private business, health care providers, citizens and the state—will study the coming federal changes and hold hearings on how the state should respond. The Coalition has also proposed that we create healthplan purchasing cooperatives to help small businesses provide health insurance for their employees. I urge your support for this important measure.

For the Department of Corrections, Wayne Garner, who I think you will agree is off to an impressive start as our new commissioner, gave me a budget that was not just flat, but actually was lower than the present budget.

But in that budget, we are doing some significant things. We are opening another 876 new prison beds and increasing county jail subsidies for housing state inmates from $15 to $20 a day.

Year before last, we worked together to do something that needed to be done for those men and women who risk their lives every day to keep our highways and communities safe. We gave our state troopers and GBI agents a five percent salary increase, you will remember, on top of their regular pay raise. This year I want you to help me do the same for our correctional officers who risk their lives daily dealing with our most dangerous incarcerated criminals—five percent on top of the regular four percent proposed for all state employees, so that correctional officers will get a nine percent salary increase this year.

We can do all three of these things—open new beds, increase the jail subsidy and fund this special salary increase—through redirection. We have reduced administrative overhead and streamlined the non-security functions of the department, freeing up more than $20 million in existing funds.

The story is similar with the GBI—a slight decrease in the bottom line, but you will find numerous instances of redirecting funds to beef up critical functions and speed up services for local law enforcement agencies.

As you may recall, last year we began to add a specialist in domestic violence to the staff of each of our GBI regional offices. These special agents are trained to handle all aspects of spouse, elder, and child abuse, including methods of questioning victims, witnesses, and the accused. This year I want to increase the number of specialists from eight to 15, which virtually provides statewide coverage.

A new forensic lab is being opened to serve Northwest Georgia. And we are adding some staff to the main lab. All these things, keep in mind, are being done with redirected funds.

In the Department of Public Safety, we are redirecting 29 existing troopers out onto our highways, and we are using redirected funds to establish nine travel teams to issue driver's licenses in the 107 counties that have no facilities.

Juvenile crime is the most troublesome area of law enforcement today, and we have almost doubled the budget for this department during my administration. We will have more than doubled it before I'm through. This session, we will add over 1,000 new beds for juvenile offenders across both budgets—a 75 percent increase in our capacity.

But once again, budget redirection is helping us respond efficiently. Gene Walker got in there, like I knew he would, and took a firm hold on one of the most challenging departments in all of state government.

He did some careful evaluation, and one of the things he found was that the Community Treatment Centers were ineffective in reducing juvenile recidivism, so we are redirecting 56 positions into court services, primarily to reduce the caseload of service workers.

Even education, which is the top priority in this budget and the primary recipient of the funding increases, is nevertheless a full participant in budget redirection. Linda Schrenko, our hard-working and forward-thinking superintendent, is leading the way in cutting back administrative overhead with what she's doing in the Department of Education. You will remember the central office was cut last year at her direction, and we're cutting it again this year again at her direction.

Local systems, if they had the will, could do the same. If you take the number of children that are in our public schools and divide it by the number of state-paid educators on the payroll, you come out with a ratio of one educator for every 15 children. Actually, it's a little lower than 15 children. So, we've got a lot—an awful lot—of educators on the payroll.

I am working very closely with Superintendent Schrenko, and I urge you to put aside partisanship and help her reject the status-quo mentality of the educational establishment, which, I regret to say, fights change more than any group I know of.

We are also doing budget redirection within the Quality Basic Education formula itself, shifting funds from lower priority areas to higher priority areas. Of the $78 million in additional funds for maintencane and operation and to pay the Medicare portion of teachers' salaries—$32.6 million of that is new money. The rest comes from redirection within the QBE formula.

The University System is redirecting $45 million of existing funds from lower priorities to higher priorities. All of the general fund improvement items for the Department of Technical and Adult Education use existing funds that have been redirected from within the department.

There are many, many instances of redirection in this budget—over $627 million worth—far too many for me to list. But I hope these examples give you an idea of how we are using budget redirection to make state government more effective and more efficient.

But as Georgia's population and economy continue to grow, we are anticipating some revenue growth for next year, even with the tax cut and the coming economic slowdown that is inevitable. We are projecting 4.9 percent revenue growth in the upcoming year, and the budget does contain some new expenditures, mostly for education.

I have already mentioned the 6 percent salary increase for teachers in our schools, colleges, and technical institutes, and the four percent pay raise for state employees.

As our general population grows in record numbers, so does our school population. So we need to add $131 million to the QBE formula for next year, primarily to address enrollment growth, as well as provide $93 million in bonds for new construction and renovation in 38 school systems.

The department's budget also includes $11 million in bonds for new libraries in eight counties. We're going to build them, but I hope you will look closely at the library funding formula, because I think we need to consider slowing down this spending. We've built 184 libraries in Georgia in the past 10 years. Perhaps we need to pause and take a hard look at just how many more we actually need, and where.

Most of the new funding in the Department of Technical and Adult Education goes to open and staff the new facilities and satellite campuses we have been building in response to record enrollment growth.

We are also adding full-time adult literacy teachers and computers in another 25 counties. My goal, as you may recall, is to have at least one full-time adult literacy teacher in every Georgia county. With this expansion, we will have covered 133 counties, leaving only 26 more to go. And I hope to be back next year with those.

Last year, 21,200 Georgians got their GEDs, one of the highest state totals in the nation. This year our goal is 22,500. I want to thank Jean DeVard Kemp and Shirley Carver Miller and all the others out there who are responsible for these record-breaking numbers.

The lottery provides $49 million to build five satellite centers in Appling, Early, Polk, Union, and Crisp Counties; to renovate institutes in Habersham, Thomas, and Cobb Counties, and to provide computers and training equipment for new facilities. After they open, we will then have 15 satellite facilities, along with our 37 technical institutes—a total of 52 campuses around the state.

Here is another area where I believe we've about reached the saturation point. We now have a facility where you can learn a skill or a trade with a HOPE scholarship—within 30 to 40 minutes driving time of nearly every person in the state. Any more any time soon would be too many. And I do not plan to propose any more satellites during this administration.

I also want to spend $1.4 million to bring our technical institutes on-line with the massive electronic library we have already established for the University System. This state-of-the-art, $10 million electronic library is based at The University of Georgia and operates off of a computer platform at Georgia State University. It allows us to make more efficient use of our library dollars by providing every institution in the University System with more resources than any one of them could afford alone. I want our technical schools to share in it also.

University System enrollments also continue to grow, thanks to the HOPE program, which is making college affordable for more Georgia families. We are the fourth largest public system in the United States, with more than 200,000 students in degree programs. That is absolutely wonderful, but an additional $19 million is needed for the system formula.

And $79 million in bonded construction addresses needed new buildings at Valdosta State, Southern Tech, Savannah State, Dalton College, Floyd College, The University of Georgia, and flood construction at Albany State. These funds will also repair fire damage at UGA's Brooks Hall, renovate a building at Brunswick College, and improve the drainage system at South Georgia College in Douglas.

The Regents budget also includes $23 million for eight special initiatives that build on the solid base we established last year with the funding of student-centered, technology-driven initiatives that benefit all institutions in the system.

We are going to upgrade our teaching faculty at the 30 non-research institutions by providing professional development and creating a master teacher program. And we will use lottery funds for a model classroom for the master teacher program at each one of these 30 institutions. We are also going to expand our distance learning programs, provide for some special renovation and rehabilitation, and expand our traditional industries research initiative.

Included in the lottery funds for the University System is $16.4 million for the Equipment, Technology, and Construction Trust Fund which, as you may recall, is matching money to leverage private contributions for our University System institutions.

Lottery funds will also provide equipment for the Georgia Research Alliance. Our six Research Alliance universities are doing more research than those universities that make up North Carolina's Research Triangle. We are beginning to see the long-term return on our investment. New, start-up companies are beginning to spin off to produce Research Alliance discoveries and inventions, which have been featured in publications from *Business Week* to *Popular Science*.

Major high-tech firms like Avian Farms, Rhone Merieux, and Rayonier are moving to locations all around Georgia to take advantage of our superior research programs.

Other economic development projects in this budget include another $100 million for our economic development highways and funds to complete the construction of Container Berth 7 at the Garden City Ports Terminal in Savannah.

The Port of Brunswick, as you may recall, has been seriously handicapped in its development, because we could not dredge the channel deeper than 30 feet without undermining the piers of the Sidney Lanier Bridge. The $20 million to complete the replacement for the Lanier Bridge is in the supplemental budget. So in the big budget, I want to provide $550,000 to match funds from the federal government and the Georgia Ports Authority for a study on deepening and modifying the Brunswick channel. I want to make Brunswick, Georgia, an attractive, world-famous, first-class port.

Finally, there are some special expenditures in the two budgets of this legislative session that we have never had before, and won't have again for a long time to come. They fulfill the state's security obligations for the 1996 Summer Olympics.

We are participating in a coordinated security effort involving the Atlanta Committee for the Olympic Games and federal, state, county, and city law enforcement agencies. It will involve over 2,600 personnel from state agencies, including nearly 2,400 sworn law enforcement officers.

Two-thirds of the Olympic venues are on state-owned property. And we are responsible to provide security at and around those venues.

This special appropriation begins in the supplemental budget, which contains $9.5 million to contract in advance for housing and food for these security personnel and to do some specialized training. The big budget contains just over $12.2 million for security costs during the Games themselves. We expect that the revenue bump we get during the Games will offset the cost of this security. It will be about a wash.

You will also find some one-time money in this budget to keep our welcome centers open for longer hours during the Olympics and do a special events promotion called "Georgia Tourism on Parade." Barcelona has sustained a 25 percent increase in tourism since they hosted the Olympics four years ago, and we are trying to do the same in Georgia. I have also recommended that we provide the 20 percent state match to draw down federal funds for a new welcome center on I-20 at Augusta, replacing the old center built in 1969.

My over-riding goal as Governor is to make the government of Georgia work for the people of Georgia, and that is what this budget does. It addresses the needs and issues that our citizens care about. It makes government leaner. It makes government more efficient. It enhances education with over one billion new dollars. But at the same time it provides for the biggest tax cut in state history.

Kris Kristofferson, the Rhodes scholar and great country music song writer who went on to become a Hollywood actor, recently released a new album. I buy all of his stuff, because I've always found he has something to say. He's got a song on there—not in the class of his "Help Me Make It Through the Night" or "Me and Bobby McGee"—but its title caught my attention. A song called "Slouching toward the Millennium." And I suppose that describes how some people view our impending encounter with the 21st century.

In Georgia, however, we are not slouching. We are "Striding Toward the Millennium." 1996 is the year of opportunity for this state. It is the year of the Georgia Olympics—the opportunity of a lifetime, of several lifetimes, to showcase Georgia to the world.

When the world spotlight shines on Georgia in a few months, we are going to show them a state that is beautiful and friendly, vibrant and healthy... a state where people and businesses want to be... a state that is not slouching reluctantly toward the millennium, but a state that is striding confidently and boldly to embrace the future.

# Georgia Press Association

*February 1, 1996*

I'd like to begin by giving you a quick run-down of Georgia's scorecard: Jobs are up; welfare rolls are down. Literacy is up; crime is down. Teacher salaries are up; state taxes are down. International trade is up; the number of state employees is down. The reserves are full. Lottery funds for education just passed the one billion dollar mark.

Georgia has been the fastest growing state east of the Rocky Mountains for the past four years in a row, and we just passed North Carolina to become the 10th largest state in the nation. And when the eyes of the world are on us next summer, we are going to put on the best Olympic Games the planet has ever seen.

That, distilled into the 30-second sound bites that rule the world you work in, is what makes Georgia a state where people and businesses want to be.

I'm very pleased to be with you again. I always look forward to it. I'd like to talk to you about something I consider myself an expert on: the news media. You know, you spend 365 days a year telling me how to do my job, so I'm going to spend a few minutes on this one afternoon telling you about yours.

Seriously, you have a tough job. Believe me, I understand that. You must daily confront a variety of complicated issues and deal with them on a tight deadline. The business side of your operation complicates your lives even further. You can talk all you want about the high-minded ideals of the news media as the fourth estate and the critical role that you are intended to play in giving citizens the information they need to participate in a democracy. That is an important role, and you have a right—a duty—to perform it. The news media must play its part in maintaining a free society. But in reality, in this new media age, you and I both know that the news is not driven at all by what people need to know in order to be responsible citizens. It is driven by marketing and market shares, by sensationalism, and by the profit margin on the bottom line.

That's not a knock, that's a reality. Many of you in this room probably don't like it—some of you have told me you don't. But it's one of the realities you face in your business, just like I face them in mine. Like it or not, you are caught up in a media age, where everything has to be distilled into 30-second sound-bites, and where morbid curiosity rather than intellectual substance is what sells advertising. And you just don't or can't spend time or ink on the issues that really matter.

If you find that frustrating, so do I. The state budget is more than 500 pages long, and I worked virtually every day for three months putting it together. It cannot be understood, let alone explained in 30 seconds or a couple of column inches, but it is at the heart of the General Assembly; it is at the heart of state government. It has more influence on what happens in state government than any other bill that could ever be passed, and if you are to do a reasonably responsible job of explaining it to your audience, then you need to invest some time in learning to understand it yourself. So this afternoon, I am going to spend my time with you talking about the budget—not so much its numbers, but what I'm trying to achieve with it.

The news media always tend to fixate on the bottom line—how much is the state budget, and how does that compare to last year? How much is this or that department's budget, and is it increasing or decreasing? Those are the obvious and immediate questions, but I believe it is more important to know what the money is being spent for and why, than it is to toss around a couple of numbers. So I am going to try to break through the 30-second sound-bite barrier—to go behind the numbers and get you to give some thought to the underlying goals that are driving the budget.

If you go to the capitol and look around, you will mostly see people with limited agendas. You will see legislators, who look at everything in terms of how it affects their particular district. You will see lobbyists, who look at everything in terms of how it affects their particular special interest. You will see department heads, who look at everything in terms of how it affects their particular area of state government.

The Governor is unique among the mix of people over there, because it is the Governor who is charged with keeping the interests of the entire state in mind. It is the Governor who ought to be looking broadly across all of the issues and expenditures. It is the Governor who must establish priorities among them. It is the Governor who ought to have the breadth of vision to say, we will best serve the future needs of this state as a whole if we emphasize these particular issues and expenditures, even if it is at the expense of other issues and expenditures.

That is what I am trying to do. I am using the budget as a policy tool to shape and direct state government. And that is why you need to understand more than just a couple of numbers. To inform, you must first be informed yourself.

Over 200 years ago, this nation was founded on a belief in limited government. But over the past several generations, government has been increasingly called upon to intervene in more and more social and economic problems. As a result, government has grown dramatically, with too little thought given to the question of just exactly what role government ought to play, or to the long-term costs and consequences of a government that keeps getting bigger and bigger. Today, many have come to see government as the problem, and not the solution. They often see waste and inefficiency. They see too many of their hard-earned tax dollars being spent with little result for themselves. And yes, despite all the good things I listed at the beginning of my remarks, the media dwells on the negative.

Let me state three facts, three givens: (1) Our citizens want better service from government on the issues they care about. (2) They are not willing to pay more to get that service, because (3) they are not convinced that they have been getting value for their tax dollars. So I am working deliberately to identify the important responsibilities that government should undertake, then deliver those vital services efficiently and effectively with a minimum burden on our taxpayers.

I have four initiatives directed toward reforming state government. First, the reason private business is cost-efficient, is because it has someone looking over its shoulder who has a direct personal financial stake in it. So in state government, I'm trying to cultivate a stronger sense of financial responsibility to the taxpayers. My goal is to collect just enough tax revenue to do our proper job with efficiency, and no more. We have just enacted the third tax cut of my administration in the form of removing the state sales tax from groceries. It is the largest tax cut in state history—$500 million a year by the time all four cents are off.

My second initiative is a major revision of the State Merit System, to make our state workforce more efficient and effective. Despite its name, the Merit System is not about merit. It does not reward good workers; it only provides cover for bad ones.

When it was established over 50 years ago, we were in need of a professional workforce, free from patronage. But today, the Merit System hamstrings state government by slowing the hiring of essential employees and making it nearly impossible to fire bad employees. I want to create a modern system that makes state government more effective by recognizing and rewarding employee productivity.

My third initiative is privatization. I have created a public-private, bi-partisan commission that is looking at every single state agency with two questions in mind: First, where can we make more efficient use of our resources by out-sourcing administrative support functions? This means looking at the privatization of functions like food and janitorial services, building maintenance, the collection of delinquent taxes, and other administrative support services.

The second question is: What functions by right belong in the private sector and ought not to be in state government at all? We are looking at privatizing facilities like the Evergreen Resort and Conference Facility and the Olympic Tennis Center at Stone Mountain Park; the Lake Lanier Islands Resort and Water Park; and the lodges and conference facilities at Unicoi, Amicalola Falls, and Red Top Mountain State Parks.

Privatization also gives us a chance to do some comparing with the private sector and find out how cost-effective we really are. For example, I have proposed privatizing a state veterans home after comparing it to a privately managed facility that has 169 fewer employees and spends 50 percent of our cost. I have also proposed that we privatize three new state prisons, which will give us the opportunity to see how the operating costs of our state-run prisons stack up against the private sector.

Finally, the initiative that is most important of all for you to understand—what I call "budget redirection." What it means is taking the money we already have and redirect it do more. Every single state agency is working with me to cut administrative costs and programs that are out-of-date or not producing results.

But it is not enough simply to make state government trim and lean. More importantly, the money that is freed up is redirected to the top-priority programs of our citizens and taxpayers, like education. The budget I have proposed for next year redirects more than $627 million in existing funds away from lower priorities and puts it into higher priorities. And in the process of streamlining our administrative operations, we are reducing the state payroll by a net of 902 jobs. We are actually eliminating several hundred more positions, but they are offset by the opening of new prisons.

You all know that familiar old proverb: Give a man a fish, and he eats for a day. Teach a man to fish, and he eats for a lifetime. That captures the primary goal of budget redirection. I am shifting money toward the things that will provide for the long-term well-being of Georgia and prevent problems from developing in the first place, rather than simply spending more and more money to paste bandaids over them after they're already here.

My top priority, of course, is education. Georgia is leading the nation with our prekindergarten program for four-year-olds and our HOPE Scholarship Program for students at our colleges and technical institutes. And we must continue to press forward in these areas, as well as improve student achievement in our classrooms at all levels.

Yes, we've got to address the severe shortage in beds for juvenile offenders. But it is more important to put more money into programs like prekindergarten, which will help to prevent juvenile delinquency in the long run. And instead of spending money to make life more comfortable for prison inmates, I'd rather use that money to increase teacher salaries, so that we can hire the best teachers for our children, and give them the education and skills they need to make a successful, legitimate life for themselves.

Yes, the DHR budget is lower for next year than it was this year—less than one-half of a percent lower. (And so is the DOT budget, by the way—its general funds were cut by 14 percent.) But what you need to understand, is that 75 percent of the DHR reduction is simply adjusting for actual caseloads and is not a cut in services. For example, the biggest single reduction in DHR is the result of more than 6,000 families coming off of the welfare rolls since August of 1994.

Our welfare reform initiatives and our WorkFirst program are proving successful. And we are going to continue to emphasize work. We are redirecting 140 staff away from determining eligibility to get onto the welfare rolls, and putting them into the Work First program to get people off the welfare rolls. And we will help with daycare for 7,000 children. The DHR budget also reflects a shift away from institutional beds, which are more expensive, toward community-based services, and, even more importantly, toward education and prevention.

Even education, which gets the lion's share of funding increases, is not immune from budget redirection. We are redirecting funds within the Quality Basic Education formula away from low priority areas and into high priority areas that directly affect the classrooms of Georgia.

Government cannot do everything; it cannot do all the things we used to think it could. Virtually all of the lobbyists and citizen groups in the halls across the street are there on behalf of valid causes. But the reality is that even if we doubled state taxes, we still would not have enough money to do all the things they want us to do. We simply have to establish some over-riding priorities and live by them in the budget. My priority is to teach fishing rather than to hand out fish.

# Democratic Party Training Academy

*February 25, 1996*

I am absolutely delighted that the Democratic National Party is sponsoring these Campaign Training Academies, because I believe that 1996 can be a year of real opportunity for Democrats.

Today, as we watch Newt Gingrich's negative ratings soar to new heights, as we watch the Republican presidential campaign grow increasingly negative and vicious, it is kind of hard to believe that just over a year ago, political columnists were writing the obituary of the Democratic Party—crushed, they claimed, by an invincible Republican juggernaut, that was unstoppable in its bid to take over the country. Who would have thought, even six months ago, that today we Democrats would be the ones with ring-side seats, watching the Republicans fight bitterly among themselves, calling each other extremists, socialists and—losers, as we Democrats have done so often in the past—to our detriment.

But before we get to gloating, before we get too sure of ourselves, let me emphasize to you that there is a very critical lesson to be learned here. And it behooves us as Democrats to pay attention and learn it well.

Listen to these words from Republican Senator John McCain of Arizona: "The Republican presidential campaign has departed from our basic themes. It has hurt us some and confused the voters."

Too many times, too many Democrats have done just that. We departed from our basic themes. We forgot the clear middle-class tradition that our party was built on, and we went off, sometimes on futile tangents, taking roads some loud, vocal interest group wanted taken, and it ran us in the ditch and got us sidetracked from our real purpose as a party.

You know, when was I growing up in the mountains of North Georgia, there was nothing more treasured than a good hunting dog. A first-class coon dog or fox hound was the envy of the town. The family might not have a car. Mama might have had but one good Sunday dress. There might not be any ham meat in the smokehouse. but if a man had a good dog, he was in pretty good shape. You know what makes a good huntin' dog? One that will stay on the trail; one that stays focused on what it's really after, and does not go off chasing every rabbit that comes along.

My friends, I'm going to tell it to you like it is: Our party has chased too many rabbits in recent years, just like the Republican Party is in danger of doing now. Too many times, we have been the proof, just like the Republican Party is in danger of proving now, that, to paraphrase Pogo, the real enemy often turns out to be ourselves. As my Mama used to say, long before it became a line in a country song, "If you don't stand for something, you'll fall for anything."

This year we Democrats have a clear opportunity to earn the trust and respect of the voters again, but we must stand up and fight for the things that are important to them.

Ever since the days of Jefferson and Jackson, Democrats have stood for the family farmer who plants his own crops and bales his own hay; the small businesswoman who stays open late and calls her customers by their first names; the young family starting out, scrimping and saving to buy a home; the older couple, holding hands as they rock on the front porch, drawing strength from each other.

These are our people, and we are their party. When they sit up late around the kitchen table, it is not because they are worried about school prayer. They are up late trying to balance the checkbook. Scrimping and saving in an effort to pay for daycare and at the same time put a little back for college. Scrimping and saving in an effort to make ends meet on a fixed retirement income.

Today, too many of our people have gone too many years without anything much to show for it. They're working harder and making less. They're pretty darn angry about it, and I don't blame them. The Republicans tell these folks that the reason they are stuck on an economic treadmill is because of "them." "Them" the immigrants. "Them" the women. "Them" the blacks. "Them" the liberals. "Them" the government. Them, them, them. Whatever happened to "We the People"?

The real story of what happened to "We the People" is that the Republicans sold us out, with a generation of trickle-down economics that blew the deficit sky-high, drove poverty through the roof, and squeezed the middle class like a lemon at a county fair. They gave themselves the goldmine, and they gave the rest of us the shaft.

The Democratic Party grew up around the economic issues that concern working Americans most deeply. That is the common bond that unites us, and we are the losers when we allow ourselves to be distracted by "rabbit" issues that divide us.

So my message to you today is to stay focused on the issues that shape the daily lives of American families. If you feel a need to reduce that message to three words, like the Republicans did with their Contract with America, try these three words: "On Your Side."

Putting government back on the side of hard-working middle-class families is not a new idea. But it is a good one. It's a proven and powerful one. And it is true to the traditions of the Democratic Party.

When I was growing up in the shadow of the Blue Ridge Mountains, my mother used to point to the one and only paved road through our valley—a narrow little strip that disappeared winding its way through a distant gap. She'd say, "You know what's so great about this place? You can get anywhere in the world from here!"

That is true of our Democratic Party. For millions of Americans, we have been the only road out of poverty, the only road that connects the country that we are to the country we can be.

But we must continue to blaze that trail, pave that road, and not veer off into the ditch or onto a rabbit trail.

If we are true to that vision, then history will look back to 1996 as the year when Democrats came together and worked together to make a way when many thought there was no way—to build a road of opportunity for every American, a road built by a government that has gotten off your back and gotten on your side.

# Supreme Court 150th Anniversary

*April 9, 1996*

Justices, judges, members of the legal profession, ladies, and gentlemen. I am honored to address this highest court of the State of Georgia on the occasion of your 150th anniversary.

I am not an attorney. But rather, I am a student and teacher of history, and that is the perspective I bring to this special celebration.

When this court was formed 150 years ago, the foremost voice in American letters was Ralph Waldo Emerson. In the course of a lecture at Harvard, he noted that the eyes of human beings have been placed in their foreheads and not in what he called their "hind-heads."

It is human nature to be continually looking forward to tomorrow with hope and anticipation. Looking back to yesterday requires a deliberate effort to turn one's head. But it is worth the effort, because a knowledge of history makes an indispensible contribution to wisdom. Or as Churchill once put it, the futher back you look, the further ahead you can see.

You who today sit on the bench of the Supreme Court of Georgia comprise without doubt the most youthful court in a 150-year-old tradition. You are a young old court. And so it is worth your while to stop on this occasion and deliberately turn your head to look backward over the history of this institution.

You are also without doubt the most diverse court to occupy this bench in 150 years of history. In fact, this is one of the most diverse State Supreme Courts in United States history. I, for one, believe that diversity adds to the richness, the strength and the energy of this court, and in the end will bring it closer to wisdom and truth.

Someone once said that if two people always agree, then one of them is useless. If two people always disagree, then both of them are useless. But if diverse perspectives can sit down together and reason together with intelligence and integrity, then there is an opportunity for progress to be achieved.

More than any other nation on earth, ours was created out of respect for the law. We had the first written Constitution—it is the oldest document of its kind in the world. And in it, we proclaimed that this would be a nation ruled by laws, and not by human whims. Our Constitution made the citizens of this nation the masters of the state, and not the other way around, and I do not believe that any of us would willingly change that for any other judicial system in the world. We created a written code of laws, and we put our faith in the interpretation of those laws by the judicial system to resolve our most basic disputes.

The Constitution of Georgia designates this Supreme Court as the court of exclusive appellate jurisdiction in a number of areas, ranging from the interpretation of the State

Constitution to habeas corpus cases to contested wills and divorces. And it directs all other state courts to consider your decisions binding as precedents. That in itself is a weighty obligation.

But I believe that for you who occupy its bench today, the heaviest burden the Georgia Constitution places on the shoulders of this court is the responsibility of regulating the entire practice of law in this state. And I believe that one of your most important tasks today is to restore public confidence in our system of justice.

We live in a time when courtroom proceedings have come to compete with soap operas and talk shows as TV entertainment. We also live in a time of over-reliance on litigation—a time when people seem to respond to hardship and even just inconvenience by looking around for someone else to hold responsible for it, preferably someone with deep pockets.

Here in the United States, we have the heaviest concentration of lawyers on earth—many times more lawyers proportionately for our population than nations like England or Germany or Japan. We have a lot more lawyers and a lot more litigation, but I am not sure that we have any more justice. By resorting to litigation at the drop of the hat, we have made justice more cumbersome, more expensive, less equal than it ought to be. Like the proverbial mills of the gods, our courts grind extremely slowly. But unlike the mills of the gods, their grinding is not always perceived to be sure.

Right now I believe you would be hard-pressed to find a majority of citizens who feel that the judicial system and legal profession consistently hold the law to the highest standards of impartiality, honesty, and equality. There is a very real sense among our citizens that to be deserving of the name, justice must become faster, fairer, more sensible, and more certain.

In this nation, we have placed an enormous power in the law. It is critical that judges and lawyers and the collective judicial system they serve, be engaged in a genuine search for truth and justice, and not in a quest, either perceived or real, to twist the power of the law to serve their own ends. The biggest challenge facing this court as it regulates the practice of law in Georgia is to ensure that our legal system lives up to its noblest tradition of honesty and impartiality, not only in public perception but also in reality. So that all people stand equal before the bar of justice.

I know you understand the responsibility of the Supreme Court of Georgia to serve justice. In agreeing to serve on it, you have dedicated your lives to this cause. Your responsibility to justice is older than the 150 years of this court. It is older than the Constitution or the Bill of Rights. It is older even than the tradition of common law. It goes back to the roots of our Western heritage, to the words of the prophet Amos: "Let justice roll down like waters, and righteousness like an ever-flowing stream."

True justice has its roots in a higher law than is found in the Official Code of Georgia. Even more fundamental than cultivating a respect for the law, is cultivating a respect for what is right. I happen to believe that justice and righteousness go hand in hand, and that it is not possible to have one without the other. Judges and lawyers, just like politicians and legislators, whose service is based purely on intellect without recognizing that higher moral law, are as likely to end up serving evil unintentionally as they are good.

I began by quoting Ralph Waldo Emerson, and I am going to close with him. After the death of his young son, he penned a difficult essay called "Experience," in which he was looking hard for reality amid the web of illusion. And he wrote, "Without any shadow of doubt, amidst this vertigo of shows and politics, I settle myself ever firmer on the creed that we should not postpone and refer and wish, but do broad justice where we are."

That is the abiding task of this court, throughout 150 years of history and for the future—to do broad justice where you are.

# Coca-Cola Scholars

*April 25, 1996*

I'm delighted to be here with you and share this special evening as we honor the 150 outstanding Coca-Cola Scholars of 1996. Carl Sandberg was referring to students just like you, when he wrote of "the human reserves that shape history."

I also want to congratulate the Coca-Cola Scholars Foundation on the 10th anniversary of this unique scholarship program. Ten years ago, the Coca-Cola Bottlers commemorated Coca-Cola's 100th anniversary by joining with the Company to create the nation's premier corporate-sponsored scholarship program. The Bottlers have a long tradition of leadership and service in their communities, and this program carries that tradition forward, not only by helping young people and their families with the cost of college, but by instilling that same tradition in them as well.

And tonight I join with all of you in saluting Crawford T. Johnson III, for his inspiration for the Scholars Program and for his leadership as chairman of its Foundation. This program truly demonstrates the power of an idea.

We live in a world where the sound of progress is no longer the ring of pounded steel, but the silent flow of digital data, as information, news, and even money shoot around the globe at the speed of light. We live in a world where computers leverage the human mind like industrial machinery leveraged human muscles just a generation ago—a world in which brains have replaced brawn as the first requisite for a good job.

But we also live in a world where poverty, crime, and dysfunctional families are becoming more worrisome, and growing numbers of people are in danger of being left behind as the level of literacy needed to function fully in society continues to rise.

As a nation, we are beginning to feel a little like Tantalus of Greek mythology. If you remember his story, he was condemned to stand in clear cool water that receded whenever he stooped to drink. Just above his head were branches full of luscious fruit that receded whenever he reached up to pluck it. Technology seems to hold out the promise of improving our quality of life so tantilizingly close. Yet we often seem unsure of our ability to reach out and fully grasp it.

Education is the solution to that dilemma. Education is the key to reducing crime and welfare, the key to promoting understanding and tolerance, the key to generating economic development and creating jobs. Yet at the same time that education has become essential to our economic health and our quality of life, the cost of college is rising out of reach for more and more families. That's why I created in Georgia a HOPE Scholarship Program that opens the doors of our public colleges and universities, tuition-free, to all Georgia students who graduate from high school with at least a B average in their academic subjects.

But government cannot do it all. It will take all of us working together to ensure that educational access and opportunity is available to all who have earned it. And tonight I especially want to commend the Coca-Cola Bottlers and Company for taking the initiative to be a partner in this great endeavor.

Coca-Cola is a home-grown Georgia company that started right here in an Atlanta drugstore. Over the course of a remarkable history, it has become one of the most widely recognized trademarks in the world, as well as one of Georgia's and America's most respected corporate citizens. What has made Coca-Cola so valuable as a corporate citizen is its ability to look beyond its own bottom line, to the understanding that the quality of its own corporate life depends upon the quality of life in the United States, and then to invest wisely in the resources on which our future quality of life depends—the young people who will be the leaders of tomorrow.

The Coca-Cola Scholars Program is such an investment. The benefits of this program will accrue not so much to The Coca-Cola Company itself, but will be found in the leadership and service that Coca-Cola Scholars increasingly bring to educational institutions, communities, and businesses all around the nation. When you read through "The Leader" and see all the things that Coca-Cola Scholars are doing as they move through college and on into their professional careers, you can see the beginnings of a powerful return on this investment.

I congratulate each one of you students who have been chosen as 1996 Coca-Cola Scholars. It was stiff competition. There are usually more than 10 applicants for each one of these 150 scholarships. So you are clearly the cream of the crop, and you deserve to be recognized for your hard work and to be given credit for your achievements.

You were chosen not only because you are smart in the academic sense. You were also chosen because you possess character, leadership gifts and the potential to make a difference through service to others. You have been chosen not only for a high honor, but also for a high calling. This scholarship will do more for you than hold down your college debt for the next four years. It will develop your personal skills for leadership and service. And it will catch you up in a network of Coca-Cola Scholars, business leaders, activists and others whose ideas and dialogue will help to move this nation forward.

So tonight, even as the thrill of being chosen as a Coca-Cola Scholar is filling you with pride and excitement, I want to take just a few minutes to look ahead with you to the challenges you face as you seek to fulfill the high calling of this honor.

I've always loved that great quotation from Teddy Roosevelt: "The credit belongs to the man—and I would add woman—who is actually in the arena, whose face is marred by dust and sweat and blood; who strives valiantly; who errs and comes up short again and again—who at best knows in the end the triumph of high achievement; and who, at the worst, if he fails, at least fails while daring greatly. So that his place shall never be with those cold and timid souls who know neither victory nor defeat."

So dare greatly, my young friends. Don't be timid, and don't be afraid to fail sometimes.

You know something I've never failed at? I have never choked up while singing in front of an audience. You see, I've never had the guts to try to sing in front of an audience. I have never been willing to take that risk. Only those people who try something run the risk of failure.

The main choice most of us make, the most important choice, is at what level we shall fail. Each of us chooses the level of our failure. In baseball, some make major league errors and some make minor league errors. But the only ones who make no errors at all, are the ones who don't play the game. In life itself, the same options are open.

From there, let me note that failure is a great teacher, the best one we'll ever have. Consider this: The only way you ever learned to walk was by failure. If you had waited until you were sure you would not fall to take that first step, you would still be wearing little high-topped white shoes with unscarred soles. The only way you ever learned to walk, or read, or add, or play the piano, or use a computer was by trying, failing and trying again!

Whatever it is, failure will teach it to us, if we let it.

One more thing: Failure never has to be final. To fail is not to be defeated. Take John Grisham. Today all his books are best sellers, but his first book was rejected by publishers twenty-five times before it was finally printed. He rejected the rejection! Abraham Lincoln failed to be elected eight times out of eleven. But he was elected three times. And it was the latter two that we remember him for.

What we call real failure is not the falling down, but the staying down. That great quotation from Teddy Roosevelt came out of his own personal experience. When he was told that he was too near-sighted to serve in the military, he organized his own civilian Rough Riders, stashed 11 pairs of thick glasses in his saddle bags, and took off for Cuba, the Spanish-American War, and San Juan Hill. He rejected the rejection!

The University of Berne turned down a Ph.D. dissertation as being "fanciful and irrelevant." The young physics student who wrote the dissertation was Albert Einstein, who rejected that rejection!

When Jackie Robinson became the first African American to play in the major leagues, he was booed and taunted by fans and players alike. But he continued to step up to the plate and let his bat speak for him. He rejected the rejection!

The rhetoric teacher at Harrow wrote on a 16-year-old's report card, "A conspicuous lack of success." That student was Winston Churchill, who rejected the rejection!

Years later, when he was invited back to Harrow for commencement, he made the shortest commencement speech on record. He looked out and said simply, "Never give up; never give up; never, never, never give up."

Tonight we celebrate your success in being selected as Coca-Cola Scholars. You are an elite, smart bunch—truly the cream of the crop. And we all congratulate you on this important achievement. But it will be perseverance and determination in the face of failure, more than anything else, that will provide the power behind your ideas, and enable you to succeed in the high calling that is yours as Coca-Cola Scholars.

So do not be a cold and timid soul. Dare greatly. Reject the rejection. And never, never give up!

# Georgia Association of Broadcasters

*June 8, 1996*

It is a real honor to be named the Georgian of the Year for 1996. I am humbled to be weighed in your scales and found deserving. And I am proud to join a long list of distinguished Georgians who have been awarded this honor.

As long as we've all left the state, I thought this might be a good opportunity to take a step back and look at the bigger picture of Georgia from an outside perspective. When you do that, you discover some pretty remarkable things about Georgia... things to be proud of.

Of course, one of those things is that next month we will host the 1996 Olympics. With more than 11,000 athletes and 2 million spectators, these Games will be the largest peace-time event in world history. This is the opportunity of a lifetime—of ten lifetimes—to showcase Georgia to the world. And we have been working hard to take advantage of that opportunity.

We are using the Olympics as a springboard to to greater prominence in international athletic competition. The world-class sports facilities and international sports relationships that we have built will enable us to host a wide range of international athletic competitions for many years to come.

We are also using the international visibility of the Olympics to promote Georgia as a travel and tourism destination. Barcelona sustained a 25 percent increase in tourism after the 1992 Olympics, and we want to do the same. And if you get to Atlanta this summer, stop by the Welcome South Visitors Center. It is phenomenal.

Third, Operation Legacy is a public-private partnership that is leveraging the Olympics for economic development. Over the past two years, it has brought ten groups of executives from 302 companies to Georgia for several days at a time to show them what is so special about this state that we were chosen to host the Olympics. Fifteen Operation Legacy companies have already announced new facilities in Georgia, creating over 2,200 new jobs.

One of the industries Operation Legacy has targeted is of special interest to you— high-tech communications and electronics. You may not realize this, but Georgia already has the significant cutting-edge research and high-tech industry we need to be a world leader in communications. And 45 of the top 50 electronics companies in the world are already located here.

Georgia is the state where the modem and IRMA board were developed... the state where the first windows-based computer software was unveiled... the state of the first nationwide satellite cable TV signal and the first mobile satellite uplink. Georgia is the state of the first commercial application of fiber-optic cable, and today we have a 150,000-mile statewide fiber-optic network, that is continuously growing. Atlanta has four times more fiber-optic trunk lines than New York City, and it lies on two major fiber-optic corridors—one along the eastern seaboard, and the other beginning in Chicago and continuing through the Caribbean into South America.

We are working very deliberately through the Georgia Research Alliance and the Georgia Center for Advanced Telecommunications Technology to expand and develop our expertise.

This summer we are going to showcase it to the world by putting on the most technically sophisticated Olympics in history, and in conjunction with those preparations, Operation Legacy has been courting the electronics and telecommunications industries.

As you can see, Georgia has been working hard to make the Olympics work for Georgia.

But we also continue to do what we were doing before the Olympics were ever announced—creating new jobs at a break-neck pace.

Georgia has been the fastest growing state east of the Rocky Mountains for the past four years in a row. And before any of you attribute that simply to Atlanta and the Olympics, let me emphasize that employment in Georgia's smaller cities and rural areas grew by 3.4 percent last year—twice as much as economists were expecting and faster than every other entire state in the region. Per capita income in Georgia's rural areas has been growing faster than in our cities during the first half of the 90s.

An obvious reason for Georgia's economic strength is our great location on the Atlantic seaboard. It gives us a time overlap with Europe's business day. It has enabled us to develop one of the premier ports on the Atlantic. Last year Savannah handled more than 13 million tons of cargo.

At the same time, we are 125 miles closer to Chicago than New York is. We are within two hours flying time of the majority of the U.S. population and withing two days ground-shipping time of the majority of U.S. consumer and industrial markets.

Another reason for Georgia's economic strength is that state government is investing in the future—both in high-tech infrastructure and in our richest resource of all, our people. We understand that a skilled workforce will be critical for the 21st century. So we created the most comprehensive prekindergarten program of any state in the nation. And we are the only state that's even close to making it available to every family that wants it.

We also have the nation's most far-reaching scholarship program. It is called HOPE. And whenever I describe it to business executives from other states, you can hear the gasps of amazement. HOPE is so significant that it has recently gotten national attention from the President. We can be proud that Georgia is on the forefront, leading the way in higher education.

Any Georgia high school student who graduates with at least a B average in their academic subjects, can get free college tuition and a book allowance at any Georgia public college, or they can get $3,000 a year to attend any Georgia private college. Keep that B average, and those scholarship benefits continue through all four years to graduation.

We also know that although most of the jobs of the future will not need a college degree, many will require technical training beyond high school. So students who don't have a B average or don't want to attend college, can get the same deal for a diploma program at a technical institute—free tuition and a book allowance.

In the two and a-half years since the HOPE Scholarship Program began, we have provided over $231 million in scholarship assistance to nearly 198,000 Georgia students.

We are also investing in state-of-the-art technology to serve our citizens. Georgia is setting the world standard with what the *New York Times* has called the most sophisticated telemedicine program in the nation. Tiny high-tech cameras and recording devices are attached to all sorts of medical equipment, to bring instant medical care from experts at the Medical College of Georgia into 40 hospitals around the state. By the end of this year, it will be 60 hospitals.

We also use this network for distance learning. It connects nearly 300 educational institutions around the state. And up to eight of these sites can be interactive at one time. In addition, Georgia was the first state in the nation to have a satellite dish at every single public educational facility, and the first state to own a transponder on a Telstar satellite to send out the programming. As a result, we lead the nation in producing educational programming, and in the number of schools and students who use it.

Georgia proudly recruits new industry, and we work eagerly with incoming companies to meet their needs in locating here. But at the same time, we are also devoted to home-growing our economy over the long haul. Existing industries can get the same tax incentives for creating new jobs and the same Quick Start employee training when they expand, as new companies get when they move to Georgia. We also provide tax incentives to help our existing industries with the cost of investing in technology, and providing job re-training, education, and child care for their employees.

So you see, when you take a step back and look at Georgia from down here, it really is a great place to visit, to live, and to do business.

I know that the Georgia Association of Broadcasters has helped to make it that way! I thank you for that, and I join you in looking forward to the Olympics next month and to keeping Georgia strong in the 21st century.

# Olympic Torch Arrival in Georgia

*Savannah, July 9, 1996*

On behalf of all Georgians, I am honored welcome the Olympic Torch to our state and to the final stage of its proud journey. This is a great moment for Georgia. As this torch moves around our state, excitement and enthusiasm for the Olympics will build to the exploding point.

But before we get caught up in that wonderful frenzy, let me say this: The *only* reason the Olympics have come to Georgia, is because one man dared greatly and worked without ceasing to realize what many thought was an impossible dream. Billy Payne has worked harder and longer, and with greater single-minded determination than any athlete who will compete in these Games. He is the biggest Olympic hero Georgia will ever have. And a gold medal would be small change compared to the magnitude of the great gift he has personally given to this state.

It was a high tribute for Atlanta to be chosen first to represent this great nation, and then to be the host city for the 1996 Olympics. And for the past 74 days, we have been repaying the trust and faith that America showed in us, by sharing the Olympic Torch with America. Since it arrived in Los Angeles, this flame has journeyed across 15,000 miles through 42 states. It has traveled on cable cars in San Francisco, along the original route of the Pony Express through Nebraska, in a jazz parade in New Orleans, in the shadow of the Statue of Liberty in New York Harbor, to the South Lawn of the White House. It has been carried by runners and horseback riders. It has traveled on bicycles and canoes, on trains and ferries, all polished to within an inch of their lives.

This torch has seen America. It has shone upon much that is great about our nation and our heritage. And America has seen this torch. Ten thousand American heros have carried it in their hands, and millions have witnessed its passage. Young and old alike have driven for miles to cheer and wave home-made torches and banners... to sing our national anthem and watch with tears in their eyes and a lump in their throat. They have been caught up in the spirit of the Olympics, and they have shared in the deep honor and pride that we in Georgia feel.

Today, as we welcome the Olympic Torch to Georgia, we thank all the Americans who have shared in its keeping and sped it on its way with their heart-felt wishes. And we pledge to do all of them proud as we host the 1996 Centennial Olympic Games on their behalf.

I especially want to thank the men and women of the Georgia State Patrol who have been the guardians of this flame on its long journey. They have presented themselves in a way that has made us all proud to be Georgians.

For the next ten days, the torch will make its way by foot, by bicycle, and by boat, over more than 1,800 miles of this great state. It will pass beneath live oaks draped with Spanish moss, and through the piney woods and the fertile farmland of South Georgia. It will cross the rolling hills of the Piedmont, and pass in the shadow of Brasstown Bald Mountain.

As the torch travels through our state, for a brief moment in time every Georgian will have a chance to participate in hosting this special symbol of world unity and peace. And I encourage all Georgians to participate in their local celebrations and witness this Olympic Torch firsthand.

After it has made virtually a 360 degree turn around Georgia, the Olympic Torch will arrive in the capital city of this state and of the South, to enter the Olympic Stadium in the opening ceremonies on July 19th. For 17 days, this flame will burn above the Olympic courts and playing fields, as the best athletes in the world put aside all differences of race, nationality, language, religion, and politics to celebrate the highest levels of human achievement and sportsmanship.

As Teddy Roosevelt once put it, they will strive valiantly, with faces marred by dust and sweat and blood. Many of them will experience the pain of coming up short, but none of them will ever be found among those cold and timid souls who know neither victory nor defeat.

This torch is a reminder that, although we may never be Olympic athletes, each one of us still faces challenges and opportunities in our own lives. And we can choose to meet them in the spirit of the Olympics.

So, as we welcome this Olympic Torch to Georgia, let us remember the high ideals that it embodies, and join with Americans all across this great land and with people around the world in celebrating all that is best in the human spirit.

# Dedication of the GCATT Building

*July 17, 1996*

The first thing I want to say is that I am not a scientist, and I don't pretend to understand the technical aspects of the research that will go on in this remarkable building. Rather I am a historian, and I look at this research center and our growing prominence in telecommunications from that perspective.

If you look at the 25 largest cities in the United States, virtually every one grew up around some natural resource. Most of them are port cities—Boston, New York, Philadelphia, and Miami on the East Coast; Seattle, Portland, San Francisco, and Los Angeles on the West Coast; New Orleans and Houston on the Gulf; Chicago on the Great Lakes.

The few that are inland can also be explained, for the most part, by major natural resources. Dallas has oil; Denver has mining. Kansas City and Minneapolis are markets for the rich grains of the Midwestern prairies. And Washington, D.C., of course, is our nation's capital.

Of the 25 largest cities in the United States, only Atlanta has no natural, logical reason for its existence. Atlanta was built on sheer human ingenuity and persistence, and the resource around which this city has grown up, is purely man-made transportation infrastructure and a knack for knowing how to leverage it.

Its very first expression, of course, was the railroad. In the 1830s, three railroads came together in a remote spot out in the Georgia woods. They formed a major junction that linked the East Coast with the Midwest, and Atlanta grew up around that railroad junction.

A century later, Atlanta was in the vanguard of the next generation of transportation, building an airport in the early days of commercial aviation. In 1940, Atlanta had the nation's busiest airport with 41 flights a day.

Two decades later, we became one of the few American cities to be located at the intersection of three major interstate highways.

Today, on the threshold of the 21st century, transportation is taking yet another leap, this time into cyberspace and onto the information superhighway, as telecommunications technology makes location increasingly irrelevant. And true to our historical roots, Atlanta is once again deliberately building the infrastructure we need to establish prominence in this newest form of "transportation."

In two days, the biggest single event in world history will begin here in Atlanta. It will also be the greatest single telecommunications event in world history. Because in the process of putting on the 1996 Olympics, Atlanta will present the world with a vision of 21st century telecommunications technology in action. A more important Olympic legacy than a swimming pool here or a stadium there, will be the telecommunications infrastructure that these Games have given us.

In preparation for the Olympics, Atlanta increased its cellular capacity by eightfold, making this the best city in the world for wireless portable phone connections. We already had three times more fiber-optic trunk lines than New York City, and the Olympics will leave us with more broadband fiber-optic connections than Manhattan— another essential piece of 21st century infrastructure that high-tech industry requires. Our new Integrated Services Digital Network provides internet connections several times faster than conventional modems, at a cost that is among the lowest anywhere.

The Olympics have given us a technological leg up. And this new telecommunications research center positions us to build on it, and continue to run out on the cutting edge of telecommunications technology.

This state-of-the-art research center, with its labs, high-tech demonstrations and incubator for new ventures, is magnificent in its own right. But it also serves as an icon for our vast telecommunications infrastructure and expertise.

You can see rail yards and highways and runways. You can see cars and ships and trains and planes. But you cannot see a satellite or a digital network. Telecommunications infrastucture is largely invisible. This research center is tangible evidence that Georgia has the both resources and the determination to become the global center for advanced telecommunications in the 21st century.

The Georgia Center for Advanced Telecommunications Technology, like its parent body, the Georgia Research Alliance, is a public-private partnership that brings together academia, private industry, and state government.

State government's role is to provide seed capital at the front end—funding to build this research center, matching funds to provide endowments for the eminent research scholars who will work here and to equip their labs. Because we believe that the collaborative research and incubator programs that the academic and industrial partners carry out in this building, are the engine that will power our telecommunications industry to world prominence.

In addition, the Governor's Development Council—another public-private partnership between industry and state government—has adopted global leadership in telecommunications as one of its goals in guiding the development of Georgia's public economic policy.

Someone once said that the biggest sin is not failure, but low aim. That's one sin we are not going to be guilty of. Our aim is high: By the end of the first decade of the new century, we intend to be the premier center in the world for advanced telecommunications. We have the infrastructure; we have the industrial base; we have the intellectual capital. We have the resources.

And in this magnificent building they will converge with a synergy that is greater than the sum of their parts, to carry Atlanta and Georgia forward to world leadership in advanced telecommunications in the 21st century.

# Acceptance of the Blue Key Award

*The University of Georgia, September 20, 1996*

I am humbled to be chosen to receive the Blue Key Award, and to receive it together with Dick Yarbrough, a remarkable man whom I have admired greatly for a long time, is a special pleasure. I also extend my congratulations to Kathy Rogers Pharr, as recipient of the Young Alumnus Award, and to Maggie Hodge, Andrew DeVooght and Julie Mickle.

Being chosen for this high honor and as your keynote speaker, gave me a chance to step back from the day-to-day details of being Governor and reflect on higher education as a historian and as one who is at heart a teacher. Perhaps it's genetic, for I am the son of two teachers. Whatever its source, a commitment to education runs deep in my soul. My goal as Governor has not been some short-term political gain, but a long-term educational gain.

I want us to establish in this state a culture of higher expectations. I want the question to be not "whether" to go to college, but "where" to go to college or technical school. I want Georgians to move into the new millennium with more productive careers and as better citizens.

Throughout American history, education has always been an over-riding preoccupation, and we have always steadfastly refused to allow other crises to distract us from it. In fact, it seems that unsettled times have often given us the push we needed to improve and expand education.

Two years before George Washington was even inaugurated, the Continental Congress passed a law requiring every new township to set aside land for a public school. Even as the Civil War swirled around him and our nation's Capitol was often in peril, President Lincoln signed the Morrill Act, creating a system of land-grant colleges.

Right in the middle of World War I, Congress took time to pass the Smith-Hughes Act—sponsored by two Georgians, Hoke Smith and Dudley Hughes—to establish a new system of vocational education. With World War II raging on both the European and Pacific fronts, Congress passed the G.I. Bill, assuring over two million returning veterans the chance of an education.

See what I mean? And we are the inheritors of those traditions. All that was strong and iron-hearted in the past has come down to us, and we must use our time to meet the challenges of our day, just as those who bequeathed it to us used theirs.

Today, as we stand on the threshold of a new millennium, we are in the middle of one of the greatest shifts in world history. Not only has our economy become global in its scope, but the technology all around us is changing by the day. There is more computer power in the Ford Taurus we now drive to the supermarket, than there was in the Apollo 11 rocket that Neil Armstrong flew to the moon.

Today, the combined forces of changing technology and global competition are bringing about a transformation that literally dwarfs the industrial revolution in its impact. These powerful forces are changing more than just our jobs. They are changing the neighborhoods we live in. They are changing the institutions that shape our lives, and even our hopes and dreams for the future.

Since the birth of this nation, the defining elements of American society have been the idea of opportunity for all and the freedom to seize it and work to make our dreams come true. But today, for the first time in our history, people aren't so sure about their ability to do that. While some see this as a time of profound opportunity, for many others it is a time of profound insecurity—a time in which the very plates of the earth seem to be shifting under their feet.

The difference—the difference between those who see opportunity and those who see insecurity—is education.

Consider these facts: Fifteen years ago, the typical employee with a college degree made 38 percent more money than the employee with only a high school diploma. Today that gap has widened to 73 percent. Half of our population today is working harder than ever before and making less money, and half of the people who lose their jobs today will never, ever find another job in which they will do as well. The unemployment rate for high school dropouts is now about 10 percent. For those with a high school diploma, it is half that. For college graduates, it is one-fourth that.

So you can see, Education doesn't matter just a little. It doesn't even matter just a lot. It matters most of all. Education is everything.

Increasingly, it is post-secondary education that is everything. A high school diploma is increasingly losing its economic value. The median income of young men ages 25-34 with a high school diploma has fallen by $14,000 over the past two decades. In the economy of the 21st century, students with only a high school diploma will be worse off than the dropouts of this century. So, what a high school diploma has become today, is only a ticket to the post-secondary education or training that will give you value on the job market.

See why I said in the beginning that I want to create a culture of higher expectations in this state? I don't want the question to be "whether," but "where" to go to college or technical school. Two years beyond high school must be expected. It must be a given. Today as never before, higher education is the key to economic growth and development. Higher education is the most important economic infrastructure a state can have.

In Georgia, we are on the right track, and headed in the right direction. Our citizens are becoming better educated than ever before. In 1949 when I finished high school, only one out of five Georgians were high school graduates. Twenty years later, in 1970, we were up to two out of five. Today, almost four out of five of our citizens are high school graduates.

Between 1970 and 1990, the percentage of Georgians with at least one year of college more than doubled, and the percentage of Georgians with a college degree has almost doubled. Minority southerners now complete high school at the same rate as white southerners, and the percentage of minority southerners with college degrees nearly tripled in the past 25 years.

But while we've been climbing up the mountain, the mountain itself has been growing. A lot more Georgians have college degrees, but it's still only 21 percent, instead of the 30 percent we need.

One of the most encouraging trends in the past decade is that the number of our high school students taking the college prep curriculum has almost tripled, and Georgia is now outstripping the national average.

Here at The University of Georgia, last fall's freshmen averaged 1108 on the SAT—a UGA record that was about 200 points above the national average. And this institution is ranked by *U.S. News and World Report* as among the top 20 public universities in the nation.

But these days, technology is changing so fast that you can't just go through college once and be done with it. The shelf-life of a technical degree is now down to five years. This reality of lifelong learning means that we're going to have to adapt to the needs of growing numbers of older, non-traditional students.

Many still have this image of college as a place full of 18-22 year-olds. But today, four of every 10 students in the University System of Georgia, as well as around the nation, are over the age of 25. The percentage of college students over age 35 has doubled in just the past decade and is going to keep growing.

It's not just enough to keep up a well-trained workforce. We also have to be on the cutting edge of research and innovation, and that is the second economic development function of higher education. Half of all basic research in the United States today is conducted at our universities. It is where polio vaccines, heart pacemakers, digital computers, municipal water purification systems, space-based weather forecasting, and disease-resistant grain and vegetables, just to name a few, have been invented.

University research has become critical to economic development, and the classroom and the research lab must be more closely connected than ever before. A great challenge for university faculty must be to become more adept at combining those two roles.

The future will belong to those that can put hand-in-hand: one, the ideas that will drive technology forward, and two, the educated workers who can make something of those ideas.

Here, the South in general and The University of Georgia in particular have been doing well. The National Research Council ranked nearly a fourth of the South's doctoral programs in the top 20 in the nation in their particular fields. The University of Georgia conducts the largest volume of research of any American university that does not have an engineering or a medical college.

Tonight, I have deliberately focused on the growing economic significance of higher education. It is absolutely critical to the future prosperity of this state. But I want close by saying that we must also never mistake technology for culture.

At the same time I have been emphasizing that higher education prepares students to "earn a living," I also want to make it clear that by itself, earning is not living. We need to educate students not only to earn, but also to live. That is the higher calling of higher education.

You see, our students are not only tomorrow's employees. They are also tomorrow's citizens, parents, customers, and neighbors. And higher education must enrich their ability to function in those capacities as well as on the job market.

The business of higher education is more than mere information. The business of higher education is knowledge. And unlike information, knowledge cannot be poured into the minds of students like water into a glass. Knowledge is not a destination; it is a process. It is learned and accumulated over a period of time through continuous study, thought, and experience.

I believe that being "educated" means that one has learned to think, to reason, to compare, to analyze. I believe that "educated" persons are continually shaping and refining their mental visions, judgments, and tastes.

Which brings me full circle to where I began—because as the shelf life of technical information becomes ever shorter, those thinking and analyzing skills are coming to be in ever higher demand in the workforce. Employers today want workers who are continually re-evaluating what they know, continually learning new things, and continually integrating what they learn with what they already know.

As we look to the 21st century, we must continually strengthen and enhance our higher education programs to meet the demands of a technology-driven global economy. But while we are doing that, we dare not forget that higher education is about more than money. And what you do here on this campus must be as essential to living as it is to earning.

# Legislative Biennial Institute

*December 10, 1996*

I always look forward to being on this campus. It's where, 40 years ago this summer, straight out of the Marine Corps, still wearing military-issued glasses, shoes, socks, and underwear, with bedsprings and mattress on an old Chevy, with a pregnant wife and a baby in diapers, we started a new life in a prefab building less than 200 yards from where this Georgia Governor stands today.

I love this university, and I have watched with pride as my alma mater, under Chuck Knapp's leadership, has risen to new heights of excellence and national prominence in academics and research. This is a great university that we all can be very proud of, and Chuck Knapp's legacy is one that will live as long as there is a University of Georgia. As they said about the architect Christopher Wren, if you want to see his monument, look around you. Thank you on behalf of all of Georgia. Shirley and I are going to miss you and Lynn very much. Good luck and God speed, my friend.

It was 36 years ago that as newly elected state senator, I came to Athens for my first prelegislative seminar. I've been back every two years since then, like a swallow returning to Capistrano. But I want you to know that I am not tired, not weary, faint-hearted or burned out. There is not a freshman legislator in this room who is looking forward to the first bang of the gavel with any greater anticipation than I am. I can't wait for the buzzer to sound.

My own preparations for the coming session have been underway for months. I gave my department heads their marching orders for budget preparation last summer before the Olympics ever began. For the past three months, I've spent hundreds of hours, hunched over a table like some bookkeeper wearing a green eyeshade, working with an able OPB staff, trying to make all the numbers work out.

In a few weeks, you will have a chance to get into those numbers, and I encourage you to do so. No one understands better than this ol' creature of the legislature, that the Governor advocates; the General Assembly appropriates. I respect that.

So, as we look ahead to the session in January, I want to take a few minutes to talk to you pretty directly about how I approach the budget process. The first and most important thing I think we must never forget is that there is no such thing as "government money." There is only "taxpayers' money." As that great American patriot Thomas Paine, who had some thoughts about taxes, wrote, "It is not the produce of riches only, but of hard earnings of labor and poverty. It is drawn even from the bitterness of want and misery."

That is the classic definition of taxpayer money, "the produce of hard earnings, drawn even from the bitterness of want and misery." It is those kinds of Georgia taxpayers who foot the bill for state government, and, as you probably learned in your recent campaign, they are not at all convinced that they have been getting good value for their tax dollars.

Next month, the halls of the Capitol will be filled with folks, trying to get some of those "hard earnings" for one thing or another. By and large, they're good folks, working on good projects, highly motivated folks. You've probably already heard from many of them—they are the ones who suddenly became your best friends the morning after the election. While many of them have legitimate interests, we can never forget that they always, always speak on behalf of their own special interest and not on behalf of the taxpayers of Georgia. What's more, we could double taxes in this state—we could triple taxes, and it still would not satisfy them. So, in this Christmas season, I would remind you that Santa Claus cannot meet all requests. Neither can the taxpayers of Georgia.

Government cannot do everything, not even many of the things we used to think it could, and I am convinced that we must be very deliberate about identifying the priorities that the taxpayers want accomplished with their money, and then focus on doing those things as efficiently and effectively as possible. Together, we have made progress toward that end in the past six years. We have become more clearly focused on priorities like education, job creation, and providing the prisons we need to keep violent criminals behind bars.

We have also become more disciplined about our spending. We are using budget redirection to constantly shift funds away from low priorities and toward high priorities. We are using privatization to shift into the private sector the functions that either belong there or can be done more efficiently there. I am continuing those efforts in next year's budget.

Last session we enacted the largest tax cut in Georgia history when we removed the state sales tax from groceries. In the months since then, I've heard from a few folks who now wish they had that money to spend, and sadly lament the fact that we ever made that cut. The truth is—and don't let anyone tell you different—Georgia is in sound financial shape. We ended the last fiscal year with a comfortable surplus. Every single reserve fund in state government is full. Among them, our reserves now total nearly $550 million, and unlike most Georgia governors, I will leave those reserves full and untouched for the governor who comes after me.

So, that food tax cut was not in any way irresponsible. It is never irresponsible to make state government more clearly focused on what the taxpayers of Georgia want it to do. What was irresponsible, was a spending system that had been on auto-pilot for way too long—a spending system that was milking the taxpayers of this state for more money than was needed to provide those basic services that our taxpayers are willing to pay for.

Of course, there are going to be some hard choices in this session and in the future. But if you don't like hard choices, my friends, you are in the wrong business, because hard choices are what governing is all about. You and I were elected by the voters of Georgia to lead this state on their behalf. And a very important part of that leadership is knowing when to say "No," and sometimes even, "Hell, no!" to special interests, and having the guts to do it.

I'm not going to get into all the details of next year's budget until I present it to you next month. But let me say a few things about it: Of course, it will be balanced, as the federal budget should be, and it continues to be based on the most conservative revenue estimate, to make sure that it stays in balance as the year progresses.

Second, it reflects another revenue cut of $152 million to accommodate removing that third cent of state sales tax from groceries, which will go into effect next October. The following October the fourth cent will come off, with another revenue cut next year of $129 million.

Third, it includes the 6 percent salary increase for teachers. Some of you may recall that I began my second term by saying that I want Georgia to be able to compete nationally for the best teachers we can get. I pledged four consecutive salary increases of 6 percent each year over the course of my second term. This is the third, and I'll be back next year with the fourth straight one.

Fourth, I have built an additional $4 million for repair and maintenance into the University System formula. We now have the fourth largest university system in the country, and we must continually address the fact that many of the buildings on our campuses are quite old and in need of some major work.

Then fifth, the budget includes a bond package that keeps our debt ratio at about half of our Constitutional limit and is consistent with the criteria of the Debt Management Advisory Committee. That bond package includes $126 million in capital outlay for the University System at 16 campuses— and yes, Chuck, it includes your parking deck. Again, we are saddened by the fact that you won't be here to see built. This will bring the total amount of capital outlay for the University System under this administration to $833 million at 32 campuses. And we've got another year to go.

Education is the passion of my administration, and it's not just because I am a teacher by profession. It is because a strong education system is the most critical economic development infrastructure that a state can have. My goal as Governor has been to establish a culture of higher expectations for this state. I want the question in Georgia to be not "whether," but "where" to go to college or technical school. More than half of the new jobs that are being created today require education beyond high school. We have got to begin regarding two years of education or training beyond high school as a minimum, as a given.

So far, with your help, we have created in Georgia the nation's largest and most comprehensive prekindergarten program for our four-year-olds, and the nation's largest and most comprehensive scholarship program for our college and tech school students. Now, our attention must be increasingly drawn to what happens in between prekindergarten and higher education... in the classrooms where education actually takes place.

Here in Georgia, we have greatly increased education spending per student in recent years, even adjusted for inflation. Average pupil-teacher ratios have been dropping. But student achievement has shown only slight improvement, even considering factors like the increasing number of students whose first language is not English.

When I point this out to educators, they say that, despite the increases, we still aren't giving them enough money. Good results, according to them, always cost a couple hundred or even a couple thousand dollars more per child than they get. Now, they may be right. I don't think so. I think it's largely a myth that greater spending automatically insures more quality education. But you see, we really have no way of knowing. Because our accountability system measures the performance of individual schools, while the Quality Basic Education formula provides state money to school systems. The way it is right now, it's difficult to connect the performance of a particular school with its level of funding. And I am beginning to conclude that the question of who controls that money and who makes the decisions about it at the local level, might be related to performance.

I don't know how many of you get out and visit the schools of your district. I recommend it. I try to devote time on a regular basis to school visits, especially to our schools of excellence around the state. I want to see what educational excellence looks like in its working clothes. And I'm beginning to sense a pattern that is also reflected in some education research. It is this: When the decisions about money take place in the central office of the school system, principals and teachers at the school level often have no idea of how much is being spent and for what at their particular school. If you ask those principals to guess, they often cannot come within 50 percent of the correct amount. If you don't believe me, go home and first thing in the morning, before the central office has a chance to call them, ask your local principal what the budget is for his school. You will be amazed.

But let me quickly point out that it is not the principal's fault. Most of them are kept in the dark and have no real authority over the schools they are responsible for running. Those principals who do know how much money they have to spend and can make decisions about how to use it, are often able to achieve substantial savings in areas outside the classroom and shift those funds toward direct services to students. For example, principals who can hire and supervise their own janitors, rather than having it done by the central office, often get more work out of fewer janitors, saving money that can be used in the classroom. Teachers who can buy their own supplies, will get them cheaper across the street at K-Mart or Wal-Mart, and without the time lag or paperwork of requisitioning them from the central office.

An observation: Show me a high-performing school, and more often than not, I'll show you a principal who has or takes control. Show me a low-performing school, and more often than not, I'll show you a school where all decisions and problems are usually referred and deferred to the central office.

I have begun to think more and more about the connection between performance at the school level, and control over resources. And I invite you to start thinking with me along the same lines. Perhaps, working together, we can come up with something that might improve the situation.

Now, let me take a few minutes to talk about another important issue we are going to have to deal with in this year's session, and that is welfare reform to come into compliance with the new federal law. Let me say that I welcome this opportunity to change another spending system that was on that auto-pilot for too long, and a system that was failing the very people it was meant to help.

I grew up with the core value that the fruits of labor come only for those who first labor for the fruits, and I will bring you welfare reform legislation based on that premise and built into the budget. It is "tough love" at its very best. And one of your former colleagues and a native of this city, Michael Thurmond, is largely responsible for what I think will come to be regarded nationwide as the best approach that a state has come up with.

Now some are going to scream that it is too hard; others will scream that it is too lenient. Which leads me to believe that it is pretty well balanced between compassion and toughness. Its most important feature is the emphasis on work. And I would remind you that before Congress and the President ever got around to it, Georgia had already retooled our welfare program to do just that. During the past two years, our WORK FIRST program has reduced Georgia's welfare rolls by more than 20,000 families, or 68,000 individuals, saving the taxpayers of this state $52 million.

This new plan carries us even farther in that same direction. Its message is that if you want to get an education and a job—if you want to become independent and self-sufficient, we will be there to help you do it. But we are not going to tolerate those who are not willing to work. We are not going to tolerate those who are not willing to accept parental responsibility. And we are not going to tolerate those who are not willing to live within the law.

This new welfare plan goes back to the original intent when welfare was first created—temporary assistance for needy families to prepare themselves to get back to work, and not an ongoing entitlement program. Under the proposal I bring you, cash assistance will be limited to a total of four years, and the family cap provision is reduced from 24 months to 10. That is the time limit after which no additional benefits will be provided for the birth of additional children.

We will have a program designed to reduce out-of-wedlock pregnancy among welfare recipients, involving counseling and education. In cases where children are born, we will demand that recipients establish paternity and obtain child support from the fathers of their children.

The first time anyone is found guilty of a drug felony or serious violent crime, their assistance will be terminated forever. They will never be able to get back on welfare.

However, the real strength of this plan is not its penalties, but its incentives and assistance for people to become self-sufficient. Teen mothers will be required to stay in school, but we will provide child care assistance for all of them. We are going to target adult recipients under age 26 for assistance to complete their GEDs. Parents will be required to take an active role in their children's education. They will be held responsible for their children attending school regularly, and they will be required to participate in parent-teacher conferences. If they don't take this responsibility, their assistance ends. We are going to provide assistance with transportation and other necessary support services to assist recipients in finding and holding jobs.

But this plan also recognizes that some recipients, because of old age or disability, are simply unable to work, and it provides a hardship exemption for them. And it goes beyond federal requirements in providing cash assistance to legal immigrants for one year.

It's a tough approach, but it is also a hopeful approach. We are saying to those on welfare, we have faith that you can work and be self-sufficient just like the rest of us. And we are going to help you do that.

In addition to welfare reform, I will have a number of other bills to lay before you for your consideration. Among them will be, once again for the seventh straight year, a strong DUI proposal. Georgia's DUI laws are still not tough enough. Too many people still drive drunk. Those who are caught are still not punished enough.

In order to fight drunk driving among younger drivers, I will ask you once again to reduce the allowable blood alcohol content to zero for drivers under age 21. And this session, in order to reduce accidents and fatalities involving teenage drivers, I will ask you to consider what will be called the Young Drivers' Safety Act of 1997.

It will provide for a graduated driver's license program for 16 and 17-year-olds, which would give these teenagers a driver's license only under certain conditions, such as requiring them to pass a driver's test, to be accompanied by an adult if they drive between 1:00 and 6:00 a.m., to remain crash and conviction free, and to make all passengers in their cars wear seat belts.

Domestic violence—that is violence that occurs in the home—has become a major problem in this state. And I will have legislation for you to consider that makes an act of violence in the home a serious criminal act, and includes a tough minimum mandatory sentence for those who assault spouses or family members.

I will also submit a bill to you that allows a parent or employer of a drug user to sue the drug dealer for damages resulting from drug abuse.

Currently the State of Georgia has one of the highest high school drop-out rates in this country. This is a drastic problem, and we must begin to deal with it more forthrightly. So the budget will contain a dropout program that will include bounty hunters, yes bounty hunters, and a dropout "diploma" that the student and parent have to sign, indicating that they understand the dire consequences of dropping out of school.

As Governor, I am going to make a call once a day to a parent whose child has dropped out. And you will also receive a regular list of the drop-outs in your district, so that you can make some calls or visits and use your considerable powers of persuasion. We will begin this in 10 or 12 of some of our worst counties. If it works like I expect, we will expand it to more counties the following year.

There's more—these are only a few of the bills that will be included in my legislative package. I look forward to working together with you on them. During the session, my door is always open to legislators. I especially want to get to know you freshmen legislators, and I want you to get to know and understand me. I very much want to work with all of you.

I know I've made a long speech—it will get you ready for my State of the State Address next month. In closing, let me say that I didn't become Governor to make the Democratic Party better. I became Governor to make Georgia better. Regardless of what political party you belong to, I trust that you share the same commitment—to make Georgia better.

I want change, growth, and reform for Georgia. That's what the people want, and if we work together, we can respond and deliver, and make Georgia better. In the meantime, I wish all of you a very happy holiday season. And get some rest, because, come January, you're going to need it.

# 1997

# Supplemental Budget Address

*January 7, 1997*

I am pleased to see all of you back after what I hope was a wonderful holiday season. I join you in looking forward to the 1997 General Assembly, and preparing for what I hope and expect will be a productive session.

I want to begin this discussion of the Fiscal Year 1997 amended budget by emphasizing that state government in Georgia remains in sound financial shape. I'll tell you a week early: the State of the State is good. Our reserves are completely full; together they total nearly $550 million.

During the past fiscal year, revenue grew by 8.5 percent, which was stronger than the low-range revenue estimate of seven percent on which we based our financial plan. As a result, when FY 96 ended last June 30th, we filled the Midyear Adjustment Reserve to its statutory limit of $104 million, and, even with that, we still had a surplus of $216 million.

In addition, good, tight, stingy management on the part of our state agencies has yielded a savings of $126 million in appropriated funds which, with my encouragement, they wisely did not spend. That gives us a total of $446 million in available general fund money. In addition, we also have $134 million in surplus and lapsed funds from the lottery, bringing the total fund availability to $581 million.

But hold it. Don't start spending it in your mind. You will note that the amended budget before you actually spends only $118 million in general funds, plus the lottery surplus, for a total of only $252 million in new expenditures—less than half of the available funds. So, let me begin by explaining what I have done with the money that is not being spent here. I have set aside the bulk of the general funds available—$331 million out of the $446 million—for two purposes.

First, I have set aside $129 million to assure a surplus of at least this much in FY 99. I have done that by lowering my revenue estimate. The reason I'm doing that is to make sure that we are able to cover the removal of the fourth and final cent of state sales tax from groceries. So if you see anyone who is still under the mistaken impression that the state could not afford that tax cut, tell them to relax, the money for it is already in the bank.— in the bank, guaranteed by the FDIC, and drawing interest.

Next, just like we did last year, the remaining $202 million is used to pre-pay debt service that is due in FY 98. Using these surplus funds to reduce our debt, rather than starting new programs in the supplemental budget, is the wise and frugal thing to do.

While I'm talking about what is *not* in this supplemental budget, let me also mention that it contains no additional money for the Olympics. We provided adequately for our responsibilities with the appropriations of last session, so, ladies and gentlemen, the state's books on the largest peacetime event in world history are closed.

Now, let me outline a few things that are in this budget. This year, as every year, the bulk of the supplemental budget goes to education. The entire lottery surplus plus most of the general funds—a total of $231 million out of the $252 million in new expenditure—goes for education.

Most of the general funds—$91 million to be exact—goes to our K-12 public schools. Specifically, it goes into the enrollment-based Quality Basic Education funding formula, to catch up with enrollments for the current school year and reflect the actual number of students our schools are serving.

In addition, I am proposing that we provide $1.6 million for middle school incentive grants to a dozen systems who have qualified for this program.

Then $1.3 million is needed to provide year-end bonuses for 29 schools with a total of more than 1,000 certified educators. These schools were successful participants in our pay-for-performance program last school year. As you may recall, Georgia's pay for performance program invites the teachers at any school in the state to set concrete goals for improving student performance, and then work together to achieve those goals. Schools that have reached their goals at the end of the school year, receive $2,000 per educator, no strings attached. The teachers who earned that money, vote on how to use it.

The $134 million from lottery surpluses and lapses are used for two purposes in this budget. Nineteen million dollars will catch up funding for prekindergarten, so that our funding levels reflect the actual enrollments and program needs that are out there—similar to the mid-year adjustment we provide in K-12 school funding.

This is a program we can all be very proud of. CNN did a special on Georgia's pre-K program on "Future Watch," and will feature it again in about two weeks on a program called "Parenting Today." Peter Jennings, on the ABC Evening News, devoted a five-minute "Solutions" segment to it. It was also featured on the "Jim Lehrer Report" on PBS. In addition, more than a dozen states have requested information on our prekindergarten program, to say nothing of several countries. Ireland is extremely interested, and Zimbabwe is sending a representative to Georgia to examine it firsthand. You see, we really have a *preschool* program, not a baby sitting service.

The remainder of the lottery surplus is used for one-time items: $63.5 million provides special construction money for rapidly growing school systems, providing funding for the full $100 million entitlement level. $28 million goes to the unique and highly successful Georgia Research Alliance for sophisticated research lab facilities and high-tech equipment so that our research universities can be on the cutting edge in promoting economic development. And $16 million is for equipment at new technical institutes and satellites.

We are rapidly approaching the time where Georgia will have a technical school within a 40-minute drive of every citizen in the state. This access, in combination with the HOPE Scholarship Program, gives every Georgian the opportunity to learn a skill and prepare to join our growing, educated workforce. There will no longer be any excuses for anyone who wants to work not to get the skills or education it takes to get a good job.

In other general fund expenditures, I am recommending $4 million in Corrections, to enable us to move forward with contractual agreements for two private prisons in Coffee and Wheeler Counties. Another $4 million will cover the start-up costs for 768 beds at five existing prisons. An additional $2 million will cover the food, medical and clothing costs for these new units and other new beds added throughout the system.

The Department has greatly expanded its capacity by double-bunking cells that had been single-bunked—in effect adding the equivalent of almost two new prisons without doing any construction. That's why I think the third one we are considering, may not be needed immediately.

One of the biggest problems inmates bring with them to prison is a lack of education. No one understands that better than I, and no one wants to do something about prison education more than I. So please get this straight. We are not cutting the opportunities for prison inmates to get an education. We are expanding them.

For several years, our prisons have had teachers on the staff, working during the regular day. However, under this administration, every able-bodied inmate is now out working during the day. So this budget reflects a shift from hiring teachers who work during the day when most prisoners are elsewhere, to contracting with teachers to provide evening classes. And we are going to augment those teachers and classes in a significant way with distance learning.

There has been a change, a drastic change, in the way knowledge is now delivered in the 1990s. For centuries, people went to school for knowledge. Now, knowledge can be delivered to them, and that kind of teaching can be individually tailored to go as slow or as fast as the person has time or ability. I am proposing $783,000 to put eight more prisons on the GSAMS distance learning network, and we are also going to have GED tapes available at every prison.

Think about this with me for a moment: Each year, more than 20,000 law-abiding Georgia citizens get their GED. Most of them do it while holding down a full-time job, and many raising a family at the same time. They get up early and watch GED classes on public TV before eating breakfast and getting their children off to school. They attend evening classes and then stay up late studying. Now I don't know about you, but I don't think it's too much to expect a convicted criminal in prison to put out the same kind of effort that thousands of our hard-working citizens do every day to get their education.

If you don't believe me, ask them. Listen to what they have to say—those average voters and taxpayers in your district, and not those who have a vested interest in the program—and you'll see they support what we're doing. These law-abiding citizens do it on their own. They are not stroked and begged and spoon fed. Why should criminals be?

The combination of evening classes and distance learning, will significantly increase the number of inmates who receive educational services and greatly expand the educational opportunities that are available to them, and at the same time save $8 million. So don't shed any tears here, folks. We are in the business of using taxpayers' money wisely, and the prison teachers whose jobs were abolished will get first shot at the contracts, before they are opened up for anyone else.

I am also recommending $3 million to continue the conversion of the Wrightsville adult prison for use by the Department of Children and Youth Services, to address the overload of juvenile offenders.

In human services, we continue our emphasis on community-based care as an approach that is both better for the client and more efficient for the taxpayers of Georgia. You will find an $11 million transfer from Human Resources Community Services into Medical Assistance to provide the state match for federal funds to expand community services. Most of the funding will be for mental health and mental retardation slots in community-based programs, but 761 community care slots for the elderly are also included.

There is also almost $15 million in transfers from mental health hospital services to community-based programs. This will fully fund services for the chronically mental ill, or CMI, in the Clarke, Gwinnett, and Thomas County service areas. It will also expand CMI services in the Fulton, Cobb, DeKalb, Troup, Lowndes, Glynn, and Ware/Bulloch county service areas.

We continue our efforts to privatize functions that can be appropriately or more efficiently provided by the private sector. You're going to see it continue for the duration of this administration. The budget for the Department of Human Resources includes further savings relative to the Veterans Nursing Home in Milledgeville, now that this privatization project is underway. It also includes the purchase of private services in the Independent Living Program and for sensory disabled clients, and the privatization of community care assessments in Augusta, Dublin, and Macon.

Let me pause here and talk philosophically about the supplemental budget. Those of you who have been around for a while, have heard me say many times that the supplemental budget should be used primarily to make needed adjustments to existing programs, and that all new initiatives ought to be placed on the table together in the big budget for next year. I have always believed that, and I still do. That is why $202 million of the surplus is used to make debt payments ahead of schedule.

However, the supplemental budget before you makes what I think are two necessary exceptions to my general philosophy and way of doing things. When you hear about them, I think you'll understand why.

The first is the Revenue Department. Many of you have been concerned about the organization and operation of this department, as I have been, and I have appreciated your advice and direction as we have considered how to reorganize it in recent years. We recently hired an outside consultant—the nationally respected firm of KPMG Peat Marwick—to study the Revenue Department of this tenth largest state in the nation, and to make recommendations for its complete overhaul and modernization, to make it more effective and more efficient.

A few weeks ago, we received the preliminary report of this "Blueprint for Modernization" for the Revenue Department. And I have asked the consultants to be here tomorrow, so that you can hear from them directly, firsthand, and ask them any questions you may have. But, let me just say today, that the urgency of some of these needs require that we begin the revamping process as soon as possible. So this amended budget includes $15 million to begin addressing twelve of the most pressing priorities recommended in the first report.

The entire reorganization and modernization process will take several years, and we will continue it with a $6 million appropriation in FY 98. To delay would mean to allow some problems to get worse as well as to lose savings we could begin to realize—savings I can tell you right now we will need some day in the not too distant future—and I think that when you hear from the consultants tomorrow, you'll see very clearly that these investments are the wise thing to do.

The second major initiative is in the budget for the Department of Human Resources. It is called Temporary Assistance for Needy Families, or TANF, and it will completely replace Georgia's old AFDC entitlement program. The federal government implemented its new requirements for welfare and changed its funding process to a block grant at the start of the federal fiscal year last October. It is to our advantage to get our new state program underway as soon as possible, rather than wait until the next fiscal year. So I am proposing a revised welfare budget that reflects its implementation as of January 1st, 1997.

Let me say that I welcome this opportunity—and I know most of you do, too—to change a spending system that has been on auto-pilot for too long, and that was failing, and failing badly, the very people it was meant to help. We now have third generation welfare recipients on the rolls, and when you look at their lives, there has been little improvement if any over the way their grandmothers were living. In Georgia, we are simply going to stop putting checks in the mail month after month, year after year. Cash assistance in this state will be limited to a total of four years.

Instead we are going to have a program that is "tough love" at its best. In Georgia, we're going to focus, we're going to fixate on two things: One, helping people get the skills for the jobs they need to become self-sufficient; and two, pregnancy prevention, especially among teenagers. As a requirement for receiving benefits, we are going to demand more personal responsibility from recipients, especially by living within the law and being parents of children.

It's a tough approach, but it is also a hopeful approach. We are saying to those on welfare, we have faith that you can do it. You can work and be self-sufficient just like the rest of us. We are going to help you do that. We are going to grant you that opportunity. We are going to smooth the path from welfare to work. But we are going to insist that you be like the woman in Proverbs who rises while it is not yet light, works, and eats not the bread of idleness.

Let me emphasize that the TANF section in this amended budget does not reflect an increase in funding for welfare—spending will remain roughly at the same level. What it shows is how the existing level of spending is being plainly reorganized to focus on preparing people to become self-sufficient and leave the rolls as soon as possible.

Georgia is ahead of many states in this regard. Some time ago, we restructured our welfare program to put a greater emphasis on work. Our WorkFirst program, together with a strong economy, has already reduced our welfare rolls by 20,000 families over the past four years. Think of that for a moment: 20,000 families for whom the American dream of bettering yourself by your own efforts is now within reach. And it is saving taxpayers $52 million.

This budget reflects our expectation that this new TANF program, combined with our WorkFirst program, will continue to reduce the rolls, and free up nearly $22 million...An amount that will be shifted into programs like GED education, assistance in finding jobs, teen pregnancy prevention, and removing the disincentive for two-parent welfare families.

You notice that I did not include more money for child care among those programs. Certainly that is critical, but unlike most states, Georgia was ahead of the curve in the increases we have been providing for child care to enable recipients to attend school or work. Presently we are in the enviable position of already having enough resources committed for child care at least through the next fiscal year. We're probably one of the few states that can say that during this time of transition. However, you will find funds in next year's budget to enable our county-level DFACS offices to do a better job of coordinating child care and determining the eligibility for it.

A major, major component of TANF will be preventing teen pregnancy. The reality is that we have a lot of sexually active teenagers out there who, if they become pregnant, will go on the welfare rolls. So teen pregnancy prevention is also welfare prevention. We are going to start our teen pregnancy prevention efforts in this budget using federal funds, and then in next year's budget, we will fund them, and fund them broadly, from the Indigent Care Trust Fund.

You will also find that we are dedicating some funds from our substance abuse block grant to target substance abusers who need treatment to turn their lives around so that they can get and hold a job.

One particular item that I want to draw your attention to, is a one-time appropriation that uses federal welfare funds to create a rainy-day reserve of $12 million. That should not really surprise you, because, as you know, I'm a great believer in rainy-day reserves. I can remember the day when I could have used one, and I want to leave you and my successor on fiscally sound ground. So, I'm putting $12 million, which is about 2.5 percent of the total amount we anticipate spending in the first year of this new program, into reserve.

Our federal funding is capped under the new block grant and will not go above a certain level. So I believe it is fiscally responsible to create a reserve, in the event that some future economic downturn increases the rolls to the point of putting a strain on this program. Please do not spend this reserve. We don't have to spend it, and the time may come, it will come sooner or later, when TANF will need it.

That federal cap also means that we cannot afford to waste any of our welfare funds, or have recipients who abuse or take advantage of the assistance they are receiving. I, like you, want to ferret out and track down fraud and abuse. So this supplemental budget includes $1.2 million, and my big budget will contain another $1.6 million to hire 50 new investigators to prevent fraud and abuse in new and recertified welfare cases. This will double the number of Georgia's investigators.

I have also proposed that Georgia provide assistance to legal immigrants for up to 12 months. And yes, this is above both the federal requirements and the federal block grant, and thus will require $1 million in state funds. We will also remove the disincentive for two-parent families, so that eligibility can be more simply determined and does not encourage fathers, as it absurdly has in the past, to leave home.

These changes are the beginning of a whole new era in welfare in Georgia. A more complete picture will emerge with the presentation of the FY 98 budget and the accompanying legislation. It is a long-overdue change. Years from now, it will be looked upon as an historic turn-around. For me—and I trust for you—it is an opportunity of a lifetime to end welfare as we know it. It is an unprecedented opportunity to make welfare work to the benefit of its recipients and to the satisfaction of the taxpayers who foot the bill for it.

There's a lesson here if we will learn from it. We must never get ourselves into such a costly entitlement program again, and we dare never allow ourselves to forget whose money we are spending in this budget. It is not ours; it came from the taxpayers of Georgia. This is their government, and as their Governor, I am leaving no stone unturned in my efforts to make it do what they want it to do.

I know that all of you share that goal, and I look forward to working with you to achieve it. Together, you and I have got a lot of work to do this session. I'm confident that as always, you'll do you part, and I want you to know that I'll strain and struggle and do my utmost to do my part to keep Georgia's star rising.

# State of the State Address

*January 14, 1997*

Thank you, Lieutenant Governor Howard. Speaker Murphy, members of the House and the Senate, members of the Supreme Court and Court of Appeals, members of our Consular Corps, ladies and gentlemen.

I am pleased to come before you this morning and report that the State of the State of Georgia—host of the greatest Olympics ever, home of the heavy-weight champion of the world and the newest member of the Baseball Hall of Fame—the State of the State of Georgia is great!

We are now the tenth largest state in the nation. We are a place where people and businesses want to be. In the six years since January 1991, Georgia's population has grown by 13.5 percent. We have been the 7th fastest growing state by percentage, and by number of people, only Texas, California, and Florida added more.

Even more significant, the number of jobs in Georgia grew by 22 percent during the same time. Georgia's unemployment rate has been dropping over the past five years to its lowest annual average in more than two decades. The pay's getting better, too. In 1995, our per capita income reached 94 percent of the national average, and our total personal income has increased by 37 percent since 1991.

Atlanta's growth has been especially strong, and the Olympics were an important contributing factor. For the past several years, we were focused on the 1996 Olympics as Georgia's chance for international attention and name recognition. I can stand here today and say that the 1996 Olympics here in Georgia were indeed the largest peacetime event in world history—bigger than the prior two Olympics combined, bigger than the Games will be in the year 2000. Six of every ten people on the planet watched them on television. Our name is known.

Our state public safety personnel performed magnificently last summer. It was a superb team effort, and our officers showed the world just how great Georgia is. To paraphrase Churchill, it was their finest hour. Dozens of Georgia communities hosted teams, and the venues around the state were outstanding. Many of our citizens continue to be in personal contact with athletes around the world.

I personally met with hundreds of foreign dignitaries and business executives who came to Atlanta in conjunction with the Olympics, and we will feel the positive effects on our growing international trade and investment for many years to come.

But, even as the Olympics were dominating the news of the day, Georgia was quietly garnering attention throughout the nation and around the world for another achievement that some might have thought as unlikely as hosting the Olympics—education.

Barely had the athletes left town and the banners been taken down, when CNN turned its attention to a "Future Watch" special on our prekindergarten program, and they will feature it again in about a week on a program called "Parenting Today." Peter Jennings, on the ABC Evening News, devoted a five-minute "Solutions" segment to it. And it was also featured on the "Jim Lehrer Report" on PBS.

A dozen states as far away as Alaska and Hawaii have requested information. Connecticut flew our program director up there to get a firsthand report. England and Ireland want to know more, and Zimbabwe is sending a representative here this month to see it in action.

The HOPE Scholarship Program was generating a high level of amazement and interest around the nation, even before President Clinton set out to emulate it on the national level.

Our P-16 Council is also getting a lot of national attention. At last count, more than 15 other university systems were trying to figure out how to copy it.

Imitation, they say, is the most sincere form of flattery, and it is great for Georgia to be in a position where others want to imitate our education programs. But there is more to be done, and that is why we are here, at the start of a new legislative session.

I am now in the late autumn of my political career, my administration as Governor, and my life. It is a time when one reflects and thinks seriously about what is really important, what really matters. In my own life, it is my family. Today Shirley and I are celebrating our 43rd wedding anniversary. She has been the motor and mainspring of my life, the wind beneath my wings. We are looking forward to the arrival of our second great-grandchild next month. Then in April, our oldest grandson will turn 15 and want to start driving.

As I have been preparing for this, my seventh session as Governor, I've been thinking a lot about what's important in the State of Georgia. And I come back to the same thing—the family.

The family is the fundamental building block of our communities and our society. It is what holds us together and makes us strong, stable and productive. The unifying theme of the bills and budget I will bring to you in the coming days, more than anything else, is to protect and promote Georgia's families.

My grandson Justin, who is coming up on 15, loves cars. We go to the Atlanta 500 together, and his heros are Dale Earnhart and Bill Elliott. He is going to need a little "tough love" as he learns to drive and gets out on the highway.

It terrifies me to realize that one out of every 24 Georgia teenagers was involved in a vehicle crash last year;179 of those teenagers were killed. They'll never have a chance to get a HOPE scholarship or thrill their parents with a grandchild. They're dead. Vehicle crashes are the leading cause of death between the ages of 16 and 20.

So I will bring you the Young Driver's Safety Act to provide a gradual process by which young drivers earn full driving privileges. It would work like this: At age 15, Justin's age, those who pass a written test and a vision test can get a learner's permit. They can only drive if a person over age 21 is beside them in the front seat, and all passengers are wearing seat belts. There would be zero tolerance for alcohol in these young drivers.

If that 15-year-old has had no wrecks, no moving violations and no illegal use of alcohol or drugs by the time they turn 16, they may take a road test. If they pass it, they get an intermediate permit. The driver with an intermediate permit could drive alone except between the hours of one and 6 A.M., when they would have to be with an adult over age 21, going to work or in a medical emergency. All passengers would be required to wear seat belts at all times, and there would continue to be zero tolerance for alcohol.

Then at the age of 18, if their permit has not been suspended within the prior 12 months, and if they've had no wrecks, no moving violations and no illegal use of alcohol or drugs within the prior 12 months—then they receive a regular driver's license, still with zero alcohol tolerance until they reach age 21.

This bill sends a clear message to teenagers and their parents that driving is not a right. It's a privilege that has to be earned though responsible behavior.

I'd also like to point out that if we fail to adopt zero alcohol tolerance for young drivers by October of 1998, we will lose $16 million of our federal highway funds the first year, increasing to $32 million the second year.

As Governor, I have talked with many families whose loved ones were killed by drunk drivers—parents who have lost an infant or a teenager, children who have lost a father or mother.

I've talked with the family of a police officer who was run over and killed while on duty. Anyone who spends five minutes with any of these families, will understand why, for the seventh year in a row, I will bring you a bill to strengthen our DUI laws.

Like last year, this DUI bill has four parts: First, the nolo plea. Incredible as it may sound, a nolo plea, which is nothing but a way to get around admitting guilt, clears your criminal record and gets your suspended license back. If anyone other than a lawyer or a drunk can explain that to me, I'd like to hear it. And so would the general public. I am proposing that even with a nolo plea, your driver's license remains suspended for the time provided by law.

Second, provide for mandatory jail time—at least 24 hours for the first offense and 72 hours for the second.

So many things I've brought to you over the years have come from my long life of hard knocks and experience. I know what it's like to grow up in a single-parent family, because I did.

I know it's possible to learn some "corps" values at boot camp, because I did. I know what it's like to want to go to college and get a special scholarship that makes it possible, because the G.I. Bill did it for me. I also know what it's like to spend the night in jail on a drunk charge, because I've done that, too.

So again, this old voice of experience who's been there and done that, says: Put those drunks in jail and let them see what it's like; let them discover how miserable and degrading it is, and how good that sunlight feels and how good that fresh air smells the next morning.

Third, once again I propose we impound the license plates from the vehicles of habitual offenders, since taking their driver's licenses isn't enough to keep these dangerous, unguided missiles off the road.

And fourth, privatizing the use of interlock ignition systems as a condition of probation.

These systems that keep someone who's drunk from starting up that unguided missile, have proved effective in other states, but are getting little use in Georgia because cities and counties are required to buy the equipment.

Innocent Georgians are being slaughtered on our highways; Georgia families are being cruelly ripped apart by drunk driving. Georgia's DUI laws are still nowhere near tough enough.

With every ounce of my being, I beg you to put aside partisan interests, give up the defense of legal loopholes, and give Georgia's citizens the protection they need and deserve.

Probably the best news for our families today is that 3.6 million Georgians have jobs—more than at any time in our history. We've seen phenomenal job growth—an average of over 2,000 new jobs a week since 1990. Last year industrial investments totaling nearly $6.3 billion were announced in Georgia. They will create over 33,000 jobs. According to *Forbes Magazine*, Georgia has created more new jobs than all but two other states. And a recent report by Dun & Bradstreet said that Georgia is "the biggest winner (ranked #1) in the battle to retain companies and jobs."

Dun & Bradstreet attributes much of our success to Georgia's "moderate tax rate," and during this administration, we have cut taxes for Georgia's families. First giving them a break on their state income tax and now removing the state sales tax from groceries. The third cent will come off in October, and the final cent next year.

There's no question that our Department of Industry, Trade and Tourism has done a significant job in this expanding economic development. But like all of us, they can always do better. So we are going to reorganize the Department to continue improving coordination among our economic development initiatives.

The state was a partner in the public-private Operation Legacy, which used the leverage of the Olympics to bring CEOs from more than 400 companies around the nation to Georgia. So far, 18 new locations have resulted from this effort, creating over 3,000 jobs. I want to continue Operation Legacy as a public-private partnership under auspices of a stronger state industry marketing effort in the Department of Industry, Trade and Tourism.

I also propose that we bring the Governor's Development Council under the Industry and Trade umbrella in a new Strategic Planning and Research Division. We will continue to encourage regional planning initiatives, with a $2.5 million grant program that supports multi-county, regional collaboration for economic development.

Despite all of this economic growth and all the new jobs, we still have too many Georgia families that are unemployed and need help. We are going to do that with a completely new welfare program that began two weeks ago on January 1st. It is called Temporary Assistance for Needy Families, or TANF.

We are going to stop the decades-old practice of simply putting checks in the mail, month after month, year after year, in some cases generation after generation. Cash assistance in Georgia will be limited to a total of four years.

Instead, we are going to focus on two things: One, helping people get the skills for the jobs they need to become self-sufficient and support their families. And two, pregnancy prevention, especially among teenagers. We are going to provide assistance with transportation and other needed support services to help recipients find and hold down jobs. We are going to require teen mothers to stay in school, and we will provide child care for their babies. And we are going to target adult recipients under age 26 with assistance to complete their GED. Parents will be required to take an active role in their children's education, making sure they attend school and participating in parent-teacher conferences.

It's a tough approach, but it is also a hopeful approach. We're saying to those on welfare, we have faith that you can work and be self-sufficient just like the rest of us.

We began restructuring our welfare program in Georgia some time ago to put more emphasis on work. I reported to you in last year's State of the State, for example, that the Macon DFACS office at that time was steering more than a third of its welfare applicants into jobs rather than onto the welfare rolls. Our WorkFirst program has already reduced our welfare rolls by 20,000 families over the past four years, saving taxpayers $52 million. So we're already farther along in this respect than many other states.

In addition to helping people get the skills they need for productive employment, the second major thrust of TANF is pregnancy prevention, especially among teenagers. It takes only a few broad brush strokes to paint a picture that explains why the problem of teen pregnancy has grown so disturbing, and it goes to the heart of the family. The common denominator you find among pregnant teens, rich or poor, from all different socio-economic categories, is the absence of a father in that teenager's home.

Second, even if we could wave a magic wand and render every single teenage male in Georgia sterile, it would reduce teen pregnancy by only 25 percent. Third, fully 60 percent of the girls who have had sex before age 15 say they were pressured into it against their will. The old traditional stereotype of two kids getting carried away in the backseat of a car no longer holds. Too many of our teenage girls are emotionally vulnerable because they have no father at home. And this is very important—they are being exploited by men in their 20s and 30s. In general, the younger the girl, the greater the age gap between her and the father of her baby.

That is why I worked so hard last year to pass a law requiring a minimum prison sentence of 10 years for anyone who is 21 or older and has sexual relations with a child under age 16. It's also why we are working so hard to identify fathers and force them to support their children.

This year, we are going to approach the problem of teen pregnancy from another angle as we reform Georgia's welfare program. The plain fact is we have a lot of sexually active teenagers out there who, if they become pregnant, will go on the welfare rolls. And once they get on the rolls, unwed teenage mothers tend to stay on the rolls significantly longer than average. Pregnancy prevention is welfare prevention. It is that simple.

TANF includes five initiatives to combat teen pregnancy. The first is to create 15 clinics in non-traditional sites, like DFACS offices, substance abuse centers, and even housing projects.

They will be concentrated in communities that have a combination of high teen pregnancy rates and high welfare caseloads. I also want to expand the family planning services in county health departments, and we are going to fund more outreach and mentoring workers at the county level.

Finally, we are going to expand two successful, community-based pregnancy prevention programs. One is targeted at teenage males, and it is already in operation in 15 Georgia communities. The other is Grady Hospital's abstinence-based program for teens called "Postponing Sexual Involvement."

These changes are the beginning of a whole new era of welfare in Georgia. It is a long overdue change, and it is an opportunity to make an historic turn-around... ending welfare as we know it and creating a program that works to the benefit of its recipients and the satisfaction of the taxpayers who foot the bill for it.

As Shirley and I celebrate our 43rd anniversary today, I think of the many Georgia families who are not as fortunate, because they are being torn apart by domestic violence—violence of spouse against spouse, parent against child, child against parent. It happens more than 15,000 times a year in Georgia. Last year there were over 30 fatalities.

Far too often judges let them off with a slap on the wrist for inflicting serious injury—broken bones, even permanent disabilities. I'm tired of allowing people to regard their own family as possessions that they can knock around as they wish in the privacy of their home.

Last year we passed our very first criminal family violence law, recognizing "family violence battery" as a misdemeanor. That was a step in the right direction, but it was only a baby step toward where we really need to be.

I have another bill to recognize the family violence crimes of assault, aggravated assault, and aggravated battery, in addition to the "family violence battery" we created last year. It provides for stronger penalties, requiring mandatory jail time ranging from five days to five years, depending on the severity of the act and the number of prior offenses.

You always hear the argument that mandatory minimum sentences interfere with a judge's discretion, and that may be true for some things. But family violence is so volatile and unpredictable, and I believe we need a mandatory minimum sentence, even if it is only a short time for the first offense, to get the attention of those who abuse their own families.

Family violence is one of the factors that has brought nearly 17,000 foster children into state custody. The pressure is unrelenting to find more foster care placements, often with little advance notice. But the urgency of placing children coming into foster care, often keeps us from giving enough attention to getting children out of foster care as they become eligible for adoption.

As a result, too many children are stuck in foster care for too long, and too many of them end up being "aged out" of the foster-care system as teenagers. They are left to navigate life completely on their own with no home or family, and many of them end up in shelters for the homeless.

As a short-term response, foster care is absolutely essential, and we are deeply grateful for the families who provide it. But it should not end up being any human being's entire childhood. That's why we've created a separate Office of Adoptions within the Department of Human Resources, and on Thursday, I am going to tell you about several initiatives to promote adoption and assist foster children who are "aged out" of the system.

As the Millers look ahead to a new arrival next month, we are praying, like all families, for a healthy baby. But, like all families, if there is a problem, we want to find out about it as quickly as possible. So I'm asking you to expand my Children First Program, which we started with your help in 1992 to screen newborn babies. Right now we are screening about a third of our newborns for problems that put their health and development at risk.

I want to screen every baby born in this state to ensure that we identify at birth every at-risk child. Then we will track them from birth until they enter prekindergarten at age four. Medical research clearly shows that those first three years, when a lot of crucial developments occur, have a long-lasting impact on a child's health, well-being, and ability to learn.

Identifying at-risk newborns, and then tracking them to make sure they get the special services they need during those critical early years, is a wise and humane investment. It will enable our children to grow up healthy and ready for school, and it will save us a lot of money in the coming years.

One of the most pressing concerns of Georgia's families today, and one of the most important responsibilities of state government, is public safety. The first thing I want to say on this subject is that I hope you will immediately pass a bill that I will bring to you to fix the "two strikes" law. Last year legislation was passed that unintentionally removed rape and aggravated sodomy from the list of violent crimes under the two strikes law. This bill will restore them.

Georgia has been among the states who have led the way in enacting legislation on child support collection, sex offender notification, and victim compensation. Widespread action by the states is now being reflected by new federal laws in these three areas, and I will bring you bills to bring Georgia's state laws into conformity with federal law, providing for seamless enforcement.

Above and beyond the legal requirements for public notification about sex offenders, I want to announce today that Georgia is establishing a state-of-the-art, automated calling center for registered victims of all kinds of crimes. It is called VINE, which stands for Victim Information and Notification Everyday.

Whenever an offender is released, the system will automatically call all of the registered victims of that inmate. It works the other direction, too. Any registered victim can call in at any time from any phone and get a status report on their offender. It gives Georgia's victims a chance to be pro-active in protecting themselves and their families.

Illegal drugs continue to be a significant problem for too many of our families, and I believe we need to become as creative in our approaches as drug dealers are if we are to stem the tide. So I'm going to ask you to pass a drug dealer liability law. I want Georgians who are harmed by illegal drugs to be able to sue the drug dealers who lit the fuse that resulted in the damage, and not only the person who actually used the drugs, but also their parents, spouses or children, their employer, and even the medical facilities who treat them. I believe all of them ought to be able to sue drug dealers to recover their costs. This could be a start to shifting the huge cost of the damage caused by illegal drugs, back onto the dealers who are profiting from the sale of the stuff.

The other side of the coin from passing public safety laws, is dealing with the convicted offenders, and I welcome this opportunity to say a few words about that. If there is any one clear message from the citizens of Georgia, it is that they do not want us to coddle criminals, and the Miller Administration is not going to. This is a governor who believes that the root cause of crime is criminals.

Today, you can enter a Georgia prison, and you will find the inmates clean-shaven and orderly, their cells and dormitories Spartan, and the facilities neat. You will not find a cleaner place in the state. I've seen floors you could eat off of. But today it would have to be a cold sandwich at lunch. Regular searches have sent a clear message to inmates that weapons and contraband simply will not be tolerated, and if you want to tear up property, you have to pay for it. We have also ended the process of letting criminals out of prison to go have a good time just because a holiday has come along.

The Medical College of Georgia is going to begin providing inmate medical care. Their sophisticated telemedicine system will save taxpayers the cost of unnecessary transportation of prisoners. The money we spend for inmate health care will stay in Georgia and be reinvested in medical education.

Taxpayers have benefited from a law, which you passed last year, to assess inmates a $5 fee to see a doctor or dentist. If it's an emergency, or they are indigent, or the prison staff orders them to go, then it's free. This has really cut back on the number of those claiming to be sick to avoid work detail.

Our prison inmates rise early in the morning, and walk four and a-half miles. Then they work eight-hour days, and in the evening they may work on their GED. For several years, some prisons have had teachers on the staff, some costing up to $82,000 a year, working during the regular day.

However, as I just pointed out, under this administration every able-bodied inmate is out working all day. Very few inmates are around to take their classes. So we are reorganizing our prison education program to contract with teachers to provide evening classes. And we are going to augment their efforts with distance learning technology. This change will greatly expand the number of inmates who receive basic education, and at the same time save $8 million for our taxpayers.

We have also privatized the constitutionally mandated responsibility to provide legal services to indigent inmates. In doing so, we have saved taxpayers $600,000 a year with no reduction in the quality of legal services.

What is wrong with all that I have just described? I don't think anything is. Unfortunately, there are a number of folks—some of them well-meaning—who want us to treat criminals like victims, and victims like criminals.

The truth of the matter is that despite more inmates than ever before, escapes are down, use of force to restrain violent prisoners is down, and complaints by inmates about prison staff are down. That's the bottom line, and Wayne Garner is responsible. I support him; I'll bet your constituents support him, and you should support him, too.

There's always room for improvement, and I welcome your help. I won't oppose the 100 percent or 85 percent, or whatever you want to do to make the sentences longer. But if you're looking for a criminal justice issue—make sure you look in both directions. For violent crimes in this state, there is less than a 50 percent arrest rate. And for property crimes, like burglary, and robbery, the arrest rate is only about 15 percent!

Folks, you can't have a prisoner to parole if there's never even been an arrest. Until this problem is dealt with, there will continue to be places in Georgia where one cannot walk or live without fear. And the voters at the coffee clatches and Rotary clubs will still be complaining.

Georgians also care about the natural environment. And I want to mention two issues briefly. First, I am going to bring you a bill to create a Coastal Zone Management Program. Georgia is the only ocean-front state that does not participate in this 24-year-old program. It would bring additional federal funding into our state to help protect our natural resources, and it would give us more authority to review and approve federal activity along our coast. No matter what anybody tells you, it will not add any new restrictions or bureaucratic layers, but instead would require greater cooperation among existing agencies and programs.

Then second, an issue we have been dealing with for several years—the allocation of water among Georgia, Alabama, and Florida. We three states have been in formal negotiations for some time now, and we have come up with two interstate water compacts: One between Alabama and Georgia for the Coosa, Tallapoosa, and Alabama River Basins, and one among Georgia, Alabama, and Florida for the Chattahoochee, Flint and Apalachicola River Basins.

These compacts are now before the state legislatures of each of these states for ratification, and since we do not have a compact to provide for interstate conference committees, they can only be adopted without change. I believe these compacts are fair to all the states involved and protect Georgia's interests. I join with the Speaker and Lieutenant Governor in asking for your support and early passage of these compacts.

I would also like to thank Speaker Newt Gingrich publicly, as I have privately, for his crucial help with these compacts. What he did Saturday was incredible, and I'm deeply grateful. Our Attorney General Mike Bowers has also been of tremendous help. This is truly a bi-partisan effort.

I know I've been talking a long time. And I've only mentioned briefly the issue I care most about—the passion of the Miller Administration—education. It comes back to the family again. Parents are their children's first teachers, and we must never forget it. Then our schools become partners with parents in helping our children grow and learn.

One of my goals for education, as you already know, is to make Georgia's teacher salaries competitive on the national market, so that we can hire and keep the best teachers possible for our kids. I made a commitment to provide a six percent salary increase for Georgia's teachers every year for four consecutive years. My goal was to put Georgia's teacher salaries at the top of the region and at the national average.

With your help, we have already enacted the first two increases. We are passing other states, and we are on track to achieve our goal to be able to compete nationally for outstanding teachers. With your support, we are going to continue.

I'm going to talk more about my goals for education and how the budget moves us toward them on Thursday. So until then, I'll close by saying that I want and need your help. For some of you, we've been together a long time. I've enjoyed the ride with you; it's been a good one, and we'll soon be getting off this old highway up at the next exit ramp.

You've probably already found out, as I have, that as life shortens, misgivings magnify. Let's not miss this opportunity, and later be sorry we did. For those of you whose exit is way on up the road, but who have worked with me for a few sessions, I want to say thank you. We've made an enormous difference. Together we've made some landmark decisions, and we now have the opportunity to further that progress.

For those of you who are just starting out, I want to draw your attention to the bipartisanship that has accompanied some of our most significant accomplishments in recent years. I want very much for that spirit to continue, and I will bend over backwards to do my part. Jean Monnet once said that all people of great achievement are ambitious. But the key question is whether they are ambitious to be, or ambitious to do.

My friends, please join me in being ambitious to do.

# Budget Address, Fiscal Year 1998

*January 16, 1997*

If this speech had a title, it would be "A Forced March to Reality," and if it had a musical score, it would be "The Bridge on the River Kwai"—not to be confused with the bridge to the 21st century.

Tuesday, I reported that the State of the State is great. Jobs are up, unemployment is down. Our economy is strong, at least by comparison to most everybody else's. Today I am pleased to add that state government's finances are equally sound. But I also want to emphasize to you that it didn't just happen. And it will not stay that way unless we are vigilant. Left to their own devices, expenditures never creep down. They always creep up, especially in government, where there is rarely competition to provide an incentive to hold them down. The only reason the state's finances are in good shape today, is because we have deliberately worked over the years to keep them that way, especially the last six years.

When I became Governor, I was faced with a slowing economy and no money at all in the state reserves. We began "a forced march to reality," and we have kept right on marching—right through the budget that is before you today. Until the day I leave office, we will still be marching, because the citizens of Georgia need and want better services from government on the things that are important to them. But right now they are not willing to pay more taxes to get those services, because they do not believe they are getting maximum benefit for the taxes they already pay. So we are constantly focusing our attention on the results we want to accomplish with those tax dollars.

In this administration, we do that with a process called "budget redirection." Every year, I require each department head to evaluate their ongoing programs, and identify at least five percent of their budget to be cut from low priorities and redirected to high priorities. Once they identify that five percent, they don't always get to keep it in their department. There might be a higher priority somewhere else.

Last year, we used budget redirection to shift nearly $600 million. This year we are redirecting another $350 million. That is almost a billion dollars in cuts across two budgets, that were redirected to other uses. This is how we have been able to make significant, long-term investments in education and economic development, while at the same time cutting taxes.

We also continue to privatize aspects of state government that ought to be in the private sector or can be done more efficiently by outsourcing them. Our very first initiative—the War Veterans Home in Milledgeville—is successfully saving taxpayers $7 million a year. The resort hotel and water park at Lake Lanier Islands is now under private operation, and will bring more than $315 million into the state treasury over the course of the lease. Bids are about to be awarded for two private prisons in Wheeler and Coffee Counties, which will save millions each year.

But I didn't want to do privatization just to save money, I wanted to change the culture of state government. When it makes sense and saves money to privatize something or to outsource support services, that should be standard operating procedure. It should not take a special privatization commission to do it.

We are also reforming welfare and Medicaid, which both involve massive amounts of our taxpayers' money. On Tuesday I described how we are overhauling welfare to make it do more, and I'm going to get back to it again a little later in this speech.

In Medicaid, we are implementing some of the recommendations of the Georgia Coalition for Health in this budget, and we are aggressively seeking out fraud. We have convicted 40 Medicaid providers for fraud, and 30 more providers have been indicted and are awaiting trial. We've scared the hell out of some folks, and you can see it in a noticeable drop in their billings.

Fraud and abuse in this program were rampant. I happen to think that it is an issue that deserves national attention. Increased access to health care is important—we all know that—but so is cost containment. It is another "forced march to reality."

We are also re-examining our reimbursement rates, and moving toward managed care, which is quality care at a lower cost. As a result, we have flat-lined the Medicaid budget. That is significant, because Medicaid used to be the Pac-Man of the budget, consuming more than its fair share of available funds, and taking up an ever larger portion of our budget.

We have also flat-lined the growth of state employees. If you exclude bed growth in Corrections and for juvenile offenders, the number of state employees is down 2 percent since I became Governor. It had been increasing at a rate of 10 percent every two years before I took office.

Most of our taxpayers are scrimping and saving to make ends meet. They've got dreams of what they'd like to accomplish with the money they earn. We have no right to take any more money from them than we need to give them the results they are looking for. So as we have made state government more efficient, we have cut more taxes. We have cut taxes by a total of nearly $700 million during this administration.

Right now, we continue to remove the state sales tax from groceries—not only the biggest tax cut in Georgia history, but one of the largest tax cuts by any state in recent years. The budget before you today accounts for the cost of removing the third cent of sales tax on October 1, and the supplemental budget sets aside an additional $129 million to cover the cost of the fourth and final cent next year. So the money is now in the bank to cover the full cost of this tax cut.

Speaking of money in the bank, we have rebuilt our reserves from absolutely zero when I took office, to nearly $550 million. We have steadily built up our Revenue Shortfall Reserve, which is our "rainy day fund," from zero to a full statutory balance of $313 million. It has taken discipline to set that money aside, but our "forced march to reality" kept us on track. Today our reserves include not only the rainy-day fund and the Midyear Adjustment Reserve, but also two lottery reserves. If we really and truly are fiscally responsible, as we like to say we are, we will establish a $12 million reserve for our new state welfare program. I intend to leave all of these reserves completely full for the next Governor.

The strong management we have exercised enables us to emphasize the state's top priorities in the budget for Fiscal Year 1998. Its total of $11.8 billion represents only a

4.6 percent growth rate over the FY 97 budget. It includes a $508 million bond package that keeps our debt ratio at about half of our Constitutional limit, where we have kept it for years, and is consistent with the criteria of the Debt Management Advisory Committee.

The most important priority for our future is education. So let me start there. Georgia's lottery continues to provide a significant source of revenue—to date, more than $2 billion. On Tuesday I told you about the incredible national and international attention our prekindergarten program is generating, and when you open your budget today, you will find lottery funds to keep it at around 60,000 children.

Since the HOPE Scholarship Program began in September 1993, it has benefitted 234,000 Georgia students at a cost of $291 million. Students who did not have a B average or did not go to college straight from high school have been able to earn a HOPE scholarship by compiling a B average over 90 quarter hours, or two years of academic work. With this budget, I propose reducing that to 45 hours, or one year.

Of the technology funds, close to $40 million, which is $30 per FTE, will go to local schools to be used at their discretion either for equipment or technology training for teachers. Another $25 million will provide teacher technology training for our schools.

Georgia's lottery for education has become a national model not only because of what it has done, but also because of what it has not done. It has not supplanted any general fund money for education. In fact, at the same time we have been implementing these lottery programs that are the envy of so many states, we have also been increasing not only the general fund dollars going for education, but the proportion of the budget we devote to it. In FY 94, when the lottery started, we were devoting 50.1 percent of the budget to education. In the budget before you today, nearly 54 percent of the general funds are devoted to education. Then the lottery is on top of that.

Of course, this budget contains the third six percent salary increase for teachers, keeping us on track to make Georgia first in the Southeast and competitive on the national market. Remember, the whole point of raising salaries is to have the best teachers in our classrooms.

Continued enrollment growth in our schools means we need to add $116 million to the Quality Basic Education formula.

And I want to make a more deliberate effort to tackle one of the toughest problems we've got in education in Georgia: dropouts. Most educators will tell you that today you can spot a potential dropout by the third or fourth grade. Prekindergarten is going to help with that, because our children will enter school ready to learn. And they will be less likely to fall behind early. But in the meantime, I want to do something about the students who are falling by the wayside.

Very few dropouts stop to consider how it will affect their future life. Our challenge is to find a firm but gentle way to send a wake-up call to those students and to their parents. To make them stop and think about what they are doing. I'm ready to try just about anything to see what might work.

In Oregon, they have a dropout diploma that the students and their parents sign that reads: "By signing this disclaimer, I show that I realize I will not have the necessary skills to survive in the 21st century." In North Carolina, Governor Jim Hunt last week had a high school student at his inauguration who had instituted a "no dropout pact" with his ninth grade classmates.

We have got to have more information about what happens to these kids. Do they find a job sometimes? Are they just hanging out on the streets? What's the time frame before some of them end up in our criminal justice system? How many of them quickly see the light and begin to work on a GED? We know that half of the GEDs earned in this state go to Georgians under age 24.

Georgia is fortunate to have a lot of retired military personnel living in our state. They could be a lot of help with these youngsters, working with them on a part-time basis. And I still like the idea of the governor or a legislator showing enough interest to be personally involved in these young lives. We need some answers. So, I want to pilot a dropout prevention program in eight school systems, which will be laboratories where we can try out innovative ideas.

Superintendent Schrenko proposed that we redirect $60 million in existing funds within the QBE formula, to reduce the class size in our high schools from 23 students to 20 students. I agree that this is a good idea. Another $5.3 million is for a new school data system, so that when we redirect existing money to fund a high school class size of 20 students, as we're proposing, we can follow up and find out whether class size actually goes down in our local schools, or whether that money gets sidetracked somewhere along the way, which I have a sneaking suspicion it does.

Then in the University System budget you will find $2 million for a new initiative called Partners in Success. None of us—not you nor I—like having to spend money on remedial education. It's paying for something we already paid for once. This program will reach down into our high schools to improve students' readiness and reduce the need for remedial work after they get to college.

An economics professor at the University of Illinois recently posed this question: Which investment pays a better return on the dollar—a 30-year treasury bond or a college student? If you said a college student, you're right. That is why I believe education is the best economic policy there is.

My goal as Governor has been to create a culture of higher expectations in this state. I want the question for our students to be not "whether" to go to college or technical school, but "where" to go. Thanks to the HOPE Scholarship Program, that is possible.

We now have the fourth largest university system in the nation, and it continues to grow. So the budget adds $23.5 million to the system's funding formula for enrollment growth. We also need space on our campuses to put all these students. So in next year's budget, I am recommending $126 million in bonds for 20 construction projects at 17 campuses, which will bring University System construction to nearly a billion dollars in this administration.

The marriage of education and technology is where the future lies. Our massive electronic library called GALILEO, already provides a cost-effective way for units of the University System to share library resources. Then it provides access to those resources for all our technical institutes and all our regional public libraries. GALILEO has been getting heavy usage. In November, it marked its one-millionth log-in.

In this computer age, I think we've got to expand access beyond GALILEO. So I propose to make Internet access available to every single one of our K-12 schools—from Waleska to Willacoochee—all 1,818 of them hooked up to the Internet. Also all 157 public libraries, all technical institutes and all public colleges and universities in Georgia. Through the PeachNet computer network of our University System, even the smallest and most remote school or library will have access not only to GALILEO, but also to the other resources available on the Internet. We're talking about something historic here. It is a coordinated attempt by all of our educational systems to work together and provide equal and systematic access to the Internet.

In addition, I am recommending $8 million in lottery and general funds to upgrade technology in the University System and to provide training for future classroom teachers and faculty members to use it well.

Georgia's University System has become a national trend setter in building economic development partnerships with private sector business, and the Georgia Research Alliance is an economic development partnership that is producing results. Since the Research Alliance was formed in 1990, sponsored research at its six member universities has nearly doubled. The number of Georgia firms sponsoring research has increased by almost four-fold. Time and time again as I recruit industry and talk with CEOs around the world, I've seen the assets of the Research Alliance make a big difference. So in addition to the lottery-financed labs in the supplemental budget, I want to provide for two more eminent research scholars in the big budget.

Textiles, forestry, and food processing have been the backbone of our manufacturing economy, and with a little help they can continue to thrive in the high-tech economy of the future. So you will find a total of $8.4 million for our Traditional Industries Research program, which serves them.

Our economic development partnership called ICAPP—the Intellectual Capital Partnership Program—is the first of its kind in the nation. It identifies specific workforce needs in specific Georgia communities, then focuses University System resources on educating Georgians for those jobs. ICAPP is helping Columbus meet a greater workforce demand for computer analysts, and is helping Augusta residents laid off from the Savannah River plant.

Our technical institutes also make a significant contribution to our economy. Of last year's tech school graduates, 83 percent went straight into jobs that were directly related to their program of study. Most of the rest went on to further education. Enrollment of credit students at our tech schools has increased by nearly 50 percent in the past six years. It is now at an all-time high of more than 43,000 students.

We are in the final stages of the most extensive technical education expansion in Georgia history, and with the completion of the facilities that are presently under construction, Georgia will have a technical school within a 40-minute drive of every citizen in the state. This kind of access, in combination with the HOPE Scholarship Program, gives every Georgian the opportunity to learn a skill and prepare to join our growing, educated workforce. Over the next two years, I want to bring the local tech schools in Atlanta and Savannah into the state system.

Over the course of this administration, Georgia has become one of the top states in the nation in the number of GEDs our citizens are earning. Shirley's worked hard on adult literacy, and I'm proud of her efforts. More than 20,000 Georgia citizens now get their GEDs every year.

More and more Georgians are finding from personal experience that what you learn determines what you earn. This budget completes a three-year initiative to put an adult literacy teacher and computer lab in every county in Georgia.

Sooner or later in politics, the obvious becomes apparent. That is what has happened with welfare in this country. So as of January 1st, the old AFDC entitlement program in Georgia was completely replaced by a new program called Temporary Assistance for Needy Families, or TANF. Michael Thurmond has done a superb job in developing this program that concentrates on helping people get the skills and jobs they need to become self-sufficient, and on pregnancy prevention, especially among teenagers.

The bottom-line expenditure of state funds is virtually unchanged. What changes, and changes drastically, is how that money is spent. We anticipate that the new TANF program, combined with our WorkFirst program, will continue to reduce the welfare rolls, and the money that is freed up will be used for the programs I described to you Tuesday.

More than $16 million will be added to enhance the education, job training and job placement efforts as part of our welfare reform. The pregnancy prevention initiatives begin in the supplemental budget, and continue with $3.5 million in this budget. And for the first time, $1 million from our substance abuse block grant is dedicated to get pregnant and postpartum welfare recipients off of drugs. $2.7 million will strengthen child support enforcement. Georgia has doubled our annual child support collections over the course of this administration. It doesn't solve the welfare problem, but it helps.

Unlike most states, Georgia was ahead of the curve in the increases we have been providing for child care to enable recipients to attend school or work. We are in the enviable position of already having enough resources committed for child care at least through the budget that is before you. But I am recommending $3.5 million in this budget to give county-level DFACS offices the staff they need to monitor this child care, and make sure quality care is reaching the families who really need it.

Our federal funding for welfare is capped under the new block grant. It will not go above a certain level. As I have already said, I believe it is fiscally responsible to create a $12 million reserve. That federal cap also means that we cannot afford to waste any of our welfare funds, or have recipients who abuse or take advantage of the assistance they receive. I, like you, want to ferret out and track down fraud and abuse. So this budget includes $1.7 million for 50 new welfare investigators to double our efforts.

On Tuesday I explained why the State of Georgia needs to be more pro-active in encouraging the adoption of more than 1,000 of our foster children who are eligible. Today I'm going to tell you how we do it. I propose $1.2 million to contract with private adoption agencies for the placement of children. Then to make adoption possible for more families, I want to increase the adoption supplement per diem to the same level as for foster children—$10.50 per day—for families who need financial assistance to adopt a special-needs child.

Another $2.8 million in the supplemental budget will enable us to set up a statewide tracking system to keep up with the 17,000 children we have in state custody. Then for foster children who are "aged out" of the system, I recommend $1.5 million for an independent living service program to teach foster children age 16 and above the skills they need to manage on their own. The program would also assist foster children who want to go on to college but lack the financial support a family provides.

Mental health provides a great example of what budget redirection means. Too many of our severely emotionally disturbed children are being hospitalized, when they could be treated in the community if services were available. To date this administration has provided $17.6 million for community-based SED services—including $1.4 million in this budget to complete Phase One services in Whitfield, Walker, Sumter, Emanuel, and Bulloch County service areas.

We also have chronically mentally ill patients in our state psychiatric hospitals who could be treated in their own communities, with better result to them and lower cost to taxpayers. In the supplemental budget, I propose that we redirect $14.7 million from hospital-based services to community based services, fully funding CMI core services in Gwinnett Clarke and Thomas County services areas, and expanding services in seven other areas.

Our shift to community-based services is also reflected in my proposal to close the Brook Run institution. I know how controversial and emotional this issue is. But if you look at the hard question of what's best for the most people, I do not see how you can help but agree. To keep Brook Run operating, with its heavy cost, really keeps many of those who need help right now from getting it. Basically, we can take the same level of funding and serve over 500 individuals in the community, compared to only 326 at Brook Run.

Public safety is an important area where our citizens are looking for results, and we continue our quest to keep violent criminals behind bars for a long, long time. Our "forced march to reality" through budget redirection is helping us achieve this goal. Across the remainder of this fiscal year and into next fiscal year, we are going to open more than 3,800 new prison beds.

In addition to expansions at five existing prisons, we are increasing the capacity of our existing prisons by double bunking cells that have been single-bunked, which is giving us more than 1,800 new beds without the cost of building anything. You will see, it costs only $2.5 million in operating funds to make these additional beds available.

One of the most alarming aspects of corrections is the surge we are seeing in violent crime by teenagers and even younger children. The number of juvenile offenders coming into DCYS custody has more than doubled in just the past five years. It has created incredible stresses and challenges for our Department of Children and Youth Services, which by the way we propose to rename the Department of Juvenile Justice. Gene Walker has done an outstanding job, as I knew he would.

We have to provide bed space for these troubled kids. So I am asking you to fund 611 new beds, bringing our total capacity to almost 4,000 beds, and I want to move forward with the new Youth Development Center in Sumter County, and an expansion at the Macon YDC.

For the GBI, I want to help local law enforcement officers fight crime by giving them access to crime labs on a regional basis. I propose upgrading and expanding our facilities in Columbus and Macon. The Macon expansion will include a morgue, which will give us four sites with autopsy capacity—one each in north, south and middle Georgia in addition to Atlanta.

I also want to expand our DNA database for sexual assault cases, establish a statewide registry of violent sexual offenders, and notify local authorities when they are released from prison.

Each and every day, I focus a lot of my attention on economic development and creating jobs. Education is important; we all agree on that. So is a good transportation system, and we have one of the best. Few states have the network of airports that we do—not just the world-class Hartsfield, but all over Georgia—and our highway system, for two years in a row, has been rated first in the nation by The Road Information Program in Washington, D.C.

We've got to keep investing in it. I am proposing another $110 million in bonds to continue our work on the economic development highway network. Then $28.5 million in motor fuel tax revenues is for the off-system State Fund Construction Program.

The DOT budget also includes $3.2 million for upkeep of the dredged areas of the Savannah Harbor, which brings us to another critical piece of our transportation and economic development infrastructure—our ports at Savannah and Brunswick. The Port of Savannah is one of the premier ports on the Atlantic coast, with service by more than 50 different international shipping lines. Last year over 13 million tons of cargo moved through that port. I am recommending $27.8 million in bonds to purchase two more cranes and expand Berth 13 at Ocean Terminal in Savannah. As usual, the Ports Authority will pay the principal and interest on these bonds.

Talking about creating jobs, I want to say this: Across this country, the convention industry is very competitive. If we want to remain one of the nation's leading convention destinations and keep those jobs that go with it, we must plan ahead. Several of our regular trade shows have now outgrown our existing space, and may soon be moving elsewhere. So you will find $10.5 million in the budget to plan and design Phase Four of the World Congress Center.

This expansion will attract half a million additional visitors to Georgia each year. It will have an economic impact of $1 billion, generate tax revenues of $53 million, and mean up to 19,000 new jobs. So, folks, you may do with this what you wish. But for me it boils down to this: Either we protect our investment and capture these additional economic benefits for Georgia, or we pull the plug on our convention industry and lose its economic benefits to our competitors.

In the area of natural resources, I am proud to report that Preservation 2000 achieved its goal of preserving 100,000 acres of natural land. We have now turned our attention to the streams and rivers which are a critical, but vulnerable natural resource. I created RiverCare 2000 to acquire sensitive river-corridor properties, and work together with local communities and private landowners to improve the management of this critical resource. Under natural resources, you will find a proposal of $10 million in bonds to continue our acquisition of natural land in our river corridors.

In addition, we need to devote $1.4 million to establishing adequate total maximum daily loads for 423 segments of our rivers and streams. This addresses a court ruling against the federal Environmental Protection Agency.

I've talked a lot about what we are going to do with state revenues in this budget. Let me talk just a little about collecting those revenues. Our taxpayers expect us to be efficient and effective in what we do with their money. They also expect us to be efficient and effective in collecting their money and making sure all taxpayers pay their fair share.

The problems that have emerged in recent years in the Revenue Department make it clear that our management structure and processing systems have fallen behind the times. So last summer I created a public-private steering committee of business and government executives for the overhaul of this department. We hired the nationally respected firm of KPMG Peat Marwick to give us a long-term "Blueprint for Modernization." They will complete this study next month.

It is already clear that we need significant changes in management approaches, technology, workforce preparation within the Department and privatization of several functions. The complete overhaul will take several years, and it is going to require a significant expenditure of funds. The supplemental budget includes the first installment of $15 million, and this budget for next year has another $6 million. It is a wise investment that will pay for itself through greater efficiency and more effective collection of back taxes. In fact, it will start paying for itself before it is even fully implemented, and will recover its entire cost soon after the changes are completed.

Thank you for listening to another long speech, and thank you for not "falling out" during the "forced march to reality." This march has not been a exercise for the timid and faint-hearted. It's not easy to resist the siren's song of simple answers. But we have discovered that tightening the belt is great for focusing the mind. Unlike some governmental entities, this state is not a "citadel of champagne wishes and caviar dreams." Rather, for us, it's a new day with a new way, and I believe the people of Georgia appreciate it.

# Armed Services Luncheon

*May 6, 1997*

This old Marine sergeant is proud to be here and pleased to join with you in honoring Celestine Sibley. She is a remarkable woman who keeps alive so many of our good southern qualities—a patriotic fervor for this great country of ours; a genuine, friendly interest in people; a love for words and ideas; a respect for history and traditions; a joy in the beauty of growing things, and a practical, down-home common sense. I am proud to be here with you to honor Celestine today and thank her for helping us to put things in perspective and remember what is really important in life.

I helped her put something in perspective once. We were doing a book signing together, and when it was scheduled to start, no one was there. Celestine smiled with her usual grace and said, "The worst thing in the world is to have a book signing and no one show up." To which I replied, "No, the worst thing in the world is to have a political campaign rally and no one show up." Knowing a great deal about both book signings and campaign rallies, Celestine knew exactly what I meant.

We are also here today, of course, to pay tribute too the men and women who serve and have served in our armed forces, and well we should. You have a rich and wonderful history that dates to earliest colonial times, and you have been essential in making this great nation what it is today.

It has been more than a century since a war was fought on American soil, but our men and women have stayed busy in other parts of the world, defending liberty, fighting aggression, and sometimes simply keeping the peace long enough for people who are at odds to find peace with each other. And I am proud to have this opportunity to thank you for what you mean, not only in the far corners of the world, but here at home.

Like many of you, I have just come from the dedication of "Sweet Eloise," the refurbished B-29 bomber that is going on display at Dobbins Air Force Base. It took me back to my earliest memories of America's armed services... to the early days of World War II. I remember Pearl Harbor. I was about ten years old when my mother brought my sister and me down out of the mountains, and went to work at the old Bell Bomber plant. Still hanging on the wall in the living room of our house in Young Harris today is a picture of a B-29 with the name "Birdie Miller" embossed on it—a gift of appreciation from the plant to my mother when the war was over and she took us back home to the mountains.

But my most vivid memories of the armed services, and the ones that continue to have a significant impact on my life to this day, are not those few years of childhood, but the few years I spent in the Marine Corps. I've written a little book about it called *Corps Values: Everything You Need to Know I Learned in the Marine Corps.*

In the course of one season of the calendar, boot camp turns sometimes aimless youth into proud and self-disciplined Marines who have well-honed senses of self-esteem and dedication to themselves, their mission, and their country. The differences of economic classes and prejudices of race and religion which they brought with them, have been transformed into respect for others and an ability to follow orders to achieve mutual goals.

Recently, our nation has been deluged with debates and oratory about the need for a renewal of "family values." This debate has been highlighted by some rather pointed and sometimes personal exchanges on what those values should be and how best to inculcate them into our children as guiding principles for successful lives. Whether it takes a "family" or a "village"—or, as I strongly believe, both—I do know that the values young people learn as part of growing up must be defined, refined, and etched into their personalities and characters.

I remember my trips onto and out of Parris Island as if they were yesterday. I recall with clarity the thoughts I had about what I learned and what I must do to make those values a positive force in my life thereafter, regardless of what course it might take. Those values are: neatness, punctuality, brotherhood, persistence, pride, respect, shame, responsibility, achievement, courage, discipline, and loyalty.

I believe these are values that should be common to all people regardless of the color of their skin, the tenets of their denomination, or the places of their residence. I submit it is the only basis upon which diversity can coexist with commonality, and all people can pursue individual goals for themselves while contributing to the general well-being and advancement of society as a whole.

Allow me to elaborate on two or three of these important values. Brotherhood: I am a living, breathing example of how the Corps refocuses the vision of the individual to the big picture of life and his place and mission in it. I was a "hillbilly" in the broadest sense of that derisive term. I came out of the Appalachian Mountains of North Georgia, an area of the purest Anglo-Saxon stock that can be found, and I had a harsh mountain twang to match.

The Marine Corps mixed me with young men of all types and classes—first-generation sons of immigrant parents who talked about growing up in "Sout Chicargo," products of the poverty of the Hamtramck part of Detroit, the disdainful youngsters of the "Big Apple" who never let anybody forget they were from "Noo Yack," blacks from the ghettos and white boys from Alabama, Georgia, and Mississippi who were still fighting the Civil War just like they learned from their granddaddies, Texans with double first names, Midwesterners who trusted everyone and New Englanders who trusted no one. We also had a few Hispanics and even two native Americans, who were called "Indians" then.

Our platoon was a microcosm of the entire United States of America, a little domestic melting pot housed in one crowded quonset hut. We were all in it together and it did not takes us long to get over our mutual suspicions of each other and realize that we were all going to sink or swim, perish or survive together. At that particular time in 1953, not a one of us probably had any notion of who Dr. Martin Luther King Jr., was. But even if we could not articulate the thought then, we would come to understand during the next 12 weeks what Dr. King meant when he later declared, "We must live together as brothers or perish together as fools."

Four decades have passed and the military services are now the most integrated part of America. In present-day society in this country, race is more polarized than it has ever been; and the military services are the best example we have where men and women are getting along and achieving side-by-side, regardless of skin color, racial origin, or cultural or religious background.

As one who has seen firsthand how integration works in the Marine Corps, I cannot help posing the question for myself and all citizens: Shouldn't that tell us something about the correctness of the way the military deals with the problem and the obviously wrong way that society-in-general is going about coping with it?

Respect: As harsh as it may sound, the only way I can describe the pervading philosophy of life which seems to motivate some of our younger citizens is "Hooray for me and to hell with you." Too many in our post-Cold-War society display a total lack of respect for anything and everything—self, peers, elders, superiors, society, government, law, and values—asking only, "What's in it for me?"

We see this attitude manifested every day in many ways—lack of respect for one's country, institutions, and the flag; lack of respect for one's parents and teachers; lack of respect for laws, be they speed limits or tax obligations; lack of respect for God and His Commandments; and in a number of other ways that allow one to feel good for the moment or to gain an unearned advantage over others.

If any one lesson drummed into the minds and hearts of recruits in Marine Corps boot camp could be characterized as paramount, it is that of demonstrating proper respect in every facet of human existence. The lesson begins with respect for authority which, in the case of the recruit, is the Drill Instructor, whose every word and inflection is to be heeded and acted upon, regardless of how the individual may feel about its wisdom or appropriateness.

It extends to the flag of our country—the symbol of freedom and opportunity for which millions have given their lives. The flag is not merely a piece of cloth to be used as clothing or desecrated by burning. It is the embodiment of the thousands of names on the Vietnam Wall, and the personification of my father who fought in World War I and the many friends of mine who were killed in Korea. I believe just as strongly that citizens should always stand at attention, place their right hands over their hearts and thank God for that flag and the nation for which it stands, just as I believe they should bow their heads, close their eyes, and join in the appropriate way for all prayers to Almighty God.

It is disgraceful enough when spectators in the stands at athletic events slouch, talk, and stuff their faces with hot dogs while the "Star Spangled Banner" is performed, but it is outrageous that the athletes on the field—the idols of our children and the spenders of the millions of our nation's dollars paid them for their sporting skills—do the same or worse. Disrespectors like basketball star Chris Jackson who refuse even to stand on such occasions, deserve to be booted out of the country which gave them the opportunity to rise from poverty to get college educations and make millions of American dollars.

To my mind, there can be no 50-50 Americans—only 100 percent Americans. Theodore Roosevelt, in a speech to the troops at Camp Union in 1917, declared, "The man who has not raised himself to be a soldier, and the woman who has not raised her boy to the a soldier, neither of them has the right or is entitled to the citizenship of the Republic." Harsh, but true!

Shame: Oh I can hear it now—the psycho-babble of those over-educated, well-meaning professionals whose reality quotient soars about 20,000 feet above *terra firma* as they analyze and condemn my "Neanderthal" views on the subject of shame. They will insist that I do not know what I am talking about and that my experiences as a child and a

Marine have warped my personality and distorted my views of life. Well-intentioned people will say that I want to bruise the tender egos of children and to thwart the efforts of experts trying to rehabilitate offenders by talking to them about how society has let them down, instead of teaching them that bad things happen to people who do bad things, and that the way to avoid having bad things happen to them is not to do bad things.

What objectors to using shame to promote desired standards of public conduct fail either to understand or to admit is that humiliation is a powerful motivational force. It was not the whipping at school, but the humiliation of receiving it, that once prompted good and acceptable conduct in public schools. Shame stings, and the sting stays with the individual so stung. I submit such stings are a powerful menas of shaping behavior.

While I am alarmed by what could happen in society of present trends continue to erode our values, I do believe with William Faulkner, who declared in his acceptance speech for the Nobel Prize in 1950, "I decline to accept the end of man." Man, said this Southern genius of the pen, alone among the creatures of the earth "has a soul, a spirit capable of compassion, sacrifice and endurance."

It is that distinction that I learned at Marine Corps boot camp. It is that distinction which I strongly believe will set those of us who care what happens to civilization back on the road of the pursuit of the basic values of life which I had to learn the hard way in boot camp.

There was a news photograph I recall from the days of college demonstrations against the Vietnam War which made an enduring impression upon my mind, one that I carried with me over the years and remember to this day. It was of a protesting student carrying a sign with the words, "Nothing is worth dying for." I did not believe that to be a true assessment of most Americans then, nor do I believe it to be accurate now. Surely, if there is nothing worth dying for in our America, then there is nothing worth living for here, either. If I did not believe that before going to Marine Corps boot camp, I most certainly was a believer after I graduated.

It is a truth I want to see indelibly impressed upon the hearts and minds of all young Americans growing up today. It is one which has kept me living, working, striving, and persevering over the years. And I am convinced it is one that will be the salvation of our nation and its coming generations if we will but impart its values to them now. Now, while there is yet time to save us as individuals and as a nation.

# Atlanta Regional Business Coalition

*May 8, 1997*

I am pleased to be here. I think. When I speak to a group, I like to propose solutions, promote ideas, be positive. But on the subject you are meeting on, I have none—at least none that I think are acceptable in this day and time. Nevertheless I want to begin by thanking you for joining with Ray in this Regional Business Coalition. You've got a very tough row to hoe, and Ray asked me to be pretty direct in talking about it, so I will. I think I already have.

I believe strongly that metro Atlanta today is at a critical juncture, and like you, I am extremely concerned about its future direction. So I want to commend you for coming together to form the Regional Business Coalition in an effort to seize the moment.

Last summer, we hosted the biggest peacetime event in world history—the 1996 Olympics. Millions came. Six out of every ten people in the world watched on television. They all now have a much better idea where Atlanta is. They can recognize some of our landmarks. They have something of a feel for what Atlanta is like. And as I have traveled on trade missions and met with international business leaders since the Olympics, I find that Atlanta is still vivid in their minds.

The question before us now, is how to capitalize on this vast international name recognition while we have it. What can we do to keep the name "Atlanta" from fading from the world's conversation? Or even worse, to keep from having a negative reputation as a place where economic development is stagnating because of our inability to deal with air and water quality or transportation.

The international name recognition that Atlanta still enjoys provides us with an opportunity to elevate our aim, and try to move this city to a higher plane. But to accomplish that—and this is why I sounded so pessimistic a minute ago, well, not really pessimistic but realistic—to accomplish that, narrow local agendas, racial politics, and turf-guarding are going to have to be dealt with. We've got to sit down together, and really talk and listen to one another. We've got to set a joint agenda for this region and work together to achieve it, and that is going to be very, very difficult.

There's an old country music song that goes, "Everybody wants to go to heaven, but nobody wants to die." Everybody wants metro Atlanta to be heaven. The real question is whether the will is there to put aside personal agendas and petty politics, and do what it takes to achieve that goal. That includes both the suburbs and the city. In this dance, I guarantee you, it takes two to tango, because if you don't have both the city and the suburbs at the table, I don't know how you're going to accomplish what you need to do. Believe me, I know that's easier said than done. So I'm going to tell you the exact same thing I tell my department heads: You cannot simply look out for your own interests to the exclusion of the bigger picture. If you do, you're doomed from the start. You're wasting your time and mine.

When people from around the nation and around the world think of Atlanta, they think of the whole metro area. Whether they were at Olympic equestrian events in Conyers, or at beach volleyball in Clayton County, or at the tennis center at Stone Mountain, they still considered themselves to be in Atlanta. Same way with business. The facility may be in Norcross or Mableton or Douglasville, but to that CEO from Toronto or Tokyo, it's in Atlanta.

That's how they see it, and that's how we've got to see it, too. We must get over this idea that because you're in Cobb or Clayton or Gwinnett County, you're not part of Atlanta. You are, whether your neighbors will admit it or not.

When we leave town—when our plane touches down at LaGuardia Airport—we think of ourselves as being in New York City. None of us says, "Well, here we are in Queens, as opposed to Brooklyn." Most of us can't name the five boroughs of New York City off the top of our heads, let alone tell where the dividing lines run. It is the same for Atlanta.

What's more, the problems on your agenda do not respect city or county lines. Environmental issues are absolutely critical to the growth of this region, and they must be approached on a regional level.

Metro Atlanta relies heavily on Lake Lanier for its water. But this same water is also needed for recreation on the lake itself, for hydro-electric power generation at the Buford Dam, for other communities downstream, and for barge traffic on the lower Chattahoochee. The State of Georgia recently signed water compacts with Alabama and Florida—states that also lay claim to the water of the Chattahoochee. There has to be coordination; there has to be cooperative planning if we are to meet all of these needs for water.

Another problem that, believe it or not, is even worse, is *air* pollution. Air, like water, also flows in total disregard of manmade political boundaries. Pollution from the downtown connector can be wafting through Conyers in a matter of minutes.

It's even harder to get a grip on air pollution than water, because the culprit is two million individual vehicles. Which one of you has a workforce that lives entirely within the same political jurisdiction as your business is located? Not a one of you. Your employees come to work from all over the metro area, and too many of them come with only a single driver in the car.

Some say the answer is obvious—commuter rail. I wish it were that simple. Railroads make their money moving freight. That's their business, their responsibility to their stockholders.

Passenger trains require a different track configuration than freight trains, and the railroads do not want to deal with that. As a result, to do commuter rail, we would have to do more than just buy the trains. We would have to build the tracks, and that is very, very expensive and complicated. Where does the money come from? Who decides? Given these considerations, I think the prospect of commuter rail anytime in the near future is dim, to say the least.

Others would like to believe that all you need to do is get the state to take over MARTA. You'd be surprised, or maybe you wouldn't, how many people have told me that over the years. But again, it is just not that simple. MARTA is structured by law to be supported by a local sales tax in the counties it serves. Even if MARTA were operated by the state, the voters of Cobb and Gwinnett Counties still would not pass a MARTA sales tax. And you still could not get enough support in the General Assembly from other parts of the state to change that financing arrangement.

What's more, the voters in 1992 turned down a constitutional amendment to allow motor fuel tax revenues to be used for anything other than building highways and bridges.

The metro area—and I want to emphasize that it is the "metro area" not just the city—faces severe penalties if we don't meet federal ozone requirements within the next three years.

We could lose $736 million in federal highway funds, as well as being prevented from expanding metro area highways, even using state and local money. Even worse, and it is not a remote possibility at all, we could also see restrictions placed on new businesses moving into metro Atlanta and on expansions of existing facilities.

We need people to drive less, to carpool and use mass transit, to drive fuel-efficient vehicles and to shift their commuting times to reduce rush-hour congestion. That is going to require an attitude change on the part of two million metro Atlanta vehicle owners. It will take encouragement and incentives from the entire community, and especially from you, their employers. The question is whether it will happen before the entire metro area suffers from widespread traffic gridlock, transportation restrictions, and ozone-related health problems.

During the 1990s, Georgia emerged as a national leader in job creation. Atlanta has been cited as the number one city in the nation for job creation. Georgia exports over $13 billion in products and services, and some 40 percent of it comes from the metro Atlanta region. Atlanta's opportunities are incredible, but we must actively seize the moment. If we fail to work together to manage and direct growth—if we fail to work together to address regional water, air quality, and transportation issues—we will choke and suffocate on the very growth that could have brought us greater economic strength and prominence.

All of these issues, and many others I've not taken time to address, rise above *any one* local government and require regional cooperation if any progress is to be made. They are a concern not only for local governments and public officials, but also for you as Atlanta's business leaders. And yes, the State of Georgia may well have to assume a larger role in dealing with the problems of metro Atlanta and its central city.

But at the same time, let me emphasize to you that government cannot come in and fix the problems of metro Atlanta. And I hope the point of this coalition is not simply to ask why doesn't the Governor or the Mayor or the County Commission come in and take over this or fix that.

Abraham Lincoln was right when he said that a house divided against itself cannot stand. I would paraphrase that: this metro area divided against itself will cease to prosper. Or to put it into the mountaineer's vernacular, the wheels will come off.

We are all in this together. Every segment of the community must be engaged in finding solutions. Business and government share many of the same goals. Rather than individual businesses and governments and communities operating in isolation and in disregard of their neighbors, they must step across public-private lines and sit down at the table together.

You are positioned to lead the way for two reasons. First, your employees come from across the metro area, and you do business across local political jurisdictions. You are better positioned to see the big picture than local politicians are. And second, when you come together as a business community, you can speak and act with a tremendous amount of power. Politicians and office holders will listen to you if you speak with one voice, and speak *forcefully*.

I will end as I began. You are all individuals who have become very successful in your line of work. You're not used to failure. You know what it is like to solve difficult problems and make hard choices. I tell you in all candor, you have never faced a problem like this one, but it is one that must be dealt with for the sake of the future economic vitality of this region and the quality of life for your children and grandchildren.

I wish you luck and remind you again that it all comes down, quite frankly, to two things: race and turf-guarding. Find out how to deal with them and the rest will be easy.

That is what this new Metro Business Coalition is about, and why it is so important. I thank you for taking time to come together and wrestle together with the problems the metro area faces. I hope that the day will come when this coalition is regarded as the group that actually began to move Atlanta to a higher plane as one of the world's great international cities.

# Young Harris College Commencement

*June 8, 1997*

Someone once defined a commencement speech as unsolicited advice to a group who has their mind on something entirely different. I believe that's right. There's not a single person in their audience who is here to hear me—maybe Shirley. They are here to see *you* reach this milestone in your life. But my job, I guess, is to make a speech, and your job is to listen. So let me get started, and if you finish your job before I finish mine, I'll hurry and try to catch up.

The poet Robert Frost was once asked, "What is it that makes a great place?" And he answered, "The first thing you've got to have is a good piece of geography." We have a good piece of geography here. There is no more beautiful spot that Brasstown Valley with Crow's Gap, Double Knobs, Three Sisters, and Brasstown Bald; a campus with the mingling of the heritage of Susan B. Harris Chapel, Sharp Hall, this Clegg Auditorium and the Goolsby Center.

Yes, Young Harris College has a good piece of geography. But that is not all it has. Young Harris College has soul. That is why it is different from any other educational institution in the world. I would not attempt to explain this indefinable quality. I do not have to, you feel it. You feel it especially strongly today. For each of us it is different, but with similarities.

For many of us, it's where we discovered the value of work, the significance of God... where we discovered ourselves, the pursuit of excellence and the thrill that stays with you all of your life of having an inspiring teacher. It's where friendships develop that will never be forgotten. It's where hearts spoke to hearts and the joy of lasting love began. YHC is all these things—and more. They have combined to make you wonder for the rest of your lives how empty your lives would have been without your experience here on this campus.

Most all of the good things in my own life started here. In fact, my life started here. I was born in the shadow of this campus to the dean and the former art teacher. I was admitted as a student in the Academy in the mid-40s, feeling small and insignificant amid the surge of returning GIs from World War II and sophisticated seniors from far-away places like Ellijay. And I was carried through my early days on this campus not by my own ambition or self-confidence, but by the sheer strength of my mother's will, and the charisma and caring of an English teacher named Edna Herren, who opened doors to the world that this mountain lad had never even imagined.

But I'm not here to talk about my life. I want to talk a few minutes about yours and what may be in store for you when you leave this college and this valley. Today we celebrate your achievement, and well we should. This is the culmination of a lot of hard work, stress and expense. You are to be congratulated and you deserve to be praised.

But take it from this old voice of experience... an alumnus not only of YHC but of CHK—the College of Hard Knocks. There will come a time next week, next month, next year, when this time of euphoria will turn to ashes. You'll be knocked down, you'll be disappointed, dare I say it—you will fail. So let me spend a few minutes talking about that subject so you may be ready when that time comes.

Perhaps first I should tell you something I've never failed at—I've never choked up while singing in front of an audience. You see, I've never had the guts to try to sing in front of an audience. Only those people who try something run the risk of failure. The main choice most of us make, the most important choice, is at what level we shall fail. Each of us chooses the level of our failure.

In baseball, some make major league errors, some make minor league errors, and some make no errors at all, because they don't play the game. In life itself, the same options are open. So, if you are able to be satisfied in life with saying nothing, doing nothing and being nothing, then, I can guarantee you that you will never fail.

From there, let me note that failure is a great teacher, the best one we'll ever have. Consider this: the only way you ever learned to walk was by failure. If you had waited until you were sure you would not fall to take that first step, you would still be wearing those little high-topped white shoes with unscarred soles. The only way you ever learned to walk, or read, or add, or play the piano, or use a computer, was by trying, failing, and trying again! Whatever it is, failure will teach it to us, if we let it.

One more thing: Failure never has to be final. To fail is not to be defeated. I think that's why I like the game of baseball so much. Where else can you succeed only three or four times out of ten turns at bat and still be an all-star? Hank Aaron hit more home runs than anyone who has ever played the game. But he also hit into more double plays than anyone who has ever played the game.

Anyone ever heard of John Grisham? These days everything he writes is a best seller, and made into a movie almost immediately. Such was not always the case. The first book he wrote and sent to a publisher was rejected. He sent it to another publisher. It was rejected. He sent it to another. Rejected. Twenty-five times until it was finally accepted. Even then, the publisher only printed 5,000 copies, because they didn't want to take a chance. What if he had accepted that first rejection and given up?

Abraham Lincoln failed to be elected eight times. But he was elected three times. And it was the latter two of those that we remember him for.

Some of you have been applying to go on to another college. And you know what it means to be on pins and needles, waiting and watching the mail for that important letter of acceptance. Well, let me tell you about a student who had applied to several colleges and after he had received several rejections, he wrote this letter:

"Dear Admissions Officer: I am in receipt of your rejection of my application. As much as I would like to accommodate you, I find I cannot accept it. I have already received four rejections from other colleges, and this number is, in fact, over my limit. Therefore, I must *reject your rejection*, and I will appear for classes on September 18th."

I like that. It may not have worked for that particular student. But this approach has and does work in many a life.

Teddy Roosevelt is one of my favorite Americans. When the Spanish-American War broke out in 1898, Roosevelt tried to join the army and was rejected. They politely told him he was too old and he couldn't half see. He went out and organized a group of civilians, called them the "Rough Riders," stored 11 pairs of glasses in his saddle bags just in case he broke a few, went to Cuba and stormed up San Juan Hill and into the history books. You see, he rejected the rejection.

Later he wrote those wonderful words, "The credit belongs to the man—and I would add woman—who is actually in the arena, whose face is marred by dust and sweat and blood; who strives valiantly; who errs and comes up short again and again... Who at best knows in the end the triumph of high achievement; and who, at worst, if he fails, at least fails while daring greatly. So that his place shall never be with those cold and timid souls who know neither victory nor defeat."

The University of Berne turned down a PhD dissertation as being "fanciful and irrelevant." The young physics student who wrote that dissertation was Albert Einstein, who rejected that rejection.

Or take the young girl whose family had to flee their home in Czechoslovakia first when Hitler invaded and again when the Communists took over, and who got her first paying job at the age of 39 when her husband left her with three daughters to raise. Her name is Madeleine Albright, and today she is America's first female Secretary of State.

Any of you every heard of Kris Kristofferson? You can see him in movies on TV every now and then. But I knew him for his music. He wrote some of the great songs of the 60s and 70s. He wrote "Why Me, Lord?" He had been a Rhodes Scholar, but wanted to be a song writer. Went to Nashville and worked as a janitor in a music studio—sweeping up, emptying ash trays, hoping he'd have a chance to pitch a song to an artist. Finally he got Johnny Cash's attention. He recorded a song called "Sunday Morning Coming Down"—the first of many Kristofferson hits.

I mention him because he wrote a great song about what I'm trying to say to you. It was called "To Beat the Devil." The "Devil" is failure. He's got wonderful lines in it about "lonely being more than a state of mind" and "when no one stood behind me except my shadow on the wall." He ends it with: "You still can hear me singing to the people who don't listen to the things I am saying, hoping someone's going to care." And then another verse—"because I don't believe that no one wants to know."

The rhetoric teacher at Harrow wrote on a 16-year-old's report card, "A conspicuous lack of success." That student was Winston Churchill, who *rejected* the rejection. Years later, when he was invited back to Harrow for graduation, he made the shortest commencement speech on record. He looked out at the students and said simply, "Never give up; never give up; never, never, never give up." He *rejected* the rejection.

This afternoon is a magical moment for each one of you, together with your parents and teachers. All of you are thrilled, excited and proud. But at various times for the rest of your lives, there are going to be disappointments. Your dreams will be shattered. You will be set back, knocked down.

And when that happens, as it inevitably will, remember the words of the Apostle Paul to the Corinthians: "We are afflicted in every way, but not crushed; perplexed, but not driven to despair . . . knocked down, but not knocked out."

Remember always: You can reject the rejection. Dare greatly and don't be a cold and timid soul. Continue always to sing to those who don't listen. And never, never give up.

# National Press Club

*November 7, 1997*

I was five years old when President Franklin Roosevelt stood on the steps of the Capitol here in Washington, looked south and said, "I see one-third of a nation ill-housed, ill-clad, and ill-nourished."

I grew up in that South, a region shackled by segregation and plagued by ignorance. But that South is no more. To use a phrase coined in Georgia, it is "gone with the wind."

In fact, today, if you were to separate out the South—I'm not advocating that, we tried it once. But if you were to separate out that "one-third of a nation," its economy would rank as fifth largest in the world, and by the year 2000, the South will surpass the Northeast in population.

At the hub of this vibrant and growing region is Georgia, a state that got tired of being poor and backward, and has been working with great determination to change itself. To move up from trailing the rest of the nation to leading it.

Today I come from a state whose economy has out-performed the nation's every year since 1991, some years by more than 80 percent, a state with 1,578 international businesses, a state that was one of the first to open overseas trade offices 25 years ago, and now has eleven of them. And only New York, Chicago, and Houston have more Fortune 500 headquarters than Atlanta.

I come from a state that has created more than 2,000 new jobs every week since 1991, a state that last year led the nation in high-tech job growth. And they are not coming because we have cheap labor or because we are building rail sidings. One of the main reasons they come is because Georgia is a world center of telecommunications.

Allow me to take a moment to give you a little history. If you look at the 25 largest cities in the United States, virtually every one grew up around some natural resource. Most of them are port cities—Boston, New York, Philadelphia, and Miami on the East Coast; Seattle, Portland, San Francisco, and Los Angeles on the West Coast; New Orleans and Houston on the Gulf; Chicago on the Great Lakes.

The few that are inland can also be explained, for the most part, by major natural resources. Dallas has oil; Denver has mining. Kansas City and Minneapolis are markets for the rich grains of the Midwestern prairies. And Washington, D.C., of course, is our nation's capital.

Of the 25 largest cities in the United States, only Atlanta has no natural, logical reason for its existence. Atlanta was built on sheer human ingenuity and persistence. And the resource around which it has grown up, is purely man-made transportation infrastructure and a knack for knowing how to leverage it.

In the 1830s, three railroads came together at a remote spot out in the Georgia woods. They formed a major junction that linked the East Coast with the Midwest. And Atlanta grew up around that railroad junction.

A century later, Atlanta was in the vanguard of the next generation of transportation, building an airport in the early days of commercial aviation. In 1940, Atlanta had the nation's busiest airport with 41 flights a day. Almost 60 years later, it is now one of the largest and busiest in the world.

Now, on the threshold of the 21st century, transportation is taking yet another leap, this time into cyberspace and onto the information superhighway. And true to our historical roots, Atlanta is once again deliberately building the infrastructure we need to establish prominence in this newest form of "transportation."

Fiber-optic cable was developed in Atlanta, and the world's largest fiber and cable manufacturing plant is located there. Atlanta not only has three times more fiber-optic trunk lines than New York City, but it is located at the most significant fiber-optic intersection in the western world—where a major fiber-optic corridor that runs along the East Coast intersects with another major corridor that begins in Chicago and runs on through the Caribbean into South America.

High-tech companies are also coming to Georgia because they know they will find the skilled, educated workforce they will need in the 21st century.

You see, I come from the state that has HOPE, the nation's most far-reaching scholarship program. My goal as Governor has been to create what I call a culture of higher expectations. I want the question in Georgia not to be "whether" to go to college or a technical institute, but "where".

In Georgia, unlike any other state in the nation, if you graduate from high school, public or private, with a B average in your core academic subjects for grades 9-12, you get free tuition, fees, and a book allowance at any public college in the state. If you choose a Georgia private college, you get a $3,000 scholarship for your freshman year. Keep up that B average, year by year, and that free tuition or that scholarship continues through all four years of college.

HOPE has nothing to do with race or income level. It is strictly merit-based. You give something, you get something. It is a strong incentive for students to achieve. It is a strong incentive for parents to be involved in encouraging their children to do well in school. And you see it work.

Also, in Georgia students who don't have a B average or decide not to go to college, can get the same deal for a diploma program at a technical institute—free tuition and fees, and a book allowance. There is a modern public technical school within 40 minutes driving time of every citizen in the state.

Unlike the other 49 states, where the rising cost of tuition is sinking families deeper and deeper in debt, in Georgia, 97 percent of the in-state freshmen at both Georgia Tech and the University of Georgia pay no tuition at all.

We are the tenth largest state in the nation, but we have the fourth largest public university system. In the past four years since HOPE began, a quarter of a million Georgia students have received this level of financial assistance.

Here's another thing about it. In some states, minority enrollments in colleges and universities are declining. In Georgia, we have more minority students enrolled in our University System than ever before, and they make up a larger percentage of its student body than ever before. Before HOPE, 18 percent of our University System enrollment was minority. Four years later, more than 21 percent is minority.

But in addition to high-tech infrastructure and an educated workforce, technology-based companies also come to Georgia to get the research they need to stay on the cutting-edge. Georgia is one of the top two states in the nation in state funding for research and development.

At a time when many universities are seeing sponsored research decline as the U.S. Defense Department moves into a post-Cold War era, Georgia's six major research universities have doubled their sponsored research during the 90s and are on track to pass a billion dollars a year by the year 2000. And the number of Georgia companies investing in research has increased fourfold.

The primary reason is the Georgia Research Alliance, a public-private partnership of academe, state government, and private-sector industry, whose board is dominated by private industry. The Research Alliance not only conducts its own research in areas that will drive our economy forward, but stimulates additional research as well.

State government's contribution to the Research Alliance has not been to build technology parks, as many other states have done, but to make what I consider to be an investment of seed capital at the front end. The state has helped to build and equip the sophisticated labs that research requires, and create endowments for two dozen world-renowned research scholars to head up those labs. We consider the labs and research scientists to be the engine that drives the process.

The telecommunications arm of the Research Alliance is the Georgia Center for Advanced Telecommunications Technology, or GCATT. It is just over a year since I used a laser wand to cut a visually simulated ribbon, opening the GCATT research building. But already more than 300 scientists and engineers are working there. GCATT is not only spinning off new companies—it has 14 start-up companies in its incubator right now—but it is also a magnet that attracts existing telecommunications companies.

Of course, new high-tech jobs are often created in start-up businesses, which require venture capital, and the Southeast, led by Georgia, has now passed the Northeast in the amount of venture capital generated. Last spring 500 venture capitalists from around the nation met in Atlanta to hear proposals for 58 start-up companies, of which 28 were from Georgia. This was the first time this venture capital group met anywhere outside of Boston or Silicon Valley.

I also come from a state that leads the nation in its use of telecommunications for education and medical services, so that a cutting-edge computer software company can grow and thrive in the little town of Hahira, deep in rural South Georgia, because the skilled workforce they need is being trained by distance learning through classes and super-computers located in other parts of the state.

In dozens of rural hospitals across the state, local doctors can connect a tiny, sophisticated camera or audio recording device to medical equipment, allowing specialists at the Medical College of Georgia, many miles away, to care for patients through what the *New York Times* has called the most sophisticated telemedicine system in the nation.

Georgia was also the first state to put a satellite dish at every single public school, college, and technical institute, and we now lead the nation by several measures of producing and using distance-learning programming.

We are also one of the few states to have systematic Internet connections and local dial-in access for every single public school, college, technical institute, and public library in the state. You can walk into the tiniest, most remote branch library in rural

Georgia and have full access to the Internet.

We also have a hard-wired, statewide interactive network connecting public schools, tech schools, and colleges. Up to twelve sites can be interactive with each other at the same time.

This network is also connected into our Export Assistance Center, which has international video-conferencing capacity with those eleven overseas trade offices I mentioned earlier. Business leaders from anywhere in the state can do face-to-face international business from home.

I come from a state that has more than 60,000 four-year-olds enrolled in a prekindergarten program that this month will receive one of the ten Innovation in American Government Awards, funded by the Ford Foundation and administered by Harvard University.

We all know how important early childhood is. Volumes have been written about it, as have cover stories in news periodicals. White House conferences have been held. Yet Georgia is the only state in the nation that provides free prekindergarten for every four-year-old whose parents want it.

In an era when our national parks are underfunded and deteriorating, I come from a state that has preserved more than 100,000 acres of natural land since 1991. A state that last year created he first major urban park in the nation in more than 25 years.

I come from the state with the toughest laws in the nation on violent crime. In Georgia, it is not three, but "two strikes and you're out." We have a list of what we call the "seven deadly sins"—murder, rape, aggravated assault and similar serious violent crimes. On the first offense, you serve a mandatory minimum of ten years before you have a chance of parole. The second time you commit one of those crimes, you are in prison forever. And in our prison system, each able-bodied inmate works forty hours a week and walks four miles every day.

I come from a state—the only state in the nation—that has done away with the old hide-bound civil service system for state government employees in which many employees felt a job was an entitlement and pay raises automatic. In his best seller, *The Death of Common Sense*, Phillip K. Howard struck a chord with the absurdities of a Civil Service System in which government workers think they've got a guaranteed job for life.

In Georgia, as in most states and here in Washington, we had a situation where it could take two months to fill a critical position, and a year and a-half to fire a bad worker, because of a mountain of endless paperwork, hearings and appeals. When the bad ones are kept on and even given the same pay raise, resentment grows among good employees, and managers are discouraged and even intimidated.

So in Georgia, we abolished that antiquated ox-cart. Today agencies have flexibility in hiring and firing. Employees undergo regular performance evaluations and are paid based on performance.

Once shackled by segregation, our state legislature now has the largest number of black members of any state. We are the only state with a black attorney general, and over the past seven years I have appointed more blacks and more women to the judiciary than all the other prior Georgia governors put together.

I know that by now you're probably thinking, "Here's another Governor bragging on his state." And to some extent you are right. But I would like to remind you that, as Dizzy Dean would say, "If you've already done it, it ain't braggin'."

Quite simply, and in closing, Georgia is a place where people and businesses want to be. And what I want you to understand is that Georgia has made this kind of progress because our attention is focused on the issues that really matter to our citizens— improving education, creating jobs, preserving the environment, and making government more effective and responsive.

That is why these programs, like most of the programs of my administration, have been supported by Republicans as well as Democrats. I even changed the all Democratic State Board of Education, which is appointed by the governor, to be a bipartisan body, and I appointed my former Republican opponent for governor to be its chair, because I respect and value his coalition building abilities.

In contrast, this city stays tied up in partisan knots.

As one who comes from that world beyond the Beltway, let me assure you that when the average American family sits up late around the kitchen table, they are not worrying about how many calls Bill Clinton made from the White House, or who he hugged on videotape. They are worrying about how to balance their checkbook, and how to pay for quality child care and at the same time save for college when tuition continues to spiral upward. They are worried about jobs, education, and crime.

They don't want more government or less government. What they want is for government to work for them, addressing the issues that matter to them in ways that they can see and appreciate.

That has been our focus in Georgia. That is why we have been able to make significant and visible progress. And I am deeply grateful to have this opportunity to tell you a little about a state that is ready for the 21st century.

# 1998

# Supplemental Budget Address

*January 5, 1998*

I hope all of you had an enjoyable, restful holiday season, and that you join me in looking forward to the New Year and the coming legislative session.

As the budget document before you indicates, Georgia is in very, very sound financial shape. We finished the last fiscal year with a comfortable surplus. Tight-fisted management by agency heads lapsed an additional $49 million. We were able to cut another $43 million because of our success with welfare reform. All of our reserves are full, and will be that way when the next Governor takes office.

So, I can tell you one week early that the state of the state is strong and vibrant! The total amount of additional funds in this budget, in state general funds, not counting the lottery, is $715 million. That includes $524 million of surplus, $111 million in the Midyear Adjustment Fund, $49 million from agency lapses and $25 million from excess motor fuel tax collections.

The purpose of my remarks today is to tell you what is in the amended budget document. But in order to get to that, let me begin by telling what is *not* there. First, I have set aside $152 million—a huge amount of money to deal with a huge problem—a whale of a problem that every state and every private business is dealing with. That amount will appear in a special supplementary budget bill that will be introduced on the first day of the legislative session.

As I'm sure you are aware, all computer-owners everywhere are faced with the dilemma of internal computer calendars and clocks that will expire on December 31, 1999—which is now a little less than two years away. This is a worldwide problem that experts project will cost as much as $1 trillion to fix. The cost to the U.S. government is expected to be $30 billion. State governments altogether are expected to spend more than $2 billion, and the $152 million I'm setting aside will probably have to be added to next year.

It's a complicated problem for state government because many of our computer systems swap data with federal and local government computers. Programmers will have to hash out hundreds of compatibility issues along the way. Another complication is the limited number of computer technicians who can fix the problem. Private industry, facing the same dilemma, is devouring this labor pool, making computer programmers hard to find and luring government technicians away with bonuses and higher salaries.

So, you see, we are faced with both a time crunch and a potential personnel shortage. To wait and pass the buck, or in this case millions of bucks, to the next governor would be too late. To wait even until next fiscal year could be too late. That's why I want to use a fast-track bill to gain a little extra valuable time to make sure our programs are reconfigured and tested before January 1, 2000.

Second, as I'm sure you also know, the unified Democratic agenda for the coming session includes a $205 million income tax cut. This is a far-reaching tax cut benefitting 5.2 million Georgians and reducing the taxes of the average family of four by $168, or 15 percent. The proposal is to raise both personal and dependent exemptions to $2,700, bringing Georgia in line with the new federal tax law.

The plan also raises the deduction for senior citizens over age 65 from $700 to $1,300. This is the second income tax cut by this administration to provide special relief for the elderly.

We are approaching a time when one of four Georgians will be elderly, and we must not forget this generation who fought our wars, taught our children—who are our fathers and mothers and ourselves to be.

You have heard me say over and over that I believe government ought to collect only what it absolutely must have to provide the services taxpayers need, and return the rest to the taxpayers. I am proud to say that this is just what we've done. This is the third major tax cut of this administration. Taken together with the income tax cut of 1994 and the removal of the state sales tax on groceries in 1996, it will mean we will have enacted the three largest tax cuts in Georgia history for a total of nearly $900 million. Folks, you should be very proud of that; very few states can make that kind of statement.

We want this tax cut to begin four days ago, January 1, 1998, and the supplemental budget reflects the fact that the revenue loss will begin in the latter part of the current fiscal year.

I also have gone ahead, as we've done before, and allocated $200 million of this money to prepay some of our state debt. I believe this is a prudent use of these funds, rather than starting up ongoing programs in the supplemental budget.

After accounting for the year 2000 computer problem, the tax cut, the debt payments and the $25 million in motor fuel taxes that under our Constitution belongs to the Department of Transportation, we then actually have $311 million from general funds and expenditure cuts to be appropriated.

I don't have to tell this group that my top priority is education. And that is why my recommendation is to use $217 million, or 70 percent of this amount for education. I especially want to call your attention to a one-shot education initiative that I propose we fund over this budget and FY 99.

Georgia is among the nation's leaders in the amount of money we have spent on educational technology for our schools and libraries. You know the list: satellite dishes at every school, computers in our classrooms and CD-ROMs in our media centers, Internet connections at every school and public library in this state—well over a half-billion dollars for educational technology from the lottery alone.

Now the time has come in my opinion to take a giant step forward with another important piece of learning equipment. It is a wonderful educational tool: compact and portable. It never needs batteries or a power source. It never crashes or needs rebooting. Its clock will not expire on December 31, 1999. You can scan it optically. It will register information directly into the brain. It has a browse feature that allows you to move instantly to any page, either forward or backward.

It is portable. It is durable. It is affordable. And the fact is that while we have been focusing our attention on outfitting our schools and libraries with the technology they had to have, we have at the same time been shortchanging them when it comes to that most fundamental learning tool of all—a book.

So I am proposing that this year we buy one million new books for school media centers and public libraries. You will see the first $10 million for this initiative in the supplemental budget of the Department of Technical and Adult Education to purchase 600,000 new books for our public libraries. Then in the big budget you will find funds to purchase another 400,000 books for our school media centers, also using some existing state funds. I also want to begin a summer reading program for our children in this budget.

One of the largest education expenditures, as always, is to provide our schools with additional funds to cover enrollment growth in the new school year. This mid-year adjustment of more than $78 million is required under the enrollment-driven Quality Basic Education formula.

I have proposed another $79 million in lottery funds for special construction in 45 of our rapidly growing systems who are scrambling to find places to put all their students. Then another $35 million goes to local school systems for a one-time adjustment as counties change to a year-round schedule for vehicle tags. The switch to a year-round tag schedule means that school systems will lose some of the money they otherwise would have received during the current school year. So I have proposed a one-time expenditure to offset the loss. By next school year, the year-round system will be in full effect and provide them with an even stream of revenue throughout the year.

My proposed budget also includes $11 million to continue the implementation of the new financial and student information system. This new system gives us information by school rather than by school system, so that we will know, when we appropriate funds, if the money reaches the individual school and its classrooms, or gets side-tracked somewhere in the bureaucracy of the central office.

Closely intertwined with education is economic development, the one thing I spend most of my time on. Not a day goes by that I am not doing something on job creation, and we have created more than 2,000 new jobs every week in Georgia since 1991. We are a national leader. Our state economy has out-performed the nation's every year since 1991, some years by more than 80 percent.

But I am still not satisfied. There is room for improvement and more help is still needed, especially in the rural areas of this state. So I want to draw your attention to a $35 million proposal from the unified Democratic leadership. As CEOs consider Georgia for a new plant, the proximity of an airport that can handle corporate jets is high on their list. The importance of this access will become increasingly significant to economic development in the future, especially for rural economic development.

For many years, we have been appropriating small amounts of matching money for upgrading airports, but we have had no comprehensive, overall statewide plan, no grand strategy. So we recommend funding a one-time appropriation of $35 million to upgrade 27 strategically located airports, giving them the runway length, terminal facilities, and fuel and maintenance services required by corporate jets. With this critical investment, as you can see, every Georgia community will be within a 45-minute drive of a top-level general aviation airport.

The other economic development item I want to mention is $42 million for the Georgia Research Alliance. It surprised a lot of people around the nation and even in this state, when last year Georgia ranked first in the nation in high-tech job growth. In noting our top ranking, the American Electronics Association cited the Georgia Research Alliance, with its expanding research engine, for both attracting and creating new jobs.

Georgia has moved up rapidly. In 1992, we were 19th in the nation in the amount of state funding we put into research and development. Only four years later, we had jumped to third place. Today Georgia is one of the top two states in the nation, and with this supplemental budget, we will become the undisputed national leader. Don't think this goes unnoticed. Last spring 500 venture capitalists from around the nation met here in Atlanta to hear proposals for 58 start-up companies, of which 28 were from Georgia. This was the first time this venture capital group had ever met anywhere outside of Boston or Silicon Valley.

I also want you to know that not all this money is being spent in Atlanta or Athens. The Research Alliance just met in Tifton to open a new, state-of-the-art agricultural research lab, which it funded. This lab provides comprehensive services to farmers on everything from seed that is biogenetically engineered to resist disease and pests, to technology that will make sprayers more precise in applying fertilizer and pest control, to cropping techniques that minimize topsoil erosion.

What has made the Georgia Research Alliance so successful in attracting and creating high tech jobs, is its ability to attract top-flight international research scholars. This budget includes matching funds to create endowments for three more of these eminent scholars, bringing the total to 27. The demand is such that the private match for the state funds is already in place. In addition to the endowments, what has made the Alliance successful in attracting these new superstars is the level of cutting-edge research equipment we offer them. Few other states can match it.

Now, the next important thing we must do is to develop commercial applications from the research that is coming out of those labs. And that is what much of the money in this budget is for. In biotechnology, for example, we have the labs and the researchers who are making the novel discoveries and getting patents on them. But turning those discoveries into marketable products is being done by California companies.

So, I propose we build three technology development centers, designed to incubate and nurture new high-tech companies, so that we will be able to handle the commercialization of our own research break-throughs. Once we do that, the Research Alliance will truly become an economic engine for all of Georgia.

We know it can be done. We used that kind of model for GCATT, and within a year of its opening, it was already incubating 14 new companies. This is not some abstract theory or some academic projection. At least one of these three new facilities I am proposing is already filled with commitments from eager companies before it is even off the drawing board.

If we are to compete in the 21st century, our economy must become increasingly technology-based. That is critical and that is why with this budget, we will have appropriated over $200 million for the Georgia Research Alliance. I consider it one of the best investments this administration has made.

Another important investment is $4.9 million for an animal science arena at the University of Georgia, which is a high priority with the agribusiness community, the Board of Regents, and the University's excellent new President Mike Adams.

One of the most pressing environmental issues facing Georgia is clean air. The greater metro Atlanta area is what the federal government calls an "ozone non-attainment area," which means that its air does not meet mandatory federal air quality standards. If we continue to fall short of these standards, Georgia will not only lose some $600 million in federal highway funds, but see restrictions placed on new businesses and expansions of existing facilities in these 13 counties. You know we can't let that happen.

So, by executive order I have created the Voluntary Ozone Action Program, or VOAP for short, which requires every state agency with employees in metro Atlanta to participate. By this coming summer every state agency will have a plan to reduce their single-occupancy vehicle trips by at least 20 percent. Whenever there is an ozone alert, they will implement their plan to help reduce air pollution. Our long-term goal is to do that all summer every summer, whether there is an ozone alert or not, so that every state employee carpools or takes mass transit or telecommutes at least one day a week as a common practice. I have also sent letters to the other governmental units in the metro area and to the 100 largest employers, asking them to do the same thing.

We already know that it works. In 1996 Atlanta hosted the largest peacetime event in the history of the world at the height of the ozone season. Yet not once during the Olympics were we out of compliance with federal ozone regulations because of our own voluntary action.

My budget proposal contains $1 million in state funds for a major public education campaign and for the monitoring of daily ozone levels.

The most commonly proposed long-term solution for metro Atlanta's air quality problems is commuter rail, and, while it is very, very expensive, the time has come to begin to move in that direction. The line with the most potential riders and the easiest and least costly to build, runs from Atlanta through Gwinnett County to Athens. The federal government will share the cost of the environmental analysis that is needed before this line can be built. But I propose that we pre-fund the federal share of the cost in the supplemental budget, enabling us to move forward with the environmental and design work. This should speed up the process and allow construction to begin as early as the year 2000, with completion in the year 2002.

A second inter-city rail line from Atlanta to Macon, as you know, is also in the planning stages, and we have already funded the environmental studies for it. But be forewarned—the environmental issues on this line will take longer than the Atlanta-Gwinnett-Athens line.

We must also upgrade our vehicle emission inspection program. Emission inspections have always been handled by the private sector, and we want to continue that. But right now there are not enough inspection stations with necessary equipment to test for the new, tougher federal standards. I have proposed a $6 million in this budget to offset some of the cost of the needed equipment, so that we can get the worst polluters fixed or off the road as soon as possible.

In human services, the most significant thing you will find in this budget is in Temporary Assistance for Needy Families, or TANF for short—the comprehensive new welfare reform program we began a year ago. Georgia is a national leader in welfare reform. We were ahead of the federal government with innovative approaches that were already reducing our welfare rolls, before the new federal guidelines opened the door for major reform.

Today, one year after we began TANF, we can see that our efforts at reform are succeeding. A year ago we budgeted for a TANF caseload of 120,000 households, and some thought we were being optimistic about getting that many people off of the rolls. But by the end of the current fiscal year, we expect to be down to about 90,000 households—25 percent lower than our original estimate.

That has freed up a significant sum of money, and I am proposing that we use most of it to expand our efforts to help welfare recipients become employable and find jobs. You will see nearly $11 million for "Welfare to Work," which will draw down matching federal funds. This is a comprehensive and cooperative effort by three state departments— Technical and Adult Education, Labor, and Human Resources—to help welfare recipients understand the demands and expectations of the workplace, learn job skills and find jobs.

Then another $15 million will be used to expand the number of day care slots for welfare recipients moving into the job force, and $7 million will provide increased transportation services.

Since we began our efforts to reform welfare three years ago, we have reduced Georgia's caseload by over 50,000 households. But the first ones off the rolls were the most employable. Those who now remain are the longer-term recipients with the lowest skills and the least work experience. It will be more difficult to make them employable, so we are stepping up our efforts to help them become self-sufficient with these plans for their work skills, their transportation to work, and day care for their children.

Public safety is another important concern that is reflected in this budget proposal. Serious and violent crime by juveniles continues to rise, and it is a struggle for the Department of Juvenile Justice to find places for the growing flood of young offenders committed to their care. To meet that pressing need, this amended budget contains a total of 550 new juvenile beds. We want to speed up construction of the new Muscogee Youth Development Center, which will have 150 beds, expand the facility at Eastman by 300 new beds, and add 100 beds total at two Regional Youth Development Centers in Gainesville and Marietta.

This budget also opens three more new adult prisons—Washington, Wilcox, and Smith in Tattnall County—which will provide 576 new prison beds. With these, the total number of new prison beds we will have opened the past eight years during this administration will pass 20,000—a record high in Georgia history.

Finally, we are continuing the process of modernizing our Revenue Department. Peat Marwick provided us with a "Blueprint for Modernization," and we are now moving into Phase Two of its implementation. I don't like big supplemental budgets, but this one I submit to you today has been well-thought-out and is fiscally responsible. It has the proper balance between investments and tax cuts, and that balance is important. We must never do anything to jeopardize that triple triple-A bond rating that we worked so hard to obtain. I recommend this budget to you, and look forward to working together with you to keep Georgia's star rising.

# Budget Address, Fiscal Year 1999

*January 13, 1998*

I come before you today to present the final budget of my administration. A budget, as I see it, is both a reflection of the state's priorities and a tool for implementing them, and I want to begin by thanking you for the careful consideration you have given to the previous budgets I have laid before you. We have not always agreed on exactly what should be in those budgets, but I have always had a great deal of respect for your positions. And I am always mindful that while governors may advocate, it is legislators who appropriate.

It was almost four decades ago that I first sat in this chamber as a legislator and listened to a Governor explain his budget. He had not been into it three minutes before I was thinking of how I would have done it differently. I know how you think. I have sat where you sit.

But today we cannot think of the Georgia of nearly four decades ago. We must think of the Georgia four decades in the future. Together we have set a course for this state that has met the very highest tests of fiscal responsibility.

When I took office as Governor in 1991, our rainy day reserve fund was bone dry. Today its cup runneth over. And for the first time in many years, it will be full for an incoming Governor.

This year, Georgia became one of only a handful of states to have Triple-A bond ratings from all three of the top bond rating services in the nation—a "triple triple-A." These outstanding ratings are a reflection not only of our ability to manage debt responsibly, but also of our willingness to establish clear priorities and invest wisely in the critical infrastructure and resources Georgia needs to prosper in the future.

But one thing about progress—there's always more of it to be made. As you look through this budget report, you will find something new. As we implemented budget redirection to focus our resources on priority programs that work, we have also begun what I call "results based budgeting." For every budgeted program, you will see in writing the results that state agencies are hoping to achieve. I believe that putting our expenditures and our anticipated results hand-in-hand will help us do a better job of meeting the needs of Georgia's citizens.

The budget before you for Fiscal Year 1999 totals $12.5 billion. Of that, $11.8 billion is projected to come from taxes and fees, which is a 6.6 percent budget increase; $530 million will come from lottery proceeds; and $149 million will come from the Indigent Care Trust Fund.

This budget reflects $334 million in tax cuts: $129 million from removing the final cent of state sales tax from groceries, and $205 million from the income tax cut proposed by the unified Democratic leadership.

This tax cut proposal, which would take effect January 1st of this year, would increase the standard exemptions for both individuals and dependents to $2,700. The proposal would also raise the deduction for citizens over age 65 from $700 to $1,300. It will be the second time this administration has provided income tax relief for Georgia's senior citizens.

This tax cut will touch every Georgia citizen who is represented on a personal income tax form—an estimated 5.2 million people. It will reduce the tax bill for a family of four by $168. This is a 15 percent income tax cut. It will be the second largest tax cut in Georgia history, surpassed only by the removal of the state sales tax from groceries, which, as I said, we are simultaneously completing in this same budget. When you add in the income tax cut of 1994, we will have enacted the three largest tax cuts in Georgia history within a five-year time span. Together they provide nearly $900 million in tax relief for Georgia citizens.

In your budget document, there is a bar graph that shows how the money in this budget is distributed. As always, the largest share is devoted to education and I am proud to say that during this administration we have not only increased the number of dollars the state devotes to education, but also the percentage of the budget. Education accounts for 56.5 percent of this budget. If you add in capital outlay, it is more than 57 percent. Some of it, of course, is due to the lottery. But exclude the lottery, and we have still increased both the dollars and the percentage of the general fund money that goes to education.

Children learn in the classroom, and if we want excellence in the classroom, we must be able to compete for the best teachers. So the largest expenditure in this budget is $275 million to provide the fourth consecutive six percent pay raise to teachers in our public schools, technical institutes, colleges and universities. This fulfills the pledge I made four years ago.

Our public school teachers' salaries now are the highest in the Southeast, and, according to the Southern Regional Education Board, we are now poised to overtake the national average in the 1999 school year. If all the local systems had done their part, we'd already be there.

There is also $3.7 million for our teacher Pay-for-Performance program, and it has been exciting to see this program grow. Any school that wants to participate, sets its own goals at the beginning of the school year for improving student achievement. If they achieve those goals by the end of the school year, they receive an award equal to $2,000 for each teacher at the school. And they get to decide how to spend that money, no strings attached.

This budget also includes a 15 percent salary supplement for all Georgia teachers who become nationally certified. This will be the largest supplement given by any state in the nation.

For the past several years, we have been concentrating on funding educational technology, and the lottery has provided more than $600 million for satellite dishes, classroom computers, media center CD-ROMs and Internet connections in every school. That was important. It was technology that our schools and libraries had to have. But while we have been spending these hundreds of millions of new lottery funds needed for technology, we have not increased funds for that most fundamental learning tool of all—a book.

So I am proposing that in this legislative session we buy one million new books for school media centers and public libraries. The supplemental budget has $10 million to purchase 600,000 new books for all our public libraries. This budget includes $5.2 million, which, combined with other existing funds, will buy 400,000 books for our school media centers. One million new books; it's a good investment!

This budget also contains close to $20 million to provide grants for reading programs for our children. During the past three years, the Department of Education has piloted "Reading 1$^{st}$," a very successful in-school reading program that includes specific training for teachers, high-quality materials and time that students devote exclusively to reading. It has been a high priority of Superintendent Schrenko and the board. This budget builds on that fine program with $9 million for 500 more schools to implement "Reading 1$^{st}$" in the early grades.

We want to complement it with an after-school initiative that will start about fourth grade and go through middle school to catch up with those kids we missed. We have already been providing some funds to support after-school programs for middle-schoolers, who otherwise would be latch-key kids who might be tempted to get in trouble if left to their own devices. These after-school programs are usually a combination of academic time for homework and community service. We want to provide grants to after-school program providers, both public and private, to include a reading program, and we hope that the availability of these funds will stimulate additional providers to undertake after-school programs for our children.

During this administration, public school enrollments have increased by more than 20 percent, and next year it will take an additional $118 million just to catch our Quality Basic Education formula up to enrollment growth. We also need classrooms for all of these students. So I am recommending over $114 million for construction in 35 school systems in this budget, which is in addition to $79 million for construction in 45 systems in the supplemental budget. Operating costs continue to rise for our schools, so $9 million is included to provide an increase of $7 per student in the maintenance and operation funds under the QBE formula.

Enrollments at our University System institutions also continue to grow, and an additional $10 million is needed to fund the formula for another year. A great University System requires a great faculty. When I took office, Georgia's faculty salaries ranked fifth among the southeastern states. Since then, we have raised faculty salaries well over 33 percent and now stand poised to rank first.

These salary increases have helped us retain outstanding faculty like Anne Hudson of Armstrong Atlantic State University, the 1996 National Faculty Member of the Year. It has also allowed us to attract the best and brightest new faculty. The National Science Foundation, for example, ranks Georgia Tech number one in the nation in attracting top new young science faculty. MIT comes in second. And the Georgia Research Alliance has lured 24 eminent scholars to Georgia to help with high tech economic development.

These fine faculty members are finding more and more students to teach. When I took office, the University System enrolled 180,000 degree students. Today it enrolls over 205,000.

We've added 25,000 students, the equivalent of another Georgia State University. That's like adding the combined populations of those two great Georgia cities of Americus and Eastman!

I'm especially proud that we've increased opportunities for African-Americans. In that same time period, their enrollment increased from 28,000 to 45,000—an increase of 56 percent. African-Americans now represent 22 percent of our student enrollment. This encouraging trend promises to help Georgia have a bright economic and social future.

Our students have done us proud: Ivy Cadle of East Georgia College was named by USA TODAY as a 1997 first-team All USA Academic Team member—one of only 20 students in the nation. UGA student Rob Sutherland and Georgia Tech student Ayodele Embry were winners in 1996. Amy Lucas of Middle Georgia College won the highest honor awarded to a student athlete by the National Junior College Athletic Association for her combination of a 4.0 grade-point average and championship tennis.

Christopher Richardson graduated from Savannah State University with a double major in math and chemistry, and received $330,000 in scholarships to finance his graduate studies toward a doctorate. And the University of Georgia boasts two recent Rhodes Scholars—Scott Herschovitz in 1998 and Rob Sutherland in 1996. Only 32 Rhodes Scholars are selected nationwide each year.

These students have studied in new and newly renovated buildings. When I became Governor, the University System was receiving $12.9 million a year for renovations and repairs; today, it receives $41 million. If you approve the capital outlay in this budget, we will pass the $1 billion mark in new construction for the University System during this administration.

We've also established distance learning classrooms which have made possible everything from telemedicine to degree courses in remote locations. We now have degrees offered entirely by computer. In every corner of this state you can find an electronic wonder called GALILEO, which has become a national model. It is a working electronic library system that has already recorded over three million hits while other states are still wondering what to do. There is $6 million dollars in the budget to upgrade technology infrastructure, including a million dollars to train University System faculty and staff in the use of technology.

You are all aware that the University System is raising its admission standards. This budget includes $2.8 million for "Partners in Success," a program to prepare students, beginning in high school and even in middle school, to be able to meet those higher standards.

Seventy percent of the jobs being created do not require college degrees, but do require technical skills. So, early in this administration, we set a goal of a tech school facility within 45 minutes driving time of every Georgia citizen. With the opening of the satellite facilities now under construction, we will achieve that goal. Now we must equip and staff these new facilities as they open and begin to serve our citizens.

In the future, I'd like it to be where students don't even have to leave home for technical education. So, there is $500,000 in the budget to begin creation of a virtual technical institute. Web-based instruction will allow students to interact with teachers and classmates from their computers at home or at work.

We have also achieved our goal of having at least one full-time adult literacy teacher in every county in Georgia, and we are turning out GED graduates by the thousands. But we still have a long way to go, because we started out with a high proportion of adults who never completed high school. I want to continue to expand our adult literacy programs by hiring 110 part-time instructors to improve the delivery of instructional services in local communities.

As I mentioned earlier, we are anticipating $530 million in lottery proceeds for next year, bringing the grand total of education funds from the lottery to more than $3 billion—money for programs and improvements we would never have otherwise had.

Two hundred eighteen million dollars is for our award-winning prekindergarten program. This amount provides for an additional 2,000 slots, and expands the assistance for pre-K families who are at risk.

The HOPE Scholarship Program is allocated $213 million. Beginning this school year, home schoolers who finish their freshman year of college with at least a B average, will be reimbursed for the cost of tuition, fees and the book allowance at a public college, or the $3,000 HOPE scholarship at a private college. Then, beginning with their sophomore year, home schoolers will be on the same footing as all other HOPE scholars.

The final category for lottery funds is educational technology and special capital outlay, which totals $91 million: $28 million will provide our schools with an allocation of $22 per student to be used for equipment or technology-related teacher training; $18 million will provide equipment for those new technical institute satellite facilities I have already mentioned; and $15 million goes into the Equipment, Technology, and Construction Trust Fund of the University System. This very successful matching fund enables our colleges and universities to leverage private donations in a dollar-for-dollar match.

I also want to continue our efforts to leverage private funds to endow faculty chairs at our colleges and universities. We began doing that for eminent scholars at our research universities, and it has proved a good way to help attract top-flight faculty. I believe our other University System units can do the same thing. So I proposed $2 million in matching funds in the supplemental budget to endow two faculty chairs at Macon College, and one each at Columbus State University and Armstrong Atlantic State University in Savannah.

As Governor, I spend most of my time on job creation. Not a day goes by that I am not doing something to try to get more and better-paying jobs in Georgia. And I have constantly wrestled with how to better address the unique characteristics and needs of the various parts of this diverse state of ours.

Over and over, in dozens of regional meetings, I have listened to the advice of local public and private leaders. What I am proposing in this budget is the result of what I have heard. It is the largest single allocation of state resources in Georgia history to assist rural areas with economic development and to provide comprehensive, one-stop economic and community assistance at the regional level. It is a joint effort between the Departments of Community Affairs and Industry, Trade, and Tourism, and the funding is divided between these two departments.

We are in the process of identifying 11 state economic development regions that will cover all of Georgia outside of metro Atlanta. Each one will have an economic development team whose core will be two employees from the Department of Community Affairs and two employees from the Department of Industry, Trade, and Tourism. One of them will focus on workforce development.

Other state agencies like Labor, Technical and Adult Education, the University System, Defense and Human Resources will all cooperate and coordinate their economic development efforts in the region through the regional team. Communities and businesses will no longer have to work independently with five or six different state agencies, but can go to one place in the region for the state economic development resources they need.

Georgia is one of the top two states in the nation in the state funds we invest in research and development. Largely because of that, we led the nation last year in the creation of new high-tech jobs. I proposed $42 million in the supplemental budget for the Georgia Research Alliance to expand and strengthen our ability to commercialize the discoveries that come from those research labs.

Today, our focus shifts to the companion program of the Research Alliance—the Traditional Industries Program. First, you should know that there is no other program like this one anywhere in the United States. Many states are investing in high-tech research, but no other state has the kind of broad-based, ongoing research program serving their traditional manufacturing base that Georgia has.

Historically, three manufacturing industries have formed the bedrock of Georgia's economy: pulp and paper, food processing, and textiles and carpet. Combined, they employ a quarter of a million Georgians—nearly half of our manufacturing workforce. The Traditional Industries Program is a public-private partnership in which each industry identifies problems that are critical to their competitiveness, and then works closely with faculty at Georgia colleges and universities to solve those problems. Let me briefly give you three practical examples.

Currently, Georgia manufacturers use warehouse pallets made of wood that weigh about 67 pounds. But now, new federal safety regulations mandate that no pallet can weigh more than 57 pounds. So Traditional Industries researchers developed a new composite material from plastic and carpet and textile waste scraps that is as durable as wood, but much lighter in weight.

Another: Wastewater is an important problem for all of these industries so our researchers designed and helped install a closed-loop wastewater treatment system at a textile mill near Griffin. It is the first of its kind, and has helped cut the mill's wastewater discharge in half.

You may also remember the recent alarm over beef that was infected with E-coli bacteria. Here in Georgia, researchers have developed a new cattle vaccine against E-coli, and they are working with the FDA right now to get it on the market.

These are just three examples of the practical ways in which the Traditional Industries Program is serving the pulp and paper, textile, and food processing industries of Georgia. You will find more than $7 million in this budget to expand the activities of this important research program, bringing the total state investment to more than $34 million. And remember, these funds are matched by private sector investment from the companies who benefit from the research.

A fundamental part of the state's role in economic development is maintaining our infrastructure, and we've done a good job. Our highways have been ranked first in the nation, and I have proposed another $135 million to continue expanding our network of four-lane economic development highways.

Once again, to ensure that the large trucks on our highways meet all state and federal safety regulations, I recommend ten new enforcement officers who will be assigned to monitor trucks in high traffic areas, something that is greatly needed. The federal government will pay 80 percent of the cost, so we need only $157,000 in state funds.

You will also find over $17 million for our ports for navigation improvements at Savannah, and for the preliminary study and design work on channel deepening projects at both Savannah and Brunswick. Brunswick's channel is only 30 feet deep, far less that most ports on the South Atlantic. Savannah's channel is now at 42 feet, but our toughest competitor, Charleston, has begun preparations to deepen its channel to 45 feet, and we can't let them get ahead of us.

I am again recommending $10.5 million to plan and design phase four of the World Congress Center. Right now, this facility is one of the top five convention centers in the United States, and it generates a lot of money for the City of Atlanta and the State of Georgia. But the demand for floorspace from supershows is growing, and if we want to remain one of the nation's leading convention destinations and keep those jobs that go with it, we must build that fourth phase. It is as simple as that.

Finally, in infrastructure investment, there is another $20 million in bonds to provide water/sewer loans to local governments throughout the state, increasing our revolving loan fund by $180 million during this administration.

In the area of human resources, the most important program in this budget proposal is the new Children's Health Insurance Program—CHIP for short. It will leverage federal matching funds, and could provide health coverage for as many as 228,000 Georgia children.

Here's how it would work: CHIP will expand Medicaid coverage for pregnant women and children from birth to age five, up to 200 percent of the federal poverty level, which is $32,100 a year for a family of four. This expansion will cover 24,000 more of our youngest children plus 1,700 pregnant women.

Children ages six to eighteen will continue to be covered under Medicaid, as they are now, up to 100 percent of the federal poverty level, or $16,500 for a family of four. Then, school children with family income between $16,500 and $32,100 for a family of four, will be covered under private health insurance plans administered by the Merit System. The premiums will run about $7.50 a month or 25 cents a day. This could cover 88,000 children who are presently uninsured.

Finally, parents of all other uninsured Georgia children whose income is above $32,100 for a family of four, will be able to buy into the private health insurance plan at cost.

Some people have asked, "Why don't we just do a Medicaid expansion?" Let me try to answer that. By using both Medicaid and private insurance, we can get the best of both worlds. I believe that for three reasons: First, according to teachers, dental and vision problems are among the health problems that interfere most with learning. Designing our own insurance plan allows us to incorporate dental and vision care and other preventive services school-age children need for learning. At the same time, Medicaid will give our youngest citizens the type of services they need in their first five years of life.

Second, we can offer a private insurance package to those 116,000 Georgia children who are above 200 percent of the poverty level, but nevertheless lack health insurance. This option would not be available with a Medicaid expansion, and the health of these children is important, too. Third, federal funds for this program are expected to decrease four years from now. This plan anticipates future changes and has long-term durability and adaptability.

Its implementation will require the Department of Medical Assistance to expand its existing program for pregnant women and preschool children to include families up to 200 percent of the poverty level. And I wanted the Merit System to be involved with the insurance program, because they have a track record of providing health insurance for 500,000 state employees, public school teachers, and their dependents.

It has not been easy, but the thrust of this administration has been to contain Medicaid costs, which during the years before I became Governor had been rising at the astronomical rate of 10 to 15 percent a year. I also wanted to curb Medicaid fraud, which had become a disgrace.

We have reduced Medicaid cost increases to about 2 percent a year, which is in line with inflation. And we have recovered over $6 million in fraudulent claims from 61 fraud convictions since 1994.

For every one dollar we have spent on fraud investigation, we have returned eight dollars to the state treasury, and in the process we have discouraged a lot of contemplated fraud. There are hundreds of millions, perhaps billions of dollars being lost on fraud on the national level, and it's outrageous that more is not being done about it.

To continue Georgia's momentum on dealing with fraud and abuse, I am including $3.5 million in this budget to create a 50-person fraud and abuse unit, which will have as one of its chief responsibilities detecting the fraud before the claims are even paid. As a result of these cost-saving measures, we have been able to expand Medicaid coverage for children three times during this administration, including this latest expansion for our tiniest citizens.

While I'm on children, I want to tell you about another initiative I'm proposing and am very excited about. We know that a baby's brain continues to form after birth, not just growing bigger as toes and fingers do, but developing microscopic connections responsible for learning and remembering.

At birth, a baby has 100 billion or more neurons forming more than 50 trillion connections, or synapses as they are called. Which sounds like a lot. But during the first months of life, the number of synapses increases 20 times to more than 1,000 trillion. This amazing growth allows a baby to do all kinds of miraculous things, from focusing its eyes on an object to shaping the word "Da-da."

The new research on brain development in babies is unbelievable. *Time* devoted a special issue to it, and I recommend its reading. I have a lot of research I'd be glad to share with you. Enrichment clearly makes a difference in brain development.

In October we had an early childhood development seminar for teachers, medical professionals, staff of our state agencies that work with children, and businesses with products and services for tiny customers. It was fascinating.

Why am I telling you all this in a speech that is already far too long? Because I want to propose something extraordinary that I don't think any other state does, and it is this.

Research shows that reading to an infant, talking with an infant and especially having that infant listen to soothing music helps those trillions of brain connections to develop, especially the ones related to math.

There is research that links the study of music to better school performance and higher scores on college entrance exams. There's even a study called the "Mozart effect" that showed after college students listened to a Mozart piano sonata for 10 minutes, their IQ scores increased by nine points. Some argue that it didn't last, but no one doubts that listening to music, especially at a very early age, affects the spatial-temporal reasoning that underlies math, engineering, and chess.

So I propose that the parents of every baby born in Georgia—over a 100,000 a year—be given a cassette or CD of music to be played often in the baby's presence. It's not a big-ticket item in the budget—only $105,000—but I believe it can help Georgia children to excel. I have asked Yoel Levi, the world-famous conductor of the Atlanta Symphony, to help me with the musical selections for the tape, although I already have some ideas. For instance, here's one that a Georgia baby might hear. That, of course, is Beethoven's "Ode to Joy." Now don't you feel smarter already? Smart enough to vote for this budget item, I hope.

As I reported last week, we have been very successful in helping Georgians move off the welfare rolls and into the job market—a decrease of 57,000 households since we began welfare reform, and a 25 percent decline in just the past year. However, the ones who remain on the rolls are those with the fewest skills and the least work experience. So we want to use $30 million of the savings to expand the Welfare-to-Work program for hard-to-place recipients, and provide child care for an additional 12,625 children.

This budget also includes more than 16 million new dollars—the most ever—to improve foster care and expand adoption, which have been two major efforts of this administration. Last fiscal year we placed a record high 744 children for adoption, and our new State Office of Adoptions has doubled the number of private adoption agencies it has under contract to place children. It has created one of only seven Websites in the nation to showcase Georgia's waiting children to a wider audience of prospective parents. A major part of our program is to place 550 special needs children.

We also continue to improve and expand our community-based services for the mentally ill and mentally retarded. Nearly $15 million is redirected from state hospitals into community services, in accordance with the hospital reallocation formula to provide services for the mentally ill and for substance abusers.

When I became Governor, community-based services for severely emotionally disturbed children, or SEDs, were available in only two counties. But with this budget, services for severely emotionally disturbed children will be available in every county of the state.

When I became Governor, less than half of the state had any community-based services for chronically mentally ill adults or CMI. With this budget, CMI services will, for the first time, also be available statewide.

As a result of these expanding community-based services, admission to our 10 state mental hospitals has declined by 28 percent. This is why we will be able to close the Georgia Mental Health Institute, freeing up $22 million—$12 million will be used to complete statewide CMI funding, and $10 million will go for needed services at the remaining state hospitals.

During this administration, we have also increased the number of community placements for mentally retarded citizens. Slots under Medicaid waivers have risen from 119 to over 2,500.

As promised, the money from closing Brook Run was first used to fund community placements for residents, or other institutional care for those too fragile to go into the community. Then, after providing for all 326 Brook Run residents, we were able to offer community-based care to 206 additional persons with mental retardation who, before, were not even being served.

In addition I am proposing that we continue our community-based services for the elderly. In this budget, $5.5 million will provide services for an additional 2,000-plus individuals under Medicaid and over 900 elderly clients who are not Medicaid eligible. During my administration funding for services for the elderly has increased over 80 percent.

Early in this administration we started the Family Connection, which provides a structure for local communities to coordinate their resources to meet the needs of at-risk families. Each local community tailors its efforts to meet its own particular needs. It has worked well, so we have been gradually expanding the Family Connection until, with this budget, it will be active in every county of the state, making a difference in the quality of life for families and children who are at risk. This is another $3 million well spent.

As violent crime by juveniles increases, we are struggling to find places to put all of the juveniles committed to our care. My supplemental budget contains 550 new juvenile beds, and in this big budget I am recommending nearly $23 million to annualize those beds and open more—a total of almost 1,200 new beds at six facilities. I am also recommending planning funds for a new RYDC in Albany. These new and expanded facilities will bring the number of YDC beds to over 3,300 and the number of RYDC beds to nearly 1,500 by FY 2001.

But we must do more than just lock up juveniles. So I propose over $2 million to expand education programs, giving all children in the RYDC system five and a-half hours of education every school day.

This budget contains the $600,000 needed to match $1.6 million in federal funds for the Department of Defense's Youth Challenge Program. The 9th class of 186 students graduated last Saturday. These funds will serve another 350 students next year.

Once again, the Corrections Department budget opens more new beds. Ten million dollars will annualize the operating cost for 1,344 new beds opening at five new prisons—Wilcox, Washington, Smith in Tattnall County, Macon, and Coastal. Another 1,500 new beds will come on line as three new private facilities open in Coffee, Charlton and Wheeler Counties. And another $2.4 million will annualize the operating cost of 768 new beds for Pulaski State Prison and Augusta State Medical Prison.

The opening of all these beds brings the total number of new prison beds we have made available during this administration to 20,717. That is a Georgia record. Make no mistake about it, were it not for this dramatic increase, it would be pointless for anyone to even talk about abolishing parole.

I want to further expand inmate access to educational instruction, so there is a million dollars for 17 existing prison-based distance learning sites and seven new sites. Remember all those editorials and dire comments about how it wouldn't work when we moved education programs to the evening after the prison workday was over, and added distance learning? Today I am pleased to report that in the first six months, inmates utilized virtually all of the distance learning hours we made available to them. They did it mostly in the evening, after the prison work day was over.

There has been a 75 percent increase in the number of those participating in classes, and a 58 percent increase in the number of inmates taking the GED exam. Next year, with the addition of these seven new sites, we expect GED exams to double compared to a year ago.

There is also $2 million to hire another 80 probation officers to allow the department to place more emphasis on supervision of the highest risk probationers.

As violent crime increases, so does our need for improved facilities at our crime labs. In the supplemental budget, I recommended funds to double the number of counties with terminals for our AFIS computer system. These terminals allow law enforcement officers to do automated fingerprint checks and to tap into the state's database of criminal fingerprints. In this budget, there is $1.2 million for a morgue building adjacent to the State Crime Lab. It is greatly needed to relieve overcrowding at the lab and allow medical examiner services to be expanded.

Two years ago, I announced the successful completion of Preservation 2000, which has preserved over 100,000 acres of wildlife habitat, beautiful natural features, and green space for the enjoyment of our citizens. Then we immediately began RiverCare 2000, to protect more of Georgia's river corridors. In this budget is $20 million in bonds for RiverCare, bringing the total state funding for this program to $43.4 million.

Much of this money will purchase tracts of land along the Chattachoochee River between White County, where it is a clear, rushing mountain stream, and Muscogee County, where it forms the boundary between Georgia and Alabama. I don't have to tell any of you that the Chattachoochee is one of the most abused rivers in the nation. This initiative will help promote water quality, protect wildlife habitat, limit development in flood-prone areas, and provide public access for boating, fishing, and other recreational uses. It could also, and this is very important, leverage significant amounts of private, local, and federal money for protecting this important river corridor. The state will work closely with local governments, the federal government and national organizations like The Conservation Fund, The Nature Conservancy, and the Trust for Public Land, in this major effort to preserve the mighty Chattahoochee.

Along with this funding, you will find bonds in the budget for the construction of the West Georgia reservoir, because the water supply needs of the western part of the state are growing increasingly critical. We are all aware that this project presents some environmental considerations, so there is specific language dictating that all state and federal regulations, including the water compact recently approved by Congress, must be met before the bonds are sold.

Speaking of Georgia's waterways, as more Georgians take to the water, we have been experiencing an increase in boating accidents. DNR will ask you to strengthen the law on reckless boating and boating under the influence of alcohol or drugs, but we also need to be able to enforce the law. So you will find funding in the Department of Natural Resources for 20 more law enforcement officers to patrol our waterways.

I also want to strengthen the Environmental Protection Division with 26 new positions to improve the management of our water resources and implement our water compacts with Alabama and Florida.

Last, but certainly not least, this budget includes funds for the second year of Georgia Gain, a pay-for-performance system for state employees. This system allows us to base salary increases on merit and performance. The days of automatic, across-the-board increases in Georgia are gone. We now have a process which allows us to reward and retain high performers.

This has been an extremely long speech, even by Miller standards, and I can tell that I am about to be drowned out by the music of growling stomachs, which, unlike Mozart, is not likely to make us any smarter.

So I close with one of my favorite quotes from Abraham Lincoln, speaking to his legislature, "The dogmas of the quiet past are inadequate to the stormy present. As our case is new, so must we think anew and act anew." On the cusp of another General Assembly, on the cusp of another century, on the cusp of a new millennium, we in Georgia are called to think and act not from the dogmas of the past, but to continue our vision of the future. That, my friends, is what this budget does.

# State of the State Address

*January 15, 1998*

Lieutenant Governor Howard, Speaker Murphy, members of the General Assembly, members of the Georgia Supreme Court and Court of Appeals, members of the Consular Corps, ladies, and gentlemen.

Over the holidays, Shirley and I got a great present. A dear friend gave us two eight-week-old yellow lab puppies. One is named Thomas B., the other is named Pierre. And I have the papers to prove it.

One of them is a little rambunctious and has a bit of a temper. The other is thoughtful and reflective, even polite. You can guess which one is which. I've already had to cuss 'em a time or two, and Shirley keeps telling me, "Why don't you just try being a little nicer to them."

These dogs will be with us for many years, and the friend who gave them to us thought it would be poetic justice for Shirley and me to get up every morning and go to bed every night, probably for the rest of our lives, taking care of Thomas B. and Pierre. I may have to let Shirley handle Thomas B.

Seriously and very sincerely, I want to begin my last State of the State Address by paying tribute to these two very good and very able men who have presided over the House and Senate during my time as Governor. Without any doubt, they are the best presiding officers in the country. Both love this state deeply and both hold passionately to their beliefs. I have much respect, admiration and, yes, great affection for both of these men. Because of their work, Georgia is a better place and I have been a better Governor. It has been one of the great privileges of my life to have worked with Tom Murphy and Pierre Howard all these years. From the bottom of my heart, I thank you both.

This past Christmas, for the 65th straight year, a family of Millers sat around an open fireplace in the old rock house in Young Harris. There were four generations of us. Shirley and I were the oldest. Our two sons, Murphy and Matt, and their two wives, Susan and Katie, were the next generation.

Eight-year-old twins, Andrew and Bryan, teenager Justin, and my granddaughter Asia and her husband Shane Martin were still another generation. And then their two sons—Jacob, almost four, and Joshua, ten months—were the fourth generation.

Quite a tribe; we filled up the entire room. Amid the wrapping paper and ribbon, amid the oohs and aahs, the obligatory thanks and the genuine surprises, I remembered back to the Christmases past and I thought of the Christmases yet to come. I did not need Jacob Marley's ghost or Tiny Tim to tell me how richly blessed I truly am.

I was just a little older than my great-grandson Jacob when the President of the United States stood on the steps of the United States Capitol, looked south and said, "I see one-third of a nation ill-housed, ill-clad and ill-nourished." That was the South I grew up in. But it is not the South my grandchildren and great-grandchildren will grow up in.

Today, that "one-third of a nation," by itself, has an economy that is the fifth largest in the world. By the year 2000, the South will surpass the Northeast in population.

Georgia is leading the way. Our economy has outperformed the nation's every year since 1991, some years by more than 80 percent. We have created more than 2,000 new jobs every week since 1991, and last year we led the nation in high-tech job growth. Georgia is now truly an international location, home to more than 1,500 international businesses. The rest of the world has discovered what we already knew: There is no better place to live, work, or raise a family than the State of Georgia.

That's the Georgia those next generations will live in. And the state of that state— today and I think for years to come—is excellent.

As a student and teacher of history, I've always been comfortable with facts and details, words, dates and numbers. And I can think of many nights I've spent under this gold dome, working on budgets, crafting legislation, looking for the right word or phrase or idea that would forge a compromise or pass a bill.

You all know exactly what I mean. You are faced with it, too: large amounts of data you must wrestle with, long pages of words and numbers you must pore over, making sure that the bill does what you really intend. It is so easy to get bogged down in the minutia of state government, to just tune out while listening to long budget messages like the one on Tuesday, to lose sight of the forest, to lose sight even of the trees.

But one thing is certain: what we do in this building is important. What we do here is vital to the daily lives of real children, real families and real communities. The words contained in any bill translate into real lives. The numbers in any budget represent real people.

Those numbers I spout so easily—299,000 HOPE scholars, 60,000 four-year-olds in prekindergarten, 2,000 new jobs every week, two strikes and you're in for life, 57,000 families off the welfare rolls—they are more than just statistics. Each number is a human being we have touched, and each touch is like a pebble tossed into the water, rippling through that person to touch their family, their community, their state. Behind each number is a face, a life, a promise, a future.

So today, I want to *show* you something of what we have accomplished together, not just *tell* you. Today I want to bring you face-to-face with those to whom we've lent a hand. Just as I saw it with my own family on Christmas morning, I want you, today, to see Georgia's present and look into the eyes of Georgia's future.

As a father, grandfather, and great-grandfather, I understand the deep desire that all parents have for their children to succeed, and the sacrifices that all parents make to help their children. For years, parents all over Georgia had been urging their children to do well in school, and scrimping and saving and doing without in hopes of being able to send their child to college or to a technical school.

Then HOPE was born. In 1993, the State of Georgia entered into a covenant with those parents and their children. We said to all the children of this state: You study and you work hard in school, and HOPE will be there to help you go to college. You give something, you get something—one of life's most important lessons.

We helped Georgia families realize their hopes and dreams for the future. Now, almost five years later, HOPE achieves an historic milestone. Today, the HOPE Scholarship Program reaches the 300,000 mark—300,000 individual students from every corner of this state, from every kind of community, have earned free tuition at our state colleges or scholarships at our private colleges.

And today we have the honor of having one of those scholars with us. I am very pleased to introduce to you the 300,000th HOPE scholar, Miss Lauren Stripling of Newnan, Georgia. Lauren, will you please stand.

Lauren has a younger brother and an older sister, and I'll bet with three children, the HOPE Scholarship has come in handy when it comes to the family budget.

Lauren graduated from Newnan High School with an outstanding 3.8 grade, point average, while at the same time playing Varsity soccer, working on the school paper and holding down a part-time job. Now she attends the University of Georgia, and has earned a perfect 4.0 this past summer and fall quarters. She told me she is thinking of majoring in history education and becoming a history teacher.

Lauren, from this old history teacher, I hope you do it. We need people like you in our classrooms. Thank you for coming today.

Let me add one footnote. We've touched this family before. Lauren's older sister was a 1994 HOPE scholar and graduated in three years at UGA... all on HOPE. And I hear her younger brother is on track for a HOPE scholarship as well.

Folks, these three children in the Stripling family are a living, breathing legacy that we should all be proud of. By your support of the HOPE scholarship, each one of you has made a difference to the Stripling family and to tens of thousands of other Georgia families.

The HOPE Scholarship Program is not the only innovation that has caught this nation's attention. In 1996, we embarked on another journey. We took Georgia where no state has ever gone before. At that time I compared it to Columbus sailing off into the unknown on the Nina, Pinta and Santa Maria. We became the first state in the history of this nation to offer prekindergarten, free of charge, to every four-year-old whose parents want it. We are still the only state to do that.

Study after study documents that the impact of pre-K lasts well into adulthood, with higher education levels, greater earning power, stronger commitment to marriage, and lower incidence of welfare and crime. In the long-run, pre-K students are more likely to stay in school, achieve higher test scores, and graduate better prepared for further education or the workforce.

More than 185,000 Georgia children have already benefitted from pre-K. What an incredible investment in our children and in our future.

Now I want you to see with your own eyes where that investment is going. I want you to look into the eyes of Georgia's future. Would you please welcome the pre-K class of Debbie Cost and Norma Luster from The Children's Center at All Saints.

Never doubt that providing pre-K for those children is one of the single most important investments we can make. Their head start will change the face of Georgia and the face of the South. Of that I have no doubt.

The pre-K program reflects my philosophy of education: Not just some, but every Georgia child should enter school ready to learn. Not just some, but every Georgia child should have equal opportunity. Not just some, but every Georgia child deserves a head start. The pre-K program achieves that.

Now I want to brag on my wife of 44 years as of yesterday, Shirley Miller. For many years Shirley and I realized that the problem of illiteracy was costing Georgia both economically and educationally.

Educationally, we were faced with the fact that nearly 30 percent of our adult population had never completed high school. In some counties, it was more than 50 percent. Economically, we discovered that over half a million adults in our workforce were functionally illiterate, costing Georgia employers over $2 billion a year.

But, even more important, behind those cold numbers are warm bodies: good, caring, decent people trapped in the darkness of illiteracy.

Shirley Carver Miller was determined to do something about it. She wanted this as her project. When she began in 1991, less than 70,000 adults were enrolled annually in literacy programs. Today, more than 100,000 are enrolled. When she began in 1991, only 13,000 Georgians were earning GEDs each year. Today, 21,000 earn their GEDs and a $500 HOPE scholarship voucher to continue their education.

When she began in 1991, only a few of Georgia's 159 counties had full-time adult literacy teachers. Today, every county has them, and more than 1,100 computers have been placed in literacy labs statewide to assist those instructors. State funding for adult literacy has tripled to almost $12 million annually.

Now I want to brag on two heroes: Willie Almond, Jr. from Franklin and Carrie Porter of Fort Valley. Will both of you please stand.

Willie Almond has an amazing story to tell. He runs a lawn service and landscaping business in the city of Franklin. Fighting dyslexia since childhood, Mr. Almond quit school before he learned to read properly and had no plans to ever go back.

With the help of adult literacy instructors and his wife, Sarah, he can now read whatever he wants. But he didn't stop there. He worked to bring a countywide literacy program to Heard County, so others could be helped, too. And he still didn't stop there. Ladies and gentlemen, as of January 2nd, let me introduce you to Franklin, Georgia's first African-American city council member of this century: Councilman Willie Almond, Jr.

Carrie Porter's middle name is "Determination." This woman doesn't understand the concept of giving up. She had to quit school after she became pregnant. She worked as a cook at Warner Robins Day Care Center for 17 years while raising four children.

Then in 1993, Mrs. Porter entered an adult literacy center in Peach County and earned her GED. But she didn't stop there. In September of 1995, she enrolled at Georgia College in Milledgeville, and has now earned an associate degree in child development.

Remember I told you she was a cook for the Warner Robins Day Care Center for 17 years? Please meet the new director of the Warner Robins Day Care Center, Mrs. Carrie Porter.

Thank you both for being here today.

The State of Georgia has done a remarkable job of helping Lauren and Carrie and Willie, and thousands like them. But Georgia also has an obligation to protect our citizens as well.

So, I'd like to tell you a more somber story. We all know that DUI has been a plague on our streets and highways, that it has caused unnecessary death and bloodshed. Too many lives have been lost. Too many families have been shattered. Too much pain has been felt.

DUI criminals—and that's what they are, criminals—can terrorize any one of us at a moment's notice. They vicitimize at random. Each and every one of us is at risk the moment we get into a car or even walk down the sidewalk along the street. It can strike anyone, anywhere, anytime. And it can be prevented. That is why drunk drivers have found no mercy during the Miller Administration.

But I had a more personal motivation as well. Back in 1992, Mr. Charles McManis was living in Jonesboro, and the first week of the session, he came to my office. I'd never met him before, and today is the first time we've spoken since that meeting.

He walked into my office and handed me a framed photograph—this portrait of his daughter, Katherine Sue. She had just been killed by a drunk driver at the age of 21. Mr. McManis talked not as constituent to Governor, but as father to father. Heart to heart. He asked me to keep this photograph in my office as a reminder of the terrible cost and terrible consequences of DUI. With tears in his eyes, he asked me not to forget about his daughter, and to please stop it from happening again.

Mr. McManis has come all the way from Dandridge, Tennessee, to be with us today. Thank you for doing that, and would you please stand.

Mr. McManis, I want you to know that up until the moment I removed it to bring it here with me today, I have kept your daughter's portrait on display in my office every single day since our meeting six years ago. This photo affected me. No longer was DUI just another political fight to win. No longer were those terrible DUI statistics just numbers. I had this face in front of me. Every single day I walked into my office, she was there.

Many people, visiting my office, have seen her picture and asked if she were my daughter or granddaughter. And each time I've told them this story. Today, I'm telling our whole state. I cannot begin to comprehend the loss of a child to drunk driving—I won't even pretend to. Here was a young woman, full of life and promise, gone forever because of a stupid, senseless crime.

So each and every year I asked you to take another major step forward toward making our highways safe from drunk and drugged drivers. And you responded. In 1997, we passed one of the toughest DUI laws in America: Mandatory jail time for drunk drivers. No keeping your license by pleading nolo. Confiscation of license plates. Zero tolerance for minors.

That is the kind of DUI protection the law-abiding drivers of Georgia deserve. Because of our work for these tougher penalties, my hope and prayer is that there will be fewer drunken killers on the road.

Thank you, Mr. McManis for bringing your daughter's picture to my office and for being here with us today.

Now let me tell you about some individuals who could not be here today. Thanks to your help, we passed "two-strikes and you're out"—the toughest crime law in the nation. Thanks to that law, there are 1,710 violent criminals who could not be here today, or anywhere else, because they are locked away in Georgia prisons.

Those 1,710 criminals were convicted under our "two-strikes" law, and they are going to serve every year, every month, every day, every second of their sentences without parole. And let me tell you something else. Collectively, those 1,710 thugs were responsible for more than 9,800 crimes, including over 4,900 violent crimes. But thanks to the two-strikes law, they are no longer a threat to the law-abiding people of Georgia. This year, we're going to do more.

We have not only made our human environment safer, we have also taken major steps to preserve our natural environment. One of our biggest success stories has been Preservation 2000, our program to protect more than 100,000 acres of natural land.

As I am speaking, television viewers are looking at some of the gorgeous natural features that Preservation 2000 has saved—places like Little Tybee Island, Tallulah Gorge, and Smithgall Woods. You in this chamber are looking at someone shaped by that rugged land, because your Governor is very much a product of the North Georgia mountains. I am so fortunate for that. I grew up surrounded by the spectacular beauty of the mountains. It is a part of me wherever I go.

We created Preservation 2000 with very ambitious goals, some said too ambitious— to protect 100,000 acres of wildlife habitat and natural areas, and save it for future generations. And we succeeded. We preserved land in some 50 counties from Dade and Walker in the northwest, to McIntosh in the southeast, from Rabun in the far northeast corner to Decatur in the far southwest corner. From the coast to the mountains, Preservation 2000 touches every part of the state.

This land is our common gift, a wonderful gift that God gave to all of us, and now a gift we treasure and nurture and pass on to our children and to generations yet to come. And this year, we will do even more.

On January 14, 1991, after I had taken the oath of office as Governor of this state, I talked about the people to whom my administration would be dedicated: The small business owners, the bold entrepreneurs, the family farmers, the senior citizens, and, as I put it then, the "young families struggling to afford day care now and save for college later."

I went on: "It is to every family that works and saves and sometimes comes up a little short at the end of the month, that this administration is dedicated." I summed it up by saying, and I quote, "The central purpose of the Miller administration will be to prepare Georgia for the 21st century. Education is the most important part of that purpose. Without it, nothing else can save us. With it, nothing else can stop us."

Today I am proud to say that with your good help, I have kept that faith. I have fought that fight—although I've still got some fight left in me—and I am preparing to finish the course.

So now, as the pages turn on the final chapter of my career as a public servant, I remember how it was in that first chapter of my life, growing up in that remote valley, in that same house in which we just celebrated Christmas.

On summer nights before the TVA dammed up the Hiawassee River and brought electricity to the valley, after the moon had come up over Double Knobs and the lightning bugs were blinking, while the frogs croaked down at the creek, and the katy-dids sang, and every once in a while a whippoorwill's lonesome cry could be heard, I remember after my mother had finally quit working and was getting us quiet and ready for bed, I remember we'd play a game.

The game would start when the headlights of that rare car would penetrate the darkness, maybe once every half-hour, on the narrow strip of cracked asphalt across the ditch in front of our house. We'd stare as the headlights would disappear and then reappear as it made its way around the steep curves and finally across Brasstown Mountain. We'd count and we'd see how long it took from the time it went by the house until its taillights disappeared through the distant gap and it was no longer a part of that one and only world I knew.

It was often at this time that my Mother would laugh and say, "You know what's so great about this place? You can get anywhere in the world from here."

That world has turned many times since I first traveled that narrow road through that gap and out of that valley. It has been a long road with many twists and turns, ups and downs, bumps and wrecks. A road that finally carried me to the highest office of the tenth largest state in the nation, to all the continents and famous cities of the world, into the Oval Office of the White House and onto Air Force One, to Madison Square Garden, where I spoke to 20 million people through a medium unknown and unimagined when I was a child watching those cars and playing that game.

And so I close my last State of the State Address, knowing that once again my mother has been proved right. One could get anywhere in the world from that little mountain valley—and back again. And I've always wanted that to be true for every child in Georgia.

Everywhere I've ever been was on my way back home. I want to thank the people of this great state for entrusting to me for eight years your Office of Governor. I hope I have served you well. And I want to thank my very special staff who has served me so well.

Thanks to all of you—my family, my friends, and my God—it has been one heck of a ride.

But we still have work to do. So let's get at it.

# National Council on Competitiveness

*Massachusetts Institute of Technology, March 12, 1998*

Thank you, President Vest. It's good to be here, and I am especially pleased to be sharing this Round Table with Governors Paul Cellucci and John Engler. I just got to know Paul a couple weeks ago at the National Governors Association, but I have served with John Engler for seven years, and I consider him one of this nation's truly great governors. I not only admire—I envy some of the things he's done in Michigan.

Each one of us is the CEO of our state. We administer annual operating budgets in the billions of dollars. Georgia's is $12.5 billion. If you took any one of our states separately, it would be within or near Fortune's top 100 businesses in the world. So we are CEOs of a right large business, and like any competitive business, we are determined to run out on the cutting edge of innovation... innovation in creating programs that promote research, intellectual capital, and participation in the global economy.

And we are successful at it. In Georgia that is reflected in our high ranking from the Batelle Institute for state investment in technology initiatives, and in our designation last year as the leading state in high-tech job growth by the American Electronics Association. So I'm very pleased to have this opportunity to tell you about some of the programs that have helped propel Georgia into the forefront.

I consider higher education to be the most important economic development infrastructure there is, for research and for workforce development. Georgia is one of the top two states in the amount of state funding for research and development, so let me begin by telling you briefly about two of our programs—the Georgia Research Alliance and the Traditional Industries Research Program.

It is important to note that they are both partnerships among higher education, private industry and state government, and they are both clearly focused on generating economic development in particular industries. They are both clearly industry-driven. They are both sharply focused on the needs of the specific industries they serve, but at the same time broadly applicable in their results.

The Georgia Research Alliance includes six research universities, public and private. Private industry dominates its governing board, but the practical cooperation of the six university presidents is what has made it successful. Early in my administration, the Research Alliance identified three high-tech fields with strong future growth potential, in which one or more of the six member universities was already doing research. They are advanced telecommunications, bio-technology and environmental technology, and the Alliance promotes and coordinates research that will attract firms, spin off firms, and generate growth in these industries.

Over the past seven years, state government has invested over $200 million in the Research Alliance. These funds have matched private funds to endow chairs for 27 eminent research scholars who have been recruited worldwide, and to equip, even build the sophisticated labs their research requires.

This state investment has generated another $500 million for the Research Alliance from the private sector and the federal government. Over and above this, sponsored research at the six member universities has doubled in dollar value, and the number of Georgia companies sponsoring university research has quadrupled.

We have two incubators that house spin-off firms, and they are bursting at the seams with fledgling businesses. So, we are about to build three more.

We are now attracting venture capitalists as never before. Last year, the South overtook the Northeast in venture capital invested, with Georgia leading the way. Monday morning I will welcome 400 participants to Atlanta's second annual Venture Capital South conference.

The second partnership I want to tell you a little about is what we call the Traditional Industries Program. It targets three manufacturing industries that account for almost half of our manufacturing workforce. They are textiles, pulp and paper, and food processing. These industries have been around for a long time in Georgia. But they know that if they are to compete in a global economy, if they are to meet new environmental and safety standards, they must virtually reinvent themselves with advanced technology.

Again, the Traditional Industries Program is a public-private partnership. Partnerships have been the strength of my administration, and I strongly believe that is what the future will require. These industries identify practical problems that are critical to their competitiveness, and then work closely with faculty at Georgia colleges and universities to solve those problems. And state funds are matched by private investment from the companies who benefit from the research.

As we have created research partnerships like these, we have found that the federal government will sometimes join in as a fourth partner.

But it is not just enough to have ideas and innovations. You must also have an educated workforce that can do something with them. So my goal as Governor has been to establish in Georgia what I call a culture of higher expectations. I want the question not to be "whether" to go to college or technical school, but "where."

That's why we created the HOPE Scholarship Program in Georgia. The *Los Angeles Times* and others have called it the most far-reaching scholarship program in America. It's based on merit, not income level. It also teaches one of life's great lessons: you give something, you get something.

Here's how it works: Every Georgia student who graduates from a Georgia high school, public or private, with at least a B average in their academic subjects, can get free tuition, mandatory fees and a book allowance as a freshman at any Georgia public college. If they choose a private Georgia college, they get a $3,000 scholarship. If they keep up that B average, year by year, through college, these scholarship benefits continue through all four years. In Georgia it's possible to go through all four years of college without paying one cent of tuition, and getting help with fees and books besides.

Those who don't have a B average or don't want to go to college can get free tuition and a book allowance for a diploma program—that's usually 18 months or a two-year program—at a post-secondary technical school.

In the past five years, more than 300,000 Georgians have received scholarship assistance totaling over $500 million from HOPE.

We also created another program that has received national attention. It is called ICAPP. That stands for Intellectual Capital Partnership Program. Again, it's the first of its kind in the nation. ICAPP gives corporations an opportunity to be active partners with the University System of Georgia by investing directly in programs designed to meet their specific needs for a college-educated workforce. ICAPP provides financial aid to speed up the education process, in return for a commitment from students to stay in Georgia to work.

For example, Columbus, Georgia, has a great demand for college graduates in computing, because it is home to numerous information technology companies, including one of the largest credit card processors in the world—Total System Services. So Columbus State University is a partner with this company in an ICAPP project designed to educate 400 computing majors a year for the next four years. Total Systems advertises the program and pays for aptitude testing and employee screening at the beginning of the education process, then guarantees a job offer at the end.

Then finally, in the area of access to the global market, I want to mention the Export Assistance Center in Atlanta, which is the first fully integrated state-federal center in the nation. It provides comprehensive services to business of all types and sizes.

Federal partners include the U.S. Department of Commerce, the SBA, and Eximbank. State partners include our Departments of Industry and Agriculture, Georgia Tech, and the Small Business Development Center at The University of Georgia. BellSouth is a private-sector partner, enabling the Export Assistance Center to offer international interactive tele-conferencing capabilities.

The center is also hooked into our statewide telecommunications network, which includes all of our 34 public colleges, universities, our 34 technical institutes, and some 200 public schools. This means that businesses anywhere in Georgia have local access to live teleconferences with state trade representatives based all around the world. Georgia, by the way, has 11 trade offices.

These are but five of the more significant and innovative things that we have done in Georgia to promote competitiveness. Again I am pleased to be here with these two great Governors, and I am looking forward to gathering new ideas from them and all of you about how we can do even more.

# Richmond College Commencement

*The American International University in London*
*May 14, 1998*

It is an honor to be invited to speak at commencement during the Silver Jubilee Year of Richmond College, and I am humbled to receive an honorary degree from the American University in London.

As a historian, I am especially interested in the unique relationship between the United States and England. I am told that history books in this country don't dwell too much on a little dispute between our nations over a tea tax a couple of hundred years ago. That's as it should be, because we have much more that is in common.

Georgia was founded by a good Englishman: James Edward Oglethorpe. I have made several pilgrimages to England in the company of other historians and fans of Oglethorpe, to visit his home, his college, the port from which he set sail, the seat of his district in Parliament, and the church where he lies buried. I was preceded in my own travels to England by my father, who attended Kings College. I have visited there as well, to walk the halls where he once studied.

Our laws are based on English law. Our views on democracy and capitalism have much in common, and over the years since we settled that little affair in the 1770s, we have stood shoulder to shoulder, time after time, on the battlefields of the world in defense of democracy.

We even share a common language—although now that you've heard my accent, which comes from the Appalachian Mountains and has been described as more barbed wire than honey, you probably agree with Oscar Wilde that "the English and Americans are two peoples *divided* by a common language."

We also share a common commitment to education, and I ask you to think with me about education this afternoon. I am passionate about education. Perhaps it's genetic, for I am the son of two teachers. More likely it is because I know first-hand where an education can lead.

Education was the vehicle that took me down the long road from the isolated Appalachian Mountain valley where I was born to the Governor's office of the tenth largest state in the United States. My goal as Governor has been to create in my state a culture of higher expectations. I wanted the question in Georgia to be not "whether" to go to college, but "where."

I pushed for a state lottery to provide the resources, which was no easy task in the American Bible Belt. I know England has introduced a national lottery that is doing many good things. I was especially pleased to hear that part of it is now dedicated to education, and I'd like to think that an article your own Sir Cyril wrote about our Georgia experience had a little bit of influence.

I used the money from Georgia's lottery to create three new education programs. The HOPE Scholarship Program is the most far-reaching scholarship program in the United

States today. Any Georgia student who does well in their academic subjects through high school, can get free tuition and a book allowance at any public college in the state, or scholarship assistance at any Georgia private college.

I also began a prekindergarten program that has made Georgia the first and so far the only state to offer free prekindergarten to every four-year-old whose parents want to enroll them. I note with pride that Prime Minister Blair has just recommended a similar program here.

The money that remained after these two programs were funded, I invested in educational technology, recognizing that in the new millennium at least 90 percent of the jobs will require technology skills, compared to 60 percent today, and about 5 percent when I got out of college.

The goal of all of these programs is to provide high-quality educational opportunity, and that is what we celebrate here today—the high quality, unique education that has been yours here at Richmond College.

That education has given you two of the greatest treasures a person can own. One, of course, is intellectual curiosity. Someone once said that your real education is what is left after you've forgotten everything you were taught in the classroom. Or, as Tom Peters put it, "Victory in the brain-based economy will go to the perpetually curious."

We are awash in a sea of information whose tides are rising so rapidly we are tempted to fear drowning. But much of it is short-lived. Those of you who studied computing, science, or engineering, will find that the shelf-life of the technical information you've learned is probably about five years, in some cases even less. That's exciting, yet frightening.

So, the business of higher education is more than mere information. The business of higher education is knowledge. And unlike information, knowledge cannot be poured into your mind like Earl Grey into an English teacup. Knowledge is not a destination; it is a process. What your future employers will value most in you is not the facts and data you have memorized, but a questing and inquisitive mind that is skilled in decision-making and problem-solving; a mind that looks at the same things everybody else sees, but finds something more; a mind that is not only comfortable with change, but anticipates it and even seeks it out; a mind that forms the foundation for lifelong intellectual inquiry that will serve you well, not only as a job skill but also in giving meaning, direction, and richness to your life.

Which brings me to the second treasure Richmond College has given you. This college is a microcosm—a visible, tangible icon—of that amorphous, invisible global village that technology has made of the world. Here a thousand students from a hundred countries come together not only to study, but also to learn to live together... to learn not merely to tolerate their differences, but to enjoy and appreciate them.

Here you have learned to find "unity in diversity." You have been exposed to a broad spectrum of human experience in practice as well as theory. And you have learned to live with confidence and grace on the balance point between the expression of your own ideas and a thoughtful respect for the perspective of others. In short, you have been prepared in a very special way to take your place in the diverse, multi-cultural contexts that increasingly characterize our world.

These two treasures, intellectual curiosity and multi-cultural sensitivity, have already brought each of you to this special day on the threshold of your careers, and they will carry you wherever it is you want to go.

Congratulations on your achievements. Use your the treasures of your education to enrich your lives and to live out your dreams.

# Excerpts

# Armed Services

We are here to express our support and appreciation for the young men and women from Georgia who answered their country's call and put their lives on the line in the Persian Gulf. They have destroyed an aggressor's vain glory, and have brought an end to a tyrant's pillage of the people and resources of Kuwait.

Edmund Burke once said that "the only thing necessary for the triumph of evil is for good men (and women) to do nothing." When Saddam Hussein marched his troops into Kuwait, he thought the whole world would watch that evil and do nothing. When the United Nations spoke, he took those words to be empty rhetoric, like so many of his own. He figured that a country that tolerated free speech and debate about war would certainly not have the spirit and unity to fight and win one.

But what Saddam Hussein and all other tyrants fail to understand is that the very same freedom that allows us to speak openly and debate issues is what unites this nation and what lies at the root of our iron resolve to fight oppression by the likes of him. To paraphrase our pledge of allegiance, it is our deep commitment to liberty and justice for all that makes us "one nation, indivisible."

We have worried and prayed about the courageous young men and women who have been in harm's way, and we are intensely proud of the job they have done. One of the best moments of my week was seeing the headline on Thursday's paper announcing that the first troops of the 24th Infantry Division had begun the journey home to Fort Stewart. They truly earned the name "victory division" with their race across the desert to block the retreat of Iraq's Republican Guard—a race which General Norman Schwarzkopf called "an unbelievable move" and which military strategists will recall and replay for years to come.

But their action and our victory was a team effort, and many other of our fellow Georgians also did their part with courage and valor. As we welcome the 24th Infantry Division home, let us also hold in our thoughts the 700-plus Georgia Army and Air National Guardsmen who remain in Saudi Arabia, helping to clean up after the war. Some of them have been in the sands of the Arabian desert since the very outset of this operation. Our armed forces, active and reserves, have earned the honor and glory that a thankful nation should bestow, and I am proud to be a part of this celebration of our collective pride.

I would also lift up before you yet another very special group—those who will not return to their loved ones from the Persian Gulf. They made the supreme sacrifice for their country, and theirs are names which will be entered on a roll call of honor that goes back to the founding of this nation.

God bless our troops. God bless our fellow Georgians. And God bless this nation.

*—Gulf War Rally, March 9, 1991*

I have a friend named Bill Anderson, a great songwriter who a few years ago wrote a song entitled "Where Have All the Heros Gone." Well, I know where one is—and today we honor him. It's great to know that real heroes still walk among us, and it's good to know that there are those who still remember, half a century after the beginning of World War II, 40 years after the start of the forgotten conflict in Korea, a quarter century after Americans marched into the quagmire called Vietnam.

America's Medal of Honor is a symbol of unusual human courage above and beyond the call of duty. The medal is a tribute to perhaps the only thing truly noble in the horror that is war: The deliberate, conscious decision of one man to sacrifice himself so that others around him might live. In the 128 years of its history, 3,416 men and one woman are listed as having earned the nation's highest decoration for valor. Nearly two of every three of those Americans did not live to see their award.

You know it is politicians who order nations into war. Sometimes out of ignorance, or grand design, or national interest, maybe even greed or anger or lack of any other alternative. But soldiers do not fight for politicians. They fight because of loyalty to those who stand with them, those who share the discomfort, the terror, the boredom, the insanity, and the suffering.

The Korean War has sometimes been called America's forgotten war. That's a shame. America and the world were caught off guard on June 25, 1950, when 90,000 North Koreans invaded South Korea. The highly trained, well-equipped Communists easily swept aside the South Korean Army and swiftly captured Seoul.

Backed by a United Nations resolution, Americans war dispatched to drive the Communists out of South Korea. It seemed an easy task. Even the Allied commander, Gen. Douglas MacArthur, predicted a quick victory. "Home by Christmas" were three words often heard.

But untold horrors lay ahead. Today, only a fraction of the American population can remember the places that for three years made headlines and are burned into my memory: Inchon, Chosin Reservoir, Heartbreak Ridge, MiG Alley. More than one million Americans fought in Korea, and more than 35,000 were killed there. In the "forgotten war" 131 Americans were named recipients of the Medal of Honor. Only 37 of them lived to wear it. We honor one of those few today.

The battle at "Frozen Chosin" was epic. In the biggest shock of the war, 300,000 Chinese Communist soldiers crossed the Yalu River from China into North Korea and trapped 8,000 members of the 1st Marine Division at the Chosin Reservoir. There was only one way out: an icy road that twisted around steep mountains. If the Chinese gained control of it, all of the Marines would be annihilated.

Lt. Col. Raymond Davis was a 35-year-old Georgia Tech graduate with already two Silver Stars for heroism in Korea and the Navy Cross, our second highest award, for gallantry on Peleiu.

He commanded a battalion of Marines faced with an apparently impossible assignment: To get to the Marines on Fox Hill, link up with them, or the thousands still at the reservoir would be doomed.

That afternoon, in 24-below-zero weather, the battalion began struggling up the side of a steep ridge. Davis's men climbed 1,000 yards before the Chinese opened up with machine guns and mortars. The Marines kept clawing their way inch by inch up the icy slopes, battling enemy soldiers who seemed tucked into every crevice. Atop the first ridge, the men's sweat froze on their eyebrows and beards. they put their wounded on stretchers and pushed on.

When darkness fell, they continued. Many fell asleep on their feet and slumped to the ground when the long line paused. "Get them up!" Davis shouted to his noncoms as he walked about kicking the bottoms of his men's boots. "Get them back on their feet!" The men rose and trudged toward still another ridge. All along, snipers picked at the slow, exposed line, but there was no time for the Marines to stop and fire back. With 100 pounds of gear on their backs, the men dragged themselves uphill. They went downhill by sliding on the ice. Davis was so numb that three times he forgot a compass reading taken only moments before.

At 4 a.m., this great Georgian halted his unit. The battalion was close to Fox Company, but had lost radio contact. Trying to reach Barber's unit in the dark without communication might get them caught in a crossfire. They would rest until daybreak. As Davis started to nap, a sniper's bullet pierced his sleeping bag, grazing his head. He tried again to sleep.

By first light, there was still no radio contact with Fox Company. Davis feared that the unit had been overrun. Then came word from his radio operator. "Colonel," he announced, "we've got Captain Barber on the radio." As the two officers talked, still hundreds of yards apart, both fought back the tears. Late in the morning, Davis's battalion arrived atop Fox Hill. The Chinese had lost the battle for Toktong Pass.

Within hours, two Marine battalions were moving south through the pass—away from the frozen Chosin. Many icy miles and more bitter fighting lay ahead before the Marines would reach the port of Hungnam, but the stand at Toktong Pass had opened the way. In five days, Fox Company had killed 1,000 of the enemy. Only 82 of the 220 Marines were able to walk off that hill.

In two weeks, the 1st Marine Division moved over icy roads and ridges through eight Chinese divisions. The Americans brought out all their wounded, dead and equipment. On the way, they killed 25,000 of the enemy. The Marines lost 730 of their numbers.

A highway named in your honor, sir? A wonderful tribute to you, sir. But so inadequate for what we and all Americans owe you. God bless you, sir. And God bless America.

*—Dedication, General Davis Medal of Honor Highway,*
*September 24, 1991*

––––––––––

It is a great honor for me, as a veteran of the United States Marine Corps, to be part of these ceremonies proclaiming Veterans' Day in Georgia. This special day is an honor we bestow upon our veterans. It is a pause from our daily routine to remember their courage in the face of danger, and to pay tribute to their commitment to liberty and justice, and their devotion to their country.

This year Veterans' Day has a special significance. Last fall at this time, tensions were escalating in the Persian Gulf. This troubled region of the world was becoming a magnet, drawing American troops, ships, planes and other military resources toward it.

Political unrest in another part of the world, which often seems remote and far away from our daily lives, suddenly became very personal and troubling to our innermost hearts. Once again we tasted the bitter dregs of war. Once again we said the painful farewells and sent our loved ones off to face danger. Only this time, our sisters and daughters went along with our brothers and sons. Fathers and mothers went, too.

So on this Veterans' Day, we honor all of our veterans, but we especially thank the men and women who answered their country's call and put their lives on the line in the Persian Gulf during the past year since we last celebrated this special day. They destroyed an aggressor's vain glory and brought to an end a tyrant's pillage of the people and resources of Kuwait. They have earned all the honor and glory that a thankful nation can bestow.

In the commemoration of that victory, we also pause especially to remember and honor those who made the supreme sacrifice for their country. We remember in sadness those who did not return to their loved ones from the Persian Gulf this year, and those who did not return from Vietnam, from Korea, from Europe and from other war-torn parts of the world where they went in defense of liberty. Their names are written with reverence on a roll-call of honor that goes back to the founding of this nation. And our hearts go out to the loved ones who feel the pain of their loss more keenly on Veterans' Day.

Finally, we remember our veterans-to-be—our troops on duty all around the world. Our thoughts are with them on this special day as they stand ready to defend liberty and fight aggression.

—*Proclamation of Veterans' Day, October 24, 1991*

More than 200 years ago, 13 scruffy little colonies declared their independence from England. In so doing, they began a war for which they had no army. So farmers left their fields, blacksmiths left their forges, teachers left their schoolrooms, cobblers left their lasts. They were all volunteers, and together they became a military force that was unified not by matching uniforms, but by devotion to and passion for a common cause.

That rag-tag army of volunteers won the war, laying the groundwork for the founding of a great and powerful democracy. They also laid the groundwork for a tried and true American tradition of volunteering in times of emergency to protect life and property and assure the survival of our democratic way of life.

That proud American tradition of volunteer militia leadership in time of emergency continues today in the Georgia State Defense Force.

—*Present Georgia Defense Day Proclamation, January 30, 1992*

The defense presence in Georgia has been so strong—for so long—that we may have taken it for granted. If so, the complacency came to an end late this spring, when four Georgia facilities were added to the list under review by the Defense Base Closure and Realignment Commission. Thanks to a lot of hard work on short notice by our congressional delegation, our base personnel and our communities, Georgia escaped significant reductions in this round of base closings. But the experience made a lot of us realize how much we would lose of one of our facilities actually closed. As the saying goes, nothing concentrates the mind like the sight of a hangman's noose.

While our minds our still concentrated, it's time to begin preparing not only for the next round of base closings scheduled for 1995—but indeed for the role our bases can play in our defense structure, our economy and our society, for years to come. That is why I am today announcing the Georgia Defense Initiative—a statewide effort to coordinate the resources we have in our base communities, our industries, our educational institutions—to build on the enormous strengths of the military presence in our state.

This effort really began back in June at the base closing hearings at the Fox Theater, when Senator Sam Nunn talked to me about the need for a more coordinated approach to the process of making Georgia's case to the Commission in the future. We agreed that the presentations made that day represented an example of brilliant broken-field running—but that a game plan would be helpful next time around.

One objective of the Georgia Defense Initiative will be to help our base communities prepare for the 1995 base closing process. But we must also recognize that the best way to tell our story in 1995 is to write some new chapters in 1993 and 1994. To ensure a broad, comprehensive effort to build on the military and civilian capabilities in and around our bases, I will assign the Georgia Defense Initiative to the Governor's Development Council, the public-private partnership responsible for strategic planning at the state and regional levels.

The initiative will have three major thrusts: First, to provide a statewide focus for efforts to increase high-technology spinoffs from our existing bases and defense industries. Second, to coordinate long-range planning between our civilian and military sectors, so that base communities, the regions that surround them, and the state as a whole are doing everything possible to build on and strengthen the military missions undertaken in Georgia. Third, to get ready for 1995 and to ensure that any base subject to review for possible realignment or closure enjoys strong state support and every available resource, including up-to-the-minute data on the cost of closure and the advantages of maintaining missions in Georgia.

I have assigned this initiative to the Development Council, because it is uniquely positioned to link short-term and long-range base planning with the economic resources of Georgia's various regions. The Council has a close working relationship with the Georgia Chamber of Commerce, the Georgia Research Alliance, our public and private colleges and universities, and state and local governments. The Development Council also directs the Georgia Corporation for Economic Development, a private entity that can raise and deploy private funds to promote the Council's agenda.

We are now looking into the possibility of creating a special restricted fund under the Corporation for Economic Development to support the Georgia Defense Initiative with staff and other resources. To advise the Governor's Development Council on the design and direction of the Georgia Defense Initiative, I will create by executive order a Military Affairs Coordinating Committee, composed of representatives of Georgia bases, base communities, business executives, and technical experts.

I am pleased to tell you that retired General Edwin Burba, former Commander in Chief of the U.S. Army Forces Command at Fort McPherson, has agreed to serve as Chairman of the Military Affairs Coordinating Committee....

With the advice and support of General Burba and the Military Affairs Coordinating Committee, the Georgia Defense Initiative will for the first time provide a statewide framework for strengthening the links between our bases, our communities, our resources, and our strategic planning. It will not—and let me emphasize this—in any way duplicate or supplant the strong local and regional efforts already underway to promote military-civilian cooperation, such as those sponsored by the Greater Atlanta Military Affairs Council, the Robins Twenty-First Century Partnership, the Fort Benning Civilian-Military Council, the Friends of Moody Air Force Base, and other groups supporting Fort Gordon, Fort Stewart, and the Marine Logistics Base in Albany.

The initiative will also draw on several existing state-level resources, including the defense conversion task force headed by Labor Commissioner David Poythress and the legislative study committee on base closings chaired by Senator Sonny Perdue. The Georgia Defense Initiative will promote teamwork among these efforts, while supplying a statewide "vision" to ensure that our preparations for 1995 are consistent with the long-range missions of our bases and the long-range needs of our people.

Teamwork and vision. These are the qualities that have made our defense facilities so valuable to the national interests of the United States. These are also the qualities that must characterize our efforts to keep those facilities intact and in touch with future needs.

Today those who owe so much to the hard work and sacrifice of Georgia's military personnel salute you with words of commitment and thanks. But we salute you best with our deeds. I call on all Georgians to join with the political, business and civic leadership of this state, in making this salute to our men and women in uniform a sustained commitment of our time and talent. We can add new chapters to the remarkable story of military-civilian cooperation in Georgia—if we begin writing them today.

*—Salute to the Military, September 27, 1993*

———

As we dedicate this Korean War Memorial, we pay tribute to the 740 Georgia veterans killed during the Korean War. We pay tribute to the unnumbered Korean War veterans who have passed on in the 40 years since that war ended, and to the 115,000 Korean veterans who still walk among us.

Someone once said that in the long course of world history, freedom has died in many ways. Freedom has died on the battlefield; freedom has died because of ignorance and greed; but the most ignoble death of all is when freedom dies in its sleep.

Freedom did not die 40 years ago on those battlefields halfway around the world. No, it was revived and given new life and breath in the victory that was won there. The purpose of this memorial is to keep freedom from dying in its sleep, by providing us with a permanent reminder of America's so-called forgotten war.

Our nation—our cities, homes, schools, churches, cemeteries—have stood unscarred by foreign foes for many, many long years, and we are in danger of becoming complacent about the freedoms we have. We have grown accustomed to traveling freely from city to city, from state to state. Our speech is uncensored. We worship our God according to the dictates of our own conscience. It's tempting to forget that neither peace nor liberty is ever guaranteed or can ever be taken for granted.

Every coin has two sides. Yes, democracy means freedom for every citizen, but it also means that every citizen is the holder of a public trust. Woodrow Wilson, who was president during World War I, said that "freedom and free institutions cannot long be maintained by any people who do not understand the nature of (them)."

The will and courage to die if necessary for our country and what it stands for, is what will keep freedom alive and well in each successive generation. If that shadowy host of the 740 Georgia veterans who died during the war and now lie beneath the sod in Korea and here at home—if that shadowy host of heros could speak to us on this special day, they would tell us to be proud of our country, to be proud of what we stand for, and never to take it for granted. That is the message of this memorial, the message that will keep freedom alive.

—*Korea War Memorial Dedication, November 11, 1993*

———————

I am a veteran of the Marine Corps, and that experience molded my character and instilled values in me that I carry with me to this day. Military service teaches you the value of personal discipline. It teaches you not to duck or sidestep difficult challenges. It teaches you to persevere.

It teaches you the value of unwavering comradeship and loyalty. It teaches you that true respect and honor come as a result of dedicating yourself to a valiant and worthy cause that is much bigger than yourself.

The heroes whom we remember today faced hardship, risks, dangers, and ultimately death with a courage that was deeply rooted in a love for the United States of America. They paid the ultimate price to assure our freedom and our future, and they died with faith in their hearts that we would never forget them, that we would never forget their courage in the face of danger, their loyalty to the United States and their devotion to preserving the homeland they loved.

On this special day, in this solemn moment, we pause to pay tribute to their heroism in combat and to join with their families in holding them close in memory. These fallen heros gave everything they had to buy the gift of freedom for all of us who are alive today. Today, on Memorial Day, we pause to say thank you.

—*Memorial Day Service, May 30, 1994*

———————

Our Vietnam veterans have often been ignored, sometimes even maligned for their participation in America's longest and most controversial war....These young heros went halfway around the world to the steamy jungles of Southeast Asia, and there they gave everything they had on behalf of the United States of America. They died with faith in their hearts that we would never forget them ... that we would always remember their courage in the face of danger, their loyalty to the United States and their devotion to the homeland they loved....

On this special Memorial Day, let us take this solemn moment to say to all our sons and daughters, our fathers and mothers, who were the fallen heros of Vietnam: We love you for what you were. We honor you for what you gave. We will never allow ourselves to forget what you sacrificed. And today we pause with a full heart to say thank you on behalf of the nation to whom you gave so much, but who let you down for so long in the years that followed.

—*Memorial Day Service for Vietnam Veterans, May 30, 1994*

---

Fifty years ago today, dawn found a broad wave of Allied landing craft along the coast of Normandy, followed closely by larger boats with tanks, artillery, and other heavy weapons. As they approached the beaches, Allied fighter planes were swarming through the air, and naval bombardment was detonating the large mine fields the Germans were counting on to hold off invaders.

By this time in the evening, exactly 50 years ago, the Allies had established firm footholds along the coast of Normandy, and by the end of the first phase of the invasion three weeks later, 27 Allied divisions had landed on the continent with nearly one million men, 177,000 vehicles and more than 500,000 tons of supplies. The tide had turned in the biggest war the world has ever known.

Those D-Day heros whom we remember today faced hardship, risks, dangers, and even death with a courage that was deeply rooted in honor, duty, and a love for the United States of America... Those fallen heros gave everything they had to buy the gift of freedom for all of us who are alive today. In this solemn moment, we pause to pay tribute to their sacrifice and to join with their families in holding them close in memory.

On this special anniversary day, we also pause to thank and honor all of our veterans who were part of that historic invasion. You were part of a cause that was much larger than one day on the beaches of Normandy. D-Day not only turned the tides of World War II, but set world history on a course that is still being played out today.

Shirley and I are honored to have all of you here at the Mansion and to join with the USO in saluting all of our veterans who were there for that very special moment in world history when D-Day launched the Allied invasion of France and the retaking of the continent.

—*D-Day 50th Anniversary, June 6, 1994*

---

As you know, Georgia's military bases rank among the very best in the nation. And we are grateful to General Edwin Burba, who chairs the Governor's Military Affairs Coordinating Committee, and who has helped us orchestrate a very effective effort to tell our story and demonstrate just outstanding our bases are.

Many states view military bases primarily as economic assets, and they emphasize the importance of their installations based on what the military does for them. In Georgia, we are keenly aware of the 42,000 civilian jobs our bases provide and of the $9 billion in military investment that comes into our state each year. That is a very important part of our economy, and we are very grateful for it.

But our commitment and support goes deeper than numbers of jobs or dollars. Rather than calculating what the military does for Georgia, we ask what we can do to support the military. Here in Georgia, we are committed to upholding the superior military strength of the United States of America. We are committed not only to standing proudly beside our military installations, but also to providing them with the community support and skilled civilian workforce that enables them to make a unique and irreplaceable contribution to our national defense.

I was in England a few weeks ago to commemorate the 300th anniversary of the birth of James Edward Oglethorpe, founder of the Colony of Georgia. As I thought back to the birth of this state, I realized anew that Georgia understood, from day one and perhaps better than any other colony, how important it is to have a strong military force.

Oglethorpe successfully built a new colony on a piece of land that had been in contention among the English, French, and Spanish, to say nothing of several Indian tribes, for the prior 200 years. To the north were his fellow English in Charleston and on up the Atlantic coast. To the south were the Spanish in what is today Florida. Georgia was the buffer between them.

The Colony of Georgia was not even 10 years old when Spanish troops marched northward in 1742, intent on expanding their territory. And the newly formed Georgia militia was the first line of defense. At the Battle of Bloody Marsh on what is today St. Simons Island, Oglethorpe and his little Georgia Militia turned the Spanish back. It was not only a military victory of the moment, but it was also one of those defining events that take on greater significance in retrospect, because they shape the course of history.

Had Oglethorpe not defeated the Spanish, they may very well have swept on northward, catching the Colony of Carolina unprepared. No one knows where that story might have ended, but the American South might be speaking Spanish today were it not for Oglethorpe. And the United States may never have emerged as one of the great powers of the world.

But Oglethorpe was a military leader of great vigor and courage, who never asked his troops to do anything he himself was not willing to do. After tangling with him and his troops, the Spanish retreated to Florida and never again attempted to dislodge the English colonists from American soil.

Ever since then, we in Georgia have understood not only the importance of our military forces, but also that we as a state can make a difference in the course of events if we do our part with courage and commitment.

It has been more than 250 years since the Battle of Bloody Marsh, and more than a century since a war has been fought here on American soil. But it has not been a time of inactivity for our military forces, because political unrest and uprising always seem to threaten one part of the world or another. The Persian Gulf, Somalia, Haiti, Bosnia and the Middle East have all been hot spots in recent years. It's anybody's guess where and when our armed forces might be called upon next—to defend liberty and fight aggression, or simply to keep the peace long enough for people who are at odds to make a truce with each other.

Georgia is proud to support the United States Army in that calling, and we look forward to continuing to be partners with you in your quest to promote peace, liberty and justice around the world.

*—Accept AUSA National Award for Distinguished Service, October 24, 1996*

Later this month we will celebrate Memorial Day, and we will remember all those who fought and died with honor to preserve and protect the freedom we Americans cherish. But today we honor a different army, another group of patriots who made a different, but very significant contribution to World War II. Today, as we unveil and dedicate "Sweet Eloise," we remember and honor the hard-working Georgians, many of them women, who worked at the old Bell Bomber plant, now Lockheed.

The entire B-29 project cost $3 billion, and was the largest military undertaking in American history. The first bulldozer scraped the ground on this site in March of 1942, and began what was the largest construction project in the South. Some worried that this site was too close to the coast, and planes from aircraft carriers in the Atlantic could bomb it. But that fear was offset by the availability of a workforce. Many in that workforce were women, and this was the first major industry to bring women in on an equal basis with men, creating the "Rosie the Riveter" character.

It was the largest plant of its kind in the world—40 acres under one roof. At its peak it had over 28,000 employees, and in the four years it was in operation, it built 668 of these B-29 bombers. This was one of five plants around the nation that together built nearly 4,000 B-29 aircraft during World War II—aircraft that played a very important role in the Allied air attacks, both in Europe and in the Pacific. Back in 1924, General Billy Mitchell was court-martialled for saying that air power could win a war without land invasion. But the B-29 proved him right, because it enabled us to defeat Japan without ever landing troops there.

It is a special personal honor for me to be part of this celebration, because my mother was one of those women who helped build B-29 bombers here in Marietta. Of course, we saved newspapers, flattened tin cans, and reused the grease in the frying pan like everybody else, but my mother had a patriotic fervor to do more to help win the war.

I was about ten years old at the time, and my mother came down out of the North Georgia mountains with my sister and me in tow, and went to work as an inspector at the Bell Bomber Plant. She always considered her real contribution to the war effort to be her work on the B-29. Still hanging on the wall in the living room of our house in Young Harris today, is a picture of a B-29 with the name "Birdie Miller" embossed on it—a gift of appreciation from the plant to my mother when the war was over and she went back home to the mountains.

She is among those whom we remember today, together with Eloise Strom, another former Bell Bomber plant employee who put up the seed money to restore this plane. And it is named in her honor.

There are only about two dozen B-29s remaining in the world today, so it is a special privilege to have one of them here in Georgia. This particular B-29 was originally made in Wichita, Kansas. And she is a tried and true veteran, with a long military career. "Sweet Eloise" flew 27 bombing missions in the Pacific during World War II, plus a number of missions to deliver supplies to prisoners of war. Although she was hit several times by enemy fire, she never suffered serious injury, causing her crew to refer to her as "sweet."

After the war, she came home to Warner Robins for a rest, then was reconfigured and sent to England to fly spy missions in Soviet-controlled air. She was finally retired, old and weather-beaten, to Florence, South Carolina, where she suffered damage from Hurricane Hugo.

But thanks to the efforts of Georgia's B-29 Super Fortress Association, the Air Force Museum has given this B-29 to the 94th Tactical Airlift Wing here at Dobbins Air Force Base. And thanks to the efforts of the Georgia Department of Technical and Adult Education, she stands here today, refurbished and reassembled as a tribute to those who served their country by building B-29s here in Marietta at the Bell Bomber Plant.

Tech students who were learning truck-driving skills, drove to South Carolina and picked up the plane. Georgia's Adjutant General Bland helped to arrange equipment to load and unload the parts of the plane at either end of the journey. The plane was divided into seven sections, and each section went to a different state technical institute. There students studying aircraft mechanics restored and refurbished the various parts. The nose cone was the first part to be completed, and over the past two and a-half years, the remaining six sections have made their way here from around the state. They were assembled by units from Warner Robins and from Dobbins into the complete aircraft we dedicate today.

So this is not a Marietta project, it is a Georgia project, the result of teamwork by people from all across the state. Just as people were recruited from all over the state to build the B-29 more than 50 years ago, so people came together from all across the state in the 90s to restore and rebuild this aircraft. Today we celebrate the result of their hard work. Together they have given us a tribute, not only to a special aircraft in our history, but also to a special time in our history when the citizens of this state came together and pulled together to make this nation and our world a better place to live. This B-29 reminds us that we need to recapture and renew that same spirit as we face the challenges of our day.

*—Dedicate Restored B-29 bomber, Dobbins AFB, May 6, 1997*

---

My father served in the Army in combat overseas during World War I, and one of my earliest memories as a child is wearing his coat with the sergeant stripes. It dragged on the floor and my arms did not extend but about half-way down the sleeves.

It was in the spring of 1917, when World War I had been underway for almost three years, that the U.S. Secretary of War called in General John Pershing and asked him to lead America's troops into the war. "Black Jack," they called him.

At that time the U.S. Army numbered just 135,000 men. But within a few months over nine million more had volunteered, and they began to be called into service by number. The first division of the American Expeditionary Forces set sail for Europe in mid-June. By the end of 1917, American troops were landing in Europe at a rate of 50,000 a month, and historians today agree that they turned the tide from stalemate and possible defeat into an Allied victory on the Western Front.

The first American artillery shot was fired on October 23, 1917. I have a brass shell-casing my father brought back. Soon American regiments were in the trenches all across Europe. Life in the trenches was cold and damp even in good weather, and when it rained, the trenches flooded. Snails crawled out of the walls, rats made nightly visits, lice were rampant.

Although an effort was made to place these inexperienced American "doughboys" in quiet sectors, nonetheless the grim toll of war was soon felt not only at the front, but also in lonely homes all across this nation where loved ones grieved.

The Americans fought so well, that by August of 1918, the commander in chief of the Allied Forces called for a separate American Army to be formed. That fall 22 American divisions stretched along the Western Front in northern France from Verdun to the Argonne Forest. They decisively defeated 46 different German divisions, representing 25 percent of the enemy's forces on the Western Front. On November 11, 1918, an armistice was signed and World War I ended, almost a year to the day after the American Expeditionary Forces had suffered their first casualties.

The doughboys on the Western Front accepted victory quietly—too cold and wet and worn out to be boisterous. The reality that the war was over began to sink in when they realized that they could climb out of the trenches to light fires in the open and sit around them to get dry and warm. And when then looked up and down along the front and saw the fires of other regiments, they began to believe that the end had actually come.

More than 100,000 Georgians served in the American forces during World War I. Nearly 2,000 were killed, and another 2,500 were wounded. For most of my lifetime, many of those veterans were still with us. They were a living presence in our Georgia communities, and their stories about places like Verdun and Paris and Flanders kept the First World War alive in our national consciousness and memory. But eight decades have now gone by since that war was fought, and the number of veterans still among us here in Georgia has dwindled to less than 100.

We now need to find other ways to keep alive their memories and remember the sacrifice they made for us. So today we honor them by dedicating a special memorial that will serve as a reminder to us and to future generations of their service and their sacrifice. They were sons and brothers and fathers who set aside their personal lives and left their families behind to respond to that call in the spring of 1917. This memorial tells their loved ones and descendants that in Georgia, they are not forgotten, but remembered with honor.

They were men of integrity, courage, and principle. They were patriots, fiercely loyal to their fellow soldiers, to the families they had left behind, and to the nation for which they fought. They left their loved ones for the trenches of a foreign land, where they were willing to give their own lives as a sacrifice to protect the lives and the freedom of those they loved. They were not lured to war by vague, abstract notions. They went to fight for the freedom of their children at play in the yard, the freedom of their parents and grandparents back home in Union County, the freedom of the small businesses their neighbors ran.

The memory of these veterans of World War I speaks to us across the years, reminding us that the freedom simply to live our daily lives and care for our loved ones is a precious treasure. They gave much and asked little. They deserve our honor and our remembrance. Today we pause to remember the gift of their lives to our state, our nation and the world, and we commemorate their service with a lasting memorial.

—*Dedicate State World War I Memorial, April 6, 1998*

# The Arts

My mother was a gifted and multi-faceted artist. Her paintings hang in my home in Young Harris. Although I did not inherit her great artistic gift, she nevertheless passed along to me a deep appreciation for art, for those who create it, and for the richness it brings to our lives.

Art is not just for artists; it is for everyone. Its intrinsic beauty and balance is capable of bringing joy into the lives of all who view it. But more than that, art is a rich part of our heritage and our identity. It provides us with an interpretive history of our past, a thought-provoking reflection of our present, and sometimes even a glimpse of our future.

In a more practical vein, I also appreciate the contribution art can make to economic development. As our economy increasingly demands a workforce that is literate and well-educated, quality of life, of which you are a big part, has become more important in attracting and holding businesses.

The watchwords of my administration are quality as opposed to quantity, and innovative change. State finances are tight and my administration will not see the kind of heady revenue growth we had in the 80s. I am going to have to keep a tight grip on the purse strings. But I don't intend to let that stop me from pursuing quality, and I am looking for new and creative ways for the state to be involved in the arts and humanities.

I do not want the arts to languish during this time of tight state finances. In fact, I want to use this opportunity as your Governor to promote and strengthen the arts, and I think that there are more ways that the state can be a catalyst for the arts than simply providing cash grants.

For example, encouraging the arts in rural areas of the state. We have been providing grants to send performing groups from Atlanta out on tour—but some might say that this is the same mentality as sending missionaries out to the less fortunate. I'd like us to look for more creative ways to foster home-grown arts activities in rural areas of the state.

At the same time I was cutting $40,000 out of the budget for the Governor to purchase artwork, I was borrowing an original sculpture from a businessman to display in my office. I cite this very rudimentary example simply to indicate my interest in pursuing creative ways of forging private-public partnerships in the arts and humanities.

—*Georgia Citizens for the Arts, January 29, 1991*

---

We are in an unprecedented time of belt-tightening in Georgia. We took the belt to the last hole during the 1991 General Assembly, and we still face the possibility of cutting new notches. But Chesterton once said that art is the signature of the human race. The arts are part of our identity as a people. They also speak to what is noblest in the human spirit, and they nourish our lives in ways that are just as important as physical nourishment.

I am a historian, and history is replete with examples of how the arts were preserved and encouraged during much more difficult times than the ones we face. During the Great Depression, Franklin Roosevelt found ways to employ artists in arts-related activities, just as he did others in building roads and dams.

When the Germans were about the capture France during World War II, the French Underground spirited thousands of paintings and sculptures out of the Louvre into hiding in rural haylofts, cheese caves and wine cellars. There was no time to catalog what went where, but when France was liberated, every single piece of artwork was returned.

The lesson of history is clear. The arts are not a frill. They are an essential, and we dare not ignore them even when times get tough. I see this time of tight finances as an opportunity to break out of old ruts—a time to look anew at how we can leverage what money we do have, to get the most out of it for the arts.

The arts really need to be a part of all of us. A partnership of public and corporate support for the arts broadens their base and allows all citizens to participate in the arts. This broader support for the arts is more than just a civic-minded contribution on the part of state government and the corporate sector, it is also an investment in our economic future.

The arts are a critical part of our effort to create the educated workforce and offer the quality of life that modern industry demands. They enhance our tourism industry and increase economic indicators like real estate value.

These advantages need to be shared throughout all of Georgia. Some of you come from Gainesville, Albany and Tifton, where active arts councils are making a difference, and I commend you for your hard work and dedication. All of us need to work together to stimulate the same kind of arts involvement in rural and other underserved areas of the state. Together with you and with Betsey Weltner, we will rise to meet the challenges facing the arts in the 90s and set this state on a new course for the next century.

*—Georgia Council for the Arts Reception, April 18, 1991*

---

I could stand here today and tell you how art is the signature of humankind and a rich part of our identity. But I'm not going to. I could explain how art provides us with an interpretive history, a thought-provoking look at the present and even a glimpse of the future. But I'm not going to. I could emphasize the need for our children to know that there is more to the arts than what they see inside a little box called a TV—that there is more to beauty, creativity, and values, than popular culture would have them believe. But I'm not going to.

What I am going to talk about, to you as the business leaders of Atlanta, is the economic importance of the arts. At the most obvious level, the arts provide jobs and income to artists and arts organizations. But that is just the tip of the iceberg.

One of my jobs as Governor is to encourage new business facilities in Georgia. When I meet with CEOs, they ask questions like, is there a good museum, an orchestra, a ballet company, an arts festival. That illusive "quality of life" factor has become vital to economic growth. Valued executives are not willing to be shunted from city to city unless an equal or higher quality of life awaits them at their new destination, and the better-educated employees demanded by new workplace technology are increasingly to be found in communities where the quality of life is high.

Cultural facilities and activities also bring money into a community from other places. They play a role in the decisions tourists make about where to go and how long to stay.

A third consideration in the economic impact of the arts is real estate. A study by the National Committee on Cultural Resources found that arts organizations and activities enhance real estate values. Eyebrows went up when Lincoln Center was built at Columbus Circle—a modest neighborhood away from many of New York's arts activities. Today the neighborhood is vibrant with offices, shops, restaurants, and residences. It is considered prime real estate.

Your contribution to the Woodruff Arts Center is much more than a charitable contribution. It is even more than an expression of good corporate citizenship. It is an economic investment in this community that will pay real financial dividends. It is not just good will—it is good business savvy. I know that each one of you is proud to be in the Woodruff Arts Center's Patron Circle of Stars, and I am pleased to join with the Arts Center in recognizing your contribution.

*—Woodruff Arts Center Reception, June 6, 1991*

———————

One of the greatest honors and pleasures of being Governor of Georgia is the chance to live for a time in the midst of one of the nation's finest collections of decorative arts from the Federal Period....

Back in the late 60s, as this Governor's Mansion was being designed and built, 70 people from across the state were assembled to form the "Executive Fine Arts Committee." Kitty Farnham, who I believe is here this evening, served on it. What a wonderful job this committee did of creating a living museum here at the Mansion.... You will find treasures that run the gamut from porcelain to tapestry, from furniture to crystal, from paintings to silver.

I'd like to mention just a few of my favorites. First, of course, is the painting in the dining room by Benjamin West, who was America's first internationally acclaimed painter. This particular painting predates the Revolutionary War.

You will find 14 pieces of furniture by Duncan Phyfe in the Mansion, but the piece of furniture that intrigues me the most is the huntboard in the family dining room. It was made in Athens, Georgia, in 1810, and it is much simpler and less sophisticated than the other furniture, which came largely from the north and copied designs from England and the continent. But it is special as one of the early pieces of furniture designed and made here in Georgia. If you did not see the wonderful collection of Derby porcelain from the late 1700s in the drawing room breakfront, you may want to swing back by there.

*—High Museum Decorative Arts Reception, December 9, 1991*

Despite the fact that money has been tight and we had to cut the budget, it has been an exciting year for the arts. I want to mention two accomplishments in particular.

Somebody once said that it doesn't take money to be creative. In fact, the lack of money often causes people to be more creative than they otherwise would be. There are a lot of creative ways to promote the arts that don't involve state funding. One that I've been personally involved in has been the series of exhibits by Georgia artists at the Capitol.

There is a large, public waiting room right outside my personal office, and dozens, sometimes hundreds of people come through it in the course of a day. We have turned this large room into a gallery to showcase an ongoing series of Georgia art exhibits. Sometimes the exhibit is organized around a theme or type of artwork, like the collection of Georgia folkart we had last summer. Other times, it is a regional exhibit, like the "Okefenokee Style" exhibit that is there right now, with all kinds of art from the Ware County area....

Although we had to cut the budget last year and those cuts were painful, I saw this time of flat revenue growth as an opportunity to take stock all across state government... a time to develop a vision of where we need to go, and lay the plans and groundwork to take us there...a time to change old habits and patterns, and to exercise some creativity and innovation in setting new ones. That has been going on at the Georgia Council for the Arts as well as in other state agencies.

The second accomplishment I want to talk about is the long-range plan for state involvement with the arts in Georgia... This had never been done before in Georgia. We simply did the minimal report required by the NEA, and updated the numbers every three years.

The old piecemeal, patchwork approach to the arts is gone, and our new, long-term plan is on the way to the printer... There were ten public hearings all across the state to gather input from citizens, and I think the Georgia Citizens for the Arts had a representative at every one. All told, about 500 people helped to shape and develop this plan. Many of you participated, and I thank you for that.

I'm not going to get into the details of the plan or we'd be here all day, but let me say one thing. The longer I'm in this business, the more convinced I become that real change does not trickle down. It percolates up. Excitement and enthusiasm, commitment and involvement do not result from state edicts that are handed down from on high. I believe that the state should spend more time encouraging local communities to gather together around their own table to make their own decisions, and then the state should help to provide some of the resources the local community needs in order to do what it has decided.

This is true for our schools. It is true for human services. It is true for the arts. It is a thread you will find woven all through this long-range plan for the arts. We want the arts to be an active, participatory grassroots effort all across Georgia, in which each community has the flexibility to develop and enjoy its own unique resources. I emphasize that to you, because the Georgia Citizens for the Arts is the embodiment of grassroots activism and volunteerism in the arts at the community level. I know that if anybody is going to stir things up in the arts at the local level, it is going to be the Georgia Citizens for the Arts.... I want to encourage your efforts in your local communities, and let you know that one of our goals at the Georgia Council for the Arts is to become more supportive of your initiatives.

—*Georgia Citizens for the Arts, January 28, 1992*

The Georgia Council for the Arts was recently notified of a grant from the National Endowment for the Arts totally nearly $100,000 for arts activities in under-served rural and innercity areas. We must match it with $25,000, which will be raised through this cultural series.

The funds will pay artists to work with two projects sponsored by the Georgia Council for the Arts: rural arts development in the Heart of Georgia area, and a cultural arts component for The Atlanta Project, which is President Jimmy Carter's massive effort to revitalize innercity Atlanta.

—*First Cultural Evening at the Mansion, April 16, 1992*

Jim Townsend was my personal friend. I loved him. I still miss him. I'm thankful that I can pull my copy of *Dear Heart* off the bookshelf and recapture the sparkle, humor and poignancy of Jim Townsend that shines through his writing. In that sense, he is very much alive and present with us, and always will be. But there are still times when I find myself wishing I could run something by him and get that famous Townsend word of encouragement.

Above and beyond his ability to use words, Jim had the gift of inspiring people, of giving them the confidence they needed to write even better than they themselves suspected they were capable of. That was a gift that he shared generously with so many of us.

I grew up in an isolated little town in the north Georgia mountains. There were no traffic lights, no railroad tracks, no lawyers, not even any bankers. But there were a lot of good storytellers. And they were my favorite people. I spent as much time as my mother allowed listening to them, and I grew up loving words.

Today we are gathered to celebrate the power and mystery of words: The ability of words to transport us beyond the reality of our day-to-day existence and into worlds they create in our imaginations. The knowledge that a well-phrased sentence can pierce the heart with more power than any weapon humankind has ever invented.

This is a power that Jim Townsend understood so well and encouraged so persuasively in so many young Atlanta writers. I cannot think of a better way to remember and honor him than by finding ways, like this award, to continue his work of encouraging writers to develop and excel in the craft of using words.

—*Townsend Fiction Prize Dinner, May 5, 1992*

---

Atlanta cannot make her mark on the world without a strong arts component. A world-class symphony, theater and art museum will put this city on the map as an economic center just as surely as they will mark it as an arts center.

—*Woodruff Arts Center Reception, June 23, 1992*

---

We tend to think of art as something that is done by a small group of unusual people who have special, innate gifts. But art is not just for artists. Art is for everyone. And it is not a luxury, but a necessity that needs to be an integral part of our educational process. Art is essential to education, because it is central not only to the preservation of the very fabric of our society, but also to the development of healthy, intelligent individual citizens. And that is what I want to talk you about today.

Biologically we are still cavemen. There is nothing of civilization contained in human genes. No language skills, no knowledge of history or literature, no understanding of the great truths of life, no comprehension of who we are or how we got to be that way—none of this is contained in DNA. There is nothing automatic about the transfer of these things from one generation to the next. Yet that transfer must be made, or we as a culture, as a people, are nothing.

The arts are the signature of humankind and a rich part of our identity. We are united as a people and a nation by the stories, myths, and beliefs that we share. Without that common base of understanding, we would perish. Those stories are told in the artwork, music, drama, and literature of this nation. When we study the arts we learn the stories of our life together, we learn about the rich heritage that gives us our unique identity as a people.

We can also learn about other cultures by studying their artwork, music, dance and literature. In fact, the arts help us to understand that truth is too big to be contained by any one culture, that there are underlying truths and principles that go beyond culture and tradition to unite humankind around the world and across the ages.

These are critical concepts to instill in our children, who are growing up in a new and global age, and will need a greater understanding and appreciation for cultural diversity.

But in addition to creating and nurturing our identity as a culture and giving us a framework for understanding other cultures, the arts also create and nurture our identity as individual persons. At the most fundamental level, experiencing the intrinsic beauty and balance of art enriches and brings joy to our lives.

Art has the additional gift of interpreting life to us. Art distills the essence of life and presents it to us in ways that can go straight to the heart of a viewer or listener. Art can give us flashes of insight and understanding about life that would otherwise take us years of daily living to discover.

But the bottom line, and the most important reason to infuse art into the elementary school experience, is what active participation in the arts does for a child. Even though very few people grow up to become professional artists, human creativity is not a special attribute that appears only in a handful of kids. It is a natural response in *all* people that is done away with only by being snuffed out. Unfortunately, that is what happens too often in our schools. In our effort to focus on academics, we exclude the arts, and creativity is snuffed out.

The creative drive present in all humans is the deepest expression of personality. It enables people to express in concrete form what is going on inside of them, providing them with a way to examine and explore their own feelings and identity. Our kids are bombarded with information from a world that is growing ever more complex. The arts are tools that help them process and make sense of it for themselves. In the course of participating in the arts, kids give form and expression to their growing understanding of the world. They shape their understanding of themselves and their environment.

Active participation in the arts also gives kids a positive outlet for emotional expression, and they gain valuable experience in tempering emotional impulses with discipline and practice. The performing arts teach them how to control and coordinate their muscles, and present themselves to an audience with a deliberate and polished poise, which builds up their self-esteem and confidence. So part of the value of the arts in education is that active participation helps our children to develop into well-rounded, mentally healthy, self-controlled, confident persons.

But the arts also support and enhance academic subjects like reading, math, science, and history. Creating art is a problem-solving exercise. You have to figure out what to do to get the results you want. You gain an appreciation for how details can be fitted together to create an overall impression and communicate a message.

Active participation in the auditory arts improves kids' listening skills. They learn to listen with greater accuracy and comprehension, and they respond better to what they hear. Active participation in the visual arts gives them a better sense of geometric shapes and spacial relationships.

Taking part in the arts cultivates higher thinking skills, like inferential linking ability and a grasp of how symbols function. Can they hear the same emotional qualities in music from the French impressionist period as they see in impressionist paintings? What does it tell them about that culture? Can they figure out the connection between the development of the camera and the expansion of other visual arts into more abstract forms? These are the kind academic and critical thinking skills that kids can learn from taking part in art activities, and they show up in the test scores of kids whose curriculum incorporates art as an integral part of their education.

Educational reform is getting a lot of attention these days. But rarely are the arts even mentioned as part of those efforts. The arts are so often considered a nice frill at the edge of the curriculum ... a luxury that you do if you have extra time and resources, but the first thing you cut if you're going to really get serious about education. Our kindergarten kids color pictures to develop their fine motor skills in preparation for writing. But the goal is staying inside the lines, not creative expression. And beyond that, art tends to fall by the wayside in our elementary school curriculum.

Here we have a model that demonstrates so well how central the arts are to intellectual development. A model that shows the direct connection between arts activities and test scores. I want to commend the Augusta Council for the Arts for its leadership in developing a program that infuses arts activities into the daily curriculum for all elementary school children....

We all want the next generation of children to understand their cultural heritage, to recognize and appreciate beauty, to have a healthy self image and be creative in their own expression, and to exercise higher-level critical thinking skills. That is what the infusion of art into the school curriculum does.

We need art to help kids come to grips with our cultural heritage, and to foster individual expression, self-confidence, and intellect, because art is what invests life with the meaning that makes the rest of human endeavors worthwhile.

—*Augusta Arts Council, November 6, 1992*

Over the past two years you have seen improvements in spite of a tight state budget— new federal grants, an arts component for Jimmy Carter's Atlanta Project, a rural arts program in middle Georgia, a young playwrights' festival. I've been personally involved—exhibiting artwork in the large reception room outside my office at the Capitol, and hosting a series of dinners at the Mansion honoring Georgia artists who achieved national prominence. I saw many of you at those dinners, and I thank you for your support.

Many of you participated in the public hearings that were held all across the state to develop a long-term plan which considers the arts to be an active, participatory grassroots effort, with each community encouraged to develop and enjoy its own unique resources....

As the state revenue picture begins to improve, we are right back in there with some new funding for the arts. My budget recommendation includes $200,000 to begin the Georgia Grassroots Arts Program. This program grows out of the long-range plan and is part of our effort to help local communities nurture their own arts. It's also going to allow for a more equitable distribution of arts grants around the state. Funds will be allocated on a per-county basis, and regional agencies will distribute them to local arts programs.

I'm also proposing $25,000 for the Historic Chattahoochee Commission, which is a joint effort between Georgia and Alabama in the Chattahoochee River basin, and $5,000 for the Georgia Folklife Program, to document and present Georgia's rich and varied cultural heritage.

—*Georgia Citizens for the Arts, January 26, 1993*

A lot of people know me as an avid country music fan, and I am that. But I am also a devoted fan of other types of music as well. Mozart is one of my favorite composers, and

I am looking forward to...the performance of "Don Giovanni" in August.

It used to be that the Metropolitan Opera of New York would come to Atlanta for a week in the late spring, and sweep Atlanta's opera lovers off their feet. But this special Opera Week is designed to remind Georgia's opera lovers that you don't need an exotic suitor from a far away place to woo you. It is possible to find happiness with the person next door.

*—Atlanta Opera Company, June 15, 1993*

———————

As most of you know, I owe my existence to art. My mother was an artist, trained at the Art Students League in New York City, and she met my father when she came to Young Harris College to teach art. Although I did not inherit her artistic gifts, she instilled in me a tremendous appreciation for the arts—an appreciation that goes beyond merely being an admirer and consumer.

For my mother, art was not something that existed in seclusion from the rest of life; it was an integral part of daily life. Yes, she painted many canvases of the beautiful mountain scenes that surrounded our home. But she also painted the trash cans of Young Harris, because she wanted the community to look a living piece of artwork. For her, the building of our rock house and the landscaping of the yard were artistic endeavors, and she was known for the beautiful flowers she grew and the special floral arrangements she created for any and every event in town.

From her I learned that art is more than a spectator sport; it is a hands-on participatory activity that ought to part of daily life in every Georgia community. The goal of this administration has been, and continues to be, finding creative ways to encourage active artistic expression all over Georgia. It's nice to have a professional symphony or ballet company visit your community for a performance, and it's great to have a traveling exhibit from a major gallery or museum come to your town. But it is even better to encourage and support and celebrate your own local artistic endeavors and make art a part of your community's life together.

That is why we developed the Georgia Grassroots Arts program, and that is why, as state revenues now begin to improve, we are focusing on the Grassroots Arts Program as we expand the budget for the Georgia Council for the Arts. We call it "GAP" for short, and it really does fill a gap.

You see, the state used to focus arts funding almost exclusively on grants to artists and arts organizations. That allowed the Atlanta Symphony to do some concerts around the state, for example, but it completely ignored areas of the state that did not have well-established artists or arts organizations that could apply for grants. So the purpose of GAP is to instigate and encourage the development of local artists and arts organizations all across the state, and especially in areas that do not now have a strong local arts presence.

I am very pleased that after the budget cuts we had to make during the recession, we were able to increase funding for the arts by 8 percent in the current year's budget. I have proposed another increase of 6 percent for next year, and I hope you will give it your support as you talk with legislators.

Important as budget dollars may be, they are not an accurate barometer of the progress that Georgia has made in the arts in recent years. Someone once said that you're often more creative when you don't have money. And I believe that we have been creative in finding ways to support that arts that go far beyond numbers on a ledger.

Specifically, I would like to thank all of you who supported and participated in the dinners we've had at the Governor's Mansion during the past two years to honor distinguished Georgia artists and raise funds for the arts. I would also like to thank all of you who have helped to arrange the wonderful exhibits of Georgia artwork that have been displayed in the large reception area outside my office since I've been Governor. These exhibits have become a popular attraction for visitors to the Capitol. I have really enjoyed being part of this effort to give Georgia artists the recognition and exposure they deserve.

These are just two examples of the creative ways we have found to support the arts that are not reflected in the budget. And I know there are many other examples in the work that all of you do at home in your own communities.

*—Georgia Citizens for the Arts, February 2, 1994*

---

Tin Pan Alley, Hollywood and Vine, and Beale Street may have gotten more publicity, but Georgia has always been the home of many famous performing artists, past and present, and we have always been a musical pioneer. The firsts in our musical heritage range from coining the phrase "gospel music" to making the first commercial country music recordings to operating the first black-owned radio station in the nation.

Georgia's music is also diverse, ranging from the classical strains of the Atlanta Symphony, to the traditional folk melodies of the Southern Appalachians, to the soul and the rhythm and blues of African-American culture.

Even the Canadian prophet and guru Marshall McLuhan who told us that "the medium is the message," knew about the Georgia music scene. He called it the hotbed, where everything starts. Truly Georgia is one of the most vibrant and most important states in America's rich musical heritage.

Today we break ground on a facility to provide permanent recognition to the outstanding artists and musical pioneers who brought Georgia to greatness as one of the leading areas of the music industry in the United States. It's fitting and appropriate that the Georgia Music Hall of Fame be built here in Macon, not only because it's a central location for the state and because it will become part of a major $30 million development here, but also because Macon is a major music center with a rich music heritage in its own right.

Macon was the home of the Allman Brothers Band, America's best answer to the British super groups who dominated rock music in the late 60s. Macon produced Robert McDuffie, one of the most brilliant violinists on America's classical scene today. Macon gave us Otis Redding, who did more to bridge the gap between black and white music than any other performer before he was killed in a tragic plane crash at the age of 26, just three days after he recorded "Sittin' on the Dock of the Bay." Macon was home to Little

Richard, who speeded up rhythm and blues to make rock and roll, wrote songs for Elvis Presley, taught Paul McCartney to sing, and helped the Beatles get started.

We have it all in Georgia—internationally known performers, major booking agencies and promoters, prominent attorneys and managers, recording studios and producers, record labels, powerful radio stations, retail chains, even manufacturing plants. Today we begin a permanent tribute to them all, a home for the Georgia Music Hall of Fame and its outstanding members, and a place where the rest of us can listen and learn about the rich and wonderful music heritage of our state.

It's going to feature state-of-the-art, interactive exhibits and media. It will teach us the physics of making and hearing sounds. It will teach us the arts and disciplines and theories that take those sounds and turn them into the music that stirs our souls. It will tell the story of Georgia music and of the Hall of Famers who made that music.

And, of course, it will give us the sounds of Georgia music itself. There will be a perpetual music festival here—an indoor village where visitors can listen to and learn about whatever type of music interests them, whether country or popular, rock or jazz or rhythm and blues...a village where visitors can visit a gospel chapel to learn about the roots of modern music in the church, or take a break in a soda shop that features Coca Cola antiques and early rock and roll music. There will even be special exhibits for children where they can make their own music.

It will also include an archive facility, with special environmental controls and storage facilities to preserve historic recordings. Each of us has our own favorite types of music, and when this Hall of Fame opens about 18 months from now, we're each going to find our own favorite places and exhibits, where we like to linger and listen. But no matter what kind of music each one of us likes best, we all like music for the same reason: It can transcend words; it can even transcend culture. It can comfort and calm; it can inspire; and it touches our emotions somewhere deep inside at the core.

When I was a boy, I spent many hours on Lee Kirby's front porch. Lee would sit on a chair with a seat made of rubber innertube pieces and play one fiddle tune after another, alternating foot-stomping ditties with mournful, wailing songs. I'd sit on the floor, leaning against a porch post and listening with complete fascination.

I can still see our old Silvertone Radio from Sears and Roebuck as clearly as if it were yesterday. It had a round, greenish dial and four knobs, and it sat on a black wooden table in the corner of the living room. We only got a few stations in the mountains at night, and often only with great difficulty, but I'd pour water on the ground or even hold the ground wire in my hand to bring in the magic of the Grand Ol' Opry a little clearer.

It was childhood experiences like that, that instilled in me a lifelong love of music from country to classical, from Milsap to Mozart, and I suspect that many of you could tell similar stories about how music touched you in a special way and came to be such an integral part of your life that your soul would starve without it. There is something about music that connects to what is important in life, something that connects to the values by which we live our lives.

—*Ground Breaking Music Hall of Fame, May 27, 1994*

———————

The first time I spoke to you as Governor four years ago, a national recession was deepening around us, and we were embarking on a series of cuts to the state budget that would total nearly $700 million. Today I am proud to be able to say that the arts grants in the state budget for Fiscal Year 1996 total $4 million—up by nearly 40 percent from where they were in FY 91.

But the most important thing I want to emphasize to you is this: As we restored cuts and added new funds for arts grants, we have not simply continued business as usual. We have also been creative and innovative, as befits a council for the arts, and begun new initiatives. Today I want to highlight two of them.

First, a brand new program called The Georgia Challenge. This is a joint effort between the Council for the Arts and the Department of Education to provide grants to local school systems for them to develop an arts curriculum for their elementary schools. What we're talking about is a sequential, K-5 curriculum that involves all students in hands-on art activities like music, drama, visual arts, and dance.

Shell Knox and her Arts Council over in Augusta have been involved for the past several years in a national model program to incorporate art experiences into the regular school curriculum for all children, grades K-5. They have discovered two important things. First, hands-on art gives children a positive outlet to deal with their own emotions, and to process and express what they are feeling about the world around them. At the same time, it helps children learn to temper their emotional impulses with discipline and practice, so that they express themselves with self-control and self-confidence.

But in addition to giving children an outlet for emotional expression and boosting their self image, participating in the arts also strengthens children's academic skills. You see, art is a problem-solving experience. You have to decide what results you want, then figure out how to put the parts together to create the overall effect that you're after. Visual arts give children a hands-on feel for geometric shapes and spatial relationships. Auditory arts improve their listening skills and comprehension. Dramatic arts improve their communication skills. What they discovered in Augusta is that when you make art an integral part of the elementary school curriculum, academic performance improves and test scores go up. That experience has been verified by other sources. The College Entrance Examination Board, for example, says that students who have participated in the arts at school score higher on the SAT.

So the budget has $700,000 for Georgia Challenge grants for local school systems to create a hands-on integrated art curriculum for their students in grades K-5. But to succeed, it will require local initiative and a local partnership of your community arts organizations with schools and business leaders. And I want to encourage all of you to get involved and encourage your community to respond to the Georgia Challenge.

The second program I want to mention is the Grassroots Arts Program. We call it GAP for short, and it really does fill a gap. You see, traditionally, state arts grants have gone to established artists and art organizations, and it *is* a wonderful thing when a state grant helps the Atlanta Symphony come to your community for a concert. But it is also a wonderful thing when a state grant helps your community develop your own arts organizations and your own artists. That is what GAP does.

As most of you know, my mother was an artist, and one of the things I learned from her is that art needs to be more than just a spectator sport. It needs to be an integral part of daily life.

The goal of the Arts Council under this administration is to invite more and more Georgians to participate in the arts by helping schools and communities develop their own arts activities. You can see that reflected in these two initiatives that I've just described.

*—Georgia Citizens for the Arts, February 1, 1995*

-----------

State government in Georgia has a long tradition of supporting the arts through grants to artists and art organizations, including the Atlanta Symphony, and my administration has continued that tradition. In fact, we have increased state funds for the arts.

But Shirley and I are also continually searching for other, more personal ways to support and celebrate the arts. Shirley serves as a trustee on the board for the Woodruff Arts Center, and every year since I became Governor, we have held a reception at the Mansion to honor the members of the Patron Circle of Stars for the Center. Many of you have been there, and we look forward to seeing you again in the spring.

This evening, we are pleased to express our personal support for the Woodruff Arts Center and the Atlanta Symphony Orchestra by serving as your official hosts.

Atlanta cannot make her mark on the world without outstanding arts organizations like our Grammy-Award-winning Symphony, and tonight as we celebrate this golden anniversary season, we congratulate the Symphony on its outstanding achievements. The 50-year history of this orchestra is a continuous journey to ever-higher levels of excellence. The Atlanta Symphony is truly a treasure that enriches our individual and community lives, and helps to make our mark on the world. The entire State of Georgia is basking in the glow of the international acclaim the Symphony has achieved.

*—50th Anniversary Concert, Atlanta Symphony Orchestra,*
*February 4, 1995*

-----------

Together we have made the arts a more important and more integral part of the life of our state, and raised awareness that every community's art is important. Together we have extended state funds to every county in Georgia and expanded our efforts to touch every age group.

We can be proud of the Georgia Challenge for the Arts educational program that provides our elementary schools with up to $50,000 a year in challenge grants to provide art programs. I want to thank the Coca-Cola Company for its contribution toward staffing this program and tracking its results.

We developed a formula to ensure equitable distribution of arts funding around the state. We can be proud of the Grassroots Arts program, which has not only seen to it that arts funding has touched every county in Georgia, but has also created and built up a network of regional arts organizations around the state. I want to recognize and thank these regional organizations for the leadership they have shown in teaching local communities how to form arts councils and how to use the state dollars they receive as seed money to leverage local dollars and promote local involvement in the arts.

It is great to have the High Museum and the Atlanta Symphony Orchestra and the many professional theater groups in Atlanta. They are what make Atlanta a world-class city, and we are very fortunate to have them here in our state. They are a wonderful resource that enables us to experience the highest levels and quality of art.

But art also ought to be important and valued in every community of this state. While we want to expose more and more Georgia citizens to world-class art in Atlanta, we also want each community of this state to encourage and support and enjoy the work of its own hands.

Art is an ongoing, creative process. In addition to admiring and learning from the work of the most outstanding artists through history, we also need to be actively involved in doing it, each of us in our own communities all across the state....

All I've done was to be a facilitator, while Georgia Citizens for the Arts and the Arts Council and all of you did the work and made it happen. I'm grateful to have had the opportunity to know you and work together with you in the quest to encourage and stimulate artwork and the appreciation of art in every community around the state.

*—Georgia Citizens for the Arts, February 5, 1998*

# The Artists

*Benny Andrews*

It has been 30 years since Benny Andrews' first New York City show at the Forum Gallery in 1962, and he is at that point in his career where the sheer weight of his credentials might obscure the man and his work.

Benny Andrews was a natural choice for this series at the Mansion to salute Georgia artists: He embodies the artist with Georgia roots whose artistic vision takes root in all America. His work is represented in all the major museums: the High Museum of Art in Atlanta; the Hirschhorn Museum at the Smithsonian Institution in Washington, D.C.; and two of New York's major institutions—the Museum of Modern Art and the Metropolitan Museum of Art. He is a recipient of some impressive awards: the John Hay Whitney and Rockefeller Foundation fellowships.

Although he could make a living just by painting, Benny enjoys teaching and is a professor at Queens College in New York.

To use one of Benny's Madison expressions, he's walking in tall grass as one of America's renowned artists. But he keeps coming back to his roots through his work, and by returning to Georgia every summer. He and his wife, Nene, an accomplished artist, have a studio outside Athens on a wooded site surrounded by pastures, very similar to the Madison countryside where Benny was born.

Growing up during the Great Depression and World War II left a lasting impression on the young Benny Andrews. Beyond these historic events, what shaped his life—week in and week out—was the Plainview Baptist Church built by his grandmother and the hub of the black community where he grew up. His father, George, farmed and also set an example as a self-taught artist willing to use any available surface—from barns to bottles—for his chalk drawings.

Benny graduated from Madison's Burney Street High School in 1948 and attended Fort Valley College for two years before enlisting in the Air Force and serving in Korea until 1954. But it was segregation that sent him out from Georgia into America as an artist. No art school in Georgia would accept blacks in the 1950s when Andrews wanted to take advantage of his G.I. Bill educational benefits. Instead, the state bought him a train ticket and paid part of his tuition to study at the Art Institute of Chicago, which *did* accept black students.

When he was profiled in *American Artists* magazine, Andrews said what bothers him most is "not being seen as a complicated individual." It's much easier, he said, "to be typecast as regional or representational or Southern or black." His own, broader view of himself is that all of his work is "of and about America, or as seen through an American's eyes."

Fittingly, he was one of 10 artists selected to design a poster to celebrate the 200-year anniversary of the signing of the Bill of Rights. That inspired his "America Series" of paintings, which depicts folks from preachers to soldiers to the K-Mart lady who represent America. *USA Today* confirms flatly, "He's doing the world next."

He can tackle the world now because his mother, Viola, pinched pennies to make sure he had pencils and paper and crayons when he was growing up. She took him to church. Most important, Benny says, his mother taught him that "it didn't matter what you had or didn't have, it was more important how you felt about yourself." That grounding frees him to bring the past into the present, to be both simple and complex, concrete and almost mystical.

He's painted the preachers of his childhood, feet firmly planted in the pulpit. Yet when he did a mural called "Flight" for Atlanta's Hartsfield Airport, he painted a bird without feet. "I made it so the bird could fly forever," he said, explaining his simple image for a complex spiritual concept.

There is no doubt he is a very complicated—and delightful and brilliant—individual. And he honors us by continuing to return to Georgia for his inspiration.

*—Cultural Evening at the Mansion, July 23, 1992*

*Chet Atkins*

Chet Atkins was born in Luttrell, Tennessee, and began playing the ukelele at an early age. By age nine, he was also proficient on the guitar and the fiddle, and was playing at Saturday night hoedowns, roadhouses, and tourist camps. But he had also developed severe asthma, so his mother sent him down out of the foggy Tennessee mountains to live with his father in Mountain City, Georgia, which became his childhood home.

It was tough for a shy young boy to come to a new school where the kids made fun of his hillybilly accent. So at first he spent a lot of his time alone with his guitar, developing the unique finger-picking style for which he became famous. His musical talent eventually made him popular at school. It attracted the girls, and the boys used his playing as a cover for their restroom craps games. When Chet would start to sing along with his guitar, it was the signal to sweep up the dice and look as innocent as was possible for 20 boys all crowded in the restroom at the same time.

As a teenager, he got a job with the National Youth Administration, and saved up for an electric guitar. There was only one problem—no electricity in Mountain City. So he went to Columbus every chance he got, knocking on the doors of people his father knew and asking if he could borrow an outlet. He played on back porches, and outside service stations and drug stores—wherever anyone would let him plug in his guitar. He soon got a job playing on Parson Jack's popular radio show on WRBL.

Then came Pearl Harbor, and his father moved to Cincinnati to help with the war effort. So a nervous young Chet Atkins swallowed hard and got on a Greyhound bus headed for Tennessee. Within a few weeks he was performing at WNOX in Knoxville on the Archie Campbell/Bill Carlisle Show. His exceptional career was launched, and the music industry would never be quite the same. Three years later, he was being heard coast-to-coast on WLW in Cincinnati. And I was listening to him as a boy up in the North Georgia Mountains, holding the groundwire of the old Sivertone radio in my hand to make the Grand Ole Opry come in clearer.

In 1947, Chet Atkins made his first recording with RCA Victor, and in 1949 he recorded his first big hit right here in Atlanta. It was called "The Galloping Guitars." During the 1950s, in addition to his own performing career, Chet Atkins also began designing signature guitars. Drawing on his boyhood experience in the school restroom, he created the first echo chamber. He began managing RCA recording operations, developing and producing many young musicians who went on to become famous.

In 1967, he won his first Grammy Award. He has won 12 more Grammys since that first one, the most recent in 1993. Also in 1967, he won his first Country Music Association Award as Instrumentalist of the Year. He has won eight more of those since that first one, and today he ranks as the artist who has won more CMA awards than anyone else in history. In 1973, he became the youngest person ever to be inducted into the Country Music Hall of Fame. In 1991, South Street in the heart of Music Row in Nashville was renamed Chet Atkins Place. In 1992, he was given special recognition with a Lifetime Achievement Award at the Grammy Ceremony. And last year, he came home to Mountain City, Georgia, to perform two benefit concerts for his alma mater, the Mountain Hill Schoolhouse.

Ladies and gentlemen, it is a tremendous honor for this long-time Chet Atkins fan to present a Georgy Award to my boyhood idol and one of country music's all-time greatest artists, and to induct him into the Georgia Music Hall of Fame.

—*Music Awards Banquet, Setpember 23, 1996*

*William Bell*

This artist had originally planned to be a doctor. But while he was in school, studying toward that goal, he got something in his blood—music. After winning talent contests, touring with a band as its featured vocalist and making records for a minor label, our honoree signed with STAX in 1962, and he enjoyed one of his biggest hits on this label. That hit was "Tryin' to Love Two."

Although William was one of STAX Records' most prominent artists in the 60's, he interrupted his career for two years to serve our country in the Army. Then in 1970, he chose Atlanta to be the home of his own record label, and he has had a powerful presence in this city ever since. He has a great deal of community spirit, and an impressive level of involvement in Georgia's music industry.

Although we recognize him tonight as a performer, he is also a composer, producer and music businessman. His wide range of his knowledge and experience is why I appointed him to the board of the Georgia Music Hall of Fame earlier this year.

In addition to "Tryin' to Love Two," William Bell has had many other hit recordings, including such memorable songs as "You Don't Miss Your Water (Till the Well Runs Dry)," "Any Other Way," "Everybody Loves a Winner," and "Share What you Got."

Earlier this year, the Rhythm and Blues Foundation presented him with their prestigious R and B Pioneer Award. He has also received the Legends Award from Ju's Blues and the Atlanta Blues Society.

—*Music Awards Banquet, September 20, 1997*

*Mac Davis*

Through the years, I have had the privilege of introducing some of the greatest Georgia music stars ever for induction into the Music Hall of Fame. But I don't think I've ever presented anyone who is more versatile than the artist I'm going to describe tonight. He began his singing career as a choir boy, and he has a number of Gold Records and best-selling albums to his credit.

But he is also a songwriter whose songs have been cut by more than 150 artists, including Elvis Presley, Nancy Sinatra, Bobby Goldsboro, Kenny Rogers, Glen Campbell, and O.C. Smith.

He has had a career in production management, first with Vee-Jay Records, then United Artists. He has been in movies, co-starring with Nick Nolte as a quarterback in *North Dallas Forty*, then later starring in *Cheaper to Keep Her*. He has had his own television variety show and appeared on stage on Broadway playing Will Rogers.

Early on, he was a ditch-digger, a gas-pump jockey, and even an employee of the State of Georgia, working at one time for the Board of Pardons and Paroles.

Of course, there is nobody in the whole world who fits that description besides Mac Davis. His aspiration was to be a songwriter, and at the age of 17, he sold his first song to Sam the Sham's manager in a public restroom in Nashville. It was called "The Phantom Strikes Again," and it earned him recording royalties of $2.42. But as Mac says, everybody has to start somewhere.

In contrast, "I Believe in Music," has been recorded by over 50 different artists and sold millions of copies since Mac first recorded it himself. He also wrote "In the Ghetto," "A Little Less Conversation," "Memories," and "Don't Cry Daddy" for Elvis Presley. Bobby Goldsboro recorded "Watching Scotty Grow," which Mac wrote about his own son whose name really is Scotty...

In the sometimes fickle world of popular music, Mac's career has made a significant and enduring mark not only on rock and roll but also on country music.

—*Music Awards Banquet, September 28, 1996*

*Lamar Dodd*

I think it's fair to say that Lamar Dodd and the arts in Georgia grew up together. So I find it very fitting that the works on exhibit here tonight range from his very first, "Boat by the Tree"—a watercolor painted when he was a precocious 12-year-old growing up in LaGrange—to one of his most recent works, another watercolor done in 1992 of an Olympic skier....

Critics and writers have had so many fine things to say about Lamar Dodd and his work that it's hard for a layperson like me to find anything new to add. Lloyd Goodrich of the Whitney Museum of American Art, summed up his career with these words:

"Quite aside from his contribution as an artist, Lamar Dodd has been an innovative art educator, creator of a major university art department, originator of many projects on behalf of American art, leading figure in national art organizations, and cultural ambassador to other countries."

As an artist, Lamar Dodd's first one-man exhibition was held at the High Museum of Art here in Atlanta in 1931. With his work now represented in every major American museum—including the High, the Whitney, the Metropolitan Museum of Art in New York, and the Smithsonian Institute in Washington—Dodd's reputation as an artist is secure. He has traveled extensively as a cultural envoy for the U.S. State Department, and in the 1960s he was among the first artists to be invited by the National Aeronautics and Space Administration to document the developing space program.

When his late wife, Mary, had open heart surgery in 1977, he turned to exploring a new frontier—the boundary between life and death, which you can see in the crucifix-like figure at the center of the intricate Open Heart Surgery oil painting on loan to us from the Georgia Heart Clinic in LaGrange.

Despite a stroke that caused a loss of motor control in his right hand, Lamar continues to paint, influenced, he admits, by his wife Annie Laurie's fresh approach and keen eye for nature as a watercolorist. You will notice that the brush strokes in his 1992 painting of the Olympic skier are as tight, clean and expressive as ever.

Lamar's reputation as an educator is equally distinguished. When he took over as head of the Art Department at The University of Georgia in 1938, there were eight students, two part-time professors and a budget of $50. At his retirement—and I use that word loosely because he is still so active—he left more than 50 faculty members, a $2 million budget, and too many students to count. He was also the impetus for the founding of the Georgia Museum.

He holds a string of honorary titles, including Regents Professor Emeritus of Art and Chairman Emeritus of the Fine Arts Division at The University of Georgia, which he earned through years of hard work that moved visual arts education in Georgia into the 20th century. But the most important thing to me about the career of Lamar Dodd is that this man—who has had such a significant impact on the arts and arts education in America—grew up in Georgia, went off to study in New York, and then can back to Georgia and stayed.

When he gave his first one-man show in New York, one reviewer wrote, "Not one scene of the Scottish moors with their purple heather. But a glorious painting of the washwoman hanging out the clothes. Not one scene of the fountains of Rome! But a magnificent thing showing the cabins of the tenant farmer. Nothing of Paris or London or Athens or Pompeii. But Georgia, Georgia, Georgia."

Although he has drawn on Georgia for his themes, Lamar Dodd's work has not been provincial. He went on to paint scenes from Paris, London, and Athens as he traveled extensively as a cultural envoy for the State Department. But in making Georgia and The University of Georgia his home, he has shown Georgia to the world and in turn exerted an influence at home that has been crucial to the artistic climate of our state and region. For that, we are deeply, deeply grateful.

—*Cultural Evening at the Mansion, June 8, 1993*

*Lena Horne*

The special performer we honor tonight was born in New York City. But we claim her as a Georgian because she spent a large portion of her early years in our state and continues to have strong roots here. She called three Georgia cities home as she was growing up: First Macon; then Fort Valley, where her uncle was dean of students and assistant to the president of Fort Valley Junior Industrial College; and finally Atlanta, where her grandparents lived.

"My mother loved Fort Valley," her daughter Gail wrote in a book about the family. She lived at the college in the girls' dormitory with her Uncle Frank's fiancee and attended a little school across the road from the college. She later "left Fort Valley for a pleasant brick house on Atlanta's West Hunter," her daughter writes.

Her grandfather edited a weekly Atlanta newspaper, and her grandmother, a native Atlantan, was a graduate of Atlanta University. She attended Booker T. Washington Junior High School, went to dancing school and in general "enjoyed the agreeable Atlanta life," says her daughter.

Our honoree began her professional career at the age of 17 as a chorus girl at the Cotton Club in New York. Later she sang with the bands of Noble Sissle and Charlie Barnet. At the age of 19, she launched a recording career that gave us some of our favorite songs—"Good-for-Nothin' Joe," "Ill Wind," "I Got a Right to Sing the Blues," and her signature song, "Stormy Weather."

She has toured widely in the United States and Europe, and is remembered for her performances in such movies as *Cabin in the Sky*, *Broadway Rhythm*, and *The Wiz*.

Many honors have been bestowed upon this gifted woman in recognition of her outstanding career achievements and her tireless devotion to civic causes. Among them is an honorary doctoral degree from Atlanta's own Spellman College.

And now, ladies and gentlemen, it is my great pleasure to present to you the newest member of the Georgia Music Hall of Fame, Miss Lena Horne.

—*Music Awards Banquet, September 21, 1991*

*George Jones*

It's especially fitting to honor George here at the Governor's Mansion, since it's really the people's house, and no matter whether he's in a mansion or a honky-tonk, George Jones has always been the people's poet. Ever since he helped me get elected in 1990, I've been trying to get George and Nancy to come here so I could give the "The Grand Tour."

He warned me when I was elected not to let it all go to my head. Well, George, after five years in office, I hope you think I'm the "Same Ol' Me" and not some phony who's "Still Doing Time."

George and I have a lot in common. We're both Marines. Both rural—very rural—Southern boys who've drunk our share of "White Lightening." We were both saved by the love of a good woman, and I want to take a moment to recognize those two women:

George's wife Nancy, and Shirley Miller. And George, I know you feel like I do: "She's My Rock" and we're glad they decided to "Walk Through the World With Me."

George's book is such a joy, because his special gift has always been to put into words what the rest of us feel. How many of us—back in the days of our wayward youth—and some of you even later—ever felt like "Tonight the Bottle Let Me Down" after singing "Bartender Blues"? Who here can look me in the eye and say he's never shed a tear to "He Stopped Lovin' Her Today"? Or asked, "Why Baby Why?" Then put on a brave front for our beer-buddies, telling them that "She Thinks I Still Care."

I cannot imagine modern country music without George Jones, without his contribution: his songs, his style, his spirit, his spunk. He truly has become a part of the fabric of this country, and it's hard to imagine how we felt pain or expressed longing before him.

Once in a while, when old country music fans like me get to talking, we think back on the greats like Hank Williams and Lefty and Roy, and we think, "Who's Gonna Fill Their Shoes?" Well, George, "The Race is On" with all these young "hunks and "hats" . But I gotta tell you I have a feeling that Hank's watching you, "From the Window Up Above." And he's saying, George, "You've Still Got a Place in My Heart."

As with any true American original, there have been pretenders and imitators. But "Once You've Had the Best," nothing else will do. So we just show them "The Door".

Of course, the minute anyone suggests to George that he slow down, he says, "I'm Not Ready Yet." I'm still "Hotter Than a Two-Dollar Pistol." I share the feeling. "I Don't Need No Rockin' Chair." You don't need no rockin' chair either, George. No you don't. What you need is a throne. Because you are truly the King of Country Music. And, God bless you, George Jones, you've "Lived to Tell It All."

*—Book Signing for George Jones, May 14, 1996*

*Robert McDuffie*

Many of you have heard me say more than once what a great influence my mother was on me. She was a gifted painter, and I am committed to the arts because she taught me that art is the signature of the human race. Robert McDuffie's mother was a pianist and organist, and she was his first music teacher. I can identify with the strong influence she had on his musical development.

Like many boys, Bobby grew up enjoying sports. In fact he once used a tape of his own playing in an attempt to fool his mother into thinking he was practicing when he was actually playing baseball. Another time, when he was about 14, he finally got his big chance to play in the starting line-up at a high school basketball game. But his mother had other plans for him that evening. She already had tickets to a recital by violinist Itzhak Perlman. Fortunately for us, Mother McDuffie prevailed. Once Perlman started to play, sports were history. An inspired 14-year-old violinist went home to practice for hours.

By age 16, he left Macon for the Julliard School of Music in New York and was well on his way to becoming the consummate artist we recognize tonight.

Many of you may have heard Bobby McDuffie perform earlier this month with the

Atlanta Symphony Orchestra, and last Sunday's Atlanta paper contained an analysis of the symphony's season that referred to his performance as having "striking individuality and integrity."

This season, he also performed with the Philadelphia Orchestra, the San Francisco Symphony, the St. Louis Symphony, and the Chamber Music Society of Lincoln Center, and he's slated to give a recital in Washington, D.C., at the special request of the United States Supreme Court. The late composers William Schuman and Leonard Bernstein both sought out McDuffie to perform their works. His performance of Schuman's Violin Concerto at his Carnegie Hall debut in 1989 earned a rave review in the *New York Times* for its virtuosity.

I have thought very highly of Bobby McDuffie for a long time—so highly that I profiled him as the most promising of America's up-and-coming young violinists in a book I wrote nearly a decade ago called *They Heard Georgia Singing*.

But there's more to Bobby McDuffie than his credentials as an artist—impressive as they are—so let me tell you a little more about this Georgia boy. He's truly devoted to introducing young people to the joys and possibilities of music. He understands that somewhere out there is another talented young boy or girl, who is going to be inspired by a firsthand performance from him, just as he was inspired by Itzhak Perlman. So he has criss-crossed the country as an Affiliate Artist in a program to showcase top performers for student audiences. He also serves on the board of directors for the Harlem School of the Arts, an oasis for talented students in elementary through high school.

During this particular visit to Atlanta, he volunteered to perform for a group of young people at Emmaus House, a community center in the Summerhill neighborhood supported by the Episcopal Church. And earlier today, he taught a master class for students at Pace Academy.

*—Cultural Evening at the Mansion, May 28, 1992*

*Lanier Meaders*

When the Folk Arts Program of the National Endowment for the Arts named Lanier Meaders a National Heritage Fellow in 1983, he was being recognized for his traditional practice of one of the world's most ancient crafts: "Turning the potter's wheel and firing earth into useful, beautiful containers." As folklorist Steve Siporin notes in his profile of Lanier Meaders as an American folk master, "Neither art, nor craft nor heritage was neglected."

In the days before home refrigeration and the proliferation of cheap glass jars and tin cans, Lanier Meaders, like his father and grandfather before him, concentrated on utilitarian vessels that people needed and used: Crocks that wouldn't leak for making sauerkraut or pickling meat; jugs for syrup; churns, pitchers, and even flowerpots.

Later, public fascination with his face jugs forced the reluctant craftsman to neglect the functional pieces and create hundreds, and then thousands, of face jugs just to meet demand. Over the years, these face jugs have evolved to become less jug-like and more sculptural to emphasize their human features. But Lanier retains a wry sense of humor about his face jugs, which he once described as being "about the ugliest thing a person can make" and as having "no earthly value at all." Of course, that's just Lanier's opinion.

Born in 1917 into a now-famous family of potters, Lanier Meaders fired up his first kiln-load of churns at the age of 17. But almost immediately the Great Depression, then later World War II, put a damper on his involvement in the family trade. In fact, Lanier did not fully resume his craft until a film crew from the Smithsonian Institution came in 1967 to film the Meaders family at work. Lanier helped his elderly parents, Cheever and Arie Meaders, complete the pottery process to be captured on film. And when his father died six months later, it was Lanier who concentrated on filling the orders coming in from the Smithsonian museum shops.

As he turned his hand to pottery, there was a sense of destiny fulfilled. As Lanier told folklorist Ralph Rinzler from the Smithsonian, "Well, it's just a trade. It's a gift that a person comes by. I could no more stop this than I could fly an airplane. I'm just into it. I'm not going to stop it; can't stop it. All of my movements, all of my work that I've done all my life has led straight to this place right here. And every time I come about it, I just get a little bit deeper into it. I'm about so deep in it now that I can't get away from it."

In January 1968, Lanier fired the new kiln he'd built for the first time. And although he'd sold his father's mule, Jason, and installed an electric pug mill to grind the clay, for all practical purposes, Lanier continued the traditional methods he'd learned as a child.

Stoneware came to England from Germany in the 1600s and to America by the early 1700s. So the Meaders family got a relatively late start for the pottery-rich region of Mossy Creek in North Georgia, when Lanier's grandfather, John M. Meaders, built his first kiln in 1892 to supplement their farm income. His youngest son, Cheever, fell heir to the pottery shop, which now bears Lanier's stamp.

The road running past the shop was graded in 1923 and blacktopped in the mid-30s, bringing hoards of Florida-bound tourists clamoring for the unique pottery. The Rural Electrification Administration brought electric power to Mossy Creek in 1936.

What didn't change was the potter's almost primal connection to his craft: hands mired in clay or measuring instinctively accurate portions of wood-ash and clay "settlin's" to create a unique dark green glaze, scavenging for just the right wood to fire the kiln, then patiently stoking the fire for hours to cure the clay and melt the glaze. Always patience as a critical ingredient in the firing, lest haste should ruin the handiwork.

As the cameraman from the Smithsonian panned the greenware drying in the sun more than two decades ago, Lanier Meader's voice on the film soundtrack noted prophetically: "Well, you're trying the preserve the old things that have been, and the things that are going out. When I go, this place will go with me, because there'll be nobody else left to carry it on. And without it, what they get here they can't get anywhere else."

Lanier Meaders is right. He comes from a unique tradition, and his stamp on that tradition has been his own. His artistry, his craftsmanship are irreplaceable, and tonight we honor him both as a National Heritage Fellow and as a fellow Georgian. His roots run so deep in the Georgia clay, that we stand in awe of this man who is both a stalwart preserver and a fearless innovator of his inherited craft tradition.

—*Cultural Evening at the Mansion, September 14, 1993*

*Edward Moulthrop*

Edward Moulthrop holds a master's of architecture from Princeton University and has studied architecture in France. He has had a long and outstanding career in architecture as a professor at Georgia Tech and chief of design for Robert and Company Associates. He has received national design awards from the American Institute of Steel Construction and the Association of Federal Architects, and he designed many buildings here in Georgia that we remember and know and admire: the old Atlanta Airport Terminal, the Atlanta Civic Center, Emory University Dental School and the master plan for Emory University Hospital, the Georgia Tech Graduate Library, the Memorial Chapel at Callaway Gardens, the Memorial Building at Stone Mountain Park, and the Stone Mountain Carillon for which he won an award.

After 45 years as an outstanding architect, Ed Moulthrop gave it up to pursue his hobby. Now, for most of us, giving up our profession to pursue a hobby would mean retiring and puttering around. But Mr. Moulthrop is even more well-known and highly regarded for his hobby than he was as an architect.

Wood turning involves shaping and hollowing a section of log as it turns on a lathe. It has been practiced for centuries, both as a practical craft by artisans and as hobby by such famous aristocrats as Peter the Great and Louis the Sixteenth. But when Ed Moulthrop does it, it becomes art.

There are several hundred professional woodturners in America today, and many more amateurs. Ed Moulthrop is one of the best. His beautiful bowls combine the skill of a true craftsman with the architect's eye for line and design, and an artistic knack for enhancing the natural beauty of the wood. The result is artwork that soars above the functional and becomes sculpture.

He favors tulipwood, especially from trees that have been struck by lightening, because the same damage that makes lumberjacks reject the tree, opens it to the action of bacteria, which permeates the wood with rich reds and purples.

Ed Moulthrop's works of art are part of the permanent collections of more than a dozen major American museums, including the both the Metropolitan Museum and the Museum of Modern Art in New York, the Smithsonian, the Boston Museum of Fine Arts, the Detroit Institute of Arts, the Houston Museum of Art, the Arizona State University Museum, and here in Georgia, the High Museum and the Columbus Museum. His works are displayed at the White House, and are part of the personal collections of such world-famous people as Steven Spielberg, Nelson Mandela, Ted Turner, Clare Booth Luce, Beverly Sills, Mary McFadden, Jack Nicholas, Queen Beatrix of the Netherlands and President Jimmy Carter.

*—Cultural Evening at the Mansion, February 11, 1998*

*Mattie Lou O'Kelle*

What a pleasure it's been for me to get to meet Mattie Lou O'Kelley tonight and to discover that she is as witty, as colorful, as down-to-earth as the pictures she paints. If you know Mattie, you know that she can be very self-effacing. Her initial response to being asked to participate in this event was to say, "Who'd pay to see me, when what I do comes as easy to me as falling off a log?"

I can't help but recognize certain similarities between this wonderful artist and my own mother, Birdie Bryan Miller. Many of you know that my mother was an artist who studied at the Art Students League in New York City. I'm here because she was adventuresome enough to travel for hours by train, then by mule-drawn stage coach to reach a little-known place in the north Georgia mountains called Young Harris, whose tiny college had advertised for an art teacher. That's where she met and married my father.

My mother believed in herself, and she had an indomitable spirit. We had a roof over our heads after my father died, because my mother, the artist, became a master artisan and built us a house with her own hands—stone by stone.

With that same indomitable spirit, Mattie Lou O'Kelley worked hard and long, picking cotton and doing other farm chores on her parents' Maysville farm. Later, she worked in a mill and sewing factory to provide for herself and her elderly mother.

She took up painting as a hobby, but she came to believe in herself as an artist. One day she boarded a bus to Atlanta with some of her paintings under her arm, and headed for the High Museum. There she met Gudmund Vigtel and showed him some of her artwork. The rest, as they say, is history.

*Cultural Evening at the Mansion, August 18, 1992*

*Eugenia Price*

Eugenia Price was the only daughter of a dentist, and, aspiring to follow in her father's footsteps, she enrolled in Northwestern Dental School in Chicago at the age of eighteen. But she was also born with a love of words and a gift for putting them together, and she dropped out of dental school to become a writer. However, it was many years before she began writing the novels that introduced so many readers worldwide to Georgia's historic coast.

She spent more than a decade as a broadcast writer and producer, first for radio then television. When she finally published her first book, it was a work of inspirational non-fiction called *Discoveries*, and she is the author of 26 devotional and inspirational books.

She was 20 years into her career as a writer—she was nationally and internationally known for touching readers with her insights on life, faith, and service—when, on her way to Florida for a promotional tour, she discovered St. Simons Island and the story of Anson Dodge, which became the basis for her first novel, *Beloved Invader*. This book was the first of more than a dozen novels, set along the Georgia and Florida coasts during the 19th century. They set a standard for historical novels of the South and earned her the 1978 Governor's Award in the Arts.

To make her novels historically accurate, she did a tremendous amount of research on her own, and supplemented it with assistance from historians, librarians, professors, and other researchers. In fact, her use of archives and libraries around the country earned her an award from Georgia archivists. But her real gift was making that research come alive. Her readers get caught up in the emotions, observations, wisdom, and follies of her characters, who are so true to life, that one reader even wrote that she prayed for the characters in those novels.

For the last several decades of her life, Eugenia Price lived in Georgia on her beloved St. Simons Island. It was here that she completed the final editing on her last book, *The Waiting* Time, just weeks before her death from heart failure on May 28, 1996. In all, she sold more than 20 million books worldwide before her death.

*—Cultural Evening at the mansion, February 11, 1998*

*Byron Herbert Reece*

Byron Herbert Reece... cannot be with us in person tonight, but his powerful and sensitive spirit still shines for us in his poetry. Were he not beyond the reach of song, as he so poignantly put it, he would have been 75 years old last Monday.

He was the epitome of the artist with Georgia roots: a north Georgia mountain farmer who used his time behind the plow and his closeness to the rhythms of the earth and its seasons to shape his poetic rhythms and images.

As all of you know, my own roots run deep in those same North Georgia mountains. As I boy, I knew "Hub" Reece as a neighbor and friend. He was tall and gaunt with hollow cheekbones and a shock of hair that, unless freshly combed, hung down upon his forehead. He lived on Wolf Creek at the base of Blood Mountain, not far from where Lake Vogel is now. It was an isolated spot. He and his brother and sisters walked four miles down the valley each day to Choestoe Elementary School. Union County High School in Blairsville was nine miles away.

The young Reece nurtured himself on the King James Bible and the mountain ballads and hymns he heard at home and at church. These resources later stood him in good stead as an artist.

For many years my Uncle Fletcher and his family were the Reeces' closest neighbors. "Hub" Reece would often come to their house after plowing a mule all day, and sit on the floor, reading. I was a frequent visitor there, too, and I was drawn to this quiet, intelligent, mild-mannered young man. Once he discovered that I was interested in insects and, on the next visit, gave me a book on insect life. On the flyleaf he wrote, "Dear Zell: I hope this book won't outlast your interest in its subject as it did mine. In any case, it will acquaint you with the insect world, an interesting and varied world indeed. It sometimes is good for the human family to recall that if an insect had a fifth as much brain power as the human being, we would have been vanquished long ago! Sincerely, Byron Herbert Reece, Jan. 6, 1946." At that time I was aware that he wrote poetry, but I was more impressed by his skills with a mule, his knowledge of nature, and his intense devotion to protecting the environment.

Professor W. L. Dance at Young Harris College recognized and encouraged "Hub" Reece's talent, and when a visiting scholar introduced the young poet to the ballad form in 1939, Reece knew immediately that he had found the ideal framework to express his own experience.

This remarkable man, who thought of himself as a farmer first and a poet second, was "discovered" by the great author-poet Jesse Stuart from reading one of his poems in a magazine. Stuart wrote to Reece, offering encouragement, and in 1945 his first book of poetry, *The Ballad of Bones*, was published by E.P. Dutton. He was plowing when the advance copies of the book arrived at the farm on his 28th birthday.

*The Ballad of Bones* immediately thrust Byron Herbert Reece onto the literary scene. The influential *Saturday Review* described the book—with its title poem based on the 37th chapter of the Old Testament book of Ezekiel—as "full of tragic beauty." By January of 1946, the book was in its third printing.

*The Ballad of Bones* was followed in 1950 by a novel, *Better a Dinner of Herbs*, as well as a second volume of poetry, *Bow Down in Jericho*. Two more volumes of poetry were published to national acclaim—*A Song of Joy* in 1952 and *The Season of Flesh* in 1955. And the north Georgia farmer was called out of the mountains to meet his public. He served as a distinguished lecturer at the University of California and at Emory University.

Yet financial reward never followed. Even though he was eventually awarded two Guggenheim fellowships, "Hub" Reece constantly struggled to make ends meet and support his elderly parents. He also battled with his own tuberculosis, and the time he spent in the hospital for treatment was like being in prison for this mountaineer.

Advised by his publisher that he'd profit by moving to an urban center, Reece responded, "The north Georgia countryside is as good a place as any for a man to wrestle with the angel of his aspiration and loneliness."

In 1955, he published his last book, *The Hawk and the Sun* and went back to Young Harris College to teach. On June 3, 1958, he put one of his favorite pieces of music on a record player and shot himself. He was 40 years old.

A monument to him now stands on the side of Blood Mountain in a shady cove not far from his home on Wolf Creek. And on that monument are these words which he wrote:

From chips and shards in idle times,
I made these stories, shaped these rhymes.
May they engage some friendly tongue
When I am past the reach of song.

—*Cultural Evening at the Mansion, September 21, 1992*

*Ferrol Sams*

Rural Georgia is the often-inexplicable world Ferrol Sams described in his first novel, *Run with the Horsemen*. "Sambo" was 58 when he first attempted to capture his memories of growing up on a Georgia farm during the Great Depression. In a recent interview in *Atlanta Magazine*, he recalled that he finally hit on one good sentence: "The stride of the man matched that of the mule in a one-plane dance down a cotton row." He built on that one sentence to discover the rhythm, the pace, and, finally, the voice that speaks through our greatest southern writers.

That voice echoes through his Porter Osborne trilogy—*Run With the Horsemen*, *Whisper of the River*, and *When All the World Was Young*. It earned Dr. Sams honorary doctorates of letters from both of his alma maters—Mercer and Emory Universities. And it has earned him a national audience for his tales about a southern boy coming of age....

Despite all the fuss and the fame, Dr. Sams continues to see patients every day in his Fayetteville clinic. This is fortunate indeed, for the many Fayette County families have come to rely on him and his family over the years for their well-being.

It is also fortunate for those of us who love to read and to laugh that he also continues to write and create characters like Porter Osborne.

*—Cultural Evening at the Mansion, June 25, 1992*

*The Skillet Lickers*

It was early 1924. Fiddlin' John Carson had just cut the very first country music record for Okeh Records, and the recording giant Columbia was looking for a piece of the action. Where they looked for it was Walton County, Georgia. They invited a chicken farmer named Gid Tanner to come to New York. He brought along his friend, blind Riley Puckett, and they became the first rural southern artists to record for Columbia.

Afterward, Gid Tanner came back to Georgia and gathered up a wild group of musical geniuses into a string band called the Skillet Lickers, that played its way to national fame. Their string band style incorporated elements of what we know today as jazz, bluegrass, western, and rhythm and blues. And their broad appeal gave new respectability and popularity to "hillbilly" music. Of course, that was nearly 70 years ago, but the spirit and the sound of the Skillet Lickers is still alive and well today.

The Tanner family has fiddlin' in their blood. Gid Tanner taught his son Gordon, who also became an outstanding musician, and made fiddles as well as playing them. Gordon's son Phil began playing back-up guitar to his father's fiddle, then graduated to lead fiddle himself. And Phil Tanner is the leader of this band of Skillet Lickers today.

That's not the end of the Tanner line, either. Phil's son Russ has moved increasingly into the band's lead fiddle spot, and his great-grandfather's blood runs true in him. When Russ cocks his head back over his fiddle, he is Gid Tanner come back to life.

Joe Miller has come right on through with the various generations of Tanners. He played with Gid Tanner and Riley Puckett back in the 30s and early 40s, then with Gordon Tanner, and now with Phil and Russ. He earned the nickname "Smokey Joe" in the early 40s. When he played, his fingers moved so fast that smoke seemed to be rising from them.

Fleet Stanley is the grandson of Dacula fiddler Rob Stanley, who was a mainstay at the old Atlanta Fiddle Conventions and also played with Gid Tanner and Riley Puckett. As a child, Fleet learned the guitar from his Aunt Roba, who was the first female country music singer to be recorded.

Doug Landress is the great-nephew of Bud Landress who played with the Georgia Yellow Hammers. He got involved with the Tanners as a high school friend of Phil, and played in jam sessions in the "chicken coop" music room behind Gordon Tanner's old house in Dacula.

Julian McDaniel is a long-time friend of "Smokey Joe" Miller's who originally comes from Barrow County. He has been playing the harmonica since he was a boy, and has been jamming with rural musicians and playing square dances all his life.

I've left Art Rosenbaum for last, because he is the only one of the group who doesn't go way back with the Tanners or similar rural north Georgia groups. In fact, he's a Yankee who only showed up in the South less than 20 years ago. But he's a southerner in his heart, and he can't help it that he was born somewhere else and finally found his way home about 20 years ago. Art is a devoted folklorist who picks a mean banjo in an age when good old-time banjo players are hard to come by. He is also a gifted artist who teaches at The University of Georgia.

—*Cultural Evening at the Mansion, August 30, 1994*

*Alfred Uhry*

Alfred Uhry has said that he wrote "Driving Miss Daisy" about illiteracy. To me, the play is about friendship and the fact that down underneath the distinctions of race, class, and gender, we are human beings who need each other.

Set against the backdrop of the exploding civil rights movement, it depicts the trust that developed between two characters as they struggled not just with illiteracy, but also with the emerging questions of racial equality and justice.

In some respects, it is a very simple play. Yet it has said so much to so many people. And when the world took note of Alfred Uhry's play, and later, his movie, it took note of Georgia and gained a little better understanding of who we are.

That process was a perfect example of why the arts are so essential. They interpret our history and express our identity. They hold a mirror to society, and all who look into it are challenged to think of themselves and of others in new ways.

Alfred Uhry is a third-generation Atlantan. In "Driving Miss Daisy," he mirrored a unique moment in our history, and it has come to have a very special meaning for many Georgians. Alfred was graduated from Druid Hills High School in 1954 and from Brown University in 1958. Then he moved to New York City, where he taught school and developed a career as a lyricist. He created the book and lyrics for "The Robber Bridegroom," for which he received nominations for a Tony and two Drama Desk awards. And he co-wrote Samuel Goldwyn Jr.'s film hit, "Mystic Pizza."

"Driving Miss Daisy" was his first play, and it won him a Pulitzer prize. Shirley and I saw this wonderful play, starring Mary Nell Santacroce, at the Alliance Theatre. I'm sure many of you did, too. It was adapted into a screenplay and made into a motion picture, which has been shown all over the world and which won an Academy Award in 1989.

Though he could easily live a celebrity's life in New York, with weekends at The Hamptons and lunches at Le Cirque, Alfred has made a commitment to help young people, especially young people with talent and an interest in playwriting. You see, Alfred Uhry is not a Pulitzer prize winner who just happened to be a teacher along the way. He is a teacher who just happened to win a Pulitzer prize along the way. He is teaching a screenwriting course at New York University. And he is president of the Young Playwrights Festival, a program that goes out into public schools, encouraging students to develop theater skills.

—*Cultural Evening at the Mansion, April 16, 1992*

# Economic Development

Atlanta is one of the few cities in the nation where three different interstates converge. And presently, we are a third of the way through a major highway construction effort for 2,700 miles more of four-lane roads. Atlanta is also a major air center, with direct air connections across the nation and beyond to Europe, Latin America, and Pacific Rim nations in Asia. Many of these international flights connect with the 34 foreign countries who have over 1,350 business facilities located in Georgia.

Our port at Savannah is the premier shipping center on the South Atlantic. It accommodates the world's largest freighters, and offers top of the line facilities, from containerized shipping to refrigerated storage to computerized customs processing. Brunswick, our second port city, is not far behind.

And, of course, railroads. Atlanta grew up as a rail center around the point where three rail lines converged. It is still a major rail center, with a large piggyback yard.

In addition to this kind of excellent infrastructure, Georgia is a center of finance and commerce with progressive interstate banking laws and offices of about 30 foreign banks.

One of the important things that makes Georgia so attractive to business is our environmental permitting procedure. We have consolidated all federal, all state, and all local permitting in a one-stop process with a single set of documents. And we pride ourselves on our rapid turn-around time—90 days versus as long as two years elsewhere.

Many of you have heard of North Carolina's famous Research Triangle. Well, in all modesty, let me point out that we have the Georgia Institute of Technology, the University of Georgia and Emory University who in combination do more research. Also, Emory University and the adjacent Centers for Disease Control are a major medical center, and we have an incubator for fledgling high-tech firms on the Georgia Tech campus.

Georgia also has a statewide network of 32 post-secondary technical institutes. They offer a host of technical programs, and they also offer Quick Start. Georgia originated this on-site employee training program for new and expanding businesses. During the last six months, we've trained 12,000 employees at over 100 companies, and during its existence Quick Start has trained 125,000 employees for more than 1,600 different businesses.

Most of the Fortune 500 companies have facilities in Georgia—many of them regional headquarters, some of them national and international headquarters. Georgia is home to a lot of small businesses, too. Eighty percent of our manufacturing firms have fewer than 100 employees, for example. That is because we nurture small businesses.

*World Finance Magazine* called Georgia the 12th best managed state in the nation. And our bond rating is Triple A. Our top-bracket corporate and personal income tax rates are 6 percent, generally matching or lower than our neighbors, and our motor fuel and sales taxes are also among the lowest.

We are very proud of our network of partnerships in Georgia—partnerships between levels of government and partnerships between business and government. This unique public-private relationship has made Atlanta the third busiest convention city in the

United States. The state built and operates the Georgia World Congress Center, one of the nation's largest and most complete convention facilities. At my recommendation, the legislature added $75 million to this year's budget to further expand the Center. The Georgia Dome, a 75,000-seat domed stadium is presently under construction next to the World Congress Center. It represents a unique partnership between the state and private business, and will be completed in August of 1992.

Government and business share many of the same goals. In Georgia, we understand that, and we are working together to make it happen. We created over 800,000 new jobs in Georgia in the last decade, and we're on the way to doing even more in the 90s. We invite you to be a part of it.

*—Red Carpet Tour, April 9, 1991*

---

Transportation is clearly a critical ingredient for economic development, just as arteries are essential to the functioning of the human body. Roads alone will not guarantee jobs. We must have a more comprehensive approach to transportation in itself.

This department used to be referred to as the Highway Department, and even though the name was changed some time ago, the focus was not. Transportation is highways, but it is also mass transit, waterways and ports, air and rail travel. And all of these modes of transportation must be balanced and coordinated with each other.

The days are gone when we can solve Atlanta's rush hour traffic problems by adding more lanes to metro-area expressways. There is no more room for that, and other solutions are called for.

Rail is a tremendous way to move both products and people between population centers. Georgia is the biggest state east of the Mississippi and our commercial centers are spread out. We need to take a new look at the role rail can play in connecting them with each other and with other parts of the country. The ports in Savannah and Brunswick will never achieve their potential, if our rail and highway networks are not designed to provide good access and distribution.

We also need better relationships with the federal government on the one hand and with local governments on the other, if we are to make maximum use of our transportation resources, which is a must in this time of limited revenues.

Finally, we are in an era that calls for a new understanding and approach to the political process. The way to progress is not through fights and stand-offs between bitter opponents, which can only be resolved when one prevails and the other is knocked out. Rather, the political process must enable the parties concerned to sit down together, find their common ground, then move forward to address problems in ways that are acceptable to all of them.

These are things that must happen in Georgia and in the DOT if we are to move toward economic prosperity in the 21st century. It is no longer enough to understand how a bridge is built or how asphalt is made. Today's transportation decisions call for a new, more comprehensive understanding of transportation and a new level of cooperation with the other players in the economic development game.

*—Swearing-in Wayne Shackelford as Transportation Commissioner,
October 31, 1991*

---

A decade or two ago, manufacturing jobs started to move around the globe, seeking places where wages were even lower than Georgia's. Instead of exporting products, we started exporting jobs, and American manufacturers were soon competing against imported goods in what used to be their exclusive domestic markets. About the same time, the microchip appeared on the scene, catapulting electronics into a whole new and pervasive era, and ushering in the information age.

Today's political, economic, and technological trends send a clear message that we are in a time of watershed change, and with it is coming dramatic and sometimes painful adjustments in many aspects of business and personal life.... The impact of these sweeping, worldwide changes has been particularly dramatic for manufacturing, which was at the heart and soul of the industrial age. Manufacturing must now undergo major change in order to compete in the international rigors of a high-tech age, and it is feeling the strain.

In 1970, almost 30 percent of Georgia's jobs were in manufacturing plants. Today, manufacturing accounts for less than 20 percent of our workforce...

Not only has technology become more complex, but the speed with which it changes has also increased dramatically. American industry used to put new technology into place, then coast for long stretches of time on its competitive edge, while it waited for the rest of the world to catch up. We'd wait to buy new equipment until the old stuff wore out, and we'd still be able to beat the competition. Once we had trained our employees on that equipment, they were squared away for years and years. Today the rest of the world catches up with a new technology within a year, and we Americans are not always the first to put that new technology into place any more. Increasingly we are the ones who must do the catching up.

There is no doubt about the superiority of our higher education system and the research that is going on at American universities. Why else would 40 percent of our graduate students and 50 percent of our PhDs in math, engineering, and computer science be coming here from other nations? Where we have lost ground over the past two decades is in the practical application of our research.

Advanced technology and its application require an intense level of research and development. At the same time, however, corporate profits have become tighter, because plant technology is increasingly expensive and needs to be replaced on a shorter cycle. At the very time that industry needs a higher level of R&D, they have less money to do it. And, wonderful as the free market economy is, one of its few short-comings is a tendency to encourage short-term profits over long-term development. So other nations have gained an edge over us in the practical application of our own research.

Talk to people in the electronics industry, and they will point to the Pacific Rim's application of American research. Talk to the textile industry, and they will tell you that Europe has taken over the lead in producing manufacturing equipment.

That is why we are here today. That is the purpose of the Fuller E. Callaway Jr. Manufacturing Research Center—to take back the competitive edge in the practical application of our own research into products that will compete on the international market, and to offer our manufacturers a modern, streamlined, efficient way to produce a quality product....

Georgia's manufacturers are clearly a tenacious bunch. But with the Manufacturing Research Center, we will do more than simply survive in these difficult times. The MARC gathers up Georgia Tech's research expertise from various disciplines and focuses it on manufacturing in ways that connect directly with industry and with the students who tomorrow will work in those industries. In so doing, the MARC will make Tech a national center of excellence in manufacturing. The MARC will put Georgia Tech and the State of Georgia out on the front lines of helping American manufacturers to regain their competitive edge on the world market.

*—Dedication of Georgia Tech Manufacturing Research Center,*
*November 8, 1991*

———————

The recent movie, "Doc Hollywood," drew humor from the plight of rural communities that have no access to the kind of specialized, state-of-the-art medical care that is available in our cities. But the problem itself is not humorous at all. It means that someone who suffers a heart attack in a rural town might die, when a person in the city might get to a specialist in time for his life to be saved. The doctors in this part of Georgia know first-hand that sick people have died on the way to Augusta from their hometowns out in the country.

I lived most of my life in an isolated, small town, Young Harris, so it's a great thrill for me to be here today to help the Medical College of Georgia kick off this telemedicine program. MCG has always led the way in the use of modern technology, but with telemedicine, the college is using technology to make specialized care available in a rural community more than 100 miles away.

This program is truly amazing. Even 10 years ago, the idea that doctors in Augusta could peer down throats, listen to heartbeats, and see and talk to patients in Eastman— 130 miles away—would have been unthinkable. Telemedicine not only will save lives; it will save money. The expense of transferring a patient from a community such as Eastman to Augusta is far greater than the cost of seeing that patient via the Telemedicine network.... This is a program that will save lives and will be a model for others.

*—Telemedicine Demonstration, November 13, 1991*

———————

In this age of advanced technology, a relevant university research program will benefit already-existing industries, attract new industries in that field, and spin off new firms. Georgia already has a strong base on which to build. In 1989, our leading research universities ranked fourth of the 17 southern and border states in total research and development spending. Emory University, Georgia Tech, and The University of Georgia combined, attract more in research contracts than the fabled Research Triangle in North Carolina.

I believe that we in Georgia must build on this base and make the decade of the 90s the decade of technology. We must promote its development and harness its potential for economic growth. The public and private sectors must come together, in partnership, to develop a technology policy for our state and steer a course for Georgia into the 21st century.

I intend to do two things to move us in this direction. First, I will create by Executive Order a Governor's Advisory Council on Science and Technology Development. It will be composed of public and private sector leaders who are knowledgeable in technology needs and opportunities, who understand current technologies, and who can identify emerging technologies that connect with our industrial strengths and needs.

Second, in conjunction with the Georgia Research Alliance, which is composed of Georgia's major public and private research universities and the state's leading technology business executives, I will propose a public-private partnership to expand research programs in three critical areas: environmental technologies, new telecommunications, and genetics.

Each of these three areas holds great promise for Georgia. They are not only areas in which we already have an industrial base, but they are three of the fastest growing and highest paying fields. Total investment in these areas in 1990 was $44 billion dollars.

The environmental technology effort will coordinate research at the University of Georgia, Georgia State, and Clark-Atlanta in areas like toxic waste clean-up and the prevention of air pollution.

The new telecommunications thrust will involve Georgia Tech and the Medical College of Georgia in research that combines broadcast, computer, and telephone technology. We are going to be on the leading edge of a digital revolution, which is going to affect everyday life in dramatic ways—fundamentally changing the way we pay our bills or even get medical care. Last week I spoke briefly at the Medical College of Georgia press conference kicking off the telemedicine program with the City of Eastman. Using telecommunications technology, doctors at the Medical College in Augusta can diagnose and offer treatment advice for patients in Eastman. This technology will improve access to medical care in rural areas without requiring patients to travel or cash-strapped rural hospitals to purchase expensive, specialized equipment.

Third, genetics, which is changing so rapidly it is hard to predict where it will go. Genetic research covers a broad range, from the diagnosis and treatment of medical diseases to enabling farmers to grow a tastier yet more disease-resistant ear of corn.

All six of Georgia's major research universities will undertake a cooperative research effort in this field, for which investment is expected to increase 20-fold in the next decade. I will ask the advisory council I mentioned earlier to guide state policy in promoting research and investment in these three areas. And next session I will recommend to the General Assembly that we invest $3.75 million in state funds in a comprehensive program to provide the research base for them at our universities. But these state funds will only be available at the point where they are equally matched by private funds. This program will be a true public-private partnership, and I believe that, through the work of the Research Alliance, the commitment is there in the private community to raise the matching funds.

Before you can attract research contracts from the federal government or the private sector, you have to have a critical mass of expert researchers and adequate labs and equipment in place. That is the purpose of these funds. It is seed money to expand our infrastructure in these three areas, so that we have the physical capability to attract the research dollars.

These are not pie-in-the-sky research programs with no practical application. They are programs that connect with existing industry in Georgia; programs that will attract jobs, create jobs, and spin off jobs. It is estimated that this investment in recruiting scholars and improving labs to expand our research efforts in these three areas will generate 5,000 new jobs in the next decade through industrial expansions, relocations, and spin-offs. They will be high-skilled jobs, the kind that themselves hold potential to spin off additional investment, creating even more jobs and opportunities.

It is a modest investment, but I believe it holds great promise for this state. The people of Georgia are every bit as good, smart, and hard-working as the people of California or Japan. The difference is that they have been willing to invest the seed money and devote the time. They have mustered the political courage to move ahead—to take a calculated risk that put them on the leading edge of industry research.

I believe that Georgia is willing commit itself to a public-private program of investment in technology research in areas where we have some expertise and an industrial base. We, too, can move out on the cutting edge of industrial technology by the end of the next decade. It's time to be daring, to take a calculated risk, if we are to meet the challenges of the next century.

*—Georgia Chamber of Commerce Prelegislative Forum,*
*November 19, 1991*

---

Since World War II the U.S. government has been committed to free trade and the growth of a world economy. It was this commitment that has led to the growth of European and East Asian economies, and it laid the groundwork for an acceleration of world trade that in the decade of the 1980s averaged 6 percent a year.

Now, with the emergence of market economies in Eastern Europe and the formation of larger and more open trading markets in Europe and North America, we will see within the next decade the development of a truly global economy. The world economy will be far more integrated across national boundaries and the volume of trade will be far greater than anything we could have imagined a few years ago.

Even though it was the United States that was instrumental in bringing about this global economy, many of our companies are not prepared to compete in this new world market. Because the United States offers such a large domestic market, American companies have, until recently, largely ignored the growth opportunities in world markets.

A little history: In the 1960s when world trade was only $50 billion, the U.S. economy was strong both domestically and in world markets, and U.S. exports represented 25 percent of total world exports. Today, world trade exceeds $1.5 trillion and the U.S. portion has dropped to 15 percent. Germany now exports more than the United States, even though its economy is only about a third the size of ours.

So much for our national status. Let me get it closer home. Georgia ranks 16th among the 50 states in the value of products exported, but we have the 12th largest state economy. Even more significant, Georgia ranks only 44th in the percentage of its manufacturing production that is exported, and one-third of these exports come from our top two exporting industries—transportation equipment and paper products. These two industries are dominated by a few large companies. What this means is that our smaller manufacturing companies have not entered the global marketplace, and now they must if they are to grow and meet the challenges from foreign competition.

Among our greatest assets in international trade are our ocean ports in Savannah and Brunswick. They are our gateway to international commerce, because 90percent of Georgia's international cargo is waterborne. About 10 million tons of cargo went through the public and private terminals in Savannah in 1989, making Savannah the largest tonnage port on the South Atlantic coast. Brunswick handled another two million tons.

However, the greatest growth in maritime commerce over the next 10 years will occur in containerized cargo, and in that type cargo our port of Savannah now trails Charleston. In the last two years, container cargo has increased over 15 percent and the Georgia Ports Authority is poised for a major expansion of its container facilities.

Georgia has an outstanding record of attracting foreign investment. More than 900 foreign companies have offices in Georgia—328 have their U.S. headquarters in Georgia and 30 percent have manufacturing operations in Georgia. Foreign companies have about $8 billion invested in property, factories, and equipment in the state. Georgia has more Japanese companies than any other state except California. State and local governments have committed substantial resources in recruiting and attracting this investment—about $5.5 million annually for state government.

By comparison, Georgia's export effort is very modest. The export promotion budget for the Department of Industry, Trade and Tourism is about $550,000. State funding for all of the export programs administered by six state agencies or universities is about $1.6 million. At the local level, Chambers of Commerce and economic development agencies are oriented almost totally toward recruitment. Only a handful have an export program.

I want to change this situation. We need to become as successful at exporting as we have been at recruiting. We need to ensure that Georgia's international commerce flows through our ports and not the ports of other states. I am going to work to ensure that Georgia companies have every advantage possible to participate in international trade and export activities. With the globalization of the economy, our future economic prospects depend on our strengthening our position in international trade.

To accomplish these goals, I will recommend to the General Assembly the most significant international trade initiative in Georgia's history. Over the next few years, this initiative will require a significant state investment, but it should generate more than $3 billion in increased economic activity and create at least 25,000 new jobs by the year

2000. This initiative is focused on trade, but we must have a broader perspective than just trade. We need to use this initiative to make Georgia one of the international business centers of the world.

—*Georgia Chamber of Commerce Prelegislative Forum,*
*November 20, 1991*

———————

Before we look ahead to the 21st century, let's look back at the 19th. You see, I am a historian by profession, so I'd like to begin with a little history. In 1836, the State of Georgia built the Western and Atlanta Rail Road line. It began in Chattanooga, where it tapped into major lines serving the Midwest, and it came south to a nondescript little spot in the countryside. The chief construction engineer Stephen Long predicted, "The terminus will be a good location for one tavern, a blacksmith shop, a grocery store and nothing else." What a surprise Mr. Long would have if he could see the terminus of his rail line today.

You see, the lure of direct rail access to Chicago and the Midwest soon had coastal rail systems laying track toward the Western and Atlanta line, and that little terminal town of Atlanta that nobody thought would amount to much, very soon grew into a bustling rail center. Today some 100 trains head out of here daily in all directions, connecting with virtually every destination east of the Mississippi.

Another transportation milestone came a few decades ago when Georgia became one of the first states in the nation to complete its interstate highway system. Three major interstates converge on Atlanta. Combined with a fourth interstate route linking Atlanta with the port of Savannah, these highways were a magnet for trucking firms. Today the State of Georgia is served by 83 Class-A scheduled motor freight lines.

Our ports at Savannah and Brunswick are a third major transportation resource. Served by more than 100 steamship lines, they handle 12 million tons of cargo a year—90 percent of Georgia's international cargo.

Of course our fourth transportation resource is Hartsfield International Airport, with daily non-stops to 150 American cities and direct air service to nearly 30 cities abroad. Nine all-cargo air carriers serve Georgia, moving more than 600,000 tons of air cargo a year.

It's evident that we have four strong transportation resources in Georgia: roads, rail, ports and air service. The task before us is how to put them to the best possible use in the 21st century. A quick look at how things are shaping up for business in the next century may help us.

The world economy is reconfiguring itself into the "global village" that Marshall McLuhan predicted several decades ago, and we've fallen a little behind the curve in getting ready for it.

One of the characteristics of a large country like the United States is a large domestic market, which has allowed us to ignore the rest of the world far longer than we should have. Manufacturers in the smaller nations of Europe and Asia have been much quicker to adopt an international marketing mindset than we have, and that is especially true for

Georgia.

Georgia has the 12th largest economy among the states, but we rank 44th in the nation in the percentage of our manufacturing production that is exported. If we are to grow and prosper, we must break out of that domestic mindset and break into the international mindset, the international market. Being competitive in the future means not only competing with the imports here at home, but also getting out there in the world market with our own products.

We are fortunate in that at the same time we are in need of broader economic horizons, international trade opportunities are breaking wide open. As the dust begins to settle on the political upheaval in the Soviet Union and Eastern Europe, it is clear that they are hungry for expanded business ties with the West.

The single most important factor in luring international business to Georgia is transportation. This global community in which we now live increasingly demands quick, efficient movement of people and goods. In Georgia, we have several challenges to overcome in our efforts to do that.

First is the adequacy of our transportation infrastructure. We are going to deepen the Savannah Harbor, complete a sixth container berth the Garden City facility and upgrade two container cranes to handle larger ships. This is the first stage of a major investment in our ports during the 90s that will allow us to double our container cargo tonnage and expand our other cargo capacity. It is mandatory if we are to be a leading international port on the Atlantic coast, and I am absolutely committed to it.

Second, air transportation. While attention always focuses on Hartsfield here in Atlanta, it is important to remember that Georgia has 103 public airports, and eight others in addition to Atlanta handle commercial flights. I recommended and the General Assembly concurred that we update our statewide airport systems plan with a major study, taking inventory of existing airport facilities and assessing our needs for the next 20 years. We are going to begin by evaluating our air service and air cargo needs, so that we can address our facility needs within that context....

Now that our great system of interstates is in place, we are concentrating on our other major four-lane arteries. We've mapped out 14 economic development highways, and the first two—Corridor Z across south Georgia and the Appalachian Highway in north Georgia—are completed. The next two to get priority will be U.S. Highway 27 running from Chattanooga to the Florida line and the Fall Line Freeway across central Georgia from Columbus to Augusta.

We also have areas of severe highway congestion. I-75 north of I-285, and the northern arc of the perimeter each carry more than 215,000 vehicles a day. I-85 north of the perimeter carries more than 180,000 vehicles a day. We have expanded these highways as much as we can, and we have taken their intersections to the ultimate engineering marvel of "Spaghetti Junction." It is time to move on to passenger rail....

Passenger rail is also part of the solution to the second challenge we face in preparing transportation for the future, and that is pollution. Atlanta has very little industrial air pollution. Our primary pollution source is automobiles, and despite the fact that virtually all cars now use unleaded gas, our levels of air pollution remain high. If we are to control air pollution in Atlanta, we need to promote car pooling with HOV lanes and provide alternate transportation to the automobile.

It is an exciting time to be involved in transportation in Georgia. It is clear that we have our work cut out for us, but it should also be clear that we are moving forward aggressively in all modes of transportation.

*—Georgia Freight Bureau Transportation Summit, April 14, 1992*

---

Many people look at the word "small" in the phrase "small business," and jump to the conclusion that small business is only a small part of Georgia's economy. The truth is just the opposite. Small business is a large part of Georgia's economy. Most of our businesses are small.

By contrast, state government is big business. With more than 100,000 employees, state government is one of the biggest businesses in Georgia. The idea of doing contract business with the state can look pretty formidable to the many small businesses who are out there.

It is in the small business community that you will find the vast majority of businesses that are owned and operated by minorities, and their growth and stability is critical to the economic well-being of the entire state.

Last November, I appointed the Small and Minority Business Development Advisory Committee to help us increase the number of minority firms doing business with state government. Today we move forward with the second step in the form of an executive order directed at all state departments and agencies.

When the House Study Committee on Minority Participation in State Government was putting together its report, it looked at the contract information that is now being centrally collected in the Department of Administrative Services Purchasing Division. The data showed that only two percent of the state's contracts are going to minority contractors. But that was an incomplete picture, because it included only certain types of contracts. Construction, for example, involves large amounts of money and lots of contracting and sub-contracting, but it is not included in the data now collected by the DOAS Purchasing Division.

So one of the things this Executive Order does is expand the reporting process on contracts. Starting with the new fiscal year on July 1st, the DOAS Purchasing Division will be sent copies of all state contracts awarded, not just certain types of contracts. This will give us a more complete and accurate picture of the level of minority participation in state government.

But I want to make this very clear: This Executive Order goes beyond simply finding out what exists. It is also aimed, it is primarily aimed at improving the level of minority contracting with the state. I am directing all state agencies to step up their efforts to get information out to the minority business community on the state bidding process and its opportunities. Not only must minority participation be encouraged in all bid documents, but I'm also asking that we advertise bid opportunities more widely in the minority community. We are also going to increase the level of awareness among majority businesses of a tax credit that is available to them if they sub-contract with minority firms.

This Executive Order also directs every department and agency in state government to designate a person to serve as a liaison to the minority business community. The name, address and phone number of this person will go on all bid documents. And this person will be available to provide one-on-one assistance to minority businesses in helping them learn the ropes and understand how the bidding process works.

It is important to recognize a problem, as we have done with the need to nurture minority businesses. Once you acknowledge a problem, it is important to take the next step of identifying knowledgeable sources of information and advice, as we have done with the Small and Minority Business Development Advisory Committee.

Now, many people mistake that second step as the end of the process of dealing with the problem. But it's not with me. The place where the rubber hits the road is the third step, which is taking action based on what you have learned from the first and second steps. Today, we move forward with the third step. With this Executive Order, we begin the process of actually changing the way we do things in an effort to improve the level of minority participation in the state contracting process.

*—Signing of Executive Order on Minority Business Contracting,*
*April 16, 1992*

---

Economic growth must become more consistent and balanced across the state. Those of you who are familiar with my career know that I have always been an active promoter and supporter of Atlanta. Making Atlanta into a major international city is an important effort that will benefit the entire state, but it's a two-way street. It is not possible to dump the entire state economy into Atlanta and leave the rest of Georgia as a barren, economic wasteland. It's also true that as the rest of the state goes, so goes Atlanta.

*—Georgia CEOs, June 12, 1992*

---

For years, the gospel for growth here in the South was chasing smokestacks. We relied on low wages, unskilled labor, rail sidings, and unregulated use of natural resources to lure factories and distribution centers away from other parts of the country. But, as MIT economist David Birch discovered in a landmark study of Dun & Bradstreet data representing 82 percent of all private-sector employment, the big difference between a growing state or region, and a stagnating one, is not how many existing jobs they lure in from other places or lose to other places, but how many new jobs they create.

The economic growth cycle is not unlike the biological growth cycle. New companies are born small, and after that early critical stage of becoming established, they undergo a growth spurt—a time when sales and employment grow rapidly. But that same growth is what turns smaller, younger companies into larger, older ones. They, in turn, can play a parenting role in encouraging innovation and the spinning off of the next generation of new young firms, starting the process all over again. If our economy is to grow, it is critical that we encourage innovation and entrepreneurship to develop....

As Governor of Georgia, my primary responsibility is the well-being and prosperity of all Georgians, and that requires careful attention to economic growth. The goals of my administration are first, to steer the general course of economic development toward balanced growth around the state; second, to provide support, services, and expertise to local communities, enabling them to nurture their own local economies; and third, to work more closely in partnership with business....

Every company can grow and excel; every community can take control of its destiny and achieve it. They key is to be willing to aim high and aim well. Some of the traditions of our beloved Dixie have encouraged us to "look away" when times change—to "look away" to powerful outside forces to come in and generate growth for us, to "look away" to a proud but tragic past rather than ahead to the future.

Now it is time to stride out proudly and confidently. It is time to view the future not as something that must be endured, but as something we can direct to our purposes. It is time to view change not as something we must react to, but as something we can create.

*—Council of Growing Companies, June 17, 1992*

----

In Georgia we have a disparity that many of you also share: The depth and breadth of professional services is much greater in our urban areas than in our rural areas. As our economy demands a more skilled workforce and as quality of life becomes a bigger factor in generating economic health, economic growth has focused on our urban areas. And we are seeking ways to overcome that disparity and generate more balanced growth across the state.

The problem is particularly acute in education and health care, and those are the two areas that we have begun to address with telecommunications technology....

Through a telecommunications network called distance learning, students in one part of the state will be able to join an advanced class that is going on in another part of the state or even around the nation. Take rural White County, in the North Georgia mountains. This little community has just succeeded in attracting a Japanese business. So, in a pilot project this spring, a handful of high school students in White County were studying Japanese with a teacher based in Nebraska. Their French teacher, who supervised them and learned along with them, was as excited as they were. Video technology with interactive audio capability brought them an educational opportunity that otherwise would not have been possible in their little town.

In another example that I personally experienced, small groups of students at four different high schools formed a single class with one teacher, using a telecommunications set-up that was interactive in both video and audio. One of the participating schools had only one student, and could never have hired a teacher and offered that course on its own. These are just two examples of more than 50 pilot projects going in Georgia schools during the past school year.

We have also piloted the use of interactive audio and video technology via hard-wire networks and satellite for teacher training programs, rather than requiring teachers to travel to a central location.

We are using similar telecommunications technology for what we call telemedicine, which brings the expertise of urban medical specialists into small, rural hospitals many miles away. Last fall I stood beside experts at the Medical College of Georgia in Augusta, while they examined a patient's X-rays, listened to his heartbeat, and consulted with his doctor. Now, there's nothing unusual in that. What was unusual was that the experts were in Augusta, and the patient and his doctor were in Eastman, more than 130 miles away in rural south Georgia. They communicated through interactive video carried by telephone cables...

What makes our state unique is the "Georgia Distance Learning and Telemedicine Act of 1992," which I believe to be landmark legislation and which may prove to be one of the most important and far-reaching acts of my administration. It calls for the development of a consolidated, integrated, statewide, shared-use telecommunications network for educational and medical purposes....

We were fortunate to have $50 million available from a telephone over-earnings case. We brought together the telephone company and the appropriate state agencies, and hammered out an agreement whereby the State Department of Administrative Services would develop the physical, statewide network to serve educational and medical needs.

The legislation also created a governing board, which has begun to meet, and which will set state policy and award funds for equipment and start-up costs to communities who apply for access to the network; but before any of the funds are awarded, a total implementation plan for distance learning and telemedicine will be prepared. This comprehensive plan will consider both the technical needs of the network itself and the educational and medical needs to be served by the network. It will ensure that we make the best possible use of our available funds and properly position ourselves for the future.

Educators, medical professionals and communications experts are all excited about the potential of distance learning and telemedicine. Our goal is to improve the quality of life in rural Georgia by using telecommunications technology to make an array of educational and medical resources available that otherwise would be found only in our larger urban areas.

*—National Governor's Association, August 3, 1992*

---

I was in Japan last fall on a trade mission, and I met with the CEO of a high-tech company that was looking at Atlanta as a potential site for a new facility. The company's site selection committee had not included Atlanta on its list, but the CEO added it because he happened to know about two eminent research scholars at Georgia Tech whose work related to his company. That is the point of the Research Alliance. High-tech companies should not have to stumble inadvertently on the fact that Georgia has the intellectual infrastructure they need. We should be promoting it.

As I travel the world on trade missions like the one to Japan, I meet with business executives who are looking at Georgia or whom we want to be looking at Georgia. Technology plays an important role in those trips. We seek out and cultivate technology-based companies that complement our own in an effort to develop import-export ties in future-looking industries that may eventually mature into capital investment.

We have begun an expanded trade initiative in the Department of Industry, Trade that targets particular industries, including high-tech industries like telecommunications. At the end of August, I was the first Georgia Governor to go to Singapore, for example, and the focus of my efforts was to begin to cultivate several electronics companies that are potential purchasers of Georgia products....

Technology is a powerful instrument of change. It can improve productivity, shorten response time to market demand, lower production costs, and even make physical location irrelevant. The future success and prosperity of our state and its citizens depends upon our ability to develop and use technology. Our ability to create a technology-based economy here in Georgia depends not only on research and development, but also on communicating with each other, working together, and making the best possible use of the resources and capabilities we've got.

—*Science and Technology Council Conference, September 28, 1992*

---

We are living in a time when it is no longer a simple question of whether a small or medium-sized company chooses to dabble in exports on the side. It is a matter of functioning successfully in a world economy. Today the price of a gallon of gas at the corner gas station is set by events in the Persian Gulf, and local manufacturers are finding that their standards of profitability, even here on our domestic markets, are set by the prevailing wages for labor halfway around the world.

As I've traveled on trade missions, I have been struck not just by the savvy, born of experience, with which small businesses of other countries function on the world market—but also by the amazement they express at the inexperience and naivete of their American counterparts. They expect American small businesses to be much more knowledgeable and adept at international trading than we really are, and it's going to be increasingly harder for us to catch up....

By the year 2000, the world economy will be far more integrated across national boundaries and the volume of trade will be far greater than anything we could have imagined just a few short years ago.

Against that backdrop, let's take a look at Georgia. Ninety percent of international cargo is waterborne, and Georgia is home to two major ocean ports at Savannah and Brunswick. The Georgia Ports Authority has offices in Athens, Greece; Oslo, Norway; and Tokyo, Japan, as well as in Chicago and New York. Georgia contains the offices of 15 career consulates, 31 honorary consulates, 19 foreign trade and tourism offices, and 13 foreign chambers of commerce. Twenty-eight international banks do business in Atlanta in 25 different currencies. We have the resources to be a world trading center. The question is whether Georgia businesses are going to take advantage of those resources, or whether this state is just going to be a port-of-call for the products of other states.

Right now, Georgia has the 12th largest state economy among the 50 states, but we rank 16th in the value of products we export. Even more significant, Georgia is a major manufacturing state, but ranks 44th among the 50 states in the percentage of our manufacturing production that is exported. A third of our exports come from two industries—transportation equipment and paper products, which are dominated by a few large companies. What it all boils down to is that our smaller manufacturing companies have simply not entered the global marketplace, and now they must if they are to grow and meet the challenges from foreign competition....

Exporting is not a quick or easy undertaking. The list of potential complications is as long as your leg: Tough competition, a maze of paperwork, shipping headaches, communicating in other languages, special packaging for shipping, electrical voltage differences, financing across currencies, arranging for service after the sale, and just getting paid—to name a few. You have to be serious, and you have to be committed. You have to do your homework, and you have to plan for the long-term. But the sales potential of exporting is tremendous....

That is why my Georgia Rebound program, passed by the General Assembly earlier this year, includes the most significant international trade initiative in Georgia's history. It is a two-pronged approach, designed to ensure the ongoing prominence of our ports, and to increase the volume of Georgia exports flowing through those ports. We need to become as successful at exporting as we have been at recruiting.

Georgia Rebound combines $63 million in state funds with $25 million from the Georgia Ports Authority to expand and improve our ports. We are expanding significantly our facilities for containerized cargo, which is the fastest growing segment of the shipping business because of its easy transfer among various modes of transportation. We are also deepening the Savannah Harbor to make it accessible to the largest cargo ships.

The second part of the Georgia Rebound trade initiative is to strengthen our international trade involvements and give Georgia companies every possible advantage to export. This effort is focused in the Department of Industry, Trade and Tourism. We have upgraded the trade program in the Department to a separate division with its own deputy commissioner....

We are going to expand this Division over the next few years to offer export assistance for additional product types, and to help Georgia firms take advantage of the new North American trade agreement with Canada and Mexico. We will soon be hiring a Georgia trade representative for Canada, and I want to bring a trade representative for Mexico on board in the near future.

Over the past few years, the Department has reorganized its export program to target three industry groups with great export potential—forest products, consumer goods and apparel, and computer software and equipment. Georgia Rebound expands that list with a new export effort targeted at agricultural and food processing machinery. We kicked off this AgriTech program last month at the Sunbelt Agricultural Expo, and we will be adding more new areas of product emphasis in the future.

—*International Trade Expo, November 10, 1992*

---

For most of our lifetime, the 21st century has seemed far away—a remote, futuristic time inhabited by science fiction stories. But the 21st century will be upon us in only seven years, and it is going to be much different than the 20th century was. The world order of the 20th century, forged by two world wars, is ending, and a new configuration is emerging in Europe, the Soviet Union and the Middle East. At the same time, advanced technology has truly turned the world into a global village....

In the 20th century, we realized economic growth by offering rail sidings, a low-skill low-wage workforce and unregulated use of natural resources. But these days, businesses want much more than a glad hand, a rail siding and a water tower with "We Want Industry" painted on the side. They are just as likely to want good schools, safe streets, and quality health care as they are a spec building. They are just as likely to want clean air and water and environmentally sound waste systems as they are the unregulated use of natural resources. Most important, they are even more likely to want a skilled workforce than they are low wages.

—*Columbus Chamber of Commerce, November 19, 1992*

———————

Beginning today, we are going to develop a strategy for our economic future through a new public-private partnership, the Governor's Development Council. This Council will not be just another advisory body, or just another one-shot "blue-ribbon panel" that will make a report and then fade into memory. It will be a working group with an ongoing responsibility for guiding Georgia's economic development efforts, and fostering teamwork across all the traditional boundaries of government agencies and business organizations...

Some of you may be asking yourselves, why make this change now? Why are we messing with a system that has worked in the past? Is it broke, and if it ain't, why fix it?

Make no mistake, Georgia is currently second-to-none in the quality of its leadership in economic development in its overall climate for business, in its spirit of government-business partnership and in its record of accomplishment. The engine of our economic development effort ain't broke—it just ain't adequate to take us on down the road ahead. You can build the best and fastest automobile imaginable, but with all pistons firing and the throttle wide open, it can't keep up with the most rickety airplane. In my judgement, that's where we are today. We have the best vehicle for yesterday's economic race, but a new race on a new track is about to begin.

There are three fundamental changes transforming our economy that make a change in our strategy for development as inevitable as the change of seasons. First, the emergence of a global economy makes a hash of all our traditional distinctions between domestic and foreign investors, and also between existing business and out-of-state prospects. In just a matter of years, virtually all our goods and services will be subject to international competition either at home or abroad, and we just can't pretend that economic development is a zero-sum game in which we attract new business while everything else remains the same.

Second, the emergence of a knowledge-based economy turns all the old assumptions that we have made about our workforce completely upside down. We used to win over investors with a large supply of low-wage, low-skill labor. Tomorrow's investors will want high-skill labor, and they'll pay high wages to get it. If we continue to market ourselves as a workforce bargain basement, then we'll wind up competing with third world countries for those jobs at the bottom of the barrel. That's a contest we would probably lose and couldn't afford to win.

Third, the emergence of an information-driven economy short-circuits the old process of leisurely marketing our state one prospect at a time. Fiber-optics networks span the continents, and billions of dollars can move in seconds from Berlin to Tokyo to Atlanta. The pace of investment decisions is increasing so rapidly that many investors know more about us than we know about ourselves. While there will always be an important place for one-on-one recruitment, we must realize that all the marketing in the world will no longer compensate for an inferior product.

These transformations in the economy have profound implications for everything we do in economic development. In the past, we thought of development as something we brought in from outside our borders. In the future, we must think of development as something we produce from within, but that links up with emerging trends in every corner of the global economy.

In the past, we gave virtually all our attention to out-of-state industrial prospects, and succeeded brilliantly in attracting their investment. In the future, we must pay more attention to the businesses we have already attracted, and to helping others start up and expand. Eight out of ten new jobs in our state are produced by existing business expansions, and we can no longer act as though we do not have a legitimate stake in their success or failure. In particular, we must ensure that any business, however small, that has any capacity for exporting is shown how—in practical terms, from the export license to political risk insurance.

In the past, we assumed that traditional banking practices would supply all the capital we needed for credit-worthy investments in our economy, and we do now boast a vibrant financial community here in Atlanta. In the future, we must find ways to finance smaller and less traditional efforts, and in particular, we must do something about our alarming lack of venture capital for innovative new businesses.

In the past, we thought of our infrastructure for development as roads, sewers, water storage tanks, and site improvements, because that's what individual prospects cared about most. In the future, we must pay more attention to our schools, our training facilities, our capacity to supply health care and recreation, and yes, our ability to manage our environmental resources, and our overall quality of life, because that's what businesses are now looking for in making investment decisions.

In the past, we thought of incentives to development as fairly simple bottom-line inducements, like tax abatements, freeports, subsidized financing, and site-specific improvements. In the future, we must understand that the changing needs of businesses will change the relative value of incentives, with workforce training assuming a special importance...

In the past, we treated all new jobs as being equal, and we maintained an almost superstitious fear of any sort of targeting in our marketing efforts. In the future, we simply must choose to concentrate on high-value-added industries, in part because that's where the high-wage jobs will be found that are critical to our standard of living, and in part because we must build a base of such industries before we can attract or stimulate others.

In the past, we scrupulously avoided any geographical targeting in our economic development efforts, on the theory that if we tried to tell prospects where to go, they'd tell us where we could go, and look elsewhere. In the future, we must help each of Georgia's many regions, not by dragging investors in for a quick look, but by identifying each area's unique economic potential and then building up its capacity to achieve that potential.

Finally, but very importantly, in the past we allowed a whole host of state agencies to take on various development functions with hardly any coordination. In the future, we must look at the billions of dollars such agencies spend, and the thousands of employees they deploy, as strategic investments bound together by a strategic plan. That's much of what this whole effort is about: We absolutely must insist on a common philosophy of development—a full sharing of information and a complete elimination of turf consciousness and institutional prerogatives—because we're all in this together and we all serve the same people.

When you look at this list of necessary changes, and there are others that could come to mind as well, it's obvious why this state needs a new comprehensive strategy for development, and a new organization to draw it up. Developing methods of aiding existing business—locating sources of venture capital, expanding our concept of infrastructure, examining our incentives—identifying high-value-added clusters of industry and technology, analyzing our regional needs, pulling together state agencies, and weaving all of these factors into a strategic plan built on public-private partnerships....

Those of you with a major stake in the current approach to development will have to share the limelight with others, and give up long-cherished turf—but you have an even more important role on a larger playing field. Community leaders will have to recognize that it's no longer enough to hold a Developer's Day and paint "We Want Industry" on the water tower—that each community's schools, health facilities, quality of life, and yes, race relations, are now important factors in development. But by assuming this broader responsibility, community leaders will become masters of their own economic destiny.

Political leaders, myself included, will have to take on a much larger responsibility for economic development than just showing up for ribbon-cuttings and counting up the jobs. But if we take our responsibility seriously, we'll have a chance to make Georgia a growing and prosperous community for generations to come.

Business leaders will have to stop thinking of themselves as passive recipients of development efforts, and begin taking their proper place as full and leading partners in a statewide strategic initiative. If they do accept full partnership, they can make this state America's trend-setter in government-business cooperation....

We are the best in America right now, but we cannot continue business as usual and expect to remain number one in a changing world. In the game of economic development, we're the national champs—but from now on, we are playing in the World Series. So let's get ready to play and to win.

*—Georgia Economic Development Association, November 23, 1992*

Georgia has come a long way in the past 10 years. We've attracted new businesses, and many of our home-grown industries have flourished. We were selected host to the Democratic Convention in 1988, the Super Bowl in 1994, and the biggest honor of all— the 1996 Olympics...

But despite our success, we can't sit still if we expect to prosper. Will Rogers once said that even if you're on the right track, you'll get run over if you don't keep moving. The 21st century beckons, and we've got to get ready.

Each business represented here today began as a dream, and each dream came true through hard work, sound judgment and a little bit of luck. You and I know that Georgia is a great place to make business dreams come true. Your presence here attests to your faith in our future.

Unfortunately, Georgia's promise is starting to look like the world's best kept secret—at least if we believe a recent cover story in *Business Week*. It was called "Hot Spots," and it profiled the nation's hottest places for high technology. It wasn't so much what was said in that story as what was left out. Georgia didn't show up anywhere in the article. That bothered me—bothered me very much—because I know that Georgia has the potential to be the next hot spot in new technology.

Part of the problem is perception, and I believe we can fix that. But you can't have sizzle without the steak. We have to admit that a large part of the problem is also rooted in reality. But we can fix that, too. In fact, we've already begun.

Two years ago, we formed the Georgia Research Alliance, a consortium of private industry and Georgia's six major research universities. The state has put $15 million into the Research Alliance for physical and intellectual infrastructure—seed money to expand targeted research programs, enabling them to attract major contracts.

Next, I created the Governor's Advisory Council on Science and Technology to develop and implement a state technology policy, and to foster communication and cooperation among industry, higher education, and government on technology concerns.

Third, we are launching a new comprehensive, integrated, strategic economic development initiative for Georgia. It will be guided by the Governor's Development Council, which is a public-private partnership.... One of this council's tasks is to increase venture capital and management expertise for Georgia's young high-tech firms.

It's no secret that the future lies in technology development, and if we work together, we can make wise choices that will create the kind of future we want for our companies and for our state. This is an exciting opportunity for all of us, and I want to thank you again for taking time this morning to learn more about how we can invest in the future through the venture capital initiative.

—*Venture Capital Breakfast, November 30, 1992*

In the long course of human history, there have been four communication developments that have revolutionized the world. The first was speech. The second was writing. The third was printing. We are now in the midst of the fourth, which is telecommunications. Here in Georgia, we are deliberately positioning ourselves to become a world leader in electronics and telecommunications research, technology and manufacturing.

*—BelTronics Ribbon Cutting, February 26, 1993*

———————

One of my primary responsibilities as Governor of Georgia is to promote economic growth. We have launched a bold new approach to economic development under the Governor's Development Council, and high technology is a very important part of it. We are going to target promising high-tech fields for growth and expansion, and help that process along by making more venture capital available. We are also going to help our traditional industries—textiles and apparel, pulp and paper, and food processing—to use advanced technology to become more competitive. We are going to expand our export assistance, helping even the smallest business with export potential....

There are a number of different high-tech initiatives within this new economic development framework. First, I have made the state a partner in the Georgia Research Alliance, together with Georgia's six major universities and private industry. The Research Alliance coordinates and promotes practical research at its six member universities, that has potential to generate economic growth, spin off new companies, and attract cutting-edge industries to the state.

But before you can attract R&D contracts, you must first have the labs, equipment and eminent researchers to use them. So the role of state government is to provide crucial seed money for the necessary research infrastructure. The state budget for next year includes $22 million for the Research Alliance for labs and equipment, and to create nine endowed chairs for eminent research scholars. It will be matched by more than $60 million in federal and private funds. In the two years since I became Governor, the total investment in the Research Alliance has surpassed $130 million in state, federal and private funds.

Technology also plays an important role in the expanded trade initiative we have begun in the Department of Industry and Trade. We are targeting particular industries, including high-tech industries like telecommunications. In August, I was the first Georgia Governor to go to Singapore, and the focus of my efforts was to begin to cultivate several electronics companies that are potential purchasers of Georgia products.

But as we develop import-export ties, we have an eye on the future, looking for companies that enhance our technology mix and building relationships that can eventually mature into capital investment.

Yet another initiative is the Governor's Advisory Council on Science and Technology Development, which has a threefold mission: To develop a science and technology policy for the state; to a generate a strategy to put it into place; and to foster communication and cooperation among industry, higher education and government on technology concerns. The Council has been gathering data on what kinds of advanced technology exist in Georgia, who is using it and how. This data will be the foundation for a strategy that enhances our strengths and addresses our needs. But it will also help Georgia's technology companies become more aware of each other and network with each other.

If computer hardware and software companies know each other and talk to each other, they can create a level of synergy that moves both of them forward. Research professors with a good sense of what companies are developing what new products, can help the Department of Industry and Trade to match up importers and exporters. There are so many ways in which communication among industry, higher education and state government can benefit all of us...

I believe that if we work together and seize our opportunities, we can become the masters of our own economic destiny and make Georgia a growing and prosperous place for generations to come.

*—High Tech Month Breakfast, April 5, 1993*

---

I'm going to tell you just like it is: Quality jobs flow to quality locations. It is that simple. All the marketing in the world isn't going to compensate for an inferior workforce or mediocre schools or inadequate quality of life.

We must have in this state a new, broader, longer-term definition of infrastructure that goes beyond roads and sewers, to include resources like schools, health care, recreation and cultural facilities, and environmental resources. Because that's what businesses now look for in making investment decisions.

Further, as many of you know so well, the competition is also changing in the area of incentives, and the Governor's Development Council is taking a close and careful look at how our incentives will have to change if Georgia is going to stay competitive.

We also know that the ongoing health of the businesses that are already here is extremely important. After all, eight of ten new jobs are created within existing businesses. To compete in a global economy, our traditional industries must incorporate advanced technology, upgrade their workforce skills and solve pollution problems efficiently. Of course, there are no ground-breakings or ribbon-cuttings when an existing industry quietly expands, or a troubled industry turns it around and doesn't close down after all. But if we're so busy concentrating on out-of-state recruitment that we don't take time for our traditional industries like textiles, pulp and paper, and agriculture, we're going to lose jobs faster than we gain them.

In today's economic climate, growing jobs at home requires some of the same things as attracting them from other places—good schools, a positive business climate, targeted infrastructure improvement, coordination and planning in our development efforts....

We have to have a comprehensive strategy that fits all of the state's investments and many programs into a big picture like pieces of a jigsaw puzzle. The Department of Industry, Trade and Tourism, the Department of Transportation, the Department of Natural Resources, the Department of Community Affairs, the Office of Planning and Budget, the Georgia Ports Authority—these are some of the many state agencies that are pieces of that puzzle, that must fit together, must work together to form a complete picture of economic development.

Private development organizations like the Chamber of Commerce, the Council of Economic Development Organizations, and the Georgia Economic Developers Association are also pieces of the puzzle...

Until now, there has been no common philosophy of development among all these organizations, no common strategy to coordinate their efforts, no structure that brings them together. In fact, they rarely have the opportunity to talk to each other. Again, that is the job of the Governor's Development Council—to bring all these diverse but crucial pieces together to form the big picture.

At the same time as we need a broader statewide vision for economic development, we also need a much sharper focus on what each region has to offer. Different parts of Georgia have different industrial mixes and economic realities. Achieving balanced growth throughout the state requires us to be much more sensitive, more aware, than we have ever been before to regional economies and local economic issues.

We want to achieve the same goals in each part of the state—to assist existing business, to encourage new home-grown business, to attract prospects, to expand trade opportunities, and to improve infrastructure and quality of life—but each region of the state has its own unique characteristics. Exactly what is needed to make those things happen, is different from one part of the state to the next. What is needed to support existing industry here in west-central Georgia, for example, may be completely different from what is needed to support existing industry in Coastal Georgia or the mountains of North Georgia.

So we have identified 11 economic regions within the state, and during the next few months, I'm going to bring members of the Governor's Development Council to meet with and listen to business and community leaders in each region, to focus on the particular characteristics of that region—its strengths and its weaknesses.

During the 1980s, broader demographic and economic trends converged to favor the Sunbelt, and Georgia was able to grow simply by riding the wave. But we no longer have that advantage. The competition is no longer just Tennessee and Tallahassee. It's also Toronto and Taiwan. Economic success in the 21st century will come from knowing what must be done and doing it in a coordinated way with a well-thought-out plan.

Building an economic development engine that meets the standards of this new race will not be easy. But it must be done. And I believe that if we take the initiative and work together, we can make this state fly.

*—Governor's Economic Development Conference, May 19, 1993*

---

Many of you are familiar with the narrative poem about the six blind men who encountered an elephant. One felt the trunk and concluded that an elephant was like a snake. Another grabbed the tail and decided that an elephant resembled a rope. The third was brushed by a flapping ear and felt the breeze, and he assumed that an elephant was like a fan.

The fourth put his arms around one of the elephant's legs and concluded that an elephant resembled a tree trunk. The fifth grabbed a tusk and decided that an elephant was like a spear. And the sixth, stretching his hands along the animal's side, decided than an elephant was just like a wall.

Each one of them thought he had the elephant pegged, that he now understood elephants. But they were all wrong, because each one assumed that his particular piece was all there was.

I've been reminded of that story lately in the context of launching a major effort to reforge Georgia's approach to economic development. In the past, some have said that all we needed to do to generate growth was build a four-lane highway or a spec building. Others said we ought to concentrate on marketing and recruiting out-of-state prospects. Still others wanted the focus to be on helping the industries we already have. And because Georgia did grow rapidly during the 1970s and 80s, they all thought they were right. But, in fact, each of those things is just one part of the elephant.

What actually happened in the 70s and 80s was that Georgia was the lucky beneficiary of larger trends that favored the Sunbelt over the Rustbelt. We could just sit back and wait for the phone to ring, as jobs and people came south, and growth was bestowed upon us. Now, those days have gone with the wind. As physical and political barriers to the flow of information come down, the world is becoming a global village, and the future will be one of keen competition in a world economy.

In the future, economic growth will come to those who not only work hard, but who also work smart—those who have organized their resources for the maximum effect and are deliberately moving forward in a carefully planned way. Economic development in Georgia will be a white elephant unless we understand all of its parts and know how they fit together to make the whole animal.

Of course, one of the primary parts of that economic development elephant is its legs—transportation. We are moving from a consumption-driven economy to an export-driven economy. This global village in which we now live increasingly demands quick, efficient movement of people and goods. Transportation is highways, but it is also air, rails and ports. And all four of these legs—all four of these modes of transportation must be coordinated with each other for the elephant to move well.

*—Gwinnett Boy Scouts, May 26, 1993*

---

Two months ago, I brought the Governor's Development Council to Macon for the very first in a series of economic development forums in each of Georgia's economic regions, and I emphasized that one of the Council's primary goals is to provide state support for regional initiatives that target and promote future-oriented, technology-based industries.

This evening here in middle Georgia, we have a perfect example of what that means and how it works. Georgia's aerospace industry, which is concentrated in middle Georgia, is a growing, technology-based industry that we want to encourage and support. Doing that well takes broad-based cooperation across the region, and between the region and the state, which is exactly what is happening right here, right now.

Last year we began a $5 million expansion of our aerospace training programs, coordinated among the four state technical institutes in this region, and we will continue to expand these workforce training programs. Next I worked closely with this region in presenting a solid case to the Base Closure Commission to keep the Warner Robins Air Force Base alive and well.

We are now addressing the need of our large, primary aerospace companies to have a larger contingent of local suppliers. We began by inviting several aerospace suppliers on our annual statewide Red Carpet Tour, which is designed to introduce Georgia to industrial prospects. I met them personally when I hosted a dinner for the tour members at the Governor's Mansion.

The enthusiastic response from those Red Carpet Tour participants resulted in the creation of a regional group called "Team Georgia." Team Georgia is made up of the 20 counties that form the middle Georgia economic development region, and five additional counties on the edge of the region. This broad-based regional body is working with the aerospace industry and 10 statewide economic development entities, including utilities, banks, and the State Department of Industry, Trade and Tourism, to attract aerospace suppliers to Georgia.

Following the Red Carpet Tour, Team Georgia went to Los Angeles, which is where the aerospace industry grew up and is still concentrated. There they put on a seminar about opportunities in Georgia for aerospace suppliers. That seminar attracted more than 50 participants, and many wanted to know more.

The two-day Silver Carpet Tour, which gets underway this evening, is the next step. We've invited aerospace suppliers to come visit Georgia's large aerospace companies like McDonnell Douglas, Northrop, Boeing, Lockheed, and the Warner Robins Base, and learn firsthand about the opportunities to do business here, and we are pleased to welcome 110 participants on the tour, representing 75 companies.

When you've got a growing, future-oriented industry and a commitment at the regional and state levels to support it, then you've got a great product to sell on a tour like the Silver Carpet Tour, and you're going to get results...

Georgia's aerospace industry is expanding and building for the future, and the middle Georgia region is working together and in cooperation with the state government and statewide development organizations to help it grow. It is partnerships like these—between government and industry, within an economic region, and between that region and state government—it is partnerships like these that create the energy and synergy that make our economy thrive.

—*Silver Carpet Tour, July 28, 1993*

---

The partnership between state government and the tourism industry must go deeper than a tourism impact study here and a welcome center there, and I want to take a few minutes here today to tell you where I'm coming from. I firmly believe that the role of government is not to compete with private industry or duplicate what private industry is doing, but to give private industry incentives and opportunities to grow and develop. It is a partnership. Let me give you two examples from the tourism industry of what I mean.

First, Jekyll Island, which is owned by the state and managed by a state authority. Marketing studies have clearly shown that if Millionaires Village is to revive, Millionaires Club must first become an active and vibrant centerpiece. So we're trying to achieve that. But the state, through the Jekyll Island Authority, is not trying to develop the Club and Village itself. Instead, we are working to make private development possible.

A private developer who works with historic properties was found to take on the Club. And a lease was negotiated with a low base payment for the first eight years to give the Club a chance to get up and running. A public-private funding package was put together, and federal historic preservation tax credits brought into play, to make renovating the Club financially feasible for a private developer to do.

A similar approach is being used to the stately homes of Millionaires Village. The Jekyll Island Authority is making basic repairs to the exterior of the mansions, bringing them to the point where they can be leased and restoration continued by the leaser. In other words, the goal of the state is to provide the ground-floor incentives that make it possible for the private sector to come in and develop Millionaires Club and Village.

A second example is a project that I've been personally involved with up in the mountains of Towns County. We've had some good tourism development up there with the beautiful Fieldstone Inn and the Hunt-Allen Shoney's project. But if we are to build the critical mass of tourism resources we need for the mountains to be perceived as a vacation destination, we need a large, first-class resort as a centerpiece.

I worked for many years to try to get a private developer to come in and do a large resort that would anchor the tourism industry up there, but nobody was willing to do it. So the state got involved to provide some incentives that would stimulate private development, and what is under construction up there right now is not a state park.... I repeat, not a state park. It is a Holiday Inn Crowne Plaza Resort that is being built by the Atlanta firm of Stormont Trice. The state's contribution has been to provide the land, and to use our bonding capacity to provide a low-interest loan for part of the construction cost, which will be paid back fully and completely from the income of the resort.

Once we made those incentives available, we were able to interest Stormont Trice, which is a private corporation with an excellent reputation for building and operating hotels and resorts, including three others in Georgia. Once Storemont Trice had designed a high-quality resort and golf course, Holiday Inn came to realize that it would meet the high standards required for a Crowne Plaza Resort. And once it's fully operational, the Brasstown Valley Resort will create about 200 jobs and generate more than $12.7 million a year in economic activity—with a lot of it coming in from outside the state.

As some of you know, Cherokee burial mounds were uncovered in the process of building the golf course. Again, the by-word has been cooperation. An archeological survey has identified all potential burial sites, and the golf course has been redesigned to avoid them. We are now working in cooperation with the Cherokee Nation to move forward with building the golf course.

As a result of the state's willingness to provide some stimulus at the front end, we have a major private tourism project underway that would never have happened if the state had not been willing to start the ball rolling. Rather than competing with the tourism industry, we provided an opportunity for private development to take place.

*—Governor's Tourism Conference, September 16, 1993*

———————

All the trade leads, all the international contacts, all the tailor-made inducements, all the hard-boiled negotiating—all those marketing efforts will not bring one single job to Georgia unless our communities are prepared for development. The product behind the sales pitch, the steak behind the sizzle, the reality behind the glossy brochures—that is what the All Star Community program is designed to address.

This program is the brainchild of the Community Developers Forum, a partnership of statewide organizations who work in economic development. It includes the University System of Georgia, the municipal and county commissioners associations, and the Georgia Departments of Community Affairs and Industry, Trade and Tourism.

The program's design is simple. Communities in the program ask themselves the same kind of questions that potential investors will ask—questions about their resources, their leadership, their infrastructure, their goals, their strategy to meet those goals, and their determination to achieve their dreams.

In effect, the State of Georgia asked the private sector to "preach what they practice" by helping communities understand what they look for when they evaluate potential sites for facilities. But the ultimate objective for All-Star communities is not just to make themselves attractive to investors from out of town, out of the state, or out of the country. The ultimate objective is to discover their own potential for home-grown jobs and development...

Human nature being what it is, there will always be people who try short-cuts to success. But economic development is like baseball—it is a test of our mettle over time. To get in the playoffs, you have to know what must be done and do it with both excellence and consistency over the long haul. In baseball, an occasional pitcher will try to win with illegal pitches. In economic development, an occasional community will try to lure investors with exaggerations and false promises. But whenever you try to win with "sucker pitches," it is inevitable that you will eventually lose your grip on the situation, and lose the game.

For more than a century after the Civil War, the South aimed to make ourselves as attractive as possible to Yankee capitalists—to build a good lightning rod, then hope that lightning would strike in the form of a relocated factory, distribution center, or service facility. We relied on low wages, unskilled labor, rail sidings and unregulated use of natural resources.

Today, however... no Georgia community can sit back and wait for the phone to ring. Communities must be more aggressive than they used to be—not just in their marketing, but more importantly in developing the assets that businesses need. We must grow our own industry in many parts of this state—by exporting our goods and services, by attracting tourists, by processing our own agricultural products, and by keeping local industry healthy and growing. Georgia communities must take control of their own economic destinies.

Now some of you who were at the regional forum for the Governor's Development

Council in Savannah are probably thinking, "This guy's singing the same tune now that he did at the Development Council meeting back in July." And you're right. The Governor's Development Council and the All Star Community program are two pieces of the same puzzle. Healthy, balanced economic development all across the state does not come from the top down. It has to be built from the bottom up. It has to start at the community level... and once a community understands what it wants to accomplish and what it needs to do to achieve that, then that community will become an active voice in its region, helping to influence the way the state directs its resources.

There are two elements of the All Star program that are of special value, because they take traditional development concepts and adapt them to today's needs. The first element is the establishment of a leadership base that is broad and strong enough to sustain a long-term community development effort. In the days when a community built a rail siding or a spec building, then tried to get an outside industrial prospect to come in and use it, their development team was made up of bankers, chamber of commerce leaders, the mayor, a few key merchants and perhaps a leading land-owner or two. Today, however, the decisions that affect a community's development potential are much more varied. If you want to be able to count on having all of your critical assets in place, you need a much broader leadership team. For example, today's potential investors are looking for facilities and services that are the responsibility of local governments and school boards. So the All Star Community program makes local governments a key part of the leadership team, and the strong attendance today from both the City of Vidalia and the Toombs County Commission is an important sign of teamwork.

There's another feature that is absolutely essential to building a broad leadership base, and I am especially pleased that you are aware of it here in Vidalia. Today, sound economics, like sound morals, indicate a more inclusive approach. You cannot have true leadership without aggressive efforts to break down racial and cultural barriers. Like it or not, our economy is growing increasingly international. If we want to compete, we have to offer levels of education, health care, environmental safety, and public safety that meet global standards, and we have to be more aware and sensitive to other cultures and customs around the world.

Today's global investment prospects tend to consider racism a stupid waste of resources and a threat to human progress. A lack of inclusiveness on your leadership team leaves them wondering what barriers they might encounter if they decide to move to your town. But there are bigger and better reasons to become more inclusive than just to please a foreign investor or two. By the year 2000, half of those entering the workforce will be minorities. If we do not bring minorities into the economic mainstream, we are all in big trouble. Our own development resources, from schools and health facilities to solid waste disposal and good roads, involve a contribution from every single citizen.

Once you have broad leadership, then a second crucial element of the All Star program will put that leadership to the test, and that is the creation of a long-range, comprehensive plan for your community's future. Until recently, long-range planning for development seemed irrelevant to many Georgia communities, since development decisions were viewed as being in the hands of individual investors rather than the hands of the community. Today long-range planning is absolutely essential to economic development... No community's economic base can be taken for granted. Every element of community life that affects its development potential must be carefully weighed. The types of development and their optimal pace must be chosen—and, most of all, a careful and realistic strategy for achieving success must be prepared.

There's also another reason for Georgia communities to undertake long-range, comprehensive planning—it's the law. The Growth Strategies legislation of 1989 aims at establishing comprehensive plans at the local, regional, and, ultimately, state level to ensure that all our decisions are made in full view of their consequences for economic growth, for our natural resources, for our system of government. This legislation does not tell a single Georgia citizen or community what to do or how to live. What it *does* tell us is that we are all going to sink or swim together. All of us must consider how our actions affect each other, and then we must work toward a consensus of how we will make progress together.

That is the purpose of the All Star Community Program, as it helps individual communities like this one to evaluate and plan for economic development. And that is the purpose of the Governor's Development Council, as it builds a state economic development plan from the bottom up—a plan that is based on helping Georgia's regions and communities achieve their development goals.

*—Vidalia All Star Community Ceremony, November 9, 1993*

---

The Governor's Development Council recently adopted a blueprint to build Georgia a new economic engine for the 21st century. An important part of that plan is to broaden our efforts from recruiting new industries to also include support for existing industry. Existing industry creates eight of ten new jobs, and I believe they deserve equal treatment when it comes to incentives.

The public-private team that has been created to work on this aspect of our economic development plan is called Georgia's BEST—the Business Expansion Support Team. Georgia's BEST has six goals for existing industry: 1) To coordinate our support programs; 2) To create a modern service program; 3) To offer financial assistance for small and medium firms; 4) To help with employee training; 5) To develop a system that matches Georgia products with potential markets; 6) To help Georgia firms expand their exports.

My economic development legislation for 1994 is designed to give Georgia's BEST the tools it needs to achieve those goals. To help existing businesses expand, I have proposed a system of tax credits for creating new jobs and for investing in new plants and equipment. Georgia's counties would be divided into three tiers based on their relative economic strength, and companies in the poorest areas of the state would get the biggest stimulus to expand. The tax credits are also larger for investments that involve pollution control, recycling, or defense conversion activities.

Then to improve the quality of our workforce, I have proposed tax credits for retraining hourly or assembly line workers to use new equipment, and for setting up child care centers so that parents can go to work on new jobs.

*—Georgia Chamber Existing Industry Council, February 16, 1994*

———————

Georgia is one of the nation's top poultry states at a time when poultry has emerged as the world's favorite high-quality, low-cost protein source. Today poultry is a $10 billion industry in Georgia. It is our biggest and fastest-growing agricultural industry. It accounts for more than a third of our farm income and a quarter of our food processing industry, both by product value and by employment....

Georgia's growing food processing industry is a very important part of bringing economic development to rural areas. As lifestyles become more complex, consumers want foods that are quick and easy to prepare. Thirty years ago, 83 percent of Georgia's broilers were marketed whole, and only 17 percent were cut up or otherwise processed. Today, those percentages are reversed, with 85 percent of our broilers processed and only 15 percent of them marketed whole.

So Georgia agribusiness is expanding and rising to meet that opportunity. We are processing more and more of our own agricultural products, and that creates jobs and adds value to our economy.

*—Ground Breaking for Cagle Poultry, March 3, 1994*

———————

Georgia's textile industry is as old as this state, and it's part of the bedrock on which our economy was built through the years. But at the same time, this industry is as new as the 21st century, as it takes full advantage of advanced manufacturing technology. When you were facing the toughest international competition in history, many expected you to go belly-up. Instead you went through a dramatic transformation and reshaped yourselves into a successful, cutting-edge industry.

We're trying to follow your example in state government—using advanced technology to improve our schools, expand our adult literacy programs, and revolutionize the way we deliver medical services to rural areas.

*—Georgia Textile Manufacturers Association, May 6, 1994*

———————

My goal as Governor is to make this state the top state—the hot spot for economic growth in the 21st century. So in addition to careful fiscal management in the present, we are also planning for the future, laying the groundwork for the sound business climate, and the skilled workforce we need to sustain long-term, balanced economic development across the state.

Of course, a big part of that is for economic developers in both the public and private sectors, at both the state and local levels, to talk together and work together and use their resources in complementary ways. That's why we convene this Governor's Conference on

Economic Development each spring, and that's why the Governor's Development Council is developing a long-range state plan that recognizes the unique economic strengths and needs of Georgia's different economic regions. It's called "Building a New Economic Engine for the 21st Century: Strength from Diversity."

Many of you participated last summer when I brought the Council to each of the 11 economic regions to learn about your strengths and your needs, and we are developing programs and legislation based on what you told us.

One of the things you told us about was incentives. So we created Georgia's BEST— our Business Expansion Support Team—which recognizes that most new jobs are created by existing businesses, and they deserve the same kinds of incentives that we use to attract new businesses.

We offer an income tax credit when companies move to Georgia and bring in a group of new jobs. But Georgia's BEST also offers that same tax credit to existing companies when they expand and create a group of new jobs. Georgia is the only state in the Southeast where a business that has operated in the state for at least three years, becomes eligible for an income tax credit when they make a major investment. Tax credits are also allowed when existing Georgia businesses retrain employees to use new technology, or even when they offer child care to their employees. We also provide a tax exemption on the purchase of new manufacturing equipment and of primary material handling equipment for large-scale new or expanded warehouses.

We've got new companies coming to Georgia because of the jobs tax credit—like Cargill Poultry which is building a $38 million complex in Macon and Dooly counties, creating 1,000 jobs and requiring 80 growers. Or Motorola, which cited our jobs tax credit as an important factor in their decision to move their Energy Products Division to Lawrenceville, bringing in 100 jobs and creating up to 900 more in the next few years.

Georgia's BEST tax incentives are also helping Georgia's existing industries grow, like the Target Warehouse in Tifton, which just announced a 480,000-square-foot expansion. In March, I spoke at the ground breaking for the Cagle Poultry expansion in Camilla. It will create 1,500 new jobs. And right here in Augusta, the Olin Corporation will benefit from a tax exemption when electricity accounts for more than half of the cost of the materials it takes to make a product.

*—Governor's Development Conference, May 18, 1994*

———————

What our challenge is and what I am working very hard to do is build growth into a balanced pattern all across the state, a pattern that brings strength to every part of the state, not just metro Atlanta. A very important part of that effort is developing and expanding our food processing industry in rural areas of the state, because the food processing industry not only creates needed jobs that fit well into our rural communities and add value to their economy, but processing our crops locally also gives our farmers more market options and advantages, and greater economic stability.

You know, science fiction imagined a 21st century in which our daily diet consisted of manmade pills and chemicals, and all our clothes were made of artificial fibers. But reality has turned out to be just the opposite. Today, on the eve of the 21st century, people want their food fresh-grown and their fibers natural.

Georgia agriculture is as old as the state and is the bedrock on which we built our economy starting in colonial days. But it is also as new as the 21st century, with new crops growing in Georgia's fields, new packing and processing plants operating in Georgia's farm communities, and new marketing opportunities opening up around the world.

—*Ribbon cutting, Morris Blueberry Processing Plant, May 26, 1994*

Ever since James Edward Oglethorpe sailed up the Savannah River and docked at Yamacraw Bluff 260 years ago, Savannah has been a maritime center. But who could have imagined, even 50 years ago when the Georgia Ports Authority was established, what the docks would be like today.

Who could have imagined, 50 years ago, the gigantic freighters from more than 100 different countries that now make their way up the newly dredged, 42-foot channel that we just dedicated last month.

Who could have imagined, 50 years ago, the towering container cranes that unload those ships, or the gigantic refrigerated warehouses that keep perishable products cool, or the vast fleets of vehicles that await pick-up at Brunswick.

Who could have imagined, 50 years ago, that the customs and docking paperwork, then typed on Remmingtons with carbon paper, would now be lodged in a sophisticated computer system.

And who could have comprehended, 50 years ago, the sheer volume of the nine million tons of cargo that now pass across the docks each year.

The Georgia Ports Authority has come a long way in the past 50 years, and the next 50 years look just as exciting. As political barriers around the world break down, international trade is growing by leaps and bounds, and 95 percent of it is water-borne. Also, over the next 50 years, America's water-borne freight is expected to shift so that a greater concentration of it comes through South Atlantic ports. We are positioning our ports to make sure Savannah and Brunswick get their full share of that increase.

But the ports belong to all of Georgia, and they contribute to the whole story of Georgia's economic success. Sixty-three thousand jobs all across the state connect directly to what goes on at those docks, and those jobs have a net economic impact of $7 billion a year that touches every corner of our state. Our ports are the gateway to the markets of the world for products from all over Georgia. Billions of dollars worth of carpet from north Georgia, kaolin from middle Georgia, agricultural products from south Georgia flow through our ports on their way to world markets.

What it all boils down to, is that in a future where international trade is on the rise, our ports are a gateway to Georgia's prosperity. Today, as we congratulate the Georgia Ports Authority on its 50th anniversary, we celebrate a past that successfully built one the premier ports in the world, and we stake our claim for a future in which businesses all over Georgia, both large and small, take full advantage of the opportunities presented by a growing world trade market.

*—Georgia Ports Authority 50th Anniversary, August 16, 1994*

---

It is glorious to be part of the communications industry at a time when the information age is unfolding around us. If you are also in Georgia, then you have the best of all possible worlds. Now, some of you may be thinking that I'm just another Governor, bragging on his state. But as Dizzy Dean used to say, "If you've already done it, it ain't braggin'."

Tonight, you are in the state where the modem and the IRMA board were developed... the state where the first windows-based word-processing software was unveiled. You are in the state where the first mobile satellite uplink was produced... the first state in the nation to put a satellite dish at every single public school, every state college and every technical institute, and to own a transponder on a Telstar satellite.

You are in the state of the first commercial application of fiber-optic cable... In a state that has a 150,000-mile fiber-optic network, and in a city that has four times more fiber-optic trunk lines than New York. You are in the first, and as yet the only state to deliver actual, insurance-reimbursable medical care by telecommunications.

You are in the state that has come to be the first-choice location of an increasing number of New York and Los Angeles film-makers. You are in the home state of CNN and Turner Broadcasting, of Cox Broadcasting, Bell South, Equifax, and Scientific Atlanta... The state of IBM, Denon, Kodak, UPS, AT&T, MCI, and GTE. In fact, 45 of the top 50 international electronics companies can be found right here in Georgia.

You are in a state with a significant presence—in private industry and in university research—of all the technologies that are now converging on the cutting edge of telecommunications—from computers to consumer electronics, from satellites to fiber optics.

And here in Georgia, these technologies are coming together with a particular energy and intensity, because we are deliberately working to make this state a world center of excellence and expertise in communications.

We have what we call the Georgia Research Alliance. It is a partnership among our six research universities, state government, and private business. It's our equivalent of North Carolina's Research Triangle. But unlike North Carolina, which put its resources into building industrial parks, Georgia is investing in the labs and the endowments it takes to attract the most eminent research scholars in the world, because we are determined to be a driving force in the development and application of new communications technology.

The Georgia Research Alliance has two dozen major communications research projects underway at five universities in areas like signal compression, optical switching, and virtual reality techniques. We are building a state-of-the-art research facility for them, adjacent both to Georgia Tech and the Turner Broadcasting System.

Also housed in this building will be a major, national research center to develop faster, cheaper micro-chips for consumer electronics. Its goal is to help the United States  .

capture 40 percent of the world market for consumer electronics during the next decade, creating literally millions of jobs.

The bottom line is that you are in a state that not only dares to dream bold dreams, but also has leaders with the courage and the tenacity to go after those dreams and make them come true.

Georgia is a pro-business state, a very pro-business state that cultivates unique public-private partnerships to realize our goals. A pro-business state that not only welcomes and nurtures technology and innovation, but uses it to build the future...

It is clear that the economy of the 21st century will drive on the information super highway. So in Georgia, when we look at the 1996 Olympics, we see more than just 17 days of world athletic events. We see the most thrilling communications event in world history. And the long-term legacy that we are determined to realize from the Olympics is much more than a stadium here and a swimming pool there. We are preparing for the Olympics by building an astounding communications infrastructure, and we are aiming for an enhanced reputation as a world center for communications.

*—Operation Legacy: Telecommunication Industries, January 31, 1995*

Another important tool in our economic development toolbox is BEST. When it comes to tax incentives, where Georgia stands out is not in giveaways for incoming industries, but in support for our existing industries. Some states may care about you just long enough to get you there. But here in Georgia, we are working to home-grow our economy. And we devote just as much attention to the ongoing vitality of our existing industries as we do to attracting new ones....

In Georgia, we have focused our sights and our economic development efforts on the long-term, because when you have a solid economic foundation of infrastructure and educational opportunity and ongoing tax incentives for existing industries, then you don't have to give away the store up-front to attract new industries to your state.

*—Governor's Economic Development Conference, May 17, 1995*

When you think of the American aerospace industry, you need to think Georgia, because the aerospace industry in Georgia is both significant and growing. The number of aerospace companies in Georgia has increased by more than 50 percent in the past three years. We now have more than 150 firms, including 15 of the top 20 aerospace and defense contractors in the United States. These companies employ more than 40,000 Georgians, and their defense contracts total more than $4 billion a year. So you can see that Georgia is one of the largest and liveliest centers for aerospace business and technology, and an important reason why is our positive business climate.

Georgia is the fastest-growing state east of the Rocky Mountains, and a national leader in job creation. New businesses coming into Georgia like our location, which is on the Atlanta seaboard where our business day overlaps with Europe's. But at the same time, Atlanta is 125 miles closer to Chicago than New York City is. In fact, two-thirds of the U.S. population is within two hours flight time from Atlanta, and two-thirds of the U.S. markets—both consumer and industrial—are within two days shipping time from Atlanta.

Businesses also like our transportation connections, from the international airport in Atlanta, which offers nonstop flights to Paris and many other European cities, to the ports of Savannah and Brunswick, which process more than 10 million tons of cargo a year.

They like our one-stop environmental permitting process that takes about 90 days, compared to up to two years in some other states.

They like our QuickStart program that provides on-site training for the new workforce they hire. Georgia is the only state in the United States that has no dollar ceiling on the amount of training Quick Start will provide.

They like our education system, which begins with a prekindergarten program for four-year-olds and ends with the most far-reaching scholarship program in the United States. It's called HOPE, and this school year it provided nearly $70 million in scholarship assistance to Georgia students at our colleges and technical institutes. Businesses know they will find a skilled and educated workforce in Georgia.

They also like our state-of-the-art telecommunications infrastructure. Georgia has a 150,000-mile fiber-optic network, and Atlanta has four times more fiber-optic trunk lines than New York City.

And they like the fact that in Georgia, we continue care about them and work with them after they've come. We work hard to home-grow our economy, and we devote just as much attention to the ongoing vitality of the businesses we already have, as we do to attracting new ones.

*—Reception for Aerospace Firms, Paris Air Show, June 14, 1995*

---

I believe the Research Alliance is pivotal to the economic future of Georgia, because it leverages the research capabilities of our universities into increased economic development. The potential of the Research Alliance is already being felt throughout the state. GRA reflects well on higher education in Georgia, adding to its image and helping us recruit top scholars in other areas as well the ones you address, and the promise of coordinated, industry-focused research has helped Georgia attract new businesses.

I was in Paris in June and met with officials at Rhone Merieux—the global leader in animal vaccines. Two weeks later, I joined them in announcing plans to expand their operations in Athens—relocating a business they purchased in Kansas to Georgia, rather than the other way around.

Rayonier—a major international timber and pulp supplier—is moving its research center from Washington State to a $10 million state-of-the-art facility at its plant in Jesup.

A poultry genetics firm called Avian Farms chose sites in Savannah and Screven

County for its new international headquarters, research labs, and production facilities. Georgia beat out highly competitive sites in three other states.

Our telemedicine program is getting attention for being out on the national forefront, and the Olympics are a great opportunity to showcase our broader expertise in telecommunications.

As these examples demonstrate, GRA's impact already reaches well beyond the vicinity of its member universities to many other parts of the state, and I am grateful for that.

The state has provided $24 million of the construction cost of the GCATT building, and I'm looking forward to being at the ground-breaking. In addition, we have appropriated a cumulative total of $81 million for endowments and research labs. Bill Todd says it has leveraged more than $200 million in private and federal investment. That is a great short-term return, and it is one of the reasons why my budget recommendations for the GRA have sailed through the General Assembly. But we must also stay focused on the long-term return, and move forward to fulfill the potential of the Research Alliance as a high-tech economic stimulator for Georgia's industries.

You university presidents with athletic teams know that when you hire a new coach, you have to give him several years to recruit and build up the team and get it working. But there comes a time when you and your alumni start looking for and expecting some results out on the field on game day. It's the same for the Research Alliance. We have been in a recruiting and building mode, and I know that takes time. But the time is also coming when we need to get the ball in the end zone.

*—Georgia Research Alliance Board, September 1, 1995*

---

Agriculture is the bedrock on which Georgia's economy was founded, and our agribusiness industry is both as old as the history of this state and as new as the 21st century. In 1733, when James Edward Oglethorpe and his little band of English settlers first set foot on the soil of what was to become the Colony of Georgia, they had plans for all kinds of exotic crops, from olives to citrus to mulberry trees for silkworms.

The most practical one turned out to be cotton, and Georgia's first cotton crop was harvested a year later in 1734. Cotton is still part of our agricultural picture today. Since the one-two punch of genetics and modern technology knocked out the boll weevil, cotton has been on the rise in Georgia. Some 1.5 million acres were planted this year, making us one of the nation's leading cotton-producing states. We have 63 cotton gins in operation, with plans on the drawing board for 14 more.

But cotton is just one of a diverse range of crops that generate nearly $5 billion in cash receipts for Georgia farmers each year. When you add in food processing, agricultural chemicals and equipment, and all the many other related industries, Georgia's agribusiness is a $38 billion industry. It forms the largest sector of our state economy and involves 18 percent of our population.

Among the 50 states, Georgia ranks first in peanut and pecan production, second in poultry and eggs, and third in cotton acreage and peach production. Let me give you a couple of examples that will give you a feel for the magnitude represented by those rankings. Georgia leads the world in the production of peanuts and grows 40 percent of the peanuts used in the United States. Or take poultry. In the course of a day—one day— Georgia produces 18 million pounds of chicken and 13 million eggs, of which 8 million will be eaten and 5 million will be incubated to hatch into broilers.

Georgia is best known for our traditional "P" crops—peanuts, pecans, peaches, and poultry. But our farm base is very diversified. Winter-cropping got us into rye, and we now rank first among the states in production and acreage.

The number one crop in Colquitt County is cabbage—just one of a great range of fruits and vegetables that are grown in Georgia. Many of them are marketed at the State Farmers Market here in Atlanta, which is one of the finest fresh produce markets of its kind, and sells about $266 million in Georgia produce each year. And although we just began producing blueberries a few years ago, Georgia growers already fly them overnight to appear on Europe's tables the day after they are picked.

Speaking of Europe, Georgia exports nearly 20 percent of our crops, foods and livestock. If you add in other agricultural products like machinery and chemicals, our annual agribusiness exports total several billion dollars.

We are also processing more and more of our own crops here in the state. As your briefing book indicates, we expect food processing to be one of Georgia's fastest-growing manufacturing industries over the next decade. Take poultry, for example. Thirty years ago we marketed 83 percent of our broilers whole and processed 17 percent of them. Today, those percentages are reversed. We process 85 percent of our broilers—some of them all the way to nugget form.

Many of our food processing industries are located in rural areas, where they can take full advantage of our jobs tax credit, which is higher for less-developed parts of the state.

*—Operation Legacy: Agribusiness, September 11, 1995*

———————

There is an unprecedented level of partnership on the federal side of this center with the Department of Commerce, which is the lead federal partner, the Small Business Administration and Eximbank. It is very exciting for the State of Georgia to have the opportunity to join with these federal partners in creating the very first completely integrated state-federal Export Assistance Center. Our state component also includes many partners such as the Department of Industry, Trade and Tourism, Georgia Tech, the Department of Agriculture, the Small Business Development Center, and on the private side, Bell South.

For our part of it, we are going to operate a toll-free phone line for Georgia businesses to call, and we have hooked this center into our interactive GSAMS telecommunications network that connects nearly 300 sites around the state... We are also going to develop international video-conferencing capability, enabling Georgia businesses to interact directly with state trade representatives and business clients around the world. And we are installing a state-of-the-art database of export information at every one of our 34 technical institutes around the state, and an equal number of chambers of commerce and business organizations. It's called the Georgia International Trade Data Network.

Our goal is work together with the federal staff to offer one-stop export assistance to Georgia businesses, no matter where they are in the state or in the process of exporting. For businesses that are totally new to exporting, we will find an extension course or a distance learning outlet in their community to give them the background they need to begin. For businesses that have done their homework and are ready to cut their first deal, we will hook them up with somebody who can guide them through that process and help them find the financing they need. Even businesses that are veteran exporters will be able to make new contacts in emerging hot markets through this Export Assistance Center.

Georgia is locating new trade representatives out in emerging markets like South America, South Africa, the Pacific Rim, and India, to help make those contacts, and we are going to develop video-conferencing capability with them.

Our goals are to expand the quantity and value of Georgia's exports, to expand the number of Georgia firms that export, and to expand the number of international markets where we are active.

*—Open Export Assistance Center, September 28, 1995*

---

Conventional wisdom would say that after the Olympic torch is extinguished at the closing ceremonies, Georgia's economy will go flatter than a punctured balloon. But if you read the *Wall Street Journal* a week ago, you already know that our post-Olympic slowdown is expected to be so brief that if you blink you'll miss it. We are simply going to go back to doing what we were doing before the Olympics were ever announced— creating new jobs at a break-neck pace.

*—Red Carpet Tour Dinner, April 9, 1996*

---

We are extremely fortunate in Georgia to have a strong corporate community made up of businesses of all sizes—strong not only in terms of your economic health, which makes our state economy strong, but also strong in the sense of your corporate citizenship and the outstanding contributions you make to your communities.

Although we attract a lot of new industry, most of Georgia's industry is existing industry that has been around for a long time. It forms the bedrock of our economy. That's why my administration has put such a strong emphasis on making sure our existing industry stays healthy. The reason we created Georgia's BEST was to give our existing industry the same kind of tax incentives that are offered to incoming new industry. And we keep on making BEST better. We keep up with how it is working and who is benefitting from it, and each year we introduce another bill in the General Assembly to fine-tune it a little more and make it work a little better.

We expanded Quick Start, Georgia's leading employee training program for incoming industry, so that it is now available to existing industry when you expand and create a block of new jobs. We created a special research program to help our traditional industries, like agriculture, pulp and paper, and textiles. And we have the nation's first full-service Export Assistance Center to help Georgia's businesses expand into the international market.

Last week, I participated in several announcements of new industry moving to Georgia, including the biggest investment announcement in state history. The large Korean conglomerate Sunkyong announced it would invest $1.5 billion to build the world's biggest polyester film manufacturing plant here in Georgia.

I know that it's always the new business announcements like these that get all the attention. Remember all the fuss in the news when Mercedes moved to Alabama? At that very same time, Georgia was busy capturing a commitment from General Motors to retool the existing Doraville plant, which had been slated to close, for the production of a new minivan. The number of jobs saved plus the number of new jobs created in the GM plant conversion was about three times greater than the number of new jobs Mercedes brought to Alabama. Yet, because the GM plant was "existing" industry, the news media paid very little attention.

But "new industries" have an incredible knack for turning into "existing industries." You stop paying attention for a minute, and before you know it they're not new anymore. That's why we are with you for the long haul in Georgia. Some states may care about you just long enough to get you there. Georgia goes on caring about you as your business grows and changes over the years.

And you know something? That long-term commitment that we make to you—our existing industries—has turned out to be a pretty good recruiting tool to attract the new ones. They know that a couple of years down the road, they are not going to be wondering what they're doing in Georgia. They will know exactly what they're doing here—they'll be existing business that are growing and thriving in the most pro-business state in the nation.

—*GEDA Existing Industry Awards Luncheon, April 15, 1996*

---

I am not a scientist, but rather a student and teacher of history, so this afternoon I'm going to begin with a little history. It was about 60 years ago here in Georgia. Richard Russell was Governor. The Great Depression had been underway for several years, and our economy had sunk to a pretty low ebb. The state was full of southern pines, as it still is today. But they were useless from an economic perspective, because their resin and pine gum prevented them from being pulped.

Dr. Charles Herty of Savannah was working on a solution for that problem. And out of a deep concern for the worsening economic plight of Georgia's farmers, Governor Russell provided state funds for Herty's efforts, supporting the start of what is today the Herty Foundation. Dr. Herty was able to develop a successful pulping process for southern pines, and the immediate return on that state investment was to give Georgia farmers a new cash crop, enabling many of them to weather the depression.

But, more significantly, the long-term return was to launch pulp and paper as a major industry in Georgia, and today this state is the nation's largest tonnage producer of paper and fiberboard. In fact, if Georgia were a nation unto itself, we would rank among the top ten producers of the world.

From that beginning nearly 60 years, this public-private partnership between the State of Georgia and the pulp and paper industry has grown into the marvelous facility that surrounds us here today. The state has invested $25 million in capital improvements for the Herty Foundation, which has helped to leverage $85 million in private industrial support for pilot and development projects. That has made the Herty Foundation the largest pilot-scale development center for pulp and paper anywhere in the United States.

That is something to be very proud of, but the real economic return on this investment is a growing industry that is full of high-tech equipment. Herty has conducted lab and pilot projects for 90 percent of Georgia's pulp and paper industry, testing answers to questions that range from fiber supply and quality, to recycling existing paper, from improving processes to addressing environmental concerns. And the Herty Foundation does not work in isolation, but is a partner with the Paper Science and Technology Institute at Georgia Tech, which is the largest research organization for pulp and paper in the nation. Herty is also a partner with the University of Georgia, Georgia Tech, Georgia Southern University, Valdosta University and others in Georgia's traditional industry research initiative for pulp and paper.

The Herty Foundation takes what scientists in these research programs discover, and develops and tests it for successful commercial application by the pulp and paper industry. Together, these institutions give Georgia a pulp and paper research and development powerhouse that enables Georgia's pulp and paper industry to compete against Sweden, Finland, Japan, and Canada in the international marketplace. Georgia's pulp and paper exports have doubled in just the past two years. Last year we exported nearly $2 billion dollars worth—making pulp and paper products this state's number one export.

Pulp and paper are considered one of Georgia's older, traditional industries, but the mills are as new as the future and full of computer-controlled advanced technology. We know that as this industry relies more and more on advanced technology, it is looking for a workforce that is better educated and has stronger skills than ever before. The first requisite for a good employee is no longer brawn, but brains. The key to the continued strength of Georgia's industries...the key to generating economic development and creating jobs, the key to our future prosperity and quality of life... is education....

When electronic communications technology like the computer and the modem began to emerge, some envisioned a future in which paper was obsolete. What has actually happened is that the demand for paper has increased. But even if those pundits still turn out to be right, and we are headed for a paper-free 21st century, the pulp and paper industry will still be an integral part of Georgia's economy, because the raw materials and the machinery, the processes and the techniques of this industry are adaptable to many other products beyond office stationery.

The Herty Foundation has been recognized for its work on NASA heat shields, nitro-cellulous paper for the Army, and composite structures for products as diverse as computers, aircraft, and cars. For example, Herty adapted the pulp and paper process to produce synthetic filters for automobile air bags, and a plant is on-line here in Georgia to produce them. There may well be no paper at all on the Starship Enterprise a century from now, but in all likelihood parts of the spaceship itself will have been made by Georgia's pulp and paper industry... a traditional industry that runs out on the cutting edge of the future, because the Herty Foundation is helping it adapt to new, higher value products even before the old ones have a chance to become obsolete.

*—Dedicate Laboratory, Herty Foundation, April 29, 1996*

———————

The University System of Georgia has begun a series of regional meetings to listen to business leaders and learn how the University System can be a better partner to them... You can see the result in the new initiative we just began by the University System called ICAPP, which stands for Intellectual Capital Partnership Program. It is the first of its kind anywhere in the United States.

Nearly 30 years ago, Georgia led the nation with the creation of our Quick Start program. Through our technical institutes like Augusta Tech, Quick Start provides specialized employee training for new and expanding manufacturing industries. It has been widely copied by other states. ICAPP takes the general idea of Quick Start and applies it to college-level education. It will focus the resources of our University System directly on the actual needs of Georgia industries for an educated workforce in specific fields and at specific places.

Let me give you a specific example: The Augusta community has been experiencing something of an economic shake-up related to the Savannah River plant, and a lot of people are being laid off who have both natural abilities and education in math and science. At the same time, Georgia's workforce demand for experts in mainframe computer programming and analysis is much greater than University System of Georgia is presently meeting. Last year, the entire University System graduated about 780 computer majors. But when we surveyed the biggest 30 companies who hire computer experts, we found that their workforce needs are in the thousands, and that does not even begin to address the needs of small and mid-sized companies where the rapid growth is.

So Augusta College is a participant in an ICAPP project, which will address the need for a workforce of trained computer and business analysts who are experts in mainframe computers. We believe this ICAPP project is an exceptional opportunity to help a group of Augustans who have skills and abilities in math and science, to shift gears and move into a related career where there is a great workforce demand.

*—Leadership Augusta, May 9, 1996*

———————

As you can see, Georgia Tech and the City of Atlanta are busy getting ready for the Olympics. Some of our visitors have wondered if we'll get all the construction done in time, but what you need to understand is that Atlanta is always under construction. It's just a little more intense than usual right now. We'll take down the scaffolding and clean up everything before the Olympics begin. Then after the Games are over, we'll get the scaffolding out again and put it back up and go back to building again.

It's the same kind of mind-set you have to have in manufacturing these days—always looking ahead with anticipation, always building and changing.

Georgia has been a strong manufacturing state for the best part of the 20th century. We are proud of that distinction, and we are even prouder of the fact that the manufacturing sector of our economy continues to be strong. Last year, nearly 800 companies announced new manufacturing facilities in Georgia—an investment of more than $3 billion that will create about 20,000 new jobs.

We believe that a strong, vibrant manufacturing base is the foundation on which a healthy economy is built. Because manufacturing is what creates wealth. It takes resources and adds value to them by making them do something more, and that is something that services, even high-tech services, simply cannot do. Charging a fee for swapping financial assets around does not create any new wealth, not even when it's done by satellite or fiber-optic cable at the speed of light.

*—FAIM Manufacturing Conference, May 13, 1996*

The original Ringgold Visitors Center was built 32 years ago. It was not only one of Georgia's first visitors centers, it was also the very first center to be built anywhere along I-75 in any state. It was designed to handle 150,000 visitors a year, which was considered adequate at the time. But the very first year it was open, it had 172,500 visitors. It now routinely hosts two million visitors every year, and with the Olympics in Georgia this summer, I expect this center will post an even higher total for 1996. So you can see why a larger facility was absolutely essential, and this new center has come in the nick of time.

The Ringgold Visitors Center was originally built to put out the welcome mat for traffic coming into the state on I-75, by providing a clean and user friendly place to take a break from the road and learn more about Georgia's vacation destinations. The center continues to fulfill that mission for thousands of people every day. It has given out more than a billion road maps and made tens of thousands of hotel reservations.

But I would venture to say that the people who have the most vivid memories of this center, remember it for other reasons than clean restrooms or a wealth of travel brochures. Over the past 30 years the Ringgold Visitors Center has repaired more than 6,000 automobiles, reunited more than 2,000 families and been the site of several weddings.

Our visitors centers are a very important component of the state's efforts to promote tourism in Georgia. Georgia was a leader in building some of the very first visitors centers in the nation, including this one, and we continue to be a leader in the use of visitors centers. With 11 centers statewide, we rank second among the states in both the amount of money we put into our centers and the number of staff we hire to operate them.

But that investment has paid off. As the Ringgold Center demonstrates, our visitors centers are attracting many times more travelers than we ever envisioned when we first started building them. In fact, more visitors stop at Georgia's visitors centers than any other state in the nation. In addition to providing a clean, attractive place for highway travelers to take a break from their journey, our visitors centers also serve as the "front door" to Georgia. It is often the friendly hospitality they experience at a visitors center, that gives travelers their first impression of what Georgia is really like, and introduces them to the attractions we have to offer. And that is what makes many of them start to consider Georgia as a possible destination for a future trip.

Nearly 60 percent of those 2 million visitors who now stop here each year, are headed for destinations in Georgia, rather than just driving through our state on their way to somewhere else. That's how tourism has become a $13.6 billion industry in Georgia... an industry that employs nearly 386,000 Georgians and pays them nearly $9 billion. It creates more than $1 billion in state revenues from sources like the sales tax and the income tax paid by those employed in the industry.

One of the special attributes of tourism, is that it brings millions of dollars into Georgia from outside the state. In fact, if the tourism industry were to suddenly shut down, each taxpaying Georgian would have to kick in nearly $400 to compensate for all of the government revenues that now come for the most part from money travelers bring into Georgia and spend here.

So you can see why my administration is building three new visitors centers—this one, one on I-85 at Lavonia which just opened ten days ago, and one on I-20 in Augusta—and why we are devoting another half-million dollars to a repair program at the remaining centers.

*—Dedicate Ringgold Visitors Center, May 13, 1996*

---

If you look at the numbers for the State of Georgia, they're pretty impressive. We have been the fastest growing state east of the Rocky Mountains for the past four years in a row. But before any of you attribute that to Atlanta and the Olympics, let me emphasize that employment in Georgia's smaller cities and rural areas grew by 3.4 percent last year—twice as much as economists were expecting, and faster than every other state in the southeast.

Last year we had a record $5.3 billion in industrial announcements. More than $3 billion of that was in manufacturing, which is the bedrock of our economy, because manufacturing is what creates wealth. That $3 billion in manufacturing investment will be made by nearly 800 firms, most of them existing companies that are expanding.

1995 was also a banner year for trade. Georgia's exports increased by 23 percent, reaching an all-time high of $12.4 billion in value. Unlike the nation as a whole, Georgia has a trade surplus. The value of the goods we ship out is hundreds of millions of dollars higher than the value of the goods coming in.

But I think we all would agree that there is still room to improve on those numbers. In addition, we know that statewide numbers can sometimes disguise inequities among economic regions within the state or cover up problems.

We also know that economic development is teamwork. The state cannot come in and do economic development for you or to you. The initiative, the leadership, and a lot of hard work must come from within each of Georgia's economic regions... from local governments in the region, local chambers of commerce in the region, local business leaders in the region, all working together.

Back in 1993, the Governor's Development Council held a series of regional economic development meetings around the state, and we asked each region to create its own economic development strategy. Then we used those regional strategies as the base on which we built the state's first economic development strategy called "Building a New Economic Engine for the 21st Century: Strength from Diversity."

The Council is now evaluating and updating our state strategy, and we have begun another round of regional meetings. We want to hear from you again on what your major issues are today and for the future.

*—Governor's Development Council Hearing, Statesboro,*
*May 20, 1996*

Some of you have probably heard me say before that small business is big business. Not only are the majority of Georgia's businesses small, but small business is also where two-thirds of Georgia's jobs are and where most of Georgia's new jobs are created. What's more, every business, no matter how big, was once a small business. It was their success as a small business that enabled them to grow up over time into a big business. So the stability and the growth of our small and minority businesses are critical to the economic health and well-being of the entire state.

The opportunities for small and minority businesses are greater today than ever before. The University of Georgia recently released a study documenting that the buying power of black Georgians has grown by almost 70 percent, just since 1990. This year, black Georgians are expected to have $26 billion in spendable income after taxes. They now control one of every six dollars spent in this state, and that creates a strong and attractive market for Georgia's minority businesses.

In fact, Georgia economist Jeffery Humphreys says this state probably has the most attractive minority market in the nation, so this is a very special time of opportunity for minority businesses. We've increased our support for these businesses. The University System of Georgia now maintains a continuously updated general directory of small and minority businesses throughout the state.

The University System also provides several programs through its minority colleges to supply direct one-on-one assistance to small businesses and entrepreneurs, and to facilitate the two-way flow of trade between Georgia and Africa. Next month, I will be the first Georgia Governor to undertake a trade mission to Africa, where Georgia is opening a new trade office.

In addition, we are working hard to make this a special time of opportunity for minority firms to do business with state government. My administration has deliberately opened the state contracting process to small and minority businesses, and we also encourage the big businesses we contract with to subcontract with minority firms. In fact, there is a state income tax credit for companies doing business with the state, when they subcontract part of the job to a minority firm.

Back in 1992, I issued an Executive Order directing state agencies to work harder to increase the participation of minority businesses in the state purchasing process. At the same time I set up a system of reporting, in which state agencies now send quarterly progress reports on minority bidding to the Department of Administrative Services. I am pleased to report that the number of minority vendors solicited and the number of minority bids received have been steadily increasing. By 1996, more than a third of the minority firms that were solicited, bid on state purchases, and a record high level of over $102 million in state contracts was awarded to minority firms....

The state's procurement process was originally established in the 1930s, and it remained largely unchanged until last year, when we passed a law to reform and streamline it. It had gotten to the point where the cost of processing paperwork for some small purchases was more than the purchase itself. Under the new law, the threshold where the bidding process kicks in has been raised to $2,500, allowing state agencies to make more small discretionary purchases. That allows them to target more small and minority firms.

State agencies are also encouraged to use our new state procurement cards for these smaller purchases. The procurement card is a special NationsBank VISA card that connects to a state account. It saves time and paperwork, both for the vendor and the state, by eliminating requisitions and invoices.

The new law also establishes a centralized state registry of firms around the state who are interested in bidding on state contracts. It is called the Georgia Procurement Registry, and it is used to advertise bid opportunities to vendors and invite them to submit bids.

In addition, the state opened a pilot homepage on the Internet last fall, that provides a list of state bid opportunities of $10,000 or more, so that potential vendors can go to their computer and find out about bid opportunities by the product or service needed, by the state agency that needs it, or by the date the bidding process will open. Even if you do not have Internet access at home or at your business, we will soon be providing every single public library in the state with Internet connections.

We believe that if we open the state bidding process as wide as possible, it enables more vendors to compete, and in the process it will give Georgia citizens the best value for their tax dollars....

I know that you are working hard every day to make your business succeed. Together, you small businesses form the foundation of Georgia's economy and Georgia's future.

*—Governor's Small Business Conference, May 30, 1997*

I am proud to report that Georgia tourism continues to grow, with increases in expenditures, increases in new jobs, increases in new product development, and increases in state and local revenues. 1996 was a banner year, when nearly 43 million visitors came to Georgia. They spent almost $15 billion, supporting over 445,000 jobs and creating nearly 60,000 new jobs that paid Georgians $9.9 billion. And state and local tax revenues generated by tourism reached the $2 billion mark.

Now, before anybody is tempted to attribute all of those terrific numbers to the 1996 Olympic Games, let me point out that many areas of the state experienced losses last July, in what is usually an optimal time of year for tourism. The tourism benefits of the Olympics were offset to some extent by the fact that their presence scared a lot of non-Olympic tourists away, causing a mid-year slump. It was a strong beginning, and then a post-Olympics rebound toward the end of the year that gave us our strength.

What that means, I believe, is that the Olympics have had a very positive impact on Georgia tourism, as we hoped, but it was a little more indirect than we had anticipated. The Olympics gave Georgia a high profile and boosted our recognition and attractiveness as a vacation destination, as we expected, but many visitors chose to adjust their vacation schedules to avoid the gridlock that was predicted during the Games themselves.

We are now three-fourths of the way through 1997, and we are expecting another strong year. Our expectations are based not only on the heightened awareness and afterglow of the Olympics, but also on the new tourism infrastructure that has been opening across the state.

The new Georgia Music Hall of Fame opened last September in Macon and is reporting record attendance for its first year, with an average of 6,000 visitors every month. As a result, the Hall of Fame will not operate at a deficit for its first year, as was predicted, but is expected to make more than $400,000. The historic Douglass Theatre, which is right across the street from the Music Hall of Fame, is now open and featuring African American legends like Otis Redding and Ma Rainey.

In Columbus, the newly restored Liberty Theater is also open and featuring African American legends, and the Challenger Space Center is open as well. In Augusta, Fort Discovery is now open. Up in the mountains of North Georgia, an excursion railroad is about to begin running between Blue Ridge and McCaysville. And in South Georgia, the Prisoner of War Museum at Andersonville is on schedule to open later this year.

So we are developing an increasing large and diverse tourism product in Georgia. The key is gong to be consumer marketing, to let tourists know about all the activities and experiences we have to offer.

—*Governor's Tourism Conference, September 10, 1997*

We have traditionally thought of economic development as a collection of straight-forward tasks that could be done independent of each other—building a rail siding, an industrial park or a spec building, or working to attract a specific company to a specific site in Georgia. But as we now look ahead to the 21st century, we know that this approach will no longer work. It will not be enough simply to update that same old mindset. It will not be enough to call it a technology park instead of an industrial park. It will not be enough just to shift our recruiting focus to high-tech companies instead of low-tech companies. The mindset has to change. The structure has to change. What we do and how we go about it has to change.

Economic development for the 21st century has grown a lot more complex, and a piecemeal approach just won't work anymore. In today's high-tech, rapidly changing, global economy, there are many complexities, many factors that must be considered together. We can no longer be content with just courting individual prospects, one at a time. Telecommunications technology short-circuits that. Today investors often know more about us than we know about ourselves. They can reject us before we even know we're on the list, let alone have the opportunity to make a pitch.

What business is looking for has also grown more complex. As I meet with business executives around the world, I find they are more interested in a skilled, educated workforce than they are in a cheap one. They are more interested in clean air and water and environmentally sound waste systems than they are in a rail siding....

The big picture has grown even bigger, much more complex and much more volatile. Where we need simplicity today is not in the tasks that we undertake, but in the process we use to do them.... We can no longer afford to have a whole bevy of public and private organizations all going their own independent ways. We can no longer afford to be so fractured and scattered in the way we approach economic development.

As the tasks become more complex, the process must become more simple. We need the channels of communication to be clearer and more direct, and we need a much wider and greater variety of working partnerships. Make no mistake about it—the competition between states is keen. There is no room for turf-guarding, for working at cross purposes, for duplication of resources. The competition is also quick, and we must be able to respond to clients, customers and prospects with a flexibility and a nimbleness that is possible only through close, close collaboration.

*—Board of Industry Trade and Tourism, September 16, 1997*

---

Atlanta and Georgia sort of snuck quietly onto the technology scene while everyone was busy paying attention to Silicon Valley in California and Corridor 128 up by Boston, and even Research Triangle in North Carolina. Some people would probably be surprised to learn that for a time back in the mid-70s, Atlanta was home to one of the only two computer stores in the entire United States. It was called "The Computer Systemcenter" and it was located on Piedmont Road in the same shopping center as the

Limelight nightclub and the "disco" Kroger.

Back in those days, the growing presence of advanced technology in Georgia was almost as surprising to Georgians as it was to anyone else. Today, there is nothing quiet or unexpected about technology in this state. In fact, during the first half of the 90s, this state was second in the nation in high-tech job growth, and in 1996, we moved into first place.

—*Technology Month Luncheon, October 17, 1997*

# Education

## Lottery

Nine years ago, on March 27, 1982, I spoke at the GAE meeting in Savannah, and I said these words to you about education funding: "The only way we're going to see a significant improvement in this area is to somehow find a new source of revenue for education. It's going to take some creativity and some insight to find it, and it's going to take some courage for a candidate or office holder to recommend it. But it's something I think we have got to be working on."

And I did work on it. As a result, the citizens of Georgia will be able to vote on a lottery in November of next year. I am not personally enamored of lotteries. I want a lottery simply because I see it as that new source of revenue for education I promised to search for a decade go.....

Let me get one thing straight. The money that comes in from the lottery will not supplant funds already going for education. The Constitutional Amendment itself specifies that the money goes into a special fund to be used for new programs that we otherwise could not afford. That fact cannot be changed in the enabling legislation.

*—Georgia Association of Educators, February 15, 1991*

---

As you all know, I have long supported a lottery with the proceeds going for education. The General Assembly passed it last session, and in November of 1992, that question will appear on the General Election ballot. In the coming session, we will go ahead and introduce the enabling legislation for two reasons. First, it will give the public a chance to know the details of what they are voting on before they vote. Second, it will expedite the implementation of the lottery after the constitutional amendment is passed. We'll be able to hit the ground running and have the money coming in as soon as possible, probably about April of 93.

So, today, let me use this time to explain how the lottery will work. Georgia's lottery will be strictly a business organization. We are not going to take state tax revenues away from other programs to operate it. It will be run by a board of proven business leaders, not state bureaucrats. Everything will be done on a bid basis.

The net proceeds will be targeted at three critical unmet education needs in Georgia. I want to divide 90 percent of the lottery proceeds about evenly among three things. First, equipment and special capital outlay needs in K-12 and in higher education. Second, voluntary programs for our preschoolers, where learning is so important. And third, scholarships to bright students who might otherwise not be able to afford to attend college.

Finally, we are going to set up a reserve with the remaining 10 percent in acknowledgment of the fact that lottery proceeds can fluctuate, and we want our programs to be consistent.... Like true love, the course of the economy is never smooth. Economic growth ebbs and flows, and as it does, so will tax revenues and lottery proceeds. Therefore, we need to assure a consistent level of funding for these lottery programs that carries across the dips and swells in the proceeds, and the way we are going to do that is by establishing a reserve fund.

*—Georgia Chamber of Commerce Prelegislative Forum,*
*November 14, 1991*

---

One of my biggest disappointments in more than 30 years of politics has been the way some education leaders have either tip-toed quietly through the tulips all around (the lottery), or some cases, strongly opposed it... Here is the first creative new source of revenue for education in my and your lifetime. Here is a chance to start three major, new educational programs to help our kids.... To take us from the bottom to the top among the states in some significant measures. Don't misunderstand me. I'm not mad at you. I'm mad at Georgia always lagging behind the rest of the nation. I'm mad at our slow rate of progress in education in Georgia.

Of course, the lottery is not a panacea for education. I have never said it was. It is simply our best and last change of the 20th century to make a dramatic difference in the lives and futures of Georgia's children.

Lotteries are not new. They date back to the birth of this nation. We fought the Revolutionary War with cannons bought with the proceeds of a lottery set up by Ben Franklin. Lottery proceeds paid for the roof under which the first regular Congress of the United States met. Here in the South, lotteries were used to raise funds for the Civil War.

Thomas Jefferson once said a lottery "is the fairest tax of them all, because it taxes only the willing." That's the point Georgians need to understand: the alternative to creative revenue sources like the lottery is taxes, and folks, in the climate we live in today, taxes ain't much of an alternative. While statistical evidence shows that only a minority of poor people will play the lottery, all of them pay taxes. When they stop at a gas station or walk into a grocery store, every Georgian will have a choice about whether to buy a lottery ticket. But they have no choice about paying taxes. Regardless of whether they buy any lottery tickets, their four-year-old kids will still be eligible for prekindergarten. Their high school seniors will be eligible for scholarships, regardless of whether they ever buy any lottery tickets at all. The lottery gives the people of Georgia a choice; taxes do not. And the lottery gives their children a chance—a chance for a better education and a better future.

Georgia is one of only 16 states that don't already have a lottery, and that has allowed us to learn from the experiences of others—Florida, for example. Those who compare Georgia's lottery to Florida's are either ignorant of the facts or have deliberately chosen to ignore them. Florida's lottery was supposed to benefit education, just like Georgia's. But there's where the similarity ends. They are as different as night and day. Not only was

Florida's language much less restrictive than Georgia's, but Florida had no new educational programs designated in law to be funded with lottery proceeds. Georgia's lottery proceeds will not go into the general treasury, but into a special trust fund, a completely separate budget class that by law is designated for three specific educational programs: prekindergarten for four-year-olds, scholarships and tuition grants, and school construction and equipment for our classrooms.

If the lottery is passed, I am going to have those programs up and running as quickly as possible while I am still Governor. Once they are underway, you know as well as I that it would be political suicide for anyone to try to cut them off.....

Contrary to what lottery opponents may imply, you cannot build a barbed-wire fence around Georgia and keep gambling out. The absence of a state lottery in Georgia will not stop Georgians who want to play a state lottery. They will simply continue to cross the state line—or send couriers when they can't go in person—spending millions of Georgia dollars to buy Florida lottery tickets. Right now, millions and millions of lottery dollars are being drained out of this state—dollars that we could be using to benefit our own children. I want to plug the drain and keep those dollars in Georgia.

Let's face it: Georgia's preschoolers are just as bright and eager as any in the nation. But by the time they graduate from our schools—your schools—they're ranked among the worst in the country. Too many of our five-year-olds enter school unprepared to learn. Too many of our classrooms are ill-equipped; and too many of our high school graduates can't afford to go to college.

*—Georgia Superintendents Association, Oct 29, 1992*

---

After a year of campaigning on the lottery in 1990, and two years of hard work to put it into place, it is a great personal pleasure to come to this day when the Georgia Lottery corporation actually begins its work.... The constitutional amendment that was passed by the voters of Georgia last month, and the enabling legislation passed by the 1992 General Assembly, create a covenant with the citizens of this state that the lottery proceeds are to be used exclusively for educational purposes. I am committed to upholding this constitutional and legal covenant.... The budget recommendations that I will make to the General Assembly for the upcoming fiscal year, will clearly apply the lottery proceeds to the three new educational programs specified in state law: prekindergarten, scholarships to our colleges and technical institutes, and special equipment and capital needs.

The other part of the Georgia Lottery for Education—the operation of the lottery itself—is the responsibility of this Board of Directors for the Georgia Lottery Corporation. In that task you, too, have a covenant with the citizens of Georgia. Not only must the lottery be run as efficiently and effectively as the best private-sector business. It must also be run honestly, ethically, and with integrity above reproach.... Georgia law created the lottery as a public corporation which would function independently of the rest of state government and be free of any political interference, which means that once I have administered the oath of office to you today, I will remove myself completely from your decision-making process.

—*Charge to the Lottery Corporation Board, Dec 15, 1992*

_____

Although Georgia is the 35th state to have a lottery, our is unique in the nation because of the careful way its proceeds have been targeted.

The first thing we knew from other states is that the lottery should not be regarded as a panacea for major problems. It is not a meat-and-potatoes revenue source, but a dietary supplement, and that is acknowledged in what we expect the Georgia lottery to do.

Second, I wanted to guarantee that Georgia did not repeat what happened in Florida, where lottery funds, which were earmarked for education, simply replaced general treasury money with no total increase in educational benefits. Georgia's Constitution not only dedicates the lottery proceeds exclusively to education, but also holds the lottery proceeds separate from the normal stream of state revenue.....

The third thing we learned from other states is that lottery proceeds will surge and taper off. So we designed our lottery to accommodate that. Ten percent of the anticipate proceeds are held in reserve, and only two of the three programs funded by the lottery entail ongoing programs. The third involves one-time expenditures and can expand and contract as needed.

Beyond prize money and operating costs, every since cent that the lottery earns in Georgia is going into...three carefully targeted, important new educational programs: prekindergarten for at-risk four-year-olds; scholarships for college and technical institute; and technology for our schools. These three programs have already been developed in detail; the groundwork for their operation has already been laid. In some cases, we have even begun pilots around the state in anticipation of the lottery. So that there will be virtually no lag time until the programs are up and running.

—*Downtown Atlanta Partnership, July 12, 1993*

_____

# Hope Scholarship Program

All parents want their children to succeed and to have a better life than they did. There are thousands of Georgia families who understand that college holds the key to personal success for their children. They have been urging their kids to do well in school, and scrimping and saving along the way to send them to college. In the meantime, tuition costs have been rising, and, sadly, too many of our families are realizing that their savings have left them too rich to qualify for most college aid, but too poor to actually pay the high cost of college.

—*Georgia Superintendents Association, Oct 29, 1992*

_____

What we've had is a system where the rich could afford whatever college they wanted, and the poor could qualify for federal assistance. But middle-income families found themselves with too much money to qualify for aid, but too little money to pay the bill on their own. HOPE begins at the point where the federal low-income Pell Grants end, and helps middle-income families to send their children to college or technical institute.

*—Downtown Atlanta Partnership, July 13, 1993*

_____

Of course, Georgia's population does include parents who graduated from college and who are raising their children and saving their money under the firm assumption that their children will go to college, too. But if Georgia is to continue to run out in front of the nation and the Southeast in jobs created, if we are to have the educated workforce we need for the future, we must reach beyond this group, and attract Georgia students who will be the first generation in their family to attend college... students who did not grow up with saving for college firmly fixed in their family budget and traditions... students who have been afraid to dream of college, because they don't think they'll ever be able to afford to go there... The HOPE program is an incentive for these students to work hard and keep their grades up in high school, because if they do, they can dream about going to college and know that their dream will come true.

*—Gordon College, August 18, 1993*

_____

The American Dream has always been that if you work hard and play by the rules, you can go places, you can be somebody. That's what the HOPE Scholarship Program is about. It's not about income levels; it's about giving young students an incentive to study and work hard in school, by rewarding their achievement with a chance to get the education they need for the jobs of tomorrow—jobs they can build a future on, jobs they can raise a family on. HOPE takes those important traditional values of discipline, hard work, and rewarding achievement, and uses them as the base for an exciting new educational opportunity that is aimed at the future.

HOPE is the most comprehensive and far-reaching state scholarship program in the nation. It astounds people from other states when you tell them that in Georgia, virtually any student who graduates from high school with a B average can get their tuition, mandatory fees, and books paid at a state college or university. If they keep a B average each and every year through college, they can have that scholarship renewed for all four years. If they choose to attend a Georgia private college, they can get $2,000 a year in scholarship assistance.

We are getting calls from other states all around the nation, wanting to meet with us and find out more about HOPE. They want to know how we did it. Colleges and universities in the states around us are particularly envious. I hear Clemson is trying to find a way to move the state line to the other side of their campus.....

I believe that HOPE is going to make a profound difference in Georgia as we move toward the 21st century, a difference that is absolutely critical to our future.... As our businesses and industries race toward the 21st century, they are undergoing rapid technological change, and the key to the thousands of new jobs that are now being created in Georgia is education. The education requirements of the average job are rising steadily and will soon pass two years of college or technical training. More than ever before, what you learn determines what you earn.

Georgia, unfortunately, does not have a strong tradition of sending its young people to college or to a technical institute. The HOPE Scholarship Program is coming right at the very time when Georgia's education level and workforce skills need to make a quantum leap forward. I believe that HOPE is the springboard that will give Georgia the educational momentum we need to prosper in the 21st century.

*—College Financial Aid officers, June 1, 1994*

HOPE's benefits begin long before those students darken the doorway of their first college class. One Georgia journalist quipped that the program was named for the emotion that parents experience on report-card day. Parents of high school students and even middle school students are more involved with their children's education, because they want their children to earn the good grades it takes to become a HOPE scholar.

*—Met Life Teacher Survey Discussion, Washington, D.C.,*
*November 29, 1995*

One of HOPE's biggest constituencies is not the students at all, but their parents. HOPE hits parents where they feel it—right in the pocketbook. It is a powerful incentive for parents to be involved in their children's education... to encourage them to do well...to stay on their case about studying and completing assignments. As the enrollment numbers show, we had a lot of parents out there who wanted to send their kids to college, but couldn't afford it. Now they can.

HOPE is also beginning to exert a powerful influence on our high schools. In determining eligibility, HOPE starts tracking everybody's grade point average down in the ninth grade. That is an incentive for students, counselors and teachers to start thinking ahead to college early on, when students still have a chance to compile the strong academic record they will need for college.

Critics of the HOPE program say they expect it to foster grade inflation—that soon every Georgia student will graduate from high school with a B average. Actually, grade inflation was around for a long time before HOPE. What HOPE did, was expose it in a major and systematic way, like never before. HOPE follows the vast majority of our top-tier high school students into college and watches how well they do. For the first time, we can see exactly how many of them are not able to sustain their B average under the rigors of college work and lose their scholarship benefits, and public pressure is coming bear on high schools statewide to turn out graduates who are better prepared for college.

In addition, the University System of Georgia is engaged in a comprehensive drive for excellence that involves raising the admission requirements at our public colleges over the next few years. HOPE's incentive for higher student achievement is working in tandem with the raising of college admission standards. It's like the track coach who slowly raises the high jump bar, while at the same time providing incentives for his athletes to jump higher.

HOPE also supports our drive for excellence in higher education by making Georgia's public and private colleges more competitive in recruiting top students. HOPE is keeping most of our brightest and best in the state. This is not a scientific survey, but every June I invite the valedictorians from every single high school in the state to a big party at the Governor's Mansion. I personally greet each student and their parents, and one of the things I always ask them is where they are going to college. My first year in office, 1991, I'd say 40, maybe even 50 percent of these top students were going out of state to college. This spring, I'd say about 15 percent were going out of state.

So you can see that HOPE is having a direct and powerful influence on all three of the critical constituencies involved in making education work—students, parents, and schools. It starts even before they get to high school, and continues on up through college.

*—ECS, July 3, 1996*

-----

## Prekindergarten Program

I sat and heard the Readiness Panel yesterday say that there is a vast difference between kids who have been to preschool and those who have not. Five-year-olds who do not know their numbers and letters or even colors, and who have not developed social and communication skills, are already far behind when they walk in the classroom door on the first day of kindergarten. Most will never catch up. Most will drop out.

The majority of three-to-five year olds in Georgia's low and middle income families are not in preschool. Georgia's Head Start program focuses only on four-year-olds from families who are below the federal poverty level, and it serves only a fraction of them. That is why preschool for four-year-olds is one of my top priorities and will be again next session. We have got to get the rest of our at-risk preschoolers into educational programs.

*—Governor's Conference on Education, October 18, 1991*

-----

A recent study by the Carnegie Institute found that 40 percent of Georgia's kindergarten kids are at risk when they walk in the door on the first day of school, and it's interesting note that the percentage of Georgia kids who drop out of school is about the same. Most of these children are weighed down by poverty, hunger, health or emotional problems, abusive homes or violent neighborhoods—problems that get in the way of learning. Yet education is the single best solution for them, and it is a fact that participation in a quality prekindergarten program creates the framework for success as an adult.

In a study begun in 1960 in Ypsilanti, Michigan, young children in a low-income neighborhood were divided into two groups—one was sent to preschool, the other was not. Then they all went to the same elementary school, and their lives followed a predictable pattern from then on. Those children have been closely tracked over the years. At the age of 27 there was still a distinct difference in the lives of those who attended preschool. As 27-year-old adults, those who went to preschool had higher income and education levels. They were more likely to have a stable family and own a house. They had required fewer social services, and they were less likely to have been arrested for any reason. The cost of sending them to preschool was repaid many times over in savings to social service and corrections programs and in the higher level of tax revenue they generated.

This fall the first phase of Georgia's prekindergarten will begin at 129 sites, and we hope to add at least 30 more communities early in 1994. These programs are as different as the communities where they're located. In some places, it's a class of four-year-olds at the local school. In others, it's an expanded Head Start program, or a non-profit program in the educational wing of a church. In every case, the local community decided what would be best according to their own needs and resources, then made a proposal to the state. And in every community, a caseworker will make sure that the families of these four-year-olds are getting the services they need.

—*Downtown Atlanta Partnership, July 13, 1993*

---

I don't believe that it's mere coincidence that Georgia's dropout rate is about the same as the percentage of kids who are struggling in kindergarten. I suspect that the 40 percent of five-year-olds who are at risk when they start kindergarten, are pretty much the same 40 percent that eventually drop out of school. What each of you is doing with four-year-olds and their families in your communities is the first and most important step in reducing our dropout rate....

We started with youngsters who are at risk, because they are the ones who need it the most. But I want to continue to expand it and carry it forward in the direction of a statewide voluntary prekindergarten program for all four year olds—at risk or not.

I want to point out two things about Georgia's prekindergarten program that are unique, because they illustrate some of the broader changes I am working on in education. First, we are not handing down any cookie-cutter models from the state level. Each local community makes their own decisions about the structure and shape of their prekindergarten program. Each of your programs is unique, because each one was developed by a team from your community to make the best possible use of your resources to meet your needs.

Of course that kind of freedom to make decisions brings with it a high level of responsibility. It's easy to sit back and criticize the decisions that somebody else has made. It's a lot harder to get out front yourself and try to make things happen. That's why we're having this conference. In addition to giving you financial resources for your programs, we also want to help you with the ideas and the knowledge and the networking you need to make your program a success.

The second thing that makes Georgia's prekindergarten program unique is the way it brings community resources together to address the full spectrum of needs that face our four-year-olds and their families. I believe in partnerships, because whenever we work together and coordinate our resources, it becomes possible to take what we have and make it do something more. In the case of prekindergarten, cooperation can do more than simply make each of you more effective in your own jobs as prekindergarten teachers or case workers or public health nurses or whatever. When all of your efforts come together and you intervene in coordinated ways in the life of a family that is at risk, a synergy happens that breaks into their old pattern of family life. That's how you really make a difference in the life of a four-year-old who is at risk—not just by teaching school readiness skills, but also by tackling the underlying problems that prevent our children from getting those readiness skills in the first place.

In closing, I'd like to go back to where I began and emphasize again that if we really want to improve education, we need more than new programs. We need old values. Disciplined students. Involved parents. Committed teachers. I may be old fashioned, but I believe that when it comes to education, children have to study, parents have to care and teachers have to inspire. There's no government program that can force all that to happen. But I believe that programs like prekindergarten set the stage for it to happen, and as an old school teacher, I can tell you there's no stopping a child when it does.

*—Georgia Prekindergarten Conference, June 13, 1994*

---

Right now Georgia leads the 50 states with the most comprehensive prekindergarten program that serves the largest percentage of four-year-olds, both at risk and not at risk. I am committed to providing prekindergarten for every four-year-old whose parents want it.

The Office of School Readiness will strengthen prekindergarten by bringing together the various functions that address and affect this program from the Departments of Education and Human Resources. At the state level, we will be able to give our four-year-olds the concentrated attention they deserve, as well as streamline our operations. At the local level, prekindergarten programs will have one central point of contact with the state, reducing confusion and eliminating red tape, so that they can focus more of their time and attention on our children.

*—Bill Signing Ceremony, Office of School Readiness, March 29, 1996*

Georgia has the most comprehensive, most extensive prekindergarten program in the United States, and we are the first state to make prekindergarten available to all parents who want their four-year-olds to attend. In some senses, we are like Christopher Columbus, sailing into uncharted waters where no one else has ever gone, and I want to thank all of you all for being part of the crew on the Nina, the Pinta and the Santa Maria.

I am firmly convinced that we are not going to come to the edge of the world and fall off, which was the prevailing opinion when Columbus set sail. I believe this journey is going to take us to a New World. We are seeing the signs of it already.

We have begun tracking the children who were in prekindergarten during the 1993-94 school year. In first grade, they took their first Iowa Test of Basic Skills, and beat both their Georgia peers who did not go to pre-K and the national average. They also have better attendance records, and 96 percent of their parents say they can still see the difference that pre-K made.....

Of course, the critics of Georgia's prekindergarten program want to write it off as merely a baby-sitting service. But you are proof that they are wrong. You are teachers in the truest sense of the word, and you are serious about getting Georgia's four-year-olds ready to learn in kindergarten and beyond. You are here because you want to understand the best and most appropriate ways to get kids ready to succeed in school.....

The only group of people who are more enthusiastic than you teachers about prekindergarten is the parents. This month is registration time for next year, and this is the only state program I know of where citizens get up out of bed in the middle of the night and take their lawn chairs and blankets and line-up outside prekindergarten facilities to be first to register and make sure their children get a slot.

Last fall we asked Georgia State University to do a survey of the parents of pre-K kids to see what they like about prekindergarten. It was resoundingly clear that parents understand that you are not only providing their children with the foundation for academic success in school. But you are also teaching them many other skills that are essential for normal, healthy development, like social skills and how to make friends.

They are confident that you are doing a good job. They like interacting with you as teachers, and they feel that you are a team with them in helping their children develop. Many of them said they have learned strategies from pre-K teachers that are effective at home, and that they have increased the time they spend in activities with their children as a result of what they learned from pre-K teachers.

That is why we want you to know what works, based on actual, practical experience, in providing appropriate learning experiences for four-year-olds. This training conference is like a cookbook to a chef. The point is not to school you in a particular pre-K curriculum, but simply to give you the best proven practical ways to teach science activities, math readiness activities, social development—proven recipes and cooking tips for teaching children basic pre-K skills and concepts.

Teachers and teaching assistants are the backbone of educating our children. I may have laid the preliminary groundwork with the politicians and bureaucrats to get prekindergarten underway, but you are the ones who make a difference in the lives of our four-year-olds. In the process, you are the ones who have led this program to the national and international recognition it has received. For a brief nine months, you hold in your hands our hope for the future. I know you give those children your devoted care.

*—Prekindergarten Teacher Training Conference, April 25, 1997*

## Education Technology

Let me tell you briefly about another exciting education bill that I initiated in this year's General Assembly. It's going to set up the best distance learning program in the nation. Here in Georgia, we have been struggling for years to find enough math and science teachers, and we've come to realize that it's a problem nationwide. They are simply not available. But even if they were, we've got a lot of small, rural systems that do not have the numbers of students or a big enough tax base to hire teachers for advanced courses in math, science and foreign language.

So we're going to try something new. We're going to set up a satellite network that will allow students in small, rural systems to join advanced classes offered by our larger urban systems. A student in Mitchell County might be part of a class in Russian that's being taught in DeKalb County. Or a small group of seniors from Dawson County might take physics with a class in Marietta. I do not exaggerate. This program has the potential to revolutionize education in rural Georgia.

*—PAGE Academic Excellence Banquet, March 28, 1992*

It is not enough just to buy the computers. Our teachers must also know how to make the best possible use of this educational tool. They need to understand the hardware and the software, to direct appropriate use by students and track their progress, and to assimilate the computer into the curriculum together with the other teaching tools and methods they use.

This is an important skill to incorporate into our teacher training programs. But it's even more vital for the teachers we have in our classrooms right now. The personal computer is so much a part of our daily lives, that it's easy to forget that it was invented only a decade ago. Nearly two-thirds of Georgia's classroom teachers were trained and developed their style and methods before the personal computer came into existence. So at the same time we are bringing computers into Georgia's classrooms, we must also give Georgia teachers the skills they need to make the best use of this wonderful resource.....

These Education Technology Centers represent a partnership not only between the University System and the State Department of Education, but also with private industry... (They) will give teachers and administrators hands-on experience and training with educational technology, as well as demonstrating state-of-the-art hardware and software. Thanks to the Georgia Lottery for Education, and especially to the generosity of our private industry donors, our statewide network of Education Technology Centers for teachers will be up and running inside of a year, enabling Georgia schools to take a quantum leap forward in using technology to better serve our children.

*—Open Valdosta State University Education Technology Center,*
*July 1, 1993*

———————

My primary goal as Governor has been to improve education and create new opportunities for Georgia's students to learn. That's why I created Georgia's pre-K program to get our four-year-olds ready to learn, and the HOPE Scholarship Program to assist Georgia students with the cost of attending college or technical school.

Distance learning technology is another way that we have enriched and expanded the educational opportunities of Georgia students in very significant ways. Distance learning comes in several different forms, and I am proud to say that Georgia is a leader in all of them. We were the first state to put a satellite dish at every single public school, college and technical institute, and one of the first to own a transponder on a TelStar satellite to send out programming. We now lead the nation by several measures of producing and using satellite-based distance learning. We are also one of the few states to have systematic Internet connections and local dial-in access for every single public school, college, technical institute, and library.

The Conservation Action Resource Center here at Zoo Atlanta is part of yet a third kind of distance learning. It is an interactive, televideo-conferencing system that communicates over high-speed telephone lines. It is called the Georgia Statewide Academic and Medical System or GSAMS for short. It is a partnership that includes the State of Georgia and Bell South.

GSAMS connects all of Georgia's public colleges, universities, and technical institutes, plus about 400 of our public schools. It also connects resources like hospitals and Chambers of Commerce and Zoo Atlanta. Up to twelve different sites can interact with each other at the same time. GSAMS brings medical expertise to Georgia's rural hospitals. GSAMS allows Georgia business people to talk with our eleven trade offices around the world. GSAMS enables students to join a class that is being taught in another part of the state.

And GSAMS takes Georgia school children on "virtual field trips," not only here to Zoo Atlanta itself, but to many other exciting places, because GSAMS sites can be connected not only to each other, but to other video-conferencing systems around the nation and the world.

*—Dedicate Zoo Atlanta Conservation Action Resource Center,*
*April 23, 1998*

## Teachers

In the play, *A Man for All Seasons,* the British Lord Chancellor Sir Thomas More is confronted by an ambitious young man looking for the way to fortune and fame. More advises him to become a teacher. "A teacher?" says the incredulous young man. "Why? And if I were good, who would know?" More says, "Your pupils, your friends, God—not a bad public, that."

He was right; it wasn't a bad public in those days and it still isn't. But education's public has grown much broader since *A Man for All Seasons* was written. Fate has set the modern world on a course that places a heavy load of responsibility on teachers and schools. The future of our nation's economy, the continuation of our level of prosperity, and our position of world leadership rests squarely on your shoulders.

Your students are your product, and the consumers of that product are the nation's business community. Your consumers will tell you that performance is the ultimate test. That is true for your human products just as it is for technology, and the performance of our high school graduates has this nation's business community scared. Corporate America is now spending $210 billion a year to educate and train their employees. That's about $30 billion more than the nation spends for its primary and secondary schools. True, some of that is for in-house technical training, but a lot of it is remedial work in basic skills that our schools have failed to teach.

The past few decades have been tough on our schools... tough on our teachers. At the same time the massive challenge I just described has been mounting up before you, the nation has been changing in ways that have made your job harder. Many of your students have only one parent in the home, and teachers often do not get the kind of parental cooperation and support they used to.

As society has grown more complex, so have its problems. Many of those problems fall to our schools to address. In addition to the three R's, we have asked you to teach drug education and sex education. We have asked you to take the lead in counteracting our historic tendency to discriminate against women and minorities. We have asked you to give special attention to at-risk students, handicapped students, and other students with special needs. Yet our school day and school year are no longer than they ever were. As a result, much of this social education has come at the expense of academic skills rather than in addition to academic skills.

We have also not given you a level of reward and recognition that is commensurate with the magnitude and importance of the task you face. The next few years are going to produce increased expectations of you and increased pressures on you. But the next few years must also provide increased incentives for you and increased rewards to you....

(Here are) three issues that affect you personally. First, the Governor's Task Force on Teacher Pay for Performance. You ask any type of business anywhere in this country how they get their employees to turn out a good product, they will all tell you the same thing: Provide incentives, evaluate performance, reward good work, weed out the worst. This approach is a matter of course in just about any business or profession except teaching. In teaching, we have an operation where no one is rewarded for success and no one is punished for failure.

I am not proposing that we get rid of the present salary schedule, and I do not have any preconceived notions about how pay-for-performance ought to work. But I am convinced that great teaching must be rewarded in the same ways as great performance in any other business or profession. There will never be enough money to pay our good teachers what they are really worth as long as we insist on paying all others the very same thing.

Second, teacher certification. I am convinced that the only way to get certification on the right track is to reorganize it from a whole different perspective. I have a bill before the General Assembly to do just that. The whole certification process will be moved out of the Department of Education, so that the Department focuses its attention on curriculum and services for our schools. Teacher certification will be placed under a reorganized Professional Standards Commission with a new board that I will appoint. This is a much smaller agency whose entire attention can be focused on assuring professional quality. The purpose is not to ease up on the professional quality we expect from our teachers, but to get rid of the obstacles that keep many qualified people out of the classroom.

We have teachers moving into this state who would like to continue teaching in Georgia, but can't because certification is so cumbersome. We have men and women out there with impeccable academic credentials—some of them also with years of success in another profession—who are drawn to the classroom in search of a new professional challenge. Our colleges and universities take advantage of such people, but unwieldy certification requirements have kept them out of our public schools. Isaac Stern, for example, could not teach music at Northside High School. I couldn't be certified to teach Georgia government.

Third, testing. This week State Superintendent Werner Rogers and I announced a new system of accountability to assess student learning. Its goals are twofold: First, to reduce the excessive number of tests that are now administered, relieving you of some of that burden and allowing us to downsize the testing apparatus of the Department. But at the same time, we will test greater content mastery and a higher level of thinking skills. The modern work force demands a higher level of skills from our students, and we need to step up our efforts to meet that demand.

These three issues—performance pay, certification, and testing—address the integrity of the teaching profession. And let me stop right here for a moment and talk about that to you heart to heart, as one teacher to another. Yes, I consider myself a teacher, and I consider teaching a profession. As a teacher, I consider myself a professional. The realities of today's world call teachers to a higher level of professional excellence and intensity than has ever been demanded of you before.

I, Zell Miller, have a deep confidence in the ability of our teachers to rise to that challenge. But I don't think the public does, given the academic shortcomings of job applicants and the resistance teachers have already demonstrated to professional standards. If you want the public to regard you as professionals, to be willing to pay you as professionals, to have faith that you will perform as professionals, you will have to demonstrate your own ability to perform in the classroom and the ability of your product—your students—to perform on the job.

Our brightest young people are being attracted to investment banking and big law firms instead of teaching. Now I don't have anything against bankers or lawyers—my wife is the former and my son the latter. But their role is to provide essential services to our society. Neither one produces anything that drives our economy forward. Teachers, on the other hand, are responsible for generating the most critical of all products demanded by a modern economy—the literate worker....

We are going to have to make changes if we are to find and keep enough quality teachers. We must increase not only the compensation and rewards, but also the professionalism and the level of respect in the community. They are intertwined....

My parents were both teachers. My sister is a teacher. As I said, I think of myself as a teacher, and I expect to return to the classroom when I leave public office. Whether you believe it or not, I feel a special kinship with you.

The Miller Administration is dedicated to improving education. That is why I got into politics in the first place, and now that I have reached this office, I intend to use this opportunity to make as much progress as I possibly can to prepare our educational system for the 21st century.

*—Georgia Association of Educators, February 15, 1991*

---

When I was inaugurated Governor, the guest of honor, seated in the center of the front row, was a teacher of mine from Young Harris College. Edna Herren influenced my life in profound and pervasive ways that continue to have an impact on me after all these years. You can have all the national and state reform initiatives you want, but a good teacher is what will change your life forever.

Even though I've been away from the classroom for a while, I've tried to retain my teacher's perspective on education. As a former—and future—teacher, I know that the heart of the education process is the relationship of teacher, student, and subject matter in the classroom. I am convinced that you will never improve education unless you do something that touches that relationship in the classroom.

So the mission of my administration is to create opportunities: Opportunities for teachers and schools to innovate and create new and more effective working models of education. I want to give you the opportunity to shake out of the rut of allowing rules and regulations to dictate your decisions, and go back to drawing on the strengths and commitment that got you into teaching in the first place: Your love for children, the thrill of seeing their eyes light up and the wheels turn in their minds, your belief in their ability to learn if they are challenged in appropriate ways.

*—Teacher of the Year Conference, May 8, 1993*

---

# Technical and Adult Education

Early in this century, a maverick car manufacturer named Henry Ford pioneered a system of mass production that became the standard for American industry. The idea was simple: Break complex tasks down into a number of simple, rote actions which an unskilled worker could repeat over and over again, with machine-like efficiency. Based on this model, America developed a thriving economy that offered decent-paying, assembly-line jobs for low-skilled workers—jobs that enabled them to buy houses, raise families, and drive nice cars, all without a high school diploma.

Then in the 1970s came the imports, and suddenly American manufacturers had to compete with goods produced overseas where wages were lower and labor was cheaper. Production costs had to be cut, and many American manufacturers began to send their jobs overseas. Today over 700 American companies have manufacturing facilities in Mexico, Singapore, and Taiwan that employ 350,000 people. There are many, many more companies who contract with overseas manufacturers for products, on which the American company then just puts its brand name. Because of all this, American productivity has slowed almost to a standstill, and many low-skilled workers have found themselves out of a job.

Other forces also were at work in the global economy at the same time. Products were becoming more sophisticated; the process of manufacturing more complex. New products were being introduced more frequently, and quality was becoming more important to consumers. Not only was labor too expensive, but the old Henry Ford system was too cumbersome and inflexible to meet these new market demands.

Let's face the reality of the situation: The cold, hard fact is that our low-skill, high-wage manufacturing system, designed nearly a century ago, is no longer an option. It is no longer possible to drop out of school after the eighth grade and earn a good living with strength, sweat, and strain. Muscle power has become a low-wage commodity. The only way for high-wage nations like us to succeed in our modern, global economy is to send the Henry Ford model the same way as the Model T, and move to manufacturing systems that are more efficient and complex than low-wage, low-skill countries are capable of.

The rote tasks of low-skill assembly-line workers are being taken over by new, computerized equipment. In some cases, one single piece of sophisticated machinery can replace as many as a dozen people. What's more, the middle manager who supervised those dozen assembly-line workers is gone, too, and the decisions that used to be made by the supervisor are now made by that lone front-line worker who operates the new machine.

It requires a new breed of front-line worker—one with a higher level of skills and abilities. One who understands how both the process and the equipment work, and can make sound decisions based on that knowledge. If Georgia is to prosper in the future, we must make the transition from a low-skill, labor-intensive industrial base to a high-skill, technology-based economy. That is the bottom line.

My friends, it is not merely a step forward that we must take, it is a quantum leap ....

We dare not leave today's illiterate adults behind as we move toward the 21st century, not only because of the severe limitations to their personal lives, but also because we have got to have them in our workforce. Eighty-five percent of the workforce of the year 2000 is already on the job. It is clearly a case of needing to dance with the ones who are already out on the dance floor.

That is why we must work toward a higher level of literacy among today's workers, and that is why one of the first legislative acts of my administration was a tax credit for workplace literacy programs, making Georgia one of the first states to offer tangible incentives for businesses to help their employees toward literacy.

*—Technical and Adult Education Literacy Conference,*
*March 19, 1992*

---

We used to consider literacy as a social issue. Reading was nice for parents and grandparents to do with children, but their livelihood didn't depend on it. But those days are gone with the wind. Today's technology demands more brains than brawn, and adult literacy has now become a matter of economics—a matter of an individual's ability to earn a living and a company's ability to hire a skilled workforce.

The Census Bureau recently took at look at their 1990 data to see how education correlated with income, and they put out a report called "What's It Worth?" In hard dollars, here is what they found education to be worth: High school drop-outs are earning an average of $492 a month. High school graduates are earning an average of $1,077 a month. College graduates are earning $2,231 a month.

Think of it! High school graduates are now earning more than twice as much as drop-outs, while college graduates earn more than four times more money than drop-outs.

It is not that those with education are earning so much more, but that those without education are seeing a dramatic drop in their earning power as the literacy level demanded by the average job increases. From the mid-70s to the mid-80s, the average earnings of males, ages 20-34, who had dropped out of high school, plummeted by 35 percent. Between 1973 and 1988, unemployment among high-school drop-outs increased by 24 percent, while unemployment among college graduates declined.

We have a growing population of adults who face chronic unemployment because they do not have the education or skills to get a job. At the same time, many Georgia businesses are going out of state to recruit skilled workers....

HOPE has an incentive for drop-outs who go back for their GED. GED recipients can get a $500 certificate for books and fees if they continue their education at a college or technical institute. And if that GED recipient goes into a diploma program at a technical institute, HOPE would pay their tuition.

But that's not all. Another component of the lottery expenditures is an unprecedented effort to bring technology into our education programs. I have proposed that we use $1.6 million in lottery proceeds to purchase computers for adult literacy. These funds will connect providers on a network, enable us to address the literacy needs of handicapped persons, assist the Satellite Literacy Project, and give small businesses access to literacy training for their employees....

But I'm not counting on technology entirely. There is nothing like a real live person to encourage you and answer your questions when you're trying to learn. Some of the neediest parts of the state are isolated, rural areas, where illiteracy is common, but it is hard to find enough qualified volunteers to tackle the problem. I think that Georgia ought to have at least one full-time adult literacy teacher in every single county, and I want to reach that goal over the next two years. For next year, I have recommended $2.7 million from the general treasury to hire 68 more adult literacy teachers.

Whenever your hear somebody say that Georgia leads the nation, it's usually in something undesirable. But I am proud to say today that Georgia continues to lead the nation in the provision of the Adult Basic Education Tax Credit for employers who sponsor or provide educational programs leading to a GED for their employees.

Nearly 100 employers are registered with the Department of Technical and Adult Education for this tax credit.... I worked with IBM to create the Governor's Awards for Achievement in Workplace Learning to reward Georgia companies who make a significant contribution to literacy among their employees. More than 130 companies have qualified for awards in the two years since we created it. The Gold Award recognizes companies with basic skill development programs for their employees... The Platinum Award honors companies whose entire workforce has reached at least an 8th grade level in reading and math.

—*Technical and Adult Education Literacy Conference,*
*February 26, 1993*

---

Traditionally, high schools have focused on students who are college bound. Those students take a demanding academic curriculum, and are counseled on how to choose a college and be admitted. But the remaining 60 percent of high school students have too often been benchwarmers, just marking time until graduation.

It's not so much that schools haven't cared about these kids. It's more that they didn't used to need a strong arsenal of skills. In the 1950s and 60s and 70s, they could get a low-skill job in a labor-intensive plant or a mill and still earn a decent living, or if they were naturally good with a wrench, they could become a mechanic at the local garage. But by the 80s, that had begun to change, and today, in the 90s, most of those low-skill jobs have gone with the wind.

Industries now require more skills and a higher level of performance from their employees. Even the cars of today feature high-tech electronics, that require specially trained mechanics to maintain. Here in Atlanta, the education level required by the average job is rapidly approaching 14 years. All of our students need strong academic skills, not just those who will go on to college, and Georgia's 32 post-secondary technical institutes have been working with the high schools in their catchment areas to create a Tech Prep track.

In Georgia, we're proud especially proud of two unique assets that are helping us to develop a strong Tech Prep program. As some of you may know, Georgia recently began a state lottery. Now that's not unusual in itself—we were the 35th state in the nation to do it. What is unique is that Georgia's lottery proceeds are specifically designated for three new education programs, above and beyond our normal education funding. One of those programs is HOPE—Helping Outstanding Pupils Educationally. Beginning this fall, HOPE is paying for the tuition of every single student enrolled in a diploma program at every single post-secondary technical institute in the State of Georgia. Cost is no longer an obstacle to prevent Georgia students from getting on the Tech Prep track and getting the job training they need to succeed in the workforce.

Second, in Georgia, we deliberately give high school juniors and seniors a chance to try courses at colleges and technical institutes. Not only do we give them high school credit for such courses, we also transfer the per-pupil education funds from the state education funding formula with them to help cover the cost. This flexibility to blur the line a little between high school and technical institute is an asset to Tech Prep as we work toward a seamless transition between these two levels of education.

We cannot sit idly by and allow our young people to mortgage their own future as individuals as well as the future of our economy. We must provide them with opportunities to get the education and jobs that will make them personally successful, and at the same time drive our economy forward.

—*National Tech Prep Network Conference, September 27, 1993*

---

More than ever before, the future of this state and the prosperity of its citizens lies in education, because more than ever before, what you learn determines what you earn.

As our economy races toward the future, business and industry are undergoing a rapid technological evolution. Jobs that require no skills are disappearing, and the earning power of Americans with no training has been declining over the past 15 years. High school drop-outs have seen their wage rates literally collapse and their unemployment rates soar.

Many of our drop-outs left school because they weren't interested in going to college, and they didn't see any connection between what was happening at school and getting a job. That's why I have a proposal before the General Assembly right now to begin a Youth Apprenticeship program for high school students. This program is designed for students who want to get out of school and start earning money. It is going to expose them to the workplace while they are still in school, so that they begin to understand firsthand that holding a job requires skills and responsibilities on their part. Then it is going to help them learn those skills and responsibilities that will be required of them in the workplace.

From the perspective of employers, the program is designed to graduate high school students who are better prepared to be effective on the job. It is also designed to mesh with our post-secondary technical institutes, because during their time as apprentices, a lot of high school students are going to see for themselves that the good job opportunities take some additional technical training.

But back to the kids who drop out of school. The realization that a good job now requires education and training has not yet had an impact on our drop-out rate. Where the shift in the workforce toward skilled jobs is reflected right now is in our GED students.

Not only has the number of GED graduates been steady increasing in recent years, reaching nearly 18,000 last year, but more than 60 percent of Georgia's GED students are under the age of 25. A third of them are under the age of 19. The point of realizing just how critical education is, comes soon after our kids have dropped out of school when they're trying to find a job. That's when they begin to see firsthand how badly they have handicapped themselves by limiting their education. That's when they begin to realize that without education, their future is a dead-end. And it doesn't take long before a lot of them are back at the books in a GED program.

*—Technical and Adult Education Literacy Conference,*
*February 25, 1994*

As our economy races toward the future, business and industry are undergoing a rapid technological evolution. This evolution is creating more job opportunities than it's closing off. But the key to this new, emerging breed of jobs that is coming to dominate our employment growth is technical skills. The old industrial hierarchy of an army of unskilled workers orchestrated by lower-level supervisors who are overseen by middle managers is rapidly breaking down. Our factories and mills are being run by teams of skilled problem-solvers who oversee computerized machinery.

For example, take the average Ford Motors plant. In 1990, only 18 percent of its manufacturing functions were controlled by computers. Today—just four years later—82 percent of its functions are controlled by computers. This technological conversion of the past few years is why American car manufacturers are now moving aggressively on the world market, while Japanese and European manufacturers are still mired in an international recession. It also means a lot of unskilled jobs have been taken over by machines in the past four years, and Ford is now looking to hire trained technicians to monitor and adjust the computers—jobs that pay more than $30,000 a year.

Or take another example. A new breed of truck driver is emerging who not only delivers complex machinery to clients, but has the skills and tools to custom-assemble it on the spot. The growing demand is not for truck drivers per se, but for technicians who drive a truck as part of the job.

Jobs that require no skills are disappearing, and the earning power of Americans with no training has been declining over the past 15 years. High school drop-outs have seen their wage rates literally collapse and their unemployment rates soar....

Georgians understand that, and they are knocking on the doors of our technical institutes in record numbers, seeking training for the jobs of the future—jobs they can build a life and raise a family on.

*—Vocational Education Legislative Breakfast, February 17, 1994*

## Education Commission of the States

We must be clearer about our program outcomes and more rigorous about our program evaluations.... Educators are not geared toward measurable outcomes, and even ineffective programs have entrenched constituencies, but we must become more critical of outcomes as we cut and reconfigure existing programs. And we must build evaluation mechanisms into the new programs we carefully develop with our limited resources during the 90s.

*—July 19, 1991*

———————

The problem, as I understand it, is primarily that our approach to education has changed very little during the past 25 years, whereas the world in which we live has changed dramatically.

Our schools have been doing a good job of serving a culture that no longer exists. Our challenge is to take a system that has not kept up, and re-form it for the 21st century.

We've been working on it pretty hard for a decade now...We've had "A Nation at Risk;" we've had "America 2000." They have helped to identify problems and set broad national goals. But the fact is, most of it has been coming from the top down.

Education policy makers get together at conferences like this one. We have substantive sessions and discussions, and it's great. We go home feeling good. But does it make any difference in the classrooms of our states?

As a former—and future—teacher, I know that the heart of the education process is the relationship of teacher, student, and subject matter in the classroom. Until change touches that relationship, I don't care what else we do, true education reform will never be realized. So the mission before us, the mission of my administration, is to move on to the next stage of education reform, which is creating tangible opportunities: Opportunities for students, opportunities for teachers and schools to innovate and create new and more effective working models of education.

There are two characteristics I want to see develop in Georgia's schools, that I believe will truly bring about change and opportunity. And I realize that not all of you will agree with me.

First, I want to see our schools belong to their local communities, and not to state government.

Children are not educated in the Governor's Office or the Department of Education. After observing it for a number of years, I have concluded that decisions made in any place far removed from the classroom, usually serve the internal convenience of the bureaucracy rather than the real needs of students.

All of you are respected education leaders, but I think you will agree that the true education leaders, the ones who really make the difference, are the teachers and principals, and the parents and community leaders at the level of the local school. They are the ones I want to see now step forward and become the decision makers. I want to see the lines of communication run across organizations in the local community, and not just up and down inside the educational bureaucracy.

Second, in my opinion, we must change our sense of purpose, and we must change the ways in which we evaluate progress. For years, the way we have measured progress has been to list programs and to count noses. If the programs existed and the kids showed up, we considered the job well done. In IRS fashion, we set out to establish the official, the correct way to do education, and we created lots of paperwork and countless regulations to make sure everybody did it just right ... in the same official way.

But, it is finally dawning on us that success cannot be measured by whether you follow all the rules and fill out all the forms. Success can be measured only, only by the results you achieve.

We have America 2000. It has given us six national goals, good ones. You know them as well as I. They range from readiness to learn in our preschoolers to stronger math and science programs, from a safe and drug-free learning environment to fewer drop-outs. Okay, we all agree, so what we ought to be doing now is making and measuring progress toward those goals.

Combine these two characteristics—ownership of local schools by their communities and a focus on educational goals instead of regulations—and I believe we can create a climate in which education can be re-invented from the bottom up.

*—May 1, 1993*

---

State government has traditionally assumed primary responsibility for education, and that, I believe very strongly, is going to be increasingly true in the future. The federal constitution says nothing about education, and as Washington tightens up its own belt, I expect it to withdraw more and more from the education picture.

In contrast, our Georgia Constitution devotes an entire article to education, beginning with the words: "The provision of an adequate public education for the citizens shall be a primary obligation of the State of Georgia." Many of your constitutions probably say something similar.

As we strive to focus our limited resources on the things that our citizens want us to do, we are going to find that education is the top priority on their list, too. Parents can see that our economy is increasingly based on technology, and that the education and training requirements of the average job are continually rising. They want a good education for their children, because they know it is no longer possible to make a good life for yourself without it.

So, while our resources may be limited, this is a time of opportunity for the states. It is a time for us to become, as David Osborne is fond of calling us, "laboratories of democracy." It is a time for us to take the initiative, to step forward with new ideas in education.

The opportunity—and notice that I say "opportunity," not "challenge"—the opportunity facing the states today is to be more creative with our limited resources—to take what we have and make it do something more. We must also be more critical in evaluating the results of our efforts, so that we are engaged in a constant process of discovering what works and what doesn't, and redirecting our resources toward what works.

We can no longer claim to have improved education simply because we have increased spending. We can no longer prove that our schools are good simply by pointing to the dollars per pupil that we appropriate. Taxpayers have grown suspicious that government treasuries are akin to ratholes, and one of the emerging rules of government finance these days is to demonstrate clearly to your taxpayers how their money is being used for their benefit.

In education, the taxpaying citizens of our states are looking for concrete results in the form of improved student performance. Student achievement is the bottom line, and the efficient use of our educational resources demands that they be focused on accountability and achievement in the classroom.

*—November 13, 1995*

---

I've always looked forward to ECS meetings as an opportunity to glean new ideas to take back home in Georgia, an opportunity to learn from the experience of others as to what works and what doesn't, and, yes, an opportunity to brag a little on the new initiatives we've begun and the successes we've experienced in Georgia.

But I've also experienced a frustration that has led me to set the theme of "Investing in Student Achievement" for our work together in the upcoming year....

We are all deeply concerned about education, but to what extent does it matter to a child in the first or the third or the seventh grade in a school back home, that you and I were here today? We've been talking about "reinventing education" for a decade or more, and I believe that it's time to get pragmatic about it...to take a look at what excellence looks like in its working clothes.

My goal for the coming year is to make a direct connection between what we are doing in ECS and what happens in the classrooms in our states back home. Let's be practical about what our students need to achieve. Then let's identify the incentives that actually result in improved student achievement, and let's sort out the policies and programs and expenditures that actually make a difference and improve performance in the daily lives of our students and teachers in the classroom.

I wouldn't be up here if I didn't believe that ECS can make a significant contribution to education in this country, but I am equally convinced that the only way we can realize that potential is to be firmly grounded in the reality of student achievement in the classrooms of our states.

I believe you can put everybody in the world into one of two categories: Thinkers, or doers. My goal in life is to be a doer. And my goal for ECS is that next summer at this time, we will have some measure of achievement...something we can point to that ECS has accomplished in improving education.

I look forward to spending the next year with you, concentrating on discovering and sharing and implementing, in our states, the programs, policies, and expenditures that will make a difference where it really counts—in our classrooms and in the lives of our students.

*—Assume National Chairmanship, July 3, 1996*

---

How do you make sure what you do at the Capitol affects teachers and students in the right way? This is one of the rare instances when the easy and obvious answer is also the right one: Go out into the classroom and ask them.

I know that sounds flip, but I'm serious. Too many education experts are out of touch with the real-life, work-a-day world of students and teachers, and the educational landscape is littered with the corpses of reform efforts which did not accomplish anything because they had nothing to do with life in the classroom.

In fact, the first question you ought to ask is not whether what you are doing has the right effect on students and teachers, but whether it has any effect at all. If it doesn't, you need to stop it right there. A chemistry professor from Georgia State University said recently that she was invited to meet with an education task force that was formed to address the problem of getting women to major in science and math. She went because she wanted to ask the task force what the point was. At Georgia State, half of the undergraduate science majors are women, 58 percent of the math majors are women, and 40 percent of the math and science graduate students are women. Those percentages are continuing to rise. Here was task force of education experts, talking about how to solve a problem that did not exist out there in the classrooms and labs.

A direct, practical, real-life awareness of the classroom, and the teachers and students who work there is absolutely essential. But it is so easy to lose that connection.

*—November 22, 1996*

---

We are good at trying things. The year-end report is full of examples of innovative state programs that are underway across the nation. I strongly encourage you to read about them, because there are too many for me to describe here.

We do less well at identifying the things that don't work and trying something else instead. A recurring refrain that crops up again and again through the pages of this report, is that education policy leaders are not really very good at collecting data and evaluating it, and then steering their resources away from unproductive initiatives and toward the ones that work. Despite states' growing investment... in a variety of creative ways, there is little or no systematic evaluation of how or whether they actually affect student achievement. The mindset of public budgeting seems to be incremental—just keep on putting a little more and a little more into what you've got, without stopping to weed out what doesn't work.

In Georgia, we have an ongoing policy called "budget redirection" that requires all state agency heads to set goals for their programs, evaluate the results, cut money from those that are not productive, and shift it into those that are. A couple of years ago, we completely cut a program that served juvenile offenders who had been released from state custody. It was a program that sounded good on paper—a community-based program with a noble purpose—to reduce the recidivism rate among juvenile offenders. Who can argue with that? And from an administrative perspective, it was running smoothly. But when we looked at the results, we found that recidivism rates for kids who went through this program were not any better than for kids who didn't. That program was not making any difference at all. It was time to stop and use those resources to try something else.

I have to wonder, as I look at all of the many education programs we all have going in our respective states... How often do we claim success based on the fact that a program has a noble goal and is running smoothly, without ever stopping to evaluate the results?....

That is why as chairman I chose to focus on "Investing in Student Achievement" in the hope that this year might serve as something of a reality check, reminding all of us of the central importance of creating policies and programs that focus on the classroom and provide incentives to do things that actually make a difference.

It takes discipline to keep your sights clearly focused. Over the past year, I've often heard that Georgia is the exception because we have all that lottery money to fund our prekindergarten program for four-year-olds and our HOPE Scholarship Program for students at our colleges and technical institutes. But most of you also have state lotteries. Most of you have that same revenue source that Georgia does. The difference is that Georgia exercised the discipline to keep those revenues clearly focused on education.

As the Ferguson study found, investing in teacher quality is the most effective way to improve student achievement. So we are now in the process of increasing Georgia's teacher salaries by six percent a year for four consecutive years, enabling us to attract better quality teachers. The money to do that comes from the general treasury. It takes discipline to find it—some of it is money we have shifted away from unproductive programs—but it is a very high priority, so we cinch up our belt in other places to do it....

It is no longer possible for educators to operate on faith alone. When it comes to education initiatives, we must take as gospel that New Testament scripture that says, "By their fruits ye shall know them." The test of a good initiative must be in the results it produces. To be worthy of the name, education reform must make a difference in the classrooms of our schools. It must be firmly grounded in the reality of the classroom, and it must produce tangible improvements in student achievement.

*—July 11, 1997*

---

## Other Excerpts

I want to mention a change I proposed earlier this week: A constitutional amendment to require that all local school superintendents be appointed and all boards elected. This is going to be a tough, up-hill fight... and I intend to pursue it. There is no room for local politics if our schools are to achieve the level of excellence demanded of them. There is no room for patronage.

*—Georgia Association of Educators, February 15, 1991*

---

Every child can learn. However, not every child learns in the same way, and not all approaches to education are equally good for each student. Further, students do not learn at the same rate in each subject or at the same rate as each other. Senate Bill 417 is designed to give our high school juniors and seniors a choice, and to encourage them to find an educational arrangement that meets their individual needs.

Presently under Quality Basic Education, high school students may take courses at colleges or post-secondary schools. However, local systems, which must first approve such arrangements, do not seem to encourage them, and the high school credit given for such courses does not recognize their true value. Further, the cost of courses at a college or technical institute must be borne by the student, effectively eliminating this option for low-income students.

S.B. 417... provides that state money shall follow the student, so that state funds available for the education of a particular student would go to the source of that education on a pro-rated basis, determined by credit received. Second, one year of full-time college credit (45 quarter hours) would be equated to one year of high school credit, with lesser amounts pro-rated accordingly. Third, rather than approving such optional arrangements, the role of the local school would be to provide counseling to students and their parents, giving them the information they need to make wise choices. Colleges and technical institutes would retain the right to decide whether to accept the students.

*—Press Conference on SB 417, February 27, 1991*

---

I've found from experience that trying to achieve (education) goals... through political means is kind of like playing gin rummy. You know what your overall objectives are— what you have to do to win—but you don't have any control over the cards that are dealt to you. The challenge is to keep your sights on the goal and be flexible and creative in using whatever resources you are dealt in each hand to move as far toward those winning objectives as you can.

*—Professional Association of Georgia Educators, March 16. 1991*

---

The point of this conference is not to make a press announcement or file a report. Voltaire once described his fellow Frenchmen as railing against the injustices of their day, then eating their dinner and going to bed. We must not congratulate ourselves over a great conference and then just go home. We must make this conference different!

As I see it, our real work begins now, with the conclusion of this conference. It's easy to be for education. It's harder to make meaningful recommendations, and it's harder still to actually achieve them.

But the main lesson we must all carry with us from this conference is that fundamental change that leads to a lasting commitment to our kids and their education begins in your communities. We learned that in the 1980s—and at this conference—that top down education management simply doesn't work.

No child was ever educated in the Governor's Office or the state department or even in the county school offices. Children are educated in schools and communities, not in bureaucracies, and it is from you, the teachers, parents, and business leaders, that education change must spring.

*—Governor's Conference on Education, October 20, 1991*

---

While we're talking about constitutional amendments on the ballot next November, let me mention another one. It would result in elected school boards and appointed superintendents.

School boards are policy-setting bodies, and need to be accountable to the communities they serve. At the same time, we want local boards to recruit the best professionals in the nation to run our schools. Those professional superintendents need to devote their full attention to educating our children, without having to spend time campaigning, raising money, and messing around with politics. This amendment is part of improving the quality of our schools and the future of our children.

*—PAGE Academic Excellence Banquet, March 28, 1992*

---

Research tells us that kids remember 10 percent of what they hear, 20 percent of what they see, 40 percent of what they discuss and 90 percent of what they do. Yet we still stand the teacher up in front of rows of desks and assume that if the kids are quiet while the teacher's talking, they must be learning.

Meanwhile, as our economy has become more global, the quality of our education is being measured according to worldwide standards. Students from other countries run rings around our students, and our standard of living is declining to match our standard of education. We are having trouble competing on the global market, because our wages are too high to attract low-skill industries, and our skills are too low to attract high-paying industries. If we are to maintain our standard of living, the most critical thing we must do is upgrade the education and skills of our workforce, and that means improving our schools.

We are going to do it, but we are going about it in a new way, a way that is different from prior education reforms in this state. In some senses, we are completely upending the process and standing it on its head....

For too long, we have labored under the assumption that there is a single, "right" way to do education. All we had to do was find that "right" way, then enact a pile of rules and regulations at the state level to make sure that everyone in all of our schools did it. We have given that approach our best effort. What we learned in the process is that a school can follow all the state rules and regulations to a "T", and still not be a very lively, stimulating place where students learn and excel. So, as we move toward the 21st century, which is only eight short years away, we have set out to change our schools.

There are three things we are working toward, three characteristics we want to develop in Georgia's schools. First, we want our schools to belong to their local communities, not to state government. We want local school and community leaders to be the prime movers in changing and improving education. Our students are the whole point of education. They are both the consumers of this service and the products of the process. But when education is run from the top down, the decisions are made by people who are far removed from the students. As a result, decisions tend to serve the internal convenience of the bureaucracy, rather than responding to the needs of the students. You as local school leaders get caught in the middle. You are stuck trying to meet the needs of students according to rules and regulations that often have no relevance to students' needs and in some cases even thwart the meeting of those needs.

Last year, Georgia won a Ford Foundation award for having one of the ten top innovative government programs in the nation, and I found it interesting that the judges for that award said they never see innovations that have resulted from somebody at the top coming up with a good blueprint and making everybody follow it. Innovation and creativity are not legislated from on high. They bubble up from the bottom, from ideas that people try locally when they are encouraged to make their own decisions....

Our real education leaders are teachers and principals, but they are also parents and community leaders. When all of these people are given the opportunity to work together and make decisions about their local school, exciting things start to happen.

The second characteristic we want to encourage in our schools is a sense of mission and purpose. The decisions you make about your school should be guided not by state rules and regulations, but by the goals and objectives you want to achieve.

And third, hand in hand with making decisions based on achieving your goals, is measuring the progress you make toward accomplishing those goals. For all of its regulations, government pays very little attention to the results of its efforts. One of my greatest frustrations as Governor is the inability of state bureaucrats to tell me whether programs are accomplishing what they were created to do. Programs that aren't doing what they're supposed to do, just keep on keeping on.

Along with the opportunity to try new things comes the responsibility to evaluate them. If it works, then do more of it, and if it doesn't work, then for goodness sakes stop doing it and try something else.

In the school of the 90s, local school and community leaders take the initiative in striving for excellence, and in finding creative, innovative ways to motivate their students and improve student achievement. These local education leaders are continually evaluating the results of their efforts, expanding their successes and changing the things that turn out not to work out as well as they expected.

From your perspective as local school leaders, it probably sounds pretty exciting, but also a little nerve-wracking. After all, it's always easier to sit back and let somebody else make the decisions and assume the responsibility, rather than getting out front yourself and trying to make things happen.

If we are going to expect local school and community leaders to take responsibility for educational progress, we also need to provide the training you need to rise to the occasion. The point of the Governor's School Leadership Institute is to empower you with the vision, knowledge, and confidence you need to take charge of your school. How do you inspire your community leaders and your staff? How do you shake out of the rut of allowing rules and regulations to dictate your decisions and go back to drawing upon the strengths and commitment that got you involved in education in the first place—your love for children, the thrill of seeing their eyes light up and the wheels turn in their minds, your belief in their ability to learn if they are challenged in appropriate ways? How do you decide on what outcomes are important; how do you go about setting up the process to achieve those outcomes; how do you evaluate your progress?

Committed educators, parents, and community leaders have the best interests of their children at heart, and I have faith that if they get the training they need, they will make sound decisions; they will come up with creative ideas that connect with their students; they will make their schools a vibrant and exciting place. And that is what will improve education.

Now that I've talked about how we want education to change at the level of the local school, let me talk about how the role of the state needs to change. State government should provide general direction and set general standards for the results we want our students to achieve, so that there is a basic level of consistency in the skills and abilities of our graduates. But when it comes to the way in which those results are achieved, state government must be less of a watchdog and more of a resource and facilitator for local schools.

Instead of new state rules and regulations, what you are going to see from my administration is new models of relating between the state and local schools. This Leadership Institute is an example. Instead of making your decisions for you, we are training you to make your own decisions. It is not just a one-shot thing this week. You will be back for follow-up sessions in subsequent years, and from the participants in these institutes, we will build networks of local educators who are devoted to positive change.

Georgia 2000 is another model. More than 50 communities have contacted my office about Georgia 2000, and more than 25 have begun to form local partnerships. I hope many of you are involved. Georgia 2000 gives us clear, measurable goals that we want to reach in the eight years remaining in this century. But the decisions on how to reach those goals are made by community-level teams that include teachers and school administrators, but also involve parents, business leaders, other community groups and volunteers.

The state-level Georgia 2000 organization serves as a resource. It provides information to local teams on services that are available from the state. It gathers and shares information on innovative ideas that are working in other places, and brings local 2000 teams together for regional networking. If local teams decide they need specially trained staff, Georgia 2000 arranges it with an organization called Cities in Schools.

A third model is the reorganization of the Department of Education's regional offices to work with individual schools, taking a team approach to solving problems and overcoming barriers to achieving their goals. The bottom line is that state government is reconfiguring itself to become a resource and provide services and opportunities to Georgia's local schools, to support you in your quest to find innovative, creative ways to improve education....

It is not going to be easy, either for you as local school leaders or for us at the state level, and the hard part is not coming up with the new ideas; the hard part is overcoming the old habits. Old habits are like old jeans; they're comfortable, and we keep wanting to slide back into them.

But it is time for a new vision of how our schools operate. I have confidence in your ability to make sound decisions about education for your school and your community.

Along with the responsibility of making decisions for school, I want to give you the freedom to try new things, the resources and opportunities you need to achieve results, and the incentives and recognition that give you credit for your accomplishments.

—*Governor's School Leadership Institute, July 19, 1992*

---

Back when I was in your shoes, I once stood up in front of the Susan B. Harris Chapel of Young Harris College—a setting similar to this—and read the class prophesy. I can no longer remember any detail of it. I cannot even remember what I prophesied for myself. But I suspect that it didn't come true. I took physics in college. Today I know nothing of physics. I took mathematics. Today my wife keeps my checkbook straight. The only thing I remember about calculus is that the final exam asked me to find "the evolute of a cissoid." I still remember that a cissoid is a figure eight, but today I have no idea what an evolute might be.

The point I am trying to make is that unless you are one of those few devoted and fortunate souls who knows right now that you want to be a doctor or an engineer or a lawyer or a dentist or a minister—unless you know right now exactly what you want to be and are saving up every day's little teaspoonful of knowledge toward that goal—you will probably forget most of what you learn in college.

Those of you who think you know what you're going to do or be when you graduate, you'd better listen, too. Because it may well be that you only think you know. I know a banker who majored in agriculture. One of the best writers I know graduated from law school. I myself was a school teacher before I got side-tracked into politics.

What, then, is the use of investing eight percent of your life in learning things you are not going to remember? What can college do for you?... College can increase your curiosity and your discontent, and if it does, then it will have been worth the investment of these precious years.

Those are two things every baby is born with, although babies have to develop a little ability to get about the place before they can exhibit it. I want to make a point of that.

Do you know how you learned to walk? By trying and failing and trying again. One day you raised your diapered bottom up off the floor and tried to take a step. You fell down. You tried again. You fell down again. You kept on trying over and over again, until you finally made it to the sofa or your mom's arm. If you had waited until you knew you could walk before you tried, you would have never taken that first step. You would still be wearing those little high-topped white shoes.

You learn by trying and falling down—failing—and then getting up and trying again. That's how you learn to catch a baseball or run a computer or play a musical instrument.

But, back to my toddler. She is a bundle of curiosity and discontent. She wants out. She wants in. She wants up. She wants down. She pulls everything off the table, and gets the pots and pans out of the cupboards. She pokes a nail file into the electric socket and blows all the fuses. She eats things she shouldn't and lights matches. She turns her parents hair gray with a constant tide of questions. What is this? What makes that? Who says so? Why? What will happen if I do this?

This curiosity and discontent is born in all humans. And, granted some equivalent in brains, it makes the final difference between great people and mediocre ones. The persons who do not lose their curiosity and discontent are almost always bound to be successful. The persons who do lose them are almost always bound to remain on the level they had reached when they lost them.

Just name your own great person, whomever you admire most. You will find in them vast curiosity combined with great discontent. Take Lincoln if you wish. Napoleon. Churchill. Marie Curie. Charles Dickens. Thomas Edison. Rosa Parks. Kris Kristofferson. A diverse group. Their only two common denominators and curiosity and discontent....

What happens to people? What puts the dimmer on curiosity and discontent, until millions of people finally develop a mere cow-like existence—grazing on the morning headlines, chewing over old tired second-hand opinions? It's the same thing that happens to the baby. Her social group cracks down on her. Just like her mother stopped her from pulling out all the pots and pans because it would be too much trouble for her to put them all back, so the neighbors, the village, the town discourage any discontent and any curiosity that tends to be greater than the comfortable average.

The social group pretends that progress and change is either evil or funny. All rich people got rich by being money-grubbers, they say. All inventors are crackpots who wear thick glasses. All artists starve in attics. All politicians are crooks. All professors are absent-minded. A child who tries to learn something in school is a "dweeb," which I think is the latest synonym for somebody we used to call a "grind."

You who still have your discontent and curiosity alive know exactly what I mean. You live in a wonderful place on this campus. Leonardo da Vinci is your neighbor. Shakespeare is just across the way. Madame Curie would be glad to go over her experiments with you. All the great men and women who ever lived are here, waiting to arouse your curiosity and discontent anew. So that never again in your life will you be satisfied with your lot and the lot of humanity. Never again will your curiosity permit you to sit idly by while a question remains unanswered that you might be able to find the answer to.

Back when I was Lieutenant Governor, I once circulated a questionnaire to all

Senators, asking them why they went to college, what they expected to get out of it, and whether they got what they wanted or not. Nearly 80 percent admitted that they went to college mostly because their friends were going, but here and there was one who wanted to increase their curiosity and discontent. None of them said that, of course. They said things like "to broaden my horizons," or "to get a better appreciation for the finer things of life," or "to get more self-confidence," or "to absorb new ideas" or "to gain perspective." But they mean the same thing.

A great number who went to college without any reason for going answered that they got little or nothing out of it, which shows that college does not really do anything for you. It merely gives you the opportunity to do something for yourself.

One man gave as his reason for going: "A blond in my high school biology class was going, so I went along." What did he get out of college? Not the blond. She married somebody else.

But the most interesting part of the survey was the answers of those who did not go to college at all. Although they did not say so directly, it was obvious that all of them thought they had missed something important. That's another little thing college can do for you—free you from the illusion that you may have missed something....

One of my friends was being interviewed for a job with an advertising agency some years ago, and they had a psychologist talk to their job applicants. The psychologist asked, "Did you finish college?" "Yes," my friend said, and started to tell where and when. But the psychologist interrupted. "I don't care where and when. I'm only interested in whether you finished, because the chief value of college to me is that it establishes work habits—a person who has demonstrated an ability to finished a major project once it has been started."

Here's probably the place to give you my formula for success. I mentioned Thomas Edison a moment ago, and this is what he said: "Most people miss opportunity, because it dresses in overalls and loves to work"....

College can be the greatest intellectual banquet ever spread before anyone, so don't sit through the banquet eating peanuts and popcorn. Don't go off into one of the side shows and miss the main tent. Don't consider college your last few remaining days of freedom before the grind of adulthood. Don't devote your college days getting ready to live. Live now.

You will never be more alive than you are at this minute. Treat yourself to new friendships. Don't lock yourself in a room and don't lock yourself in your own mind. Develop a little fun and a little trouble. Find something to be enthusiastic about; find something to be indignant about. Then do some of both.

Don't ignore life, for life moves away from you at the rate of one hour every 60 minutes. Life moves away from you one day every 24 hours.

—*Spellman College Convocation, November 10, 1992*

---

Georgia is the third state in the nation to create what are called charter schools, which operate completely free of state regulation. Charter schools empower local educators and parents to develop working models of new approaches to education in our classrooms. They can take the initiative, for example, in changing the way the day is structured, or the way classes are organized and the methods that teachers use.

We are encouraging teachers and parents to draw up a plan that specifies how the school will go about achieving the six national education goals, and how they will measure their progress. It is a contract between the school and the state, renewable every three years by the State Board of Education.

In addition to the choice that charter schools provide, we have another choice in what we call Next Generation Schools. To help schools with the cost of innovation and change, we created a fund to provide a one-third/one-third/one-third match of state, local and private-sector money for one-time grants to schools to help them with some major change.

We also have established the Governor's School Leadership Institute to give local school leaders the skills and know-how they need to bring about innovation and positive change. With this program, the state serves as a broker, and we bring in experts from the Center for Creative Leadership in Greensboro, North Carolina, to do the training.

We have created an organization we call Georgia 2000. It is statewide and is composed of local 2000 groups, which support the schools in their own communities and help them achieve the six national education goals. Georgia 2000 is a resource that provides information about available services, brokers staff training from an organization called Cities in Schools, shares information about ideas that others are trying, and helps local partnerships to network with each other.

As the result of a constitutional amendment passed last fall, communities will have the right to elect school board members to set policy, and those elected representatives will have the opportunity to search out the best professional talent to manage their schools....

I'm a history teacher by profession, and I've always taught my students that this country was created as a nation where the power was in the hands of the people, a nation where individual initiative was encouraged and rewarded, a nation where people believed that they could make things happen, rather than simply have things happen to them. I've tried to impress upon my students that this nation was not built by the efforts of a government bureaucracy, but through the personal initiative of individual Americans in their own neighborhoods and in their own communities.

I have become convinced that that is the only way education reform will ever truly be realized—by the initiative of real people—teachers, students, parents, community leaders—in their own neighborhoods and communities. My goal as Governor of Georgia is to give Georgia communities the opportunity to take back their schools—to move education decision-making and problem-solving out of the bureaucracy that has been more of a problem than a solution, and back into the communities where real, live people teach and learn. State government should not be a watchdog that enforces the rules. It should be a resource that helps schools and assists communities to overcome barriers and lift themselves up to a better future.

*—Northeast School Improvement Conference, April 26, 1993*

All the programs and all the money and all the new ideas in the world will never be enough to improve education if we fail to give our kids and our teachers a safe environment for learning and teaching. I am afraid that in the not too distant future we will know that school has started when we hear the sound of gunshots and will measure the pace of the school year by the deaths of students.

We all know school violence is a real and growing problem. This summer, national pollster Lou Harris talked to 2,500 middle and high school students around the country. Here is what he found: 15 percent of those kids had personally carried a handgun at some point during the prior 30 days; nine percent had shot a gun at another person; 39 percent had had a personal acquaintance injured or killed by gunfire.

In Georgia we hear tragic stories from our campuses nearly every week. Less than three weeks ago at Harper High School in the inner city of Atlanta a 15-year old student shot two other students in the school cafeteria, and one died. Just up the road in suburban Duluth a 16-year old student was accused of pointing a semi-automatic pistol at another student at school. In Columbus seven 6th graders were arrested for bringing weapons into the school and plotting to hurt one of their teachers. Even in rural Dublin school officials had to hire uniformed police officers to patrol the halls of their junior and senior high schools in response to several incidents in which guns were confiscated and shots fired.

These stories and these statistics are unbelievable. They are not only unbelievable, they are also morally unacceptable. School violence is not a city problem. It's not a rural problem; it's not a white or a black problem. It is a Georgia problem, and it is our responsibility—as public officials, parents, business leaders and educators—to solve it. Students should be carrying books, not guns, to school. We can have the best teachers and educational equipment around, but no one can learn when they are nervously wondering whether the bully who threatened them in the hall packs a gun.

We need, we have to, we must, make schools safe. To do that, we must address two problems in our schools: the presence of weapons and the presence of violent, disruptive students. I will attack this critical issue head-on with a six-point program designed to make schools safe. It is comprehensive, and it goes beyond schools themselves, because youth violence is such a pervasive problem. My six point plan to make our schools safe includes:

1. Urge schools to involve local law enforcement officers, parents and community leaders in developing a safe school plan. Then I will recommend $10 million in lottery proceeds in my supplemental budget to help purchase metal detectors, monitoring devices, and other equipment for schools that need them to implement their safe school plan.

2. Create violence-free safety zones around school sites, similar to the drug-free zones we now have, where violence, misbehavior and loitering will not be tolerated and will be punished more severely.

3. Increase the penalties for handgun assaults on students and teachers and for possession of weapons in school safety zones, and require incidents of assault or possession of weapons to be reported to the police immediately for investigation and prosecution.

4. Encourage local systems to establish alternative schools for students who

constantly disrupt classrooms, but have not committed an offense that would send them into juvenile court. This will allow teachers to concentrate on teaching students who want to learn, rather than simply on classroom control.

5. Ban the possession of handguns by those under age 18, and make it a felony for anyone to furnish them with a handgun. If you want to keep weapons out of schools, the way to do it is keep them out of the hands of students altogether. It would apply across the board with limited appropriate exceptions like hunting, target practice or direct parental supervision in controlled settings.

6. Finally, we must fundamentally change our system of juvenile justice in Georgia so that the truly violent young offenders, the most hardened of our youthful offenders, will never again disrupt a public classroom.

Back when our present juvenile justice system was first created, a juvenile delinquent was a youngster who stole hubcaps, shoplifted, ran away from home, or painted graffiti on public property. Our present system did not envision the problems we see today—teenagers shooting people and committing rapes; young hoodlums running gangs and terrorizing neighborhoods, and showing little or no remorse when they're caught.

Youth who commit such violent crimes should not be in school. Students who want to learn deserve a safe environment that is free from bullying, harassment and violence. Nor should these young ruffians be mixed in with less violent or non-violent offenders in a detention facility.

These are tough hoodlums; they require tough measures. These are adult crimes; they deserve adult treatment.

That is why I will introduce legislation to require that youth between the ages of 13 and 17 who commit certain violent acts such as rape, murder and aggravated assault, be tried and prosecuted in adult court. Right now judges and prosecutors only have the discretion to try such crimes in a juvenile or adult court. If these youthful offenders are convicted, I will propose they be given an adult sentence in a special youth facility run by the Department of Corrections. This approach will ensure public safety and, at the same time... free the juvenile justice system and the Department of Children and Youth Services to concentrate on the young offenders they were created to serve....

But neither government nor schools can solve this horrible problem by themselves. The ultimate solution lies in strengthening our families and the values and discipline that are impressed upon our children. Some good old-fashioned discipline tempered by the love and caring that kids require would in themselves go a long way toward solving some of the problems we see.

As Proverbs says, "Train up a child in the way he should go, and when he is old he will not depart from it." That will happen only when parents, schools, churches and synagogues, and community organizations have the opportunity to work together and reinforce each other.

—*Governor's Conference on Education, October 25, 1993*

---

We all want to improve education. But we all also know that all the new programs and ideas in the world will never be enough if we fail to give our children and our teachers a safe environment that fosters teaching and learning. So we are implementing comprehensive plan to do that. It's like a three-legged stool.

One leg of the stool is getting weapons and violence out of our schools. We have banned the possession of handguns by anyone under age 18 and enacted tough penalties for attacks on students and teachers. We urged Georgia's schools to sit down with parents and local law enforcement officers, and develop their own school safety plan. Then we provided funds for whatever security equipment our local schools had decided they needed to be safe. And we're getting tough with teenage punks who commit adult crimes, trying them as adults and sentencing them to a separate youth facility run by the Department of Corrections.

The second leg of the stool is helping our children with their frustrations and fears, and strengthening their values. We are putting the first state-funded counselors down into the elementary grades to help our teachers deal with problems that get in the way of learning. We worked with the highly-regarded Scholastic Magazine to develop special education materials on drugs and violence, and we recently had Safe Schools Week. We're also expanding DARE—Drug Abuse Resistance Education—which brings law enforcement officers into our schools to teach kids about the dangers of drugs.

Today, we are here at DeKalb Alternative School to talk about the third leg of the stool, which is creating a school environment where teachers can concentrate on teaching rather than class control, and students can learn, free from disruption. A South Georgia high school principal with more than 1,400 students has said that if he could just get about 27 of them into an alternative school, he would have a completely different place. He is now going to have a chance to do that with the help of state funding.

But alternative schools accomplish more than simply removing those students who disrupt classes or do not function well in a normal school setting. Alternative schools give these students the special setting and special help they need to learn and succeed and complete their education.

I put $16 million in the budget to help local school systems with alternative schools, and we invited every system in the state to sit down with local parents and community leaders and develop an alternative school plan that meets their particular needs.

This afternoon, Superintendent Werner Rogers will present the State Board of Education with a list of 81 alternative school projects representing 113 school systems all around the state. They are as unique as the communities who drew them up. Some are located in schools, others are in other community buildings. Some will function during the school day, others will be open in the evenings and on Saturdays. Some are large systems with more than one facility like here in DeKalb, others are joint projects, like the five smaller systems that are working together to create one school. But they all represent a collaborative effort at the local level to help youth who have special needs and problems.

Here at the state level, the process has been a broad and open partnership, with private-sector expertise from Cities in Schools and input from the Partnership for Excellence in Education, as well as participation by the State Departments of Education, Human Resources, and Children and Youth Services.

Government can never take the place of parents in raising children. Government can never take the place of families and churches and synagogues in teaching values. But what I believe government must do is provide opportunities and encouragement for families and communities to work together, and strengthen and renew the ties that bind. That is what we are doing with alternative schools. We are encouraging local communities to take the initiative and work together to help their children with special needs, and we are providing the resources they need to do it.

—*Announce Alternative School Grants, May 11, 1994*

During my time as Governor, I have made a point of visiting schools and talking with educators all across the state, and I've learned a lot from listening. One of the biggest frustrations I've heard from our classroom teachers is that more and more students are bringing more and more personal problems with them to school—problems that get in the way of learning, problems that teachers are simply not prepared to deal with. And one of the goals of my administration is to put together a support network of resources in our local communities to help our children and their families deal successfully with those problems, including the presence and temptation of drugs.

DARE is a very essential part of that network of resources that support our children and their families. Former first Lady Nancy Reagan was criticized for being too simplistic when she advised, "Just Say No." Her critics were wrong. No is a two-letter word whose meaning is perfectly clear. It is simple. It is just not easy. We need to give our children the knowledge and instill in them the moral values that will help them in the difficult task of saying that simple, little, two-letter word.

That is why my administration has doubled DARE's capacity to train law enforcement officers, adding $1.2 million to DARE since 1991. That's why we have expanded the program from the elementary grades up into middle school, to provide continued support and reinforcement to our children as they approach adolescence. With this group of DARE graduates, Georgia will have 302 specially trained, veteran law enforcement officers working in 129 Georgia school systems.

As law enforcement officers, you deal daily with the devastating consequences of drug abuse. You see firsthand how drugs can ruin lives and destroy the potential of our youth be become happy, productive citizens. You are uniquely qualified to come into our schools and help our children understand the horrors that await them if they yield to the temptation to get into drugs.

But DARE does much more than give our children information about the dangers of drugs. Through DARE, they learn the skills they need to say no. Beginning in elementary school before they have ever experimented with drugs or alcohol, DARE teaches children how to make decisions based on personal values. They learn interpersonal communication skills. They learn how to resist peer pressure. They learn positive ways to deal with anger, disagreements and other personal frustrations that can sometimes lead to drug use. And as they interact with uniformed officers in a positive, helpful way, these young children also gain a greater respect for the law and the people who enforce it.

DARE is an important part of our efforts to make our schools safer, healthier and better.

*—Graduation for DARE Officer Training, August 26, 1994*

---

I'm an old history professor—and may be again—so I'd like to begin with a little history. Even as we look ahead to the future, we are standing on the shoulders of the past—a past in which a lot of able people have worked hard to build up and develop the University System of Georgia and bring it to this moment.

Back in the sixties, when I was teaching at Young Harris College and taking winter quarters off to come down here and serve in the Georgia Senate, we were defining progress in the University System in terms of geographic access. We created colleges and built campuses to make higher education geographically accessible to more Georgians.

Then when I was Lieutenant Governor, we moved to a new stage and a new definition of progress in the University System—enrollment growth. Now that the campus facilities existed, we were concerned about critical masses of students, and the rapid enrollment growth at some of our University System units is what first brought Georgia into the peripheral vision of the national higher education scene.

During my first term as Governor, we defined progress in the University System in terms of financial access. We created the HOPE scholarship program, and Georgia is now the only state in the nation where a student can go through all four years at a public college without paying any tuition or mandatory fees, and get $100 each quarter to help pay for books. We also expanded technological access, so that every one of our campuses now has satellite connections and is also on a statewide interactive network.

We come to this day with a strong record of making higher education accessible to a wide range of Georgia citizens. And I am very proud, as I know you are, of the national attention we have begun to receive as a result. We were proud when Georgia Southern University was designated the fastest growing college or university in the nation. We were proud when the *Chronicle of Higher Education* ranked Georgia first among the 50 states in increased state funding for higher education during the past two years. We were proud when the *New York Times* called the telemedicine program coming out of the Medical College of Georgia the most sophisticated in the nation. We were proud when the *Los Angeles Times* called the HOPE scholarship program the most comprehensive program of its kind in the nation.

We are now the fourth largest and one of the fastest growing systems in the nation. We've proved we have the students. With our record-setting funding increases, building campaign, technology and HOPE scholarship program, we've proved we have the resources. Now the time has come when we must prove that we know what to do with the students and the resources.

So as we begin the next stage in the development of the University System, the definition of progress changes once again. That new definition, as outlined in the vision statement recently adopted by the Board of Regents, is that, as we continue to build on our tradition of providing access and support, we are going to place more emphasis on quality and excellence. We are going to lift this University System to a new level of national prominence that goes beyond the size of our enrollment or the level of our funding to recognize the quality of our faculty, students, and programs.

*—Inauguration of Chancellor Stephen Portch, October 12, 1994*

---

The place where local control has really got to happen is not in state government, but in local communities, because what makes local control really work is parents attending parent-teacher conferences and PTA meetings and school board meetings, and volunteering at their child's school. What makes local control really work is individuals and businesses in your communities, getting involved in mentoring programs and youth apprenticeship programs, and building effective partnerships right down at the school level.

You understand that. You are not here tonight because you sat around and waited for state government to come and improve your schools for you. You are here tonight because you took both the initiative and the responsibility to strive for excellence in your own schools.

*—Schools of Excellence Banquet, April 13, 1995*

---

I want Georgia to continue going places where we've never been before...to continue to be progressive and innovative and creative...to continue to try new things and undertake new initiatives. I want us to be able to fill a child's mind and a child's soul as well as we can fill a prison cell. I want us to be able to educate a promising young person as effectively as we can incarcerate a violent one. Because if we do a good job of filling the minds and souls of our children, and educating our youth, we will not have to spend as much taxpayers' money on prison cells.

That's why education is and will continue to be my top priority. It addresses so many of the other challenges we face, from crime to welfare, and especially economic development and job creation....

Some are saying today that if we reform welfare, build prisons, crack down on crime, cut government and cut taxes, we will have done our work. They are not entirely correct. Those are important things to do, and I am doing them. They are all part of my agenda. But make no mistake about it—I believe, if that is all we do in Georgia, we will not secure the kind of future that our children can have and deserve to have. You see, I believe we must do more than respond to people's fears. We must also respond to their hopes and their dreams. We have to respond to their potential.

I may be old-fashioned, but I believe that when it comes to education, children have to study, teachers have to inspire and parents have to care. And as an old school teacher, I can tell you that when all that comes together, there's no stopping a child.

*—Star Student Banquet, May 2, 1995*

Ever since the Pilgrims arrived on the Mayflower ten generations ago, parents have dreamed of a better future for their children and worked hard to make that dream come true. Our belief in that dream—the American dream—is the common bond that unites this nation and makes the United States so exceptional among the nations of the world.

Today, on the threshold of the 21st century, the magic that makes the American Dream come true is education. Education, more than anything else, is the legacy that will make a better life possible for our children and grandchildren.

We face an urgent choice: We will either compete with the Japanese and the Europeans in the brain race, or we will end up competing with Third World countries that offer little but strong backs and low wages. That is why education has been and will continue to be my top priority as Governor of Georgia.

—*The Walker School, August 27, 1995*

Last week several executives from the big international Korean conglomerate of Sunkyong were in my office at the Capitol to announce a $1.5 billion manufacturing investment in Georgia. It was the largest single economic development announcement in state history, and it involves the construction of the largest polyester film manufacturing plant in the world.

At that press conference, a TV reporter asked Mr. Chey this question: Out of 70 sites in 16 states that were considered for this plant, why did Sunkyong choose Georgia? I remembered the economic mission I had made to Korea, and I beamed when I thought that he might say Georgia was the only state whose Governor made a personal visit to the company headquarters.

Then I thought he might say that it was my budget recommendation, approved by the General Assembly, to provide $7.5 million for the site and its development.

What he actually said, was that Sunkyong chose Georgia because they were impressed with our commitment to education and workforce development. He was right. Because education is where it all begins. The key to reducing crime and welfare, the key to generating economic development and creating jobs, is education. And that is why education is my top priority as Governor.

That's why I created the prekindergarten program for our four-year-olds, and Georgia has the most comprehensive program of any state—serving proportionately more of our four-year-olds, both at risk and not at risk, than any other state.

That's why I created the HOPE Scholarship Program to open the doors of our colleges and universities and technical institutes to Georgia's students, so that any student at any Georgia high school who graduates with at least a B average in their academic subjects, can get free tuition and a book allowance at any public college or university in the state. If they don't have a B average or don't want to go to college, they can get the same deal at a technical institute—free tuition and a book allowance.

That's why we are putting technology into our schools in amounts unheard of just a few years ago, and creating new initiatives like the P-16 Council to improve education all along the way from prekindergarten through four years of college.

But simply providing education programs like these is not enough. Because, as all of you business leaders know so well, customer satisfaction is the bottom line that can make or break you. If your product or service is going to be a success, it has to do what your customers need and want it to do.

Our students are not only the consumers of the University System; they are also its product. And you are the customers who need and use that product. We have an obligation to them and to you to offer educational opportunities that lead to a career for the student and provide a skilled workforce for you in industry. That means we need to be closely attuned to your needs and to the ongoing trends and changes in your workforce. We also have research and service programs in the University System for which private-sector business is the customer. What we are engaged in right now is doing a little research to find out what our customers need and want from the University System of Georgia.

Thirty years ago, Georgia set the standard for on-site employee training when we listened to industry and created the Quick Start program, which trains workers for incoming and expanding Georgia industries. We recently listened again, and created a new, cutting-edge partnership between private business and the University System called the Intellectual Capital Partnership Program, or ICAPP for short. Its projects bring the education resources of the University System to bear on specific workforce needs.

The reason we are here today is to listen to you. Does your industry struggle with a particular problem that could be improved or solved if the system would help out with a little practical research? As your business changes, will you need more computer majors or more business graduates, and are you wondering where they're going to come from?

We want to learn about the needs of the business community of this region for workforce education, for practical research, for service programs, and together we are going to look for creative ways to meet those needs.

*—University System of Georgia Listening Forum, April 18, 1996*

----------

All around the nation, education policy experts are pondering how to achieve greater excellence in higher education, and at the same time increase access. Here in Georgia, I am proud to say, we are doing just that. Our University System institutions are turning up and rising up on the lists of the best institutions in the nation. Our strong enrollment growth outpaces the national trends. All the while, you are raising admission standards, so that the quality of our students is going up at the same time. I am proud that the HOPE Scholarship Program is there to support your efforts by encouraging students to work hard and strive for excellence all through high school and then on through college.

When I read about our University System in *USA Today*, the *New York Times*, the *Wall Street Journal*, the *Chronicle of Higher Education*, and *Education Week*... when I hear Georgia touted as a national model for the trends that will take higher education into the 21st century, it makes me very proud, and it should you, too. As you know, I'm a long-time observer and student of the University System, and I believe that the system is now in the best shape of any time in history.

—*Board of Regents, University System, September 12, 1996*

---

The words "the American Dream" touch something deep inside each one of our hearts. For those of us who are parents, it is the eternal hope that our children will inherit an America that is even greater than the one we grew up in. For our children, the American Dream means having the opportunity to go as far in life as their abilities will take them. Anyone in America can aspire to be a doctor, a teacher, a police officer, a Governor, even a President. But the only way you can actually get any of these important jobs, is if you have the opportunity to acquire the education and the skills you need. The key to the American Dream is education."

—*Towns County Partners in Education, April 30, 1997*

---

Over the course of the past four decades, I have been blessed with the opportunity to watch, up-close, three generations of little ones—my own children, grandchildren and great grandchildren. I was always amazed, during this period of their lives more than any other time, how quick and agile their little minds were, how they absorbed like little sponges everything they saw and heard (and some things you might not want them to absorb).

It fascinated me, so I read everything I could find on the subject. It is what led me to create Georgia's Prekindergarten Program for four-year-olds. I was spell-bound by *Newsweek*'s special edition on how a baby's brain is built. As chairman of the Education Commission of the States, I found like-minded interests, so we held a conference in Georgia on brain development and how tiny children learn. Bear with me please, while I tell you briefly some of what I've learned and why we're here today.

The ear is the first sensory organ to develop. Unborn babies begin to hear just 16 weeks into pregnancy. That is pretty much the unborn baby's only stimulation from the outside world as its brain begins to develop. Research suggests that sounds have a direct connection to brain development. The first sound unborn babies hear is their mother's heart-beat and the corresponding rhythmic whoosh of blood in the placenta. By the time it is born, a baby's hearing is so sophisticated that it can differentiate between a recording of its own mother's prenatal womb sounds and the sounds of another baby's mother. Newborns also recognize the emotional content in the recording of their mother's womb sounds and respond with movements and changes in their own heart rate.

We know that a baby's brain continues to form after birth, not just growing bigger as toes and fingers do, but developing more and more microscopic connections that will be responsible for learning and remembering throughout life. At birth, a baby has 100 billion or more neurons forming more than 50 trillion connections, or synapses as they are called. But during the first months of life, that number increases 20 times to more than 1,000 trillion.

It is these mental maps—the patterns and connections that are made and reinforced in the brain during the early months and years of life—that form the basis of our intelligence. Research shows that reading and talking with an infant, and especially having that infant listen to soothing music, helps those trillions of brain connections to develop, especially the ones related to math.

What underlies our spatial reasoning skills is our ability to detect and predict patterns. That is what musical melodies and harmonies are—sequences of sound patterns that strengthen the brain's ability to process information and identify patterns in it. As early as four months old, babies will react to changes in melodies; they can detect notes that are out-of-tune, and they can sing a pitch that you've sung to them when they are as young as six months old.

The brain has two lobes, or hemispheres. Analytical, logical, and language skills are found on the left hemisphere, while visual, direct perception, and creativity are located on the right. People are sometimes called right or left-brain thinkers, depending on which type of thinking comes more naturally to them.

Music, however, engages both hemispheres. Its creativity and its ability to evoke the emotions engages the right hemisphere of the brain, but the mechanics of deciphering melody, rhythm and pitch intervals belong to the left. People who receives musical exposure and training early in life when their brain circuits were still developing have a larger "corpus callosum," which is the bundle of nerves that connect the two halves of the brain.

So music promotes the ability to join the logic of the left with the insight of the right. In fact, some researchers suspect that music's bilateral effect on the brain may make it a higher function than language, which is located on the left side of the brain—a more advanced, sophisticated way of knowing, analyzing, synthesizing and communicating than words.

I'd had the idea of somehow exposing Georgia babies to music in the back of my mind for more than a year, but I couldn't see how to do it. Then I was at the hospital the day my granddaughter took my second great-grandchild home. She was given this big bag of samples—diapers, wipes, baby formula, baby food. A light bulb went on in my head. I thought, we could put a CD or a tape in here with a little information for the parents about how they could begin to build their baby's brain through the power of music....

This CD and cassette will go home from the hospital with every baby born in Georgia for the next 12 months, and I hope their parents will play it often. It's an easy thing they can do to help Georgia's little ones to begin to develop their brains through the power of music.

This is how I put it to the parent on the CD:

"It really works!

"Einstein knew it.

"So did Galileo.

"They knew that there was a direct relationship between music and math. What many studies have shown since, is that the connection begins in infancy and can be increased by a baby hearing soothing music on a regular basis.

"A six-month-old infant can tell whether the music is harmonious or not.

Microscopic connections in the brain responsible for learning and remembering are enhanced through listening.

"That, my dear parent, is why Sony Music and I wanted you to have this recording. Play it often. I hope both you and your baby enjoy it—and that your little one will get off to a smart start."

—*Press Conference, June 24, 1998*

# Environment

## Preservation 2000 / RiverCare 2000

Preservation 2000 is one of my top priorities as Governor. It is one of the most important, ambitious, and far-reaching programs of my administration. Acquiring 100,000 acres in three years will be a big challenge, but I intend to rise to meet that challenge with your help.

We've already gotten started. A private benefactor, who has asked to remain anonymous, has donated $1 million for the purchase of Little Tybee and Cabbage Islands near Savannah. The state will add to this generous contribution from the Non-Game Wildlife Fund, an income-tax check-off program we began several years ago. As Twain noted, they are not making barrier islands anymore. Little Tybee and Cabbage Islands are the last two on Georgia's coastline that are still unspoiled but also unprotected.

This purchase sets the tone for Preservation 2000—a public-private partnership to buy and protect vital and unique areas of this state—and I will continue to seek out private donations of funds and land from citizens, corporations, and foundations.

I want to acquire a variety of properties spread across the state and across several types of use, including hunting and fishing lands, unique natural areas, and state parks. The state has already identified hundreds of properties through its Natural Areas Program and Heritage Inventory Program that we should be attempting to acquire. Groups like the Nature Conservancy have also identified properties the state should acquire.

Your job as the Advisory Council for Preservation 2000 is to work with the Department of Natural Resources and the environmental community in establishing guidelines and criteria for the purchase of property. I want you to weigh factors like the unique features of a site, the need for increased natural areas and outdoor recreation in the region around it, and the potential threat of development on the site.

I also need your help in promoting the public-private partnership idea and in developing a volunteer base. If you know of donors or potential donors of either land or money, please let me or my staff know. And I want to hear your ideas on other ways the state might be involved in protecting land beyond outright purchase.

I am going to look to you for advice, support, and help over the next three years. If we work together in a concerted effort, then history will look back on the first part of the 90s as a time when Georgia took a giant step forward in preserving this unique and diverse state for our children and their children.

*—Swear in Preservation 2000 Advisory Council, June 24, 1991*

Georgia has one of the richest, most diverse environments in the nation. Yet we have preserved only seven percent of our land area. We rank in the bottom half of the southeastern states in our recreation land per capita. Our goal ought to be to preserve 20 percent. In the Piedmont, where more than half of the state's population lives, only two percent of our land is in parks and forests.

Mark Twain once said, "Buy land—they're not making it anymore." And that is exactly what I intend to do. One of my most ambitious undertakings as Governor is Preservation 2000. It is a public-private partnership whose purpose is to acquire 100,000 acres of land over the course of my administration. A mixture of public and private funds will be used to acquire land as recommended by an advisory council of conservationists and respected community leaders.

In choosing sites for purchase, the council considers factors like unique natural features, the need for increased natural areas and outdoor recreation opportunities in the region around the site, and the potential threat of development on the site....

The Preservation 2000 Advisory Council and I will continue to seek private funding for this effort. I will also take advantage of our great bond rating and the present low interest rates for the purchase of some new natural areas.

Two million dollars for debt service in next year's budget will give us $20 million in bonds to purchase land. And we will use the state appropriation to leverage even more in private contributions. I will continue this pattern over the remainder of my administration, as we work toward the Preservation 2000 goal of 100,000 new acres for recreation, for hunting and fishing and for conservation.

*—Georgia Chamber of Commerce Prelegislative Forum,*
*November 20, 1991*

Today I am signing into law House Bill 1392, which authorizes an increase of $1.50 in hunting and fishing licenses. These funds will underwrite the debt payment on $20 million in bonds to buy land for Preservation 2000....For each of the next two years, I will seek another $20 million in bonds for the purchase of natural land, for a total of $60 million in state funding....In return for a modest increase in hunting and fishing licenses, the people of Georgia will receive an enormous increase in the acreage held back for hunting, fishing, recreation and wilderness protection.

*—Bill Signing Ceremony, March 11, 1992*

We've already preserved nearly 40,000 acres, and we've got another 43,000 acres under negotiation. The sites are spread across the state from Rabun and Walker Counties in the north, to Glynn and Coffee Counties in the south, and they include natural areas, parklands and wildlife management areas.

So far, we have committed $40 million in state bond funds for land purchases. We've received private donations of nearly $1.4 million, plus almost a million dollars from sources like the state income tax check-off and the federal government.

Environmental protection is a much bigger job than state government alone. It will take all of us working together if we are to preserve the earth as we know it for future generations.

—*Nature Conservancy of Georgia, September 9, 1993*

As of this week, Preservation 2000 has acquired or placed under option 56,000 acres, with another 55,500 acres under active negotiation, for a grand total of about 111,500 acres. These sites are spread all across the state in 58 different counties, from Dade and Walker in the northwest to McIntosh in the southeast, from Rabun in the far northeast corner to Decatur in the far southwest corner.

It is land for hunting, fishing, boating, hiking, camping, and bird-watching. It protects cave entrances and wetlands, and wards off encroaching development. It restores and protects the habitats of rare or endangered plants and animals. It preserves scenic views and offers opportunities for environmental education.

Even when we were in a recession and money was tight, the General Assembly never questioned the importance of acquiring land for Preservation 2000, because the support from the Georgia Wildlife Federation and other environmental organizations was so strong and so solid.

This land is a wonderful gift for all Georgians to enjoy, and an incredible legacy for their children and their children's children. And I've added $1 million to the budget every year for the past three years for enhancements at Georgia's public fishing and wildlife management areas, so that these areas are properly cared for and managed for the enjoyment of Georgia's citizens.

—*Accept Georgia Wildlife Federation Award, April 21, 1994*

Today the State of Georgia will acquire the 5,562-acre Dukes Creek Woods. This will be the crowning jewel of my Preservation 2000 Program. Look around. Listen. Without a doubt, this is some of the most spectacular mountain woodland in the Southeast.

I think you all know what these mountains mean to me. They are my home. I draw strength from them, and in their beauty I find renewal....

Dukes Creek Woods has been in very good hands. Charles A. Smithgall, Jr., a noted conservationist and businessman, has protected this property and restored it. Now, through his generosity, the people of Georgia will enjoy this resource for generations. This property is valued at $21.6 million. This acquisition of Dukes Creek is possible at this time because Mr. Smithgall has donated half the value of the property to the state—a donation worth $10.8 million. The state will fund the other half of the purchase. This is an opportunity we couldn't pass up. In honor of this contribution, we will name this property "Smithgall Woods - Dukes Creek Conservation Area."

This tract includes about four and a-half miles of Dukes Creek and sever and a-half miles of other native trout streams. Dukes Creek Woods provides a home to thriving populations of deer, wild turkey, small mammals, reptiles and song birds. These woods are home to two state-protected species—pink and yellow lady slippers—and their may be others. Most of the forest is mature pine-hardwood stands.

*—Announce Acquisition of Dukes Creek Woods, August 8, 1994*

Preservation 2000 has already protected 66,100 acres, with 30 percent of its value in private gifts. Another 54,400 acres are under active negotiation for a total of 120,500 acres.

During the next four years, I am going to begin River Care 2000. Based on the Preservation 2000 model of public-private partnership, River Care 2000 will focus on protecting our river corridors and wetlands. We have already begun by strengthening our laws relative to rivers and coastal areas, and outlawing live-aboard boats. RiverCare 2000 will move us on to the next step of acquiring natural areas and historic property along the banks of our rivers. In addition to providing recreation and park land, these natural areas will enable us to do a better job of flood management in the future.

*—Nature Conservancy of Georgia, Sept 8, 1994*

The wetlands along our rivers, lakes, and coastal waters are an essential part of our natural environment. They serve as a buffer against changing water levels. They act as a filter, helping to remove pollution and impurities from the water. They provide natural holding areas from which water can evaporate into the air and seep into the soil, promoting the natural recycling of water in the environment. In short, they are an essential part of our natural habitat and are essential to our water supply.

Natural areas like this one also make other contributions to our well-being. A stroll along this wetlands walkway or through the park next to it reaffirms the words of the psalmist that green pastures and still waters will restore the soul....

It is very important for us to understand how our natural resources and systems work, and to preserve our natural environment, not only because it is beautiful, but also because it is essential to life itself. That is why I created Preservation 2000, to preserve an additional 100,000 acres of natural land in Georgia. We are very close to achieving that goal, and before the end of this year we will have protected more than 100,000 acres under this program.

One of our priorities with Preservation 2000 has been to deliberately seek out naturally occurring water features, and many of the properties we have protected include bodies of water or front on water. But we are going to do even more, because water is so critical to live in all of its forms, plant and animal. Yet it is also a very fragile resource that can easily be damaged or destroyed.

The state budget for next year, which begins on July 1st, contains $5 million to begin a new wetlands conservation program called RiverCare 2000. Like Preservation 2000, it will be a public-private partnership that uses both state funds and private donations to acquire and protect sensitive natural areas along our river corridors.

But RiverCare 2000 cannot do it all. Georgia has 70,000 miles of streams and rivers. Much of the land along their banks will always remain in private hands, and some of it will be developed to varying degrees. So it is very important that our citizens understand both how important natural wetlands are in sustaining life, and how easy they are to destroy.

—*Dedicate Rome Wetlands Demonstration Project, May 26, 1995*

I am pleased to report to you this morning that as of this moment, 99,000 acres have either been fully protected or are under contract for purchase, and we still have another 10,000 acres under active negotiation. But even as we tie up the loose ends on Preservation 2000, we are turning our attention to RiverCare 2000.

Georgia has 70,000 miles of streams and rivers, which is an awful lot of riverbanks, but much of this land is in private hands and is not available for sale, and the tracts we will be able to acquire will be much smaller than most of the Preservation 2000 properties. So RiverCare 2000 will also pursue other protection measures in addition to the actual purchase of land, like voluntary covenants with landowners of riverfront property. They might agree, for example, not to remove any vegetation within 100 feet of a stream bank.

—*Nature Conservancy of Georgia, Oct 19, 1995*

We have made many significant improvements in the quality of Georgia's rivers since the days when the waterways of northwest Georgia were rainbow hued from textile dyes, and the waters of southeast Georgia were clogged with the waste of live-aboard boats. But we still face significant challenges from growing activity in our river corridors that often gets too close to our waterways. When homes and farms are located too close, storm-water run-off carries many chemicals from lawns and fields into our rivers. When landowners disturb the soil without careful control, erosion damages both their property and the water quality as well as plants and animals. Development and other alterations to riverbanks and wetlands have reduced the populations of many native wildlife species of both plants and animals.

From our earliest history, Georgia's inhabitants settled near to our rivers, and modern development has threatened or destroyed many of our historic treasures. As we learned from Tropical Storm Alberto a year and a-half ago, unwise development of flood-prone areas can cost lives and millions of dollars in property damage.

My goal in creating RiverCare 2000 is to improve our knowledge and management of Georgia's waterways, by acquiring sensitive river-corridor property and by educating other property owners along our rivers and encouraging greater responsibility from them. To succeed, we will have to forge strong public-private partnerships: between the federal, state, and local levels of government, and then between government and businesses, landowners, the environmental community, and knowledgeable experts in the private sector.

—*Swear in RiverCare 2000 Coordinating Committee, December 4, 1995*

When I began Preservation 2000 five years ago at the start of my administration, some said it was unrealistic to try to preserve 100,000 acres of prime Georgia real estate. But a few weeks ago, we achieved that goal. Preservation 2000 has now officially preserved 100,369 acres of natural land at 57 locations; 25 are new sites and 32 are expansions of existing sites. They stretch from Little Tybee and Cabbage Islands here on the coast to Tallulah Gorge and Smithgall Woods up in the north Georgia mountains where I'm from.

—*Weekend for Wildlife, Sea Island, Feb 10, 1996*

One of the partnerships in which Georgia Power and the state have worked very closely together is Preservation 2000, preserving 100,369 acres of natural land at 57 sites around the state. In my mind, the most striking of those 57 sites is Tallulah Gorge. Two miles long and 1,000 feet deep, it is without doubt one of the most spectacular natural features in the South.

Back at the turn of the century, this was a major resort area, with hotels and a railroad station. This new interpretive center pays tribute to that era by replicating the arts-and-crafts architecture of the time when Tallulah Falls was in its heyday. In fact, some of the center's architectural details were taken directly from the old hotels and train depot that were here at the time.

Today, a century later, Tallulah Gorge is expected to become Georgia's most popular state park, once again promoting tourism and helping to stimulate the economy of this region. Soon after the 20th century began, Tallulah Gorge put aside recreation and frivolity, and focused on productivity. In one of the nation's most significant engineering projects of the time, its water was put to work to generate hydro-electric power.

Our challenge today was to find a balance among the gorge's working life, the conservation of its natural beauty, and the opportunity for Georgians to see, understand and appreciate it. So a unique public-private partnership was created between Georgia Power and the State Department of Natural Resources to develop 3,000 acres, owned by the power company, into a state park.

It was undertaken with a great deal of care for two reasons: First, the rugged terrain and the sheer drops from the rim of the gorge made safety a major factor. And second, as Allen mentioned, the rare and fragile plant and animal life of the gorge must be preserved. In other words, we have developed this park in a way that protects the visitors from the gorge and the gorge from the visitors. The Jane Hurt Yarn Interpretative Center plays a central role in that effort.

Two primary trails, one on the north rim and one on the south rim, have been designed to give visitors access to a number of scenic overlooks into the gorge. But admittance to the gorge itself is very restricted, and this center will issue permits and prepare the few hikers who are allowed to enter the gorge.

More importantly, the center will give general visitors a vicarious sense of what the gorge is like without the risks, either to them or to the gorge, of actually going down into it. It features an award-winning film that takes visitors on a breath-taking tour. And the atrium gives them a feeling of hiking the gorge as they move among simulated rock outcroppings and natural exhibits.

—*Dedicate Jane Hurt Yarn Center, Tallulah Gorge, June 28, 1996*

---

We have already begun to acquire land in Georgia's river corridors. The state's initial purchase is 5,700 acres along five rivers and two streams. The largest is more than 2,000 acres along the Ocmulgee River in Twiggs and Bleckley Counties. Then we've got over 1,500 acres in Baker County along two streams, and 742 acres in Emanuel County along the Little Ohoopee River. We're acquiring 331 acres in Hall County along the Chattahoochee where it flows into Lake Lanier, 279 acres in Madison County along the Broad River and its tributary streams, and 100 acres in Baldwin County on the Oconee River. So you can see these sites are pretty widely spread around the state.

—*Nature Conservancy of Georgia, Oct 15, 1996*

---

Today it gives me great pleasure to announce that the Oconee Rivers Greenway is the very first local partnership project to receive funding under RiverCare 2000.

Georgia's rivers and streams are in a very real sense this state's lifeblood. They supply our water and assimilate our wastes. They generate electrical power and transport us and our goods. They maintain a wide and diverse range of native plant and animal species, and carry essential nutrients that make our coastal waters such productive fishing grounds.

The archeological and historic artifacts that appear in rivers, from stone fish traps to trail crossings, show how important rivers have been since time before memory. Many a Georgia city owes its location to a river.

We have not always been as kind to our rivers as they have been to us. In the past, pollution from manufacturing and waste-treatment plants reduced water quality in many streams. Over the past 20 years, many different programs have greatly helped to reduce pollution in our rivers, and today, Georgia is fortunate to have a generally good supply of clean water. However, our rivers still face significant challenges, mostly resulting from our modern lifestyles.

I established the RiverCare 2000 conservation program in 1995 to address these important river issues, and improve our understanding and management of Georgia's rivers. More than 130 knowledgeable private citizens and public officials provide RiverCare 2000 with expertise and advice....

Better river management requires public-private partnerships. We need to give landowners better tools and more incentives to manage their land with river conservation in mind. RiverCare 2000 is working on these issues. It is completing Georgia's first comprehensive river assessment, which will be published on the World Wide Web to provide access for everyone who is concerned about river management. RiverCare will also publish recommendations on legislation, improved land-management practices and financial and other incentives for land owners. And, of course, RiverCare is using $28 million in state and other funds to acquire important riverbank and watershed lands for management by the Department of Natural Resources and local governments.

Everyone lives in a watershed, and we all live downstream from somebody else. The quality of the Oconee Rivers in Athens-Clarke County depends upon the decisions of upstream property owners over which you have little control. In turn, the communities that lie downstream from you, depend on your wisdom and management for the quality and quantity of their water....

The Oconee Rivers Greenway is a tangible way of improving river management. The green space on each side of the river filters out pollutants before they can reach the water. Trees provide beauty, wildlife habitat, and shade. Trails allow local residents to walk or cycle rather than using their cars for short errands. Interpretive materials along the trails help residents and visitors learn of the many ways the river contributes to the community....

I hope this RiverCare 2000 partnership becomes a model, and I challenge other local communities to carve out their own greenways.

—*Press Conference, Athens, November 11, 1997*

---

I am very proud that Preservation 2000 conserved 100,367 acres of natural areas, parks, greenways, and other wildlife habitat. We have now turned our attention to RiverCare 2000, and so far the state has acquired 13,420 acres along nearly 43 miles of river and lake frontage.

These initiatives are significant, both compared to previous efforts in Georgia and to efforts by other states. Nevertheless these numbers pale against the millions of acres of privately owned forest that blanket this state.

Think about it: Georgia ranks first in the nation in the production of paper and board products, and is tied for first in the production of wood pulp products. What these rankings mean, is that Georgia has a lot of forests—23.6 million acres of timberland, to be exact. Sixty-four percent of this state's land area is covered by forests. And, as Georgia's top national rankings in forestry products imply, most of that timberland is in private corporate ownership. In fact, 93 percent of Georgia's land mass is in private hands.

It is clear that any significant effort to conserve wildlife must be done in partnership with private landowners, and the Georgia Department of Natural Resources has taken an innovative approach to wildlife conservation by building public-private partnerships.

The DNR Wildlife Resources Division began a Private Lands Initiative in 1995 to promote, encourage, and provide technical assistance for wildlife conservation on private lands.

Through the Wildlife Management Area Program, nearly 230,000 acres of private land are leased to the Wildlife Resources Division to provide public recreational opportunities like hunting, fishing, boating, hiking, wildlife viewing, and birdwatching. Over half of this acreage is corporate timberland. The Farm Bill Conservation Program also helps to preserve wildlife habitat on private agricultural land.

Today we mark the beginning of another public-private partnership to promote wildlife conservation. It is called the Forestry for Wildlife Partnership Program. You see, those millions of acres of commercial forest that feed our pulp and paper industry, also provide extensive habitats for Georgia's wildlife. The Forestry for Wildlife Partnership Program will encourage and help corporate landowners to incorporate wildlife conservation efforts into their forest management plans.

The DNR Wildlife Resources Division worked with 14 corporate forest landowners to develop the Forestry for Wildlife Partnership Program. The program is voluntary, flexible, non-competitive, and driven by its participants. It joins with DNR's other public-private partnerships to increase emphasis on multiple-resource conservation and environmental protection, and to promote the conservation of wildlife and wildlife habitat as an land management objective. Together, these partnerships have the potential to conserve habitat for a multitude of wildlife species on more than 10 million acres of Georgia land.

—*Announce Forestry for Wildlife Partnership Program,*
*April 24, 1998*

---

# Pollution

Not long ago the Environmental Protection Agency released a ranking of the states by the amount of total pollutants they generate and by the amount they release into the environment. Georgia was in the top half of the states both in the amount of waste we generate and the amount we release into the environment. Louisiana, once the number one state in producing pollutants, cut the amount of waste it generates nearly in half from 1987 to 1989. New Jersey, a state that is often the butt of pollution jokes, releases less than half the waste into the environment that Georgia does.

It is clear that the only really safe way to handle toxic pollutants is not to produce them in the first place. It can be done. The production of toxic pollutants can be reduced, and they can be disposed of in a responsible manner. It must be done, and I intend for it to begin during my administration as Governor.

To that end, I initiated legislation, which the General Assembly passed, to reconstitute the Hazardous Waste Management Authority and to broaden and change the focus of its mission. In reconstituting the Authority, I removed the politicians, and I made it clear that my appointments to this body would be professionals—scientists, engineers, and environmentalists, who would make decisions that favor the environment instead of political constituencies or special interest groups.

The new law also makes clear that your job is no longer merely selecting a place to dispose of our waste. While that continues as part of your responsibility, your priority is now to attack the problem at its source—reducing the amount of hazardous waste we generate....

Georgia is a special and wonderful place, from its white sand beaches where sea turtles lay their eggs, to the cool forests and rushing trout streams of its mountains. Those treasures are in our keeping, and our well-being depends upon the kind of job we do. If we work together in a concerted effort, then history will look back on the first part of the 90s as a time when Georgia took a giant step forward in reducing destructive wastes and preserving this unique and special state for our children and their children.

*—Swear In Hazardous Waste Management Authority, July 23, 1991*

---

Despite all of our efforts over the past 25 years, the earth is scarred, worn and over-populated. Its people continue to lay waste to its wetlands and forests at a rate that has accelerated rather than declined. Plant and animal species are being obliterated with increasing speed. The ozone layer is thinning rapidly, the levels of carbon dioxide in the atmosphere are increasing. The amount of damage that has happened just in my own lifetime is frightening, and at times I wonder whether we have doomed our children to extinction along with so many animals, plants, forests and wetlands.

While we have made progress, we are clearly far from resting on our laurels. If we are to have a chance at saving the earth for future generations, immediate and dramatic action beyond what we have done in the past is called for....

We have identified environmental technology as one of three areas of concentration for the Georgia Research Alliance. The demand for environmental technology is going to increase tremendously in the future, as we work to reduce and treat waste, and to deal more effectively with environmental crises like chemical spills or radioactive leaks. Analytical services and the development of cutting-edge products to address tighter environmental controls have enormous potential to generate jobs and economic development. I understand that, and part of the reason why I want Georgia to be a center of expertise in environmental technology, is because I want this state to enjoy all of the new jobs and other economic benefits that will result.

But we cannot limit our concern with environmental technology to inventing gizmos or techniques to use with smokestacks or the water released by industry or sewage processing plants. Environmental considerations must permeate a much broader sweep of our research and technology development. Environmental considerations must be present in the technology and processes we develop for industry.

How can our industries reduce the waste they generate? How can they recycle their waste into other uses? What other products can be made from industrial wastes? Can we make the recycling process more efficient for the glass, paper, plastic, and aluminum saved by individual citizens? As we develop improved manufacturing processes and equipment for our traditional industries—textiles, food-processing, and pulp-and-paper—can we cut down on the amount of water these industries take from the environment? Can we find ways to reuse dye batches or bleaching solutions to minimize chemical waste? Find more energy-efficient drying processes?

We need to look at air quality not just from the perspective of smokestack filters, but also in terms of reducing emissions by lowering energy consumption and using alternate energy sources. How can our industries build a greater level of environmental sensitivity into their planning for new products and the development of new materials? Finally, how can they do all these things in a cost-effective way that allows them to compete in an increasingly difficult global market?

Here's another vital question: How can we manage our natural resources in way that is sensitive to their preservation and at the same time allows our economy to flourish? We need sophisticated management systems that reconcile the competing demands on our water systems. We need agricultural practices that prevent erosion and the leaching of nutrients from the soil, and control pests in ways that are ecologically safe.

The environmental challenges of the future are tremendous, and they must be met and met quickly if the planet as we know it is to survive.

—*University System Research Symposium on the Environment,*
*May 9, 1992*

---

You have obviously been working hard, and I want to thank you... for your determination to help make Georgia a better place... You have some great ideas and recommendations, and it has helped us a lot to hear them.

As I listened to your presentations, it was clear to me that you are right on target in identifying many of the problems we must solve, but I also got the feeling that you tend to think these problems can be solved simply by passing a law. What I want you to understand is that laws are only the beginning. They are only the skeleton for a lot of other things, and by themselves, they are not enough.

For example, it is not enough to have a law that says you must recycle. You must also have a place for people to take their glass, paper, plastic, and aluminum, or you must have special recycling containers for everyone to put out on the curb, and trucks to collect it all. Then you have to have manufacturing plants where you take all of these things to make them into other products. Stores must be willing to sell those products, and you and your families and friends must be willing to buy them, so that the companies that make these products and the stores that sell them don't go out of business. So you see, a successful recycling program takes much more than a law. It takes a lot of time and money and careful planning.

We can start by changing the laws. This year we have passed laws about old tires, laws about cleaning up old dumps, laws about helping local governments to do more recycling and improve the ways they deal with garbage. But the bottom line is that all of us have to change our own everyday habits and behavior. Most people just put all their garbage out on the curb and forget about it. But there is no garbage fairy. All of that garbage is piling up in landfills, and we are running out of places to put it. If we are really going to make a difference, we must change everybody's habits and lifestyle.

My Office of Energy Resources has given some money to Jim Higdon for a statewide publicity campaign called *Georgia's Future: Don't Waste It*, and to train teachers and students like you about the importance of managing our garbage properly and preserving the environment. But we need your help.... As you leave, I want to ask you to take your ideas and your message back home to your families, your class and teachers at school, and your community. Everybody needs to learn how to change their own lives by recycling and reducing waste, just like you.

*—Children's Environmental Council, November 16, 1992*

---

Prior to 1972, Georgia had no laws on solid waste disposal. We had 400 open municipal dumps, but only one sanitary landfill in the entire state. Odors, scavengers, rats, flies, and wild dogs proliferated at those dumps. When the dumps got full, we simply set them on fire. It was a cheap way to control volume, but it didn't do much for air quality.

Then came the Georgia Solid Waste Management Act in 1972, and all of the open dumps have now been replaced by 181 permitted landfills. However, while we've been improving solid waste management over the past 20 years, garbage has been multiplying faster than wire hangers in a dark closet. In 1972, municipal garbage was being produced at a rate of 2.8 pounds a day per person. Today, it's 4.5 pounds a day per person—even higher in urban areas. In one year, Georgia's household waste would make a stack 40 feet high, that filled up one side of I-20 from Atlanta to Augusta.

The solid waste issues facing us are not only complex and costly, but they also operate on several levels that sometimes conflict. At the level of legislation and long-term planning, we want comprehensive management that protects the environment and produces facilities that are compatible with surrounding land uses. But the *unwritten* laws of garbage tend to get in the way of comprehensive solid waste management. They include:

1. Everybody wants you to pick up their garbage, but nobody wants you to put it down.

2. My county's garbage is better than your county's garbage.

3. The issue of where to locate the new landfill always needs still more study.

4. *Everything* can be recycled, so the life of a landfill is not an issue.

5. The life of a landfill is always half as long as the consultant said it would be; twice as long as you told the neighbors it would be; and just long enough for you to get out of

office.

6. Garbage never *elects* anyone to public office, but it can *un-elect* you.

There are also political, socio-economic and emotional issues. Some of you worry that local governments will be forced out of the landfill business and left at the mercy of private-sector mega-landfills. You may be right. All over Georgia, citizens are fighting new county landfills just as hard as they fight new private sector landfills. These battles over landfill siting are part of the crisis we face.

Georgia recently did a thorough analysis of solid waste management around the state. Then the General Assembly undertook a comprehensive revision of the 1972 Solid Waste Management Act. The 1990 Georgia Comprehensive Solid Waste Management Act provides a sound framework and requires management strategies at both the state and the local/regional levels. And we are continuing to address this problem within that framework....

We cannot change what is past. Old landfills that continue to be hazards must be cleaned up, and the state stands ready to help with the economic burden of doing that. However, we must also minimize our future clean-up liability by moving quickly to reduce waste, recycle, and properly dispose of the waste we do generate. I am extremely pleased with the passage of the constitutional amendment authorizing the Georgia Environmental Facilities Authority—GEFA—to make low interest loans to local governments for recycling, composting, and solid waste disposal facilities. This fund can help save tax dollars by allowing communities to share voluntarily the costs of public solid waste management facilities....

A significant part of Georgia's solid waste problem is scrap tires. Georgians toss out 6.5 million a year, and as one of only four states that did not regulated them, we were attracting huge numbers of tires from other states. Many legitimate landfills refuse to accept old tires, so they were often dumped illegally in rural areas. This year we have a new law that bans whole scrap tires from landfills by 1995 and levies a dollar-per-tire fee at retail sale to clean up illegal tire dumps, support local tire abatement and management programs, and fund research on reuse and recycling....

I am proud of Georgia's laws, of our accomplishments, and of the example we set through programs like Keep Georgia Beautiful and the recycling program for state agencies. Georgia is also a leading state in providing markets for recycled paper, glass, plastics, and metals. I appointed the Recycling Market Development Council to further promote these markets. Now both state and local governments must set a good example by buying recycled products.

But even the best programs, slogans, and laws will not solve our solid waste problems unless all of us also change our own lifestyles. We have become a throw-away society, and we are running out of places to throw it. The United States has five percent of the world's population, yet we generate more than 25 percent of its trash. Every hour, we use 2.5 million plastic bottles. Every two weeks, we throw away enough glass to fill both towers of the New York World Trade Center. Every three months, we throw away enough aluminum to rebuild our entire commercial airline fleet. Every Sunday, we kill more than a half million trees, because we did not recycle 88% of the previous Sunday's newspapers. And every year we send 24 million tons of leaves and grass clippings to landfills, then turn around and buy fertilizer with phosphates that pollute our water.

I am firmly committed to the concept of state and local planning. And I believe that local governments should have primary jurisdiction over solid waste management. But with that authority comes a responsibility to the three R's: reduce, reuse, and recycle.

Let me close by thanking you again for coming to address the solid waste challenges we face and help us set a course to meet them. Together we can find practical solutions that will make Georgia a better place to live, work, and play.

—*Solid Waste Management Conference, November 16, 1992*

---

The Environmental Protection Division and many of you who are here today have been working together over the past 13 years or so to decrease the industrial pollutants that contribute to Atlanta's ozone problem, and because of all of your efforts, the release of industrial toxins has been greatly reduced, often at significant cost.

We are now turning our attention to another major contributor to air pollution— vehicle emissions. This is a tough one, because virtually all of Atlanta's citizens contribute to the problem. It is much easier to pinpoint a handful of industries and use technology to control their emissions, than it is to change the way several million people conduct the miscellaneous activities of their personal lives. But every single one of the millions of people who live and work in metro Atlanta has to breathe, and it is in everyone's direct personal interest to work together and contribute to making our air healthier.

As you learned this morning, state agencies are making plans to reduce the pollution caused by their vehicle fleets, both by purchasing new vehicles that burn cleaner fuels and by converting existing vehicles to alternative fuels. I urge all of you to do the same.

—*EPD Seminar on Clean Fueled Vehicle Fleets, February 11, 1994*

---

Right now, the 13-county metro Atlanta area is what the federal government calls an "ozone non-attainment area," which means that its air does not meet mandatory federal air quality standards. If we continue to fall short of the standards, metro Atlanta is not only going to lose some $600 million in federal highway funds, but we could also see restrictions placed on new businesses moving into metro Atlanta and on expansions of existing facilities.

So, this morning I signed an executive order creating the Voluntary Ozone Action Program, or VOAP for short, and I am requiring every state agency with employees in metro Atlanta to participate. During this coming summer whenever there is an ozone alert, every state agency will have a plan in place to reduce their single-occupancy vehicle trips by at least 20 percent. And they will implement it. Our goal is to do that all summer every summer, whether there is an ozone alert or not, so that every state employee carpools or takes mass transit or tele-commutes at least one day a week as a common practice.

In addition, I have sent letters today to the other governmental units in the metro area and to the 100 largest employers, asking them to do the same thing. If they all participate, and I'm strongly urging them to do so, we are talking about some 200,000 employees, acting in concert to reduce harmful emissions.

We already know that it works. Last year Atlanta hosted the largest peacetime event in the history of the world at the height of the ozone season. Yet not once during the Olympics were we out of compliance with federal ozone regulations, and the reason was because metro-Atlanta businesses and employees voluntarily worked staggered hours, used public transit and tele-commuted from their homes.

We will spend $1 million in state funds for a major public education campaign and the monitoring of daily ozone levels.

*—Commerce Club Board, December 4, 1997*

———  ———

This is clearly a historic occasion, and one that has been achieved only through a great effort on the part of everyone involved. I want to begin by concurring in the remarks of my fellow governors regarding the importance of the process on which we are embarking. The parties who are involved here have invested millions of dollars in state and federal funds, and will invest millions more to develop information and technical data that will serve us well in our efforts.

We have all met countless times with our stakeholders in these river basins. Each of our state legislative bodies, as well as Congress and the President, has given us a mandate to move forward expeditiously toward an allocation formula. This commitment of financial and personal resources, and the trust it has already created among us, is unprecedented in the history of water management. It is vital that we live up to these expectations.

We know that this will not be an easy task. Seven years of study have made it clear that the interests of the participants are diverse, complex, and significant. The concerns of each party deserve the utmost respect of the others. Each of our three states has a very real and significant interest in ensuring a future water supply for domestic, agricultural, and industrial uses, in protecting the ecosystems in and around these rivers, and in providing for recreational and economic development purposes. I believe that we have in our collective grasp the potential to develop a methodology that respects all of these interests.

We have the information and technical data developed over seven years. We have the mutual respect developed in the course of that work. If we now add the political will, we can allocate the waters of these major river systems in a manner that is equitable and fair to all concerned.

Each compact offers several common benefits to all of the states and the federal government: First, and perhaps foremost, a compact provides a mechanism to resolve disputes outside the courts. Second, a compact allows dispute resolution to take place here at a basin and regional level with the federal interests fully participating as partners. Third, a compact can provide certainty—certainty of supply and certainty of rates of flow to meet in-stream environmental requirements, certainty which is not now available to any state individually.

Finally, a compact can provide for a common repository of data for all of us to share as we refine and build on our knowledge of water supply and its relationship to economic development, protection of the environment, and superior quality of life....

Georgia is absolutely committed to meeting as long and as often as is necessary, at any place and under any circumstances that are reasonable. Georgia is committed to setting out its own needs honestly and clearly, and to listening carefully and respectfully to the needs of our sister states and the federal interests. I fully believe that if we all pursue the common goal of commitment to fair and equitable apportionments, it is possible to have compact allocations by the deadline.

However, if we fail to seize the moment and agree to compact allocation formulas, we lose this certainty and we lose these benefits. Seven years of hard work will have gained us nothing. The price of protracted litigation, bickering, and ultimately looking back with 20/20 hindsight at what we might have done with this opportunity, is too great for any of us to pay....

Our three states are well blessed with water. In fact, less-well-blessed states in the West may find our dispute amusing. But we do not. We fully understand the seriousness of it and of our respective needs....

If we fail, if we blow this opportunity, we may lose all that we have accomplished to date. The compacts will become void, and we will be faced with an uncertain future. We want to avoid that, and we look forward to working with you to bring these negotiations to a successful resolution.

*—Tri-State River Compact Commission, February 18, 1998*

---

The ozone problem is a very serious one for the State of Georgia. It affects the health of our residents. It also has very serious implications for federal transportation funds. It can bring economic development in the Atlanta region to a standstill.

When you get right down to it, the solution to the problem is cultural change. That is what VOAP is about—cultural change. We are all going to have to change our personal habits, and it will not be easy. It is not easy to teach an old dog new tricks. Mark Twain once said that habit cannot be flung out of the window, but has to be coaxed down the stairs one step at a time. Your job as VOAP Partners is to help with that coaxing, one step at a time.

The individual residents of metro Atlanta must become more aware of how their personal behavior patterns create ozone, and be willing to change their travel habits with more carpooling, more telecommuting and more use of MARTA. You, our partners in VOAP, are an essential part of making that happen. You are the key to encouraging and helping the residents of metro Atlanta to change their daily habits. It is not going to be easy, but it has to be done. By putting new policies in place at your worksites and by encouraging the use of alternate transportation, you can help in a significant way to move this region to new patterns and expectations.

Someone once said that all meaningful and lasting change starts on the inside and works its way outside, and that is true. You have to want to change your habits in order to actually do it. But I also believe that sometimes you have to jump-start change. You have to provide a little encouragement and incentive to emphasize its importance and help people want to do it.

The goal of my Executive Order creating VOAP was to jump-start something in Atlanta that all of you would embrace and that would make the residents of this region more aware of the choices in their daily lives that contribute to the problem.

—*VOAP Partners Breakfast, April 28, 1998*

# Eulogies

*Luke Carver, April 9, 1992*

The ranks of the true mountain men are growing thin. They are a vanishing breed, a species rapidly becoming extinct. Television, four-lane highways, shopping malls, the modern high-tech world has just about done away with them. And we will not see their kind again.

Luke Carver was a true mountain man...100 percent authentic, the genuine article...with the bark on. He was not packaged; you got what you saw. He did not pretend.

He knew and loved these mountains and their people. All his life, he hunted these hollows and fished these streams and lakes. He cleared the new ground in Rail Cove and farmed its land. He loved these mountains and was in agony when he was away from them very long.

Luke loved his politics, national, state and local. I bet he didn't miss an election from the time he became old enough to vote. He kept up with it daily, read it, talked it, participated in it, worked it on the precinct grounds. Those of us who knew him know that he was highly partisan..."born a Democrat" as we say around here. The only person more partisan than Luke was Mama Bea, his wife of many years. And the family had wonderful, heated, loud, animated, opinionated arguments around the kitchen table, on the front porch and around the spring that would go on for hours.

I've never been real sure exactly if Luke ever thought I was good enough for his daughter—that's the way fathers are—but I know this: He loved the fact that I was in politics. And that encouraged me very much.

Most of all, Daddy Luke loved his family...how he loved his family! The more it grew with the new babies and in-laws, the better he liked it. And they loved him back. He spent his time with them, teased them, took great pride in their achievements and had a way of communicating with them that most older people don't have with younger people. He was the family patriarch. We idolized him. As the song goes, we thought he walked on water. Each member of our family knew that Luke deeply and sincerely cared for them.

We—and others—were always spellbound by his storytelling. About catching a moonshiner, or cutting down a still, or tunneling through a mountain, or winning a big poker hand. Wherever he is right now, it won't be long before he'll start telling one of his stories and others will gather around as he weaves his web.

His leaving us will leave a deep void in the lives of this family. He was the big, strong white oak in our forest.

Our love for him—and his love for us—kept a large and diverse and widely scattered family together. We will miss him very much, but we will never forget him. He was of these mountains and of this valley. And he will always, always be with us.

---

*Charlie Jenkins, March 2, 1993*

As Governor, I've gotten to do a lot of things that as a boy growing up in these mountains, I would never have even dreamed of. I sat in Ted Turner's box with President Carter and watched the Atlanta Braves win a National League championship. I visited the Baseball Hall of Fame in Cooperstown with Hank Aaron. I've become good friends with Mickey Mantle, walked around in the clubhouse with him and out onto the playing field at Yankee Stadium.

For one who has worshiped the game of baseball since I was a boy, these were heady, wondrous times that I could never have imagined that I would ever experience. But when it comes to baseball legends, when it comes to boyhood heroes, it is not a Mantle or an Aaron that touches my soul and sends shivers of excitement up my spine. No, my boyhood heroes were not named Mickey or Willie or the Babe. they were named Quentin and Hoyle, Tom and Skud, Arnold and Charlie.

Charlie...to this day I can shut my eyes and see that graceful, magnificent, remarkable athlete. I can see that smooth, effortless fielder at first base. I can see him pitching...throwing what in our day we called a drop—when it would get to the plate, it would drop straight down, like it had rolled off a table. The catcher was as bewildered with it as was the batter at the plate.

I can see that unique left-handed batting stance, the bat held kinda higher in the air, the knees almost together, the right knee facing the pitcher to cock back before stepping forward, uncoiling like a whip and sending a line drive screaming into right field. I can see that half smile and the twinkle in his eyes after a particularly good play or good hit...Not arrogance or cockiness, but more of a nonchalant, self-assurance that seemed to say: I know how to play this game, boys.

Yes, in the mirror if my mind I can see my heroes do things that I'd never seen before or seen since. I saw Tom Jenkins, Charlie's brother, bunt a baseball...with the end of a bat. In basketball, I saw Hoyle Bryson at a jump ball at the foul line routinely jump and tip it into the goal...a feat, to me, more amazing than any of the slam-dunking today. And whether you believe it or not, I saw Charlie Jenkins take a broom stick and while holding it in both hands, jump over it. While that was sinking in, he would jump backwards over it, still holding it in both hands without turning it loose.

I remember those things as if they were yesterday...although more than 45 birthdays have come and gone. In those days, I measured my life by the spring and by the summers I didn't want to end. My boyhood heroes were majestic figures, gods in flannel uniforms with Frank Abernathy Funeral Home or M.C. Hood General Merchandise on their backs. This boy became a man and in between played baseball with Charlie's sons: Charles, Ed, and Kenneth. And they weren't bad themselves.

But there was only one Charlie Jenkins, and my early life would have been so empty without him and Tom, Hoyle, Quentin, Arnold and the others. I simply cannot imagine growing up without them, and I thank God for the life of this good man, Charlie Jenkins, and that his life touched my life in such a meaningful and unforgettable way. I'm thankful that I was able to see this extremely gifted athlete in action, and especially, I'm thankful that he was my friend.

Charlie Jenkins was of these mountains and of this valley. And he will always, always be with those of us who were fortunate enough to have known him.

---

*Edna Herren, July 8, 1994*

I speak today for all those students whose lives were touched by this remarkable woman.

Edna Herren was first, last, and always a teacher. A teacher unrelenting in her demands, but with extraordinary magnetism - dramatic, spellbinding in the way she made the personalities in English literature come alive. I go back and read the same passages that she once read to us and the realism, the drama, the emotion are just not there. I read Chaucer and Beowulf and they are boring and plodding now, but when she read them they lived so vividly you'd get goose bumps.

What a teacher! What a teacher! She had the wonderful ability to make each one of us feel so very special—that we were somebody. Or could be if we'd just listen to her and work hard. For years, I lived with the impression that she directed most of her attention to just me. In an egotistical way, I felt I was so special that she gave me all of her undivided attention. I thought how fortunate I was that she had singled me out. And then, as I met others over the years who felt the same way, I realized that was her magic: She made you feel like you were hers. You! You were so important to her.

What a gift! What a gift! She gave it in abundance to so many, many of us. So, for all of them, for all of us, I say thank you. Our wonderful friend. You blessed our lives. And you did, especially, bless mine. I took every course you taught. I joined every organization you advised. I tried to debate because of you, although I was absolutely terrified to speak in public.

During most of my teenage years—and beyond—my goal was to please you. Later, I compared every other teacher I knew to you. I compared myself as a teacher to you. I compared every woman to you. I compared my mother to you. I compared my wife to you.

You were my life's yardstick, and to this very day something deep inside me says I must measure up to your expectations. You will be forever with me.

---

*Cap Hicks, August 22, 1994*

The full measure of a person's life has nothing to do with those things most of us consider to be important: length of life in years, accomplishments achieved, massing material fortunes, honors garnered by the bushel baskets full. The truth of the matter is that the measure of a person's life is found in none of these. The true measure of a person's life is found not in the obvious things most people consider to be paramount.

A man is recorded in the Bible to have lived 969 years and the commentary on that long life was, "And he died." The length of the long years was not distinguished at all. "He lived and he died," a sad epitaph for one who lived longer than anyone else has before or after him.

The way you measure the true value of a person's life, I believe, is by what the person gives to others not in what he gets from others. Cap Hicks gave to others. He gave to others in abundance. Cap Hicks gave to each one of us here today. He loved helping people. He loved to have a project to be working on. He loved cutting through the bureaucracy and getting a constituent satisfied. He loved showing new legislators how the system worked. He loved doing for others. That is what he lived for.

As we all know, Cap had his own style. In politics—I guess in other things too—but you notice it more in politics, you meet a lot of fence straddlers, mealy mouthed, wishy-washy folks.

Cap detested this and didn't have one ounce of timidity in his loyal body. You've seen it. You've done it and so have I: someone would start talking about someone you really liked or were close to and you'd feel awkward, shift from foot to foot, clear your throat. But, just stand there and take it, saying nothing. That was not Cap's style at all. Right quickly, with no hesitation, Cap would say, "You're talking about him, you're talking about me. He's my friend!"

Cap Hicks loved a good fight. Whether it was an election or a vote in the legislature, he was very competitive. He was very combative, and I loved it. Some of you laughed at the highway sign dedication when I said, "We were a bad combination in that both of us were too anxious for combat. It was true. Neither would counsel the other to go slow.

Cap Hicks loved laughter and a good story. No one could tell a story with the embellishment and mimicking like Cap. He was as good as I've ever seen, better than anyone on TV. And, he could see and remember the funny things of history. He could pick out the humorous in the midst of boredom. He could cut through the pompousness of politicians. See humor in sometimes very serious situations. He was a master at that.

Cap Hicks was a patriot. An old fashioned one. Most of his friends and acquaintances never knew because Cap kept this to himself. But Cap Hicks was a hero. A legitimate war hero. The Silver Star is the nation's third highest award for heroism and valor in combat.

Marvin W. Hicks was a Silver Star winner, but he never told you or me. He fought for his country in World War II, 28 months in the European theater, 35 combat missions as an 18-19 year old aerial gunner on a B-24. We had him out to the Mansion for the 50th Anniversary of D-Day. Other veterans were there. We sang old World War II songs and he had a great time...

If a person's life is measured by what he gives to others and not in what he gets from others, Cap Hicks' life was very successful, very meaningful. He gave to Governors, Lt. Governors, Speakers, judges, legislators, commissioners and countless constituents. They all got that one-track, undivided, go-for-the goal attention. He gave to his country. He gave to his community. He gave to his family and his friends. And we will never, ever forget him...

His spirit is in that Capitol. His ghost walks the third floor of that Capitol.

Somewhere up there Saint Peter has had a good chuckle and old Marvin, Holloway, John Riley, and all the others are getting caught up on the latest gossip and some of

Cap's stories.

God, bless him and welcome him home, and thank you for allowing him to come our way and touch our lives.

---

*Mary Olmstead, November 21, 1994*

Mary Olmstead was a very dear friend of Shirley's and mine, and we were deeply saddened at her passing. She reminded me of Ruth in the Bible. Ruth was devoted to her family and friends. She always put their needs ahead of her own. And her family and friends loved her dearly.

That was true of Mary to the very end of her life. Even when she wasn't well...when she was in pain and knew she didn't have long to live, Mary continued to devote herself to the care and support of those she loved.

I will never forget stepping off the plane in Macon just two weeks ago from today—on the last stop of our fly-around on the day before the election—and there was Mary at the airport to greet us and show us her care and support. Then again the next day, she came to Atlanta with Tommy to be with Shirley and me during that nerve-wracking time of watching the election returns come it. She stayed with us well into the night. She wasn't well. Her health was failing. Anyone else would have stayed home in bed. But Mary came to be with us.

She continued to devote herself to others right up to the end. She was strengthened by the depth of her love for those she cared about, and we were strengthened by the magnitude of her caring. I will never forget the love and loyalty and friendship she gave so generously to Shirley and me.

Like Ruth of the Bible, Mary was married to a leader, a man of position and authority in his community. Like Ruth, Mary gave her husband her loyalty and help and support in his responsibilities. And, behind the scenes, they had a very special, loving relationship with each other. As Ruth said in the Bible, "Whither thou goest, I will go; and where thou lodgest, I will lodge; thy people shall be my people, and thy God my God."

Like Ruth, who put in long days gleaning in the fields, Mary worked hard. In addition to raising her family and renovating her own historic home, she devoted herself to this community, helping to preserve Macon's rich heritage. And what Ruth's husband, Boaz, said of her is also true for Mary: All the city knows that she was a woman of great worth.

Shirley and I join you in paying tribute to the life of Mary Olmstead, and to the love and care which she gave so generously to us. Like you, we will miss her very, very much. And she will continue to live and to touch our lives in the very special memories we all have of the many times she was there for us. The times when she put our needs ahead of her own, and reached out to give us her very special love and care.

---

*Mickey Mantle, August 20, 1995*

Seeing Gary Cooper play Lou Gehrig in the movie *Pride of the Yankees* did it for me. After "the luckiest man on the face of the earth" speech, I was hooked. So, at an early age I became a die-hard New York Yankees fan, one of only a few, I guess, in rural Georgia.

I followed the team religiously; I saw Joe DiMaggio, Charlie Keller, and Tommy Henrich at old Ponce de Leon as they came through during spring training in the 1940s. I even got Keller's autograph (and DiMaggio's 50 years later). So when the "Comet from Commerce," Mickey Mantle, came up in 1951, I immediately became an ardent, adoring fan of this gifted young god.

I got to see him play, too, his first year in the majors. My Aunt Mary took me to New York that summer as a graduation present for finishing Young Harris College. She told me that we would get to see the Broadway play "Oklahoma" and the Statue of Liberty. I wanted to see Yankee Stadium and Mickey Mantle. So, while the others took the sight-seeing bus, I went to see my "Field of Dreams." To say that it was an unforgettable experience is an understatement. Mantle beat out a drag bunt that day, and for 44 years I've told the story over and over again about how he could fly.

They sent him down to Kansas City about a month later. He wasn't hitting. Deeply disappointed, he wanted to quit the game, but after a talk with his father, he began hitting again. He came back, and he never left again until that day in 1968, when, after playing with pain for years, that magnificent body would no longer respond as he thought it should, so he took off his uniform and went home. But he never really left our public consciousness, and he never will—not as long as they play the game of baseball.

I saw Mickey play only once more, this time at old Comiskey Park when as a Marine I was stationed at Great Lakes, Ill. I followed his career daily, poring over every box score, reading every article, watching every game on TV.

So, you see, it was a dream come true when I finally got to meet the legend himself in Greensboro one warm Georgia day in 1991. I went to Lake Oconee to a golf tournament, wanting to see him close up, maybe even get to shake his hand and tell him what a fan I was. I figured it would mean nothing to him, because he had heard that from a million other fans just like me. But I got to do more. Lots more. I sat around the 15th hole with him and Hank Bauer, another Yankee great and a former Marine like me. Mickey would hit a golf ball to the green, and if anyone in the foursome coming through came closer to the pin that he did, they'd get an autographed ball. Hank and I were his helpers, setting up photos and handing him balls to sign. I stayed there all day long right to the end. I was, to put it mildly, in heaven.

I could tell he was surprised that I knew so much about his career; that I, like he, came from a very small town; and that I was outspoken in my belief that the 1961 Yankees were the best team ever. As they would say in small towns like Young Harris, Ga., and Commerce, Okla., "We hit it off."

So began my friendship with Mickey Mantle. Never in my wildest imagination would I have dreamed this would happen. I came to realize, after many hours together, that this man who had been my lifetime idol from afar was also a hero up close. He was generous, thoughtful, and funny. Some brief examples of each.

Generous: There's a beautiful baseball field at Young Harris College, largely because

Mickey and Hank Aaron (another hero) did a fund-raiser where we raised $66,000 to build it. During the terrible flood of 1994, Mickey suggested that he make a donation for the flood victims in Macon. "Is $25,000 enough?" he asked. He did all kinds of things for folks, for which he did not want any credit. Just ask the people in Greene County. Then of course, the last, most generous, and most significant: An endowed chair at the Baylor University Medical Center.

Thoughtful: It was impossible for Mickey to appear in public like a normal person. He couldn't go to ball games; he couldn't eat in restaurants; he couldn't do anything without being literally hounded to death for a photo or an autograph or a handshake. Think of living with that for all your adult life. And yet, through it all, there was the smile, the graciousness, the seeking to please.

He called me from Chicago a day after being in Atlanta the night before. We had eaten in a restaurant and he had been unable to wait to pose for a picture with a man who couldn't get his camera to work. He wanted me to tell the man he'd try to do it the next time he was here. It had bothered him that the man, whom he had never seen before or would see again, might consider him rude.

He lavished gifts on me, autographed baseballs, not just from him but from Whitey, Yogi, and others. He took me to meet Willie Mays, Stan Musial, and Ted Williams. He gave me one of his bats, a Yankee warm-up jacket for Christmas, took me to his Fantasy Camp in Fort Lauderdale, and to Old Timers Day at Yankee Stadium. He helped in my campaign and wanted to be present at my inauguration: He liked winning. And without my knowing it that day, he left me an autographed inauguration program with this inscription, "Zell, I've been on some great teams and had some great wins. But this is one of the all-timers. Thanks a lot. Mickey Mantle."

Funny: He had a tremendous sense of humor—the kind athletes have when they rag you about everything, the practical-joke kind, the locker-room kind. His eyes would sparkle, his nose would squinch up and he'd give you that big, toothy grin. Even in the hospital after the transplant, he wanted to pose in a rubber mask of an old ugly man to show his friends back in Georgia how he was doing.

We had a running joke about who came from the smallest town. I once went to his hometown of Commerce and wrote him a letter on city hall stationery, which I got from the little police department, saying that I had counted the red lights and there were three in Commerce, but none in Young Harris. He immediately countered with, "but I'm not really from Commerce. I just grew up there. I was born in Spavinaw" (a spot in the road a few miles away in that hard country).

While in Commerce I went by the home where he had lived, a tiny wooden frame house with green asbestos shingles on the side. I walked in the field out behind where his daddy had taught him as a youngster to switch hit, skipping supper and working with him for hours and hours until it got dark. I cried as I thought, this is where it all started for Mickey.

I went to Dallas to see him a few days after the liver transplant. His son, Danny, took me in, because he was not allowed to have visitors. Mick showed me his stapled belly and shook his head over his shriveled legs. "Look at these wheels," he said. We talked about Georgia, the good times, the people we knew, and we made the funny photo with the mask. A nurse came in and glared me as if to say I should not be in the room. Mickey told her, "Don't worry about him; that's my daddy." When I went to leave, we shook hands, embraced, and I said, "I'll see you back in Georgia." He paused a long time as if to think about that, and softly responded, "I hope so."

As one who has had a niece die after two liver transplants, I am no stranger to the organ transplant program. Shirley and I long ago signed our donor cards. So I have been saddened by those who don't understand how the transplant program works and have said some vicious and inconsiderate things. I'd like to point out to the cynical and uninformed that Mickey Mantle gave a face to organ transplants, a famous face, a face it had never had before. There have been thousands who have become donors because they learned about it from this man. There will be many more.

That and the chair at Baylor are now as much a part of the legacy of Mickey Mantle as the statistics and the awesome talent. As Bob Costas said in his moving eulogy, No. 7 had "a great ninth inning."

---

*Stuart Lewengrub, November 8, 1995*

Stu Lewengrub was a friend of mine for more than a quarter of a century. A good man who did good work as executive director of the Southeast office of the Anti-Defamation League of B'nai B'rith. Stu's strength, devotion, and professional leadership made the ADL a strong and effective organization in this community. And more times than anyone will ever know, I called on Stu for help and advice on sensitive issues.

But our friendship was more than a professional one. He and I were both baseball trivia fanatics, and we both did our share of hosting radio quiz shows in our time, where listeners would call in and try to stump us. Most challenging of all were the long sessions Stu and I spent together, trying to stump each other with obscure baseball facts and statistics that most people neither know nor care about. He was extremely knowledgeable, and boy was he competitive, just as he was in all areas of his life.

Stu Lewengrub was a very special person, and all of us who knew him, especially B'nai B'rith, are going to miss him very much. But because he was a very dynamic person who was always a vivid part of our landscape, we also have a lot of fond memories of Stu. And I know that next time I am faced with a difficult problem in human relations, I will miss Stu. Next time I am trying to remember a bit of baseball trivia, I'll think of Stu. And I'll hear his voice again in my memory.

Shalom, my dear friend.

---

*Peter Zack Geer, January 8, 1997*

There were three things that Peter Zack loved above all—except, of course, family: The law, politics and this part of Georgia.

He loved the law. He revered it. It was in his blood. His grandfather, William Idus Geer, was an attorney and a judge. His father, Peter Zack Geer, Sr., was an attorney and a judge. And his Uncle Walter was an attorney and a judge. It was in his blood. He attended the Walter F. George School of Law at Mercer University, where he won the freshman scholarship award, delivered the annual senior address, and graduated cum laude.

He was powerful in the court room, spell-binding to watch and acknowledged as one of the great criminal lawyers in Georgia. I always thought that if I ever got in serious trouble and needed to have a lawyer, I'd want Peter Zack or Denmark Groover. Who will ever forget or cease to appreciate his prosecution of the Alday Family killers...

I was in the State Senate when Peter Zack was with Governor Vandiver. I loved his style. I heard early on the story of Peter Zack calling a department head and asking him to do something on behalf of Governor Vandiver. When the department head hesitated, Peter Zack asked him if he had heard of Executive Order Number One. "Well, no," the department head answered. To which Peter Zack responded, "Executive Order Number One says, "Damn It, Do It." I liked his style.

In 1962 he was elected Lieutenant Governor, and I served under him in the Senate. Without question, he was the best presiding officer I've ever seen. He was a lot of help to Governor Carl Sanders, who talked with him and thanked him again only a few days before his death.

In 1966, when a joint legislative session had to choose between "Bo" Callaway and Lester Maddox, Peter Zack, although he had been defeated, did such a dignified and forthright job of presiding, he received national attention. No one else could have handled that difficult and very volatile job in such a firm and fair way.

Of course, he loved this region. He loved Miller County, all the rural counties...the fertile fields and piney woods of Southwest Georgia. It is therefore fitting and proper that 65 miles of State Route 91 through this area be designated the "Peter Zack Geer Highway" by the DOT Board on January 16th. That stretch runs from the South Albany city limit across Baker, Miller, and Seminole counties, joining the Herman Talmadge Bridge (isn't that how he'd like it) south of Donaldsonville.

Peter Zack loved the people, and that love was returned. Once when he was representing a client from this area, a man of very modest means, the opposing lawyer, a little uppity, referring to Peter Zack's reputation and fees, said, "And how are you going to pay Mr. Peter Zack Geer?" That South Georgia man replied, "In butter beans and quail."

He loved this area so much, it was always difficult to get him to leave it. He could have made more money practicing in some large city, but this is where his heart always was. It held him like a dog on a leash. It was in his soul, and where he wanted to be buried.

Things end. Dramas, wars, careers, eras, loves, and lives. The mortal life of this dynamic young man—I still think of him that way: as a young man—has ended. But in the mirror of our minds, forever, we will see that intimidating presence, that erect and confident posture, that glint in his eye when he kind of "gotcha" or had made a good point.

We'll see him on the political stump with the crowds hushed, listening to every word because Peter Zack was speaking. We'll see him enjoying a drink, waiting behind a dog for a covey to rise....I'll see him riding a horse in a wagon train going up Bald Mountain. The other candidates had come to that event in expensive suits. You can guess who carried

Towns County.

Yes, he lives on, not only in our minds so vividly, but also in his son and daughter and grandchildren. So today I say to Mrs. Geer and Ada and all the family, that in all of our tomorrows, as we remember and love Peter Zack, we will remember and love you.

———————

*Joe Kennedy, June 21, 1997*

I have lost one of the best friends I've ever had—and Georgia has lost one of it's finest public servants. We will not see his like again. A big oak has fallen in the forest.

In this atmosphere where politics is becoming increasingly so uncivil and nasty—Joe Kennedy was always civil, polite, and pleasant. It was not weakness, for there was not a weak bone in his body. It was the way he was, the way he had been raised. It was just good manners from a southern gentleman.

When I heard of his death Friday morning, like you I was stunned and shocked. Shirley and I had been with him and Lalah only a week before, and, in his position as a University Regent, we were planning to be together often, spending some time with each other as we once had—back in what I call the Senate years. Those were wonderful times. We traveled together...we visited each other. I shaved and showered in his bathroom. We relaxed at the Pond House. We rode in parades.

For sixteen years, I presided over the Senate. For sixteen years I looked slightly down into that face on the front row—as close as I am to him right now. The speaker in the well would be right between us. I could always get Joe's message to me without him saying a word. It would be a twinkle in his eye—a wink sometimes—and sometimes, as quick as one of those rattlesnakes that live around here, he would go way around with a sweeping arm, pick up the microphone for a penetrating question to the speaker in the well. It would be so quick and he would be on his feet so fast, that the speaker in the well, only a few feet from him, would recoil with a step backward.

It would nearly always be one short question—Joe was a man of few words—but it would go, it would zing, to the heart of whatever the subject was. It could be so devastating that the speaker would almost panic to get out of the well and get back to his seat. It could be so encouraging that the speaker would quickly take it as his own argument as if he had just thought of it himself. Without a word, with only eye contact, we communicated in a special way.

He helped me so much. I'd get off on something, I won't mention any specifics, but there's no way it would be hugely popular in Southeast Georgia, but he'd stick with me, because I was his friend—or because he could see the big picture.

We're going to miss him around the Capitol—it will never be the same. This area is going to miss him. The University System of Georgia is going to miss him. There would not have been a Georgia Southern University without Joe Kennedy, and he was getting ready to contribute so much more in that new job as a Regent.

Most of all, his family is going to miss him. He loved you all so much, and he was so proud of you. It just radiated from him. You talk about family values. Joe Kennedy lived and breathed and laughed and cried family values.

I wish every person first getting into politics could have known and watched Joe Kennedy in action. He was so good, so able, so sincere, so filled with integrity, and so pure.

No, we will not see his like again. But because he served and walked among us, this family, this county, this state, this Governor are all so much better off because he came our way.

---

*Bill Burson, November 15, 1997*

There is a well-known book entitled *The Transformation of Southern Politics*. The name of Bill Burson is not in it. It should be. Bill Burson could have written it...in the first person. Too many people know too little about this man. He was one of the visionaries. It burned in him to do something about that "one-third of a nation, ill-housed, ill-clad, ill-nourished" that Franklin Roosevelt spoke of. And he did. He truly was one of the architects of the Georgia we know today...a Georgia no longer shackled by segregation, malnutrition and ignorance.

Today we celebrate the life of this unique individual. Brilliant. Blunt. Bullheaded. Rigid, and right. An original personality who in his own unsung, and largely unknown, manner helped to change Georgia in a profound and significant way. His life-long habit of never taking credit, never wanting credit, has left us—even those who knew him best—without a true and thorough record of his accomplishments.

Burson worked in strange and mysterious ways. A major decision, a memorable speech by a U.S. Senator, a Governor, a Lieutenant Governor, a Speaker, a Comptroller General, or a candidate—and he worked for all of them—will never be credited or remembered as a Burson contribution. But more often than not, it was. From the network of Burson, "B" Brooks and Bob Short came "wonders to behold," and to listen to. The Vandiver speech on keeping the University open was a profile in courage. The Maddox inaugural address was a surprisingly moderate masterpiece.

What I'm trying to say is that in the 1950s, 60s and 70s, his influence was enormous. Even those who knew him best, much less the general public, will never know just how enormous. But, you see, that's the way Bill wanted it, and he would be a little amused at me today for trying to sort it out and put it together. He'd have that little half-smile on his face as if to say, "It's my little secret. And that's the way I want it."

Bill Burson was a genius: valedictorian of his high school class, Phi Beta Kappa at the University of Georgia, magna cum laude graduate at age 19, and the youngest combat correspondent in Korea, cited for bravery under fire. He also commandeered—that was Burson's term for it; it was a synonym for "stole"—commandeered a colonel's jeep, painted it a different color and drove it all over the battle front, then gave it to the UPI correspondent sent to relieve him.

Perhaps one of Burson's highest compliments came from former Governor and United States Senator Herman Talmadge, who asked his press secretary Walter B. Brooks, "Who is that reporter who asks such good questions?" "It is Bill Burson of United Press International," Brooks replied. "Hire him!" Talmadge ordered. "He's smarter than you are."

Brooks did, and in so doing launched the long and successful public career of this remarkable man...

Bill was also a family man, a loyal son, a devoted husband and a loving father who took great pride in his children and spoke of them often.

Bill Burson was a good and decent man, the most scrupulous, most talented and most conscientious person I have known in Georgia politics. I consider myself very fortunate to have worked so closely with him. I will always treasure a note he wrote me the day before he died, after I had visited him for a while. He ended it with the words, "I love you, man. P.S. Excuse a sick man's scrawl."

Bill Burson, I love you too, man. And P.S. Excuse an inadequate man's tribute.

----------

*Pete McDuffie, April 7, 1998*

He made us laugh. He made us think. He spun yarns about a Georgia that is all but disappeared, and of a kind of politics that is no more. Bagby...Culver...Hodge...Cap... Pete...genuine articles. Originals, all of them. And could they play off one another. Better...funnier than anything you'll ever see on TV.

I first met Pete when he came to the Senate in 1971. I was the new Lieutenant Governor Lester Maddox's aide, and he was presiding over the Senate for the first time. Not one of his favorite jobs, I might add. It was interesting times...a unique time in Georgia politics. And Pete was right in the middle of it.... right in the middle of that stormy, tempestuous time...

Pete attracted friends like honey attracts flies, and people all over the state knew him. Mention his name, and someone will come up with their own Pete McDuffie story. He had that marvelous sense of humor, but underneath was a heart with a soft spot for anyone who needed his help. Helping people was one of his greatest talents.

Not too long ago, Pete was talking to former Senator Hodge Timmons, and he was complaining that he'd called Senator Rooney Bowen and Rooney had not called him back. Hodge, also out of political office by then, replied, "Pete, write this down. Heavies don't call lights, and you are now a light...Welcome to retirement."

To me, however, Pete McDuffie will always be a heavy. Although we mourn his loss and the empty place it leaves in our lives, when we think about him, there will always be a smile for the humor and for the genuine caring he brought into our own lives and into the lives of so many others.

We won't see his like again, and no one who knew him will ever forget him. Right now, as we leave this church, Pete is up there with Culver and Cap and Bagby having a good time. That's how he would want us to remember him.

----------

*Elmore Thrash, June 10, 1998*

We will miss this witty, funny, and good man. No one lived a more complete or fuller life. He taught us how to laugh at ourselves and not to take ourselves so seriously, and how to grow old with grace and optimism. I never knew anyone who grew old with more style and flair. Like all of you and thousands who could not be here, I loved him.

Often I would come in and he'd be waiting on me in the Governor's Office. Usually it was a word or two of sage advice, or a penetrating observation putting a different take on some controversial subject of that legislative day.

He will be missed. But that indomitable spirit will forever be with us. I'll think of him frequently as I grow older. He showed me and you how it should be done.

And the spiritual presence of Elmore Thrash will hover over that Speaker's rostrum and walk that third floor for many years to come.

Farewell, our dear friend. We will never see another like you.

# Great Georgians

## Hank Aaron

Shirley and I are pleased to welcome all of you to the Governor's Mansion for this dinner honoring a man who is one of baseball's all-time greatest players and one of my own personal bigger-than-life heroes.

Hank Aaron grew up at a time when a professional athletic career was little more than a pipe dream for minority youth. But his athletic talents caught the eye of the barnstorming Indianapolis Clowns, and then a .467 batting average drew the attention of the big leagues. And what was once an unattainable boyhood dream became a single-minded pursuit of baseball excellence that lasted a quarter of a century...a career during which Hank Aaron piled up and still holds more major league batting records than any other player in the history of the game.

Since retiring from the line-up, Hank has turned his drive and pursuit of excellence to the benefit of Atlanta, contributing to this community in countless ways. He is an inspiration and mentor to young baseball players and a tireless contributor to many worthwhile causes.

So it is indeed a privilege for Shirley and me to welcome all of you to this birthday tribute to a great athlete, a great leader, and a great man whom I am honored and humbled to call my friend.

—*Hank Aaron Birthday Dinner, February 5, 1994*

## Jimmy Carter

My personal friendship with Jimmy Carter goes back more than 30 years to when we served together in the Georgia Senate. And it was obvious to me then already that he was a most remarkable man. He became one of Georgia's most progressive Governors, and then he beat the political odds to become the first and only President of the United States to come from Georgia...

But when history looks back on Jimmy Carter, I suspect it will remember him as much for his achievements since leaving the presidency as for his four years in the White House. Unlike other presidents, who retired to private lives of comfort and ease, he has continued to crusade for a just and decent life for all people. He and Rosalynn have taught us by example that there is "everything to gain" and "how to make the most of the rest of your life." Rather than a typical presidential library of documents gathering dust, the Carter Center in Atlanta is a living nerve center for ongoing programs that serve human needs here at home and around the world.

This museum in the high school that Jimmy Carter attended, salutes his leadership through service to his fellow human beings in all of its many forms...whether as a scoutmaster in Plains, or as commander in chief in Washington...whether building houses for Habitat for Humanity in Hungary, or building democracy in Latin America... Whether teaching a Sunday school class at Maranatha Baptist Church, or brokering peace in the Middle East.

As this new museum in an old place of learning continues to teach its visitors how Jimmy Carter has made the world a better place, it will once again inspire young people...offering them the chance to sit in the same place where Jimmy and Rosalynn sat when they were young. Offering them a chance to learn from the Carters' example how one person really can change the world.

I am proud that the State of Georgia has played a small part in this project. But our contribution, and indeed this entire museum is but a small tribute in return for the inspiration and public service Jimmy Carter has given Georgia, the United States, and the world.

President Carter, on behalf of the State of Georgia, we are proud to have the privilege of knowing you and of claiming you as one of our own. We are deeply grateful for all you have done for us and for this nation. And we are pleased to dedicate this museum to you, in admiration and gratitude for what you have achieved, and in the hope and expectation that it will inspire many others to follow in your footsteps.

—*Dedication of Carter Museum, Plains, October 1, 1996*

## Lewis Grizzard

Lewis Grizzard was born at Ft. Benning and grew up in Moreland. By the age of 10, his dream was to become a sports writer and cover the Atlanta Crackers. As a shy youth, he walked into the old newspaper office on Forsyth Street in Atlanta and applied for a job. He was told there was none. If someone had told him then that he would become a famous syndicated columnist and the author of books that made the *New York Times*'s best seller list, he would have laughed. But he went on to become the "boy wonder" sports editor of the *Athens Daily News* at the age of 19, and he spent the rest of his life defying the odds again and again.

After a variety of sports writing and editing jobs, including executive sports editor of the *Chicago Sun-Times*, he came home to Georgia to stay in 1977, and in 1978 his writing found its home in a column on the news pages of the *Atlanta Constitution*. That column caught on like wildfire, and his first book, a collection of his columns, appeared in 1979. By the time of his passing, he was syndicated in 450 newspapers; he had 20 books to his credit; and he was in demand as a performer with a proven ability to captivate an audience with his humor.

He said that his mother taught him "a love of words, of how they should be used and how they can fill a creative soul with a passion and lead it to a life's work." He learned the lesson well.

He remained a down-home country boy, whose rural edges were never quite smoothed away by fame and big-city life. His subjects often came from his own daily life—his love of the South, trains, dogs, country music, and the University of Georgia; his dislike of airplanes and Yankees; his devotion to his family roots; and even his own foibles and flaws.

He was a modern-day Will Rogers, a 20th-century Mark Twain who told it like it like it was. He had a special insight into the humor and sense of the ordinary things we all experience, and a unique ability to distill the essence of people we all knew into fictitious characters. Those gifts enabled him to touch people from all walks of life, and even when they didn't agree with him, he could still make them laugh and cry.

*—Music Awards Banquet, September 24, 1994*

## Margaret Mitchell

I have always had a great admiration for Margaret Mitchell. She is not only in my book, *Great Georgians*, she is also on the dust jacket.

When an ankle injury ended Peggy Mitchell's career with the *Atlanta Journal Magazine*, her husband, John Marsh, suggested she write a book. So she thought back to her childhood, when she had spent long Sunday afternoons listening to elderly relatives refight the Civil War in their living rooms. Soon her apartment was awash with manuscript. Completed chapters were used as door stops. When she finally gave it to Harry Latham of the Macmillan Company, he had to purchase a large suitcase to carry the five-foot stack of manila envelopes.

Within four months of its publication in 1936, more than 700,000 copies of *Gone With the Wind* had been sold. It was translated into 21 languages and printed in Braille. But success and acclaim changed little in the modest lifestyle of Margaret Mitchell. She stayed out of the limelight, refused interviews, and went on living as she had always lived. So few mementos remain to commemorate the woman whose literary masterpiece has taken on a life of its own in the imaginations and hearts of countless readers around the globe.

*—Open Margaret Mitchell House, May 16, 1997*

## Billy Payne

The Olympic journey that brought us to this day was begun a number of years ago by one man who undertook it pretty much single-handedly. At the time, a lot of people thought he was crazy. The process of winning the right to host the 1996 Olympics was a difficult and demanding task. The voices of doubters and skeptics were heard in the land. But with enthusiasm and single-minded determination, Billy Payne stayed the course and overcame the odds.

*—Olympic Flag Arrival in Atlanta, September 21, 1992*

_____

Many people were amazed when Atlanta became the U.S. nominee to the International Olympic Committee. They were even more amazed when this city was actually chosen over Athens, Greece, to host the Centennial Games. But they had reckoned without a man named William Porter Payne. The *only* reason the Olympics came to Atlanta, was because this one man had a great vision and worked without ceasing to realize what many considered an impossible dream.

More than a decade ago, back when I was Lieutenant Governor, he walked into my office, and told me, as persuasively as anyone could ever have done, how Atlanta could host the Olympics in the far-off year of 1996. I was only one of many people that Billy Payne visited to lay out his vision for the Atlanta Games. Most of them thought he was crazy.

Convincing Atlanta that we could even be a contender to host the Olympics, was like missionary work among cannibals. But Billy never gave up, and the fact that Atlanta, considered a long-shot, was actually chosen, is a direct tribute to his persistence.

Once he'd won the election and Atlanta had been chosen, he took on the challenge of actually putting on the Games. It was another monumental task. Ten new athletic venues had to be built at a cost of over $600 million. Other venues had to be renovated and upgraded. Several dormitories had to be built on the Georgia Tech campus to give it the housing capacity to serve as the Olympic Village.

In full swing, the Atlanta Olympic Committee would have ranked among the Fortune 500. It had more than 1,000 employees and a budget of $1.7 billion, which had to be raised privately.

It was Billy Payne who made it work. And he did it through team building. He carefully identified skilled persons for each critical task, and devoted his energy to making them function as a team, as a well-oiled machine whose parts all worked together toward a common end.

Billy Payne worked harder and longer, and with greater single-minded determination than any athlete who competed in Atlanta last summer. A gold medal would be small change compared to the magnitude of the great gift he gave us. In Georgia, Billy Payne will always be Mr. Olympics. He is the biggest Olympic hero we will ever have.

*—NGA New Governors Conference, November 15, 1996*

_____

Two years ago, we were in the frenzy of last-minute preparations to host the biggest peacetime event in world history. Enthusiasm and excitement were in full bloom throughout the state. The Olympic dream was unfolding before our very eyes.

And in the midst of that whirlwind of activity, I would sometimes stop and think back to that day, years before, when I was Lieutenant Governor and Billy Payne came to my office to tell me his dream of bringing the Olympics to Atlanta.

At that time, the Olympic dream was so incredible, that many considered it a pipe dream. Yet Billy was so convinced it could happen, that I said at that time he might very well do it, because Billy Payne possesses in abundance the most valuable character trait a human being can have—perseverance, sheer perseverance. Billy demonstrated to all of us what that word really means.

Perseverance is what gave him the energy to keep knocking on doors and telling the dream even when people said he was crazy. Perseverance is what made him press on until he persuaded a few folks to provide a little financial backing, and Georgia Tech to provide a little computer technology.

Even after Atlanta became the U.S. entry in the international hosting competition, many people still considered it a long shot. But Billy never gave up, and in the end, that is what brought the Olympics to Georgia—the simple fact that one man named William Porter Payne never gave up.

Plenty of people have dreamed dreams that are just as grand and as visionary as Billy's was. But very, very few of them ever exercise the perseverance that it takes to make those dreams come true. That is what we pay tribute to as we honor Billy Payne with this statue. We not only thank him for the incredible gift he gave the State of Georgia in the form of the Olympic experience, but we also lift up his living example of the power of one person's perseverance to achieve what virtually everyone else considered impossible.

—*Unveil Billy Payne Statue, March 27, 1998*

## Jackie Robinson

I believe Jackie Robinson is one of the most important persons in the 20th century. If there had not been a Jackie Robinson, then there would have been no Martin Luther King Jr., who changed not only this country, but the world. And I find it very interesting that both these men were Georgians. Jackie Robinson's struggle to integrate baseball not only foreshadowed the civil rights movement, it paved the way; it laid the foundation on which the movement was built.

Jackie was born here in Grady County. I just came from the location where the house stood in which he was born. He was the son of a sharecropper, the grandson of a slave. His tremendous athletic gifts were clearly evident from early childhood. His teammate Roy Campanella said, "Jackie could beat you every way there was to beat you. He could think so much faster than anybody I ever played with or against. He was two steps and one thought ahead of everyone else."

But it was more than athletic gifts that made Jackie Robinson one of the most important persons in 20th century America. It was his character. It was not easy—and he later entitled his autobiography "I Never Had It Made." Despite being a high school star in several sports, no major colleges recruited him until he had completed two astounding years at his local junior college. At UCLA, he was the first student in school history to letter in four sports—football, basketball, baseball and track—but no pro team in any of those sports recruited him.

He went into the Army during World War II, where he first spoke out against discrimination. When he got out, he signed with the Kansas City Monarchs, one of the Negro Leagues' best baseball teams. The team made long, grinding trips in cramped, broken-down buses. At many places they simply could not find restaurants or hotels that would accept black guests.

But that did not keep Jackie from hitting .350 and running the bases as few men could. When Branch Rickey approached him about playing for the Brooklyn Dodgers, he was ready. But was baseball ready for him?

Branch Rickey knew it would take more than a gifted athlete to break baseball's color barrier. It would also take a gentleman who could hold his tongue in the face of taunts, obscenities, and even injuries, so that no one would have any excuse for trying to get rid of him.

No one was a stronger competitor than Jackie Robinson, and he was used to speaking up for his rights. So turning the other cheek was a hard challenge. But he knew he had to do it. Years later he wrote, "I had no right to lose my temper and jeopardize the chances of all the blacks who would follow me if I could help break down the barriers."

His first season with the Dodger's top farm team was a triumph. He led the league with a .349 batting average and with 113 runs scored. He stole 40 bases and was rated the best second-baseman in the league. But Jackie felt the tremendous pressure. He had trouble sleeping. He could not eat a full meal. He felt he was carrying the weight of all black Americans on his back, and that he had to make good so that other doors would open for them.

After one season with the farm team, Branch Rickey moved Jackie to the big leagues—first base for the Brooklyn Dodgers. When the Dodgers opened against Philadelphia in early April of 1947, the Phillies from the manager on down, heaped the foulest racial abuse they could think of onto Jackie. Later Jackie admitted that of all the unpleasant days of his life, this one brought him closest to cracking.

All through the 1947 season, the pressure never let up. Fans and opposing players shouted obscenities. Pitchers threw at his head. Runners tried to knock him down or spike him. Infielders kicked him or stepped on his legs when he slid. But day after day, through the 154 games of that season, Jackie Robinson played with an athletic brilliance and a personal dignity that slowly chipped away at the preconceived notions about who blacks were and what they could accomplish.

His fans also understood the significance of what he was trying to do, and they modeled their behavior after his. They knew that just like Jackie had a responsibility to hold his temper on the field, they had a responsibility to hold theirs in the stands. The by-word that spread from city to city as the Dodgers traveled, was "Don't spoil Jackie's chances."

At the time, Jackie said, "There is no possible chance that I will flunk it or quit before the end for any other reason than I am not a good enough ball player." He was a good enough ball player. In fact, he was so good, that baseball had no choice but to give him the Rookie of the Year Award, which in 1947 covered both leagues.

Once his position on the Dodger roster was well established, Branch Rickey gave him the freedom to speak out. And for the rest of his life he spoke out against injustice and unfairness, caring nothing about the popularity it cost him.

Shortly before his death in 1972, Jackie wrote, "A life is not important except in the impact it has on other lives." Today, we can only begin to guess the vastness of his impact on the millions of white Americans who had their horizons widened and the millions of black Americans who had their opportunities expanded because of his life.

Armed with athletic skills and personal determination, Jackie Robinson pressed ahead in the face of bigotry, hatred, and loneliness. And from the baseball diamond, he engaged a whole generation of Americans in a conversation on the nature of equal rights.

*—Dedication of Jackie Robinson Highway, August 27, 1997*

## Franklin Delano Roosevelt

When Franklin Delano Roosevelt first came to Warm Springs on October 3, 1924—almost exactly 70 years ago—this was a vacation resort. But he didn't come for a vacation. He came to visit a young engineer, who was using the buoyancy of the warm spring water to support him while he exercised his legs and gained enough strength to walk despite polio...

When Roosevelt returned to Warm Springs six months later to try his own hand at hydro-therapy, he found a group of fellow polio sufferers already gathered and awaiting his advice. Warm Springs was still only a vacation resort with no medical program or staff, so FDR became, in effect, the very first Warm Springs therapist in Georgia history.

Imagine how amazed and pleased he would be, if he could be here with us today and see the Roosevelt Warm Springs Institute, which grew out of his personal struggle to overcome the limits of polio in his own life....

Roosevelt's experience at Warm Springs and in the surrounding Georgia countryside gave him a firsthand, common sense feel for what the Great Depression meant in the lives of ordinary Americans in the rural South. And the reason he spoke so directly to the real needs of this nation during the Depression and the reason his programs were so practical, was because he understood the needs of his friends and neighbors here at Warm Springs and he designed programs to help people he knew....

But the best lesson that FDR can teach us comes from his own personal life here at Warm Springs and the values that characterized it. Eleanor Roosevelt said her husband's struggle with polio taught him "infinite patience and never-ending persistence" and gave him "strength and courage he had not had before." His therapist said that "he didn't really have any muscles at all. He walked on sheer determination."

*—Warm Springs Ground Breaking, September 22, 1994*

Fifty years ago, when Franklin Roosevelt died here in Warm Springs, a doctor declared him "the victim of a cerebral hemorrhage." Twenty years before that, other doctors had described FDR as "a victim of polio." But Franklin Delano Roosevelt was never the "victim" of anything. His life and his work, his causes and his crusades, are an enduring testament to the indomitable spirit of human beings, and the unconquerable will of America.

Eleanor Roosevelt said her husband's struggle with polio here at Warm Springs taught him "infinite patience and never-ending persistence," and gave him "strength and courage he had not had before." And FDR in turn gave America strength and courage we had not had before.

A man who could not walk, he was the Commander in Chief who marched freedom's forces to victory over fascism. A man born to privilege, he put the mighty power of the Presidency on the side of the "forgotten man." A man confined to a wheelchair, he put America back on its feet, after the Great Depression had put this country flat on its back. All through sheer force of his will, and a commitment to "bold, persistent experimentation."

We Georgians loved him...Loved him for bringing electricity to our remote rural homes. Loved him for bringing prosperity to our impoverished region. Loved him most of all for bringing hope to those of us born without wealth, without power and without influence...hope that the American Dream could indeed come true for us, because FDR's government would create opportunity for every American with the initiative to seize it. Yes, we Georgians loved FDR...and we love him still. After a half-century in which his memory has been lionized and his greatness universally trumpeted, FDR today is hailed as a hero by all.

But it was not always so. In his day, there were those who hated him, ridiculed him, mocked him, and even cursed him. The leading pundit of his time, Walter Lippmann, wrote that "Franklin D. Roosevelt...is no tribune of the people...He is a pleasant man...without any important qualifications for office."

Some on the right accused him of socialism, but the economic boom he began rejuvenated capitalism. Others on the left said he was too timid. But FDR straightened his back, clenched his teeth, and fought on. He knew that the troubles of his time would not be solved by an irrelevant debate between right and left, when the choice was more often between right and wrong.

He once declared defiantly, "We have invited battle. We have earned the hatred of entrenched greed." But in that process, FDR also earned the love of a grateful nation.

It is only fitting today that we honor FDR's life, and fitting too that the small shrill voices who hated him have been forgotten entirely—reduced to looking like fools and appearing only in history's footnotes.

Now, in our day and in our time, the struggles are once again titanic, and the extremists once again spew their venom. But those of us raised in the legacy of FDR know full well that if this nation truly honors the history and heritage of Franklin Roosevelt...If we remain true to that endless faith he had in working people, if we remain true to his boundless hope for America's future and his relentless quest to renew the American Dream...Then we will have fulfilled FDR's final wish, one he wrote here in Warm Springs for a speech he never lived to deliver: "The only limit to our realization of tomorrow will be our doubts of today. Let us move forward with strong and active faith."

## Dean Rusk

I am honored to be here today and join with you in dedicating this beautiful building to the memory of a remarkable Georgian who could have finished his career at any prestigious place in the world, but chose to come back to his home state and to this campus. As President Knapp noted, he considered himself first and foremost an educator. But on his way here to this Law School, he made his mark on our nation and the world.

President Lyndon Johnson, whom he served as Secretary of State, said Dean Rusk was "tough as a Georgia pine knot." Cyrus Vance, another former Secretary of State, characterized him as "a man of complete integrity and unstinting loyalty."

Born on a modest farm in Cherokee County, Georgia, Dean Rusk put himself through Davidson College, working at a bank and waiting tables at the boarding house where he stayed. But he still found time to play basketball, serve as ROTC commander, and graduate magna cum laude—an exceptional college career that earned him a Rhodes Scholarship.

At Oxford University, he studied international relations, history, law, politics, and philosophy. And he spent his vacations studying in Germany. He was there in Berlin when Hitler seized power in 1933.

After graduating from Oxford, he joined the faculty of Mills College in California, intent on an academic career...until December of 1940, when he received a telegram from the United States Government. It said, "Greetings. Report for active service." Those five words not only began a 30-year interruption in Dean Rusk's career as an educator, but they also changed the United States and the world.

In Europe as a student, then in the army during World War II, he was appalled at what he described as the "passivity of democracies in refusing to face up to...aggression." As a result, he volunteered for the controversial job of Assistant Secretary of State for Far Eastern Affairs in 1950. He played a key role in the U.S. decision to intervene in Korea, then helped to set the 38th parallel that still divides North and South Korea today.

During the 1960s, he served as Secretary of State under Presidents Kennedy and Johnson, helping to steer this nation through one of its most turbulent eras at home and abroad. Personal experience formed the basis for his firm diplomatic hand in dealing with the Bay of Pigs Invasion, the Berlin Crisis, the Cuban Missile Crisis, the Six Day War, and the Vietnam War.

Amid the tensions of the Cold War, Dean Rusk's personal negotiations led to a series of nuclear treaties between the United States and the Soviet Union. He was also the architect of programs to improve the quality of life in developing African nations, and of U.S. sanctions against South Africa for apartheid.

At home, he testified in support of the Civil Rights Act of 1964. He knew firsthand the negative attention America's racial problems were generating around the world. And he was acutely embarrassed when ambassadors and other dignitaries from African nations were denied haircuts or refused service at lunch with their international colleagues.

Today, a quarter-century after he left Washington, the nation and the world still bear the shape of his hand. Perhaps the most powerful legacy Dean Rusk left us was his example of courage in grappling with difficult issues, and strength of character not only to do what he perceived to be right, but also to assume responsibility for it.

But naming this building for him is especially appropriate for another reason. It was not among the power brokers of the world, but here among his students, where he was happiest and most at home.

*—Naming of Rusk Hall, UGA, September 21, 1996*

# Richard Russell

Let me tell you about a period in Georgia history. The economy was shaky and state revenues were slow. A new Governor—a former legislative leader—had just been elected on a platform that called for reorganizing state government to eliminate waste and achieve greater efficiency. A commission was studying the issue, and in the meantime, the Governor was squeezing state agency budgets hard to bring expenditures into line with revenues. Sound familiar? The year was not 1991, but 1931—60 years ago—and the Governor was Richard Brevard Russell, Jr.

We don't remember Richard Russell as Governor but as Senator. He was a "Senator's Senator" and his reverence for the institution and that of its members for him, even those who opposed him on the issues and had conflicting philosophies of government, was total and bordered on worship.

He was a confirmed bachelor who never contemplated marriage, nor was he ever publicly linked romantically with anyone. He regarded the Senate as his "life and work" and is the only Senator in history to have spent more than half of his lifetime in the Senate.

He worked 12-hour days, cooked his own meals, washed his own socks in an austere bachelor apartment, and indulged himself only with frequent visits with his kinfolks at the Russell family home in Winder.

The oldest son of 13 children of the Georgia Chief Justice for whom he was named, he was particularly close to his mother, Ina Dillard Russell. At his request, he was buried by her side in the family cemetery.

He began his remarkable career with election to the Georgia House of Representatives when he was 23 years old. He served that body for ten years, the last four as Speaker. He was elected Georgia's youngest Governor in history after a campaign in which he wore out a Model A Ford in a statewide automobile tour. He was sworn in by his father at the age of 33 in the middle of the Depression.

He had campaigned on a platform of "the 3 R's"—Reorganization, Redistricting and Refinancing." He began by cutting the state budget by 20 percent and reducing the number of state departments and agencies from 102 to 18. I'm not sure how many state employees got laid off in the process. He also established the Board of Regents to administer a unified University System of Georgia.

He established a national reputation for himself with a brilliant speech seconding the nomination of Franklin D. Roosevelt at the 1932 Democratic National Convention, and, of course, was elected to the Senate.

He went to Washington in 1933 thoroughly committed to the "New Deal." He served as floor manager for the Rural Electrification Act and authored the School Lunch Program Act. The latter he always regarded as his most important contribution to the country.

He became an expert on military matters, serving as Chairman of the Senate Armed Forces Committee and was the man most responsible for the development of the nation's Cold War defense establishment. When President Truman fired General MacArthur, he defused the explosive situation by holding impartial and exhaustive hearings over which he personally presided.

No American leader in any position other than the presidency ever exercised greater influence on power than did Richard Russell during his last two decades of service in the Senate. It was often said that the "only power a President has that Dick Russell doesn't is to push the button, and that no President would think of pushing it without first consulting Dick Russell."

*—Russell Dinner, September 14, 1991*

------------

## Celestine Sibley

So much of what we find in the newspapers today is about criminal activity, or about high-level intrigue and international diplomacy, or about the stars of sports or entertainment. We shudder at the crime and hope we never have to endure it. We look at the diplomats and the stars a little wistfully, knowing it's a world we'll never inhabit, but wondering what it might be like to have glamour, fame, and wealth.

Then we come to Celestine Sibley, who reminds us that all of that is not just counterbalanced, but outweighed by the richness and pleasures of our ordinary daily lives, if we will just stop long enough to notice them. With her characteristic down-home common sense and her great writing skill, Celestine points out that the greatest treasures are seldom the most expensive or glamorous. She refocuses our attention on what really matters—family and friends who care about us, the beauty in our own backyards or just up the road, contentment in the comforts of home, the gift of our heritage, and the privilege of living in the greatest country on earth.

She is a woman who lives each day of her own life to the fullest and makes the most of the pleasures it offers her. Whether she is writing about food or family or faith, about murder or mulching her garden, she has a way of touching something in the hearts of all of us. As her fellow writer Terry Kay says, her words get up off the page and follow us into our lives.

That gift has made Celestine Sibley one of the longest-running columnists in American newspaper history. But I have known her from the old days before she became a columnist, back when she was a reporter for the *Atlanta Constitution*.

Celestine began writing about Georgia politics when Eugene Talmadge was presiding over this state, and I am the twelfth Georgia Governor to feel the touch of her hands on the keyboard. Yet she stands out, almost alone, from among all the reporters who have covered state politics through the years, because she has never had an attitude, but is one of a very few who both understand and enjoy politics.

Back when she covered the Capitol, she was always fair, scrupulous about reporting exactly what she saw and heard. But she did it without ridicule or rancor, without favor or fear, and she never acted like she was superior in intellect or character. Of course she is, but she never wore a sign around her neck proclaiming it, as some reporters do.

What's more, she enjoyed Georgia politics and delighted in the foolishness and foibles of its colorful participants. She plainly liked us, and we unanimously adored her. The same knack that makes her such a good story teller in her columns, enabled her to recognize and appreciate the story tellers and raconteurs at the Capitol—politicians like Cheney Griffin, George Bagby, and Bobby Rowan.

She would laugh heartily at their jokes and stunts, but she never let the showmanship cloud her vision of what was significant. When she sat down to write her story, she cut straight through the rhetoric to the heart of the issue and told it like it was.

Her unique ability to fully enjoy the absurd while at the same time never losing sight of what is really important, is still at the heart of her writing today. Not only has Celestine Sibley written about the ridiculous and the sublime with equal skill, but this shrewd sister also knows the difference between the two and separates them as well as anyone I have ever known or read.

I can only remember one time when I had the rare opportunity to help her put something in perspective. We were doing a book signing together, and when it was scheduled to start, no one was there. Celestine smiled with her usual grace and said, "The worst thing in the world is to have a book signing and no one show up." To which I replied, "No, the worst thing in the world is to have a political campaign rally and no one show up." Knowing a great deal about both book signings and campaign rallies, Celestine knew exactly what I meant.

Celestine Sibley does not suffer from want of awards. She has won hundreds of them over the years, and she has advanced from competing for Pulitzers to serving on the juries that judge them. What's more, she seldom pays her awards much notice.

Nevertheless, Celestine, we are going to give you another award in a few minutes. Because we want you to know that your columns and books have been shining lights that have brightened the dark moments of our lives and shown us the way more times than any of us can count. And even if you don't pay much attention to the gas light that will honor you, it will still serve the useful purpose of reminding the rest of us of the great wealth you have given us and the many times your words have been a shining light that has touched each one of our lives.

—*Presenting Shining Light Award to Celestine Sibley,*
*November 20, 1997*

## Ted Turner

I am so delighted and pleased that you have chosen to honor Ted Turner at this event, because he has single-handedly done more to put Atlanta on the map than anyone else that I can think of. When this man started CNN back in 1980, the big boys of broadcasting regarded him as the "Rodney Dangerfield" of the industry. The Atlanta Braves, which he had purchased not long before, weren't getting much respect, either.

But during the past decade, CNN has become a powerful and influential international force in the broadcast industry. Not only does it reach more than 119 million households in more than 140 countries, but the very news media who once made fun of it have come to rely on it for information and story leads. The Atlanta Braves have likewise moved into the forefront of the sports world with historic back-to-back National League championships....

I am proud to know Ted Turner. I like him. I admire him. And I'm grateful for the tremendous contribution he has made to Atlanta by making this city the base of his operations.

*—ACVB Annual Meeting, February 10, 1993*

# Human Services

One of Publius Syrus' maxims is: "Good health and good sense are two of life's greatest blessings." Unfortunately, we do not always exercise the two of them in conjunction with each other.

Preventive health care is the most sensible part of medicine. For every dollar we spend on prenatal care, we save $3.50 in neonatal intensive care, according to the Institute of Medicine. That is why I am mandating immediate treatment for pregnant women who are drug abusers, and using the Indigent Care Trust Fund to expand perinatal care.

It is also foolish to ignore the problems of babies to save money, so I have recommended funding for an intervention program for developmentally delayed children from infancy through kindergarten age. And I am asking the General Assembly to pass language in the appropriations bill to authorize the use of Medicaid funds to coordinate a full range of services for the families of children who are identified by their schools as being at risk.

If health services, educational services, and other community services all come together at the right time, many of these children can and will grow up into productive citizens.

*—Medical Association of Georgia, February 2, 1991*

---

I have repeatedly said that I wanted to find new ways to solve old problems, and in my State of the State Address, I announced that I was requesting the departments of Education, Human Resources and Medical Assistance to work together and come up with a collaborative approach to children at risk.

The problems are obvious: 25percent of Georgia families live in poverty; only 61% of our children graduate from high school; we're third in teenage pregnancy; teens account for 25percent of all sexually transmitted diseases and approximately 60,000-80,000 sixth-twelfth graders are using alcohol or drugs. These problems lead to wasted lives and drain our limited public resources.

You may ask any teacher what makes a good student, and she will almost always point to a supportive, nurturing family. This is true because a student's intellectual growth is intertwined with his physical, emotional and social well-being. If we are to make education as effective as it can be, we must help families be as strong and supportive as they can be.

Unfortunately, many families are not strong. They are troubled—by illness, poverty or other stresses. They may need health care or counseling. They may need parenting advice or after school care...

The Joseph B. Whitehead Foundation of Atlanta is a Woodruff-related philanthropy long respected for its generosity in support of projects to benefit children. It is providing $5 million over two years to help 14 community projects get underway. Grants will be awarded to the participating communities, and the amount of each grant will depend on the need and the scope of each community program...

I do not have any preconceived ideas about what each model should look like. In fact, I would be delighted if the 14 communities developed 14 different models. What I am concerned about is providing improved services to children at the lowest possible cost to the taxpayer...

I have put this project on the fast track. I am asking that the local coalitions develop their plans this summer and plan to begin delivering services during the 1991-92 school year.

I have high expectations for this public and private partnership. It is the kind of partnership—public and private—that you have already seen before in this Administration; see again today, and will see many more times before this administration is over. This initiative will move us closer to our vision of a Georgia where every youngster has the best chance to develop his or her potential.

*—Announce Whitehead Foundation Grant, May 8, 1991*

We all know that our future prosperity depends on strong families with healthy, well-educated children. That's what all of us want. But the odds seem to be stacking up against us, and we are faced with the question of whether we are willing to do what it takes to get there.

At least one out of every four Georgia preschoolers is already at risk of becoming a non-productive adult. They walk in the door on the first day of kindergarten without the readiness skills they need. Most of them never catch up. Most of them eventually drop out. Look in the file of any young offender at a state youth detention center. You will find a whole litany of problems: poverty, substance abuse, difficulties at school, an unstable family situation at home. And you wonder where we were along the way in this kid's life. How did things get so far out of hand? How could we have done a better job starting back when this kid was one of those at-risk preschoolers?

A major goal of my administration is to piece together the various services for children from around state government—to stitch them into a quilt that covers our families who are at risk with a greater degree of comfort and security. Obviously, we do not have a lot of new money to throw at the problem. But, to quote Caldwell Johnson, who was one of NASA's most creative pioneers, "It doesn't take money to think. That's when you do your best thinking—when you have no money."

But thinking is only half the job. After the thinking, it is time to act—to act with boldness and creativity. To quote Caldwell Johnson again, the ultimate in creativity is not to invent something entirely new, but to take what you have and make it do something more. That is our goal—to take what resources and programs we already have for children, and make them do something more. The Family Connection enables us to do more with what we have by forming partnerships among our schools and social service agencies.

True working partnerships that percolate up from the local level, rather than trickle down from on high, take sweat and hard work and patience to achieve. They demand that we overcome our natural turf-guarding instincts. They do not fit neatly into our old bureaucratic structures and procedures.

As The Family Connection develops, you probably have run into rules, regulations, and practices that stand in the way of true cooperation. We must eliminate them. It is already clear in these early days that the partnerships being created by The Family Connection are exciting and rewarding, and they must be nurtured, not stifled.

When we get it together on the local level, then we not only maximize our resources, but we also have the best shot at fitting all the pieces together for our families who are at risk. From the families' perspective, dealing with government bureaucracy to get the services they need, will become less complicated and less threatening.

Our schools are a common denominator—all families in the community go through those doors. By making our schools a focal point for broader services, we also remove the stigma of seeking help. When the county health office is hooked together with the school nurse in providing immunizations, health screenings and nutrition education...when an after-school program brings community volunteers and recreation department employees to school to work with the kids...when teachers know how to tap into local social service agencies...then the process of getting help becomes easier for families, and we have a fighting chance at dealing with all those other factors outside the classroom that interfere with a youngster's ability and motivation to learn.

*—Boards of the Departments of Human Resources and Education,*
*December 11, 1991*

---

These days the wear and tear of daily life seems to be creating more problems for more people than ever before. Some blame it on an increasingly rapid rate of change in our modern world. But as a historian, I think back to the incredibly rapid changes in Europe in the decade or two before World War I, then again between the first and second world wars. Or, consider the saying that nothing is permanent but change—that astute observation about the universe dates back to the 6th century B.C.

What has changed is the speed at which we find out about the events that are happening around us. Fifty years after the invention of the battery in 1798, only a few scientists had any idea what it was. Today, any ten-year-old can tell you about computers, lasers and microchips. In 1805, news of Nelson's victory at Trafalgar took six weeks to reach Montreal. A year ago, we turned on our TV sets and watched the war in the Persian Gulf take place right before our eyes.

Past generations have been beset by far more disorder and confusion that we have in our world right now. The difference is that these days technology brings it all right into our own living rooms as it happens. We experience international events firsthand, that our parents and grandparents only learned about after they were over, if indeed they ever found out about them at all.

For many people, this increased awareness of the magnitude, drama, and immediacy of events going on in the world, carries over into their personal lives. They no longer feel certain of anything. Job, marriage, moral principles—all the things that usually anchor daily life seem to be threatened by events half way around the globe, and the little irritations of life, like a change in a procedure at work or the moving of the bus-stop around the corner, take on more dramatic proportions.

Modern science has given us a sophisticated understanding of mental illness and the ways in which it can be cured or controlled. But at the same time, the impact of modern technology on their daily lives is subjecting more people either to mental dysfunction or a pseudo-escape into alcohol and drugs.

From drug-related murders to the carnage caused on the highway by drunk drivers, nothing is more heart-rending than the violence and destruction that result from substance abuse. And we want very much to take constructive steps to reclaim the lives of those who suffer mental illness or abuse alcohol and drugs.

The same dichotomy is true for mental retardation. Scientific advances have enabled us to make great gains in our understanding of what causes mental disability and retardation. But scientific advances are also increasing the level of literacy and skills required to function in our high-tech world, making it harder for mentally disabled persons to achieve a level of independence.

*—Governor's Council on Mental Health,*
*Mental Retardation, and Substance Abuse,*
*January 29, 1992*

———————

Health care is one of the largest and most controversial social issues in the United States today. Medical advances and miracles seem to have soared off the charts, and so have our expectations that medicine can reverse or stave off the normal course of nature. But in the process, costs have soared off the charts as well. Millions of Americans are left with a lower level of health care than in countries like El Salvador and Rumania.

You know, if you're very poor, you can get basic health care through Medicaid. And if you're very rich, America offers you the best medical technology in the world. But if you're in the middle, as most Georgians are, you're not so lucky. Many working families of modest means do not have any health insurance provided by their employer. After they pay for health care for the poor with their tax dollars, they do not have enough money left to buy health insurance for themselves.

A 1991 study of Georgia's children estimates that more than one out of five is not covered either by Medicaid or private insurance. Those Georgians who do have private health insurance have seen the premium costs rise while the coverage shrinks. And the maximum amount that insurance policies will pay stays the same year after year, while medical costs shoot up two times faster than inflation. So if you or someone in your family gets very sick—before you know it, the insurance runs out and you are buried under medical bills that will take you the rest of your life to pay.

Medical care is also spread unevenly by geography. There are many rural areas of Georgia in which adequate medical care is simply not available. Obstetrical care, for example, is not available in 79 of Georgia's 159 counties—half of this state's counties have no practicing obstetrician at all. As a result, more than one in four births in this state is to a woman who has not received adequate prenatal care.

State government is caught between rising medical costs and declining federal support for Medicaid, which takes away our ability to set priorities. We are forced to put a disproportionate share of new revenues into Medicaid, to the neglect of other important programs like education, human services, and law enforcement.

Everyone recognizes the fact that we have a health care crisis. But we have not seen any comprehensive, workable solutions from the medical profession, the insurance industry, or the federal government. So we are struggling to make our way through a health care maze without the benefit of common sense policies that address the fundamental decisions and provide equal access to whatever level of basic care we agree on.

If we are to have health care policies that work to everyone's satisfaction, we must first understand the values on which the policies and the system need to be based. As a nation, America has grown up around a balance between the rights and privileges that individuals can expect from society, and the responsibilities and obligations that those same individuals have to society in return. An understanding of how that balance should be expressed in health care is the first step in developing policies and solutions.

What level of health care can society afford to provide for all of its citizens, and how are we going to pay for it? What is the best use of our resources? We now spend more on health care than we do for education and national defense combined. What should our priorities be? Elderly people make up one-eighth of the population, but one-third of the health care costs, and one of every five Medicaid dollars is spent during the last few months of the recipient's life. Are we spending too much money to prolong the suffering in cases where the natural course of life is drawing to a close and death is inevitable?

The purpose of this statewide Georgia Health Decisions campaign is to raise fundamental questions like these in the media, then discuss them at 300 community forums. All Georgia citizens will have an opportunity to share their experiences and frustrations, and discuss what they think is fair in the way of a health care system...

Insurance companies, employers and Medicaid all stretch across state lines, so many health care policy issues must be addressed on a national level. But that does not absolve us in Georgia from doing what we can to understand the problem and look for solutions.

—*Kick Off Georgia Health Decisions, March 23, 1992*

---

I believe it was the Reagan administration that described welfare with the phrase "safety net," referring to the net that catches circus acrobats who have lost their balance, and saves them from a fatal crash. In some senses, the allusion is apt. In these tough economic times, life for many has indeed become a high-wire act, where one misstep will send them tumbling. Where the parallel breaks down, is that after the safety net has caught them on the way down, circus performers crawl out of the net, climb up the ladder again, and go back to work. That is the dimension we have failed to capture in our welfare program—the climbing out of the safety net and back up the ladder. For too many Georgians, welfare is a dead end. They simply stay in the net and never climb back out to a productive life.

*—Charge to Welfare Reform Task Force, Aug 17, 1992*

_____

Hospitals that serve large numbers of low-income patients have been voluntarily donating money to the Indigent Care Trust Fund. The state then uses the fund to draw down matching federal Medicaid dollars. This program has helped to improve access to health care for thousands of Georgians unable to afford it, while at the same time helping the hospitals recover the cost of providing that care. The Trust Fund also has placed nurses in local schools in some parts of the state, assisted rural areas to recruit physicians, supported mammography screening, and expanded services for pregnant women and young children statewide.

New federal regulations will not allow the Trust Fund to continue in its present form. So constitutional amendment number 3 (on the ballot) provides for it to be restructured to conform with the new regulations.

Without passage of amendment number 3, we will lose more than $150 million a year in federal Medicaid funds. But, more than that, we will lose the momentum that has begun in communities across this state where hospitals, health directors, county commissioners and citizens are meeting at the table to discuss their community's needs. They are working together to identify local solutions to local problems, and the Indigent Care Trust Fund is fueling these efforts. We can't afford to slow down now—we're just getting started.

I don't think anyone in this room believes that any one program—this trust fund included—is going to solve Georgia's health care problems. We all know that's not realistic. But I also think we all recognize a vitally important, innovative step in the right direction when we see one.

Georgia's Indigent Care Trust Fund is held up across the nation as a model program—one that represents this state's determination to find answers and solve problems.

*—Coalition for a Healthy Georgia, October 8, 1992*

_____

Individual liberty is one of America's strongest traditions, and to a lot of people that means the right to do exactly as they please in the privacy of their own homes. But our tradition of individual liberty is counter-balanced with a tradition of corporate responsibility and caring for the well-being of all citizens.

Family violence is one of those difficult places where these traditions collide...where the ties that are supposed to bind families together and nurture them, get misconstrued as ownership rights. And in the course of exercising what they consider to be their personal rights, one family member ends up inflicting emotional damage, serious injury, or even death on another.

Although it takes place within an intimate group on private property, family violence is nonetheless a public policy issue. Not only does it violate the rights of its victims, but it also requires the expenditure of public monies for police services, criminal prosecution, incarceration and other forms of correction, custody settlements, foster care, and public assistance...

We have come to realize not only that the implementation of our laws is inconsistent, but also, and more importantly, that laws are not enough. As a result, we have created the State Commission on Family Violence.

The top priority of my administration in this time of limited resources is to be creative in finding ways to take what we have and make it do something more. To do that, we must step across organizational lines and gather the various interested parties at the table, to work together, and make better use of our limited resources. This is particularly critical in the area of human services.

Rather than more new programs, resulting in even greater fragmentation, we are building new models of relating among the departments and agencies and service providers we already have—so that people who are dealing with the same things come together to share information and coordinate their efforts...

For many years family violence remained hidden in the privacy of individual homes and nuclear families. But as our society now deals with a changing definition of what a family is, the issue of family violence has come into the public spotlight as never before. It is important that we use this opportunity to reach across organizational lines and make the best possible use of our resources in addressing it.

*—Swear in Family Violence Commission, November 2, 1992*

---

I grew up in a home without a father, and I know what it is to struggle to make ends meet. I could tell you personal stories about wearing hand-me-downs from cousins and collecting coat hangers to sell for a loaf of bread over in Techwood—stories some of you wouldn't believe.

But I have another list of stories just as long about how hard my mother worked and how she kept us going with her grit and determination—the kind of hard work and personal initiative that built this state and this nation. We have many citizens today who, like my mother, are working hard and struggling to get by, and I am concerned that we not cheapen their efforts and demean the precious values of family, hard work, and personal responsibility in our attempt to help those who are not making it.

Right now 30 percent of Georgia's welfare recipients are staying on the rolls for more than three years. For many of them, it's become a hand-out rather than a hand-up. So the central concept of my welfare proposals is personal responsibility...If we require able-bodied AFDC recipients to work, their children would be better off. AFDC benefits plus Food Stamps gives a family of three $6,864 a year. With the federal tax credit, 40 hours a week at minimum wage would give that family $11,740.

It is very important for you to realize that my welfare initiatives are but one piece of a bigger picture, and you cannot judge them fairly without also looking at the other pieces and how they all fit together. Let me mention some of the other pieces: Stronger efforts to crack down on absentee parents who fail to pay child support will help to keep children off of AFDC...prekindergarten for at-risk children, which will help working mothers with child care as well as preparing their kids for a better school experience...expanding our adult literacy program, and providing financial incentives for GED recipients to attend a technical institute or college...and expanding Medicaid to cover more children whose parents work in low-wage jobs that don't offer health benefits...

Welfare is a difficult and emotional issue because it brings some of our most precious and deeply-held values into conflict with each other. We value family, work, and personal initiative and responsibility; but we also value compassion, community and helping those who are less fortunate. Our present welfare system fails to strike an effective balance between those values. Because it only cushions poverty rather than helping people to escape it, it is failing both the people it is supposed to assist and the working people who are paying for it. Rather than isolating and stigmatizing welfare recipients, we need incentives, and support systems like job training and health care, that move them back into the mainstream of society.

That is the challenge I have been struggling with, and that is the challenge now before this committee: To make welfare into a second chance rather than a way of life.

*—House of Representatives Committee Hearing, February 8, 1993*

---

Seventeen percent of all Georgians are without health insurance at all, and 38 percent of our people will lack insurance at some point during this year. No telling how many more fear the loss of health insurance, afraid even to take a better job lest they flunk the physical.

For those of us who do have health insurance, the cost is eating us alive. That's true even if you are one of the rare few whose own premiums have not skyrocketed. Georgia businesses are spending more than $4 billion per year on employee health insurance. For the large employers, whose costs are easiest to track, the average annual cost of employee health plans jumped 80 percent between 1978 and 1991.

At a time when our businesses have been fighting their way out of a recession, it's sobering to realize just how many jobs and just how much capital investment instead had to be poured into higher health care premiums. Even if you don't own a business, you are still paying through the nose for health insurance, because all taxpayers are employers of state workers, whose health plans are costing more than five times as much as in 1981. In addition, taxpayers are also footing the rising health costs of Medicaid recipients, to the tune of $2.9 billion, up more than 200 percent since 1987.

If we want to keep people healthy, if we want to promote strong job growth in the private sector, if we want to hold down government spending, we simply have to do something about health care. Aas we all know, it will not be easy.

Just in your own deliberations, you have witnessed a parade, as long and loud as Mardi Gras, of interest group representatives who each deny any responsibility for the problem while blaming each other.

Some doctors say the lawyers are all to blame. Some lawyers say the doctors are all to blame. Some politicians say the insurance companies are all to blame. Some insurers say the politicians are all to blame.

Those on the extreme left of the political spectrum say the private health care market is all to blame, and call for socialized health insurance. Those on the extreme right of the political spectrum say that public health financing is all to blame, and call for pouring tax credits into an unregulated private market.

I say this blame game is part of the problem, not part of the solution. We are never going to achieve health care reform if we adopt the selfish point of view of those who are so busy scratching around in the pine straw that they can't see the trees, much less the forest...

Bringing some order and consistency to health care in Georgia is the key to holding down costs and improve access. We are not, however, operating in a vacuum. Medicaid is an enormous portion of our health care scheme in Georgia as elsewhere. Anything we propose to do that involves Medicaid must pass muster with the federal health care bureaucracy, which typically moves with the speed and grace of a brontosaurus.

*—Governor's Health Care Commission, September 13, 1993*

---

The ironic thing about the way state government is presently organized is that the departments of Education, Human Resources, Medical Assistance, and Children and Youth Services are dealing pretty much with the same population of children and families who are at risk. Yet there is very little opportunity or occasion for you to even talk to each other, let alone work together.

I asked you to join me today, because I want to introduce you to Governor's Policy Council on Children and Families...They are about to undertake a task that involves all of you and that has the potential to change the way you deliver services to Georgia citizens. So before the Council begins its work, I wanted to get everybody together so you would know one another, and to make sure all of you understand where we're headed.

All of you represent large state bureaucracies, and there are only two places where coordination among you is manageable. One is at the level of the local community, where that common population of children and families have names and faces that teachers, social workers, county health nurses, and juvenile judges know. The other is here at the level of the boards and commissioners who make the policy decisions. These are the two places where we are focusing to instigate long-range change in how we approach service delivery.

Many of you have already been involved at the very front-end of this process, as we have piloted The Family Connection and begun the new prekindergarten program with lottery proceeds. I want to commend and thank you for working together to make the initial launching of these two programs so successful.

The Family Connection and the prekindergarten program demonstrate two important and distinct characteristics that I want to bring to the delivery of all of your services:

First, local communities are given both more flexibility and authority, and more accountability. Rather than the state dictating from the top down how projects should be run and money spent, these programs call for broad-based community participation in deciding what to do and how to do it, then making a proposal to the state.

Second, there is a focus and emphasis on coordinating all kinds of services for children and families within the local community, so that the service providers, who are all working with the same target population, come together to share information and plan together, creating a seamless web of services that meet the needs of these children and families in the best possible way. It's not so much starting new programs, as it is starting new relationships that take our existing programs and make them do more....

Georgia has historically tended toward reacting to crises and putting out fires. We have never before developed a pro-active vision of what we want for our children and families. I believe it is going to be a very useful and worthwhile endeavor...

This is a big project; it is a long-term project; and it has major ramifications for the way all of your departments operate. You are here today, because I wanted to bring all of you to the table and involve you in the process right from the start...

Over the past two years, you as members of your respective boards have talked together and worked together more than at any other time in state history. I'm asking you today to do even more of that.

—*Boards of Human Resources,*
*Education, Medical Assistance, and Youth Services,*
*September 17, 1993*

————————

There are tremendous human and long-term financial costs that result when Georgia's tiniest citizens lack prenatal and preventive health care. That concerns me deeply, and that is why I have worked hard to improve Medicaid coverage for pregnant women and children.

Last year I proposed expanding Medicaid to serve pregnant women and their infants up to an income level of 185 percent of the federal poverty level—the maximum allowable under federal law. That became a reality on July 1st, and as a result, we anticipate that in the current fiscal year Medicaid will pay for the delivery of 60,000 Georgia babies—nearly half of all the births in this state.

We have also begun "presumptive eligibility" for pregnant women. In other words, when a pregnant woman first applies for Medicaid, if the preliminary indicators are that she is going to qualify, we begin covering her prenatal care immediately, without waiting for her application to go through all the red tape of the approval process.

We also have another Medicaid program called "Health Check" that provides well-baby screenings for children from birth to age five. But only a little more than one-fourth of the babies and preschoolers who are eligible for "Health Check" are taking full advantage of it. So we are working hard to make sure that every pregnant woman on Medicaid knows about "Health Check" and the importance of well-baby care. And we would appreciate any help you can give us in encouraging Medicaid moms to keep up with regular well-baby screenings.

We are also making immunizations for Medicaid babies more widely available at doctors offices through a new program that begins this month. The Department of Human Resources already has a contract with the Centers for Disease Control to purchase vaccines for our county health offices. We are expanding that to include vaccines for Medicaid babies, and we are signing up doctors who are willing to give the shots if we take responsibility for supplying the vaccine.

My wife Shirley has been active in helping to promote immunizations for infants and toddlers, and Georgia is making progress. Last year we reached an all-time high—73 percent of our children were fully immunized by the age of two. The national goal is 90 percent by the year 2000, and Georgia is working hard to beat it...

But best of all, it has been very exciting to see everyone's efforts begin to pay off. Last year Georgia's infant mortality rate for the first year of life was only 10.1 deaths per 1,000 births, down from 12.7 just five years earlier. In the latest state rankings that were released in January, Georgia has finally risen from the very bottom of the list for infant mortality, passing Alabama, Mississippi, and South Carolina last year.

Medicaid cannot do it alone. State government cannot do it alone. It takes all of us working together and each of us doing our part to reach mothers and babies with the information, services and encouragement they need to stay healthy. That is how we have made progress, and that is how we will continue to make progress.

*—Healthy Mothers, Healthy Babies Coalition of Georgia,*
*February 2, 1994*

———————

Last June we unveiled a "Ten Most Wanted" poster that had pictures of ten Georgians who were on the run. They were Georgia's ten worst dead-beat parents, who owed large amounts of court-ordered child support. They were on the run from their own families— the spouses they had once loved, the children they had created.

Over the past six months, seven of those ten most wanted parents discovered that while they could run, they could not hide. Acquaintances, co-workers, and employers saw them on the poster. One even turned himself in after he saw the poster, figuring his days were numbered.

Those parents are now paying up, like they're supposed to. They are taking responsibility for their children, like they're supposed to. And the real winner is not Zell Miller who pushed this idea, or the state workers who implemented it, or even the taxpayers of Georgia who end up supporting many of these children when their parents run out on them. The real winners are the children who are now receiving the support from their own parents that they need and deserve. Those children are what this program is all about.

Today, I'm pleased to unveil a new Ten Most Wanted poster that again will be distributed across Georgia and around the nation. The ten parents on this poster have failed to pay large amounts of child support. They have not made any payments for at least six months now, although when we last knew their whereabouts, they had the means to make those payments. They have also failed to notify the courts of their whereabouts, as is required, and we have already tried to find them through more conventional means.

Take a good look at those faces. Behind every single one of them is a child who has been abandoned by their own parent. These are the faces of parents who can afford to meet their obligations to their children, but who choose not to do so. These are the faces of parents who just don't care. These are the faces of parents who leave us no choice but to come after them in the name of their own children.

We make this public announcement and distribute this poster for two good reasons: First, we need and want the help of the news media and the citizens of this state to track down dead-beat parents and bring them to justice. Second, we need and want to make it clear that in Georgia, supporting your own children is not just a moral responsibility. It's the law, and we will enforce it. In Georgia, parents who refuse to honor their obligation to provide for their children will be treated like the criminals they are.

So we are going to distribute thousands of these posters to the field offices of every state agency and department all around Georgia. They, in turn, will work with local news media, government and local organizations to get these posters out. We are also going to send posters to every single one of the other 49 states in this nation, because many times dead-beat parents leave the state to avoid being traced.

But this poster is just one weapon in our war on dead-beat parents. Another is legislation I sponsored in 1993 requiring Georgia employers to report all new hirings. The results of that law have been as phenomenal as the results of the first poster. Since it took effect in July of 1993, it has helped us find 103,000 parents we were looking for, and we obtained court or administrative orders to collect more than $115 million from them for their children. In fact, our total collections of child support in Georgia have doubled over the past four years, and in 1994 they exceeded $250 million. That is a record I am very proud of.

A lot of that money represents a savings for Georgia taxpayers, who many times must pay welfare benefits for children whose parents have walked out on them.

But more importantly, this program is about children. It's about helping thousands of Georgia children get the support they need and deserve from their own parents. And it's about reminding parents of the responsibilities they assume when they bring a child into this world.

—*Press Conference, January 20, 1995*

---

"Local control" has become a popular slogan that is often presented as a ready solution to a variety of problems. But in reality, what local control means is you take the initiative in your community, you take the responsibility in your community, and you are held accountable for the results in your community. It is a real challenge for you to step forward and take the responsibility upon yourself for making things happen, but that is exactly what all of you have done in your communities. I am proud of you, and I want to thank you for your courage.

You represent communities with an intelligent and caring vision for your children and their families. You represent communities who have pursued that vision, and worked to make it a reality. I am pleased that The Family Connection is helping and supporting you in that quest, and I am personally grateful to you, because you are the ones who, through hard work and cooperation in your communities, have made The Family Connection a success.

This is a tough time for kids to be growing up. Our society is demanding a higher level of literacy than ever before, and the education and training requirements of the average job just keep going up. But at the same time, more of our families are troubled— unwed parents...teenage mothers...mothers who have not completed high school. Half of Georgia's new families have at least one of these strikes against them. Many have two and even all three strikes against them. More and more of our children walk in the classroom door bringing problems with them that get in the way of learning. But they are not problems that our schools can solve.

In fact, this is not a problem that can be solved by any single institution or agency or organization working alone. Not a one of you has either the resources or the capacity to do the job. So the purpose of The Family Connection is to rally a broad group of community partners to work together to help strengthen our families, enabling them to do their part in nurturing our children, freeing our teachers to focus on teaching and our children on learning.

Each one of your communities puts together your own plan to strengthen and support families that are at risk, whether through parent education, or family resource centers, or school-based health clinics, or whatever you have decided meets the needs of your community. There is no one particular model; there is no cookie-cutter mold for The Family Connection. There are no two communities in this program that are exactly alike. But each of you can take comfort in the fact that 54 other Family Connection communities are out there trying their ideas just like you are.

This conference is a chance for all of you to come together, and look around at each other, and see things here and there that you might want to take home and try in your own communities. It is also a chance for you to share your success and see the success of others, and come away feeling good about what you have done and more confident about your ability to achieve your goals.

The goals of The Family Connection are to strengthen family functioning and self-sufficiency, and to improve children's health, development, and school performance. As each of you pursues those goals in your own way in your community, I want to emphasize and reinforce couple of critical elements that need to characterize all local Family Connection programs:

First, cooperation and collaboration. When you get right down to it, you all work with the same kids in your community. The kids who are having academic trouble at school are often the same ones whose parents need to be in adult literacy classes. They are the children of poverty and unemployment. Their families are on the AFDC rolls or the Medicaid rolls. They are often the victims of untreated medical conditions or even child abuse. They are prone to teen pregnancy and violent behavior. They—either the children or the parents or sometimes both—have often had run-ins with the law. No matter whether you are an educator or a public health care provider or a social caseworker or a probation officer or a juvenile judge or a counselor with the Department of Labor...no matter what your professional capacity, if you take a hard look, you will find that all of you from the same community are serving the same kids and the same families.

Each of you touches only one part of the problems that trouble these families. It is as if each one of you holds some of the pieces to a jigsaw puzzle, and the only way that the puzzle can be put together into a complete picture, is for each one to bring your pieces to the table, sit down with one another, and cooperate in fitting the pieces together. That is how you can make a very real difference in the lives of our children and their families.

The second element that characterizes Family Connection programs is prevention. I truly believe the old saying that an ounce of prevention is worth a pound of cure. Unfortunately, many of our state programs are of necessity focused on putting out fires and responding to crises. For me, one of the most exciting aspects of The Family Connection is the potential for this program to break out of that pattern and represent an opportunity to help prevent problems before they occur. The question that needs to be always present in your minds as you shape your local Family Connection program, is: How can we strengthen our families in ways that will prevent future problems from developing?

Third, The Family Connection is results oriented. Nobody tells you what to do or how to do it. You decide what is best for your community. Your success is measured by what you achieve, not by how well you follow a particular set of rules.

And the fourth characteristic of all Family Connection programs is broad participation at the community level. Of course, you all had to start somewhere, and often the starting point was smaller than you'd like. But as you get your Family Connection program underway in your community, keep looking to expand. Keep looking to identify new places that need to be set at your table. The ability to marshall a broad base of public and political support is going to help you succeed. It is going to help you identify troubled families faster and intervene in their lives in a timely and comprehensive way.

Broad community participation creates and solidifies a single touch-point in your community for troubled families, so that they are not running back and forth among multiple offices in frustration, as they try to get the help they need. It is also going to make your Family Connection program look good in your community. When you have coordination across a broad base, that enables you to do something significant that makes a real difference. Citizens begin to feel that their community is on the ball and is taking responsibility for making things happen, and that government is responsive and really does work for ordinary people.

*—Family Connection Conference, August 7, 1995*

---

For many long years, Georgia has ranked near the bottom on a lot of the measures of well-being for children, from infant deaths to teen pregnancy, from high school dropouts to juvenile delinquency. There are no quick fixes for any of these problems. Nor can government solve any them alone, without the active participation of churches and business and community leaders.

I sponsored the legislation that created this Georgia Policy Council for Children and

Families, because we need to investigate what we can do together to reverse these trends, and I challenge this council to lead our public deliberation as we carefully weigh costs and considerations in deciding what Georgia is to do for our children and families. I charge you with a five-part agenda that flows from the work of the interim Policy Council for Children and Families, which recommended that this permanent body be established.

The first agenda item is accountability for results. Exactly what in the way of concrete results do we want to achieve, and how will we measure it? In what specific ways do we want our families to be better off? And how will we know if we have accomplished them? We are used to counting the number of home visits, or counseling sessions, or errors in the welfare rolls. But these are not measures of success or failure. Over the past several decades, this nation has poured trillions of dollars into social service programs, and citizens today are not convinced that things have gotten much better. They are looking for results that show progress...

The second agenda item is prevention and strengthening our families. In a democracy where people are given the freedom to live their lives as they choose, government is often limited to reacting. But I believe deeply in doing as much in the way of prevention as we possibly can. That is the whole idea behind prekindergarten, The Family Connection, literacy action programs, parent education programs, and so on. What else can we do to strengthen our families and give parents the skills and sense of responsibility they need to raise children, especially during the first three years of life?

Third on your agenda is budget redirection. As I mentioned a moment ago, today's taxpayers are looking for concrete results. The federal government has alerted states to be prepared for significant, in some cases staggering, cutbacks. The economic recovery we have been enjoying will slow following the Olympics next summer. We simply are not going to have much in the way of new resources. We need to do a better job not only of identifying and measuring results, but also of directing our resources toward the initiatives that generate those results.

Fourth is government reform, and let me say right now that I have high expectations in this area. The only way we are going to be able to take our existing resources and make them do something more, is to work harder AND smarter. As they are shuttled back and forth between too many offices, the citizens who need our help the most often feel that government is not responsive. How can we streamline and integrate our work to do more with less?

Finally, community-based decision-making. Churches, communities, and citizen groups must be active participants and leaders in improving the well-being of our children and families. But that can only happen if they are able to work together and make decisions together at the community level.

The charge I have just given you is great and full of responsibility. As the Good Book says, it will require you to "be wise as serpents and innocent as doves." But I know that you will work earnestly, and apply your wisdom and integrity to this task for the sake of our children.

*—Swear in the Georgia Policy Council for Children and Families,*
*December 4, 1995*

The best investment we can make in Georgia's future is to invest in Georgia's children, because our children are our future. One of the simplest, most effective and most efficient investments that we can make in the health of Georgia's children is to immunize them against preventable diseases.

Of course, we require children to be fully immunized when they begin school. But too many parents wait until then, and too many of our infants and toddlers are not getting those important early immunizations. That puts them at risk for diseases that can easily be prevented, but if they are given the opportunity strike, they can maim or even kill.

Shirley is a spokesperson for "Immunize Georgia's Little Guys," and programs like this one and "HOPE for Kids" have helped Georgia make great progress in our efforts to immunize our young children. But this year of 1996 is a hallmark year. Because the national goal for child immunization is that by the end of this year of 1996, at least 90 percent of our preschoolers will be fully immunized.

I am proud to say that by the end of 1995, more than 60 Georgia counties had already surpassed that goal of having 90 percent of their preschoolers immunized. In fact, more than 40 of those counties have already reached the ultimate goal of 100 percent of their preschoolers fully immunized. And we are very, very proud of them. But in the remaining 90-plus counties, we still have more work to do. Because our statewide immunization rate is just over 85 percent.

Almost 15 percent of our preschoolers still lack proper immunization against diseases like polio, diphtheria, measles, mumps, and whooping cough, so we need to work together and work hard...

You are here today because you care about Georgia's children. You are here because you want them to have a chance for a happy, healthy childhood that is not disrupted and possibly even permanently marred by diseases that could have easily been prevented. On behalf of the State of Georgia, Shirley and I want to express our gratitude for caring and for helping with this very, very important undertaking. Let's get out there and "immunize Georgia's little guys!"

—*"Immunize Georgia's Little Guys" Rally, April 20, 1996*

Government cannot do everything. It cannot take the place of parents and churches and synagogues in raising children to be moral and responsible adults. It cannot take the place of people in our communities working together and helping each other.

This is particularly true when it comes to substance abuse. This is a serious, complex, and pervasive health problem, and its effects often create other problems that threaten community safety and well-being like no other health condition does. While government must often respond to the public safety dilemmas, substance abuse in itself is not a problem that government alone can solve.

There is no law that the General Assembly can pass that will instill the personal responsibility and moral values it takes for a person to resist abusing drugs or driving drunk. We can make it tougher, which we have, and I'll have more DUI legislation this session. Georgia's DUI laws are still not tough enough. Too many people still drive drunk. Those who are caught are still not punished enough.

There is no state budget appropriation that will automatically provide the personal encouragement and support an abuser needs to kick the habit and stay clean...The problem of substance abuse can only truly be addressed when families and churches, community organizations and employers, all reinforce each other in calling people to take responsibility for their lives and in helping and supporting them in their efforts to do that.

We in government, of course, must do what we can. My administration has tried to be supportive of that call to drug-free living, by emphasizing primary education and prevention programs among the children and youth of Georgia.

We have more than doubled the DARE program, which brings specially trained law enforcement officers into public schools. And we now have over 300 veteran law enforcement officers working with children in three-quarters of Georgia's school systems. DARE not only helps educate our children on the dangers of drugs, but it also teaches them how to make decisions based on personal values, how to say "no" in the face of peer pressure, and how to deal in positive ways with anger, disagreements and other personal frustrations that can lead to substance abuse.

We also devote $10 million a year to our "Drug Free School" program, which includes diversion activities for youth, to keep them out of a drug-conducive environment.

The federal government is also beginning to focus increasingly on prevention, requiring us to spend at least 20 percent of our substance abuse block grant for primary prevention programs, and my budget will reflect that.

In addition, we have targeted $1.3 million from our block grant toward locating and intervention with pregnant women who are abusers, in hopes of getting their children off to a better start in life. We provided $2 million to state and local law enforcement agencies for drug prevention and eradication programs, plus an additional $1 million in state funds last year for drug counseling for prison inmates.

One of the major issues facing us in the coming General Assembly is welfare reform, bringing Georgia into compliance with the new federal legislation. The welfare reform proposal I will bring to the General Assembly puts $1 million of our federal substance abuse block grant into providing treatment for welfare recipients who need it to get their lives together and get back to work.

But more important than any of that, is for families and churches, community organizations, and leaders like all of you, and the business community in its employee policies, for all segments of community life in each one of Georgia's communities to be willing to get involved and put their shoulders to this wheel if we are to move forward in reducing substance abuse.

*—Atlanta Regional Commission Substance Abuse Conference,*
*December 16, 1996*

Let me tell you a few stories, stories that may sound familiar to you. The first one is about a program that began 30 years ago, in a time when civil rights was a new phrase in the national vocabulary...a time when Lyndon Johnson talked of a "Great Society." In a speech after the march on Selma, Alabama, he said, "These are the enemies: poverty, ignorance, disease. They are our enemies, not our fellow man, not our neighbor. And these enemies too—poverty, disease and ignorance—we shall overcome."

Oddly enough for that time, Johnson was not just advocating an unthinking handout; he believed by helping people pull themselves up, society would benefit. That was when Medicaid was created, initially to help poor women and children get medical care.

That year—Medicaid's first year—the total budget to fund the program for the entire United States was about the size of the Medicaid budget last year for just the State of Georgia. Just a few years ago, in 1990, cash benefit payments to Georgians on Medicaid totaled about $1.4 billion, and Medicaid accounted for 7.2 percent of the total state budget.

The next year—1991—Medicaid eligibility expanded, and so did its budget...increasing to about 9.2 percent of the total state budget. By 1994, only three years later, Medicaid accounted for 13 percent—nearly double what it had been just five years earlier—13 percent of a state budget that was increasingly straining at its seams. That's how much Medicaid grew in Georgia.

Seeing what was coming, I asked all of our state agencies to find what savings they could, and with some thoughtful, careful trimming, Medicaid's budget now equals 11 percent of our total state budget, or about $3 billion.

But we know more change is coming from Washington; Medicaid and Medicare are increasingly visible targets of Congressional budget-cutting and we're all feeling the pinch. Every state is in the same boat. We are all looking for ways to keep caring for children, the disabled, and elderly people who need someone to look after them. But we are all also looking for ways to do it without busting the budget. So in the last two years, we've had to make some tough choices. And I'll bet that story sounds familiar to you, too.

We've tried to make sure that everyone involved in the system shares the financial burden equally, so that the tough choices aren't harder on doctors, for instance, than they are on the hospitals or the nursing homes. And we've tried especially hard to make sure the people who need that medical care are getting the same quality care they've gotten before.

We've seen other states' efforts to rein in costs. Some make a wholesale, feet-first jump into radical reform that looks good at first blush, but then they find themselves scrambling to climb out of deep water. Other states, including Georgia, have put our toes in first to check the temperature, adjust it a little bit, and then we began to wade into it a step at a time from the shallow end. We have implemented changes gradually, carefully, incrementally, so that the impact isn't too great all at once.

Our primary-care case management plan, Georgia Better Health Care, started in Augusta and a few other Georgia counties on October of 1993, and has now expanded to more than half the state's counties. So you can see we took our time making sure it worked and getting people used to the idea. It will be available to qualified Medicaid recipients statewide by the end of this calendar year. Georgia's Medicaid HMO program began a year ago in just five counties in metro Atlanta. It is now becoming available outside the Atlanta area. Savannah, Augusta, and Macon are finding that many of their Medicaid patients want a program that can offer them more preventive care at less cost to the state.

The Department of Medical Assistance is also working to bring our payments to providers into closer alignment with what other states around us are paying. Again, they're slowly reducing the amounts paid to doctors; gradually instituting a system that will pay hospitals different rates according to the service they've provided; and encouraging nursing homes to limit the number of days Medicaid patients spend there, especially when those folks might be able to stay in their own homes instead.

One of the best success stories we've had in Georgia comes from the books of the people who fight fraud and abuse. As you may know, I established our State Healthcare Fraud Control Unit just a few years ago. The Unit works directly with DMA's own Investigations and Compliance office and with our State Department of Audits. With agents from the Georgia Bureau of Investigation and prosecutors from the state Attorney General's office, these folks have stopped millions of dollars in Medicaid fraud, convicted dozens of criminals in those few years, and they have probably frightened off more than a few other folks who might have been thinking about stealing from the state.

In just the past year, state and federal prosecutors have won almost three dozen convictions in Georgia on Medicaid fraud charges. Often, those folks convicted have been stealing from private insurers, too, and other government agencies like Medicare and CHAMPUS.

A psychiatrist in Saint Simons, on the Georgia coast, was convicted about 10 days ago of conspiracy, mail and wire fraud, filing false claims, money laundering, and even prescribing drugs to people who didn't need them. That happened on Saturday, June 28th; he'll be sentenced in about six weeks, and could end up spending 33 years in federal prison and paying a million-dollar fine.

Our investigators caught another man, one who probably worked his unique fraud scheme in several states before he was stopped here. He put together networks of people who filed claims of about $6 each. Six dollars! But he put together enough of those little six-dollar claims to defraud all of us more than $3 million in about a year. Georgia Medicaid fraud investigators noticed something suspicious, mounted up the evidence, and—working with the U.S. Attorney's office in Atlanta—brought about a guilty plea. He'll be sentenced in August.

There are more stories I could tell you: about a South Georgia pharmacist who claimed he wrote prescriptions he never did—he's been sentenced to five years in state prison. About people who claimed they had put together "clinics" to help "counsel" Georgia children who truly do need help. But instead of helping children, they were helping themselves—to the taxpayers' money. The kids they claimed they'd counseled, never got a minute of care.

Cases like these cost Georgia taxpayers $14 million in the past year. But we've caught and convicted the people who stole that money, and we'll recover as much of it as we can. Because of our aggressive prosecution of fraud cases like these, we believe we're stopping the fraud that national estimates show is costing us 10 percent of all health-care costs, and has wasted millions of Medicaid dollars that flow to criminals instead of real medical care—criminals who don't care if they hurt our kids, older people, and the disabled in their efforts to cheat our taxpaying citizens.

There's more. The staff from Georgia's Department of Medical Assistance will tell you more about Auto-Audit, a new computer system that will spot fraud before it happens. It'll screen claims before they're paid and flag the ones that don't make sense, like a psychiatrist who says he spent 100 hours with patients in one 24 hour day, and stop that money from going out at all. It's a program that began in private industry and has been used by commercial insurers for years. But we're one of the first states to use it for Medicaid claims...

Thirty years ago, history was being made when one man decided we should help each other up out of poverty, ignorance, and disease. I believe we're making history again, by making sure the programs that were meant to help people up and out, get back to doing exactly that. We can care for our children; we can make sure our elderly have someone watching out for them; and we can do that while being responsible to the people who pay the bills—the taxpayers of Georgia and the United States.

—*Medicaid Management Information Systems Conference, July 8, 1997*

---

There are some state rankings that Georgia can be proud of. Georgia's preschool program, for example, is the largest and most comprehensive in the nation, and it is getting national and even international attention. Zimbabwe is sending a representative for a firsthand look. Our HOPE Scholarship Program is also the most far-reaching in the nation, and that's not just a Governor bragging; that's what the *Los Angeles Times* and the *Chronicle of Higher Education* have said.

But there's one ranking we cannot be proud of, and that is Georgia's place at or near the top of the states in teen pregnancy. Every year nine out of every 100 teenage girls in this state get pregnant. It is a tragedy for these young girls, because it can close the door to so many of the opportunities and choices that would have enabled them to realize their potential as productive citizens. And it is a tragedy for the babies they bear, because two-thirds of them will be raised in poverty.

Teen pregnancy has been around for a long time. In fact, as some point out, the teen birthrate was higher back in the 1950s than it is today. But back then, most teenage moms were 18 or 19 and married. Today, we are faced with a significant number of pregnancies among teens under age 17, and over 75 percent of teenage moms are unmarried, compared to only 15 percent back in 1960.

Over half of Georgia's first-born babies are at risk because their mothers are still teenagers, are unmarried or have not finished high school—often a combination of all three of these factors...

I want to emphasize something that is very, very important. Government cannot solve this problem. It cannot take the place of parents and churches and synagogues in raising children to be moral and responsible adults. It cannot take the place of people in communities, working together to help each other.

There is no law that the General Assembly can pass that will instill the moral values and the personal responsibility it takes to abstain from sex or even be diligent in the use of birth control. Government cannot put half of our citizens to policing the personal lives of the other half. There is no state budget appropriation that can provide the parental guidance and emotional support so many of our teens need and are hungering for.

The problem of teen pregnancy—and it is a terrible problem—will not be solved by calling for more government action and money, although that is important. The problem can only truly be solved when families and churches and community organizations like Families First and Jane Fonda's Georgia Adolescent Pregnancy Program and the Children and Youth Coordinating Council, all reinforce each other in calling individual people to be responsible in their own lives, and in helping and supporting them in their efforts to do that...

Georgia's families desperately need your help to teach their children about responsible decision making regarding sex, about male responsibility in sex and in fathering a child, and, yes, about how to resist pressure to engage in sex.

*—Families First Pregnancy Campaign, January 8, 1997*

---

I had barely been inaugurated Governor in 1991, when Kids Count ranked Georgia last in the nation, and I made a commitment to improving the quality of life for Georgia's children and families. The first thing we learned was that if you want to touch young lives, you have to know where they are. You can't wait for them to show up to register for kindergarten. You have to go out into Georgia's towns and neighborhoods and find them. No child lives in the Governor's Office or at the Department of Human Resources. They live in Waycross and Dawsonville and Sylvester and hundreds of other Georgia communities.

Over the past seven years, we have created many new programs to find and serve Georgia's children. In 1993 and again in 1994, we expanded Medicaid to provide coverage for pregnant women and their infants up to 185 percent of the federal poverty level, and children ages one to six up to 133 percent of the federal poverty level. We are now in the process of considering our options and making plans to use the new federal funds to provide even more health coverage for our children.

We created "Children 1st" to check all newborn babies in Georgia before they go from the hospital that very first time. "Children 1st" enables us to provide information on health care, child care, parenting, and other support families might need, and identifies any little ones with problems that need to be addressed in those critical early years. Last year Georgia was one of ten states that received a grant from the Carnegie Foundation to participate in "Starting Points"—a program that makes sure that parents are ready to care for their baby when it is born.

We also began The Family Connection, a partnership between the state and local communities to improve the lives of our children and families. Each local Family Connection program is different, because each one is tailored by its community to address its own particular needs. Many of them have now been underway long enough to begin seeing positive results.

Family Connection communities are reporting lower rates of teenage pregnancy and infant mortality, higher immunization rates and preschool enrollments, lower rates of suspension and grade retention in schools, higher rates of school attendance and participation in parent-student sessions at school. We have gradually expanded this program over the course of several years from just a handful of sites to 86 Georgia counties, and I want to continue to expand it.

I also know that Georgia parents want their children to be safe while they are at work, and the latest research shows the critical importance of quality child care. So over the past seven years we've been expanding our state-supported child-care placements for low-income families. Since 1991, government-funded child-care in Georgia has increased by more than fourfold, from $26 million to $117 million.

Then when those children get to be four-years old, they enter Georgia's Prekindergarten Program, which serves 60,000 youngsters in locally-controlled programs, giving them the skills they need to be ready to succeed in school, from recognizing colors and letters, to developing social skills, to simply learning how to hold a pencil. Georgia is the only state in the nation that offers prekindergarten to all four-year-olds whose parents want it. Earlier this month our Prekindergarten Program won a national Innovation in American Government Award, funded by the Ford Foundation and administered by Harvard University.

So we have a lot of good state programs for young children, and there are many local programs in operation all across Georgia. Our challenge is to weave the threads of these programs together into a supporting web for Georgia families.

In 1995, we passed Senate Bill 256, creating the Georgia Policy Council for Children and Families. The council has established 26 benchmarks that measure how we're doing in areas like teen pregnancy and school drop-out rates. It is also working with the 86 Family Connection communities to blend and integrate state and local programs for children and make the most effective use of the resources these programs offer. The idea is to keep children from falling through the cracks between agencies and programs, and to streamline service provision, making it easier for families to get the services they need by getting the agencies who serve families to work together.

We need to imbue all of our efforts for Georgia's children with the same characteristics that the Council emphasizes: A focus on accountability and achieving results, and an inter-meshing of programs for greater effectiveness and wiser use of our resources. I believe that doing these two things will serve Georgia's children better than making an already long list of programs even longer.

So what we are trying to do now, is to gather up the programs that serve Georgia's youngest children under one large umbrella that I call "Thrive by Five." The goal is that our youngest citizens will be healthy, have stable, self-sufficient families; and start school ready to learn—in other words, that Georgia's children will thrive by the age of five. Right now we are in the process of building the "Thrive by Five" umbrella, and, like you, we are here to listen and learn from these ECS experts. But we are also here to listen and learn from you, who work with Georgia's children every day. Because it will take all of us working together, in state government and in our own local communities, to give all of our children the chance to "thrive by five"—to develop the foundation in those critical early years on which they can build a lifetime of achieving their hopes and dreams.

—*Early Learning and Brain Development Conference,*
*October 27, 1997*

———————

There is an old saying that goes like this: "Give a man a fish and he eats for a day. Teach him to fish and he eats for a lifetime." I think we have to do both. We have to teach people how to fish—how to be self-sufficient and take responsibility for themselves and their children. But in the meantime, until they are able to fish, we can't let them and their families starve. And that is where the wonderful partnership comes in that is expressed here in this room today.

Addressing and preventing hunger has to be a partnership. It has to look both short-term and long-term, and we must have hunger-relief agencies on the front lines, taking on the responsibility in their own communities on a day-to-day and case-to-case basis. You are the ones who address hunger in its most literal and pressing form...

The "State of the State on Hunger" report shows that Georgia's people and corporations are willing and ready to support our hunger-relief agencies. But it also shows that we need to work harder to raise public awareness, and to identify and mobilize the help that is willing to work on reducing hunger in Georgia.

—*"Understanding Hunger in Georgia" Symposium, November 12, 1997*

———————

Georgia's hunters have helped to lead the fight against hunger in our state for the past five years by participating in Hunters for the Hungry. Each year this program provides more than 10,000 pounds of ground venison to families in need. It is a public-private effort, sponsored by the State Departments of Natural Resources, Corrections and Agriculture, in conjunction with conservation organizations like the Georgia Wildlife Federation and the Safari Club International, and private businesses like Bass Pro Shops.

Hunger is a growing problem in the United States, and Georgia is no exception. The Georgia Food Bank uses over 25 million pounds of food to feed more than two million hungry people each year. Churches, Scouts, and other civic organizations promote food drives to help stock our food banks with non-perishable groceries. But the most difficult item to get in quantity is meat. Georgia's Hunters for the Hungry program provides one of the largest single donations of meat to the food bank. In the past four years, Hunters for the Hungry have donated nearly 12 tons of ground venison.

What makes this program is unique compared to other feed-the-hungry programs, is that it has no reliable source of income. There is no cost to hunters, which means that they are more likely to participate if they do not have to pay a fee in addition to donating the deer they shoot. But, because neither the hunters nor the state puts any money into it, the program depends on donated deer, donated refrigerated trucks, donated processing and donated everything else, for its operation. That makes expanding the program very difficult.

So last year we started the Governor's Quail Hunt to raise some much-needed funding for Hunters for the Hungry, and I especially want to thank the National Rifle Association, Philip Morris Companies, and other organizations that are participating in this second Governor's Quail Hunt. Their sponsorship and your participation have broadened the Hunters for the Hungry program, enabling more hunters to help their neighbors.

With the first hunt, we raised more than $25,000, and the funds raised by today's hunt are expected to surpass that remarkable total. These funds will help to print donation forms, provide banners to mark the collection trucks, and cover the expenses of college students who work at collection sites for Hunters for the Hungry.

In the future, funds from the Governor's Quail Hunt will be used to rent additional refrigerated trucks to allow for more collection sites, and to pay for additional processing if the volume of donated meat exceeds the donated processing capacity...

Your participation in this hunt as a hunter and a fellow Georgian not only helps to raise money for an outstanding cause, but it also helps to promote the good things that hunters are doing for wildlife conservation in their communities.

*—Governor's Quail Hunt Dinner, December 1, 1997*

# The Humanities

Georgia was one of the five original states chosen in 1970 by the National Endowment for the Humanities to pioneer the very first state humanities councils, and in 1971 the first Georgia humanities grants were made. The role of the council has changed since then. Its early focus was on public policy programs for adults who had finished their formal education. Over the years, however, the council has become more involved with educational institutions, often serving as a bridge between them and the general public. It has broadened its services to include teacher institutes, film projects, and a resource center whose materials benefit more than 100,000 people a year.

As one whose own profession and interests are in the humanities, I take great pride in my connections with the Georgia Humanities Council. I have served on its board, and I was pleased to have played a role in helping to start this annual event, separating out the humanities from the arts for special distinction.

Benjamin Disraeli, British statesman of the 19th century, once criticized the United States for putting too much emphasis on science and not enough on the humanities. He said, "By the aid of a few scientific discoveries, they have succeeded in establishing a society which mistakes comfort for civilization."

It is true that we have an orientation toward new frontiers and technological progress, but what binds us together as a society is not the fact that we all use microwave ovens or take videos home from the movie store. It is the fact that we share the same cultural heritage. Only by studying where we have been and how we became who we are, can we truly understand where we are headed.

Not to know about your own history and tradition—not to know who Huck Finn was, or what the Declaration of Independence did, or what Abraham Lincoln said in the Gettysburg Address—renders you a citizen incapable of functioning in a democracy. You have no context for participating in society, no framework to help you make wise decisions. You vote for a tradition about which you are ignorant; you pay for a government whose performance you cannot rightly judge.

If we are to improve the quality of life for all Georgians, we must improve the knowledge of the cultural heritage we share and the traditions in which we participate. That is the job you have undertaken—to remember and remind us of who we are and how we got that way.

*—Governor's Awards in the Humanities, February 21, 1991*

---

The poet Robert Frost once said, "What makes a nation in the beginning is a good piece of geography." That is what makes Georgia in the beginning—a good piece of geography. Our coastline has spectacular beaches, live oaks draped with Spanish moss and waters rich in marine life. In northeast Georgia, where I come from, the mountains offer spectacular scenery of a different sort, with expansive vistas, lush forests, and cool rushing trout streams. In between we have the stunning man-made jewel of Atlanta, with its gleaming skyscrapers and big-city excitement.

But, as Frost noted, good geography is just the beginning. The real essence of Georgia, the heart and soul of this great state, is its people. Our heritage as a people is rich with volunteerism and community spirit. This state was hewn out of the rough by volunteers—citizens who helped each other build barns and put roofs on their homes, who nursed each other through times of illness, who banded together to form volunteer fire brigades.

Modern-day Americans continue to give a lot of their time. In recent years Americans have volunteered about 70 billion dollars worth of volunteer time a year in service to their communities.

I have had a long career in politics that began as mayor of a tiny town and has now culminated as Governor of this great state. The longer I'm in politics, the more aware I become of the limitations of government. Government cannot do everything—not even many of the things we once supposed it could. A lot of what really counts in life is done by volunteers, and the value of volunteer work is much greater than its tangible accomplishments. A Georgia VISTA volunteer once said, "Volunteerism is love expressed in its purest form; idealism made practical through service."

The young people we honor today have learned that the pursuit of happiness our Constitution guarantees goes beyond acquiring the material trappings of success. It is more than a jacuzzi on the deck or a Mercedes in the driveway, and skin creams, clothes and hair styles are pretty superficial when you come right down to it.

The deeper reality of happiness is contained in that sage bit of advice we find in the New Testament: We find personal fulfillment not by focusing inward on ourselves, but by giving of ourselves to others.

*—Princeton Awards for Community Service, May 9, 1991*

---

The United States is not a melting pot. We do not boil our cultures together into one bland mass. The United States is a salad bowl. We are many cultures mixed together. But each culture keeps its unique shape. And we enjoy all of the different colors, textures and tastes.

Hispanic culture has a special place in the salad. Hispanic explorers discovered our continent, and over the centuries since then, we have enjoyed Hispanic culture, from music and art to food. Hispanic families are close-knit. Hispanic communities are proud. And those are important values for America to remember and maintain.

The number of Hispanic people in Georgia is growing. It has almost doubled in the past ten years. We want to generate greater acceptance of this growing part of Georgia's people. We want Georgians to learn more about Hispanic culture. And we want Hispanic people to be an important part of our state.

September 15 to October 15 is National Hispanic Heritage Month. Today I proclaim it Hispanic Heritage Month in Georgia, too.

*—Proclamation Ceremony, September 12, 1991*

---

"But age, alas! that cankers everything, has stripped me of my beauty and go. Goodbye, let them go, and the devil go with them! What's left to say? The flour's all gone and now I must sell the bran as best I may. Even so, I mean to rejoice!"

Those words were written by Geoffrey Chaucer, English poet of the 14th century.

The ancient Greek philosopher Socrates took time in his old age to learn to dance and play musical instruments, and he considered it time well spent. The Roman philosopher Cato set out to learn the Greek language at the age of 80. When a friend asked him why he was beginning so large an undertaking at such an advanced age, he said it was the youngest age he had left.

It is a delight for me, whose own hair is growing increasingly silver, to be here with this group of present-day Chaucers who still mean to rejoice, this group of modern Socrateses who are still learning to dance, this group of energetic Catos who still set out on great undertakings.

It's not easy being a senior citizen in a society that worships youth. All around us are messages implying that to qualify for first-class citizenship, you must be young and beautiful. Youth and beauty sell everything from soap to suitcases.

But when it comes right down to it, the only way to keep from aging is to die young. The artist Pablo Picasso, who continued to paint through a ripe old age, once remarked that age only matters when one is aging. "Now that I have arrived at a great age," he said, "I might just as well be 20."

And he was right. Like youth, age also has its own fascination, its driving forces, its vigor, its freedom from hard work, its special perspective on life, and its own brand of grace and graciousness. I like to think of aging in terms of the ripening of an ear of corn. When the silk is faded and drooping and the husk is becoming withered and dried on the outside, that is simply a sign that what is inside is full, rich, mature, and at its prime.

You are one of the richest resources Georgia has—rich in wisdom, patience, perspective, and experience. Rich in understanding of how cope with change—an understanding you gained over a lifetime of living in a rapidly changing, turbulent world. There is much we can learn from you. . .

Georgia is presently mired in one of the deepest, longest recessions we have seen in some time. Some say it is the most severe since the Great Depression. Well, you were young back in the time of the Great Depression. You started off your adult life learning how to "make do" when jobs and money were scarce. We have a lot to learn from you about the skill of "making do," which is once again needed and important...

Having a significant group of older people around is a relatively new thing for our society, and I have a sense that we haven't quite learned how to handle it well. People used to die a lot younger. At the time when you were born, only one out of 25 people were making it to age 65. Nobody did serious long-term planning for retirement, because such a thing rarely occurred.

You are the first real generation of senior citizens, and you are teaching us what the poet Thomas More meant when he wrote, "Days though shortening still can shine"... I am personally counting on your expertise and foresight, because the next group of Georgia's retirees is going to include me.

—*Silver-Haired Legislature, October 24, 1991*

---

A couple of thousand years ago, God spoke from a burning bush to a man named Moses, and promised to deliver the Children of Israel from captivity in Egypt and bring them to a land that flowed with milk and honey. Many long centuries later, however, when the Jewish people again began to gather in their homeland at the turn of the 20th century, the land that once flowed with milk and honey was barren and desolate. Centuries of neglect and erosion had turned the promised land into deserts and malarial swamps.

For the past 90 years, the Jewish National Fund has been hard at work, restoring Israel and making it once again a homeland where the Jewish people can prosper. JNF has been reclaiming arable land and planting trees; draining swamps and preparing construction sites; building highways, dams and reservoirs; and establishing parks and recreational areas.

Georgia is blanketed with southern pines, and we tend to take trees for granted. But in arid zones, the tree is truly a giver of life. Its foliage cools and shelters, its roots hold the soil fast against the desert winds. In many parts of the world, we are learning that the hard way. As nearby trees are cut, deserts have been creeping and spreading, challenging human survival in areas that were once green and verdant. The work of JNF in reclaiming arid land for farms, homes, industry, and parks is becoming a model for the rest of the world to follow.

—*Jewish National Fund, October 30, 1991*

---

I grew up in an isolated little village up in the North Georgia mountains, and I learned from personal experience that the good news and the bad news about life in a village are both the same thing: You become intimately involved with your neighbors.

You may wish you could ignore your neighbors if they do things differently than you do, but in a village you can't, because the time will come when you will need their help. So in a village, you come to terms with your neighbors, even if they have different outlooks and values, and do things differently than you.

Modern technology has made it possible to send a message around the globe in one-fifth of a second. Our world has truly become, in the phrase coined by Marshall McLuhan a few decades ago, a "global village." But the realities of village life remain unchanged. They apply to this global village of ours, the same as they did in the little town of Young Harris where I'm from.

International neighbors need to be friends, even though we do some things differently from each other, because there are many times when we need each other's help. In the neighborly spirit of the international friendship we share, I would like to thank you for your support and participation in this Friendship Force mission.

—*Friendship Force Mission, Moscow, December 20, 1991*

---

"Let justice roll down like water, and righteousness like an ever-flowing stream." The imagery of these words from the Old Testament prophet Amos is rich and evocative. The water of a mighty river rolls and surges with tremendous force, roaring through rapids, thundering over falls, driving giant turbines to generate electrical power. It sets its own course, carving away the earth at will, and with unwearying persistence it wears away even the most stubborn granite.

An ever-flowing stream has cool, clear waters that bubble with a peaceful murmur over the pebbles and rocks in the creekbed. It is a magnet for a vast variety of living things, and it refreshes and nurtures them all.

Martin Luther King, Jr. dreamed of a society where justice shapes the landscape, like the rolling waters of a mighty river. He dreamed of a society that is renewed and sustained by a continual flow of goodness and wisdom, a society in which justice and righteousness are always in motion, always at work smoothing out the rough places, again and again.

Today we pause not just to honor the memory of a great man, although we do. But we also pause to recapture the dream ... the dream of justice and goodness in constant motion among us. And we pause to renew our commitment to making the dream live on in our life together. For without our ongoing efforts, the river of justice and the stream of righteousness will run dry.

—*M. L. King, Jr. Ecumenical Memorial Service, January 20, 1992*

---

It is a great pleasure to receive this first copy of "Preserving the Legacy: A Tour of African American Historic Resources in Georgia." As a historian, I have a great appreciation for the preservation of historic structures and for the efforts of the Minority Historic Preservation Committee to call attention to African American historic sites.

The sense of place is a powerful thing. The sensory experience of actually being where history happened brings our heritage out of the realm of the imaginary and into the realm of reality. If we can stand in the very place where history happened, if we can walk the same paths our heroes once walked, and look out of the same windows through which they once looked—history comes alive. It enriches our understanding of what it must have been like for our forebears, and weaves our rich heritage into our daily lives in a tangible way.

This brochure is a wonderful tool to help us understand and appreciate the contribution African Americans have made to Georgia history. They have been an integral part of life in Georgia since colonial days, and this brochure celebrates their achievements, as well as marking the historic structures in which those achievements were realized. It is more than just a map that shows the location of each of 58 important sites that are on the National Register of Historic Places. It is a tour through history as well as a tour through Georgia. You can start down on the coast in colonial Savannah, and move through history as you travel around the state, ending up here in Atlanta with the civil rights movement. It is going to be a practical, helpful addition not only in the promotion of these historic sites to visitors, but also for our schools, as we teach our children the history of this great state.

*—Accept Black Historic Preservation Brochure, February 18. 1992*

———————

The Georgia Humanities Council provides resources and encouragement to humanities projects and activities in our schools and for the general public. It is a critical effort. As Jerry Martin noted in last year's lecture, "biologically we are still cavemen." There is nothing of civilization in human genes. None of the great truths of life, no knowledge of our inventions from the wheel to the microchip, no language skills, no understanding of history or literature—none of this is contained in DNA. There is nothing automatic about the transfer of these things from one generation to the next. Yet that transfer must be made, or we as a culture, as a people, are nothing.

Who or what is America, and how did we get to be that way? What do we believe and why? The answers to such questions are tied up in the stories of the Pilgrims in the Mayflower, of the Revolutionary War, of the western frontier... Stories of the civil rights struggle, of exploring outer space, and of all the many immigrants who have come to this nation over the years and learned its language and its customs and become a part of it.

We are united us as a people and a nation by the stories, myths, and beliefs that we share. Without that common base of understanding, we would perish. The task of the humanities is to deliberately foster the telling of the stories of our life together, to help us learn about the rich heritage that gives us our unique identity as a people.

At the same time, the humanities also help us to understand that truth is too big to be contained by any one culture. That there are underlying truths and principles that go beyond culture and tradition to unite humankind around the world and across the ages.

*—Governor's Awards in the Humanities, February 19, 1992*

———————

Celebrating the 15th anniversary of Friendship Force brings back a lot of memories for my family and me. Shirley and I were part of the very first Friendship Force mission to Newcastle, England, in July of 1977, and we served as hosts for the first Friendship Force group from Newcastle that reciprocated our original visit. We were packed and ready to go on that early Friendship Force trip to Korea that had to be abandoned in the uncertainty that surrounded the shooting down of an airliner carrying a Georgia Congressman. Just this past December, with things in political turmoil in what used to be the Soviet Union, my son Matt and I joined a Friendship Force group on a trip to Moscow. So you can see that we Millers have been active participants in The Friendship Force throughout its 15-year history.

Wayne Smith has been a personal friend of mine for a long time, and I would like to take this opportunity to thank him for his foresight, determination and hard work over the years. When he first began to organize The Friendship Force, there were those who thought he was either a little naive and idealistic, or else a little crazy. They said that the fostering of world peace and global understanding is surely far more complex than a couple of tour groups traveling somewhere for a week or two, and it requires much more expertise than ordinary citizens have.

But the endorsement and involvement of Jimmy Carter, who was then President, and of Rosalynn Carter gave The Friendship Force enough credibility to get it off the ground. And Shirley and I were pleased to do our small part by participating in that very first exchange trip.

Over the years, as I've kept in close touch with Wayne and traveled occasionally with Friendship Force groups, it has given me great pleasure to see this program grow and expand. And you know, those early skeptics were right: Wayne Smith is an idealist, and the principles upon which The Friendship Force is based are simplistic. But they are also true, because they are based on a keen understanding of human nature, rather than on an academic knowledge of international policy issues.

We all have friends who hold a special place in our lives and contribute to our happiness. We all know from personal experience what it's like to share joys and troubles with a friend and look at things from a friend's point of view. Friendship is something that every person knows about and has some experience and expertise in, and it is a very profound and powerful force in the daily life of every human around the world. The Friendship Force builds upon person-to-person friendships, which in their own sphere are just as powerful a force as official international diplomacy—and over the long-term, I suspect, even more powerful.

Shirley and I are proud to be among the 100,000 Friendship Force Ambassadors that have traveled abroad. And we proud to be among the 300,000 hosts who have had international Friendship Force visitors stay in our homes.

*—Friendship Force 15th Anniversary, March 16, 1992*

---

We live in an international age. People all over the world are learning more and more about Georgia, and we want them to. The approaching SuperBowl in 1994 and Olympic Games in 1996 are unprecedented opportunities to showcase this state to the entire world.

As we prepare for these events, it is clearly time for us to consider carefully the image of Georgia that we want to communicate. I want the world to see Georgia as a vibrant, growing state that is moving ahead, and not as a state that is entrenched, holding fast to the symbols of a time when we resisted efforts to right the wrongs of our past.

The present Georgia flag with its stars and bars was adopted in 1956, in the dawning days of the civil rights era. What we fly today is not an enduring symbol of our heritage, but the fighting flag of those who wanted to preserve a segregated South in the face of the civil rights movement.

It is time we shake completely free of that era. The old Dixiecrats have by-and-large said they were wrong. Their one-time presidential candidate, Strom Thurmond, recently supported the nomination of Clarence Thomas to the Supreme Court.

The Georgia flag is a last remaining vestige of days that are not only gone, but also days that we have no right to be proud of—days that should not be revered as one of the high points in the history of this state. We need to lay the days of segregation to rest, to let by-gones be by-gones, and rest our souls.

—*Press Conference, May 28, 1992*

---

A child can learn many things at a mother's knee. One of the things I learned at my mother's knee was politics. I grew up in the mountains of northeast Georgia, where some of the roughest and most unusual politics in the nation is practiced. Politics here is a serious business that has divided neighbors and sometimes even families through the years, in some cases, through the centuries. The representative from this county voted against secession during the Civil War. I grew up with Republican neighbors who would give me the shirt off their backs, but would never even consider voting for me.

My mother was one of the few persons the warring factions knew they could trust to be honest and fair, so she was routinely chosen to help at the polls. One of the most vivid memories of my childhood was spending election day and on into the night huddled in the corner of the "law house," as it was called, as my mother held the elections, surrounded by rough grizzled mountain men with beards on their faces and whiskey on their breath.

She also served on the Young Harris City Council for over 25 years. She was often the clerk to whom the residents of the town paid their taxes and their water bills. Most persons dropped by our house to pay their taxes, and I learned much from their choice comments to my mother about how their hard-earned money was to be spent.

My mother was twice elected mayor of Young Harris in a time when a woman mayor was a rarity, and she served as one of the first vice-presidents of the Georgia Municipal Association when it was first formed. She also broke new ground in the local courts as the first woman ever chosen to serve on a jury in Towns County.

I was once asked in my first statewide campaign what I thought of women in politics. I answered truthfully, "I never knew anything else." I grew up watching a capable woman function with success and integrity in a number of different political capacities, and I grew up understanding that an interest and knack for politics and public service is not the special domain of the male of the species.

We in Georgia have for too long limited our horizons and denied ourselves the advantages of fully utilizing the political gifts and skills of so many of our women. I, for one, think it is about time that changed.

—*Democratic Party Conference on Women in Politics, June 4, 1992*

At a time when dark and ominous clouds of resurgent racial tensions are appearing here and there across this country, it is especially fitting that we gather here today... not just to honor the memory of a great Georgian, although we do, but also to call again to mind the words of his dream, and to renew our commitment to keeping them alive.

Martin Luther King, Jr. dreamed of a time when the sons and daughters of former slaves and former slave owners would sit down together at the table in the red clay hills of Georgia. They do that more often now than ever before in the history of this state.

But we are also reminded with a frequency that is all too great, that the struggle is not yet over. We have not reached the point where we dare allow Dr. King's dream to become just a memory. For dreams, you see, are living things. It is not enough to acknowledge a dream; it is not enough to remember a dream. Dreams must be carefully and deliberately nurtured to stay alive. In the words of the poet Langston Hughes: "If dreams die, life is a broken-winged bird that cannot fly."

So we pause each year at this time to honor the memory of Martin Luther King, Jr.... to remember the many ways in which this one man changed the life of an entire nation for the better... and to renew our own commitment to his dream of a society that values individuals for their character and not for their color.

*—M. L. King Jr. Proclamation Signing, January 15, 1993*

To lot of people, an event that focuses on Georgia as a gateway to international understanding would mean a program that looks to the future and describes how the 1996 Olympics can make us a more international place as we move into the 21st century. But grappling with international understanding will not just begin in 1996. It has been part of our life and our history right from the start, as you know from hearing Dr. David Hurst Thomas describe the four-way interactions among Native Americans, Spanish, Africans, and English down on the coast some 300 years ago.

The history of this state and the nation is largely the ongoing story of an endless stream of immigrants who came here from around the world to make their homes. They fought with each other and learned from each other, and together they made us what we are today.

*—Governor's Awards in the Humanities, February 25, 1993*

More than 100 years ago, Charles Dickens began *A Tale of Two Cities* with one of the most eloquent paragraphs in English literature. You may remember it goes like this:

It was the best of times, it was the worst of times; it was the age of wisdom, it was the age of foolishness; it was the epoch of belief, it was the epoch of incredulity; it was the season of Light, it was the season of Darkness; it was the spring of hope, it was the winter of despair; we had everything before us, we had nothing before us.

It describes very well the present world in which we live—one that is as full of opportunity as it is fraught with problems. It's all in how you look at it.

Some people see only the problems—the foolishness, the incredulity, the darkness, the winter of despair. If you take that approach, you are going to conclude that you have nothing before you. You're going to feel a sense of hopelessness and alienation. You won't see any reason to get involved, because you can't see how it is possible for you as an individual to make a difference.

But if you look for the opportunities, and I think most of you in this Chamber do— or you wouldn't be here. If you look for the wisdom, the belief, the light, the spring of hope—you are going to feel like you have everything before you....

Of course, making progress always takes a great deal of work and effort and perseverance. Someone once said that "history never looks like history when you are living through it. It always looks confusing and messy, and it always feels uncomfortable."

A lot of Georgia history has been made right here in this Chamber over the past century. Here's where 18-year-olds first gained the right to vote in the United States, where the first woman U.S. Senator was chosen—legislatures elected them back then.

The process when those things happened and even last week looked confusing and messy, and felt uncomfortable. The casual observer of the process is mostly going to see the confusion and mess. But if you look more broadly at the ramifications and results over the years, the majesty and splendor of the legislative process emerges.

I have repeatedly watched the process bring people together and reconcile them. It slows down those who would hurry ahead too quickly, and pulls along those who are doing too much foot-dragging. It tempers both those ideas that are too conservative and those that are too liberal.

Each year 236 individual legislators come to this Chamber and its twin across the Rotunda, each with their own ideas of what needs to be done and how things ought to be. They are all leaders in their own local communities, and the legislative process calls for leaders. But it is not a boxing match where one idea wins by scoring a knock-out on all the others. The process gridlocks when we fixate on opposite extremes and try to force a stand-off between them. That's when the feeling shifts to foolishness and incredulity and the winter of despair. People start to think there is no point to politics and they don't want to be involved.

In the course of the legislative process, the various ideas and beliefs and viewpoints that are represented in Georgia are laid out and considered. Then we sort out the middle ground where we can all stand together. The wisdom and light and hope come when the process helps us find practical compromises that enable us to move forward with solutions to the problems we face.

So when you bring your ideas here to this Chamber, you have to expect that they will be discussed and modified and adjusted to accommodate a variety of viewpoints beyond your own.

But you have to come with ideas. You have to have a vision for what Georgia can become and ideas on how to achieve it.

I've heard some legislators say they'll just listen to their constituents and vote however their constituents want them to on whatever issues happen to come along. But, my young friends, that's not leadership; it's not even close. That's just seeing a parade going down the street and running out and getting in front of it.

The Founding Fathers of this nation were visionaries. If they had listened in their day to the timid and fainthearted voices of the status quo, our 13 colonies would never have come together as one nation. If Thomas Jefferson had not defied the cramped vision of his critics and invested the then-unheard-of sum of $15 million to purchase most of the land from the Mississippi to the Rockies, America would not be what it is today. If Abraham Lincoln had let the carping critics carry his day, our Union would have crumbled during the crisis of the Civil War and never have emerged as "the last, best hope of the world."

And now, today, we feel the challenge of our time. I have a vision for Georgia. I see the opportunities, and I believe we have everything before us. But we are going to have to work together to achieve it.

I envision a Georgia whose citizens have the education that good jobs demand in today's economy. So I have sought to lead the way with the Georgia lottery to pay for prekindergarten programs for our four-year-olds who are at risk, to put computers and satellite dishes at all of our schools, and to help high school kids go on to college and technical institute...

I envision a Georgia with a clean environment. So I have sought to lead the way with Preservation 2000, to protect 100,000 acres of natural wilderness.

I envision a Georgia whose streets are safe. So I have sought to lead the way with boot camps to turn around the lives of young drug offenders, with tougher DUI penalties to get drunk drivers off the road, and with a real life sentence without parole to keep cold-blooded murders behind bars.

I envision a Georgia whose economy is strong. So I have sought to lead the way with a stronger, broader economic development program that encourages new technology development, supports traditional industries, and expands our international markets.

Together all of these things are what will give Georgia a future. They are what will make this great state even better tomorrow than it is today. They are what will make us believe, as Dickens said, that we live in the season of light and in the spring of hope, and that we have everything before us.

But in order to have everything before us, we must be willing to get involved, to invest a lot of work and effort and determination and perseverance. If I am not willing to get involved and work for progress; if you are not willing to get involved and work for progress; then we will indeed live in an age of foolishness and incredulity, a season of darkness, a winter of despair. And we will have nothing before us.

In my 60-plus years, I have learned that there are two kinds of people in this world— no matter what age, sex, or race—two kinds: Those who ponder life and those who live it.

Teddy Roosevelt is one of my heros. He once said, "I'd rather wear out than rust out."

And he said something else that I hope you'll remember and carry with you every day of your lives: "The credit belongs to the man who is actually in the arena—whose face is marred by dust and sweat and blood—who knows the great enthusiasms, the great devotions—and spends himself in a worthy cause ... who at best if he wins, knows the thrills of high achievement, and if he fails, at least fails while daring greatly—so that his place shall never be with those cold and timid souls who know neither victory nor defeat."

*—YMCA Youth Assembly, House Chamber, April 2, 1993*

---

It is more than 125 years since the last shots died away at the end of the War Between the States. It was a brief four-year moment in our history. But the trauma and tragedy of a war in which nearly three million Americans rose up to fight against each other, sometimes even brother against brother, made a tremendous impression on the psyche of this nation and shaped its subsequent course.

The Civil War has always fascinated me, as I know it has you. I have taught that U.S. History course from colonial times up through 1865 many, many times. I always would hurry through the colonial period, the French and Indian War, the Revolutionary War, the Articles of Confederation, the forming of the Union, the War of 1812, Jacksonian democracy, the War with Mexico, and the Gold Rush and westward expansion. I'd go through all that in six weeks so that I could have the next six weeks to focus on the antebellum South, secession, and the War Between the States.

History is history, and can never be changed. But we dare not either glamorize it or forget it, lest we be doomed to repeat it. In his Gettysburg Address, President Abraham Lincoln said, "We here highly resolve that these dead shall not have died in vain."

If we are to uphold those words—if the lessons of that grave and terrible war are to remain with us—then heed must be paid to preservation. Many of the battlefields and other historic sites and monuments of the Civil War are threatened by modern development. Some have already vanished, and with their disappearance will go not only our comprehension of the geography and events of that war, but also our understanding of its causes and its consequences and effects on our state and its people.

The goal of this commission is to preserve and conserve the heritage of the Civil War—by inventorying historic sites, by encouraging their restoration and preservation, and by promoting a clearer understanding of the causes and effects of the war and the reconstruction period which followed.

*—Swear in Civil War Commission, September 10, 1993*

---

In 1836, the State of Georgia built the Western and Atlanta Rail Road line. It began in Chattanooga, where it tapped into major lines serving the Midwest, and it came south to a nondescript little spot in the countryside. The chief construction engineer Stephen Long predicted, "The terminus will be a good location for one tavern, a blacksmith shop, a grocery store and nothing else." What a surprise Mr. Long would have if he could see the terminus of his rail line today.

You see, the lure of direct rail access to Chicago and the Midwest soon had coastal railroads laying track toward the end of the Western and Atlanta line. And the little terminal town that nobody thought would amount to much, very soon grew into a bustling rail center.

From that inauspicious beginning, grew a great city that during its century and a half of life has been a focal point for this nation's two most significant internal upheavals—the Civil War and the civil rights movement... a great city that is home to the headquarters of such international giants as Coca-Cola, Delta Airlines, CNN, Holiday Inn Worldwide, and UPS... a great city that has produced such prominent Americans as Martin Luther King Jr., Margaret Mitchell, and Henry Grady... a great city with rich, world-class cultural and arts resources and organizations.... a great city that has historically provided fertile soil for black entrepreneurs, businesses, and political leaders, and a city that is growing increasingly diverse.

The story of Atlanta's growth is a moving and fascinating one... from a rough and ready rail town to a major international center, and the Atlanta History Museum is a major step forward in the preservation and telling of this remarkable story.

—*Dedication of the Atlanta History Center, October 22, 1993*

———————

My ancestors were among the earliest pioneers in the North Georgia mountains. They settled in isolation from the rest of the nation, and their life became an unchanged microcosm of 18th century language, customs, and character. If the Bard of Avon had been reincarnated into 19th century Choestoe, he would have felt right at home among the open fireplaces, spinning wheels, handmade looms, Greek lamps, and the Elizabethan English expressions that still dominated the language.

During my own lifetime, the Morth Georgia mountains were increasingly opened to the outside world through highways and tourists, and through radio and television. And the questions of whether and how the mountaineers could preserve their distinctive heritage amidst all those outside influences and changes have been of great interest and concern to me for many years....

Last year we looked at Georgia's growing role as international gateway to the world. This year we look at how we can hang onto our identity even as our world changes. These are subjects that strike at the heart of the humanities, for the humanities are responsible for sorting out and holding fast to what is important and unique in the rich heritage that is ours, to help us learn from it and carry it with us. But at the same time, it is also the task of the humanities to help us understand that truth is too big to be contained by any one culture at any one moment, that there are underlying truths and principles and common bonds that go beyond culture and tradition to unite humankind around the world and across the ages.

—*Governor's Awards in the Humanities, February 23, 1994*

———————

My own interest in this courthouse goes beyond my general love of history to a more personal level, because this is a part of the state where I've got family roots. You see, my Miller ancestors were natives of the Mossy Creek area of White County. My grandfather, William J. Miller was a child, growing up in this community, when this courthouse was new.

He went by "Bud" Miller, and he was the one who transplanted my family tree to Choestoe when he left White County to take a teaching job there. He met my grandmother in Choestoe, which is where she was born and grew up. But her family also had a connection to this community. Her grandfather left North Carolina in 1809 and brought his family to this area to live until the 1830s when Cherokee Indian territory was opened to white settlers and they moved to Choestoe.

So when I look at this wonderful old courthouse today, I imagine what it was like when my grandfather was a boy and this building was the center of legal, commercial, and educational life in White County. I imagine him coming here on errands with his parents, and perhaps attending school on the first floor. This is more than a lovely, gracious old building. It reminds me of my heritage, my roots. It brings my past into my present life in a very real, tangible way.

The sense of place is a powerful thing. Nothing brings history to life like standing in the place where it actually happened. In this case, I can see, touch, and go inside the very same building my grandfather and his parents saw, touched and went inside of more than 100 years ago. Here I can get a feel through my own senses of what life was like for them.

That is why the preservation of historic structures like this one is so important. They are what bring our history and heritage out of the recesses of library shelves and make it a part of our lives. They help us understand who we are and how we got to be that way. They remind us of the events and stories and traditions that bind us together. They are symbols of the rich heritage that gives us our identity.

The State of Georgia began its efforts to place our historic buildings and districts on the National Register of Historic Places 25 years ago. This courthouse was one of the very first Georgia buildings to be nominated for the National Register. In the years since then, we have added more and more of our historic sites to the list.

I have placed a new level of priority on state efforts at historic preservation over the past four years. In the past our State Office of Historic Preservation has been hidden away within the Division of Parks, Recreation and Historic Sites of the Georgia Department of Natural Resources. Many people didn't even know it was there. I am elevating it to full division status, both to give more clout and visibility to historic preservation and in recognition of its increasing level of activity.

This office presently administers 11 federal and state programs, and as a result of its efforts, Georgia is among the top 10 states in the nation in funding from the Federal Historic Preservation Fund. One of its responsibilities is to certify historical restoration projects for state and federal income tax credits. These tax credits have been a real incentive for historic preservation in Georgia, and we are among the top three states in the nation in our use of tax incentives for historic preservation. Georgia has had a total of 1,700 historic restoration projects representing a total investment of $500 million that have qualified for either state or federal tax credits.

Of course, the projects that qualify for tax credits are often commercial projects, and they are undertaken by individuals or private companies who pay taxes. Public buildings like this courthouse that are restored by local governments or non-profit organizations do not benefit from tax incentives. That why I created Georgia Heritage 2000. It is a state grant program to help local governments and non-profit organizations with the cost of restoring historic public buildings like courthouses, city halls, libraries, theaters, or museums, for continued public use. The first round of funding will become available this summer, and the first applications are now being sent out.

—*Dedicate Renovated White County Courthouse, May 13, 1994*

---

Throughout world history, politics and religion have been star-crossed lovers. They are perennially attracted to each other, but their relationship is most often uneasy. And sometimes, as in Ireland, Bosnia, the Middle East, the result is outright death and destruction.

In our own case, our forefathers recognized that as institutions, church and state have often tried to use each other to their own ends, with unfortunate consequences. They wisely sought to settle the matter right at the start by imposing a constitutional separation of these two institutions in the First Amendment.

But does that really mean that we ought to banish all expression of religious faith from our public life? George Washington felt that only religion could supply "that virtue of morality" which is necessary to have a free country.

In my opinion, we must both recognize and respect our differences in heritage and faith, but at same time also strengthen the common moral ties that bind us together and make democracy possible. Our challenge, as I see it is to create a society that is both tolerant and open to a variety of religious traditions and expressions, and at the same time seeks out and promotes the underlying virtues and moral values that our various religious faiths hold in common.

It is the humanities that foster the ongoing discussion of how to do that. And I want to note that the Council is presenting a series of forums around the state this spring, to explore the role of virtue and moral values in a pluralistic society, especially as it relates to our schools.

The task of the humanities is to help us to understand what is going on in society around us, and then give it deeper meaning by putting it into the broader perspective of what has happened at other times and in other places. It is a tremendous task, and I want to thank the Georgia Humanities Council on behalf of the State of Georgia for its work in providing resources and encouragement to projects in the humanities.

—*Governor's Awards in the Humanities, March 2, 1995*

---

The way mountaineers talk is fast going the way of the languages of other ancient civilizations. It started disappearing when the radio came. Later the highways brought the automobile and the TVA lakes lured the tourists and summer residents. And finally, that quaint and beautiful language was killed dead by the electronic marvel and intellectual monster that is television.

Let me give you a little history. Indulge me. The people in these mountains were descendants of the Scotch-Irish who were driven out of Northern Ireland by the Stuart Kings. They first landed in Maryland and Virginia and then migrated west as far as the hostile Indians and French would allow. When they couldn't go any further, they then moved south into the heart of the region of rugged mountains and beautiful valleys we now know as Appalachia. They were accompanied and followed by Huguenots, Pennsylvania Quakers, Palatine Germans, and various dissatisfied Protestant sects.

They were the first Americans to fall back on their own resources. Keep in mind, they settled in isolation from the remainder of the nation and the world and from all but their closest neighbors who may have been a mile or so away. Their language, their customs, their character, possessions, knowledge, and their tools were isolated with them. They all were literally suspended in time. They were insulated from the normal evolution which commerce and communication with others brings. In short, they became an unchanging microcosm of eighteenth-century thought, culture, values, and language. For more than 200 years the only changes they knew were those of birth and death.

Mountaineers possessed the Anglo-Saxon and Anglo-Celtic characteristics of love of liberty, personal courage, capacity to withstand and overcome hardship, unstinted hospitality, intense family loyalty, trust in God, and a sort of a dry, innate humor. If they had one overriding characteristic, it was independence. They developed as extreme, rugged individualists who never closed their doors, had inherent self-respect, were honest, very shrewd, knew no grades of society, and had a sort of dignity which was utterly without pretension.

If Shakespeare could have been reincarnated in Towns County in 1850-1935, he would have felt right at home. The open fireplaces, spinning wheels, handmade looms, and the Elizabethan English then spoken would have been quite familiar. Good mountain words like nary, yonder and fetch were used by Shakespeare in all his plays, and pert, atwix, and smidgen go even further back than Shakespeare. They are right out of Chaucer's *The Canterbury Tales*.

I tried to write about mountain dialect in my book. It's hard. Because mountain speech is primarily a spoken rather than a written language. If you write down 'I'm a'comin' d'reck'ly" it looks like gibberish. But to the ear, it makes perfect sense. At least it does to me.

Scholars have identified some 800 obsolete words heard in Appalachia which had their origin in Elizabethan phraseology—many of them used in almost exactly the same sense as by Shakespeare and Christopher Marlowe. As I say, some of them go back as far as Chaucer. "Holp" for help can be found in Shakespeare's, *The Tempest*. And the mountaineer who said, "I clum up that aire ridge," and city folks who made fun of him should know one could point to Chaucer as proof of the correctness of that usage.

Another common characteristic of old English is the use of certain verbs in the past tense: "throwed" instead of threw, "knowed" instead of knew, "growed" instead of grew, "choosed" instead of chose and the like. Mountaineers use "done" instead of have a lot. "I done done it" would be used instead of "I have done it;" "I done wrote it" instead of "I have written it;" and "I done said it" instead of "I have said it." All are standard mountain constructions.

Use of double nouns are, or is, especially prevalent: terms like biscuit-bread, ham-meat, tooth-dentist, women-folks, men-folks, preacher-man, church-house, kid-of-a-boy, rifle-gun, hose-pipe, kilt-dead. My mother was always referred to as a widow-woman.

One of the most universally recognized mountain idioms is the adding of the suffix of "uns" to pronouns; we-uns, you-uns. Another variation of this form is using "un" to describe people, like "He's a tough-un."

Mountaineers often use nouns and adjectives as verbs. Those are as unusual as the imagination of the speaker. "That deer'll meat me a month" and "The moon fulls tonight" are good examples. Mountaineers use verbs as adjectives: "She's the talkines' woman" and "He's the workines' man."

Mountaineers often use common words in a different way than you might think of that particular word being used, like "ashamed" for bashful, "aim" for intend, "spell" for time (stay a spell), "reckon" for think and "fix" for prepare, repair, or a condition.

Most of these are from Shakespeare and Chaucer and some can be traced to great English writers like John Milton, and Robert Burns. Shakespeare, for example, had Othello saying, "I aim to," which is one of the commonest mountain expressions of intention to do something.

Here are some more Elizabethan terms mountaineers once used a lot: "afeared" instead of afraid; "pert" instead of lively; "tetchy" instead of sensitive; "sight of" or "many a'" instead of a lot; "nigh" instead of near; "plunder" instead of possessions (He moved and took all of his plunder); "afore" instead of before; "betwixt" instead of between; "nary" and "airy" instead of neither and either; "puny" instead of sickly; "misery" instead of pain; "traipse" which means wander about.

I might point out that traipse is different from "sashay" which means walk proudly. If you ever heard "journey-proud," it means really looking forward to going on a trip. "Plum tuckered" means tired; "conniption fit" means temper tantrum. You know, here's an interesting thing: "Conniption fit" is what you have when someone does something to you. "Hissey-fit" is a tantrum where you don't get your way.

"Dark-thirty" or "first dark" for dark; "druthers" for preference; "contrarious" for contrary; "disremember" for don't remember; "het" for heated; "jubious" for dubious; "hellacious" can mean good or bad; "tote" for carry; "poke" for bag; "anti-godlin'" for crooked or not straight, "all-overs" for nervousness, and "lit a shuck" for left or departed.

Perhaps the best known of all mountain words and most used by "furriners" when making fun of us mountaineers is "hit" which is used for it. Few who laugh know, however, that "hit" is the Old Anglo-Saxon neuter form of the pronoun "he" and is perfectly good English. It is the legacy of an ancient culture rather than our ignorance.

But the most colorful and picturesque characteristic of mountain speech, I've always thought, is that it is filled with original mountain expressions, usually graphically descriptive. Many of them long since have found their way into universal American usage, and their users are unaware of their mountain origin. Let me give you just a few notable examples.

"Nothin' will do him but..."

"Rode hard and put up wet."

"Sick as a dyin' calf in a hailstorm."

"Purty as a speckled pup under a red waggin."

"His mouth ain't no prayer book."

"Vomit up shoe soles."

"On the down go."

"Rough as a cob."

"Borned tired and raised lazy."

"Warm as a grandmamma's blanket."

I'll end with two of my favorites. I once heard a man—could have been a politician—described as "sich a liar, he'd have to get somebody else to holler in his hogs." And my favorite of all. We were sitting around a pot-bellied stove on nail kegs in Homer Howell's general merchandise store. A woman who had had a child out of wedlock came in and someone made a snide remark about her when she left. Jake Carson, a grizzled old mountaineer whom I never saw without overalls and brogans, and who wouldn't eat tomatoes because he thought they were poison, summed up the essence of tolerance. He said, "Well, I ain't no judge, and there ain't enough of me to be a jury."

*—Fund-Raiser for "Reach of Song," April 8, 1995*

---

The Peabody Awards date back 55 years to the infancy of this industry, when Franklin Roosevelt was doing his fireside chats and radio was basically all there was in the way of electronic media. Television technology was on the threshold of its debut, but in 1940—the first year of the Peabody Awards—President Roosevelt held up its commercial application to allow for the formation of federal rules and regulations to prevent a monopoly. Then World War II intervened. Cable wasn't even a gleam in anybody's eye. So, to create an award for excellence in broadcasting at that early stage of the industry was truly visionary.

In the years since then, this industry has grown rapidly and in a remarkable way to prominence in the life and culture of this nation and the world. It has been gratifying to see the Peabody Awards grow in prestige and prominence together with the industry. This is a highly competitive award, with the 31 winners we honor today, chosen from more than 1,100 outstanding entries.

We are proud of the role of the Peabody Awards in stimulating excellence and creativity in broadcasting and cable, but there is more to the Peabody Awards than this special luncheon to recognize and honor the most outstanding work of the previous year. Throughout the 55-year history of this award, we have been saving not just the winners, but all of the entries, in an archive at The University of Georgia.

Over the years, the Peabody Collection has grown into one of the world's most extensive and complete archives of the history of the broadcasting industry. It contains the best work of the best broadcasters around the nation, and virtually all of the landmark broadcasts in history. It is a primary source for research by scholars of the broadcast industry, as well as for historic film footage and audio tape for use in current programming.

So to our award winners and to everyone else who entered the competition this year—your work goes down in history in the Peabody Collection as the best of the industry for 1994.

Who knows—some day, years from now, your work may become a recognized classic of the industry. Some future producer may pull it out of the Peabody Collection and bring it back to life by inserting it as a historical clip in a future program that becomes yet another outstanding Peabody Award winner.

*—Peabody Awards in Broadcasting, May 8, 1995*

---

We all know the story in the Old Testament about how the young man Moses was tending the sheep of his father-in-law, and encountered a bush that was on fire, but did not burn up. And, you remember, the voice of God spoke to Moses from the bush, calling him to lead his people out of bondage and promising to bring them to a land that flowed with milk and honey.

But, as you may also remember, it turned out to be a long, slow journey with a lot of struggle and hardship along the way. Not until several hundred pages and several biblical books have gone by and Moses has died, does Joshua finally arrive at Jericho and bring down the walls.

It was hard for the Children of Israel to keep the dream alive during all those many years of journeying in the wilderness, when it sometimes seemed like they'd never reach their goal. It was a struggle to stay focused on the vision of the promised land, and to instill it in each new generation.

Like Moses, Martin Luther King, Jr. started us off on a journey toward the promised land—a land where, as he put it, "the sons of slaves and the sons of former slave owners will be able to sit down together at the table of brotherhood." Today, like the Children of Israel, we are still struggling on the journey to reach that place, and we face the challenge of keeping the dream alive for each new generation.

So today, as we give thanks for Dr. King's life, as we celebrate the many ways in which he changed our nation and our world for the better, let us also pause to recapture his dream. And let us renew our commitment and determination to press forward together on the journey toward the promised land.

*—M. L. King Jr. Ecumenical Memorial Service, January 15, 1996*

---

The writers of our Constitution recognized that as institutions, the church and the state have often tried to exploit each other to their own ends, with unfortunate consequences, and they wisely sought to settle the matter right at the start by imposing a constitutional separation between them in the First Amendment.

Today, more than 200 years later, our society is confronted by deteriorating moral values and increasing wanton violence. We are coming to realize anew that rights must be balanced with responsibility, and that we must recapture and strengthen personal integrity and respect. So it is a very important time for us to revisit the First Amendment.

Democracy demands that we have a common set of moral values that bind us together and govern the way we live with each other. In order to allow people the freedom to live their lives as they choose, we have to be able to count on them to be honest and upright, and the challenge of the First Amendment is to create a society that is tolerant of a variety of religious faiths and expressions, but at the same time seeks out and promotes the underlying virtues and moral values that we all hold in common and that make democracy possible.

*—Governor's Awards in the Humanities, February 20, 1996*

---

Colin Campbell did not include the Governor's Mansion on the list he made for *The New Georgia Guide* of the ten best things to see in Atlanta, but it still has some interesting aspects. There's the outstanding collection of decorative arts—each piece has a story all of its own to tell. Then there's my own favorite room—the library, which has a pretty extensive collection of the work of Georgia authors. It includes an autographed copy of the book by a Georgia author that has outsold Margaret Mitchell's *Gone With the Wind*, and you can find out which author and book it is by reading *The New Georgia Guide*.....

Where in Georgia do you go if you want to see the world's smallest church or the world's largest collection of afghans? Where in Georgia was AT&T President Theodore Vail when he participated in the first-ever transcontinental telephone call with Alexander Graham Bell, who was in New York, and Thomas Watson, who was in San Francisco? Where in Georgia can you find America's only black-built vaudeville theater, where Louis Armstrong, Duke Ellington, Cab Calloway, and Bessie Smith all performed?

Where in Georgia were William K. Vanderbilt, Vincent Astor, Marshall Field, Joseph Pulitzer, J. Pierpont Morgan, and William J. Rockefeller all neighbors of each other? Where in Georgia can you find America's first miniature golf course, or the "Tour de Swamp" bicycle race, or the largest city in the largest county in the largest state east of the Mississippi River?

The answers to all of those questions and many, many more are right here in *The New Georgia Guide*, and I am very pleased and proud to accept this copy. This is not "Arthur Frommer does Georgia." There are no lists of hotels or restaurants with little stars or dollar signs to show how good or how expensive they are. This is a guide to what the real Georgia is like and where to find it...a guide to the unique identity and the soul of Georgia... a guide to its rich and diverse history and culture as well as its rich and diverse natural features.

The roots of this book go back to the 1930s, to the Depression and the Works Progress Administration, which was one of Franklin Roosevelt's alphabet soup of agencies designed to put Americans back to work and stimulate the economy. One of the WPA projects was to hire writers all across America to chronicle the geographic and cultural character of the states. The result here in Georgia was a publication called *Georgia: A Guide to Its Towns and Countryside*, which was published by The University of Georgia in 1940. That initial *Guide* did more than feed a handful of hungry writers when times were tough. It has captured the imagination of countless Georgians over the past 50 years, and this *New Guide to Georgia* recaptures and updates the spirit of that original effort.

Its timely publication coincides with the most momentous international event in Georgia history—the hosting of the Centennial Olympic Games. I sincerely hope that every international journalist who has been assigned to seek out Georgia's local color and unique features will be carrying a dog-eared copy of *The New Georgia Guide* around like a bible.

But this book is more than a guide for Olympic visitors or newcomers. It is also for native Georgians. And I for one am willing to bet that even the most savvy native will learn a few things along the way, in addition to having a good time reading it.

*The New Georgia Guide* disproves the old saying that "too many cooks spoil the broth." Because it is the result of five years of collective effort by literally dozens of historians, writers, editors, journalists, naturalists and cartographers. It was a privilege for me to serve as honorary chair of its editorial board. And I want to thank Tom Dyer and the editorial board members, who were the ones who actually did the work, for organizing and shaping and guiding the book.

Together we have produced a clear-eyed look at the state we love—the achievements and adversities, the unpleasant and the beautiful. Here in this book is Georgia: its land, its people, its past, and the challenges of its future.

*—Presentation of The New Georgia Guide, May 9, 1996*

---

Georgia is presently engaged in a year-long celebration of the 300th anniversary of Oglethorpe's birth. The highlight of the year for us is this pilgrimage to the important places in his life, like Corpus Christi College, and we appreciate your hospitality and friendship.

Oglethorpe was admitted to Corpus Christi College at the age of 18, and over the next 13 years, he kept returning this place. Corpus Christi clearly played a significant role in shaping his life and nurturing the altruism and high-minded ideals that led to the founding of the Colony of Georgia in 1733.

In addition to being a man who lived his life by his ideals, Oglethorpe was also a man of extraordinary personal courage and energy. His City of Savannah was so well designed that the unique pattern of squares, streets, and lots he planned still gives that city its charm today. In his spare time, he negotiated with Indians, nursed sick settlers, maintained relations with the English colonies to the north, and organized an army with which he defeated a Spanish invasion from the south and literally saved the colonies for England.

It was a remarkable achievement that continues to amaze us today as we look back on it, and it was complete altruism on his part. The only thing Oglethorpe ever got for his pains was to be reimbursed by Parliament for his considerable personal expenditures on behalf of his new colony.

But he set a course for Georgia that today has made us the 10th largest state in the United States and one of the strongest economically. We continue to revere him as our founder, and we appreciate this opportunity to visit Corpus Christi College and learn more about the institution that shaped his life.

*—Corpus Christi College, England, October 5, 1996*

The name of James Edward Oglethorpe and the date of February 12, 1733, are engraved in every Georgia history textbook and in the mind of every Georgia school child. About midafternoon on that day, Oglethorpe and his little band of settlers dropped anchor in the Savannah River at the foot of Yamacraw Bluff, and climbed up the 40-foot embankment by way of some wooden stairs built by a scouting party sent ahead of them.

At the top, they were welcomed by a local Indian chief named Tomochichi. After an solemn exchange of greetings, Tomochichi went back up the river to his village, and the settlers pitched four large tents for the night. Oglethorpe, true leader that he was, unrolled his blankets out in the open by the watch fire. The new colony of Georgia was officially founded.

In the weeks to come Oglethorpe had his hands full. There was a town to plan and build, and if you go to Savannah today, you will still find the charming pattern of squares, streets and lots that he laid out. There were complaints from settlers to resolve. There were Carolinians to ingratiate to the north and Spaniards to worry about to the south. Defense had to be seen to, and a treaty for rights to the land negotiated with Tomochichi.

Every time he turned around, something else awaited his decision. It seemed there were not enough hours in the day to accomplish everything he had to do. And there was nothing in it for him. The king saw Georgia as a buffer against the Spanish for better-established colonies to the north, and as way to enrich his realm. But to its trustees, Georgia was a kind of noble experiment—a place where common tradesmen and the poor and unemployed could make a new life for themselves.

It had only a few laws to uphold its high-minded ideals: no slaves, no rum or spirits, and no lawyers. The trustees, including Oglethorpe, were not allowed to hold office, own property or profit financially from the new colony. Their motto was "Not for ourselves, but others."

What was more, Georgia's royal charter gave the king veto power over any governor the trustees might appoint. Suspicious, they responded by not appointing a governor. That was fine for those who stayed home, but for Oglethorpe, as leader of the expedition, it was a manager's worst nightmare. He had all of the responsibility, but no authority.

Yet he persevered. And to this day, we in Georgia continue to be eternally grateful that Oglethorpe lived up to his family motto, which translates, "He does not know when to give up."

He single-handedly established Georgia on a piece of land that had been in contention among the English, Spanish and French, to say nothing of several Indian tribes, for the prior 200 years, and he beat back a major Spanish invasion in the process.

History has it that Oglethorpe personally led the charge that sent the Spanish packing from Georgia's St. Simons Island. And it not only ensured the survival of the fledgling Colony of Georgia, but also set the course of American history. Had Oglethorpe not defeated the Spanish, they may very well have swept on northward, catching the Colony of Carolina unprepared. No one knows where that story might have ended, but the American South might be speaking Spanish today, were it not for Oglethorpe.

Georgia historian Phinizy Spalding, who was here in 1983 to commemorate Georgia's 250th anniversary, wrote: "Oglethorpe was an exceedingly vigorous leader who possessed unlimited personal courage. He never asked his troops to do anything he himself would not do."

After tangling with Oglethorpe's troops, the Spanish retreated back south and never again attempted to dislodge the English colonists from American soil.

We regard Oglethorpe as an American hero whose courage saved the day and whose high-minded ideals set standards for Georgia that we are still trying to live up to today.

*—Meath House, Godalming, England, October 6, 1996*

Oglethorpe's place in Georgia history is extraordinary. When he set out to establish a new colony, it was a risky undertaking. Not only did he set out without expectation of any financial gain on his part, but he also risked his health, his life, and his personal fortune—not knowing until he returned to England that Parliament would be willing to reimburse him for his substantial personal expenditures on Georgia's behalf.

Georgia is a living legacy of the efforts of this great man, who set the standards for us in accord with his own high-minded ideals, and left us an enduring colony and state marked with his personal touch. The little colony he founded with a boatload of settlers, has grown into the 10th largest of all the 50 states, and an economic powerhouse that has been creating 2,000 jobs a week for the past five years.

In his day, he negotiated with Indians, kept on good terms with the other English colonies, and sent the Spanish packing when they attacked in an effort to take over the colonies. It was a lesson in international diplomacy that has remained with us, as we hosted the 1996 Summer Olympics, and as Atlanta has grown into the leading American hot-spot for international investment.

Today we are honored to join with you in commemorating the birth of your great citizen and our great founder, James Edward Oglethorpe.

*—Dedicate Commemorative Lamppost, Godalming, England,*
*October 6, 1996*

I am a student and teacher of history, and I am fascinated by the long and rich history of Native Americans in Georgia. White Georgians number the years of our history in this place by the hundreds. Native Americans number theirs by the thousands of years. It is a history that contains moments of pride, but also a great deal of pain.

Georgia's early inhabitants left us such archeological wonders as the Rock Eagle Mound east of here, the large circular ceremonial lodge at what is now the Ocmulgee National Monument in middle Georgia, the elaborate flat-topped mounds at Etowah in northern Georgia, and the shell ring on Sapelo Island along the coast.

The earliest Spanish explorers arrived in Georgia in the 1500s, and their forages through Georgia began the decimation of Native Americans through disease, military force, and the general disruption of Native American life. By the time the actual colonization of Georgia began 200 years later, the Native American population of this region had already been significantly weakened and reduced.

When James Edward Oglethorpe and his little band of English settlers arrived at the mouth of the Savannah River in 1733, they were greeted by Tomochichi, chief of the Yamacraw. The two men worked out an amicable arrangement as to the land, and became fast friends. When Oglethorpe returned to England for a two-year visit in 1734, he took with him Tomochichi, his wife, his great-nephew, and five Yamacraw warriors. Today, Tomochichi's portrait hangs at the State Capitol among the great leaders of this state, and every school child in Georgia knows about him.

The Yamacraw were one of fourteen Georgia tribes that comprised what remained of the great Creek Confederacy. My own home is in the part of North Georgia which was once the Cherokee Nation. I live near Choestoe, which in Cherokee means "land of the dancing rabbits."

The Cherokees had a sophisticated and highly developed culture. A chief named Sequoyah created a written alphabet of 85 letters for the Cherokee language, then used it to unify the Cherokee nation—first through a systematic education campaign which resulted in widespread literacy, and then by publishing a newspaper called the *Cherokee Phoenix.*

Not only were the Cherokees the first tribe in the nation with a written language, but they also established the first recorded literary prize in America by giving Sequoyah a medal and $500 a year for the rest of his life in recognition of his great contribution.

The *Cherokee Phoenix* was printed at New Echota, the capital city of the Cherokee nation, on a press that was also used to print textbooks for Cherokee students. Also at New Echota were a library and a courthouse. The Cherokee had a highly developed democratic form of government. They had a written Constitution and elected their chief. They had a legislature made of two bodies. Each October the legislature and the superior court met in New Echota to deal with tribal matters.

In fact, their government was very much like the white government that was developing for the new nation, and it must be said that the Cherokees did everything they knew to do, to live peacefully with whites, and to fit into American life while retaining their identity.

But in 1829 gold was discovered in the North Georgia hills, triggering the Georgia Gold Rush and with it one of the most painful chapters of Native American history. Despite the fact that they had worked so hard to find their niche in the new nation that was developing around them, thousands of Cherokees were rounded up and sent off to new lands in Oklahoma. A third of them died on the way. By 1851, only 321 Cherokees were left in Georgia.

At the time, American President Van Buren reported that this forced removal had had the "happiest effect." But the name the Cherokees gave it in their own language means "the trail where they cried." Today we call it the Trail of Tears. The hardship and heartbreak of the Trail of Tears can never be undone. But once again, we Georgians of today hope that we have learned some lessons from it.

New Echota and many other vestiges of the Cherokee Nation are now preserved, and Georgia law makes it a major felony to loot Native American burial sites. A few years ago, as a golf course was being developed on state-owned property near my home town, the remnants of an old Native American village—2,000 years old and more—were discovered at the site. We immediately stopped work on the golf course and consulted with the Eastern Band of the Cherokees. Together, we sent an archeologist out, not to dig up anything, but simply to determine the extent of the site. Then the golf course was redesigned to avoid the site completely. The state took the new plan to the annual gathering of the Cherokee Nation in Oklahoma for approval, before work on the golf course resumed. The site now lies untouched, and decisions about it will remain with the Cherokee Nation.

Georgia is also trying to make New Echota a place where Cherokees can once again come together and feel welcome. The Cherokee Council House has been rebuilt by the local community, and it was dedicated this summer as the Olympic Torch paused there on its way to Atlanta. Some of you who are here today, were at that ceremony, and since that dedication ceremony—within the past two months—the Cherokees have held a meeting in the rebuilt council house.

But we know we still have a ways to go. We need to continue to learn how to live together in respect for each other and for the environment we share.... There is much that the rest of us can learn about you and from you, because the issues on your agenda are issues that affect all Americans, and I think it will help all of us to look at them over your shoulder.

*—National Native America Forum, November 12, 1996*

---

I have always had a great admiration for Margaret Mitchell. She is not only in my book, *Great Georgians*, she is also on the dust jacket.

When an ankle injury ended Peggy Mitchell's career with the *Atlanta Journal Magazine*, her husband, John Marsh, suggested she write a book. So she thought back to her childhood, when she had spent long Sunday afternoons listening to elderly relatives re-fight the Civil War in their living rooms. Soon her apartment was awash with manuscript. Completed chapters were used as door stops. When she finally gave it to Harry Latham of The Macmillan Company, he had to purchase a large suitcase to carry the five-foot stack of manila envelopes.

Within four months of its publication in 1936, more than 700,000 copies of *Gone*

*With the Wind* had been sold. It was translated into 21 languages and printed in Braille. But success and acclaim changed little in the modest lifestyle of Margaret Mitchell. She stayed out of the limelight, refused interviews, and went on living as she had always lived. So few mementos remain to commemorate the woman whose literary masterpiece has taken on a life of its own in the imaginations and hearts of countless readers around the globe. I want to thank Mary Rose Taylor and Daimler-Benz for giving us back "the Dump" in tribute to Atlanta's best-known writer.

*—Dedicate Rebuilt Margaret Mitchell House, May 16, 1997*

---

My middle name is Bryan. It was my mother's maiden name. She always claimed we were related to William Jennings Bryan, and while I was never able to actually document that connection, I have always shared her great admiration and fascination for Bryan's skills as a communicator and orator.

I have also always been fascinated with the John Scopes trial. I have been enthralled with the play and the movie, *Inherit the Wind.* I must have seen the movie at least a half dozen times, and I saw the play both times it ran on Broadway—the most recent being just last year with George C. Scott playing Clarence Darrow and Charles Durning playing William Jennings Bryan.

So it was very exciting for me to discover that we have the foremost Scopes trial expert of our day right here in Georgia. As a historian, I am pleased to see somebody setting the record straight. It's an opportunity I'd like to have had a time or two in my administration. As we have made our way through the 20th century, we've seen a number of trials come and go that have been billed as the "trial of the century." Most of them have been forgotten—footnotes in the fine print of history.

But there was something about the trial of John Scopes for teaching Darwin's theory of evolution that not only captured the nation's attention 80 years ago, but continues to haunt us today. I think it's because we continue to wrestle with the same questions and tensions that were at the heart of the Scopes trial—the question of what role religion should play in public life, the question of majority rule versus individual rights, the question of who decides what is instilled in the minds of American children.

The Scopes trial story that most everybody knew, myself included, was the one that was told in the play and the movie. That, as it turns out, was the glamorized, romanticized, mythologized version. In his book *Summer for the Gods*, Dr. Ed Larson de-glamorizes, de- romanticizes, and de-mythologizes the story. He sticks to the cold, hard facts, but the result is not any less interesting. Rather, it proves the old adage that truth is often stranger than fiction.

It is a rare privilege to have a Pulitzer Prize winner here in Georgia. It is also rare to find an historian and a lawyer who can write so well. I am very proud of Dr. Larson, and of The University of Georgia. I claim bragging rights, both as an alumnus and as a Governor bragging on the flagship institution of his state.

*—Reception for Dr. Ed Larson, June 2, 1998*

# Judicial Appointments

The Judicial Nominating Commission was created about 20 years ago by Governor Carter to assist him in reviewing applications from interested candidates for judgeships, then recommending a group of up to five of the top candidates for the Governor's consideration. The commission continued through the years in pretty much the same form—five members of the State Bar by virtue of their position and five members appointed by the Governor.

Today, we break with that history and do things differently. It is my privilege to swear in a reconstituted commission, chosen through a broader selection process and containing broader representation than under any previous administration. It is time for this state's judiciary to become more inclusive while still retaining its integrity and high quality.

To that end, I have deliberately reconstituted the membership of this group to broaden the perspectives that are brought to bear in the nominating process. In particular, by mandating that the commission membership shall include both women and minorities, I want both to ensure their participation in the nominating process and to encourage qualified women and minorities to apply, knowing that they will receive due consideration.

*—Swear in Judicial Nominating Commission, February 25, 1991*

This state we live in and where many of you practice law has a wider range of people who are highly qualified for the bench than is reflected in our present judiciary. We need them in our courts.

I was convinced that if we would broaden the perspectives that are brought to bear in considering candidates, that would give the nominating process more credibility in the eyes of minorities and women, and encourage them to apply.

Two months ago, I swore in a Judicial Nominating Commission which included women and minorities, and which had been chosen through a broader selection process. That group has now participated in choosing five top-notch judges, including two African-Americans, one woman, and several relatively young but nevertheless exceptional candidates. The pool of applicants was broader and deeper than ever before, and the quality was never higher... We have already begun the realization of one of my goals as Governor—to make the state's judiciary more inclusive and more reflective of our population, while at the same time maintaining a high level of quality among our judges.

*—Judicial Oath of Office Ceremony, May 16, 1991*

Some may say that making our judiciary more representative will automatically mean lowering the standards used in the selection process and the quality of the judges selected. But that narrow view of things simply is not true. What is true, is that the closed nature of the screening process used to discourage highly qualified female and minority candidates from applying.

My approach was not to lower any standards, but to broaden the membership and perspectives represented on the Judicial Nominating Commission, because I knew that if the nominating process were given more credibility in the eyes of minorities and women, they would be more likely to apply. I am proud and delighted about the way the process has opened up under the reconstituted Judicial Nominating Commission....

*—Judicial Oath of Office Ceremony, June 6, 1991*

For too long, women and minorities have not been represented in the Georgia judicial system in proportion to their numbers. There's almost been a sign on it: "Only white males need apply." Those days are over. They are gone with the wind.

My goal as Governor was to open up the process, giving qualified women and minorities the assurance that they will get fair and equal consideration. I was convinced that we could retain a high level of quality in our judicial system while at the same time making it more representative.

And already in my administration, I have appointed more outstanding women and minorities to the judicial system than in any other eight-month period in the state's history. It is my intention to continue opening doors for women and minorities in the expectation that eventually the day will come when there is no wall left, only doors of opportunity.

Today we celebrate the opening of yet another of those doors of opportunity in the judicial system with the swearing in of Georgia's very first female district attorney.

*—Oath of Office Ceremony, September 12, 1991*

We are about to seat the first woman ever on the bench of the Georgia Supreme Court. The second African American on the Georgia Supreme Court. Georgia's youngest Supreme Court justice. The first minority woman to sit on a state supreme court bench in the Southeast. And the second minority woman to sit on a state supreme court bench in the nation.

I learned about all of these history-making precedents by reading the newspapers the day after I appointed Leah Sears to the Georgia Supreme Court. They were not on my mind as I spent two sleepless nights, sifting through the files of ten excellent candidates, remembering and replaying in my mind the interviews I had conducted, weighing the recommendations I had received, searching my heart for the right choice.

I chose Leah Sears for this position because she is intelligent, scholarly, thoughtful, disciplined and fair-minded. I knew she would bring excellence to the Court at the same time she was bringing diversity.

Allow me to quote a sentence I said early last year, at the beginning of my administration. I said that it was "time for this state's judiciary to become more inclusive while still retaining its integrity and high quality."

My approach to achieving that goal was not to change the requirements or the process by which judges are chosen—I did not want lower standards. The first step in that process was to change the membership of the Judicial Nominating Commission, including by mandate both women and minorities. I hoped that by broadening the perspectives brought to bear on the selection of judicial candidates, more qualified women and minorities would be willing to apply, confident that they would receive due consideration.

The results have far exceeded my expectations. Over the past year, the Judicial Nominating Commission has consistently recommended candidate groups of both the highest quality and greatest diversity this state has seen. That was especially true of the group of ten outstanding candidates recommended to me by the Commission from which to fill vacancies on the Supreme Court and the Court of Appeals. I could have picked any one at random, and been confident that he or she would serve Georgia well.

The justices who now sit on the bench of the Georgia Supreme Court are all excellent judges, and we are very fortunate to have them there. But they are all of the same gender and the same generation—my gender and my generation. So I did approach this appointment with an eye on diversity, looking to enrich our highest court with a fresh perspective.

Leah Sears was not the only woman in the candidate group—there were six others. Nor was she the only minority candidate or the only candidate who could bring the perspective of a younger generation. But she combined all three of these traits, of course, and even more importantly, she had a proven level of excellence on the bench. In addition, she was not appointed to her present seat on the Superior Court bench; she ran for it and was elected.

Judge Leah Sears possesses in abundance the qualities an outstanding jurist should have: intellect, temperament, and energy. I said when I appointed her that I believe this scholarly and thoughtful woman has the potential to become one of this nation's most brilliant and sensitive jurists. I am very proud to be the Governor to appoint and swear her in as a justice on the Supreme Court of the State of Georgia.

—*Judicial Oath of Office Ceremony, March 6, 1992*

---

Those of you who have been watching the judicial appointments of my administration know that I take this responsibility very seriously. I worry and agonize especially when it comes to appointing Supreme Court justices. In my mind, these are decisions that must be lifted above personal or political considerations to a higher plane.

In making appointments to the Supreme Court, my goal from the beginning has been to mold a court that reflects and balances the breadth and diversity of Georgia's citizens. I believe that in order for the Supreme Court to speak and act in the best interests of this huge, fast-growing and diverse State of Georgia, its justices must represent the variety of perspectives that exist in this state. I want a Supreme Court that is made up of very bright, very thoughtful individuals who represent the divergent views of Georgia's people and who argue with each other over the issues at hand.

With each appointment to this high court, I have tried to give the court that kind of breadth and balance by choosing someone whose intellect, temperament, strengths of character, and perspective complement the other six justices.

—*Judicial Oath of Office Ceremony, July 26, 1995*

# Law Enforcement

I come to this ceremony with mixed emotions. I am proud, on the one hand, to be part of this special and important tribute to those Georgia peace officers who have made the ultimate sacrifice on behalf of this state and their communities. But on the other hand, I am deeply grieved over the loss of these fine officers, and I wish that some year we could come to this ceremony with no new names to add to this roll of honor.

In their deaths, these law enforcement officers taught us how to live. They were persons of integrity and principle, persons who were loyal to their colleagues, who respected their fellow human beings, and who honored the laws that govern the way we live together. They taught us that to live means to stand ready to help in times of trouble, to focus on serving others, and to devote ourselves to the well-being of our neighbors and our community.

They also taught us how to die. They died with courage and with valor. They died in the midst of living out their commitments and putting others ahead of themselves.

Years ago, in his paintings Norman Rockwell portrayed the American policeman as a jolly soul, who spent his days helping little old ladies across the street and rescuing lost children. Today the realities of law enforcement take our officers into difficulties and dangers far beyond that image. Today, our peace officers have the difficult and dangerous task of dealing with the violent and brutal side of life, whether it be drug-related crime or accidents on our highways. They face horrors in the line of duty that would make the rest of us cringe and turn away.

Someone once said that the difference between a hero and a coward is one step sideways. No one understands that better than law enforcement officers. The officers we honor today met danger head-on, with no side-stepping. Their dedication to duty and their heroism in refusing to step to the side, out of harm's way, cost them all they had.

On behalf of the State of Georgia, I want to pay special tribute to them and extend our deep appreciation to their families for the service they gave to their communities and this state. I know that nothing any of us can say, nothing any of us can do will bring them back to you. But we join you in honoring them and in holding them close in memory.

—*Peace Officers Memorial Service, May 15, 1992*

---

As you know so well, making Georgia safe has become a very difficult and dangerous task. There is no quick fix; there is no magic-wand solution. You have devoted a lot of hard work and determination to it, and also a lot of personal risk and personal sacrifice. You are increasingly putting your own lives on the line to protect Georgia's citizens, and I want to recognize your efforts and thank you on behalf of the citizens of this state for everything you do for them and for the personal risk you take upon yourselves on their behalf....

Most everyone at sometime in their life has heard quoted the words of the Declaration of Independence: "We hold these truths to be self-evident: that all men are created equal, that they are endowed by their Creator with certain unalienable rights, that among them are life, liberty and the pursuit of happiness."

We all know those words. But do you know what the next sentence is? "That to secure these rights, governments are instituted among men, deriving their just powers from the consent of the governed." That is the reason we have government—"to secure," that is, to keep safe our rights. And what is the first right mentioned? Life. If government can't keep its citizens safe, it fails. It fails at its first basic purpose, no matter what other good it accomplishes.

*—POAG Annual Conference, September 13, 1994*

---

I wasn't very old when the State Patrol was born, but I've come to know a lot about those days. You see, E.D. Rivers was governor at the time, and he had been a colleague of my father's in the Georgia Senate. So, as a student and teacher of history and government, I have always been keenly interested in his administration.

The Department of Public Safety started off with 80 troopers. They received one month of training at Georgia Tech. They had 31 cars among them—gun-metal grey in color with orange lettering and bullet-proof windshields. They were state-of-the-art for their time. They had the newest automotive invention—mechanical brakes. And they cost $710 apiece.

But there was a lot those 31 cars didn't have. They didn't have radios. Troopers on patrol were signaled of accidents or calls by red flags flying at gas stations along their patrol routes.

Sixty years may have gone by on the calendar since then, but today's State Patrol is light years away from those days. You have powerful cars with sophisticated communications equipment, to say nothing of planes and boats and helicopters. The number of troopers has increased by more than tenfold, and you are better prepared for your jobs.

The problems have grown more sophisticated, too. Millions of vehicles now travel Georgia's highways at high rates of speed, and driving under the influence of alcohol or drugs is a bigger problem. Drug dealers try to take advantage of our secluded coastline and many small airstrips. But the State Patrol has an excellent record of growing and adapting to meet the changing needs of the State of Georgia and continue to ensure the safety of our citizens.

I am proud to celebrate with you today. I am proud of the outstanding job you do to keep Georgians safe, and I look forward to continuing to work with you as you enter your 70th decade.

*—Georgia State Patrol 60th Anniversary, September 28, 1997*

## "Two Strikes"

I grew up in small town, Georgia, where neighbors knew neighbors. You didn't lock your doors at night; you didn't lock your car if you were lucky enough to have one. It was safe for children to walk to school, and it was safe for teachers to teach in school. That's the world I grew up in, and for most adults in Georgia, that is what they remember as well.

Violent thugs have affected the lives of too many of us. First, of course, are the actual victims of those who choose to rob, rape, and kill. My heart goes out to each and every one of those victims and their families. But we are all touched by the violence. It is that uneasiness the late night store clerk feels in Carrollton. It is the anxiety the secretary in Savannah feels when she walks alone to the parking garage. It is the fear that shoots through the mom in Atlanta as she momentarily loses eye contact with her child in a busy mall, or that nervousness we've all shared when unknown footsteps walk behind us on any given street.

There has been a second impact as well. Good, decent, law-abiding citizens are frustrated by a criminal justice system that doesn't work, a system where a 20-year sentence really means just a bunch of words on a piece of paper, and maybe, just maybe, three years in a prison cell. Where criminals escape with plea bargains and no time. Where a system seems better at letting criminals out, than keeping criminals locked away serving their time. Our citizens simply don't feel that justice is being served. I've seen that frustration in every corner of this state. And I have the same frustration. I am frequently asked two questions: why can't violent criminals get tougher sentences? And, most important, why can't violent criminals just serve the time the judge gives them? Well, I'm here today to tell you, they should, they can and they will....

We're going to get tougher on repeat offenders. Real tough. Repeat offenders must be dealt with harshly. The people of Washington State approved a constitutional amendment which gives life without parole to offenders who commit three violent crimes in their lifetime. The federal government is also looking at this concept called "Three Strikes and You're Out."

I like baseball, but violent crime is not a game. My mother always taught me that folks deserve a second chance, and I've always believed that. But a third chance at violence, a third chance to kill, rape or commit armed robbery, is a completely different matter. Under my program, if you've been convicted of murder or any of the above listed violent crimes, and you commit a second violent crime, you are gone for life—you will never get out of a Georgia prison again. In Georgia, the rule is going to be "Two Strikes and You're Gone"....We are going to have a criminal justice system that's as tough on criminals as they are tough on us.

—*Press Conference, January 5, 1994*

The reason I have worked so hard to get tough on violent crime is because I believe in safety, discipline and respect for others, and I believe that our laws and our prison sentences must also make it clear that we expect our citizens to live by those values.... So this November, you will have the opportunity to vote for a constitutional amendment that will give Georgia the toughest laws in the country on violent crime. It's "two strikes and you're in." Here's how it works:

For rape, armed robbery, kidnaping and the like, you'll get a mandatory sentence of at least 10 years, and whatever number of years the judge gives you is what you will actually serve. For murder, we've got capital punishment, life without parole or regular life. If you get regular life, we will double the time you have to serve before you're even eligible to be considered for parole. And if you convicted a second time for one of these "seven deadly sins," you'll be sent away for life: No parole, no loopholes, no exceptions....

It's going to be a tough lesson for violent criminals of all ages to learn—that in Georgia their sentences will be long and hard, with no chance of getting out early. Once they finally do get our, their second chance will be their last chance. Some of them won't believe it until it happens to them. But it is a lesson that must be learned if we are to reverse the increasing level of violence in our society. The long time they must spend behind bars will demonstrate that we mean business when we say that we are not going to tolerate violent crime.

—*Georgia Parole Association, August 4, 1994*

---

The theme of this conference recognizes a very important truth—that breaking the cycle of violence is an interagency challenge that will take the efforts of many departments and agencies working together.

As most of you know, I believe we need to begin by getting tough on violent crime. We need to make it clear that in Georgia life is not cheap. If you damage or destroy it, the consequences are going to be heavy.

So next month you are going to find an amendment on the ballot to give this state the toughest law for violent criminals in the United States. In Georgia, we're going to make it "two strikes and you're out."

—*Georgia Correctional Training Conference, October 17, 1994*

---

## Boot Camp

One of the hallmarks of my campaign for Governor last year was boot camps for first-time, non-violent drug offenders. And there are a number of good, common-sense reasons for boot camps. First they are much less expensive to build and operate than conventional prison beds, which are consuming an ever-growing portion of the state budget. Second, many young offenders can benefit from the kick in the pants that military-style discipline provides. Third the regimen of hard work that will be part of boot-camp life will be designed to benefit the state and citizens of Georgia.

—*Signing Ceremony, Senate Bill 177, April 23, 1991*

We are going to end Georgia's early release program. That has been one of my goals all along, and I started work on it even before my inauguration. With boot camps giving us a solid intermediate alternative in between prisons and probation, the offenders who end up in prison are those who truly need to be there, and we certainly do not want to release them early. And with boot camps and new prisons giving us the additional bed capacity we need, we can keep the hardened criminals in prison where they should be.

—*Prelegislative Forum, November 13, 1991*

In the course of putting Georgia's new boot camp program into place, some of you have pointed out that the idea of shock incarceration is not new, and that is true. Nearly half of the states are using it. But what is unique about Georgia's program is the way we incorporate the boot camp idea into our broader efforts in corrections. The basic training regimen I went through at Parris Island was not an end in itself, but was designed to prepare young recruits like me to function successfully in the Marines. The purpose of military discipline in Georgia's boot camps is not simply to punish young offenders, but to get their attention—to put them into the proper frame of mind to turn their lives around.

Strict discipline and hard work are only part of the picture. Georgia's boot camps also deal with substance abuse and provide young offenders with educational programs. Boot camp prepares them for a successful period of probation or parole afterward, during which they are helped to integrate back into society as useful, productive citizens.

Georgia's Comprehensive Boot Camp Program also breaks new ground by incorporating military-style discipline into a variety of correctional programs. This is the third boot camp in the state for inmates who would have otherwise been sent to prison. We also have three probation boot camps in operation, where young offenders, who would otherwise simply go on probation, are getting the extra benefit of a boot camp experience, increasing their changes for success. And we have incorporated military-style discipline into the programs of 12 detention centers, and set up four intensive discipline units inside prisons to serve older, more hardened criminals....

On the one hand, we must make judicious use of our prison beds for violent criminals who need to be kept away from society for the full length of their sentence. On the other hand, however, we need forceful alternatives to prison that have teeth in them, if sentences are to mean anything and enhance the safety of our communities....

Georgia has been in the vanguard around the nation in developing innovative intermediate punishment and treatment programs like diversion centers, probation detention centers, and intensive probation. We are once again in the lead in using military-style boot camp discipline, not just as an add-on to our other correctional programs, but in a comprehensive way that integrates with and complements our other programs.

*—Opening of Phillips Correctional Institution, October 14, 1992*

## Driving under the Influence

One of the greatest tragedies of modern society is the carnage on our highways caused by drunk drivers. It is raw violence, often inflicting injury and death on innocent victims.... I want to get chronically drunk drivers off our highways, and I want all other drivers to curtail their drinking or plan ahead for their travel needs when they drink. Toward that end I proposed the strongest DUI legislation this state has ever seen. Although what was eventually passed by the General Assembly was not as strong as my original legislation, nevertheless I was pleased to sign it into law, because it moves us in the right direction.

The level of blood alcohol that constitutes DUI has been reduced from .12 grams to .10 grams for adults, and set at .06 grams for teens under age 18. My preference for teenagers would be zero legal tolerance of alcohol, since it is really illegal for these youngsters to be drinking.

*—Third District Law Enforcement Officers, September 23, 1991*

Every year for the four legislative sessions I have been Governor, I have asked the General Assembly to take a major step toward making our highways safe from drunk and drugged drivers. They have never been willing to take quite as big a step as I have asked them to, but every year we have made progress in the right direction....

During this administration, we have lowered the legal level of blood alcohol for drivers. We have strengthened the penalties for driving under the influence of alcohol or drugs. And with this legislation, we will require that every drunk driver's license be suspended administratively, even when it's a first offense. This bill also eliminates the nolo plea for persons with blood alcohol above .15. It requires mandatory community service for first, second, and third-time offenders, and minimum jail terms for second and third-time offenders. And it lowers the legal blood alcohol level for drivers under age 18 to .04. I would have preferred zero, since it's not legal for them to be drinking at all. But I'm glad for this move in the right direction.

—*DUI Bill Signing Ceremony, April 19, 1994*

Each and every year since I became Governor, I have proposed legislation to make Georgia's DUI laws tougher. We have increased fines and lowered legal blood alcohol levels. We have expanded administrative license suspension and restricted the use of the nolo plea. There is now community service for all offenders, mandatory jail time for second and third-time offenders, and the forfeiture of vehicles for habitual offenders.

Our newest weapon is "Star GSP" or "Star 477" on car phones. This special emergency number allows motorists to report drunk drivers to our State Patrol posts.

Because of these major advances, the number of DUI-related deaths in Georgia has declined by 30 percent during my administration. Each and every one of you deserves credit for this success. Our efforts have saved lives.

But much more needs to be done. I want to see mandatory jail time for every drunk driver—even first-time offenders. I want to get rid of the nolo contendere plea completely. And when a habitual violator is convicted of driving on a suspended license, I want to impound the license plate on their vehicle.

—*Crime Prevention Dinner, Columbus, October 5, 1994*

Each one of you comes to this candlelight vigil tonight bearing the scars and the grief of having lost someone you loved in a vehicle crash with a drunk or drugged driver. I can only imagine the intensity of your pain. I come to this candlelight vigil knowing that nothing I can say tonight, nothing anyone can ever say, will bring them back to you. We cannot restore the life of a single one of them. But I know that they live on in your minds and in your hearts. And I join with you this evening in holding them close in memory and in celebrating the precious gift of their lives among us....

One out of every three vehicles crashes on Georgia highways involves alcohol or drugs. One out of every three. The damage and loss that these crashes cause are even more significant, because DUI crashes tend to be violent, and they cause much more than a third of the injuries and deaths on our highways. There are injuries in nine out of ten DUI crashes, compared to a little less than half of the crashes where no alcohol or drugs are involved. The probability that someone will be killed is nearly 10 times greater in DUI crashes, than in crashes that do not involve alcohol or drugs....

Back in 1993, many of you joined me in working to pass legislation to provide for the use of interlock ignition systems as a condition of probation. Those who are on probation from a DUI conviction would be required to breathe into a device connected to their car ignition before they could start the car. If the device detected alcohol on their breath, the car could not be started.

These interlock ignition systems have been used successfully in other states to keep people from driving when they are drunk. But in Georgia they have not yet seen much use, because the law requires local governments to buy the equipment. I want to allow local governments to contract with private providers to supply these systems, which will make it easier for local governments and more likely for them to be used.

I also want Georgia's teenagers and their parents to understand that driving is a privilege that has to be earned through responsible behavior. So I have proposed a graduated process for teenagers to get driver's licenses. It provides for zero tolerance of blood alcohol until age 21. Georgia is one of only 13 states that still tolerate alcohol in the blood of young drivers under 21.

You understand and you care, and there is no one better than you, who speak with the integrity and the passion of personal experience, to help the General Assembly comprehend the agony that DUI causes.

There is no better way to commemorate the lives that we remember tonight, than to prevent lives from being taken in the future. So tonight, let us hope and pray for the day when the carnage of drunk and drugged driving will cease, and there will no new names to call out and no new candles to light at this vigil.

*—MADD Candlelight Vigil, January 25, 1997*

––––––––––

## Victims' Rights

This afternoon I stand in the same place where many a prosecutor and defense attorney have stood to address the court. But for this ceremony we have made an important change: We have turned the podium around to address you, the citizens of this state...

House Bill 486 allows a victim impact statement to be presented in court in murder cases. Presently, members of the criminal's family can take that witness stand and tell sad tales of how they will suffer when their loved one is put into prison for having committed murder. Judges and juries are allowed to hear their pleas for mercy and leniency in the sentence because of the duress their family will suffer with a parent or breadwinner behind bars.

The victim may also have been a parent or breadwinner, whose family is also suffering duress. But nobody stopped to consult the victim's family when the victim's fate was decided, and when the killer came to trial, they could not take that witness stand and tell how the murder of their loved one has hurt the family left behind. There was no chance for them to say that the victim was a hard-working, upstanding citizen, an active church member, beloved by family and friends, whose life did not warrant being snuffed out, whose loss will be deeply felt.

This is a situation in which criminals are allowed rights that are denied to victims. It is time we tell victims of the horrible crime of murder that the court will hear their voices, too. In the words of the late U.S. Supreme Court Justice Benjamin Cardozo, "Justice, though due to the accused, is due to the accuser also"....

I want to thank and recognize the members of Georgians for Victim Justice who have joined us here today. You are the families of murder victims—the families who have been denied access to the witness stand—the families who fear the release of the criminals who murdered your loved ones. It is your rights we recognize and protect today.

*—Bill Signing Ceremony, April 27, 1993*

---

I believe that Georgians want and deserve a justice system that is tough but fair for the criminals, and sensitive to the victims whose rights have been trampled in the committing of the crime.

Georgians worry about a lot of things, but fear of crime is one of the biggest. We have innocent people sitting behind burglar bars, prisoners in their own homes, afraid of the criminals who ought to be behind prison bars. They are afraid of being hurt or killed. They are afraid of having treasured possessions stolen or damaged, and of having the privacy of their personal lives violated. They are afraid of becoming victims in a system that seems to focus more on the rights of criminals than on them.

As the prosecutors who hold criminals accountable for their misdeeds, you are among the few champions these victims have in the justice system. I know they are grateful for your hard work, and I know you are grateful that the families of murder victims now have a chance to speak out in court.

*—Georgia Prosecuting and District Attorneys, August 3, 1993*

---

Our judicial system was created to deal with those who broke society's laws, and the question before it has always been what to do with the offender. However, over the past several decades, there has been a growing sense that the system has become too preoccupied with the rights of criminals to care about the victims of their crimes. The system seems to have forgotten that crime violates not only the law, but also the lives of innocent victims. And many of those who have been the targets of crime come to feel that they have been victimized twice—first by the criminal and then by the judicial system.

My administration has been working deliberately to bring the rights and needs of crime victims back into the picture and create a better balance....

We have also expanded services for victims over the course of this administration. We have made more than 250 grants totaling more than $4 million to victim assistance programs around the state. The next round of grants is coming in the fall. It will total $1.6 million and go to nearly 100 projects.

We have also increased the Crime Victim Compensation Program by more than 200 percent in the number of victims served and by nearly 200 percent in the amount of money paid to those victims. The money in the Crime Victim Compensation Fund comes largely from people who broke the law, which is, in effect, a form of restitution. Its largest source of income is a special fine levied on those convicted of DUI. It was created by law in 1992 in the course of our ongoing efforts to crack down on drunk and drugged driving and give Georgia the toughest DUI laws in the nation. The Fund also benefits from fees that are paid by offenders who are out on parole.

For our most helpless victims, we've got the Statewide Child Abuse Panel, which has operated under the Criminal Justice Coordinating Council since last year. This panel has improved the collection of information on child abuse and recommended improvements to the Department of Human Resources in the way child abuse cases are handled.

*—CJCC Georgia Victim's Conference, July 20, 1994*

---

Too often in America, the justice system protects the rights of the perpetrator, but does little for the victim of a crime. But we've been changing that in Georgia. Because of our efforts, today in Georgia, the victim's family in a capital felony case can appear before the court at the sentencing stage of a trial, to explain the impact that the crime has had on their lives. We have also expanded the State Crime Victim Compensation Program by 200 percent, and given more than $4 million in grants to local victim assistance programs around the state.

But again, it is a record to build on, not to sit on. The next step is a "Victims' Bill of Rights"—18 specific rights that will give crime victims the information they need and the voice they deserve all along the way in the criminal justice process.

The Victims' Bill of Rights begins by giving victims or their families the right to be notified when an arrest is made, and it keeps them informed of each step along the way: when decisions are to be made about bail or bond, when court proceedings are scheduled and then conducted, when any appeals are made, and finally, when release is considered and made.

The Victims' Bill of Rights also includes opportunities throughout the process for victims or their families to make their feelings known. It begins with the right to tell the district attorney what they think about bail or bond release. It includes the right to have input into plea or sentence negotiations, input into decisions about the defendant's participation in pre-trial or post-trial diversion programs, and input into decisions about parole.

No longer will Georgia victims be left in the dark or denied the right to be heard. I want to make the criminal justice system just as sensitive to the needs and rights of the victim as it has been to the accused.

*—POAG Annual Conference, September 13, 1994*

---

Domestic violence is an undercurrent that only erupts into public view when it reaches devastating proportions. But it occurs in as many as one of every four American families. And it's tangled up in the intense emotions of the closest of all personal relationships, which makes it hard to address and prevent.

I want to recognize and thank the Council on Battered Women, for the assistance you provide to battered women and for taking the initiative on this conference. I also want to recognize the Medical Association of Georgia, who is a co-sponsor of this conference for your domestic violence prevention campaign called "Life Preservers." I've contributed $10,000 in matching funds from my discretionary fund for The Life Preservers Guide on Domestic Violence for Physicians. It will tell doctors how to recognize when injuries are caused by domestic violence, and how to respond to these patients.

In addition to information on diagnosing and treating domestic violence injuries, the book will brief doctors on how to question patients about domestic violence and where to refer them for help. And it will outline the legal considerations that relate to domestic violence.

I believe we also need to increase the level of sensitivity and expertise that the Georgia Bureau of Investigation brings to domestic violence cases. I'm going to add a staff person in each of the 16 GBI regions with sole responsibility for investigating domestic violence. These agents will be specially trained to handle all aspects of spouse, child and elder abuse cases, including methods of questioning victims, witnesses, and the accused. And I support legislation to require our superior courts to consider evidence of family violence when they are resolving child custody issues.

In the past four years, we have made more than $4 million in grants to local crime victim assistance programs. And more than $1 million of it has gone specifically to programs for battered women and their children.

—*Council on Battered Women, October 6, 1994*

---

Another important area where we count on the CJCC is victim assistance. I especially want to thank the CJCC staff for your rapid response to the victims of the tragic bombing in Centennial Park during the Olympics. Even though it was early on a Saturday morning, you were in the office immediately after the explosion, preparing to assist the victims. You helped the State of Georgia stand tall at a difficult time, and you made me very proud.

These are important support functions for law enforcement, where we really count on the CJCC to carry the ball for us. So I am pleased to have this opportunity to thank you for your efforts on behalf of all Georgians in helping victims pick up the pieces. You help make Georgia a safer place, and we are grateful.

—*Criminal Justice Coordinating Council, November 7, 1996*

---

One of the first bills I signed into law after the legislature adjourned was Georgia's version of "Megan's Law"—bringing us into compliance with the federal law on public notification of any sex offenders moving into the community. But we didn't stop there. Above and beyond the legal requirements for public notification about sex offenders, Georgia has established a state-of-the-art, automated calling center for registered victims of all kinds of crimes.

It is called VINE, which stands for Victim Information and Notification Everyday. Whenever an offender is released, the system will automatically contact all the registered victims of that inmate. It works the other direction, too. Any registered victim can call in at any time from any phone and get a status report on their offender. VINE gives Georgia's victims a chance to be proactive in protecting themselves and their families...

On the same day that I signed our state "Megan's Law", I signed another victims' rights bill, extending the time window to apply for victim's compensation after a crime from 180 days to a year. This year Georgia's victim rights compensation program has already received a record high of 1,100 claims and awarded more than $1.7 million in compensation to victims.

Another piece of legislation that I proposed and the General Assembly passed this year has to do with illegal drugs, which continue to be a significant problem for too many of our families.

I believe we need to become as creative in our response as drug dealers are in pushing the stuff, if we are to stem the tide. So we now have a law that allows Georgians who harmed by illegal drugs or whose loved ones were harmed, to sue the drug dealers who lit the fuse that resulted in the damage, and recover some of the cost. The goal is to start shifting the huge cost of the damage caused by illegal drugs back onto the dealers who are profiting from the sale of the stuff.

I also proposed a bill to crack down on domestic violence, which is still in the hands of the General Assembly and which I will work very hard to pass next year. It is estimated that in the course of a year, 440,000 women are battered. Each year more than 7,000 women and children take refuge in Georgia's 37 shelters for battered women. Another time that many are turned away for lack of space.

Too many Georgia families are being torn apart by domestic violence—violence of spouse against spouse, parent against child, child against parent. Far too often, judges let the perpetrators off with a slap on the wrist for inflicting serious injury—broken bones, even permanent disabilities. I'm tired of allowing people to regard their own family as possessions that they can knock around as they wish in the privacy of their home.

Two years ago, Georgia passed our first criminal family violence law, recognizing "family violence battery" as a misdemeanor. But I believe it was only the first step, and a small one at that, in the right direction. I want our state law to recognize the family violence crimes of assault, aggravated assault, and aggravated battery— and to provide for stronger penalties, requiring mandatory jail time. The time behind bars would vary depending on the severity of the offense and the number of prior offenses.

You always hear the argument that mandatory minimum sentences interfere with a judge's discretion, and that may be true for some things. But family violence is so volatile and unpredictable, and I believe we need a mandatory minimum sentence, even if it is only a short time for a first offense, to get the attention of those who abuse their own families.

—*CJCC Victims' Rights Conference, May 7, 1997*

———————

# Sentencing

The sentence of life in prison is one of the biggest frauds in our judicial system today. The so-called "life-sentence" actually amounts to 11 to 13 years behind bars—in some cases as few as seven years. The families of those who have been maimed and murdered in violent crimes live in fear that in as little as seven years, the same criminal who devastated their lives will be free and on the prowl again. Victims and their families deserve better than this; justice demands better than this. That is why I proposed House Bill 485, which provides for a sentence of life in prison without parole. It is a third alternative in addition to the death penalty and the standard life sentence. It is an alternative that truly means what it says—life in prison.

Since I mentioned the death penalty, let me emphasize that I support it and have always supported it throughout my career. I believe it is a deterrent to crime. But the death penalty can only be imposed by unanimous agreement among the men and women who sit in that jury box. And in cases where the crime is heinous enough to call for its consideration, but the jury cannot quite reach a unanimous decision to impose it, the only other alternative has been a sentence that makes the offender eligible for parole in seven years.

In my mind, there is a wide gap between those two options: death or eligibility for parole after only seven years in prison. House Bill 485 provides a third alternative in between those two—a sentence of life without parole.

*—Bill Signing Ceremony, April 27, 1993*

---

In Georgia, we have strengthened our decisions about how to punish our most violent criminals. I believe we must continue the process by strengthening our punishment for lesser offenses as well. We need to take a new look at the offenses for which our system allows alternatives to incarceration. Too many criminals get away with a fine or some probation time—little more than a slap on the wrist.

I want to change that. No more just supervision with a few restrictions, and, maybe, some restitution. If you violate the laws of Georgia, I believe you should give something back to Georgia. Give something back to the community that you wronged. I want mandatory community service imposed on everyone convicted of a crime but not sentenced to prison.

Communities all over Georgia would benefit from this service. There is more than enough trash along our highways and river banks, more than enough grass to mow and weeds to cut down, more than enough graffiti to be cleaned off of buildings, more than enough local parks and recreation areas to be built and maintained, to keep those offenders busy for a long time.

I also want to change Georgia's bail laws. In cases where there is considerable evidence of violent behavior, repeat violent offenders should be denied bail during the pre-trial period. They should not be allowed out on the street while awaiting trial.

I have always been and continue to be a strong supporter of the death penalty, which the United States Supreme Court reinstated in 1973. In the 20 years since then, Georgia has executed 18 criminals. There are currently 112 individuals on death row in Georgia.

The average length of time that a death row inmate spends on Georgia's death row prior to execution is ore than 10 years. That lengthy delay between imposition of the death sentence and its execution is caused by the inmate's using judicial delay tactics in state and federal court.

I can do nothing to speed up the process in federal court, but I am committed to making the state judicial process work more quickly and more efficiently. I believe that any deterrent should be swift and sure. And the way the death penalty has been working is anything but swift.

I will propose a new law which would limit a person convicted and sentenced to death to only one appeal in Georgia. And that would have to be made within six months of their conviction. This will help those cases involving the death penalty not to get bogged down in state courts for many years.

*—POAG Annual conference, September 13, 1994*

## Juvenile Justice

Our children are the future of this great state. Those of us who are parents and grandparents understand that in a very personal way.

Over the course of my political career, I have been watching with grave concern as the number of children living in poverty has increased, as the number of babies born to drug-addicted mothers has increased, as the number of school drop-outs has increased, as the number of children who are either victims or perpetrators of violence has increased, and as the number of youngsters entering our juvenile justice system has increased.

We live in a time when a healthy economy, jobs, and prosperity increasingly depend on a well-adjusted, productive, literate workforce. Unfortunately, at the same time, the odds seem to be stacking up against us as we struggle toward that end. We must do a better job of nurturing our troubled children and preparing them to make their own way in the 21st century. It is critical that we get our act together before it is too late.

I asked the General Assembly to create this joint study committee to address two specific questions: First, how can we do a better job of preventing our children and youth who are at risk from becoming criminals? And second, are we doing what we ought to be doing to get those who have become juvenile offenders back on track?

Pick any young offender from any youth detention center and look in his file. You will find a whole litany of problems: poverty, substance abuse, difficulties at school, a troubled family at home. And you immediately wonder, where were we along the way in that kid's life? How did things get so far out of hand? How could we have done a better job of prevention in this young offender's life? And, most importantly for this committee, is what are we doing here at this YDC going to get this kid back on track?

Government tends to have an institutional mentality. We address problems by establishing institutions and putting people in them, rather than pursuing alternative treatment programs that can be individually tailored. Then we make decisions based on the ease of operating the institution, rather than on the individual needs of the people in it. I have a tremendous sense that the needs of juvenile offenders as persons are falling between the institutional cracks. I also have a sense that the agencies that ought to be working together to address that stack of problems in a juvenile offender's file, are acting independently at best, and oftentimes working at cross purposes with each other....

The easy answer to problems like this is to throw money at them. Unfortunately, that is not an option in these days of tight revenue, and I am not sure the results would be any better if it were.

*—Swear In Children and Youth Coordinating Council,*
*September 6, 1991*

Everyone in this room knows from experience that violence in America is not limited to adults. In fact, some of the most vicious crimes we see being committed today are by young people toward other young people, their elders, and even the handicapped. We ask ourselves, how can human beings do such things to other human beings?

Folks, I believe that regardless of the age of the criminal, society must be protected. So we changed the way Georgia deals with young offenders. Under the new laws I proposed and the legislature enacted, starting at age 13, teenagers who commit certain violent crimes are going to be tried as adults and receive adult sentences. And they will serve those sentences in a special youth facility, separate from the youth whose offenses are less severe.

We also realize that young lives can be salvaged. And we've increased the budget for the Department of Children and Youth Services by 14 percent in just the past two years. We have committed funds for new group homes and wilderness programs, for additional placements in community treatment centers and day centers, and for 700 more youth in the electronic monitoring program.

This year's budget also includes nearly $13 million to make improvements in state Youth Development Centers, including new facilities in Savannah and Cobb County, and a major expansion in Augusta. But at the same time, we are going to move forward forcefully to control juvenile violence, and I am committed to meeting the need for additional space.

*—Georgia Correctional Training Conference, October 17, 1994*

Back when our juvenile justice system was created, a juvenile delinquent was a youngster who stole hubcaps, shoplifted, ran away from home, or painted graffiti on public property. Judges basically had two alternatives: a regular YDC or probation. No one envisioned the kinds of problems we are facing today, and we are now creating a range of sentencing alternatives that match the range of problems we are faced with. For example, we've got a special facility for teenagers who commit certain violent crimes and are tried and sentenced as adults, so that they are not mixed in with other juvenile offenders. Then we've got some outdoor wilderness programs for youth who will respond better in that setting than in a more traditional YDC.

What you've got here in Irwin County is yet another specialized facility that is, in effect, a boot camp for juvenile offenders. These are kids who are sort of like the mule in that old story where the farmer used to have to hit him up-side his head to get his attention before he could tell him what to do. Their offenses are not serious enough to require them to be sent to a regular YDC. But they are kids who the judge feels would benefit from up to 90 days in a boot camp type of setting, as a way of getting their attention, so to speak.

Six months or so ago, we had a backlog of nearly 200 juveniles waiting for a slot in this 90-day boot-camp program. Irwin had an empty prison facility going begging because the overflow of federal prisoners you had envisioned did not materialize. Today, all of us can celebrate together. From our point of view at the state level, we are pleased and excited to have this special YDC up and running, providing us with the beds to offer a specialized alternative to juvenile offenders who the judges feel would benefit from it. We are also pleased to be able to work with Irwin County in putting this facility to good use in the spirit of your original intentions. This YDC provides 180 jobs to local community residents, and it is operated by a private provider, the Bobby Ross Group.

—*Irwin YDC Ribbon Cutting, May 11, 1995*

## Georgia Bureau of Investigation

It takes many tools to fight crime. At one end, you have to have good law enforcement officers out on the streets. And I'm proud of our Georgia law enforcement officers and the many accomplishments we have achieved together over the past four years. At the other end you have to have strong sentencing laws to put violent criminals behind bars....Of course it takes prison space to keep offenders behind bars, and I have opened more prison beds than at any time in Georgia history—13,000 new beds by the end of this year. That's a 50 percent increase since I became Governor.

But in between, you have to have the evidence it takes to convict the criminals in court. The GBI's State Crime Lab is the only full-service forensic lab in the state, and it serves every single law enforcement agency in the state. In recent years, lab tests have come to play a bigger role than ever before in providing evidence and placing people at the scene of a crime, and the demand for work by the State Crime Lab has been growing.

In the process of responding to the larger workload, we have also been working to give Georgia's local law enforcement agencies faster turn-around time and bring forensic services closer to them. We are doing that by building a network of regional crime labs. These labs provide law enforcement agencies with direct access to lab scientists during the investigation of a case, and they also provide our judicial system with direct access to lab experts as these cases go through court.

We have regional crime labs in Columbus, Macon, Augusta, Savannah, and Moultrie. But so far, northwest Georgia, which has a high caseload, has been served solely out of the main crime lab in Atlanta. Today I am announcing the sixth GBI branch lab in the network. It will be located here in Summerville adjacent to the Hayes Correctional Institution, and it will serve 20 northwest Georgia counties....

It will have a morgue and a medical examiner, allowing local investigators to be on hand for autopsies and ask questions directly. It will have a vault where evidence can be secured, and an enclosed garage to use for examining vehicles involved in a crime. It will provide full lab services, including drug identification, toxicology, serology, and criminalistic testing. We plan to have a fingerprint expert on the staff here, as well as a remote terminal that connects this lab with the Automated Fingerprint Identification System at the main lab in Atlanta. What that means is instant access to the state computer bank of fingerprints, to give the law enforcement agencies of this region fast identification of criminal suspects and of fingerprints left at the scene of a crime.

—*Announce Summerville GBI lab, September 28, 1998*

# The 1996 Olympics

It is a great pleasure to greet you, President Samaranch, on behalf of the State of Georgia, and to welcome you to our state and capital city of Atlanta. We are honored and proud to be chosen as the site of the 1996 Olympic Games, and we thank you for the wonderful opportunity you have extended to us to host the Games here in Atlanta.

The American South is known for its gracious hospitality. We look forward to extending that hospitality to the athletes, officials, and guests who come to Georgia for this event.

The ribbon cutting for the offices for the Atlanta Committee for the Olympic Games this afternoon is more than the dedication of a physical facility. It is a dedication of ourselves as Georgians to the monumental task that lies before us in preparing to host this tremendous event.

We commit ourselves to the task at hand of making the 1996 Games the best the world has seen. We look to you and the International Olympic Committee for advice and counsel. And we pledge to work together with each other, and with you and the International Committee over the next five years in the true spirit of the Olympic Games.

*—ACOG Luncheon for Juan Samaranch, April 29, 1991*

---

You who sit on this Authority come from Atlanta, Fulton, and DeKalb, from Savannah, from the World Congress Center. Each of you has your own piece of Olympic action and your own Olympic agenda. There are also many strong personalities here around the Authority table. That is to be expected. Assertiveness and tenacity are among the characteristics that made you leaders, and that is why you are here—because you are proven leaders.

But meeting the tremendous challenge before you in the next five years will require not only leadership and hard work, but also teamwork in the true Olympic spirit. And that is the point of what I want to say to you this afternoon.

The Olympic spirit is the spirit of cooperation, the spirit of give and take. It is recognizing and appreciating the skills and expertise that each member brings to this table, and then listening with respect and acting with sensitivity. It is rising above the differences among you, above your own personal agendas, and yes, above your own egos, to work on a higher plane—a plane on which everyone focuses on the goal of orchestrating every aspect of the 1996 Olympics into a seamless performance of excellence.

Our duty is to host the world's biggest event. Our challenge is to make it the world's best event. This is the opportunity of a lifetime, perhaps even more than a lifetime. For the sake of Georgia's future, we dare not miss the mark. We dare not allow internal bickering to distract us from the over-arching goal of collectively putting our best foot forward.

When all the eyes of the world are turned toward us for these Centennial Olympic Games, they need to see an Olympics that stands out against a hundred years of past events. They need to see an Olympics that sets the tenor for the next century of future Games.

It is a heavy load that rests on your shoulders. There is much to be accomplished before we will be ready to step into the international spotlight. But I am confident of your ability to carry it well, and to carry it in the true spirit of the Olympics.

*—Georgia Authority for Olympic Games, June 6, 1991*

---

I am an early riser by habit, and I usually spend the quiet of the early morning catching up with my reading and deskwork. But one year ago today, Shirley joined me, and we turned on the television to watch the suspense build toward the announcement of the site of the 1996 Olympics.

Never has a single word unleashed such an explosion of joy as did the word "Atlanta," spoken into the hush of that crowded room in Tokyo. The underdog had not only made it to the play-offs, but had emerged the champion. And with that one word, the world recognized what we knew all along in our hearts—that Atlanta was a giant among the international cities of the world. We gather today to recapture the moment, to recall the exhilaration, to recreate the thrill of victory.

But, my friends, we must go beyond wallowing in nostalgia. Being named the site of the 1996 Olympics is one thing. Actually staging the Games is something else entirely. What we celebrate this morning is the creation of expectations. What still lies ahead of us is living up to those expectations. That is a higher hurdle than any we have yet faced.

Our duty is to host the world's biggest event. Our challenge is to make it the world's best event. This is the opportunity of a lifetime—more than a lifetime. For the sake of Georgia's future, we dare not miss the mark. When the eyes of the world are upon us in 1996, they must see an Olympics that stands out against a hundred years of past events. They must see an Olympics that sets the tenor for the next century of future Games.

Meeting that tremendous challenge in the brief space of time that remains will require not only *hard* work, but also *team*work in the true spirit of the Olympics. We are called to a higher plane, above personal agendas and egos—a plane where everyone focuses on the goal of orchestrating every aspect of the 1996 Olympics into a seamless performance of excellence.

To that end, let us use this occasion to recapture the oneness of purpose we felt at this dramatic moment a year ago, and to dedicate ourselves with renewed vigor to the task that lies ahead.

*—One-Year Anniversary, Naming of Atlanta, September 18, 1991*

---

We have a chance to give the entire world the impression that here is an up-and-coming, international city that has its act together and is going places, and they'd better pay more attention to Atlanta if they want to be where the action is in the 21st century. But if we blow it, we are going to come across as a bumbling, provincial center whose attention is focused inward on internal disagreements, and who is living 50 years in the past.

The challenge is before us. For the sake of the future of the entire metro area, we dare not miss the mark.

*—Metro Atlanta Business Forum, August 12, 1992*

---

Two hundred fifty-nine years ago, a man stood here where we are now and watched a tall ship from Europe sailing up the Savannah River. It was a new experience for him. Something was happening here that had never happened before, and he was caught up in the drama and the wonder of it.

The man who stood on the bluffs watching was a native American named Tomochichi. The ship was carrying James Edward Oglethorpe and a band of settlers. And the arrival of that ship at this site changed the course of Georgia history in striking and far-reaching ways.

This morning, like Tomochichi, we have watched a tall ship sailing up the Savannah River. Once again something is happening here on the river bluffs that has never happened before—something that has the potential to change the course of Georgia history in striking and far-reaching ways. And we are caught up in the drama and the wonder of it.

Its arrival can do the same for us as Oglethorpe's did for Tomochichi: Expand our horizons and bring us into a new international world.

The arrival of this ship today may not have quite as drastic an impact on our individual lives as Oglethorpe's had on Tomochichi's. But in welcoming this flag to Georgia, we open our state to the entire world to a greater extent than ever has been before.

Barcelona, with its ancient architectural treasures and centuries-old heritage, set the mood in which to begin a celebration of the Olympic centennial. It was truly an appropriate setting for looking back over the heritage of the first century of these Games. And some wondered how Atlanta, a mere infant of a city by comparison, could offer a meaningful continuation of this historic celebration.

Atlanta has always focused its efforts on making its dreams come true, rather than dwelling on the past. The predominant characteristic of its personality has always been a vision for the future and a confident determination to overcome whatever obstacles may stand in the way of getting there. That makes it the perfect place for the Olympics to turn the corner toward its second century and the 21st century. We are going to host an Olympics that looks toward the next century and creates a new set of standards for the age of high technology.

But as we stand here where Tomochichi stood so many years ago, let's take a moment, before we leave the past, to think back and remember the way in which he played a role in changing the course of history in this great state. Tomochichi greeted the world with hospitality and grace when it arrived on his doorstep, and a new Georgia grew and thrived, because of the statesmanship and friendship he demonstrated in his moment of opportunity.

Today, it is our ship that has come in. It is our doorstep upon which the world now stands. So let us resolve to be as wise and farsighted with the opportunity that lies before us in the course of the next four years, as Tomochichi was when that other tall ship sailed up the Savannah River in his time nearly 260 years ago.

*—Olympic Flag Arrival in Savannah, September 10, 1992*

The flag of the Olympic Games has arrived in Atlanta, and we have officially become THE Olympic site, THE Olympic hosts. We are no longer waiting in line in the wings while Barcelona holds center stage. Barcelona's performance has concluded, and has been duly recognized, admired, and applauded. It is now our turn.

With this celebration, we step onto the stage and into the spotlight. We do that with great joy, relishing the opportunity that lies before us to showcase our state to the world. But we also feel some of the butterflies of stage fright in the pits of our stomach. High expectations have been laid before us, and in receiving this flag, the weight of meeting those expectations comes to rest upon our shoulders....

Our task is not unlike that of the athletes who will compete in Georgia four years from now. Like those athletes, our sights must be fixed with unwavering resolve on excelling to the utmost of our capabilities in the events of four years from now. Our plans and schedule for accomplishing that goal must be wisely laid, and we must adhere to them with single-minded determination.

*—Arrival of Olympic Flag in Atlanta, September 21, 1992*

The Olympics have given us a clear-cut deadline and a pretty tight time framework within which a lot of things need to be done. It is a real challenge to move ahead on schedule and, at the same time, allow for the kind of sensitity and input into the planning process that needs to happen, if we are to make the best long-term use of this tremendous opportunity.

But it can be done. And the arrival of this day, on which we actually break ground for the Olympic Stadium, is evidence that it is being done. I want to congratulate everyone who has worked so hard to bring us to this day.

*—Ground Breaking, Olympic Stadium, July 10, 1993*

----------

Here in Georgia we have been given a unique opportunity—to host the Centennial of the Modern Olympic Games. We have exactly three years from this day to make Georgia the very best it can be. The Atlanta Committee for the Olympic Games is well on the way to doing its part in preparing for the Games, and your local and state governments are working extremely hard to ensure that Georgia will put its best foot forward when our time at the center of the world stage comes.

You, the members of The Olympic Force, are also playing a vital role. Because of your efforts to feed the hungry, care for the sick, visit the elderly, assist in the education process and enhance and protect the environment, you are making this state a better place to live—a place that responds to the needs of its own—a place of which we can all be extremely proud.

We have undertaken a great challenge and nothing great can ever be achieved without great men and women. Your involvement makes me confident that we will live up to the challenge. In recognition of your efforts and the efforts of your fellow Olympic Force members, I have issued a state proclamation making today—July 20, 1993—Volunteer Recognition Day in Georgia.

*—Olympic Volunteer Awards Luncheon, July 20, 1993*

----------

The Olympics are much more than a few incredible weeks of heavy tourism volume and strong cash flow. They are our chance to get the State of Georgia on the lists and in the minds of travel agents and travelers all over the globe.

It used to be that when travelers from Europe and the Pacific Rim thought of the United States, the names that automatically popped into their minds were California, Florida and New York. Those were the commonly known destinations in the United States, and that's where the tours and tourists went. But now the words "Atlanta" and "Georgia" are frequently heard on the streets and in the restaurants of the world. This state is being featured by international travel agencies as "the" place to go, and it's making a difference. Did you know that even after you factor out Olympic-related visitors to Georgia, we experienced a 34 percent increase in international visitors last year?

We are going to step up our efforts to reach out to international visitors as the Olympics draw closer. The Olympics are an unprecedented opportunity for us to showcase the rich natural and historic attractions of Georgia to the world, so that long after the Olympic Torch is passed on to the next host site, Georgia will remain on the list of favorite places for international tourists to visit.

*—Governor's Tourism Conference, December 7, 1994*

----------

We like to think of the Games as the Georgia Olympics. Not only will some of the events take place in other parts of the state—such as volleyball in Columbus, rowing in Gainesville, soccer in Athens, and yachting in Savannah—but literally dozens of Georgia communities are standing ready to host your teams as they train and get acclimated to this environment in preparation for the Games.

The goal of the Georgia Olympic Training Alliance is to be a liaison between your teams and the Georgia communities who have training facilities to offer. The Alliance is ready to help you secure appropriate training facilities for your teams as you prepare for the 1996 Olympics.

You've been getting letters and phone calls and faxes from the Alliance over the past year about bringing your teams to Georgia to train in advance of the Olympics. Tonight I simply want to reiterate that invitation in person.

The 1996 Olympic Games are special to the world, because they are the centennial games of the modern Olympics. They are special to Georgia, because it is the first time in history that we have had the honor of hosting them. So we are working very hard to make the 1996 Olympics the best games ever. And we understand that a very important part of making the these Olympics the best ever is to help every Olympic team do its very best.

That's why we want to give every Olympic team the opportunity to get acquainted with our state and learn to feel at home here. We want to give every Olympic team the opportunity to train and build endurance in our warm, humid summer weather... So that when the Games begin, your teams are comfortable, acclimated, and ready to do their very best.

There are colleges and universities all around this state who are ready to offer Olympic teams the use of their athletic facilities. And did you know that one of the best world-class diving wells in the entire United States are located in the South Georgia town of Moultrie?

More than 80 Georgia communities with quality athletic facilities to offer are ready to roll out the welcome mat to your teams, and the Georgia Olympic Training Alliance is prepared to help you find a community that fits your needs. The Alliance can schedule visits for you to the communities you are interested in. The Alliance will also help you select the best community for your needs, and help negotiate an agreement with that community to host your team.

The Alliance is also working with the many Georgia communities on their list, to make sure they understand the responsibilities they will face as hosts to teams in training. Then the Alliance will stay in touch with your team during the time they are training here in Georgia, to ensure the quality of the services provided to them, and they will do it with no charge.

You see, Georgia is known around the world for our hospitality, and the reason is because we care about our guests. If you are our guest, we want to do everything we can to make you comfortable and meet your needs. That's why we're working so hard to make everyone's visit to Georgia a memorable experience.

The Georgia Olympic Training Alliance focuses on the needs of your teams as they come to train and prepare prior to the Games. Then during the Olympics, the Welcome South Visitors Center, right in the middle of downtown Atlanta, will be a central place where both visitors and athletes can find everything they need. Its specially trained staff will speak various languages. Visitors can buy tickets to Olympic events at the Welcome South Visitors Center. Everyone can buy souvenirs.

The Welcome South Visitors Center will also feature exhibits that present the unique color, flavor, culture and history of the American South. So that visitors and athletes can find out about other attractions they may want to visit in Georgia and the surrounding states. And they can make their travel or hotel reservations at the Welcome South Visitors Center. They can even buy airline tickets there.

We even have a special program for business executives who want to combine a visit to the Olympics with a chance to check out business opportunities in our state. It is called Operation Legacy, and it helps business leaders learn more about the business opportunities for them here in Georgia.

We want your teams to be in top shape going into the Olympics, and we want the summer of 1996 to be a very special and memorable event—not just in overall Olympic history, but also for the athletes who represent your country and want to be able to give you their personal best performance. Thank you for coming and spending this week in Georgia. Over the upcoming months, we look forward to welcoming your teams to our state to train and become acclimated in preparation for the best Olympic Games ever.

—*National Olympic Committees, December 14, 1994*

———————

The Olympics represent immediate opportunity for the entire state, with Olympic teams already moving into communities all over Georgia to get used to our summer weather. GOTA, the Georgia Olympic Training Alliance, is helping communities take advantage of this opportunity. GOTA helps get teams and communities together, helps to negotiate contracts, and keeps in touch with both sides to make sure it is a positive experience for everyone.

We have also designated $2 million in state funds to help communities with infrastructure to attract teams for training. For example, we helped Elberton with a rowing dock on Lake Richard Russell, and the Swedish rowing team is training there. We helped Cochran with improvements to the baseball field at Middle Georgia College, and the French baseball team is training there.

Tomorrow morning you'll have a chance to learn more about just how extensive these Olympic-related activities are. You'll be surprised at the number—at least three dozen: Belgian equestrians and cyclers in Chatsworth, British divers in Moultrie, Italian and Polish wrestlers in Valdosta, Greek weightlifters in Mount Vernon, Ugandan athletes in Tifton, and Tanzanian athletes in Ellijay.

—*Governor's Economic Development Conference, May 17, 1995*

———————

We have been welcoming many Australians to Atlanta these days, just as four years go, Georgians were flocking to Barcelona. There's a sort of camaraderie among Olympic host cities. And that is how it should be. The Olympics are too big a thing for each successive host city to reinvent the wheel, when we can be learning from each other.

If Sydney is anything like Atlanta, you are thrilled to be the host for the Olympics in the year 2000. At the same time you are a little nervous about the magnitude of the task that lies before you. In Atlanta, we are still thrilled, and we are still a little nervous. To give you an idea of the magnitude of this thing—if the Atlanta Olympic Committee were a corporation, it would be listed among the Fortune 500. It has 1,000 employees and a budget of over $1.5 billion.

We are building 10 new athletic venues at a cost of over $600 million, and renovating several other sports facilities, plus building eight new dormitories on the campus of Georgia Tech, which will be the Olympic Village. We've got all our venues on schedule and on budget. We've got three-quarters of the work done, and we're very optimistic that we going to actually pull it off.

Hosting the Olympics is a once-in-a-lifetime opportunity—actually it's more like once in ten lifetimes. We are working very hard, not only to get the Olympics venues ready, but also to utilize the other opportunities the Olympics provide. Millions of people all around the world who know very little about Atlanta and Georgia will be forming impressions and making assumptions based on what they see on television during the next 10 months. We want to impress upon them that Georgia is a place that is beautiful, a place that is hospitable, a place where businesses thrive and life is good, a place where people want to be. That is the most basic level of opportunity that the Olympic Games give their host city.

The next level of opportunity the Olympics offer is an unprecedented chance for their host site to make itself more inviting and desirable as an international tourism destination. Prior Olympic cities have focused their economic development efforts on tourism, and it's a smart idea, because disposable income and leisure time are on the rise around the world. That makes tourism the great growth industry of the 21st century. Barcelona, for example, is sustaining a 25 percent increase in tourism since it hosted the Summer Olympics three years ago.

So Georgia has a number of initiatives designed to create a strong image of our state as a travel destination for both business and pleasure. We have a $9 million international advertising campaign underway called "Georgia Global Now" that is targeted toward influential international travelers.

We have opened the Welcome South Visitor Center in downtown Atlanta. It is located right in the thick of our downtown hotels near the Centennial Olympic Park, and it is midway between the Olympic village and the major downtown sport venues. This high-tech visitors center promotes attractions and offers reservation services and tour packages that will get Olympic visitors to the places they choose to visit.

For those who arrive by air, we have just renovated and expanded the terminal at Atlanta's Hartsfield International Airport. For those who arrive by car, we are preparing our visitors centers, which are located where major highways enter the state and near major attractions.

We see a third level of economic opportunity in the sports infrastructure we are building to put on the Games. Even though the Olympics themselves may not return to

Georgia for a long time, the top-notch facilities they require will enable us to host many other world-class sports events. The Atlanta Sports Council has developed a 10-year plan that targets more than 60 different sports, and each of our other venue sites is preparing similar long-term plans for the sports they will host.

Georgia has even identified yet a fourth level of opportunity in the Olympics that no one has ever tried before. We are the first host site ever to make a deliberate attempt to use the Olympics as a springboard for general long-term economic development. For example, Georgia is already well on the way to establishing itself as a world center of communications technology and expertise.... We are building a massive telecommunications infrastructure and sophisticated computer networks that will enable us to put on the most high-tech Olympics the world has ever seen. And we will use the Games to showcase our capabilities and achieve greater recognition around the world as a center for communications technology.

We have also gathered a group of public and private partners for an economic development effort we call Operation Legacy. This group first identified the industry types that have the most potential for future development in Georgia. Then it identified the best companies within those industry types.

For the past 18 months, we have been bringing the top executives from those companies to Georgia for several days at a time to show them what is so special about our state that we were chosen to host the Olympics. By the time the Olympics begin next summer, we will have hosted executives from about 300 companies, and many of them will be coming back for the Games. Our goal is 20 new facilities with 6,000 jobs and a collective payroll of $150 million.

We are also going to use the opportunity of the Olympics to expand international trade. The day before I left on this trip, I helped to cut the ribbon on a new Export Assistance Center to give Georgia businesses one-stop assistance....

As you can tell, we see the Olympics as much more than 17 days of world athletic events. We have our eye on long-term Olympic gold. And we are working hard to win it. No other host site has ever tried to do the kind of long-term economic development based on the Olympics that we are attempting. But we believe it has a lot of potential, and we are determined to find out if it really works.

We will be glad to share our experience with you here in Sydney. But I need to warn you up-front—we are going to do our very best to make the 1996 Olympic Games a hard act to follow.

—*American Chamber of Commerce, Sydney, Australia, October 9, 1995*

---

We join you in looking forward to the historic moment when Georgia stands in the world's spotlight, as six of every 10 people on this planet watch the 1996 Olympic Games.

At the most fundamental level, we are preparing to provide security at the many Olympic venues on state property....We are also doing our best to take advantage of this unprecedented opportunity at all levels—to increase tourism, attract future world-class athletic events, expand trade and develop business relationships.

And when the world spotlight shines on Georgia in a few months, we are going to show them a state that is beautiful and friendly, vibrant and healthy....a state where people and businesses want to be....a state that is striding confidently and boldly forward to embrace the 21st century.

*—Georgia Chamber of Commerce Eggs & Issues Breakfast, January 11, 1996*

———————

I hope you are going to come back in a few months for the Olympics, because as an event, these Games are going to set a couple of world records of their own. First, with several million visitors on hand and three of every five people on the planet watching on television, it is going to be the biggest peace-time event in world history.

However, despite being the biggest Olympics ever, these Games will also be the most compact Olympics ever. Most of the athletic venues, to say nothing of the Olympic Village and thousands of hotel rooms, are located within a relatively small geographic area.

These are also going to be the most high-tech Olympics ever held, because Atlanta is a high-tech telecommunications nerve center, and we are using our expertise to put on the Games.

*—World View 90s International Media Tour, March 19, 1996*

———————

Although this new center is not something we are doing just for the Olympics, it is a great example of the opportunity that the Olympics provide. The Olympics, in this case, were a catalyst that enabled us to move out on the cutting edge of traffic management and make Atlanta a model to develop and test the high-tech traffic management system of the future.

*—Open DOT Transportation Management Center, April 11, 1996*

———————

Today the Olympic flame begins a journey through 42 states, including 29 state capitals and our nation's capital. It will come within two hours traveling time of 90 percent of the American people. On the way, it will be held aloft by 10,000 runners... runners of all ages, from all walks of life... but who all share the common characteristic of making a difference in their communities.

I believe the torch will carry with it the distinct spirit of the Olympics, generating pride and enthusiasm for the 1996 Games as it travels throughout the United States, so that when it arrives in Georgia, 74 days from now on July 10th, the torch will bring with it the goodwill and best wishes of the American people, who in the process of catching a glimpse of the flame itself, have also caught the spirit that it embodies.

The central core of this torch is made of Georgia hardwood. That core is bound with 22 aluminum reeds, representing the number of times the Modern Olympic Games have been held. The hardwood of Georgia is what gives this torch its special identity, just as the State of Georgia will give the 1996 Olympic Games their special identity. This is the first time in history that the Olympic Torch has come to the American South, and we look forward with enormous pride to welcoming the world, and presenting our region, with its unique natural and historical features, its warm hospitality, and its distinct and vibrant culture.

Just as we celebrate what defines the American South and makes us unique as a region, we also cherish the common bonds that all of us share as Americans. We Georgians are the beneficiaries of the successful Los Angeles Games, and I promise that as the host of these Centennial Olympics, Georgia will do honor to our country.

While the core of Georgia hardwood proclaims that the 1996 Olympics will be uniquely Georgian and uniquely American, at the same time the aluminum reeds remind us that these Games are also bound up in the rich and wonderful international tradition of 22 prior Olympics. We in Georgia will carry on that great tradition—remembering every past city and region that has been granted the great privilege of hosting the Games, and moving the tradition forward in a way that does them all credit.

*—Olympic Torch Arrival, Los Angeles, April 27, 1996*

———————

From the perspective of the State of Georgia, you have the most important job of anybody who has anything to do with the Olympics. Safety and security are paramount. Everything else, from the gold medals down, is secondary. Security at your venue must be so strong that no one has cause to wonder about it, and at the same time so unobtrusive that no one has cause to be inconvenienced by it. Remember the old adage, "no news is good news"? Your challenge is to make it come true. Because the ultimate goal that this team must achieve is to be so effective and at the same time so smooth, that security never becomes an issue that attracts attention to itself.

Our team consists of many members—sworn law enforcement officers from all across state agencies, ACOG staff, local law enforcement officers, federal agencies and the military, and the key to a successful public safety effort is teamwork among all of you.

Two-thirds of the Olympic venues are on state-owned property, and the state is responsible for providing security at those venues. For that task we have enlisted roughly 3,000 state personnel, including nearly 2,500 sworn law enforcement officers.

In addition, I want to assure all of you that state assets and resources are being made available to each of your venues. The state has created the Special Management Center—known as the SMC—to provide assistance at every venue in the event of a disaster, crisis or problem. The SMC, as you have learned today, has representatives from most jurisdictions throughout the Olympic arena. They will be available to support everyone in the Olympics, including In-Transit, Dignitary Protection, Bomb Management,

Intelligence, and Aviation.

The heart of the State's security effort is SOLEC—the State Olympic Law Enforcement Command. It was created to serve you as you handle safety and security at your individual venues, to serve the Olympic participants and visitors, and to serve the citizens of this state. SOLEC is the state's central command. It is SOLEC's duty to coordinate all state law enforcement operations in carrying out the state's Olympic mission.

The SOLEC Command Post reports directly to me, and it will have the final authority for all command decisions through the conclusion of all games and events associated with the 1996 Olympics. I have made it my personal mission to ensure that the State of Georgia successfully fulfills our obligations both to the Olympic participants and visitors, and to the citizens of this state. And I will be in frequent and direct contact with SOLEC in the weeks and months ahead.

I have also made it a personal mission to ensure that the State successfully fulfills our obligations to each one of you as you provide for safety and security at your particular venue. In return, I am counting on each one of you to successfully fulfill your responsibilities and obligations at your venue.

Remember, your security operations are the most important part of hosting the Olympics. The success of these Games ultimately rests on your shoulders. But I have every confidence in your ability to work together as a team, and in the ability of this team to succeed in the task that is before you.

Doing your job so well that nobody ever stops to worry about safety will not get you any headlines. But it will establish these 1996 Olympics on the cutting edge of security operations, and earn you the admiration and respect of your professional colleagues around the world.

—*Charge to Olympic Venue Commanders, April 30, 1996*

I've been looking around in admiration and remembering the ground-breaking ceremony, less than two years ago. At that time, everyone was a little nervous about the tight time framework in which so many major Olympic projects had to be completed. Today we celebrate with pride in a job well done and with confidence as, one by one, our big Olympic projects reach completion.

As the Olympic torch journeys across our great nation on its way to this very spot, we look forward with enthusiasm to welcoming the world. Here is proof that when those words, "Let the Games begin," are uttered in just a few weeks, Georgia will be ready.

—*Dedication, Olympic Stadium, May 18, 1996*

Yesterday, you attended the opening of our new Olympic Stadium. It is one of 10 new athletic facilities we have built for the Olympics at a cost of over $600 million. We have also renovated several other sports facilities. So, when this summer's Games raise Georgia's profile in the international world of sports, we are prepared to take advantage of the opportunity that provides.

Facilities like our new natatorium, velodrome, tennis center, and equestrian center, and our yachting and rowing venues give Georgia the infrastructure we need to host a wide range of world-class athletic competitions after the Olympics.

The Atlanta Sports Council has developed a 10-year plan that targets major competitions for more than 60 different sports. And each of our other venue sites is preparing similar long-term plans for the sports they will host during the Olympics.

Georgia already has a strong sports-related economic base, and we are working hard to use the Olympics as a springboard to lift our sports industry to an even higher level of prominence.

*—Operation Legacy Dinner for Sports Industry Executives, May 19, 1996*

---

The 1996 Summer Olympics, which will get underway in about six weeks, will be the largest peace-time event in world history. With more than 11,000 athletes and some two million spectators, they will be double the size of the Los Angeles Games 12 years ago. That poses a security challenge like no other before in history.

Today we come to the end of a long and detailed and painstaking planning process and begin the actual realization of those plans. Within the next week, an impressive, hand-picked team of highly trained and motivated law enforcement and public safety specialists will come together here and begin operations. They are the core of the state law enforcement team for the 1996 Centennial Olympic Games, and they will supervise and direct a massive Olympic force that involves roughly 3,000 state personnel, including nearly 2,500 sworn law enforcement officers.

They come from different agencies, but they are focused and committed to achieving one common goal—providing a safe and secure environment for the 1996 Olympic Games. Two-thirds of the Olympic venues are on property that is owned by the State of Georgia, and the state is responsible for providing security at those venues.

From my perspective and the perspective of this team, safety and security are paramount. Everything else, from the gold medals down, is secondary. I have made it my personal mission to ensure that the State of Georgia successfully fulfills our obligations to both the Olympic participants and visitors, and to the citizens of this state. I will be in frequent and direct contact with the staff here at the State Operations Center in the weeks and months ahead....

What I want to emphasize is that this center represents a level of teamwork that is unprecedented, both in state government and in Olympic history. Coordination and teamwork will be the hallmarks of this operation, and I am confident that this team will do an outstanding job of providing a safe and enjoyable environment for everyone this summer. As is so often the case in the Olympics, a combination of excellence and teamwork is what will win Georgia the gold in the eyes of athletes, officials, spectators, and Georgia citizens.

This operation can be characterized as high-tech, but low visibility. The technology you will see in this command center today is the most sophisticated in Olympic history. It allows us to make security very strong and pervasive at our Olympic venues without making them look or feel like fortified garrisons. Our goal is to make the 1996 Olympics the best ever by making security at the state-owned venues so sound that no one worries about it, and at the same time so unobtrusive that no one is inconvenienced by it without cause. If we successfully achieve that goal, it will establish these 1996 Olympics on the cutting edge of security operations, and earn this Georgia team the admiration and respect of their professional colleagues around the world.

Like so much of our Olympic infrastructure, this center will have a much bigger impact on Georgia than simply serving as the command center for the state's security operations for two weeks of athletic events. It is a long-term investment. Following the Games, this facility will become the Crisis Management Center for GEMA, the Georgia Emergency Management Agency... The Olympics have given Georgia the opportunity to develop a state-of-the-art facility from which to coordinate our response to any emergency or crisis that may come our way in the long-term.

—*Dedicate State Olympic Operations Center, June 5, 1996*

---

We believe one of the most distinctive and memorable feature of the 1996 Olympics will be the warm friendliness of Georgia's people and our tradition of southern hospitality. The focal point for that hospitality will be here at the Olympic Village, as we put out the welcome mat for the athletes and officials who are the real guests of the Games. Here is where we literally say to our most important Olympic visitors, "Our house is your house. Come in, sit down, put up your feet, make yourself at home, and let us make you comfortable."

The village will have a mayor who will officially welcome national delegations as they arrive, and present each country with a handmade Georgia quilt as a gift. Then they will be encouraged to unpack and relax in the first completely air conditioned Olympic Village in the history of the Games.

First and foremost, the village provides a place for them to rest and prepare themselves mentally and physically for competition. It includes extensive athletic training facilities and a sports medicine clinic.

But we know that the residents are human beings as well as athletes, and the village is designed to help them enjoy their time at the Games to the fullest. Dining facilities will serve a diverse international menu 24 hours a day and pack box lunches for anyone who wants them. There's a bowling alley, a theater, video-viewing facilities, a music listening center, an arcade, a health club, a swimming pool, a coffee house, and a dance club. There's a department store, a dry cleaner, a travel agency, a hair salon, a post office, and a bank. There are worship areas and ministers for Christians, Jews, Buddhists, and Muslims. There's telephone service in 20 languages, an international news stand, and computers for athlete E-mail and surfing the Internet.

When the Olympics are over, they may not want to go home.

*—Transfer Olympic Village to ACOG, July 1, 1996*

———————

This consular corps, more than any other single group, is what makes Atlanta an international city, and you are pivotal as we prepare to welcome the world.

We have already had Olympic teams from 103 countries training in 65 different Georgia communities, and I want to thank you for helping us with hosting the athletes from your countries.

In addition to the athletes, every one of you is now preparing for a large number of dignitaries and guests from your country to come to Atlanta. In the coming days and weeks, your responsibilities will be heavier than ever before.

This is a time for us to work together and help each other out in the task of hosting a record number of international guests. I want to thank each of you in advance for your efforts in helping to look after the athletes, officials and dignitaries from your country. We are counting on you to help make things go smoothly while they are here. At the same time, I want to assure you that you can count on us. The Georgia Department of Industry, Trade and Tourism will help you in any way they can with your delegations of dignitaries, and I will try to be available as my schedule allows, to meet international leaders.

If we work together and help each other, we can give our guests a memorable Olympic experience, and that will reflect well on you as well as on the State of Georgia.

*—Consular Corps, July 9, 1996*

———————

This park is owned by the state, designed and developed by the World Congress Center Authority. It is the State of Georgia's first and only urban park, and the largest urban park to be built in the United States in more than a quarter of a century. But to this day, no tax dollars have gone into the building of it. This park was made possible by the generous gifts of those who love Atlanta—the business community, the Woodruff Foundation, and the thousands of individual citizens who purchased bricks....

For the next three weeks, this spectacular park will be the crossroads of the world, where people from around the globe gather in a spirit of unity and friendship. For many long years beyond the Games, it will stand as a true Olympic legacy, a lasting tribute to the power of the Olympic spirit at work in the City of Atlanta.

*—Opening of Centennial Olympic Park, July 13, 1996*

———————

Atlanta is not an international city because the Olympics are here. The Olympics are here because Atlanta is an international city. We see the Olympics as a piece of a bigger picture. Our goal is to make our state and its capital city the world center for advanced telecommunications technology, and the opportunity the Olympics provide to showcase our technological capabilities is a step in the direction of achieving that goal.

*—BellSouth Board of Directors, July 22, 1996*

---

Georgia opened the doors of the Olympics to ordinary fans as never before, with a world record of 8.6 million event tickets—more tickets than the last two Olympics combined. The athletes responded to the fans' enthusiasm with record-breaking performances, and both the athletes and the fans had a wonderful time. Isn't that what the Olympics are about, after all? That's why I believe these were the best Games ever.

But the sheer magnitude and complexity of making the 1996 Olympics the "Games of the People" made your job all the harder. For the past several months—and for some of you it's been the past several years—you have dedicated an unprecedented level of commitment and diligence to one common cause: The safety and protection of the Olympic Game athletes, officials, and visitors, and the citizens of this state. With a total of 5,300 state and local law enforcement personnel, and 4,800 National Guardsmen, Georgia proved we were capable of holding up our end of the bargain.

It was not easy. There were long hours and hardships. I visited "Lakewood Prison" and got me a copy of the "Lakewood Prison Blues." I know how much your troops would rather have been on summer vacation or even just been able to spend evenings and weekends with their families. All of you made a personal sacrifice in order to provide a safe environment for the world to celebrate the 100th anniversary of the modern Olympic Games. And I am proud of the way the State of Georgia fulfilled its Olympic security obligations.

I was in the State Operations Center in the early hours of Saturday morning after the bomb exploded in Centennial Park. I personally witnessed the public safety forces of this state, rallying together, first to respond rapidly to this tragedy, and then to prepare for the days ahead as the Olympics continued. I was very proud of the quick response of state law enforcement personnel on the scene, to begin clearing the area even before anyone knew about the 911 call. You literally saved many lives and prevented many from being injured. I especially want to extend my gratitude and best wishes for a quick recovery to the state employees who were injured in the process of clearing the area.

The Olympics called upon state government to work together across agency lines as never before. SOLEC has involved 46 state and local agencies. Thirty-five of them loaned personnel to SOLEC for the Games. And then SOLEC worked closely together with ACOG and several federal law enforcement agencies. I have heard from a number of law enforcement leaders that the level of teamwork represented in the State Olympic Law Enforcement Command is unprecedented in state history.

In fact, it was so unprecedented that some doubted at the beginning whether it would work. But it has worked, and it has worked extremely well. The reason is because you all have gone the extra mile in helping each other and working together.

*—State Olympic Law Enforcement Command, August 12, 1996*

<br>

With over 12,000 athletes and nearly nine million event tickets, the 1996 Olympics here in Georgia were the largest peacetime event in world history. They were bigger than the prior two Olympics combined, and bigger than the Games will be in the year 2000. And six of every ten people on the planet watched them on television.

The Olympics gave Georgia a chance to showcase ourselves to the world as a place that is beautiful, a place that is hospitable, a place where businesses thrive and life is good, a place where people want to be. This community did that better than any other venue in the state. I say that from personal experience, because I came to Gainesville for the rowing competition. And I'm pleased to have this opportunity tonight to tell you how outstanding it was in all respects....

Our goal as a state was to showcase Georgia on four different levels, and Gainesville did an exceptional job on all four. On the most fundamental level, we were presenting Georgia to those billions of people around the globe who were watching on television. Most of them knew very little about Atlanta or even Georgia—and certainly not Gainesville or Hall County. They were forming their initial impressions based on what they saw on TV, and what they saw when they watched the rowing competition was the beautiful, picture-postcard setting of Clark's Bridge Park.

On the second level, the Olympics were an opportunity to make a good impression on our visitors, and increase our profile as an attractive tourism destination. Once again, Gainesville excelled. Olympic visitors found 1,000 community volunteers ready to be helpful. Over 200 homes were rented to visitors in the most successful housing venture of any venue city. NBC announcer Charlie Jones went so far as to call Gainesville the Hospitality Capital of the World. You can bet that the 160,000 spectators who visited this community spread the word about what a wonderful time they had, and many will want to come back.

The third level of opportunity the Olympics provided was a chance to showcase our world-class sports facilities and establish ourselves as a site for future international competition and athletic training. And you did that. Gainesville now possesses one of only two international rowing courses in the United States. And the presidents of both the International Rowing Federation and the International Canoe-Kayak Federation declared it the best Olympic venue in the history of their sports.

Full-scale regattas are planned annually, and a half-dozen local high schools and colleges have begun rowing programs. Rowing has been established as a Gainesville sport, and Gainesville has been established as a rowing center.

Georgia went beyond prior Olympic sites to identify yet a fourth level of opportunity that no one had tried before. We were the first site ever to make a deliberate attempt to use the Olympics as a springboard for general, long-term economic development, and I want to commend Gainesville and Hall County for your efforts in this regard.

At the state level, we had Operation Legacy, which brought executives from 302 companies to Georgia in the two years leading up to the Olympics, then brought in executives from 163 companies during the Games themselves. And Gainesville was one of 20 communities around the state to participate in Operation Legacy.

But you went beyond that with your own efforts. Hall County went into the Olympics already having some 40 foreign companies representing 10 different countries. And you also already had one of the finest industry recruitment programs in the state— one that has created one of the most solid and diversified local economies in the nation, while at the same time preserving the quality environment of Lake Lanier.

I know of no other place in Georgia that was better-positioned to use the economic development leverage the Olympics offered, and I am confident that you will continue to use this opportunity to move economic development to a higher plane in Hall County.

*—Gainesville Rotary Club, February 19, 1997*

---

It was just four and a-half years ago that Billy Payne suggested we build a park on this site to serve as a sort of living room for the 1996 Centennial Olympic Games. It was a major undertaking—the first major urban park to be built anywhere in the United States for more than a quarter of a century. Barely four months later we unveiled the master plan for a 21-acre park, and under the leadership of the World Congress Center Authority and its exceptional Executive Director Dan Graveline, construction was begun on the first phase.

As Billy predicted, it became the gathering place for throngs of Georgians and guests from around the world during the Olympics. Once the Games were over, we went back to the drawing board to plan a permanent park that would be a rich Olympic legacy and would make downtown Atlanta more vibrant by continuing to draw Georgians and visitors alike.

With contributions from the Southern Company, the Georgia World Congress Center and the Robert W. Woodruff Foundation, we moved forward with phase two of the construction. It has been a deliberate process, with construction proceeding as funds became available, and through the long winter months, some of you must have wondered if it would ever stop raining long enough to finish the work.

But there has never been any doubt in my mind that we would reach this night. One of the hallmarks of my administration has been public-private partnerships. They have been the means of accomplishing some of my most significant initiatives. From the moment of its conception to the first strains of "Summon the Heroes" tonight, Centennial Olympic Park has been an outstanding example of a successful public-private partnership.

So it is my great pleasure to be here with you, to share in this special moment in our history, and to publicly thank everyone who shared in the dream for this park and helped to realize it—each company who contributed and each individual who purchased a brick.

*—Reopening of Centennial Olympic Park, March 28, 1998*

---

# State Government

We are sailing on rough and stormy seas here in Georgia. The dark clouds of a national recession hang low over us. The waves are choppy from a federal policy of passing costs along to the states rather than curtailing spending. But here in Georgia, we are going to do more than batten down the hatches and ride out the storm. We will chart a daring course across the swells and turn our sails to catch the wind....

Not only are we going to sail through the stormy seas of this economic downturn without raising taxes, but I am also determined to give the people of Georgia a break on the taxes they pay... State government must become leaner and cleaner, so that it concentrates on providing the maximum level of services to you for every dollar of tax money you pay, rather than on preserving its own bureaucracy.

*—Clayton County Chamber of Commerce, January 18, 1991*

---

I sought the office of Governor because I felt I had a contribution to make to the State of Georgia. I have definite ideas and goals, and I have a practical understanding of how to make them work from experience in both the executive and the legislative branches. I was serious about the promises I made during my campaign to become Governor, and I have an active, vigorous agenda I intend to pursue during my administration....

As department heads in the Miller Administration, it is not enough for each of you to do a good job within your own particular department, independent of each other. We are in a time that calls for teamwork. We are putting together a jigsaw puzzle here, and each one of you is holding a piece. If we are to get it together, each of you must look beyond the colors and patterns that are printed on your own particular piece. You must also look at how your piece fits into the broader picture.

We are in a time that requires each of you to rise above being the ward boss of your own internal operation to become statesmen. Statesmen who understand how your particular operation fits together with the rest of state government. Statesmen who can look beyond your own particular wants and priorities within your department, and understand how the things that you desire fit into the broader priorities of state government in its mission to serve the citizens of Georgia.

If you watched the NBA championship series between the L.A. Lakers and the Chicago Bulls, you understand what I am talking about. Each one of those players wanted to make baskets for himself. Each one of those players wanted to run up his own point total. But in order to win the game, each one of them also had to be alert to everything that was going on around the court at all times. Each one had to be willing to pass the ball to the player with the best shot at that particular moment. In that kind of nip-and-tuck game, there was no room for either the ill-advised shots or the missed opportunities to score, that are inevitable when any one player puts his own personal goals ahead of the team.

There are outstanding, all-star players on both of those teams—the Michael Jordans, the Magic Johnsons—and yet there were games when the lesser-known John Paxson was named the most valuable player. The reason was that he had the good scoring opportunities, and Michael Jordan was willing to pass to him rather than take the shot himself.

We are in the same sort of game, folks. It is nip-and-tuck. If we are going to win, we are going to have to cooperate and work together as a team. We must all look at the bigger picture and take maximum advantage of our opportunities to score. There are going to be times for each one of you when you are called upon to pass the ball when you would rather shoot. But that is what teamwork means—a willingness to pass the ball, a willingness to fit into the bigger picture of the game strategy. That is what I am asking and what I expect from each one of you....

You are my team. You wear the jersey of the Miller Administration. And I am going to be counting on each of you to work together and carry out your part in the overall game plan. I view my election as Governor as a compact with the voters of Georgia. I expect those of you who were appointed to join me in my commitment, and those of you who were elected to share this view.

If we are to govern effectively over the next four years, we need to maintain credibility in the eyes of the citizens of Georgia. We need to strengthen and build on the trust they put in us by electing us—a trust that we will indeed follow through with integrity on the campaign promises we made.

We are still in a "window of opportunity"—a time in which we are establishing the tone and tenor of this administration—a time in which the Miller Administration establishes its image and reputation either as a progressive, pro-active on-the-ball operation, or a passive, passe, don't-rock-the-boat sort of outfit. I doubt that it is any surprise to you that I aim to be a progressive, pro-active, take-charge Governor. We are going to play hard, we are going to play tough, we are going to sweat.

And how will we know if we've won? The goal of this administration is for state government to make a real difference in the daily lives of working Georgia families. We are striving for the Georgia that can be—the Georgia that has a world-class education system; a leaner, cleaner state government; a clean environment for future generations; safer streets and neighborhoods; lower auto insurance rates; better highways and public facilities in our communities, and balanced economic growth.... We've set a rapid pace, and we are not going to slack off—if anything, the pace will intensify and accelerate....

When we gather together in the huddle and set out a play that calls for you to pass the ball, I will be counting on you to do that when you get out there on the court. When you and I and the OPB staff sit down around the table and come to an agreement as to how and where we are going to curb spending, I will be expecting each one of you to go back to your agency or department and follow through on that agreement.

As I mentioned a few moments ago, one of the primary objectives of the Miller Administration is a leaner, cleaner state government. The present economic and political climate not only makes a leaner state government imperative—it also presents a new standard of cleanliness. We are all subject to a higher standard of public scrutiny. Not only must we manage with fewer resources, but we must do it with wisdom, with integrity, and without the slightest hint of impropriety, in a more open political environment.

If we are to maintain public trust, we are going to have to demonstrate visibly that we are indeed managing the limited resources entrusted to us according to the needs of Georgia's citizens rather than the needs of our own bureaucracy. That is the standard against which we will be measured in whatever we do and say.

Innovation, creativity, and cooperation are the key to doing more with less, and I place emphasis not only on the words "more with less," but also on the word "doing." I want you to be innovative and creative. My staff and I want to hear your ideas. You are going to find yourself working more closely with me and with each other than ever before.

This is not a pick-up game on the corner playground. We are a team, and we are going to act like one. We are going to huddle among ourselves to share ideas and set the plays to take maximum advantage of the situation we face. Then we are going to go out on the court and play with the discipline and the cooperation that characterizes a good team. That is what makes a winning team, and that is what we are going to be—a winning team.

*—Department Heads Meeting, June 18, 1991*

I came into the Governor's office with high aspirations for what I want to accomplish over the next four years. After my inauguration, I spread out the cards in my hand, slowly, like a poker player. It was not jacks or better. State revenues were not growing.... My first decision was that, unlike nearly 30 other governors around the nation, I would not raise taxes. In fact, we cut taxes for working families and senior citizens with incomes of less than $20,000 a year....

If there is a positive side to these tough financial times, it is that they present us with an opportunity to make some major changes in the way state revenues are spent. One of my campaign pledges was to streamline state government, eliminating waste, and focusing attention on services to our citizens rather than on sustaining the bureaucracy. Not only have we been cutting the budget, we have also rearranged priorities, shifted money around and focused it on direct services in important program initiatives. I am striving for an unprecedented level of cooperation among state agencies and departments, and an unprecedented level of economy in state services. We will have less government, but it will be smarter government. We are going to do more, but we are going to do it with less.

*—GAEL Summer Conference, July 16, 1991*

We have two roads we can travel, two choices we can make. We can raise taxes, or we can cut expenditures and live within our means. I do not think—and I believe most of you agree with me—that it is right for the state to balance its budget on the backs of working people struggling with their own financial problems. That is why this is going to be a cutting session, not a spending session.

We're going to plow new ground this week. We've got the political equivalent of standing in front of a freight train moving at high speed, stopping it cold, and then pushing it back up the hill. We've got to stop the run-away growth in the state payroll. We've got not only to downsize state government, but to right-size it as well. This will mean some hard, hard cuts, and the termination of a large number of state employees— regrettable steps, but absolutely necessary to have a balanced budget. We need to reverse some patterns of growth and spending in government that have built up over many years. Today, with this meeting, we begin....

I did not take a meat ax to the budget. I took a scalpel. Although the final effect of these cuts is to change the numbers in the budget line-items, they are not simple percentage-based reductions to those broad categories. There is nothing "across-the-board" about them....

There are tracks from the Williams Commission in this budget. They have looked closely at just what makes up those continuation lump sums that in the past have been routinely continued from one budget year to the next with few questions asked. The result was careful, discerning cuts that are designed to streamline and update administration, bringing decision-making closer to the front lines, while always maintaining services.

When you piece together and consider the hundreds of small cuts on the list before you, they add up to major administrative reorganization in the Departments of Corrections; Education; Natural Resources; Agriculture; Industry, Trade and Tourism; the Regents and the Building Authority....

My own office is right in there with the rest of the agencies on the administrative cuts. I have eliminated a total of 24 positions from my personal staff and the agencies attached to my office. That is a 12 percent cut—one of the highest among the departments....

As you look down over the list of cuts in human services, you will see some in contracts and programs that address important health problems. There was a method in choosing them. Virtually all of them fit into one of three categories. First, we have cut the programs that either proved to be inefficient or were not getting the results that were expected. Second, we felt it was important to be consistent and fair by preserving programs that make services available statewide. This meant cutting some programs or grants that were offered just in specific communities or regions, rather than to the state as a whole. Third, we have made some cuts in grants for basic medical research, because we felt we could not justify funding them at the expense of direct services. Right now direct services have to be given top priority.

I sought election to this office as a progressive Governor with a long agenda for action: better schools, safer streets, improved roads and bridges, a cleaner environment. And I retain those goals. But sound management demands that we have a clear mission for state government and that we are efficient and effective in fulfilling that mission. My first and foremost responsibility as CEO of this state is to bring discipline to the state budget process and to set this state on a new course, to pave the way for economic recovery and growth.

I strongly believe that if we respond to this temporary crisis in a responsible manner, Georgia can move forward toward greater growth and prosperity.

—*Joint Appropriations Committees, August 16, 1991*

---

As you know, we have just been through a special session in which we cut the state budget by $415.4 million, or about six percent. That may not sound like much, but when you eliminate fixed expenses from the picture, it was a significant cut to what remained. Further, it was the second round of cuts. I had already cut the budget for Fiscal Year 91 by over $200 million....

Not only did we cut luxuries we cannot afford, such as chefs at the Mansion, personal cars, state planes, and assistant executive deputy commissioners, but we scrutinized the internal operations of state government in detail, evaluating and putting cost control measures into place.

Let me give you just one example. The budget for the massive Department of Human Resources includes hundreds of small service facilities all over the state. There is no formula for funding them, and the funding patterns have never been look at as far as I know. Each year their budgets were increased a little for inflation, and those located in the districts of powerful legislators often got a little extra added in. Over the years, wide disparities gradually opened up among similar facilities across the state. For instance, state funds for day-care facilities for the mentally retarded ranged from $6,000 to $16,000 per client per year. There were disparities in other indicators, like the proportional cost of administrative overhead. Instead of across-the-board cuts, we went in there and established ceilings and guidelines for these facilities, and brought the big spenders back into line with the rest of the state....

That is an approach that you as business leaders can understand and appreciate, and it is indicative of what you will see from the Miller Administration.... I am going to use this dormant season in the economy to do some very selective pruning and reshaping in state government, in order to set the stage for economic recovery and growth when it does come.

—*Georgia Business Council, September 19, 1991*

---

Last summer as we undertook the largest budget cut in the history of this state, it was a great relief to me to have the work of this commission underway. I deeply appreciate your willingness to speed up the process and devote even more of your valuable time to the task at hand, so that we could have the benefit of your advice as we proceeded with budget cuts. Because we had already turned our sights toward efficiency in government, we were able to use the budget cutting process as an opportunity to downsize and streamline the things that needed to be made more efficient, rather than simply doing across-the-board cuts.

I chose you for the Williams Commission because you are gifted business leaders, and men and women of high intellect, determination, and proven accomplishment. Above all, I chose you because you are not state government bureaucrats. State government is a massive enterprise, and the people within it tend to be specialists in their own little part of it. When you're used to focusing on a particular tree, it is sometimes hard to back away and see the forest....

Government and private business are interested in many of the same things, and we can do more if we combine our resources and work together. So I want one of the hallmarks of my administration as Governor to be public-private partnerships all across state government. The Williams Commission has been one of the first of these partnerships, and as such provides us with something of a model that we can learn from and use in other areas....

You taught us much from your private-sector perspective. And we hope that you gained a better sense of all the things that go on in state government—including things like federal rules and regulations and an obligation to serve all the customers, like it or not, that sometimes make us less efficient than we otherwise could be.

1991 was characterized by your timely work and our downsizing of state government—a process which will continue throughout the course of the next three years. With the guidance of your report, we will take a more business-like and efficient approach to managing state government than this state has ever seen.

—*Conclusion of Williams Commission, January 8, 1992*

---

I had campaigned on a platform that included downsizing and reorganizing state government, but doing it under the constraints of a budget crisis was not quite what I had in mind.

You see, many who talk about fat in government make it sound like waste exists in neat little pockets and packages, and they act like it is a simple matter to go in and cut it without affecting anything else.

But you know, and I know, that in reality, it's not like that at all. State employees are good, conscientious, reliable workers, and I am proud of them. We do not have groups of employees here and there who are goofing off on the job. We do not have do-nothing agencies that are easily eliminated. State employees are diligently doing what it says in their job description; they are doing what they have been hired to do. The problem is not with the people, but with the structure.

The fat in government is just like the fat in the package of ground beef you bring home from the supermarket. You know that it's in there, but it's not in a neat chunk that's easy to see or cut away with a few quick knife strokes. You separate out the fat in the process of putting the whole chunk of ground beef in a skillet on the stove and cooking it. In the end, you have not just drained off the fat, more importantly, you have transformed the whole batch of ground beef into a completely different form. You have fundamentally changed the meat, so that you can use it in ways that were not possible before you cooked it.

When I talk about downsizing government, it does not mean that I am on the look-out for employees who are goofing off so that I can eliminate their jobs. It means that I am looking at the fundamental mission of state government—at what state government should do to promote the well-being of Georgia in the high-tech, high-speed global economy of the 21st century.

*—State Personnel in Employment Security, May 13, 1992*

———————

We in state government are keenly interested in promoting the well-being of all Georgians, but that is a tremendous undertaking which government could never accomplish alone, even with unlimited resources. Religious organizations like the Salvation Army provide invaluable help in the task of caring for the citizens of this state, and you provide a very important ingredient that government lacks. You care for people on a personal level, and you are motivated by genuine love, God's love. That added dimension is so very important. There is no way that government programs can fulfill the need that all of us have for loving, caring personal relationships. That need is cared for in our biological families and in our church families.

*—Salvation Army Training Center, June 5, 1992*

———————

I began my administration by saying that I want to move Georgia forward to the cutting edge, and that to get there, we are going to have to make changes and do things differently. In the months since then, as the presidential campaign has become a vehicle for coalescing and expressing public opinion, the need for change has become strikingly clear. We are in a critical time in the management of government. The unwritten rules by which government has functioned in the past no longer hold. It can no longer be business as usual.

Taxes have about reached the limit of what citizens are willing to bear, and we still do not have the resources to do the things we once thought we could. At the same time citizens have become skeptical and dubious about government's ability to function and fulfill its responsibilities.

Not only do we in state government need a clearer sense of our mission and purpose, and of our progress in achieving it, but we also need strong management skills and a greater level of awareness of what the public needs and expects from us.

*—Kennedy School of Government Seminar for Agency Heads, June 30, 1992*

———————

Without question, matters have now improved. But, it didn't just happen. We made it happen through some very tough management, tough decisions....In some quarters, this has raised high expectations that perhaps the state is poised for a return to the kind of heady growth we enjoyed through most of the 1970s and 80s. Nowhere are these expectations more clearly mirrored than in the new spending requests which I have received from you. A total of $2.641 billion in fiscal year 1995, or, listen to this—a 31 percent increase!

That amount of spending would exceed our entire total growth over the past five years, including the imposition of a one cent sales tax increase. Folks, the total of your budget improvement requests is greater than Georgia's total budget was 15 years ago. So, I wanted to meet with you this morning for some frank and hard talk about the realities of fiscal year 1995, the budget for which I am now preparing recommendations to the General Assembly....

I want to make things perfectly clear: I have no intention of making any proposal that would increase revenues of any nature. In fact, I am earnestly seeking a way to *decrease* our people's tax burden, not increase it. So, how then do we build a 1995 budget that meets the needs of our citizens? There are two corrections to our course that we must make.

First, it is extremely important that every department head go back and reexamine your budget request, and consider more carefully your priorities in expanding services from the limited new revenues available....Decide on those few initiatives that are the most important to the citizens you serve and be able to fully justify them from every angle. Present accurate information about annualized costs if the program is being phased in. Please do not bring to the hearings a long list of spending items for discussion. If you have to have another meeting with your boards in order to get their very highest priorities, do it. If you have to reschedule your meeting with me, we will accommodate you....

You should know that it is my intention to take a very sharp pencil to your continuation requests. I do not intend to simply perpetuate the kinds of spending increases that were allowed in the past or to recommend restoration of recent budget reductions. That is just not going to happen. Beginning now, and continuing as long as I have anything to do with it, we are going to pay as much attention to the continuation level budget as to the improvements budget....

I asked each department head to list and discuss with me during budget hearings your ideas on which programs or activities in your department can be privatized, downsized or eliminated. These recommendations should be well thought out and comprehensive—and not just something you tacked on at the end to try to temporarily satisfy a cantankerous Governor. I want you to dig into the continuation budget to find the money to fund many of your needs that cannot be funded with revenue growth. Let me make this very clear, I am not talking about the kind of budget cuts that we have been making in recent years. Those cuts primarily consisted of reducing the level of budget increases already enacted. I am talking now about digging into the very bowels of government spending and finding those long-existing programs that today would rank lower in priority than some of your new proposals.

If you've just got to have some improvements, then you are going to have to help me find much of that money in your current budget. All of you must seize your own initiatives immediately and search for efficiencies, economies and other changes that will make better use of the funds appropriated to you....

The more you sift through your own budgets for such cost-saving, cost-cutting and efficient actions, the easier it will be for your departments to cope with the tight budgeting that is likely to continue through this decade, perhaps even beyond. We should be partners in making the hard choices between competing demands for limited resources within the context of a new approach to budgeting. Frankly, your original budget requests did not do that. But if you work within my new budget instructions, you will have no other choice.

Of even greater importance, we are talking here about basic changes in the way we should do things over the next several years. We can no longer continue to fund programs just because we have done so in the past. Every program, those that are very old and those that are brand new, must be scrutinized and justified. Existing programs that cannot stand the scrutiny must be abolished or reduced in size, with the money reallocated to higher priorities. I am not talking about reducing costs through the sacrifice of services. I am talking about the opposite—providing more services at less cost; or delivering a needed service in a new and more efficient and effective manner.

We have worked together well over the last three years to pull Georgia through its most perilous period in four decades. We have not pleased everyone, but we did our job. Our present economic condition is evidence of that. You helped me do it before, and I am grateful for your efforts. But now, we must reach for an even higher level of achievement. It will require even greater dedication and persistence. It will require toughness, and I realize that it will be harder than the first round of cuts....Only through mutual understanding and cooperation can we make the changes and innovations that are necessary for Georgia's future well-being. I have every confidence that you will be just as committed in this new endeavor as you have been over the last three years. If we succeed in this mission, and we must, Georgia will be a more prosperous and stronger state, and our citizens will be economically better off. I have no doubt that with your help, we will meet our responsibilities once again.

*—Department Heads, September 22, 1993*

---

When I took office as Governor, a national recession was deepening around us, and state government was in a bind: The budget wasn't balanced, and the rainy day fund was dry. So we tightened our belt. We cut $800 million from the state budget in our first year alone. We eliminated 5,000 positions from the state payroll. We took a state government workforce that had been growing by 10 percent a year for two decades, and slowed that growth to 1.6 percent for the first two and a-half years of my administration. And that growth rate would be zero, if we hadn't had to hire staff for the new prisons we opened to stop the early release of dangerous criminals.

We made the tough decisions; we exercised tough management; we streamlined state government; we kept our top bond ratings; and we saved enough to put $121 million into our rainy day savings account.

I am here today to tell you that the hard work and sacrifice of the people of Georgia and the public servants of Georgia has paid off. Our economy is picking up. By the end of October, Georgia had replaced all the jobs lost during the recession and added nearly 100,000 more. Housing starts and new car sales are on the rise. Real personal income is increasing. That's good news for your family budget, and it's good news for the state budget.

Now that the economy has turned around and state revenues are improving, we are not going back to business as usual in state government. In the old days, under the old ways, an increase in state revenues would have been treated as feeding time at the hog farm, with every politician bellying up for a share of the pork. But I promised to put business as usual out of business.

When we began the budget cutting process, I said that I viewed the recession as an opportunity to more forward on a new, long-term course that checked the growth in state government and made it more efficient. Even though the recession is over, we are going to hold to that course. We are going to do what is necessary to create safe communities and improve education for our children. But beyond that, I am proposing that we return the remaining tax revenues to the citizens of Georgia.

In my inaugural address, I dedicated this administration to every family that works and saves and sometimes comes up a little short at the end of the month and to every senior citizen who open their utility bill with trembling hands, afraid they will have to choose between heating and eating.

Today I am proposing a permanent income tax cut of $100 million for families with dependents and for senior citizens. About $83 million will go to families with children, in the form of a $1,000 increase in the allowance for each dependent. Instead of deducting $1,500 for each child, I am proposing $2,500. That will be real money in the pockets of Georgia's hard-pressed middle-class families—$120 extra for a family with two children and an income of $30,000. This tax cut will reward many of the hard-working, middle-class families who have been taking it on the chin for too long, and 50,000 struggling, low-income families, who are working hard to make ends meet and stay off of welfare, would be free from having to pay any income taxes at all, because of the increased allowance they can claim for their dependent children.

We'll be able to give a tax cut of about that same size to Georgia's retirees, many of whom are struggling to make ends meet on a fixed income. By increasing the income-exclusion for retirees from $10,000 to $12,000, we could put up to $120 into the pockets of an elderly Georgian with retirement income of $12,000 or more a year.

In total, Georgia families and senior citizens would enjoy a four percent tax reduction—the largest in Georgia history....We've invested in new schools for our children, and new opportunities for high school graduates at colleges and technical institutes. Now is the time to make another investment—a new investment in our people—a tax cut that will tell all of our hard-working families and our senior citizens that here in Georgia, we're changing the way government does business.

—*Press Conference, December 17, 1993*

As Governor of Georgia, I'm in charge of an operation that has a $10 billion budget and more than 100,000 employees, and serves a clientele of seven million citizens. But there are some significant differences between government and the private-sector. For one thing, I didn't hire and can't fire many of my department heads. They all report to their own boards of directors, and some of them were elected just like I was. Even if I have the support of my department heads and their boards, my decisions are still subject to trial by fire and water in the state legislature and the news media. Then there are the political humorists whose tradition stretches from Mark Twain to Mark Russell with Will Rogers in between.

The decision-making process in the public sector is just that—public. The very nature of democracy makes governmental decision-making slow and cumbersome, because it is done out in the open with a lot of input and influence from many different sources along the way.

Another difference is that government cannot choose a market niche and concentrate on the goods or services that it wants or needs the way you can. Some programs, like education, must overcome market niches and provide equally for all citizens. Others, like welfare and Medicaid, serve the leftover markets that the private sector does not accommodate. In essence, we get the market sectors where you can't realize a profit.

But there are a lot of ways in which our respective leadership roles are similar. Corporate decision-making is becoming less hierarchical and more diffuse, and I suspect you are leading more through communication and persuasion—the same as in the public sector.

We are both striving for greater efficiency. We face increasing expectations from those we serve, but they are not willing to pay any more money to get a better product. It doesn't matter whether the car or the camera that you produce is better today than it was 20 years ago. The critical question is how does it stack up against the Germans or the Japanese. Similarly it doesn't matter whether our schools are better today than they were 20 years ago. The critical question is how do they stack up against the Germans or the Japanese.

But most importantly, government and business share many of the same goals. You want to be successful, because that's how you pay the bills. We want you to be successful, because that's how we pay the bills. So we both want a strong and vibrant economy. We both want solid public infrastructure and a skilled workforce. We both want quality of life and an attractive environment where businesses and their employees can thrive.

These are goals that we can work together to achieve. When we put our public and private resources on the table together and use them in complementary ways, then it becomes possible to do more with less. That is why I am pursuing public-private partnerships here in Georgia to a greater extent than ever before. We have them in economic development. We have them in education. We have them in health care. We have them at the state level and at the local level and mixed up across the levels.

—Business Week *Forum, May 5, 1994*

I want to say to you, and say emphatically...that there will not be any new sources of revenue to get us where we're going. In fact, if my proposal to exempt groceries from the sales tax passes—and it has some strong support in the General Assembly and among the citizens of this state—our revenue base will narrow slightly over the next four years. In addition, at this point the economic recovery we have been enjoying has pretty much matured. It is virtually certain that revenue growth will slow its upward trend in the very near future. At best—at best, the rate of revenue growth over the next few years will be flat, and we need to be prepared for it to begin to ease up a little.

So the tenor and tone for the next four years is going to continue too be doing more with less. We are going to continue to be very tight and efficient about continuation expenditures. I want all of you to take particular note of the proposal that is now before the General Assembly to take $30 million out of the education bureaucracy and move it into direct services to students at the school level. That is the type of thinking that each and every one of you should be engaged in—searching for ways to tighten up and streamline your administrative structure, and move more of your resources into direct services to the citizens of this state.

The message from the voters in November was clear: Business as usual in government is not good enough. And we need to learn a lesson from the private sector about becoming more productive and more attuned to customer service. The taxpaying citizens of this state are the clients we serve, and let's never forget it. They are also the ones who pick up the tab for our operations. So the focus of our decisions must be on how we can best respond to their needs, rather than on what is most convenient for state employees or the administrative bureaucracy.

We must constantly reexamine our programs and missions, not only to ensure that we are being as productive as possible and delivering services as efficiently as possible, but also to ensure that the services we deliver are those that the citizens of today really want and need. We are going to continue to evaluate programs and to become more results-oriented in our evaluations. Please, please do not hesitate to propose to me any new or redirected effort for your department that would shift resources away from administration toward direct services, that would make your service delivery more efficient, or that would revise your services to make them more sensitive to what citizens need.

*—Department Head Meeting, Jan 17, 1995*

---

In January, I gave you the message about how the tenor and tone of the next four years needs to be doing more with less. As you know, "the devil is in the details," and today, I have brought you together to follow up with those practical details—to explain how that is going to happen and what it is going to mean in the way we operate state government... This meeting is unique, because for the first time in my knowledge in Georgia history, a governor has called department heads together when economic times are still good to take steps to avoid a future fiscal crisis. Usually Governors don't call their department heads together until after a fiscal crisis has already arrived and immediate emergency measures are called for. But my friends, it does not take a crystal ball to see that when your revenue growth is going down and your mandated expenditures are going up, you are on a collision course. And we are going to change course now, while we still have time, to avoid the prospect of a future financial crisis.

Those of you who are elected constitutional officers keep your ear to the ground, and you know that "business as usual" in government is no longer good enough. "Business as usual" will just not cut it anymore. We dare never forget that the taxpaying citizens of this state are our customers. They are the ones who pick up the tab for our services. And we need to learn a lesson from the private sector about becoming more productive, and more attuned to customer service. Just like the customers that private business serves, Georgians want better service from government. But they are not willing to pay more to get it, because they are not convinced that they have been getting value for their money. They expect a smaller sized government that plays a smaller role in their lives, and is more efficient and responsive them in the way it operates. That is our challenge, and we are going to rise to meet it—not just in the lip-service of our rhetoric, but in the practical realities of how we operate....

As the economy slows around us, we are going to be ready. We are going to plan ahead and be prepared by redirecting our budget process. We are going to examine and reorder our priorities to make sure that the services we deliver are what the citizens of today want, need, and are willing to pay for. Then we are going to be constantly and systematically "squeezing down" our continuation expenditures to keep them tightly focused on our priorities. And we are going to change—and change drastically—the way we deal with improvements. In the past, department heads would simply write down all the wants of the all the special interests they dealt with in a big, long, endless wish list that rivaled the letters of my six-year-old twin grandsons to Santa Claus. The process was always the same: The Governor would be presented with a cumulative improvement request that was 20 times greater than the amount of new money that was going to be available. And just like those six-year-olds discovered on Christmas morning, the gap between expectations and reality turned out to be incredibly vast. No wonder people have grown cynical about the ability of government to fulfill their expectations.

So let me set the tone for the way we're going to do improvement items by saying to you that I expect you to become a lot more realistic...a lot more realistic...even brutally realistic about your requests. The days of endless wish lists are over. Together, we're going to set some priorities for state government and some realistic limits on improvement requests. Then you are going to learn to use some discipline and some toughness and some honesty in the way you deal with your special interest groups.

We're going to get into more details about the revenue picture and the redirection of the budget process in a few minutes. But before we do, I want to emphasize that we are not going to just talk about this new approach to the budget here today, and then leave. This is something we will live with the next three and a-half years.... Let me also emphasize that I do not view this new process of budget redirection in the same light as the old budget cuts. There is nothing temporary about it. There is nothing "across-the-board" about it. This is about setting our priories in an orderly fashion, and then "squeezing down" state government so that it is tightly focused and efficient in achieving those priorities.

*—Department Heads Meeting, May 2, 1995*

---------------

We must have a state that is financially solid, because business and industry are only going to locate new plants and create new jobs in states that are financially sound. We must have new ideas and new methods for responding to the vast technological changes that are occurring daily in the workplace. We must oversee and manage state spending like a chief financial officer would run a multi-national corporation. That is the reality of the time in which we live—a time in which in Georgia the economic recovery has matured and revenue growth in the next few years will begin to flatten out—a time of commitment to a tax cut and a time when new revenue sources are nonexistent.

I believe that one of the ways we deal with this reality can be found in the private sector, where, unlike government, the profit motive requires constant vigilance, innovation, and modernization. Balancing the budget is a government function. Maximizing corporate assets to improve services, cut costs, and increase shareholder equity is a business function. I want to take a close look at those business functions, incorporate them as much possible in state government, and make them work for all Georgians.

I am announcing today the creation of the Governor's Commission of Privatization of Governmental Services. I have asked as good a department head as any governor ever had, Joe Tanner, a hard-nosed, no-nonsense administrator, to resign his post as commissioner of Natural Resources and take on this important responsibility. He will operate directly out of the Governor's office. That is how serious I am....

As you can see, I have made this nine member commission as bipartisan as I possibly can, because this is not a partisan issue. This commission will look at everything. I want to make that very clear: everything is on the table, from prisons and youth facilities to food service, printing parks, recreation—you name it—everything! Some facilities may be leased; some may even be sold. Implemented properly, I believe privatization can improve state services while at the same time save taxpayers millions of dollars.

It should be noted that the Miller Administration has already taken some preliminary steps at privatization. We hired outside vendors in the areas of computer services and printing operations. We leased a youth prison in Ocilla and a management firm is running our newest state resort in Towns County. But much more can be done. There are many things that the private sector can obviously do better than state government. There are many things that government should probably not even be in. This commission will take a comprehensive and thorough look at the ways we can privatize state operations and together, with the General Assembly, I believe we can overhaul state government and make it something that all Georgians can be proud of and our neighbors will envy.

*—Press Conference: Announce Privatization, May 2, 1995*

---------------

I have instructed this (privatization) commission to put every aspect of state government up on the table under the examining lights. There will be no sacred cows.

I want to emphasize to you that this is not some new idea that just popped into my head. Nor am I "trending" in a different direction. It began four years ago with the Williams Commission, and since then we have been exploring and piloting privatization with a number of state functions. We have privatized computer support to state agencies. Even the cleaning and maintenance at our welcome centers has been put on a private contract basis. Two of our new alternatives for juvenile offenders are operated by private providers. I was in Ocilla to visit one of them earlier this month....

What we are doing now is moving on to the next phase in this process, which is to undertake a systematic and comprehensive evaluation of all parts of state government. The commission is going to ask two questions: First, what activities are appropriate for state government, and what are more appropriate for the private sector? Have we gotten government involved in things it shouldn't be involved in? And second, how can privatization be used to make state government more efficient and effective?

*—Legislative Leaders Meeting, May 30, 1995*

Be assured that your recommendations will not simply be put up on a back shelf somewhere to collect dust. To the best of my ability, I will implement all of them without modification or delay. All around us, private business are restructuring to become more efficient in our global economy, and more attuned to customer service. Government must do the same. Your task is an important part of our overall effort to examine and reorder our priorities to make sure we deliver in an efficient way those services that our citizens truly want, need and, most importantly, are willing to pay for. You are about to embark on an historic voyage through uncharted seas. Good luck. Sail on.

*—Charge to Privatization Commission, June 27, 1995*

I think you know I'm hard to please. I set high standards for myself, for my administration and for my state. I got into government because I've always believed that government can be an agent of positive change to accomplish good for the benefit of the public. I used to teach that to my students and will again someday. I believe that each of you shares that goal. I believe that you are committed to making a difference in the life of this state. I'm not sure all of you want to change it as much as I do.

Back during the 1980s, Georgia saw unprecedented revenue growth, and state government—and I was part of it—government just ate the whole thing. It was a time, as Merle Haggard sang, of "drinking that free bubble-up and eating that rainbow stew." That was an era that is no more. It's "gone with the wind." You have got to understand that. It's gone. It didn't last long, but it seemed to have spoiled so many in state government forever.

In 1991, you will remember, the "fat boy" was faced with a crash diet, and I said at the time that there was an easy way to cut a budget, and a hard way. A right way, and a wrong way. Keeping the same old spending patterns but just at a lower level was the easy way, and the wrong way. But we've learned just how hard it is to do it the right way. Back when we began this whole process in 1991, state departments had deputy commissioners and assistant commissioners and deputy assistant commissioners and assistant executive deputy commissioners. And you know what? As the Atlanta newspapers recently pointed out, we still do.

Folks, we cannot continue to do business as usual. This cycle of unreasonably high expectations has got to be broken. The way we've done business in the past has got to end. Our long-term financial situation simply does not support a budget approach that continually seeks to create new government programs while ignoring the ongoing review of existing programs. And I think it is irresponsible to encourage high expectations among your constituencies.

The purpose of budget redirection is not to "get by" until better times arrive. It's not that at all. The purpose of budget redirection is not even to keep our ongoing expenditures as lean as possible, although that is absolutely essential to do. The purpose of budget redirection is to completely rethink our expenditures, and then eliminate or downsize those activities that are no longer useful, needed or as important as some others may be. Remember Ecclesiastes: "There is a time to keep and a time to cast away." Let me mention one other thing to you that surely has gone through your mind: this is not just some cranky Governor whose whims need to be humored temporarily. Well, cranky maybe, but seriously, the credibility of state government, and I am convinced the credibility of your individual departments and agencies, is on the line with the taxpayers of Georgia, who foot the bill for your operation. Remember—this is their government; it is not yours and it is not mine...

Many of the taxpayers who pay for your budget stay up late at night, sitting at the kitchen table with their checkbooks, worrying over how to make ends meet. They ask themselves two critical questions about every single item in that checkbook: Can we afford it? Can we do without it? Can we afford it? And can we do without it? Write that down indelibly, on your foreheads if necessary, so your employees and co-workers can see it, and you can see it every time you look in the mirror. It's our Scarlet Letter.

Can we afford it? Can we do without it? I hate to say it, and I hate to fuss, but I don't think very many of you were thinking of those questions when you requested almost a billion and a half dollars in new construction in one year. But they are the questions I have to ask as I put the state budget together, and as I search for ways that we can scrimp and save and still do an effective job of meeting our responsibilities. Look, I am the guy with the green eyeshade that has got to make all the numbers work. Not a very glamorous job. I'd rather be dedicating buildings and cutting ribbons, but making those numbers work is absolutely necessary.

Let me put it to you as plainly as I can: As I told you in May at the Mansion, the economy will slow next year and the year after, and we have to prepare for slower growth in revenues. At the same time, the federal government will be reducing the amount of federal funds we will receive for a number of programs, like Medicaid and welfare. And there will be a tax cut next session of the General Assembly. Believe me, there will be. Of course, we have to fund the most important priorities, like educating and protecting our citizens. My top priority remains education. We simply cannot afford to do everything we would like to do.

So, when I asked you to limit your improvement requests to a 6.5 percent increase, that was just defining the ballpark in which we are going to play. Few of you, maybe none, will actually see a 6.5 percent increase in your budget or anything close to it. That is why this exercise of budget redirection—of identifying at least five percent of your continuation budget that can be shifted to support a higher priority—is so very critical....

We need to be very clear as to our priorities, and then we need to squeeze every possible spare penny out of our ongoing operations and redirect it toward those priorities. Doing it now, before a budget crisis forces our hand, will minimize disruption and safeguard our ability to sustain critical state services as revenue growth flattens out. It can be done....(but) it cannot be done without a concerted effort on everyone's part; it cannot be done without all of us working together.... The time to bear down on reorganizing and streamlining is now. The time to put problem areas up on the table and wrestle with them is now. The time to work together and work hard is now....

All across Georgia, private businesses are reorganizing their operations. All across Georgia, private businesses are redesigning their products and retooling their services to be more efficient and responsive to what their customers want. We must be doing the same thing in state government. Our goal must be not only to make state government more cost-effective and efficient, but also more clearly focused on the needs and priorities of the taxpayers who foot the bill. Philosophically speaking, that should be our goal no matter what our financial situation. Practically speaking, it is an absolute necessity to restore and maintain public confidence in state government at a time when revenue growth is flattening out.

—*Department Heads Meeting, Oct 20, 1995*

---

There is an inherent danger that you have to watch out for, especially in politics. It is so easy to dream unrealistic dreams. It is so easy to dream of things the way you wish they could be rather than the way they are actually going to turn out to be. Willie Nelson warned of that with the lines, "Be careful of what you're dreaming, or your dreams will be dreaming you."

So, if strategic planning is really going to work, we have to envision the future realistically, as it is actually going to be. Otherwise it's not strategic planning; it's just wishful thinking.

—*BROC Budget Oversight Conference, November 1, 1995*

---

I am proud to be standing here with these Democratic leaders to announce that we are united in an effort to give the taxpayers of Georgia the largest tax cut in our history : a $500 million one....This is an historic day, and I don't say that lightly. Our purpose is to eliminate the state sales tax off all groceries and unprepared foods. You've heard of that before. But never from all of us and never with the cut built into the budget before hand.

This time the cut will be built into the budget. Half, or two cents, off in October of 1996, another one cent in 1997 and another one cent off in 1998. It will be a total tax cut of $500 million, the largest cut in history. And the first time—perhaps in our history— that a major tax has been completely repealed.

We're able to do it now, whereas we could not do it before, because we've exercised tough management; we've streamlined government; this state is in good fiscal health. We have a top bond rating, and we have replenished our Revenue Shortfall Reserve Fund.

We've cut taxes before in the past four years. Twice in fact. The $100 million in 1994 for senior citizens and families with kids was the largest in Georgia history—up until now.

They say nothing is certain except death and taxes. We can't repeal death. But we darn sure can repeal the taxes on the food that keeps us alive. The government already taxes us from cradle to grave. The least it can do is give us a break for dinner.... It is wrong to tax the very thing we must have to live. It is wrong to tax baby food and formula; it's wrong to tax bread and milk for our older citizens, strapped on fixed incomes. It's wrong to tax food for the middle class who are scrimping and saving to make ends meet. The elimination of the sales tax on food is the fairest tax cut of all. The cut doesn't go to certain segments of our society. It doesn't hand out breaks to special interests. It goes directly to the people. It cuts across all classes. It affects every citizen directly, 365 days a year. In an age of so much talk about tax cuts, this tax cut is by far the most progressive. Under this plan, if you eat, you win.

*—Press Conference: Announce Tax Cut Plan, Dec 13, 1995*

---

In Georgia, we are deliberately working too set priorities and streamline state government, so that it is smaller, more efficient, and more effective in addressing the issues that our taxpayers care about.... I have created a public-private, bi-partisan commission, chaired by a former Republican mayor, to examine every single state agency and make recommendations. And I am committed to taking their recommendations without modification. Some of those recommendations address how we can make more efficient use of our resources by out-sourcing administrative support functions. These functions include food and janitorial services, building maintenance, the collection of delinquent taxes, processing motor vehicle tags and titles, and other kinds of administrative support services.

Privatization is also giving us a chance to evaluate how cost-effective we really are in state government. For example, the commission has proposed privatizing three new state prisons, to see how the operating costs at our state-run prisons stack up against the private sector. They also proposed privatizing a state veterans home, after comparing it to a privately-managed facility that operates with 169 fewer employees and at 50 percent of the cost of our state facility.

Then there are projects that might just belong in the private sector rather than in state government. In Georgia, we have discovered to our delight, that privatization can have an interesting and positive impact on economic development. Let me give you an example. Our first major privatization project was the development of the Brasstown Valley Golf Resort in the mountains of North Georgia. Everyone agreed that a major resort was needed to anchor the tourism industry in northeast Georgia, but private developers all said it just wasn't feasible. Rather than get into the tourism business itself, the state contracted with the Stormont Trice Corporation of Atlanta to design, build and manage a Holiday Inn Crowne Plaza Resort. The resort is on state property, and the state provided some bond financing to hold down the interest cost of its construction. But revenue from the resort covers its operating costs and also pays off the state bonds.

The most direct economic impact of the resort is to provide about 200 private-sector jobs that would not be there otherwise. In addition, its guests generate a lot of business in the broader community, and it has begun to draw millions of dollars in private-sector investment for the construction of additional attractions and amenities. We didn't create any new state programs or hire any new state employees, and we aren't spending any state money. But by providing the stimulus that made a private resort possible, we have generated economic development and jobs in the private sector.

With that experience under our belt, we are now looking at privatizing other state tourism-type facilities, with some interesting results. For example, a major investor, who was looking for a site for a large outdoor entertainment complex, had rejected Georgia. Then we explained that we had a state-owned, 1,200-acre resort—complete with a hotel, golf course and water park—that was available for private contract. At that point, Georgia moved immediately to the top of this investor's list.

Rather than trying to do everything ourselves, privatization projects like these give state government a chance to sit down with the private sector and put our resources on the table together in a cooperative effort that benefits both.

—*National Governors' Association, February 3, 1996*

---

It is the Governor who is charged with keeping the interests of the entire state in mind. It is the Governor who looks across the length and breadth of state government, at all the various responsibilities and obligations that must be met. I am the accountant in the green eyeshade who has to make all the numbers work.

You are concerned about how many students are going to be in our public schools next year, and finding adequate funding to serve them. That is an important question, and I am looking at it, too. But I am also looking at how many inmates we will have in our state prisons and juvenile detention facilities and finding adequate funding to serve them... and how many people we will have on our AFDC and Medicaid rolls and finding adequate funding to serve them... and how many mentally ill and mentally retarded citizens need care and finding adequate funding to serve them. Yes, education is my top priority, but I cannot ignore state government's many other obligations and responsibilities....

I know that the numbers are a heck of a lot bigger, but the state budget is really a lot like your family budgets. You have certain obligations that you must meet—like the mortgage, the car payment, the utility bills. There is no compromising here. Those bills must be paid.

Then there are places where you can save a little. You can eat out less often; you can have hamburgers instead of steak. You can shop for clothes at Target instead of Saks. You can put new heels on that old pair of shoes and make them last a little longer. When you economize and save a little money here and there, then you can do something extra that ought to be done—put a new roof on your house, replace that sagging couch in the den, or pay for piano lessons for your daughter.

But while you can cut some corners here and there and save a little money to put toward priorities like these, you can never say, "Well, this year it's really important to have a great wardrobe, so we're not going to buy any groceries at all," or, "This year, we really ought to have the house painted, so we're not going to make our mortgage payments." You can save a little here and there, but you can't stop buying groceries altogether; you can't stop paying your utility bills or your mortgage.

It's the same way with the state budget. Education is my top priority. But I can't stop making debt payments or stop locking up violent criminals in order to get more money for education. These other obligations have to be taken care of, and the best I'll ever be able to do is save a little here and there and shift it toward my top priority, just like you do in your family budget.

Then suppose Grandma dies and Grandpa comes to live at your house. Or suppose a new baby is born. Or twins. Whenever that happens, you have to find the money in your budget to accommodate your growing family. It's the same with the state budget. It is great to be the fastest-growing state east of the Rocky Mountains for four years in a row, but it creates tremendous budget obligations. It means that just to keep up our existing services, we have to put more money into the Quality Basic Education formula and into the University System formula, and into health services and Medicaid and such like.

Now, suppose your family income is $50,000 a year. That does not mean you are in a position to go out and buy a new Mercedes every year. Most of that $50,000 is tied up in obligations that have to be met. After you pay the bills, you might have enough left for pizza and a movie. It's the same for state government....

If you translate (next year's state budget) back to our model family that has $50,000 in income, it would mean that even after they scrimped and saved, and ate hamburger and shopped at Target, their ongoing obligations that had to be paid would use up $48,000 of their income. They would have only $2,000 left to put toward painting the house or buying a new refrigerator or whatever extra project needed to be done. That is how tight next year's budget is.

—*Teacher of the Year Conference, May 17, 1996*

———————

A little over a year ago, I brought you all together to announce my financial plan for the remainder of this administration.... and the first thing I want you to understand is that

I am going to stay that course. Next year's budget is going to continue with redirection and privatization. Most all the economic indicators—things like unemployment rates and personal and corporate income that we use to predict revenue growth—have not changed. So, we continue to expect—we're now even more sure of it—that revenue growth will gradually slow through Fiscal Year 99. When economic growth peaks and starts to slow, then you have to be more careful, conservative and cautious about estimating your revenues than when it was on the upswing. Because as the economy slows, it becomes more wobbly, and it becomes more susceptible to jolts and shocks, which will quickly be reflected in state revenues. We need to be prepared to absorb those potential wobbles and jolts.

Those of us who were around in 1990, the year before I became Governor, can recall how quickly the Revenue Shortfall Reserve was exhausted. Those of you who were still around when I became Governor in 1991, can recall how painful it was to be confronted with a $450 million cut in the budget. I want to avoid a replay of that, and with good planning we can....

The bottom line is that, just like last year, we are not going to have enough money from revenue growth alone to address population growth and still fund my top priority improvements like education in the FY 98 budget. That's why I lowered the enhancement you could request from 6.5 percent to 4.5 percent. Again, just like last year, budget redirection will be the linchpin of our financial planning. If you want to do some new things, you have got to find the money for them in your budget.

That's why I hope all of you have been evaluating programs and cutting back or culling out the ones that are out-of-date or not producing results, because, come September 1st, and later when I go over your budget with each of you, I expect you to have identified at least 5 percent of your general funds that is redirected to higher priority areas. That is absolutely mandatory. It is a given. It is not a point for discussion. I expect you to be serious about it and to do it right. I don't want to see any slights of hand or "funny money" in that 5 percent.

Folks, I hope you can see that this is more than just preparing for slower revenue growth. It must be a new a continuous mindset—a habit of always, always looking at your budget, your own numbers, with a very critical eye—always questioning whether you really need to keep on with a particular service at a particular level or at all—always asking whether it would be more efficient and effective if you did it differently. I've said this before, and I'll say it again: this is not your money. It's not your board's money or your department's money. There is no such thing as government money. There is only taxpayers' money, earned by the sweat and toil of the citizens of this state. We owe it to them to identify clearly the vital services that rightfully belong to government as opposed to the private sector, and then to take only enough tax money from the citizens of this state to deliver those services effectively and efficiently....We cannot stop with budget redirection and privatization until we have made state government as efficient as it can possibly be. We owe that to the taxpayers of this state....

All of you received a letter from me in the spring, explaining changes I wanted to make in the budget process to focus it more clearly on accountability.... I believe it is time for Georgia to start doing a better job of gathering information that will tell me, tell you, tell the legislature and tell the taxpayers who foot the bill, whether our expenditures are actually achieving our objectives. I don't think it's too much to ask for positive, measurable results that will tell us and tell them what government has accomplished with their money. As we do a better job of evaluating and documenting our progress, we must present the results to the taxpayers of Georgia in a form that they can understand and appreciate.

*—Department Heads Meeting, July 16, 1996*

I believe citizens deserve value for their tax dollars. We do that in Georgia by investing in the future, and by establishing clear priorities as to what government can and should do, and then making government as small and efficient as possible in carrying out those priorities. I have been working with my department and agency heads—some of them might say I have been twisting their arms—to get them in the habit of continually reevaluating everything in their budgets, looking for programs and services that are outdated or ineffective and can be downsized or discontinued, looking for ways to make their priority programs more efficient....

We believe that our careful fiscal management and our investments in the future economic strength of this state—its workforce, its technology, and its infrastructure—are what will make Georgia prosper in the 21st century.

*—Green Carpet Tour, Sept 25, 1996*

The longer I'm in politics, the more aware I have become of the limitations of government. Government simply cannot do everything, not even many of the things we once supposed it could. Powerful as government is, it can only do so much. Government can help the next generation become better off, but government cannot make the next generation better. To do that requires crossing a line from "statecraft" to "soulcraft." And only people can do that for each other. Government can set goals. But only people can touch souls.

*—Towns County Partners in Education, April 30, 1997*

You have clearly accomplished your mission "to be the catalyst to cause the use of privatization to improve the delivery of public services, to make government more effective and more efficienct and to reduce the costs of government to the taxpayers."

The privatization of the Georgia War Veterans Home in Milledgeville, for example, will save taxpayers $106 million over the next ten years. The privatization of three new 500 bed prisons will save $74 million over the 20-year term of the agreement. The privatization of book stores, building and grounds maintenance, and security at our state technical institutes will save $800,000 each year. The privatization of Lake Lanier Islands will generate $340 million in cash payments to the state over the course of its 50-year lease, and the privatization at Stone Mountain will generate more than $1 billion over its 50-year lease.

Altogether, the state will either save or receive income in excess of $1.5 billion as a result of your efforts. But the matter of privatization goes beyond simply saving money. The fundamental premise on which this nation was founded more than 200 years ago was limited government, but over the past several generations, government has increasingly been called upon to intervene in more and more social and economic problems. As a result, government at all levels has grown dramatically and stretched its tendrils like kudzu into more and more aspects of life. Many came to view government as part of the problem rather than as part of the solution. So the deeper challenge of privatization, beyond making government more efficient, is to identify clearly what government ought to be responsible for.

Some of those who opposed the privatization of Lake Lanier and Stone Mountain missed the point. The most fundamental question was not who can do it the cheapest, but whether the state ought to be competing with private industry in the operation of tourism facilities. The state has no business taking tax dollars from the private sector and then using that money to compete against the private sector.

*—Final Meeting, Privatization Commission, September 11, 1997*

---

Between Labor Day and Christmas, I spend countless hours with my green eyeshade on, hunched over spreadsheets, trying to make the numbers work in the budget I will present to the General Assembly come January. I interrupted that process to be here with you today, but I'll be back at it tomorrow. It's laborious work. It's a challenge to make everything fit. But it's a labor of love that I enjoy and take satisfaction in. The one thing I've learned about money matters, is that money matters.

All of your recommendations are good. All of them would improve things. And I appreciate your help yesterday and today in sorting them out and establishing priorities. I cannot begin to tell you how important what you have done is. But when I look at them, I am not only weighing them against each other like you are doing. I am also weighing them against the other tasks and challenges that face state government.

You may decide that your top priority for funding is to hire two new project managers in the tourism division. But I have to decide whether I hire those two new project managers, or whether I hire two new staff people for children's health care. And whether, if I go with the two project managers, they will generate enough money in two or three years to do even more for health care. I will face hundreds of decisions just like that later this year, balancing needs and measuring them against what we have in total resources.

I look at economic development as one important issue among many important issues on my plate and in my budget—issues like education, public safety, health care, pollution prevention—that all also have a bearing on the future prosperity of this state.

—Board, Department of Industry, Trade and Tourism, September 16, 1997

—————

I'd like to thank each one of you for being here during some or all of the past seven and a-half years of my administration. You have worked very hard, and together we have accomplished many good things during those seven and a-half years. So the first thing I want to emphasize to you this morning is that we are not going to tarnish that record by letting up on our efforts or ceasing to pay attention during the final seven and a-half months.

So be forewarned, I am going to continue to be an active, hands-on Governor until that inauguration ceremony next January. I am going to stay on top of state government issues and on your case as department heads until the very last day of my administration. I want all of us to be above reproach in providing the next Governor, whoever he may be, with a good a good foundation on which to begin his administration.

That means, when I leave office, all reserves will be full. We will have the best bond ratings. The groundwork for a sound supplemental budget for this year and big budget for next year will have been laid. And we will have dealt responsibly with outstanding issues like the DJJ Settlement and VOAP.

*—Department Heads Meeting, May 12, 1998*

GOVERNING Magazine called Zell Miller one of the six "best American governors of the 1990's" and the *Almanac of American Politics* declared: "Few Governors have played as pivotal a role in national politics or have sounded a louder clarion call of regional leadership than Zell Miller."

President Bill Clinton stated: "In my experience, I believe that what Zell Miller has done as Governor of Georgia has affected more people personally, positively, than the work of any other governor with whom I have worked in the last twenty years."

Born in the Appalachian mountain village of Young Harris, Georgia, and reared by a single mother, he enlisted in the U.S. Marine Corps in 1953 and served for three years. He became a college professor and taught history and political science at four Georgia colleges and is the author of four books. He was elected Lieutenant Governor of Georgia in 1974 and served for sixteen years.

In 1990, he was elected the Governor of Georgia, the tenth largest state in the United States. He was re-elected in 1994. In 1992, he was the keynote speaker at the Democratic National Convention.

After taking office, his love of teaching and commitment to education resulted in one of the most ambitious agendas to improve public education in this century. *Education Weekly* put it this way: "If there were a book about education governors, Miller might just be the main character."

Governor Miller's HOPE Scholarship Program was called by *The Los Angeles Times* "the most far-reaching scholarship program in the nation." His pre-kindergarten program is the only one in the nation available to all four-year-olds and won an award for innovation from the Kennedy School of Government at Harvard.

He raised spending on education in Georgia to new highs, but at the same time cut taxes more than any Governor in Georgia history. In the 1990's Georgia was one of the leading states in job creation, averaging 2,000 new jobs each week.

Governor Miller served as chairman of the Education Commission of the States, Southern Governors' Association, Southern Growth Policies Board, Southern Regional Education Board, the Appalachian Regional Commission and the Council of State Governments.

He is married to the former Shirley Carver. They have two sons, four grandchildren, and two great-grandchildren.

# Index